NUFFIELD
ECONOMICS
& BUSINESS

Students' book
SECOND EDITION

Longman

Edinburgh Gate
Harlow, Essex

Thanks need to be given to the following:-

For case studies, articles, pictures and quotes:-
Allied Domecq
Amstrad
Andrex
Bank of England
Bluebird
British Petroleum
Britannia
BP Amoco Chemicals, Hull
Burger King
C & A
Cadbury
Calvin Klein
Channel 5
Development Organisation of Rural Sichuan, Gloucester
DX Communication
Edinburgh Bicycle
European Commission
Ford
Frizzel
Guinness
Halo
Hugo Boss
ITW Finishing Systems & Products, Bournemouth
Levi's
Lucozade
Marks & Spencer
Mars
Jack Scaife Butchers Ltd
Joseph Rowntree Foundation
Kingfisher plc
Lever Brothers Ltd, Kingston upon Thames
Mattel UK Ltd, Meridian West, Leicester
Matcon, Moreton in the Marsh
Medicash
Mortgage Express
Nissan
Nutshell Ltd, Salisbury
Ogilvy & Mather
Pepsi
Quick Snack
Radion
Richer Sounds
Roly's Fudge
Royal Shakespeare Company
S & A Foods
Sainsbury's
Samsung
Sharon Brennan's Mum
Smithkline Beecham
Somerfield Store Ltd
Sony
SWEB
Tetley
The Body Shop
The Griffin Inn
Thorntons
Tumble Home Furniture, Totnes, Devon
Unison
Village Bakery
Virgin
Vivid Imagination
Volvo
Woolworths

Contents

About this book

The resources that have been developed by the Nuffield Economics and Business Project are designed specifically to support Edexcel Advanced Subsidiary GCE in Economics and Business Studies (Nuffield) and Edexcel Advanced GCE in Economics and Business Studies (Nuffield).

This book is designed to be used alongside the Teachers' Resource Pack, also published by Longman. The two are complementary. The TRP includes:

- photocopiable activities
- advice for teachers
- data handling information sheets
- answers to some of the questions
- the Nuffield IT Investigations, which are to be found on the CD ROM which is inside the pack.

Together these publications provide a complete support system for the courses. Valuable information may also be obtained from the Nuffield Foundation website. The url is:
http://www.nuffieldfoundation.org/ curriculum/
From time to time news and new activities will be posted there. There will be information about forthcoming in-service training and any other services which can be made available.

Changes from the first edition

The main changes have been brought about by the overall respecification of A level courses, overseen by the Qualifications and Curriculum Authority. There are now three options, all of which use the joint Economics and Business approach. It was necessary also to reduce the scope of the AS course in line with QCA requirements. The result of these changes has been to alter the order in which some concepts are taught. However users of the first edition will find much familiar material in the new resources. This should make it possible to continue to use existing resources which individual teachers have developed for their own use.

Using this book

The content of this book is grouped around a series of questions. This emphasises the investigative nature of the course. Each section starts with practical context or setting that raises questions. This leads into exploration of the theories, concepts and ideas which can be used to analyse the real world.

'Your agenda' is expected to focus the reader's mind on the central questions to be addressed. In contrast, 'Work in progress' is designed to check personal comprehension and provide practice in using the ideas investigated.

We have continued to use a spiral curriculum approach. This gives great benefits in terms of the ability of students to develop an overview of the subject area at an early stage. It also means that central themes and ideas learnt early on can be reviewed later in the course so as to enhance and strengthen understanding. Students are encouraged all the way through the course to adopt a synoptic approach.

The course specifications, available from Edexcel, provide quite considerably detailed information on the requirements and course content of Economics and Business Studies (Nuffield). Every effort has been made to integrate the course content, the coverage of this book, the copymasters in the Teacher's Resource Pack and the Nuffield IT Investigations into a coherent whole. We very much hope that this will help you and that you will all enjoy the course.

Acknowledgements

Much of this edition of the Students' Book has been rewritten to fit the 2000 specifications for Economics and Business (Nuffield) now offered by Edexcel. It has been written by Jenny Wales and Nancy Wall, with a substantial contribution from Stephen Barnes, written before he left the project in late 1998. We are indebted to all those who helped to create the first edition. In particular some of Stephen Barnes' work survives in the options, as do the contributions of David Lines to the first edition.

Many other people have contributed in a variety of ways. Ian Etherington and Claire Emery each contributed to the writing of the options. Clive Ruscoe was involved in planning and writing and later read and commented on much of the book. Paul Rock helped with planning and resourcing one of the options. Sam Memory contributed several case studies.

Many people have given a great deal of time and energy to a critical reading of the book. We are particularly grateful to Professor David Myddleton of Cranfield University who read almost the whole book and made many valuable comments. Duncan Cullimore did the same for two of the options. Jo Bentham, John Birchall, Nicholas Bray, Brian Ellis, Claire Emery, Sue Hall, Sam Memory, Frank Ruffoni and Gerald Wood also gave valuable help at various times.

Other people helped us by providing information. We are particularly grateful to people in business who provided material upon which case studies are based. We would like to thank especially NTC Publications Ltd, who have allowed us to quote from their Marketing Pocket Book 2000. This is a most useful publication. (For further information, phone 01491 411000 or email info@ntc.co.uk.

The help and support of our administrator, Linda Westgarth, whose contributions were so many and so great that they cannot be briefly described, were essential to both the development work and the final preparation of the book for publication. We would also like to thank our partners, who have helped in many ways.

The publications and the course would not have come into being without the financial support of the Nuffield Foundation. This has kept the Nuffield Economics and Business Project going since its start in 1991. With these publications, the active development phase of the project comes to an end, but continuation work will still be possible.

Nancy Wall
Editor

Module 1 Objectives

Objectives drive the behaviour of us all in our many roles. In this module you will discover how objectives vary for different people in different situations. The module paints a picture of the economy and business as a whole. It shows how objectives affect business behaviour and personal choices. It examines various ways in which progress towards our objectives can be measured.

1.1 What do people want?

People have many roles. We work, we shop, we have families and friends and we vote. We may have commitments to social or voluntary organisations. We are involved in business and the economy through many of these roles. There may be conflict between them. These roles can be explored and we can identify what we want from them. This part of the module also looks carefully at some of the trade-offs that have to be made when we cannot have all we want.

1.2 What does business do?

Businesses work in a competitive market to satisfy people's wants. They use scarce resources to add value to their products. They look for profitable ways of marketing their products. They plan their activities so that they can make a profit if possible, but they may make a loss. Ways of analysing the decisions of both consumers and businesses are explored here so that we can begin to understand both their objectives and the outcomes.

What do people want?

Enquiry 1   Why be in business?

1 Getting it right

What makes the difference?

Richard Emanuel, DX communications: employs 700 people in 150 stores selling mobile phones

Richard began by selling phones door-to-door to small businesses. He accounts for his success as follows:

"There were a lot of people in the market doing a bad job. Customer service and loyalty were not relevant because salesmen would sell a phone and move on to the next customer. I knew that this was no way to build a business and add value through a better level of service. It cost me nothing but my time — and my reputation was built on ensuring that customers were buying what was right for them."

Sharon Brennan, marketing director, Taboo: a Young Enterprise company selling pocket pants

A-level students at Tiffin Girls' School in Kingston, Surrey, found that they had nowhere to keep tickets, money and keys when they went out for the evening so they devised a strategy to solve the problem. The company bought pants from a wholesaler and sewed pockets on to them! Packaged in a ribbon-fastened plastic pouch, the pants retailed at £3 a pair. The company very quickly had its first £100 in the bank.

Perween Warsi, owner and general manager, S&A Foods: produces ready-to-cook chilled ethnic food for supermarkets in the UK and Europe

Perween started in business after her home-made samosas *"flew out of the shop"* where she was testing the market. As a result she set up S&A foods, named after her sons, Sadiq and Abid. Her aim is to produce top-quality, authentic foods. The business grew and grew and now employs 500 people and has a turnover of £40 million. *"I always had a dream to be the best. That dream and a lot of hard work got me where I am today."*

Jim Anderson, general manager of operations, DeVilbiss: world's leading maker of paint spray guns

DeVilbiss was not in trouble but Jim Anderson knew that if change did not take place, it might be. Threats could come from rivals which might grow more efficient and imports from countries where labour is cheap. He reorganised the company completely so that costs fell, and he was able to cut prices. The company is now selling 20 per cent more but employs half the people it used to.

Your agenda

1. What do these businesses have in common?
2. What influenced the strategy of each one?
3. In each case what makes their business different from others in the same field?
4. What conclusions can you draw about how a business can make itself more effective than others?

Every successful business must look carefully at what people want and work out how best to deliver the goods. It is equally important to identify the strengths of the business and its staff. By putting together both sides of the story, bright ideas have an opportunity to surface and be turned into winning strategies.

Each of the businesses described above shows not only how this match has been made but also adds reasons for the success of a distinctive approach. Every business must compete for customers, so having a competitive edge is all important. If everyone involved asks 'What can we do better than the competition?', the answers will help to decide a future pathway. This means searching for sources of **competitive advantage**. For example:

● Richard Emanuel has competitive advantage because he is careful to sell the phones that people need.
● Taboo had competitive advantage because it identified an innovative product that met a need.
● DeVilbiss has competitive advantage because Jim Anderson saw the need to restructure before everyone else. This meant he could cut prices.
● S&A Foods has competitive advantage because Perween Warsi insists on high standards and develops innovative products to meet the supermarkets' needs.

Each of these examples shows how a business may have distinguishing features which enable it to stand out from the rest. These features usually fall into one of the following three categories: innovation, relationships and reputation.

Essentials

Competitive advantage is a distinctive feature that makes a business successful. It may result from innovation, reputation or the relationship with customers and suppliers. It must be hard for other businesses to copy or competitive advantage will not last very long. To get it right, a business must carefully identify the people who will buy the product. Competitive advantage may show itself in the ability of the business to charge a lower price than other similar products.

■ Innovation

Being the first with something new is a powerful way of being distinctive. For this to become a source of competitive advantage, a business must be able to:

protect its invention
or
keep ahead of the game.

A new idea that everyone else can copy will never give competitive advantage for long. If the girls running Taboo patented their product so that no one else could sew pockets on pants, they could be on to a winner.

Jim Anderson, on the other hand, was developing competitive advantage in the way that he was running the business. By overhauling the organisation, it became possible to produce more cheaply and meet customer needs more quickly. He was trying to keep ahead of the game.

Perween Warsi was on the constant lookout for new products that built on her reputation for quality. When S&A Foods moved into Chinese meals, she used Ken Hom, the famous Chinese chef, to advise the company. Although many firms produce Chinese food, Perween's mix of reputation and products that are just a bit different give her competitive advantage.

Innovation is more than just the ability to introduce new products. It involves the ability of the company as a whole to be innovative in the way people do things and think about the world. It happens when a business is prepared to:

● change the product
● change the way things are made
● change the organisation of the business.

This means that those involved must be on the alert to the world around them and not stay hidden in their burrows!

Essentials

Innovation is the introduction of new ideas. It may affect products or the way in which they are made.

Relationships

Everyone responds to being treated well by others. Customers, employees and other businesses are no exception to this rule. The business which looks carefully at the way it works with these three groups is more likely to be successful because it will be working cooperatively. This is as true of making motor cars as of selling clothes on the high street.

Perween Warsi has demonstrated the ability to work in this way with supermarkets. Customers vary between supermarkets, so it is important to get the products just right in order to meet their needs. S&A Foods and the product development staff from the supermarket companies work closely together to ensure that the correct mix is achieved. As this relationship is successful, S&A Foods continues to be asked to supply ethnic foods to the big supermarket chains.

The department store partnership, John Lewis, has always had a special relationship with its employees. The business was established as a cooperative because the staff were to be totally involved in the organisation.

When the car manufacturer Nissan set up in the UK, one objective was to establish a close relationship with its component suppliers. They worked together on achieving high-quality parts that were exactly what the company needed.

High street retailers, Marks and Spencer, have a special relationship with all three categories:

- Employees know that if they show commitment, they will be fairly rewarded.
- Customers know that their purchases will be good quality and that they can return them without argument.
- Suppliers know that, provided they meet the standards required at a price that makes sense in the stores, they will be fairly treated.

The special relationships that companies develop are known as 'architecture'. When used to describe buildings, architecture refers to the design and shape of the building. It is just the same with a business. It shows the fundamental features that hold the business together and make it successful. In a building these would be bricks and mortar or concrete and steel. In a business it is the employees, customers and suppliers.

When the economy is growing such relationships work well. They seem more difficult to maintain when times are hard. In a search for cost savings, Marks and Spencer, for example, pulled out of relationships with UK suppliers because it could buy more cheaply in the Far East.

Reputation

We can all immediately think of businesses that are successful because of their reputation.

The car manufacturer Volvo is often the one that springs to mind. You don't buy one for excitement – but you know that if you have an accident, you have a greater chance of survival. Building on this foundation, Volvo introduced a sportier range which aims to provide reputation with some excitement.

A reputation can be achieved through developing a particular image. It may come from:

- keeping prices low like Kwik Save
- appealing to the affluent like the Ritz
- ensuring top quality like Rolls-Royce
- having fun like Tango
- being sensible like Clarks.

Reputation can take a long time to build but is invaluable once it has been achieved. Richard Emanuel knew this from the start. He had watched other mobile phone businesses where people worked on the basis of a one-off sale, never worrying about the customer returning. He knew that it was important and set out to establish his reputation. Richard had the added advantage of being in the business early.

2 What is the reward?

The first answer to this question is always – a **profit**. Running a business is a challenge and therefore the people involved are looking for a reward. Profit is, in simple terms, the difference between the costs of production and the revenue from sales, but it is many other things as well.

Defining Profit

■ The difference between costs and revenue

Before a product can be put on the market, there are costs to be counted. Money must be spent on the development process. Market research must be carried out to discover whether the public will buy the good or service. The raw materials, staff and appropriate premises must be acquired before anything can be sold. There are then the ongoing costs of employing people and keeping production running. Revenue is simply the number of items sold multiplied by their price.

Once all the costs have been deducted from the revenue, the amount that is left is profit.

This provides an introduction to the idea of profit. Later, you will encounter a more sophisticated interpretation which takes into account the ways companies work and present their accounts to the world.

■ The reward for taking a risk

Business is always risky and there is no guarantee that there will be any profit at the end of the day. **Entrepreneurs**, the people responsible for making the decisions, obviously hope to make a profit, but they may also make a loss. Profit can therefore be defined in this context as: the reward for taking a risk not only at a personal level but also a risk with the money or capital which has to be invested in order to start the business and keep it going.

■ The return on the money used to run the business

If money is kept in a bank or building society savings account, it earns interest. Any money that is used to run a business must earn more than it would earn in the bank. If not, it would have been better to have left the money in the bank!

■ The signal that people want to buy the product

A business that is making a profit will know that people are buying its output. This may encourage it to make and sell more. Rising profit often sends a signal that resources should be used to increase output.

Essentials

Profit is the difference between a firm's revenues from its trading activities and its total costs. It is a reward for risk and a return on capital invested. It signals that people want to buy the product and that more resources may be used in this way.

Essentials

Entrepreneurs combine the necessary attitudes and skills to run a business. They must be prepared to take risks as this is how they earn a profit. If they fail, they will make a loss.

But is it always profit?

Point of view

Why do they do it?

> It gave Stockton the chance to change his quality of life and to include his children in the business.

said of Richard Stockton who swapped his Midlands engineering firm for a pub in the Wye Valley

> I still find clinching the deal is the single most exciting thing I ever do. It gives me such a buzz. It's more exhilarating than skiing any black run.

Eddie Jordan, owner of Jordan Grand Prix team

> It is easier to do it alone because it is very nice to feel in control.

Linda Bennett of L K Bennett clothing shops

> Businesses like ours show that there is a different way of making food that has integrity and doesn't cut corners.

Andrew Whitley of the Village Bakery at Melmerby, Cumbria, who sells bread to Waitrose and Sainsbury's

Your Agenda

1 Make a list of the motives that these people have for running a business.

2 Do any of them mention profit?

3 Do you think that they care about profit? Why?

4 What other motives can you think of? Can you think of a local or nationally known business which demonstrates each of your examples?

People run businesses in all sorts of different ways and for many different reasons. Profit is always one of them because a business will not survive without it. There are however many other reasons which may be even stronger.

The graph in Figure M1.1 shows that profit comes low down the list. Independence is much more important. Some businesses go on in the same old way for years because owners opt for a quiet life. In the end such strategies tend to fail, but they may meet the needs of the people involved.

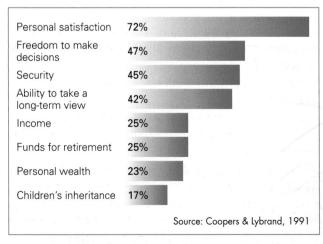

Personal satisfaction	72%
Freedom to make decisions	47%
Security	45%
Ability to take a long-term view	42%
Income	25%
Funds for retirement	25%
Personal wealth	23%
Children's inheritance	17%

Source: Coopers & Lybrand, 1991

Figure M1.1 Reasons for running a business

Mine or ours?

Making a game of it

In the early days of computer games, Ian Stewart saw an opportunity. He was working for the audio retailer Laskey's in Sheffield where he could not persuade the owners to devote enough shelf space to the wide range of games that people wanted to buy. He decided to open his own shop and found a location in the side streets of the town. To do this he needed to start up a business and raise some money. In order to establish his business formally, he had to decide whether to run it as a sole trader or set up a company.

Your agenda

Use the information in Figure M1.2 to decide the path that Ian Stewart should have taken when he set up his business. Explain your choice.

Ian Stewart certainly made the right decision! Under the name Gremlin, he started producing computer games instead of just selling them. He now runs a company which is valued at £29 million.

	Sole Trader	**Company**
Legal	– no legal formalities	– a legal structure with a separate identity from those who run it. Shareholders own the company but it is run by a board of directors
Profit	Receives all profits – profits go straight to owner	Profits go to shareholders when costs have been met
Liability	Unlimited liability – personally responsible for all losses (personal possessions are at risk)	Limited liability – if the business makes a loss, the personal people who run it are safe because they are only liable for the money that they have put into the company
Capital	Can only raise capital from own resources, such as family, borrowing from the bank	Capital can be raised by selling shares. The share holdings are known as equity
Flexibility	– free to change direction if necessary	Decisions taken by board of directors and shareholders

Figure M1.2 Deciding which way

The sole trader gains on the flexibility aspect because decisions can be made quickly. There is no head office or board of directors to consult so new ideas can be turned into reality very quickly. The main drawback is lack of financial resources. New ideas often require an injection of money and this may prove difficult. The sole trader can only draw on ploughed-back profits or people's willingness to lend.

There is also the problem of not having limited liability. If the business gets into difficulties, the person who runs it can lose everything, including his or her house and all its contents. This is often a key determinant in the decision on the type of business organisation.

Running a business requires a range of expertise. The word 'sole' means that only one person is involved. It is therefore unlikely that one person will have all the skills that are required. In a large organisation there will be experts in areas like marketing and finance. A sole trader can employ people, but not having limited liability can lead to problems if things go wrong. As the business grows it is likely to become a private company.

Another key drawback is the scale of the operation. A large company such as chemicals giant ICI can buy the materials that it needs in great quantity, which generally means that they are proportionately cheaper. Costs of production are therefore usually lower for large firms.

The sole trader who wants a holiday may be in difficulties. It is often hard to shut down a business for even a few days as customers may go elsewhere.

A company can raise money through selling shares. This means that a group of people share the ownership of the business. The shareholders in a private limited company are usually family members or a group of friends. This, of course, limits the amount of capital that may be available, but it does keep control in the hands of a small group and limits the information which has to be made available to the public. There are also some surprisingly large companies that have been kept private such as the high street clothes retailer C&A and the Virgin organisations which are still owned by Richard Branson.

A public limited company (plc), on the other hand, sells shares to the general public and large organisations that want to see their money grow in value, such as pension funds. This means that, providing the company seems to be sound, large amounts of money can be raised. Plcs can also borrow at low interest rates because lenders feel sure that their money will be returned. Almost all the well-known names, from oil and petroleum giant Shell to food and soft drinks manufacturer Cadbury Schweppes are run as plcs.

As both private and public limited companies both have *limited* liability people who invest in them have limited risk. They can only lose the money that they have put into the business. Nothing else is at risk. This means that people are much more willing to put money into such businesses. This sort of investment is done by buying shares, so if the business hits difficult times shareholders will only lose the value of their shares. The shares in a company are known as its equity.

Public companies are too large to be controlled by all the shareholders on a daily basis. To overcome this problem, the shareholders appoint directors who run the company but are answerable for their actions at the annual general meeting.

As a business grows, it is likely to change its status. The sole trader who finds that the business is expanding will usually set up a company. Many companies remain private on a permanent basis but those which really want to grow will probably go public and sell shares on the Stock Exchange in order to have access to more investment. The Stock Exchange is mainly used for buying and selling existing shares. Its existence means that more people are prepared to buy shares because it provides a ready market if the purchaser wants to sell.

1 Why become a customer?

How do people spend their money?

Item	%
Housing	17
Food	18
Clothing and footwear	6
Fuel, light and power	4
Motoring and fares	15
Household goods and services	13
Leisure goods and services	17
Alcohol and tobacco	2
Other goods and services	5

Figure M1.3   Source: ONS, *Social Trends*, 1998

Your agenda

1 In 1998 the average family was earning £290 per week after tax. Work out how much they spent on each item in the list in Figure M1.3.

2 Reorganise the list into rank order so that the largest item of expenditure comes first and the smallest comes last.

3 Explain the variations between the amount spent on each item on the list. Make a list of your reasons.

4 Use your list to create categories to explain spending patterns.

5 Put the following items into the categories: a trip to the cinema, a carton of milk, a pair of shoes, a pad of file paper, a CD, a bus pass.

6 You created the spending categories and decided what went into them. Why might other people have different items in their categories? Give some examples.

Meeting the needs ...

We can rarely have everything we want. The data in Figure M1.3 show where the bulk of people's money goes. The highest proportion of spending is on necessities that we cannot do without – housing, food, power, etc. The remainder of our income is spent on the wants, or luxuries, that we can afford.

As few people can afford everything, we all have to choose. There are choices to be made at every level. Think of the decisions that have to be made about housing, the choice of food in the supermarket, or which pair of shoes to buy. The poorest in society have hard choices to make in order to meet basic needs. The more affluent regard many things as essential and may only have to choose between a range of luxuries.

... and the wants

What shall we do tonight?

Scene: a phone call on Saturday afternoon

NICK: Hi Sam, its Nick. Got any plans for tonight?

SAM: Thought we might go to that new club. There were handouts at college. Did you see them?

NICK: I don't know if I can afford it. I've got to pay for that Economics and Business Conference next week. How much is it?

SAM: I'll just have a look on the leaflet. Here it is – it's usually a fiver, but there is a special opening offer of two for the price of one with this voucher.

NICK: I couldn't manage a fiver, but £2.50 is just about OK. Are there no parties on anywhere? That would be even cheaper.

SAM: There's the film that won all the Oscars at the new multiplex. It's really cool there – but I always want a tub of popcorn and a coke. It's hard to get out without spending ten quid. Course, its cheaper at the old cinema in town, but there still wouldn't be much change from a fiver. If only the price were lower, I'd go every week. There are so many good films on at the moment.

SAM: So what are we going to do Nick? We'll have to choose.

NICK: Well Sam, if we go to the club, I'll have a bit of money left for a night out during the week. If I do anything else, I'll be stuck at home all week. I could get that piece of portfolio work done, I suppose! Oh let's go clubbing, then at least I'm free to choose during the week.

SAM: Sounds good to me. I'll come round about eight.

Your agenda

1 Why did the new club offer half-price vouchers to potential customers?

2 What might happen if the club raised the price to £7.50 or lowered it to £2.50? Draw a simple line graph to show what might happen at different prices.

3 Is this pattern common to other products or services that people buy?

4 If Nick goes to either cinema, what does he have to give up? How does this affect his choice?

5 Why do some people opt to go to the multiplex rather than the older local cinema?

Nick and Sam have a choice on their hands. Like most students, they have a limited amount of money to spend and want to make the most of it.

Their decision involves selecting the best option from two or more alternatives or opportunities. They are seeking the optimum choice. In making this choice the next best alternative has to be given up. The value of this next-best-alternative is called the **opportunity cost** of a decision. If Nick and Sam had opted for the local cinema, the club and an outing during the week would have had to be given up. This was too much! The decision was therefore made to go to the club.

This principle has applications in every situation. The search for the optimum choice is made many times a day by people in business, in government and on their own behalf. Every decision is determined by identifying the opportunity cost of alternatives in order to seek the best solution.

The need to choose arises because there is never enough to go round. If we all got everything we wanted, the world would soon run out of resources. This **scarcity** of resources has been overcome by the development of money and price which determines how much people can have.

In making choices, there are **trade-offs**. If you decide to go on a fortnight's holiday rather than buy a car, you have traded the gains from a holiday for a year of personal transport. If you decide to go for a week's holiday and buy an older car instead, you are making a trade-off between the two. People, businesses and governments all have to make trade-offs when they make decisions.

Essentials

The **opportunity cost** of a decision is the value expected to be derived from the next best alternative decision. By making a choice, you make the opportunity cost of your actions clear.

Essentials

The **scarcity** of resources means that people cannot have all they want. As a result most resources are allocated according to the amount that people are able or prepared to pay.

Essentials

Trade-offs occur when two things cannot be fully achieved. The more you have of one, the less you can have of another.

Demand: making wants real

The desire to buy goods or services is called **demand**. In effect, this is an open request to other members of society, asking for our particular desires to be fulfilled. But since other people are unlikely to give us their resources for nothing, demand only becomes **effective demand** when backed by money.

Nick and Sam turned their wants into reality when they parted with £2.50 each to go to the new club. They were not prepared to spend £5 each, but other people might have been. If the price was lower than £2.50, many more people, who put a lower value on clubbing, might have gone as well.

Essentials

Demand means any want directed towards a particular good or service. It cannot be put into action unless it is backed by money or other items of value which might be used to exchange. Then it becomes effective demand.

For most things that are available in shops, as the price falls, people will buy more because they feel that they are receiving more benefit from spending their money in this way, rather than any other. As the price falls, the opportunity cost falls because they have to give up less in order to make this purchase.

Even at a high price there are often some people who feel that the benefit they receive is worth paying for. As the price falls, an increasing number of people enter the market and start to buy. So the **demand curve** is downward sloping. Demand curves help in the analysis of how people behave in response to price changes. Figure M1.4 shows the result.

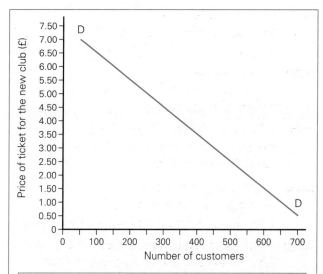

Price	Number of tickets sold	Price	Number of tickets sold
£7.00	50	£3.50	400
£6.50	100	£3.00	450
£6.00	150	£2.50	500
£5.50	200	£2.00	550
£5.00	250	£1.50	600
£4.50	300	£1.00	650
£4.00	350	£0.50	700

Figure M1.4 Demand for tickets at the new club

Demand can be measured for an individual. A more useful measure is known as market demand because it shows how purchasers in general will respond to different prices. It is produced by adding together all the individual demand. Figure M1.4 is a market demand curve because it shows the demand for everyone, not just for Nick or Sam.

Essentials

The **demand curve** shows how much people are prepared to buy at a range of prices.

Work in progress

Q
1 The data in Figure M1.5 show Sam's demand for compact disks at different prices. Plot his individual demand curve.

2 Will most people react similarly to a change in the price of compact disks?

3 What is the market demand curve likely to look like?

Figure M1.5 Demand for compact disks

4 A price change will affect the demand for some products more than others. Identify those whose demand will be relatively unaffected, and those which will be affected a great deal. Is there any pattern?

Price £	Quantity demanded per year
15	5
10	10
5	15

2. What causes the demand curve to shift?

When spending power increases ...

'Hi Sam, it's Nick here. I've got a job! There was a notice in the book-shop window saying they needed part-time help, so I went in to find out more. It's just Saturday and some Sunday afternoons. It doesn't pay a lot but at least it means that I've a bit more to spend.'

Your agenda

1 What effect is the job likely to have on Nick's demand curve for cinema tickets? Draw a diagram to show what has happened.

2 What else is likely to change demand in this way?

3 What sort of things are unlikely to be affected by a change in income?

The amount that people have to spend usually determines how they use their money. An increase in income may change the pattern. Things that they couldn't afford now become a possibility. More people will be prepared to buy compact disks, for example, as their income rises. What effect will this have on the demand curve?

The new curve (see Figure M1.6) has shifted to the right and shows that at any particular price more compact disks will be sold. Of course, if incomes fall, the curve will shift to the left, showing that fewer will be sold at each price.

The same movement takes place if there are other changes which affect demand. Fashion is an important influence. Once people only bought Levi jeans if they needed them for heavy work! Then they became the ultimate fashion item. Now they are a standard in many wardrobes, but have been copied at both the top and bottom of the market. As the fashion fades, the demand curve may return to its former position.

Some very simple factors will shift the curve. Try looking for ice-cream in the newsagent's ice-cream

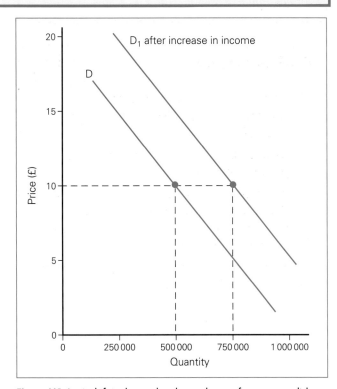

Figure M1.6. A shift in the market demand curve for compact disks

cabinet on the first day of the year that the temperature rises above 20°C! Ice-cream firms try to anticipate change but they often misjudge the moment.

The demand for a product may also be closely related to the price of something else. If the price of petrol rose to £2 a litre, people might think twice about buying a car and might increase their demand for public transport. The demand curve for cars would, therefore, shift to the left while the demand curve for buses and train travel would shift to the right. Petrol and cars are known as **complementary goods** and cars and trains are **substitutes**. Indeed, all sorts of things make the demand curve shift. Health scares can cut demand for certain food products, while hot weather can boost ice-cream sales.

Essentials

Complementary goods are used together, so if the price of one rises, demand for the other will fall.

Essentials

Substitutes can be used to replace each other, so if the price of one rises, demand for the other will rise.

Work in progress

Q 1 Can you identify some products which respond more than others to a change in income?

2 List three pairs of complements and three pairs of substitutes.

3 What products are, at the moment, facing a shifting demand curve because of a changing fashion? Don't forget that the curve can shift backwards as well.

Point of view

Toys 'R' Us has played too long

In the USA, Toys 'R' Us has hit the buffers. After years of dominating the market, the business is no longer performing and its share of the market has fallen to 20 percent. Why has this happened? Competition from giant supermarket chains has led to price cutting, but competing on price has not been enough.

In the USA there is a growing range of specialist shops selling educational and scientific toys. They also catch the market for the latest fashions among more affluent parents – who have money to spend and are in search of a combination of the right toy and the right environment. They choose to shop in bright airy places where assistants have expertise and can give advice. Toys 'R' Us no longer fits the bill.

Your agenda

1 Toys 'R' Us has lost market in two directions. Explain these changes using demand curves to show what has happened.

2 Why are people prepared to pay more in the new types of shops which are opening up?

3 Think of some other products that are being sold in this way.

Enquiry 3 Why do people work?

1 Money plus ...?

Which strategy?

The Council strategy

Composition of Council

The Council is composed of elected employees representing constituencies comprising coherent groups of the Company's employees together with nominees of the Company. An example of a constituency is the body and press shop. All employees are represented by a maximum of ten representatives. The Chairman and Secretary of the Council will be nominated by the company.

Responsibilities of elected representatives

The prime responsibility of all members of the Council is to ensure the prosperity of the Company and by doing so promote the prosperity and security of all staff.

Source: Nissan Information Pack

The Friday night strategy

'The social life here is very good. We mix a lot and the place has become a mix between a business and a university. There is a beer bust every Friday night for every store. The bars send us the bills and we settle them. There are no rules about spending limits – except don't rip the arse out of it. I believe that people should be treated with respect and, if you do that, they do not want to abuse you.'

(Charles Dunstone, founder of Carphone Warehouse)

Source: Sunday Business, 21 April 1998

Your agenda

1 What are both these companies trying to do?

2 Why do they invest time and money in such activities?

3 Why do the two companies use such different strategies?

4 Nissan's Council might not be as democratic as it seems. Why?

5 If a business wants to encourage employees to contribute effectively, what other sorts of needs might be taken into consideration?

6 How might a business set about meeting other needs?

What do people want from work?

The first answer to this question is always 'money'. It seems obvious that in order to pay for the requirements of daily life, you need a job with an adequate wage. A question which is often asked is 'What do you do for a living?' The answer given usually implies more than simply a living, as people in work usually have a wider range of needs.

You might hear people fantasise about having enough money so that they never have to work again. As work provides more than simply money, such 'lucky' people frequently find that their new life does not come up to their expectations.

What needs?

It is obvious that everyone has basic survival needs such as eating and sleeping. People's behaviour, however, suggests that we have needs which go far beyond these simple requirements. Abraham Maslow

(1908–70) was a US psychologist who, writing in 1954, proposed a hierarchy of needs to explain human behaviour:

- *Level 1 Physiological needs* – the basic essentials of life such as food and drink, warmth and sleep.
- *Level 2 Security needs* – the sense of being in a secure environment.
- *Level 3 Affiliation needs* – the desire for receiving and giving friendship and love: a sense of belonging.
- *Level 4 Esteem needs* – feeling self-respect and experiencing the respect of others.
- *Level 5 Self-actualisation needs* – the drive towards creative self-fulfilment.

These levels of need can be represented in a simple diagram – see Figure M1.7.

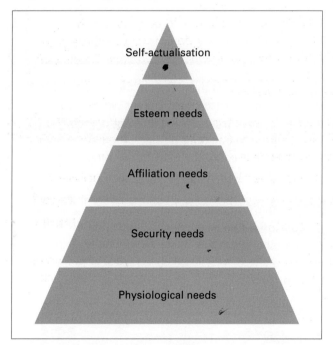

Figure M1.7 Maslow's hierarchy of needs

Physiological needs are a person's first source of motivation. Higher levels of need matter little if people are homeless and hungry. Once the first level of need is met, people look for satisfaction in other ways. A sense of security raises them to level 2. Once achieved, they are in search of the next level until they reach a level at which they feel totally fulfilled.

This analysis of needs applies directly to the question of why people work. In the UK almost all jobs provide enough income to meet physical needs.

Many jobs are also reasonably secure or at least the skill of the worker can be applied in employment elsewhere. Some jobs meet social needs while others will additionally yield the quality of esteem. Relatively few jobs go very far in meeting the highest human need: the drive for creative self-fulfilment.

There is an important message to be drawn from this theory. When people initially seek employment, they are likely to be **motivated** by needs for money and a secure job. But once these needs are largely met through holding the job, they will then seek to fulfil their higher needs (i.e. levels 3–5 in Figure M1.7). Frustration and under-performance at work are often caused by the inability of employees to fulfil their higher needs. Merely being offered another pay rise or a better contract may not be enough to encourage a person's true commitment and determination at work. However, some more recent studies do suggest that when one level of need is thwarted, then the level below may be perceived as proportionately more important.

Work in progress

Q

Look back at the opening case study:

1 Where do Nissan and Carphone Warehouse fit into Maslow's triangle?

2 Suggest three jobs where only the lowest levels and three jobs where the highest levels in Maslow's hierarchy are likely to be fulfilled.

3 What common factors are there in each of the two groups of jobs?

4 Can you see any possible weaknesses in Maslow's theory?

Essentials

Many businesses are concerned about **motivation** because the right strategy will help people to be more productive. By meeting people's needs, a business can increase commitment and therefore improve performance.

2. Speeding up?

A small skill – a big idea

Adam Smith, one of the founders of modern economics, was surprised by the way the pin factory worked.

'One man draws out the wire, another straightens it, a third cuts it, a fourth points it, a fifth grinds it at the top for receiving the head; to make the head requires two or three distinct operations; to put it on is a peculiar business, to whiten the pins is another; it is even a trade by itself to put them into the paper; and the important business of making a pin is, in this manner, divided into about eighteen distinct operations, which, in some manufactories, are all performed by distinct hands.'

In 1776, Adam Smith published this in *The Wealth of Nations*, using it to show how industry could be more efficient by using people in a different way.

Your agenda

1 One person's output of pins would be very low. How many reasons can you find for the increase in output when people take on different tasks? Explain your reasons.

2 What other industries function more efficiently when work is broken down in this way?

3 What sort of businesses might not benefit from working in this way? Give some examples and explain why.

Specialised skills

If you were stranded on a desert island, how long would you survive? Can you produce your own food? Can you make a shelter to withstand all weathers? (Your island might be somewhere off the Shetland Islands!) What about clothes, boats, radios?

A peasant farmer would be better placed to survive. In situations where people cannot trade, everyone has to fend for themselves so everyone learns all the skills. As soon as anyone grows a little more than they need to exist, trade and **specialisation** begin. People start to develop their strengths. To start with, these were very broadly defined. There were experts in house building. Today it takes a multitude of skills to build a house. If we all specialise in areas where we have an obvious advantage, it generally means that we are more efficient than other people, so we produce more. As a result specialisation leads to greater output per person.

If everyone produces the things they do best, they must barter or buy everything else. Economies do not really start to develop until **exchange** begins to happen. The ability to specialise and therefore produce more allows economies to grow richer.

This ability to specialise has been put to work by business and is known as the **division of labour**. By dividing jobs up, as they were in the pin factory described in the case study, output per head rises because people use their expertise effectively. If people are concentrating on one task, any equipment they need is used all the time so the process is cheaper and more efficient.

Essentials

Specialisation means that people make the most of their skills by concentrating their expertise in a particular field. As a skilled person produces more, output per head will rise. It can only occur when people are in a position to trade.

Essentials

Exchange refers to the process of getting the things you need by offering someone your own product and taking his orders in exchange. Money makes the process of exchange much easier.

Essentials

The **division of labour** refers to the practice of organising workers so that individuals specialise in one part of a production process. It generally leads to an increase in output per person.

■ Specialisation and production

As the idea of the division of labour established itself, it became clear that equipment could be used more efficiently by people who specialised in a particular task. From pin-making equipment to highly technical lasers, any machine that is used all day long should earn its keep. The opportunity cost of its being left idle most of the time is high – it would be a waste of resources.

The combination of people with specialist skills and the mechanisation of their work had an overwhelming impact on industrial production. These changes made the 1800s a revolutionary period for most people. The way of life and the range of products available to the ordinary family changed dramatically. As a result, the era became known as the Industrial Revolution.

Motivation and specialisation: a contradiction

Specialisation has enabled society to develop rapidly so that our way of life has become unrecognisable to that of our ancestors. Like most things, however, you can have too much of a good thing.

In the early twentieth century the style of mass production in which everyone sat on production lines and carried out repetitive tasks became the objective of industry. At first, there was novelty value and praise was heaped on the clean, efficient environment within which people worked. From the early days, however, there have been satirists who were aware of the issues. In the silent movie 'Modern Times', for example, Charlie Chaplin played an individual trapped in the system.

Work in progress

At the Nissan plant in Sunderland, the key objective was to be able to compete with Japan for new models. One of the three key areas for improvement was 'people management, development and care'. If the plant were to produce more cars per head, people were important. A survey of all 4200 employees was carried out. It showed that people wanted improved career development and more job rotation. This would reduce the monotony of some jobs by allowing people to do a range of different jobs.

At the end of the three-year programme, the plant succeeded in achieving these aims and won the next model.

Q

1   How do Nissan's UK employees appear to have reacted to the division of labour?

2   To what extent do the needs of the employees match Maslow's hierarchy?

3   How might Nissan go about meeting people's needs?

4   What are the costs and benefits to the company of doing so?

© 1999 Roy Export Company Establishment

Charlie Chaplin in 'Modern Times'

Point of view

United skills

Jim Anderson at DeVilbiss (see page 4) decided to redesign the whole business. The switch was from a functional operational style where people did set jobs to a process-dedicated one where teams of non-specialist people work in multi-disciplinary teams which take full responsibility for production in their sector or cell. Each cell is run like an independent business.

Clive Hughes, deputy cell leader in the aircap cell:

'When they said they were going to introduce these new management ideas, I *knew* it couldn't happen. I've been a manager all my life and I knew that companies that bought things in great big lumps got the best prices.'

'And,' he adds triumphantly, 'I was

wrong. This is brilliant. It's so easy. Everybody in our cell wants to run our business in a really special way. We haven't seen the bosses for a year. We control our budget. Which other workers can say that? Management never bears down on you, demanding to know why you haven't performed. We know our targets because we set them, and we know the consequences of not meeting them.'

Source: Adapted from *The Sunday Times*, 8 February 1998

Your agenda

1 In what way is this contradicting the idea of division of labour?

2 Why do you think that people are more interested in their work than they were in the old system?

3 How does this fit into Maslow's triangle?

4 Is there a contradiction between asking people to carry out very specialised, repetitive jobs and motivating them?

Most people respond to a system in which they are given responsibility and their views are taken into account. This does not mean that production has to be slowed down. DeVilbiss found that improved motivation led to increased output with fewer resources.

How much work?

One way of counting the amount of work in the economy is to measure the total income that is earned. This figure, however, excludes some aspects of the work that are carried out. What work goes on in your family which is not counted. Who does the decorating? If it is not done by members of the family, has the painter been paid in cash? Why? Do you ever look after younger brothers or sisters without pay? If you are paid, do you declare it to the Inland Revenue?

It is, of course, very difficult to estimate just how much unpaid and undeclared work is being carried out. Estimates vary. The figures in Figure M1.8 are thought by some to be conservative. They suggest that over half the

work in the UK is in what is called the **informal economy** as opposed to the **formal economy**.

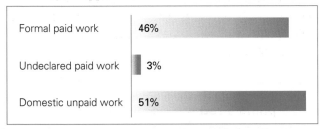

Formal paid work	46%
Undeclared paid work	3%
Domestic unpaid work	51%

Figure M1.8 What is work?

The amount of informal work varies considerably between countries. Russians, for example, are now notorious for non-payment of taxes. The implication is that the government has less to spend on the services that it provides.

Essentials

The **formal economy** includes everything that is counted in the gross domestic product (GDP), whereas activity in the **informal economy** is not included.

3 Changing patterns

Who does what?

	% of total employment							
	Males				**Females**			
	1978	**1981**	**1991**	**1998**	**1978**	**1981**	**1991**	**1998**
Distribution, hotels, catering and repairs	15	16	19	20	24	25	25	26
Manufacturing	35	33	26	25	22	18	12	10
Financial and business services	9	10	15	16	11	12	16	19
Transport and communication	9	9	9	9	3	3	3	3
Construction	8	8	8	8	1	1	1	1
Agriculture	2	2	2	2	1	1	1	1
Energy and water supply	5	5	3	1	1	1	1	-
Other services	16	17	19	19	38	39	41	40

Figure M1.9 Patterns in UK employment, 1978–98   Source: ONS, *Social Trends*, 1999

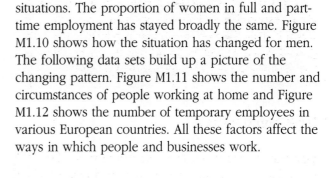

Your agenda

1 What are the main patterns of change shown in the data in Figure M1.9?

2 Are the trends the same for males and females?

3 Think carefully about how people spend their money today compared with 20 years ago. Can this explain any of the changes?

4 What other reasons can you think of for these changes?

5 How might the changes that you have identified affect people's way of life?

The world of work is constantly changing. The data in Figure M1.9 show clearly that jobs have shifted from the manufacturing or **secondary sector** to services, which are known as the **tertiary sector**. Fewer people have worked in the **primary sector**, which encompasses mining, fishing and farming, for the last 50 years.

The key trend in the labour market has been an increase in the need for people to adapt to changing situations. The proportion of women in full and part-time employment has stayed broadly the same. Figure M1.10 shows how the situation has changed for men. The following data sets build up a picture of the changing pattern. Figure M1.11 shows the number and circumstances of people working at home and Figure M1.12 shows the number of temporary employees in various European countries. All these factors affect the ways in which people and businesses work.

Essentials

The **primary sector** includes industries involved in mining, fishing and farming.

Essentials

The **secondary sector** includes all manufacturing industry.

Essentials

The **tertiary sector** includes all service industries.

A changing pattern

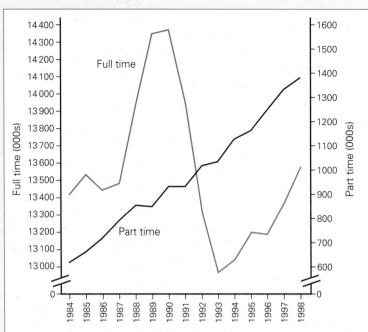

Figure M1.10 Men in full and part-time employment, 1984–98   Source: ONS, *Social Trends*, 1999

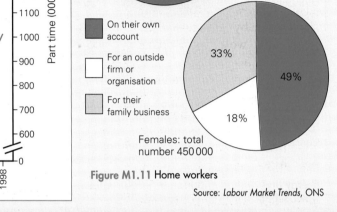

Males: total number 205 000

Females: total number 450 000

- On their own account
- For an outside firm or organisation
- For their family business

Figure M1.11 Home workers

Source: *Labour Market Trends*, ONS

Your agenda

1 What percentage of men had part-time work in 1998 compared with 1984?

2 Why might businesses want their employees to work on temporary contracts or from home?

3 How might flexible working help the economy to grow?

4 What effect might temporary contracts have on staff?

5 What other information would you like before you could make final decisions about the effects of flexible working on people and the economy?

	Males	% **Females**	**All**
Spain	32.4	35.8	33.6
Finland	15.3	18.9	17.1
France	12.1	14.3	13.1
Portugal	11.7	12.9	12.2
Sweden	10.1	14.0	12.1
Germany	11.5	12.1	11.7
Netherlands	8.8	14.9	11.4
Denmark	10.6	11.6	11.1
Greece	10.2	11.9	10.9
Irish Republic	7.1	12.1	9.4
Italy	7.3	9.7	8.2
Austria	7.3	8.4	7.8
United Kingdom	6.5	8.4	7.4
Belgium	4.6	8.6	6.3
Luxembourg	1.8	2.7	2.1
EU average	11.5	13.1	12.2

Figure M1.12 Temporary employees in Europe, 1997

Source: ONS, *Social Trends*, 1998

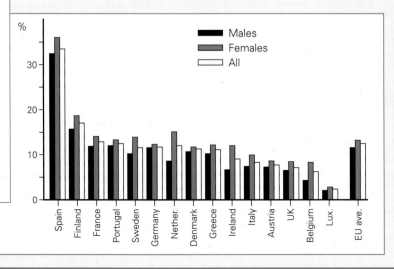

What happens to the people?

Flexibility

Martin and Gaby Allen run football schools for children from their house and garage. Martin, who runs the courses, also plays professional football. Gaby takes care of the secretarial work, promotions and marketing.

They work in pleasant surroundings, with views over the fields behind their house in Winchester. They see more of their two children because they are there when they come home from school. An important advantage is not having to pay any rent for offices.

The garage, however, is full of the equipment for the courses and the dining room is full of paperwork. Further expansion will mean a move. The main drawback of working from home is that work never goes away – you can't escape!

Source: *Workers for Freedom* by Oliver Bennet, *Sunday Times Magazine*, 31.5.97.
© Times Newspapers Limited, 1999.

Brian Pickering returned to his roots as a musician when redundancy ended his 30-year career in the oil industry. He teaches saxophone, clarinet and flute, conducts the Harrow Symphony Orchestra and is music director of the Harrow Concert Band.

He also trains in personal efficiency and advises on the setting up of career-development centres. 'I had to decide what to do with the rest of my life. My experience fell into two categories – setting up something from scratch and sorting out a mess.' Pickering set up a company to specialise in the management of change.

'The teaching took off quickly and I had no time for other work, but that was OK because I knew that it would take a while for the company to get going,' he says.

'I balance work on the basis of what I enjoy doing. I have room for more training, so I spend time networking and marketing. I belong to an excellent network of 40 people, all in different professions and we generate leads for one another. Personal development is very important. You have to re-skill constantly. You have to keep up to date with the latest software and other sorts of information.'

'I don't ever intend to retire. I enjoy the things I do. There is less security and it's different because I have had some pretty big jobs, but I would never go back; I would have to give up too much.'

Source: *Sunday Times*, 31.8.97.
© Times Newspapers Limited 1999.

Your agenda

1 In what ways are these three people working flexibly?
2 What are the advantages and disadvantages for Martin and Gaby Allen and Brian Pickering?
3 Why would some people not enjoy this style of work?
4 What sort of jobs would be difficult to carry out in this way?
5 What would be the effects of everyone working as independently as this?

The striking factor that emerges from all these data is the effect that such working practices have on people. The traditional working pattern of a 9 to 5 job, with evenings and weekends free to spend as you choose, has disappeared for many. As businesses strive to be more competitive, they have searched for ways to provide a better service, cut costs and generally perform more efficiently.

This has led to a need for a more **flexible** approach. The data show how many people are working in ways that were uncommon 20 years ago. Part-time work has become much more common. For some people, it may mean having several jobs. This portfolio approach to working life is increasingly common.

Essentials

Flexible working involves being able to carry out a range of jobs and being available at different times. It makes business more efficient because it reduces costs.

DeVilbiss, the paint spray company (see page 20), had changed its practices to create a much more flexible environment. The result was more efficient production as employees were expected to carry out a variety of tasks. The increase in efficiency, however, led to many redundancies, so people either had to look for more work in the same line or reskill. The ability and facilities for reskilling are therefore a crucial element in the move to flexibility. It may be carried out by the business itself in order to maintain morale, but if people are made redundant, it becomes the task of the government or the individuals themselves.

Work in progress

The data in this enquiry are shown in different ways.

Q

1 Look at each graph and explain why that particular type of graph has been used.

2 Look at Figure M1.9 on page 21 and suggest the style of graph that would be most appropriate to present the data.

Point of view

The contract catch

The short-term contract has become an increasingly popular way for business to organise its workforce according to its needs. People are employed for exactly the job that needs to be done – no more, no less. There are many structural savings to be made by reducing the number of permanent staff. They do not need a permanent work space. They probably have no pension rights or sick pay.

But what happens when things go wrong ...

Your agenda

1 What are the advantages and disadvantages of short-term contracts for the employee?

2 Where do people on short-term contracts fit into Maslow's triangle (see page 17)?

3 What problems does this create for the employer?

4 What might businesses do to overcome these problems?

4 What are trade unions for?

What should a trade union do?

	%
Protect existing jobs	33
Improve working conditions	22
Improve pay	21
Have more say over management's long term plans	7
Reduce pay differences at the workplace	4
Have more say about how work is done day to day	2
Work for equal opportunities for women	2

Your agenda

1 What do most people want from their union?

2 Why is there interest in the long-term plans for the business?

3 What factors might affect the power of trade unions?

Figure M1.13 Employees' views about what trade unions should try to do   Source: ONS, Annual Abstract, 1998

Trade unions first appeared in the eighteenth century. By the nineteenth century, they were beginning to be perceived as a threat to employers because, by working as a group, employees had much greater power to negotiate. Laws were passed that banned their activities for a period. Even when legal again,

ways were found of dealing with groups that were becoming too powerful. The Tolpuddle Martyrs, for example, were transported to Australia for seven years, not because they founded a union but because they were found to have taken an illegal oath!

Today trade unions play the same fundamental role

UNISON

- **Holiday club**
- **Credit card**
- **Insurance services**
- **Breakdown services**
- **Building society**

Figure M1.14 The trade union UNISON offers its members a variety of services

in the UK and do not have as many problems with the authorities. Legislation is still, however, used to curtail the extent of their power. The role of the union has changed – as the activities of UNISON in Figure M1.14 show. This union represents people who work in the public services and essential utilities such as water, gas and electricity.

As the nature of employment has changed, union membership has fallen quite markedly. This is partly because the manufacturing industries have always been strongly unionised. The fall in employment in the secondary sector has therefore naturally reduced union membership. The other contributing factor is the increasingly individual nature of employment contracts. People with individual skills are likely to negotiate their own contracts without feeling the need for union representation. Union membership stood at 13 million in 1979 and had fallen to just under 8 million by 1996.

Point of view

Shell and the environment

Large companies generally run their own pension schemes. Employees are usually included among the trustees of their pension schemes. This means that if company shares are part of the pension fund, they can vote at the annual general meeting (AGM), when shareholders can have their say about how the company is run.

Oil and petroleum producer Shell had suffered a loss of reputation because of some of its activities in Africa. Because of this, a resolution demanding improved policies on the environment was being put before the AGM.

The Trades Union Congress (TUC), which represents all trade unions, wrote to all the union members who were trustees and encouraged them to vote on the resolution. It did not tell them how to vote, but the implication was clear.

The World Wide Fund for Nature worked on persuading the financial services provider the Prudential, the largest shareholder in Shell, to vote for the resolution.

Your agenda

1. How does this action fit with the information in Figure M1.13?
2. How was this activity different from the usual trade union activity?
3. Why can working in partnership be more effective than working alone?
4. Why do you think trade unions have broadened their agenda?

The action of the TUC in this case shows how trade unions have become more involved in broader policy work than simply looking after the direct interests of their members. They are prepared to join campaigns which involve working with other organisations to change attitudes and affect issues.

Essentials

Trade unions developed to protect the rights of workers. By working collectively, members of a union have more power to negotiate than they do as individuals.

1 Tough trade-offs?

Rising prices put jobs at risk

WE NEED JOBS!

NO JOB – NO FUTURE!

UK economy falls behind

The headlines show some of the issues that have faced governments. Such problems are not easy to solve because the solutions often have side effects.

Your agenda

1 What might the government do to reduce unemployment?
2 How will it pay for the additional costs of these activities?
3 Draw a flow diagram to show your ideas.
4 Are there any disadvantages to your suggestions?
5 Try the same strategy for rising prices.
6 Are there any contradictions in trying to reduce unemployment and inflation?

The objective of any political party, once in power, is to stay there. Governments are elected and are therefore at the mercy of the electorate. If the policies do not work or are not found acceptable, a party may find itself on the opposition benches in the House of Commons. Unfortunately, for many governments, solutions to problems are not as straightforward as people might think.

The main factors that parties want to influence are:

- inflation
- employment
- economic growth
- standard of living.

Measuring change

There are standard ways of measuring these factors or indicators so that they can be compared on a regular basis:

- **Inflation** is a sustained rise in prices which is measured on a monthly basis. Its results are also clear to see in the Retail Prices Index (RPI). This looks at how the prices of a range of products which people buy on a regular basis change from month to month. It is shown as an index because it makes each month easy to compare with previous months. It works by picking one year as a starting point and calling it 100. Every change is then compared to that base year and it is calculated as a proportion of 100. For example, if 1987 is called 100, by 1998 the index had risen to 162.9, so prices had gone up by nearly 63 per cent.

- **Unemployment** has been counted by using the number of people who are claiming benefit because they do not have a job. In 1998 a second measure was added. This is known as the ILO measure, used by the International Labour Organisation to make international comparisons. It may prove in time to give a more accurate picture.

- **Economic growth** is measured by counting up the total income that is earned in the country. As you might imagine, this is a very complex procedure! Three counts are actually made – total income, total expenditure and total production. They should be the same, but there are always some adjustments to be made because of the difficulty of counting. Index numbers are often used to make comparisons from year to year.

Essentials

Inflation is a sustained rise in prices which is measured by the Retail Prices Index. Small rises of up to 2 per cent are generally thought acceptable. Large rises can damage the economic prospects of a country.

Essentials

Unemployment occurs when there are people who want to work at the going wage but are unable to find a job. High levels of unemployment mean that resources, in the form of people, are being wasted and the government has to pay high levels of benefit.

Essentials

Economic growth is an increase in the total output of the country. It is most frequently measured using gross domestic product (GDP) or national income.

■ Working with index numbers

In 1948 real GDP was £124 billion in the UK. In 1985 it was £306 billion and by 1990 it had grown to £356 billion (all in 1985 prices). To help in interpreting these figures, **index numbers** can be used. Giving an index number value of 100 to the 1985 level of GDP, then the index number value of GDP in 1948 was 40.5 and in 1990 was 116.2. Index numbers, because they are based on 100, are easier to manipulate and interpret than much larger numbers.

To convert a series of statistics to index number form, it is first necessary to call one number 100. This is the *base number*. For instance, assume that the GDP of an economy was £400 million in year 1 and then grows to £600 million in year 10. Then, if we make year 1 the base year and £400 million the base figure of 100, GDP will grow to 150 in year 10. This is because £600 is 50 per cent more than £400.

We can make any year the base year. Depending on which year we take, we get a different series of index numbers. Figure M1.15 shows the value of index numbers for GDP over a twenty-year period depending upon which year is taken as the base year.

	(£ million)	GDP		
		If Year 1 = 100	If Year 10 = 100	If Year 20 = 100
Year 1	400	100	67	33
Year 10	600	150	100	50
Year 20	1200	300	200	100

Figure M1.15 Gross domestic product calculated using different base years

It is possible to use index numbers to represent averages. The RPI is an example of an index which is used to show an average – in this case the price of a typical basket of goods at a particular point in time.

Essentials

Index numbers can be used to make comparisons between a series of large numbers. A selected point is given the value of 100 and the others are compared with it. The RPI is one of the most frequently used examples of an index.

Take care!

Index numbers will not necessarily make allowances for inflation. If, for instance, GDP in one year had an index number value of 75 and in another year 150, we could conclude that GDP had doubled in money terms. If it refers to GDP at **current** prices, we will not know how much of the change is actually just inflation. If we are told that it has been measured in **constant** prices, then we know that GDP doubled in **real** terms, i.e. output actually doubled.

Take care!

Index numbers cause confusion if they are read as absolute values. They are not.

Year	Germany	Japan	UK
1994	100	100	100
1995	101.9	101.4	102.7
1996	103.3	105.5	105.5
1997	105.6	106.4	108.5

Figure M1.16 Gross domestic product

Source: ONS GDP

Figure M1.16 shows why. It uses the patterns of growth experienced in Germany, Japan and the UK as its basis.

Which country had the highest level of GDP in 1997? The answer is that we can't tell. The GDP for each country has been called 100 in 1994, but that does not mean that each country had the same GDP in that year. The GDP of Japan could therefore be twice as much as that of the UK, or half as much – it is impossible to say from this table. But the UK had the highest growth rate of the three countries, an 8.5 per cent increase over four years. Germany, on the other hand, had the lowest growth rate, only 5.6 per cent over four years.

How does inflation affect comparisons?

- In 1948 GDP was £10 398 million in the UK.
- In 1990 GDP was £479 452 million.
- It had multiplied 46 times.
- The country's output of goods and services had not multiplied 46 times.

What had happened?

- Prices had gone up.
- A basket of goods which cost £10 in 1948 cost £160 in 1990.
- Prices had multiplied 16 times.

The figures therefore hide the fact that some of the change was caused by an increase in output, but the rest came from rising prices. It is important to know exactly what story the data are telling or they can be misunderstood.

- If data are described as current, **nominal** or **money**, inflation has not been taken into account.
- If data are described as **real**, inflation has been taken into account.

So – at 1985 prices, GDP in 1948 was £124 billion, while in 1990 it was £350 billion, only a three-fold increase.

Essentials

Real values have been adjusted to allow for inflation and are calculated in **constant prices**.

Essentials

Money values will include some inflation, being given in **current** prices. Another way of describing such data is that they are given in **nominal** terms.

Wages and prices

Are people getting better off?

Year	£
1994	325.7
1995	336.3
1996	351.7
1997	367.6
1998	384.5

Figure M1.17
UK average weekly earnings

Source: ONS, *Annual Abstract of Statistics*, 1999

Year	Index
1989	115.2
1990	126.1
1991	133.5
1992	138.5
1993	140.7
1994	144.1
1995	149.1
1996	152.7
1997	157.5
1998	162.9
1999 est.	165.5

Figure M1.18 UK Retail Prices Index (January 1987 = 100)

Source: ONS, *Annual Abstract of Statistics*, 1999

Your agenda

1 At a glance, what do Figures M1.17 and M1.18 show?

2 How does Figure M1.18 affect your views on Figure M1.17?

3 Why?

4 If prices are rising fast, what do you think happens to wage demands?

5 If wages are rising fast, what do you think happens to prices?

6 Why?

Prices and employment and output

Nothing in the economy can change without having an impact on something else. At a simple level, a rise in petrol prices has a knock-on effect on almost everything. Deliveries become more expensive, bus fares go up and the cost of running a car rises.

The data in Figures M1.17 and M1.18 showed one of these linkages. Prices and earnings are clearly inter-related. If one changes, the other will probably change too. Figures M1.19 and M1.20 look at the relationship between national income and unemployment.

The data in the two case studies above show the changes that have taken place in these key indicators in recent years. As you can see, the economy has been on a generally upward path with some blips. These blips are associated with higher levels of unemployment. The Retail Prices Index has also risen steadily but at a varying pace.

Up and down

Year	Claimant count (000s)
1987	2 192.2
1988	2 315.9
1989	1 813.8
1990	1 638.9
1991	2 223.4
1992	2 725.9
1993	2 916.8
1994	2 651.1
1995	2 327.2
1996	2 135.1
1997	1 586.2
1998	1 346.8

Figure M1.19 UK unemployment, 1987–98
Source: ONS, *Annual Abstract of Statistics*, 1999

Year	£ million
1989	661 956
1990	665 651
1991	651 789
1992	648 975
1993	664 018
1994	693 177
1995	712 548
1996	730 767
1997	756 661
1998	772 268

Figure M1.20 UK GDP, at 1995 price levels
Source: *National Institute Economic Review*, no. 3, 1999

Your agenda

1 Enter the data in Figures M1.19 and M1.20 on a spreadsheet. Include the Retail Prices Index from Figure M1.18.

2 Create three graphs showing the changes in the Retail Prices Index, gross domestic product and unemployment that have taken place between 1987 and 1998.

3 Can you see any relationships between them? Do you think there is any pattern of cause and effect?

2 Decisions, decisions ...

Unemployment under control

When unemployment rises the government can do one of two things. It can either wait for (1) the economy to take its course or (2) intervene.

Solution 1 means that more people are without jobs, which has implications for them and their families as well as the economy as a whole. People who are able to work but are not employed are a waste of resources. They could be contributing to the total output of the country.

Solution 2 means spending money on a variety of strategies to get people back to work. These strategies might involve:

- training schemes to develop new skills
- helping people to move to areas where there are jobs
- assisting employers to take on new staff
- projects which help the economy and employ people.

As these strategies mean increasing expenditure, the government has to decide how to raise the money. There are two basic alternatives: to borrow or to raise taxation. Before making a decision like this, politicians will keep an eye on the electorate. How will it affect their popularity at the next election? Much will depend on their claims in the last party manifesto.

Keeping inflation under control

In general, prices tend to rise. Most of the time they can be contained. Sometimes they get out of hand. The last time prices fell generally was during the 1930s when the whole world was in a slump and countries were producing less and less and millions were unemployed. At the other end of the scale, inflation reached a high point of 26 per cent in the UK in the mid-1970s.

Now inflation is being kept under control by adjusting interest rates. If interest rates rise, people pay more to borrow money, and think twice before adding to their credit card bill or taking out a loan. They may therefore reduce the amount they spend. If many spend less, there will be less pressure on the products in the shops so prices are less likely to rise.

There are some drawbacks to using interest rates like this:

- Businesses often want to borrow money for new developments. If interest rates rise too high, the costs of borrowing may deter firms from carrying out their plans.
- If interest rates in the UK are high, people who trade in currencies want pounds more because they will get a greater return for lending them. As pounds become more popular, the cost of buying them goes up. As a result, their value against other currencies rises. It gets cheaper to go on holiday abroad, but products that we sell to other countries become more expensive. This may hit UK industry. For countries that are members of the European single currency, the cost of holidays in the USA will change but going to Spain will stay the same.

Going for growth

Most people enjoy the benefits of a growing economy. It means more jobs, a rising standard of living and that elusive 'feel-good factor'. Politicians obviously enjoy it because they are more likely to be re-elected. That is why they have at times engineered growth just before an election.

Growth can be achieved by encouraging businesses to expand and people to spend. If it is pushed too far, prices will start to rise because people will want more and more. The economy will then be heading for inflationary problems.

Striking the balance

Every economic decision has a trade-off. 'If we do this, then ... .' Economists can often predict what will happen. The difficulty is knowing the extent of the change. Firm control of inflation may reduce demand in the economy to such an extent that people have little to spend so businesses sell little and may lay people off. Unemployment rises.

Too much government spending to reduce unemployment may lead to inflation as it puts more money into people's pockets.

It is also difficult to get these things just right because economic strategies take time to work and circumstances may change in the mean time. For example, big increases in oil prices can make many things more expensive so that people buy fewer goods and services. This might make unemployment worse. The Chancellor of the Exchequer's role is never an easy one.

Work in progress

	(base year) 1981	1986	1991	1995	1998
Retail Prices Index	100	137	185	208	220
Passenger transport prices:					
Bus and coach fares	100	139	198	252	278
Rail fares	100	137	201	246	278
Purchase of cars, etc	100	116	144	161	174
Petrol and oil	100	145	156	202	240
Maintenance	100	138	195	242	276
Tax and insurance	100	146	220	320	335

Figure M1.21 Travel costs

Source: ONS, *Social Trends*, 1999

Q

1 Why are the figures for the Retail Prices Index here different from those in Figure M1.18?

2 Why do you think 1981 was chosen as a base for the Retail Prices Index in this data set?

3 Compare the relative prices of bus and train fares over the period shown in the data.

4 Do the data tell you whether it is more expensive to travel by car or train? Explain your answer.

5 Was travelling by bus or buying a car relatively more expensive in 1997 than it was in 1981?

6 Use the data plus any economic arguments to persuade a friend into or out of buying a car.

3 But what about the voters?

What do voters want?

Scene: The Ram, Monday, 9.30pm

FRED: Hello George, just arrived? Have you seen the state of that road out there? I must have hit every pot hole in it on the way here.

GEORGE: Yes it's a right mess. I don't know why the council can't do something about it.

FRED: Oh, have you signed the petition they've got behind the bar? You know that they are threatening to close the local hospital again. Well, Brian is getting up a petition. He's got over 200 signatures already.

GEORGE: Pass it over. We can't do without that hospital. It's ten miles to the next nearest. What if I had a heart attack! Talking of heart attacks, did you see that one of the road protestors had one? I bet they took him there.

FRED: They do have a point, that lot. I used to play all over those hills when I was a kid. Can't bear the thought of it all being dug up. The bluebells would never be the same. Why can't they build a tunnel, I wonder?

GEORGE: Are you coming in tomorrow, Fred?

FRED: Yes, I'm going to pop in on my way home from work. You know it's the Budget. We can come and have a moan about taxes going up again. I'm just off to fill up the car and buy in some beer to beat the price rises. Cheerio!

Your agenda

1   Have you ever heard conversations like this before?

2   What is the contradiction in the views they are expressing?

3   Explain why the government has to decide its priorities and how it might go about this.

Fred and George's dilemma is one that faces every government. The voters want everything. Many appear to want more government spending and less taxation, without realising the contradiction of their desires.

Helping the electorate to understand these issues is a challenge for any government, either local or national. It is often done by looking at the relationship between its income and expenditure. Local government is a starting point for this.

Local government

About half the money that local government spends comes from central government. The rest is raised locally within certain constraints. It comes from local taxation in the form of the Council Tax, which is based on the value of the house you live in, and the Uniform Business Rate, which is calculated on the basis of the value of business premises. The remainder is raised from council house rents and other services which the local authority sells.

Local government is responsible for many areas of expenditure and has to decide its priorities. Different parts of the country will have different needs and therefore choices will be made accordingly.

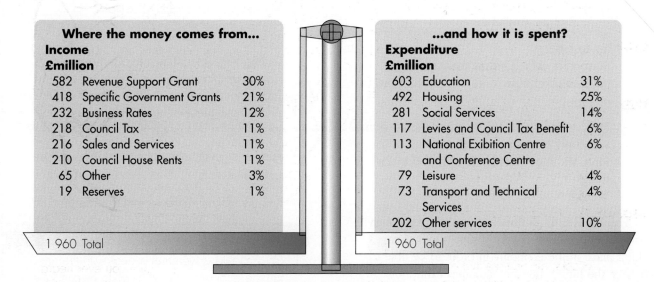

Where the money comes from...

Income
£million

582	Revenue Support Grant	30%
418	Specific Government Grants	21%
232	Business Rates	12%
218	Council Tax	11%
216	Sales and Services	11%
210	Council House Rents	11%
65	Other	3%
19	Reserves	1%

1 960 Total

...and how it is spent?

Expenditure
£million

603	Education	31%
492	Housing	25%
281	Social Services	14%
117	Levies and Council Tax Benefit	6%
113	National Exibition Centre and Conference Centre	6%
79	Leisure	4%
73	Transport and Technical Services	4%
202	Other services	10%

1 960 Total

Fig M1.22 Birmingham's budget   Source: *Budget Summary 1998/9*, Birmingham City Council

Central government

Where does it come from? Where does it go to?

Income (£ billion)		Expenditure (£ billion)	
Income tax	88	Social security	102
Corporation tax	30	Health	61
VAT	54	Housing and environment	13
Excise duties	36		
Business rates	16	Defence	22
Social security contributions	56	Education	41
		Law and order	19
Council tax	13	Transport	9
Other	53	Industry, agriculture and employment	15
		Debt interest	26
		Other spending	41

Figure M1.23 Government income and expenditure, 1999–2000

Source: *The Guardian*, 10 March 1999

Your agenda

1 Create pie graphs from the data in Figure M1.23.

2 Adjust the order of the entries so that the information is in order of size.

3 If you were in control, how would you amend the list of expenditure? Explain why and justify the cuts that you would have to make in some areas.

4 Use the idea of opportunity cost to explain how these choices are made.

5 Do the two columns balance?

6 If not, where does the difference come from or go to?

7 Why might the government decide in a particular year to:
a spend more than it raises
b raise more than it spends?

What decisions does the government have to make about the economy?

■ What are its priorities?
How much does it want to spend in total?
How much does it want to spend on each category?

■ How will the money be raised?
More spending needs more income. It can come either from:
– taxation, which means deciding which type of tax to raise
– borrowing, which means making interest payments in future.

■ What will happen to the economy?
– More spending puts money into the economy so people have more to spend.
– More tax stops people spending on other things.
– What should the balance be?

The answers to all these questions are not easy. Governments collect masses of data about changes taking place in the economy in order to be able to forecast the future, but the outcomes cannot be guaranteed. The UK economy is itself dynamic and is subject to influences from the rest of the world.

Point of view

Can we have it all?

- Macro-economic policy
- Investment
- Training
- Creation of new enterprises
- Regeneration of declining regions
- Ensuring that everyone can work to their full potential
- Coping with the consequences of family change and breakdown
- Changing the dynamics of communities where children are growing up without seeing the prospect of a job or control of their own lives

These are all critical to the future of welfare in Britain.

Source: John Hills, *The Future of Welfare*, Joseph Rowntree Foundation, 1993

Your agenda

1 How should governments deal with the need to run the economy smoothly while meeting the social needs of its population?

2 Why should a government worry about meeting the social needs of the population?

4 The European dimension

Where does the money go?

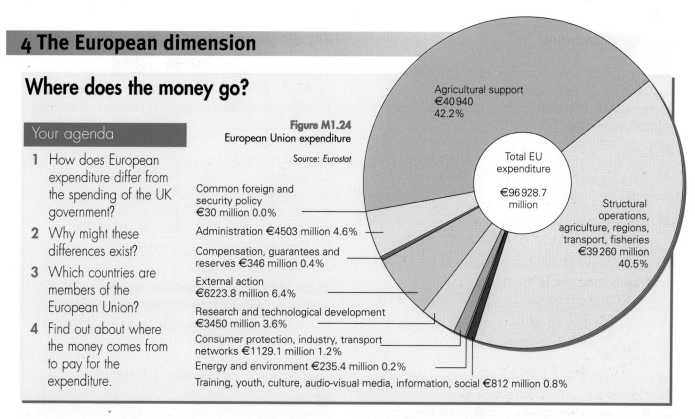

Your agenda

1 How does European expenditure differ from the spending of the UK government?

2 Why might these differences exist?

3 Which countries are members of the European Union?

4 Find out about where the money comes from to pay for the expenditure.

Figure M1.24
European Union expenditure

Source: *Eurostat*

Common foreign and security policy €30 million 0.0%

Administration €4503 million 4.6%

Compensation, guarantees and reserves €346 million 0.4%

External action €6223.8 million 6.4%

Research and technological development €3450 million 3.6%

Consumer protection, industry, transport networks €1129.1 million 1.2%

Energy and environment €235.4 million 0.2%

Training, youth, culture, audio-visual media, information, social €812 million 0.8%

Agricultural support €40 940 42.2%

Total EU expenditure €96 928.7 million

Structural operations, agriculture, regions, transport, fisheries €39 260 million 40.5%

The European Union (EU) is made up of a group of countries which came together to create economic and political security. Since it was established by the Treaty of Rome in 1957, it has grown and developed in a variety of significant ways.

How is it organised?

The EU is run by the following bodies which represent the member countries:

■ The European Council is composed of the heads of government of member countries. It meets at least twice a year.

■ The Council of Ministers meets to discuss topics in particular fields. The Chancellor of the Exchequer will meet other finance ministers to discuss the budget, for example.

■ The European Parliament is made up of elected representatives from member states.

■ The European Commission puts forward proposals to the Council of Ministers and carries out policy.

Agricultural policy

The EU allocates a high proportion of its spending to agricultural support. During the Second World War, the population of Europe nearly starved because it was unable to feed itself. The Atlantic was blockaded and imports were unable to get through. No one wanted this ever to happen again so European governments set up schemes to encourage agricultural production in order to make the continent self-sufficient. These support systems have led to overproduction in many areas and are now gently being dismantled (you will find out more about this in Do markets work? on page 121). It is, of course, very hard to reduce support to farmers who have built a living on the basis of knowing that they will be able to sell whatever they produce at a predetermined price. In countries which have a high percentage of the population in agriculture, governments are having to make tough political decisions.

The single market

The creation of a single market, in which all countries can trade on an equal basis, has led to a need to ensure that all countries play the game. A country which allows children to work in factories, for example, will be able to produce things more cheaply because wages will be lower. As a result, that country will have an advantage over others. The EU has two views on the problem:

■ It should not be allowed because no country should be able to achieve an advantage in this way.

■ It should not be allowed because children should be in school, not in the factory.

The objective of many EU initiatives is to create a 'level playing field' on which no country has any advantage. This often involves social legislation as the conditions in which people work generally affect costs of production. The environment is another area where laws determine how industry behaves.

The movement towards a single currency throughout Europe will lead to a progressive harmonisation of policies designed to control member countries' economies.

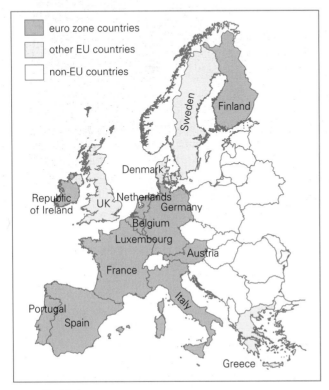

Figure M1.25 The euro zone

The single currency

The 1 January 1999 marked a great event in the history of the EU. Eleven countries took the initial steps in the transition period to the common currency – the euro.

The euro zone

The first eleven were:

Austria	Luxembourg
Belgium	Netherlands
Finland	Portugal
France	Republic of Ireland
Germany	Spain.
Italy	

Those which chose to join were supposed to have achieved certain objectives. If the single currency was to work, the economies had to be in line with each other as they would need to run similar economic policies. Participating countries were asked therefore to meet the following criteria:

■ The budget deficit had to be less than 3 per cent of GDP.

■ The government's total debt had to be less than 60 per cent of GDP.

■ Inflation had to be less than 1.5 per cent higher than the average of the three lowest inflation countries.

■ Exchange rates should be stable.

■ Interest rates should be in line with others and stable.

The key objective was to achieve stability. Businesses involved in international trade were keen because:

■ within the member countries, the stable value of the euro would enable companies to plan ahead

■ there would be no need to change money from one currency to another so money would be saved on the transaction.

Some argue that it is a political move rather than an economic one, but only the future can tell.

1. Why does business care?

A helping hand

Brownie and Rainbow Guides need your tokens...

Andrex® PUPPY APPEAL
1972-1997

...to help Andrex® raise £500,000 for Guide Dogs for the blind

Your agenda

1 What return does each of these businesses receive from their sponsorship?

2 Why do you think these businesses decide to spend money in this way?

3 How do ideas from earlier in this module help to explain their actions?

Who comes first?

Business, in general, has long considered that the needs of the shareholders are paramount. As shareholders have invested their money in the company, their reward must always be the most important concern when making decisions about how the business will be run.

There are exceptions to this rule because some notable businesses have always had a wider agenda.

Confectionery manufacturers Cadbury's and Rowntrees, for example, were very concerned about the well-being of their employees and the local community.

Quite recently, some businesses have realised that by taking a broader view of their responsibilities shareholders could benefit even more. Research in the field has demonstrated that there is a relationship between looking after **stakeholders** and benefits to shareholders.

Who are the stakeholders?

Stakeholders are all people who are affected by the behaviour of a business.

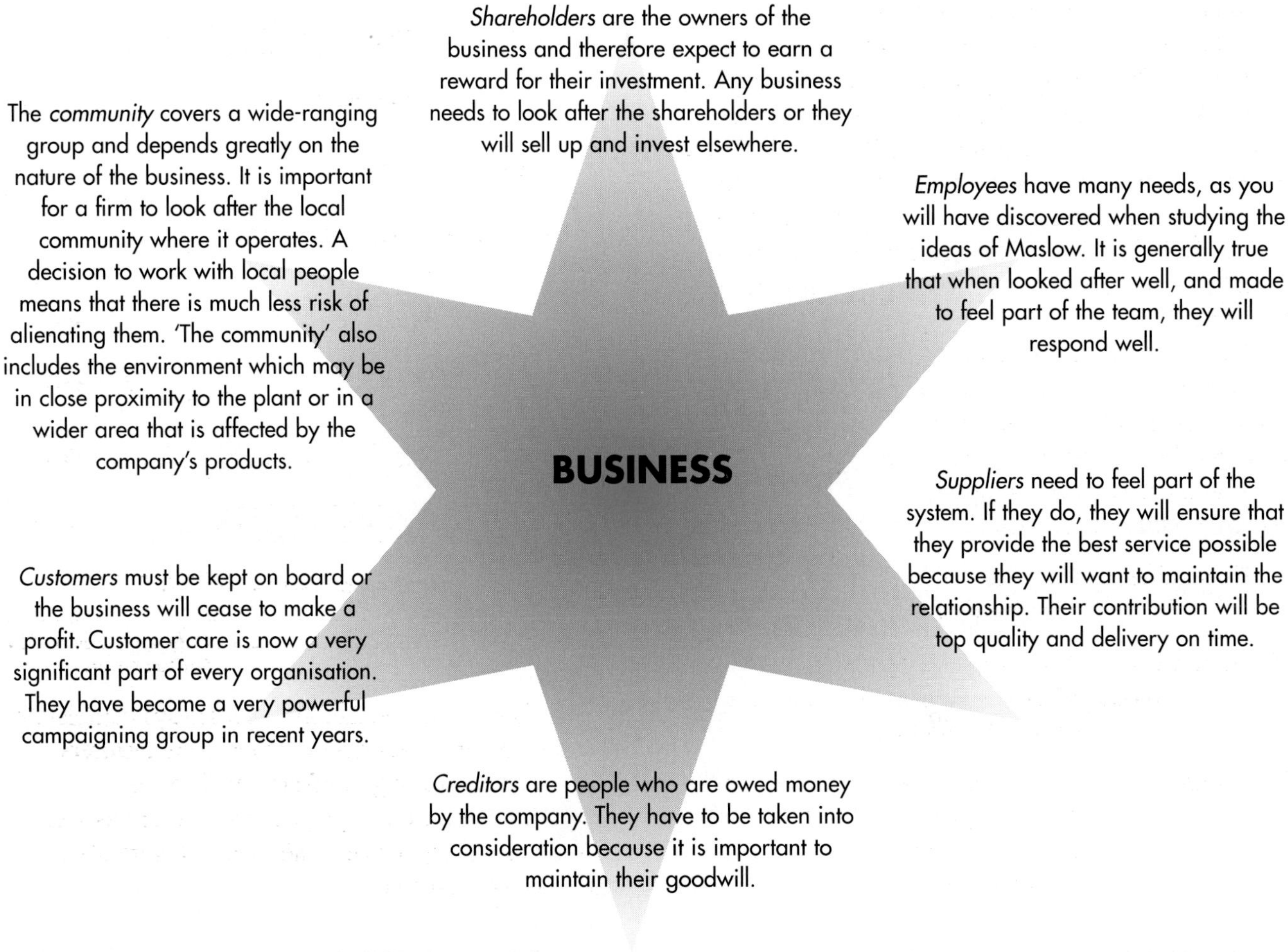

Shareholders are the owners of the business and therefore expect to earn a reward for their investment. Any business needs to look after the shareholders or they will sell up and invest elsewhere.

The *community* covers a wide-ranging group and depends greatly on the nature of the business. It is important for a firm to look after the local community where it operates. A decision to work with local people means that there is much less risk of alienating them. 'The community' also includes the environment which may be in close proximity to the plant or in a wider area that is affected by the company's products.

Employees have many needs, as you will have discovered when studying the ideas of Maslow. It is generally true that when looked after well, and made to feel part of the team, they will respond well.

BUSINESS

Suppliers need to feel part of the system. If they do, they will ensure that they provide the best service possible because they will want to maintain the relationship. Their contribution will be top quality and delivery on time.

Customers must be kept on board or the business will cease to make a profit. Customer care is now a very significant part of every organisation. They have become a very powerful campaigning group in recent years.

Creditors are people who are owed money by the company. They have to be taken into consideration because it is important to maintain their goodwill.

Figure M1.26 A business's stakeholders

In deciding who comes first, there is often a trade-off. Actions that will give immediate profit and therefore benefit the shareholders, may not be in their long-term interest. By taking a longer view and looking after other stakeholders, there may be an even better outcome.

The reputations of companies, particularly those which deal directly with the general public, are extremely easy to dent. When oil and petroleum producer Shell had environmental problems in Nigeria, its products were boycotted in Germany and a petrol station was burnt down. This is an extreme example but shows how violent consumer reaction can be. Once a reputation has been damaged, it is hard to rebuild.

> **Essentials**
>
> **Stakeholders** are all those individuals and groups which have a 'stake' in a company. They therefore include the employees, suppliers, creditors, customers, shareholders and local communities which are affected by the actions of the business.

2 Counting the kudos

It is not easy to draw definite conclusions about the impact for a business of spending time and money on investment in the community. It is much easier to be wise after the event, when things have gone wrong!

Research has shown a correlation between looking after stakeholders and looking after shareholders. In retailing, it worked particularly well. The data in Figure M1.27 show that retailers Boots and Marks & Spencer scored well on both counts whereas Sears and Burtons did relatively badly on both. The data are not up to the minute because this sort of research is not carried out annually.

The comparison was made by asking the questions outlined below about how the company had treated different stakeholders. The question of reputation was answered by looking at how each company ranked in the 'The Most Admired Company' survey in the magazine *Management Today*.

■ Shareholders – How much had their shares earned over the past five years?

■ Employees – What has happened to pay? What has happened to the number of people employed?

■ Community – What percentage of revenue did the company give to charity? What percentage of profit did the company pay in taxes?

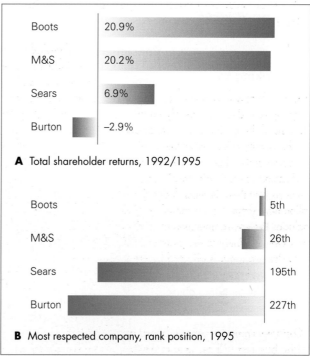

A Total shareholder returns, 1992/1995

B Most respected company, rank position, 1995

Figure M1.27 Who cares wins?   Source: Compustat Data provided by Standard & Poor's

Of course, the correlation is not always completely accurate. A similar exercise for food manufacturers shows that despite high rankings in all other categories, Cadbury's employees did not fare as well when it came to pay rises. The data in Figure M1.28 show the comparison.

	Total shareholder return	Reputation	Taxes paid % profit	Charity contribution % turnover	Salary increase	Employment growth
Guinness	19.3%	14	30.2%	0.052%	5.0%	−2.85%
Cadbury	14.3	4	30.4%	0.017%	1.25%	4.55%
Unigate	8.6%	171	26.8%	0.009%	3.9%	0.28%
Hillsdown Holdings	−4.1%	215	27.2%	0.008%	3.3%	−8.46%

Figure M1.28 Food manufacturers   Source: Compustat Data provided by Standard & Poor's

Point of view 66 99

Whose values?

	Consumers	Business
Ranking by perceived importance		
Medical/health	1	7
Education	2	1
Environment	3	4
People with disabilities	4	–
Children's disabilities	5	3
Poverty and social hardship in the UK	6	5
Housing/homeless	7	10
Animal rights and protection	8	11
Alcohol and drug abuse	9	–
Community issues	10	–
Third world causes	11	9
Youth development	12	6
Urban regeneration	13	8
The arts	14	2

Your agenda

1 Does corporate sponsorship match the consumers' list of causes?
2 What sort of areas have the greatest similarity?
3 Which have the greatest difference?
4 Can you think of any reasons that might account for these differences?

Figure M1.29 Ranking by perceived importance

Source: *The Winning Game*, Business in the Community, 1997

3 What is the trend?

There has been a growing trend for businesses to be more closely involved with their stakeholders. The growing awareness that reputation is an important contributor to competitiveness has enhanced this trend.

In today's media age, when everyone knows instantly when a business is in difficulties, and customers are increasingly vociferous, a good reputation can help a business to ride rough times.

The commitment to stakeholders may also vary according to the state of the economy and the business's profit levels. In good times, a company will probably be prepared to spend more on such activities than when money is tight and profits fall.

The size of the business will also affect attitudes. Although small organisations may sponsor the local cricket club for a weekend or provide a rubbish bin in the local shopping centre, in general their involvement in the community is substantially less.

Large organisations have the resources to look after staff on a different scale. Many big companies have elaborate sports and social clubs for example, which, of course, contribute to employees' sense of well-being. Small companies can achieve a very effective corporate spirit through different sorts of activities, but it is probably not as easy to identify how it happens.

Pressure groups have become very powerful agents for change. Many large businesses have faced criticism from them. Some companies have begun a trend by collaborating with pressure groups rather than simply rebutting the criticism.

4 Always a rosy picture?

No! No! No!

From the Springfield Argus, 12 May 1999

The cry of protestors and hoots from passing cars drowned the noise of contractors in Hill Road today. The placards carried messages from the local population – Save the Hill Road Shops – Save the Hill Road Trees – Save the Hill Road Children.

A chain of local mums and their children encircled the trees so that the saws could not get near. The trees must go before supermarket building can begin. The developers went home for the day. They could not be seen to tangle with such protesters.

When asked about the development, the supermarket company claims that there is plenty of demand for the new shop. The nearest alternative is five miles away at the other end of town. Traffic jams the local roads so a shopping expedition can take all day.

Ann Shoesmith, who lives a mile from the new site confirmed their views. 'It takes me hours to shop at the other end of town. I'm really looking forward to being able to shop here. It'll be great for me!'

Not everyone agrees.

Your agenda

1 Why does the company want to develop this site?

2 What objections do the protesters have? Why?

3 What might the company do to make the development less sensitive?

4 What is the role of local government in decisions such as this?

Local papers are full of horror stories about new hypermarkets damaging local communities, the development of office blocks rather than housing and a myriad of other activities.

Why does business do it? The profit motive is very strong so the supermarket chain will seek to establish a national network which will optimise its coverage of the country. The case study above shows the sort of issue that may be involved. There will always be some members of the community that are keen for developments to take place. It is often the case that the protesters have a louder voice than the supporters. In the end, the decision has to be made by the local authority which is expected to take everyone's point of view into account.

Issues can also arise over financial matters. There is evidence that some large organisations have a poor record when it comes to paying bills. This, of course, has a negative effect on creditors. Small firms have complained vociferously that this makes their financial situation difficult. Having supplied products, they expect to be paid in a given period of time. If nothing is forthcoming, it becomes impossible to pay their own bills.

Small businesses often have to be more careful because banks regard them as a greater financial risk and will not allow overdrafts to be extended for long. Eventually, a small business may go under if its cash flow is affected in this way.

There are many other ways in which conflict may arise among stakeholders as their interests will inevitably differ. Businesses have to decide whether they can afford the damage to their reputation which may occur if an issue becomes public knowledge.

5 Who takes charge?

There are two types of relationship between a business and its stakeholders:

■ the way that it carries out its business activities

■ activities in which business engages in order to build reputation.

These two categories are in many ways intertwined. Oil and petroleum producer BP Amoco, for example, needs to keep the local community on its side in areas where it extracts oil. It will therefore concentrate resources on activities such as working with schools in the locality or looking after the environment. This gives it a 'licence to operate' by being seen to make its contribution to the community.

Some activities are simply aimed at putting the company's name in front of the public. The multi-national drinks group Allied Domecq, in linking its name with the Royal Shakespeare Company, seeks to create an image of a high-class product to which people might aspire.

In general, most of these schemes have no negative effects on stakeholders and contribute to organisations which benefit from the link.

Occasionally, such links are identified as problematic. Cigarette companies' sponsorship of motor racing was a case in point. As cigarette advertising has been strictly controlled, it appeared that the rules were being flouted by formula one cars rushing round the track adorned with famous brand names. To contend with this problem, an international agreement was drawn up to reduce the link gradually until cars would no longer carry such logos.

The relationship between schools and business has always been carefully considered because of the fear that companies would use such links as marketing opportunities to catch a vulnerable section of the market. Most businesses have worked responsibly with educational organisations because they are well aware that regulation might lead to greater restrictions.

When such activities are undertaken with care and thought, everyone wins. The business gains in reputation and wins the respect of its stakeholders. The partner organisations gain from the support, whether financial or in kind. If relationships become exploitative, the end result will be legislation, which would be difficult to frame and might lead to the withdrawal of business from such activities.

6 Who's responsible?

Which role?

1 Identify the different roles that you can see in the pictures.

2 Can you think of any ways in which there might be conflict between these roles in terms of:

   a How the government, both local and national, should raise and spend its money

   b How business should treat its stakeholders

   c The responsibility of an employee.

3 How many roles do you have? Do any conflict? How do you decide which is most important?

Few people have only one role at any one time. It is not impossible that an individual may find conflict between his or her roles. If you work in a supermarket, the manager may demand that you work more hours than is good for your A-level course. You have a decision to make.

People have to make all sorts of decisions which reflect their responsibilities to themselves and others.

Responsibilities to ourselves mean that we make decisions about our training and employment. There are many trade-offs involved. Are three years at university worth the investment of time and loss of earnings in the short run? There are many decisions of this order which affect each of us personally. There are also decisions which demonstrate our responsibility to others and the community. Do we recycle our newspapers? Do we turn off the tap while we clean our teeth? Do we pay our taxes?

Attitudes change as time passes. Environmental issues, for example, have become much more significant during the last 30 years. Government intervention in support of the individual has been reduced. People now have to take much more responsibility for their own financial well-being as benefits and pensions provide less support.

Some areas of such decision-making are taken out of our hands because the government has already decided. If people and businesses will not act in the best interest of others, government often legislates to protect people or the environment, for example.

Individuals are responsible for providing most of their needs. However, because there are some things which people cannot or will not provide for themselves, the government raises taxes in order to meet the need. Health, education, roads and defence are all in this category. The responsibility that a government takes when it comes to spending will depend on the political stance of the party which holds power.

People and governments are constantly using opportunity cost in order to weigh up alternatives and make decisions about the future.

What does business do?

Enquiry 1   What makes a market?

1 How do markets work?

Markets and markets

A market stall

An estate agent   E-commerce

A fund manager

Your agenda

1 What do the markets illustrated here have in common?

2 What sorts of competition will the street trader and the estate agent face?

3 Fund managers don't sell oranges and mail order is not generally used for selling houses. Why do each of the markets illustrated deal in a very limited range of products?

4 Explain what the consequences will be if many people have rising incomes and want to buy bigger houses.

5 The people in the pictures deal in both goods and services. The fund manager invests on behalf of customers. The estate agent sells marketing services. Give three examples of markets which are quite different from those illustrated.

Markets come in many forms. Where there is a **market**, there are buyers and sellers. They will communicate, but not necessarily face to face. This means that a market is quite often not located in a specific place.

A deal takes place when both buyer and seller are ready to exchange something at a price they can agree on. Both of them expect to be better off as a result. Usually, the seller sets the price, though some change price quite often in response to circumstances. However, there are a number of markets where the price is negotiated. People haggle until they can agree.

The more sellers there are in any one market, the more competition there will be. Sellers watch each others' actions. If one cuts prices, the competitors will often follow suit. Competition usually means that buyers get better value for their money. Equally, a few sellers, each facing little competition, have much more freedom to decide to raise the price.

Essentials

A **market** is any medium through which buyers and sellers can reach agreement to trade at a price.

Specialisation and exchange

In ancient times, our ancestors could do most things for themselves: to a large degree families were self-sufficient. But even then within the family, men tended to be involved in food production, women in food preparation. They specialised.

Today self-sufficiency is very rare. We saw in the last unit (page 18) that most people specialise in activities in which they have some advantage. Then they exchange what they produce for other things which they need. Teachers of Economics and Business are specialised in spreading understanding of their subjects. They can exchange their earnings for food, housing, clothing and various sources of enjoyment.

The more specialised people become, the more important it is to have efficient ways of exchanging goods and services for money. Many people are doing less and less for themselves. It is very tempting to buy processed foods which save on cooking time. People who do not cook very often do not become good at it! By specialising in their line of work, they earn more and can afford ready-cooked meals. The same people may have money but little time and become energetic mail-order customers. In this way new markets spring up all the time to meet new needs.

Specialisation is very important because it enables people to get better at what they do. Their output rises and the costs of producing fall. Overall, we all produce much more by specialising. (Remember the story of Adam Smith's visit to the pin factory on page 18?) The process contributes to rising standards of living.

Having markets which work well to bring buyers and sellers together is essential in facilitating the exchange of specialised people's products. If we could not exchange our output for money, and then for goods and services, we would not specialise.

The labour market

Everyone who wants to work is a potential seller in the labour market. In practice, though, most people are in one area of the labour market where sellers specialise in a particular set of skills. The demand for their services comes from an employer who needs those skills to create a product which is itself in demand. So ultimately, demand for labour comes from customers.

People with very scarce skills can command higher rates of pay. Computer systems specialists are in considerable demand. However, if more people train in this field there will be more competition, and pay may become less attractive.

Of course, some people are special. Think of your favourite band. Its members are probably very specialised in making a particular style of music. Can anyone compete with them? If not, their pay may be very substantial, but will they retain their uniqueness and popularity in the future?

The impact of competition

Most people find they are competing with other people who have specialised in the same area. This means we compete with other people who might be capable of doing our jobs when we apply for them. Competition helps to create choices.

If you were the only person selling oranges, you would be able to put the price up and still find buyers. In fact, many people sell oranges and so they will compete for buyers by keeping their prices low. Consumers benefit. What sellers will try to avoid doing is selling the oranges at less than the price they paid for them.

Work in progress

Q

1 Give four examples of markets which are organised without face-to-face communication.

2 Think of five items which might be sold at a price agreed by negotiation between buyer and seller.

3 Why do most people specialise in producing one or a few products?

4 Why will businesses usually not sell their products for less than they paid to get or produce them?

5 Close the book and explain in your own words what a market is and why markets are important. (This is not quite as simple as it sounds.)

2 Supply and price

Deciding what to grow

For many years, Jack Mackenzie grew chrysanthemums. He had a good local market for them, selling to a number of florist shops where he could get £1 per bunch. He sent the rest of his blooms to the market in Brighton, where they usually fetched 75p. He could keep production going all the year round because he had a system of heating, lighting and blackout which enabled him to fool the plants into thinking it was their autumn flowering time, at any time of year.

Then things started to change. He found that imports from African countries and from the Netherlands were able to undercut his prices. This didn't matter with the local florists, but it reduced his sales in the wholesale market seriously. He found that the only way to sell his flowers was to accept a price of 50p. This was below his costs and made production uneconomic.

Jack decided to look for an alternative product. Lilies seemed appropriate: they required similar conditions to the chrysanthemums so he could use all his existing equipment in the same way. He could sell them for £1.50 to the florists or for £1 in the market. They were a bit more trouble to grow, but the higher price made the effort worthwhile.

After a while Jack worked out how changing prices would affect his best strategy. So long as he could continue to get £1 per bunch, it paid him to continue producing chrysanthemums for the local florists. However, they would only take 1500 bunches a week. It made sense for him to turn over the rest of his glasshouse space to producing lilies which he could sell for higher prices in both the florists and the market.

If you added up all the production from UK growers at a range of prices, you might get a result something like Figure M1.30, showing how rising prices provide an incentive to produce more.

These figures can be graphed. Notice that when we graph supply and demand, quantity is *always* on the horizontal axis and price on the vertical axis.

Price of lilies	Quantity produced per week	Price of chrysanthemums	Quantity produced per week
50p	0	50p	50 000
75p	15 000	75p	250 000
£1.00	120 000	£1.00	450 000
£1.25	225 000	£1.25	600 000
£1.50	300 000		

Figure M1.30 Price and quantity

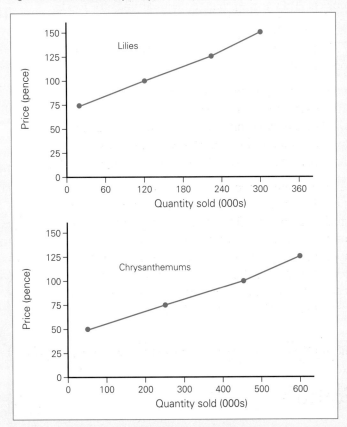

Figure M1.31 Supply and demand

Your agenda

1 Why do you think no lilies at all will be produced at 50p per bunch?

2 Explain why increasing quantities of flowers will be grown at successively higher prices.

3 What would happen if an increase in the minimum wage meant that the growers had to pay higher wages to their employees?

A product is only brought to the market if its costs of production are exceeded by its likely selling price. In other words, price – and the corresponding profit – is the incentive for a firm to supply any given product. Below 75p in the above case study, it is simply not worthwhile for the growers to produce lilies at all. As the price rises, they become increasingly profitable. If the prices of other flowers are less attractive, growers will switch to lilies to make a better profit.

The relationship between price and quantity supplied can be presented as a graph showing the **supply curve**. The supply curve is usually upward sloping, since – all other factors remaining unchanged – a higher price implies higher profit and therefore a greater incentive to produce.

It is important to notice that supply curves are constructed on certain key assumptions:

- They represent the industry or a given sector of the market and not an individual firm.
- They are based on a highly competitive market where the products of different firms are very similar and individual firms cannot influence prices.

Below a certain price, no firm is willing to supply any units of a product at all. Then a low price is reached at which the first firm finds it worth supplying a small output to the market. At successively higher prices, more firms begin to supply and existing firms supply more. We can see that higher prices are acting like a beacon in attracting firms to start or increase output. Resources are drawn into the industry.

Could the supply curve change?

Life never stays the same for long. Supposing new safety regulations come into force, requiring horticulture workers to have regular health checks. At the same time, extra safety equipment is required and this is costly to provide. The cost of growing a given quantity of flowers will rise.

What will happen to the supply curve? Costs have risen. Whatever the quantity, the price required to induce growers to produce it will rise. The supply curve will shift in the way shown in Figure M1.32.

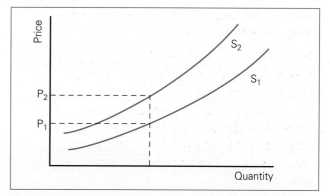

Figure M1.32 A change in costs and a shift in supply

Essentials

The **supply curve** gives the relationship between price and quantity supplied when shown on a graph. It is usually upward sloping to the right because higher prices provide a greater incentive to produce.

3 Putting supply and demand together

Footballs

During the 1998 World Cup tournament, massive TV and other media coverage helped cause a surge in the popularity of football. Demand for footballs increased worldwide. People who had never thought of playing football before suddenly became interested. This was not due to any change in their price. In fact, at any price charged, there would have been a greater quantity demanded.

Your agenda

1 How would you feel about this change if you were a producer of footballs? What would your reaction be?

2 What would you expect to happen to the price of footballs? Explain the likely sequence of events.

Think about the production of plastic footballs. Why, at a given price, do firms not produce more? Because it is more profitable to produce something else. In other words, the opportunity cost of producing extra footballs is too high, but at a higher price it becomes worth producing more footballs and less of 'something else'. For these extra units of output, price has exceeded opportunity cost (the profit on 'something else'). In effect, the gradient of the supply curve illustrates price overcoming the opportunity costs of production.

It is important now to look at demand again. At a high price for footballs, value for money is poor and consumers will want only small amounts of the product. The alternatives are too attractive. Put another way, the opportunity cost is too high. At lower prices consumers will find higher value for money in buying footballs and increase their demand. This improving value for money is, in effect, overcoming the opportunity cost of expenditure on footballs.

We can now combine the supply and demand curves in a single diagram. In Figure M1.33 there is a price at which the number of footballs people want to buy is exactly equal to the quantity producers want to sell.

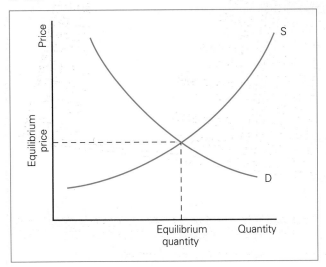

Figure M1.33 Demand and supply for footballs

This point, where quantity supplied and quantity demanded are the same, is important. It is called the **equilibrium price** because supply and demand balance at that point. Another name for this price is the **market clearing price**. We sometimes say 'The market has cleared' because everything that sellers

want to sell has actually been bought. There will be no unsold stocks and no disappointed customers.

> **Essentials**
>
> The **equilibrium price** is the price at which the amount buyers demand and the amount sellers supply is exactly the same.

> **Essentials**
>
> The **market clears** when there are no unsold stocks and no customers unable to obtain the product.

Thinking about changes – demand

When the world went football crazy, what happened to demand for footballs? We can show the consequences with a supply and demand diagram. Figure M1.34 shows demand for footballs increasing at all prices. The demand curve shifts to the right. The equilibrium price rises and so does the quantity sold.

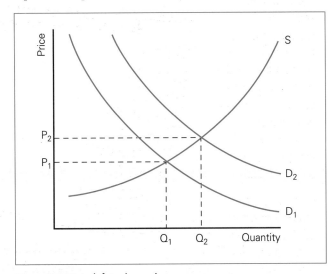

Figure M1.34 A shift in demand

Will this situation last? It is really just a short-run event, because even if demand for footballs stays higher than before, more football producers will be attracted into the market quite quickly. Competition from these new producers will drive the price back down to its original level. This will be a little above the cost of the inputs needed to produce them – just enough to give businesses an incentive to produce. We can be sure that the price will stay much the same, though the quantity sold will probably be higher.

Although a change like this may not affect price in the long run, it is still very important. What you are seeing is the market economy at work. Market forces are drawing extra resources into the production of something people want to consume in greater quantities.

The football story was all about a change in tastes or fashions. Changes in demand can equally well come from changing incomes, or changes in prices of other products. The arrival of a cheap substitute will reduce demand, shifting the demand curve to the left. A change in the price of a complement will also be important from time to time.

4 Is equilibrium always possible?

Fresh from the sea

Until 1996 Sarah Hart worked as a chef for a number of large caterers. After experience in Paris and at a five-star hotel in London, she decided to take a risk and start her own business – as a fishmonger.

Fish From the Quayside is situated in Devon, in the centre of a small but busy town with a significant tourist trade. Sarah buys most of her fish direct from local wholesalers at Brixham and Plymouth with daily deliveries fresh from the sea. The reputation of her business has been built on the quality and variety of her produce combined with personal service and imaginative advice on fish recipes.

Every day Sarah places her orders for fish based on the latest quayside prices. These are variable and largely unpredictable.

Outside the shop are large blackboards displaying the current prices of fish varieties in the shop.

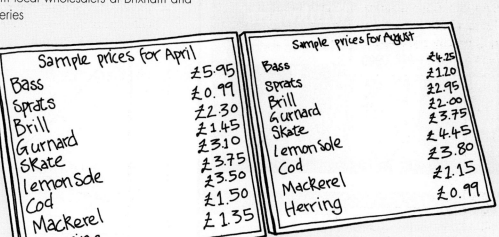

Sample prices for April

Bass	£5.95
Sprats	£0.99
Brill	£2.30
Gurnard	£1.45
Skate	£3.10
Lemon sole	£3.75
Cod	£3.50
Mackerel	£1.50
Herring	£1.35

Sample prices for August

Bass	£4.25
Sprats	£1.20
Brill	£2.95
Gurnard	£2.00
Skate	£3.75
Lemon sole	£4.45
Cod	£3.80
Mackerel	£1.15
Herring	£0.99

Your agenda

1 What specific factors might influence the demand for fish?

2 Draw diagrams showing the likely effect on price and quantity supplied if:

   a a period of stormy weather prevents many fishing boats from leaving port

   b the media carry news of a health scare connected with fish and chemical contamination of the sea.

3 Why do you think the prices vary between April and August?

Retail fish prices are quite variable. The price adjusts whenever there is a change in demand or in supply. Prices are not controlled in any way, so if supplies change, or quantity demanded alters, a price change follows. The new equilibrium price ensures that the quantity supplied and the quantity demanded are the same.

A different situation

Houses

In 1999, houses were selling very fast in London. Estate agents were begging people to put their homes on the market as they had nothing to sell. Prices were rising fast.

Your agenda

1 Why might homes have been selling so fast?
2 What would buyers need to do if they were determined to find something?
3 Can the prices of houses be set in advance?
4 What happens to sellers when no one wants to buy?

Houses are different from fish in that prices do not adjust so easily. Rising incomes make people want bigger houses. Some people who previously rented will come into the market for smaller houses. It is not possible suddenly to build more of them. People will snap up any house that comes on the market. You can see what happens in Figure M1.35. The quantity

demanded will be greater than the quantity supplied. This is called **excess demand**. In the housing market, people sometimes will say 'It's a sellers' market'. Eventually, the excess demand will go away as prices rise and some people find they cannot afford what they want, but the adjustment takes time.

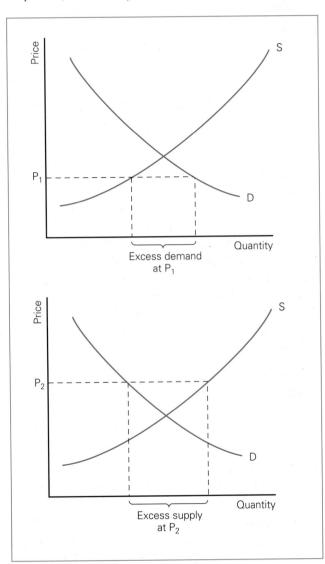

Figure M1.35 Excess demand and excess supply

The opposite will happen if many people have recently been made redundant and some of them have to sell their homes. Finding a buyer may be difficult. It may be some time before sellers decide to reduce the price. Until they do, there will be more sellers than buyers. This is called **excess supply**. Quantity supplied is greater than quantity demanded. The price is above the equilibrium level and the market will not clear.

Essentials

Excess demand – a situation in which the quantity demanded is greater than the quantity supplied at current prices.

Essentials

Excess supply – the quantity which people want to buy is less than the quantity people want to sell at current prices.

Excess supply can be seen when there are unsold stocks. Sellers will reduce prices, hold sales, or even simply hold on to their product in the hope of a change in the market. Excess demand shows itself in a shortage. Some customers will have to wait for the product.

Excess supply or excess demand both mean that the market is in disequilibrium. Usually some kind of change will take place, and a new equilibrium price will be the result. In some markets this happens quite quickly. In others, prices are sticky downwards and adjust rather slowly. Fish markets clear quite quickly: the fish are perishable and sellers will try to get rid of them, at least to the freezer. Usually, markets take time to clear.

Work in progress

Q Draw supply and demand diagrams to illustrate the following changes:

a Rising incomes affect the market for hotel beds in London. What happens to the price of an overnight stay?

b Cheap imports of good-quality cotton towels become available. What is the effect on the market for towels produced in the UK?

c Employees in the UK car industry secure a good pay increase. What happens to the price and quantity of cars sold?

d The government decides to subsidise rail travel and fares are cut. What happens to the demand for petrol?

Point of view

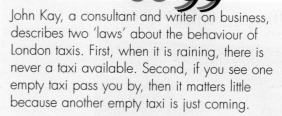

John Kay, a consultant and writer on business, describes two 'laws' about the behaviour of London taxis. First, when it is raining, there is never a taxi available. Second, if you see one empty taxi pass you by, then it matters little because another empty taxi is just coming.

These sound like anecdotes with little meaning. Actually, they are fair observations with an economic explanation. Taxi fares are not fixed by the forces of demand and supply but by the government in the form of the Home Office.

Your agenda

1 How would you explain John Kay's two 'laws' of London taxis?

2 Draw a diagram to show what is happening when there are no taxis available.

3 If Home Office control over fares was abolished, how might taxi users be affected? Why?

4 Why are excess demand and excess supply likely to develop quite often with London taxis?

1 What is value?

Buffing up value?

The car in the picture is not worth much. It probably will not sell at the asking price. Yet it goes. What is it really worth?

At car auctions, where motor dealers buy their stock, there is usually a valeting service available. Some dealers have been known to buy a car, have it cleaned and sell it in the space of an hour or so at a profit.

Your agenda

1 Has the cleaning added to the value of the car? Why?
2 Has the person who bought the car from the dealer been cheated?

What is a second-hand car worth? Someone who bought a car for £10 000 a year ago will not appreciate being told that it is worth £6000 now. A 'reasonable' figure, he or she might feel, would be £8000. Perhaps the car was originally overpriced. Perhaps the model is moving out of fashion? Maybe a few scratches spoil its appearance? The owner may feel strongly that it is 'worth' £8000, but if a buyer can only be found at £6000, then that is its market value.

Markets, in other words, decide value. What people feel something is – or should be – worth does not affect its market value. Of course, a car or any other product may have a special value to its *owner*, but if no one else feels the same way about the item, then the private sense of value remains purely personal.

It is tempting to think that some sources of value are more 'real' than others. A road-worthy second-hand car has value because it is a means of transport and other similar cars have a comparable value, but it may also have value because it is a status symbol. This source of value is not derived from anything objective that can be measured, but from the buyer's subjective *feelings*. So how does the buyer feel about a car that has grimy paintwork, dirty upholstery and a grubby dashboard? Negative feelings subtract value.

Once valeted, the car creates a very different impression. The price that buyers are prepared to pay may increase sharply. The fact that they could have cleaned it themselves does not affect its value now. Having someone clean up the car gives it **added value**. The same principle applies to almost any business enterprise.

The Rumours Restaurant

Your agenda

1 At the Rumours Restaurant, the cost of the food itself represents 15–25 per cent of the menu price. How useful is this information when thinking about:
   a added value?   **b** profit?

2 How would you imagine that Rumours adds value?

3 A customer describes Rumours as 'good value for money' after paying £8.95 for Mediterranean vegetables that might have cost £1 in the market. What exactly does she mean?

4 If restaurants add value, do supermarkets?

Added value

Any firm that does not add value will make losses and soon be forced out of business. Supermarkets add value in a wide variety of ways. Figure M1.36 shows some of the important functions which add value.

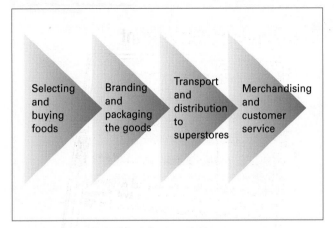

Figure M1.36 Added value in the supermarket

These value adding activities form a sequence called a value chain. In practice, each activity in Figure M1.36 can be subdivided into many more value chains that will be complex in their pattern and interaction. But the principle of always trying to add more value at less cost remains the same.

During the 1990s, Tesco and Sainsbury's were locked in a dramatic battle for supremacy in the national groceries market. At the start of the decade Sainsbury's was ahead of Tesco in terms of market share and profit margins. The company had traditionally enjoyed an enviable reputation for quality with profit margins that no other chain could match. Then, under the leadership of Ian McLaurin, Tesco launched a programme of massive expansion while driving up quality – and profit margins. To counteract the advance of Tesco, David Sainsbury was forced to sacrifice his margin advantage. But his market share was still overtaken by Tesco.

During this battle, both supermarket chains searched for new ways to add value. Marks & Spencer had already established itself as the leading supplier of high-quality ready-prepared meals. These carry a high level of added value relative to cost. Like all 'honey pots' of profit, this market soon attracted competitors. The supermarket chains such as Sainsbury's and Tesco launched their own ranges of ready-prepared meals while finding new ways of adding value to many other conventional products.

2 What adds value?

Value is added by the **factors of production**. These include labour, capital, land and enterprise (the role of the entrepreneur). Labour – or human resources – provides a prime source of added value. The amount of labour (measured by time) and the quality of that labour (measured by skill) are critical to adding value in many products, especially services. Then there is the use of capital – buildings, machinery and other equipment. Land is used to provide the necessary space in which production can take place. Finally, there is the role of the entrepreneur in combining materials, labour, capital and land in the hope of making a profit, but with the risk of making a loss. This input is also a source of added value since without the entrepreneur, the contributions of the other factors could never take place.

Factors of production are used to process raw materials or to assemble components or to provide services. A school uses land, buildings, computers and teachers to provide educational services. An accountant uses office space and a computer to help people with their tax returns and their business accounts.

Although the factors of production are *sources* of added value, they are not *guaranteed* to add value. An intricately made product requiring many hours of skilled labour may command little or no value in the market. Cost does not necessarily imply that the product has value. If there is a lack of effective demand, value will be very limited. This does mean that a product which has been very successful in the past can lose its appeal. When this happens the price will fall and the added value which it embodies may sink below the level of the costs of production.

Work in progress

 1 Explain how your local supermarket adds value.

2 Think about a local business, other than a supermarket, which you know about. Explain how it adds value, including as many of its activities as you can.

3 How do you think this business might add more value than it does at present?

Promoting the product

There are many ways of adding value. Image can be enhanced by clever promotion. This can mean that the price can rise while still staying within the range which the customer perceives as being fair. Perfumes are advertised in a way which creates the image which people want to access when they buy the product. The price they pay is the price of the image, not just of the perfume itself. Value is added by devising seductive advertising strategies.

Branding

Certain brands are recognised by customers; they will be prepared to pay more for them. The brand's position may be the result of advertising, or of being first in the market, but very often it is achieved simply by word of mouth. Consumers find out by use that the product is of good quality. The best examples of such goods are brand names that have become generic. A Hoover is a vacuum cleaner and a Kleenex is a paper tissue. Arguably, the achievement of this transfer in people's minds is the ultimate in brand management.

Brand names such as these add more value, which can be exploited by charging more without consumers feeling in any way aggrieved or cheated. They allow a higher price to be charged without reducing the customer's sense of good value for money. This links with the idea of reputation, explored earlier (see page 6).

Companies which own a valuable brand do have to be careful to maintain its reputation. The introduction of gimmicks or other short-run changes can dent the power of the brand name to evoke a sense of quality.

Work in progress

 1 Think of two brand names which have become associated with reliability in use. To what extent are they really more reliable than competing products?

2 Think of two brand names for which image is very important. Explain why they are able to charge higher prices.

3 'Adding value through brands and advertising is just adding empty froth.' Is this so?

3 Adding value and competitive advantage

Tumble Home

Angus Cumming had a degree in sculpture. However, this had not helped him to find work. In time, he began to consider furniture making. He knew he could not compete with mass-produced flat packs, but he thought that if he could find a gap in the market, he could use his skills in art and design to add value. He set up Tumble Home in Devon. He recyled timber and other materials and sold his products in an open-air market. Turnover and profits grew, and Angus was able to open a shop. It was clear that customers would pay for a product that was sufficiently special.

The main source of added value at Tumble Home is skilled labour and creative ideas. Typically, materials only cost about 20 per cent of the selling price, so the materials in a small display unit priced at £40 might cost around £8. The rest of the value is largely added by Angus.

The unique selling point of Tumble Home furniture is design: it's different. Traditional in its construction of solid timber, interesting in its use of recycled materials, modern in its striking shapes and colours – no other furniture is the same. The customers are different too. Tending to be young and successful, they are people who like to experiment. Within this niche market there is only limited competition. Habitat in Exeter does sell modern furniture, but it's expensive and less imaginative.

This means that Tumble Home can achieve fairly high prices while maintaining a steady turnover. The secret of the firm's success is its ability to produce distinctive designs that add exceptional value. Even if any competitor emerged, the flow of new ideas at Tumble Home would be very difficult to imitate or reproduce.

Your agenda

1   What is the source of competitive advantage at Tumble Home? Why is it secure?

2   Prices at Tumble Home are already quite high. What is there to prevent the firm from pushing them higher?

3   Should Tumble Home produce some cheaper furniture that will sell quickly and might increase total turnover?

Competitive advantage enables a firm to make profits that exceed the opportunity cost of the resources used by the enterprise. A source of competitive advantage is always liable to come under pressure, especially from competitors in the same line of business. A key job of business managers is always to defend and to intensify their sources of competitive advantage.

■ Charging more

Competitive advantage is quite often achieved by adjusting the relationship between product and price in the market. Tumble Home knows that its customers are trying to get away from mass-produced furniture and value the fact that each design is only produced in very small numbers. It would cut costs to produce many more of each design but it would also undermine competitive advantage and reduce added value.

The supermarket Tesco was a company based on a cost advantage. 'Pile 'em high, sell 'em cheap' was the slogan of its founder, but in the climate of the 1990s it made more sense to differentiate Tesco quality and to boost margins on the back of some product advantage. As a result, many Tesco products became more expensive to produce, but the higher price achieved was more than adequate compensation.

■ Cutting costs

It would be wrong to think that improving quality or moving upmarket is always the right strategy. Kingfisher plc owns B&Q, Woolworths, Superdrug and Comet. Each of these firms operates in an extremely competitive and price sensitive market. Certainly, quality must be adequate and at least as good as the quality offered by competitors, but a decision to greatly increase quality at the expense of much higher prices would almost certainly destroy the firm. Customers are looking for reasonable quality, but they are determined to enjoy low prices. Satisfying these preferences with strong brands is the source of Kingfisher's competitive advantage. Successful business management ensures that the balance between product and price is optimal and under constant review.

Remember that added value is the difference between price and the cost of bought-in inputs such as components and raw materials. If these costs can be cut while quality and price are maintained at the same level, the slice of added value will be increased. Costs can be cut by looking for ways of improving efficiency, for example through the use of new technologies. This is always a possible route to competitive advantage.

1 What is market orientation?

What are railways selling?

During the 1950s US railroads began to make heavy losses. Passengers increasingly were travelling by air or driving their cars down the new freeways.

In 1960 Theodore Levitt published an article in *Harvard Business Review* called 'Marketing myopia'. It became one of the most famous business articles of all time.

'What did the railway managers think they were in business to provide?' asked Levitt. The answer appeared to be tracks and trains. Wrong! argued Levitt. Railroads are selling travel. Their customers do not want tracks or trains, but they do want to travel comfortably and efficiently to their destination.

All firms need to focus not on their product but on their market. The starting point for all business activity should be the customer. Businesses should understand what the customer wants and orientate the firm to providing it.

Your agenda

1 A company produces heating oil. What is it selling?

2 'Starting with the customer.' What could this mean for a manufacturer of bicycles?

3 What lessons might this experience have for the management of a chain of hairdressers?

On a famous occasion in the 1980s, the chairman of British Rail (the state-owned railway corporation) was passed a copy of the new timetable cover for his approval. Normally, this was automatic. The cover showed a tasteful picture of a train speeding along the track. The chairman rejected it. 'We're not selling trains' was his argument. Levitt's idea has influenced managers all over the world.

■ An organisation can be dominated by its product and production process. This outlook is called **product orientation**. It means that the product is the starting point for the business: selling in the market follows. Product orientation was common in many firms until the mid-twentieth century and can still be found in some industries. It was particularly common in Britain's state-owned utilities until they were privatised (for example railways, gas, telecommunications).

■ The alternative is **market orientation**. As Theodore Levitt suggests, this moves the starting point for business activity to the market and the consumer. Rather than being driven by the needs of the production process, the firm is driven by the demands of its actual and potential customers. This in turn redefines the product. For example, a firm making sportswear might redefine itself as a producer of leisure and fashion clothing. A more product-orientated firm might focus only on the needs of the sport while failing to recognise that many of its customers value sportswear for general leisure use.

Essentials

Product orientation in decision-taking implies that the business will focus its efforts upon creating the product rather than responding to the nature of the market.

Essentials

Market orientation in decision-taking implies that the business will focus on the needs of the customer before taking decisions about the product, its price and the way it is promoted.

Investigating markets

In trying to generate profit from the use of scarce resources, every firm needs a target market. When we think of everyday products such as bread or bus journeys, the nature of the market may seem fairly obvious. Yet actually this appearance is deceptive.

Try imagining for a moment all the consumers in Britain. That is around 58 million people. Every person is unique and so has a different scale of preferences and tastes. Each person has a different amount of money, and each person is willing to spend a different amount of money on different products (goods and services). All these characteristics of all these people are changing all the time. Then think of the rest of the world ... .

Markets actually present a very complex picture. Even the production and sale of bread is full of uncertainty. What is the likely split between brown and white? Sliced and unsliced? How will sales divide between the major brands? What about specialist breads? How do sales vary by days of the week? By seasons? Over time? In different parts of the country? From different types of retail outlet? All the same types of questions could be asked about bus travel. How many passengers with what kind of tickets travel on which routes at what times? How would travel patterns change if the services were re-routed or retimed? How would ticket sales be affected by increases or decreases in the fares?

All markets are – at least to some extent – a mystery. This is a key factor in the discovery of a competitive advantage and its exploitation. Everyone has their own reason for placing value on any product, but the reasons and the products change. Recognising, tracking and understanding the true pattern of demand is the starting point for business success.

2 Researching markets

A virtual shampoo?

A New York advertising agency was taken aback when it was asked to produce the best advert in the world for shampoo. What surprised the staff most was that there was no product. How could you advertise something that didn't exist?

To solve the problem, agency staff went out on to the street and asked people what they wanted of a shampoo. They asked all the questions that they could think of. What colour, what perfume, what bottle, what label, what price? Everybody had a view; after all they all knew what they wanted from a shampoo. As a result, the advertising agency came up with a description of the perfect product and made a wonderful advert to sell it. The client was delighted, but the agency could not understand how he could use the advert when he had no product.

The answer was simple. The work that the agency had done gave him all the answers to his problem of what people were looking for in the perfect shampoo. He would now go and make it.

The man's name was Alberto. The shampoo became Alberto Balsam. The date was 1908. The shampoo is still selling today.

Your agenda

1 Why do you think this approach to product development – in 1908 – was so successful?

2 '...the agency staff went out on to the street and asked people what they wanted of a shampoo'. Which people on the street would the agency have asked? Give your reasons.

3 What problems might be faced in trying to design a 'perfect' shampoo for the new century?

The process of finding out about the potential sales for any product is called **market research**. This means investigating consumer motivation and behaviour so that products can be evaluated, sales estimated and opportunities seized. The sophistication and coverage of market research varies widely: it can mean anything from a shopkeeper informally consulting customers through to an agency carrying out a statistically defined survey involving thousands of households across the country.

Broadly, market research falls into two categories: **field research** and **desk research**. Desk research is all about using data which are already available, i.e. **secondary data**. Good market research will tap a whole range of sources which will then be analysed in some detail. This type of approach will usually contribute to **quantitative research**, which generates estimates of future sales. Desk research is normally carried out before field research because it helps to inform subsequent work.

Field research involves collecting **primary data**. This may be done using a survey, or perhaps a focus group, where a 'moderator' leads a group of people in exploring their perception of a product, brand or organisation. In-depth interviews may be included in the plan, perhaps combined with product testing. These approaches are particularly suitable for conducting **qualitative research**. Qualitative information can reveal much about consumer attitudes and behaviour. The Alberto Balsam case study shows the value of qualitative research.

> ### Essentials
> **Quantitative research** involves the analysis of numerical data.

> ### Essentials
> **Market research** involves finding out about the exact wants of customers. It includes the collection of data from published sources and the gathering of primary data.

> ### Essentials
> **Field research** is undertaken to collect information directly from individuals. The objective is to obtain both qualitative and quantitative data.

> ### Essentials
> **Desk research** is primarily concerned with assembling secondary data which has already been collected and made available.

> ### Essentials
> **Primary data** are collected directly from source by means of surveys, focus groups and in-depth interviews.

> ### Essentials
> **Secondary data** can be collected from published electronic and paper-based sources.

> ### Essentials
> **Qualitative research** is directed towards discovering consumers' genuine opinions in some detail.

3 Planning market research

Seahorses

Owned by Zoë Chapman and Tom Gambold, Seahorses offers coffees, light snacks and a small range of alcoholic drinks. It is usually busy and considered to be fashionable, stylish and slightly upmarket. The largest group of customers are in their twenties and thirties and opening hours are from 10 am to 6 pm.

To help plan development of the business, Zoë checked the prices and assessed the quality offered by her competitors, the four cafés located within 500 metres.

The Sail Loft: inexpensive; hot food, mostly fried plus sandwiches; seaside decor; very busy; appeals to families and tourists; 8am – 5pm.

Bumpers: trendy, younger customers including teenagers; pine tables and posters; coffee and snacks including burgers; no licence; fairly cheap; 10am – 5.30pm.

The Singing Kettle: traditional tea room that offers lunches; 'olde worlde' decor; popular with the elderly; loyal customers; moderate prices; 9am – 5pm.

George's Café: emphasis on low prices; greasy food; plastic furniture; takeaway trade; used by lower-paid workers – mainly men; smoking; 7am – 4pm.

Your agenda

1 To what extent does Seahorses face competition?

2 How might the information collected by Zoë influence developments at Seahorses?

3 How would you describe the data collected? Use the terms defined in the previous section (page 58).

For small firms market research is often fairly informal. Managers or owners can use their own sales records to analyse customer preferences and identify trends. More market information is often available from trade magazines, organisations such as chambers of commerce and from suppliers. It is also common for small firms to carry out their own investigative market research.

Large companies will have a significant budget for market research and normally contract out the work to a professional agency. Because market research uses scarce resources, it carries an opportunity cost to the firm and must deliver value for money. It is most likely to be effective if disciplined by a clear model such as that shown in Figure M1.37.

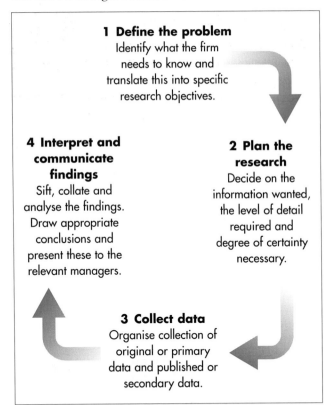

Figure M1.37 Model for market research

Defining the problem

Problem definition is very important. Unless there is a clear understanding of the questions to which answers are wanted, the research is liable to be inefficient and unfocused. For example, does the firm want to know about consumer attitudes to its existing product range or does it want to know about the features a new range might offer? The objectives of research might be:

- exploratory – in setting the scene for further research, for example, what are the key trends in the retail market for ice cream?
- descriptive – in collecting information about the market, for example, what is the age and gender profile of consumers who buy premium (luxury) ice-cream?
- causal – in evaluating how causes and effects are related, for example, how are sales of ice-cream affected by weather conditions?

Secondary research

Secondary research is normally carried out first. It has a role in preparing for the primary research: this costs more and takes longer, so careful preparation can ensure that it is sharply focused on the real issues.

Secondary data may be internal or external to the business. Internal sources include:

- accounting data, for example product sales information
- reports from the sales team
- customer records
- stock records
- customer enquiries/complaints.

Much useful secondary data are available free (for example, from libraries or the Internet). Useful sources include government statistics collected by the Office for National Statistics (ONS) and by international organisations.

Some commercial organisations, such as A.C. Neilson and Mintel, specialise in providing data for market research. They will charge for the information but it will often cost less to buy than it would for the business to do the research on its own. Trade associations and industry journals can also be good secondary sources.

Substantial market research will combine primary with secondary research to produce a comprehensive picture upon which decisions can be based.

Primary research

When investigating specialised problems that relate to the particular firm, it is often necessary to collect primary data. It is a highly skilled task to ensure that the data collected are:

- relevant to the research objectives
- accurate to the right degree
- up to date enough for the purpose
- unbiased by the method of collection.

First, qualitative research must be undertaken. This might involve using focus groups, which can establish what questions need to be included in a survey questionnaire.

Survey research is the most common method of collecting quantitative primary data. It can also be used to generate qualitative data from a large sample of people. Questionnaires – a pre-planned series of questions – can be sent through the post, asked over the telephone or used in a personal interview. Great care must be taken in designing the questions which should be clear, relevant, logically sequenced and never personally intrusive. Closed-end questions ask the respondent to select from a choice of answers while open-end questions allow answers to be freely expressed, often at greater length.

Closed-end questions tend to generate quantitative data while open-end questions are more useful in building a qualitative picture. Firms often want to discover the thoughts and feelings in consumers' minds.

For any survey to be totally representative it would need to consult every possible consumer. Although this is usually impossible, an adequate degree of accuracy can be achieved through **sampling**. This involves consulting a group of people (the sample) which will be representative of the population of the target market. The sample size must be large enough to reflect the variations in people's responses reasonably accurately. Otherwise, the sample may have a **bias** towards one particular group.

A variety of sampling methods can be used. The best known is random sampling. Then every member of the target population has an equal chance of being selected.

Once research is completed, the task of analysis begins. Usually the data form the basis of a report which attempts to answer the original research questions. This report should focus the information collected and needs to be clear in its presentation of data and conclusions reached. It must also be directed to the relevant managers within the time limits agreed.

In recent years, among large firms there has been a trend away from market research as an intermittent, project-driven, activity towards market intelligence systems that provide a continuous flow of customised information to the right managers at the right time.

Essentials

Sampling involves selecting a group of people who will be representative of the target market.

Essentials

Bias occurs when the sample is small, or not representative of the target market; the information given will not be accurate.

4 What is market segmentation?

Should Somerfield stock organic fruit and vegetables?

Although a relatively small supermarket chain, in terms of turnover, Somerfield has the largest number of stores of any food retailer in the UK. It has 10.8% of the total grocery market. Formerly Gateway, the business merged with KwickSave in 1998.

Somerfield then wanted a stronger identity and increased customer appeal. The chain had not previously been associated with the trend towards healthy eating represented by organic produce, so it needed to know the level of likely sales and how far additional customers could be won over to shop at Somerfield through the availability of this product group.

The research plan investigated the growth in sales of organic produce (secondary data) and the attitudes of existing Somerfield customers to the possibility of paying a premium price for the new range (primary data). The findings were carefully considered by the marketing department and at boardroom level. The result was a launch of organic fruit and vegetables at selected stores only.

Source: Somerfield Stores Ltd

Your agenda

1 Given that organic fruit and vegetables are a growth market, why do you think that Somerfield had not introduced these products earlier?

2 How far would the company need to be certain that organic produce will sell in sufficient quantities to be profitable?

3 How would Somerfield decide what price to charge?

Segmenting an orange involves peeling off the skin and gently pulling apart the sections of fruit inside. The concept of **market segmentation** works in a comparable way, but the process is usually less tidy.

First, what is meant by the 'market' for a product?

- Some products are aimed at a mass market, meaning that they are aimed at a very wide range of consumers. Products such as Coca Cola or Esso petrol are examples.

- Other markets can be subdivided to pinpoint more closely the type of customer demand being met. For example, the housing market might be divided into markets for starter homes, flats, family houses, retirement homes, etc. These categories could be further split: family homes might divide by numbers of bedrooms or by whether they are terraced, semi-detached or detached. Each choice may reveal a segment of the market with its own characteristics. Estate agents or builders will need to understand these market segments.

Firms segment markets so that they are better able to meet the demands of consumers and so add more value. Holiday companies offer a range of packages varying by destinations, activities offered, type of catering or length of stay. Building societies market a range of accounts, each with different restrictions and rates of interest. TV stations target different audiences by times of transmission and types of programme.

Some firms build their whole business strategy on meeting the demands of one segment in a market. Distinctive segments that attract firms of this type are called **niche markets**. Identifying a niche market and then making those particular consumers a focus for all activity can be a powerful source of competitive advantage. The ideal situation is to discover a niche that was previously unrecognised but which then grows rapidly. This often allows the firm to build a strong brand identity with a loyal but expanding customer base. Profitability is likely to be high, with competitors at a disadvantage.

Essentials

Niche markets are essentially small market segments. Suppliers are likely to face less competition within them.

Essentials

Market segmentation means that the market is divided up into segments, each of which represents different customer preferences. Product specifications and marketing strategies can then be devised to fit the wants of each particular group of customers.

Point of view

How the Sony Walkman nearly never was

Akio Morita, chairman of the Sony Corporation, had been watching with great interest the development of the Walkman. He was understandably surprised when the marketing department advised against the launch. Staff didn't think it would sell. They thought people would find the headphones annoying and therefore would not buy it. They also feared that potential customers would be put off as the machine would not record.

The chairman was very attached to this new product and was not deterred by the views of the marketing department. He decided that it should go ahead. He was right. It was an instant success.

Your agenda

1 What factors in the audio market had the Sony marketing department failed to recognise?

2 Confronted with the arguments of the marketing department, what do you think made Morita so confident?

3 How do you think the marketing department of a large and famous company such as Sony could make such a misjudgement?

4 Sony made the Walkman and with it, a world-class brand. What kind of organisation could be facing a similar problem and decide not to go ahead?

The Body Shop is a classic example with its virtual invention of the niche market for natural cosmetics. Supermarkets selling organic food in the past were catering for a niche in the market. Increasingly, the niche may grow into a segment. Somerfield found its organic produce sales grew well, allowing it to increase the number of lines rapidly.

However, niche markets also carry dangers. Sometimes they represent short-lived fashions rather than real trends. Then there is the risk that competitors will improve on the original firm's product or use their greater marketing power to invade the niche concerned. The 'me-too' product can be seen quite often.

Market research, especially when used to monitor market change on a continuous basis, is a powerful tool, but there are still conditions where it may fail to detect both threats and opportunities, as follows:

■ An undiscovered market emerges. Many needs and wants are latent: that is, until they are aroused, they are not expressed.

■ The pattern of circumstance changes suddenly and unpredictably. The past ceases to be a good guide for the future.

■ The key variables in the market are qualitative rather than quantitative. Market research can overstress quantities and neglect the complex qualities of human feeling.

In terms of audio products before 1979, the market for personal stereos simply did not exist, but with more students and younger people on the move, there was a huge latent market for the personal playback of tapes. Since most people had a tape machine at home that could record, the playback-only limitation of the Walkman had become unimportant. Meanwhile technological developments allowed a good quality of sound from miniaturised speakers. Finally, there was the potential of the Walkman to become a fashion accessory while allowing a new sense of personal freedom in the enjoyment of music. Against all the apparent odds, a winner was in the making.

5 Pitching the price

Profits and prices

Tesco plc is the country's largest retailer of food products. Its competitive advantage lies in the effectiveness of its supplier relationships, the strength of its brand and the ability to innovate ahead of rivals. The emphasis is on achieving maximum turnover with relatively slender profit margins (profit per item sold).

1998	£ million
Sales	£17 158
Profit	£934

SmithKline Beecham is one of Britain's largest pharmaceutical companies with global operations and markets. The firm's competitive advantage lies in its reputation, its accumulated research knowledge and the skills of its staff. Turnover is large, but profits need to be high in order to fund further research in the future. Long-term success depends on a continuous flow of improved products.

1998	£ million
Sales	£8 082
Profit	£1 618

Your agenda

1 Why do you think Tesco's profit is so much lower than SmithKline Beecham's?

2 Tesco could increase margins and make more profit on each sale. SmithKline Beecham could cut margins and increase sales with lower prices. Why do you think these strategies have not been adopted?

3 Both companies operate in competitive markets. However, the nature of the competition is rather different. Explain this difference and how it affects the two companies' strategies.

When a firm puts a product on the market, it must decide on the price that will best meet its objectives. Superficially, a high price is always attractive since it will ensure a higher margin of profit. But every firm is constrained by the willingness of its customers to pay. A very high price that resulted in virtually no sales would make a poor strategy. In other words, firms face a trade-off between two variables: profit and sales.

In some industries, conditions are highly competitive with little real difference between competing firms' products. This means that a high price relative to other firms will almost certainly mean very low sales. In practice, managers have little choice but to price at the 'going rate'. By contrast, a firm with a strongly individual product and a clear competitive advantage has the opportunity to earn good profits without sacrificing too much of its market share. Much depends on whether the business is competing on price or quality.

Enquiry 4   How is a profit made?

1 How do costs add up?

Rock Around the Clock

A 1950s'-style clock featuring Bill Haley on its face was Jane Andersen's creative design project at technical college. The clock sold before it was made and by the time her end-of-course exhibition was over, she found herself with orders for a dozen clocks. Before long she had produced sketches for other clocks with a rock theme (Elvis Presley, The Beatles, Queen, REM, etc.) and even before she left college, a business enterprise had begun.

Despite a high level of customer interest, the early goal was still survival. Jane had found a workshop and had purchased the necessary tools and equipment. Experience showed that it was possible to produce a maximum of 240 clocks per month. The selling price was fixed at £24. The cost of components plus an allowance for labour amounted to £14 for each clock. In addition, overhead expenses such as rent, rates, electricity, advertising and other costs amounted to £800 per month.

Your agenda

1 If Jane produced and sold 100 clocks in a month, what would be the average cost of each clock?

2 How much profit would she make on each clock?

3 How would these figures be affected if output and sales rose to 200 clocks per month?

4 What would the total profit for the month be on these figures?

Business is about combining scarce resources so that the cost of inputs is less than the market value of the corresponding output. Since every business uses scarce resources, it follows that every business must experience costs. As a business buys the resources that it needs – materials, labour, information technology, marketing and much more – it must pay market prices. Only by transforming those resources into something more valuable (i.e. by adding value) can it make a profit.

All business costs can be roughly divided into two basic types:

- **variable costs** (VC) that increase proportionately with output
- **fixed costs** (FC) that stay the same regardless of output.

Variable costs increase with the level of output and include materials and labour. Fixed costs are constant and include rent, equipment, administration, marketing costs and insurance. They will stay the same even if there is no output at all. Fixed costs are often referred to in business as overheads.

Figure M1.38 shows the costs of Rock Around the Clock. Because fixed costs do not vary with output, the line is horizontal at £800. Variable costs rise by £14 per unit. **Total cost** rises parallel with variable cost, but starting from the level of fixed cost.

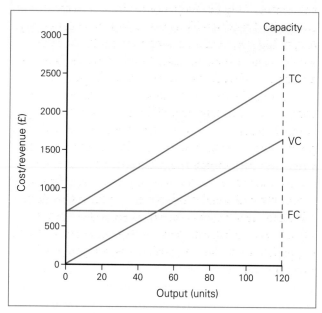

Figure M1.38 Fixed, variable and total costs

The quantity sold multiplied by the price is the **sales revenue**. Businesses sometimes refer to this as turnover.

Essentials

Variable costs grow proportionately with the level of output.

Essentials

Fixed costs remain the same at all levels of output. They may change in the long run if, for example, more buildings and equipment are bought.

Essentials

Total cost includes both fixed and variable costs.

Essentials

Sales, or total, revenue is price times quantity sold.

Work in progress

Q 1 What would Jane's sales revenue be if she sold 200 clocks?

2 If Jane found it hard to sell the clocks, would reducing the price help? What would happen to sales revenue?

3 Are there any ways in which costs could be cut?

Can the business break even?

When sales revenue is exactly equal to total costs, the level of output is at the **break-even point.** At this point there is no profit and no loss. This is shown in Figure M1.39, which combines cost and revenue. Output is measured on the x (horizontal) axis while money amounts are shown on y (vertical) axis. At an output of 80 units, total costs are exactly covered by sales revenue.

Essentials

The **break-even** level of output is where sales revenue is just enough to cover all the costs.

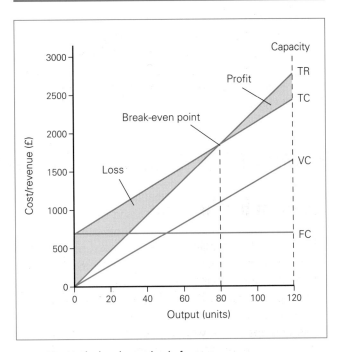

Figure M1.39 The break-even level of output

The revenue curve, like the variable cost curve, starts at the origin. If the firm sells no output, it receives no sales revenue. The resulting straight line is easily plotted.

The break-even point, by definition, occurs where total costs equal total revenue, or at the output level indicated by the intersection of the two lines. In this case, break-even output and sales level is 80 clocks per month. Below this level, losses are inevitable. Once output and sales pass this point, every clock adds £10 to profit.

Why is a break-even chart useful?
The arithmetic that underpins a break-even chart is very simple. But, as a model, it provides a way of thinking about profitability and exploring how this could be affected by changes in revenue or costs. For many business enterprises the difference between profit and loss is quite precarious. Small changes in variable cost, fixed cost, price or sales volume can quickly translate into major changes in profitability.

Work in progress

Q Explain what will happen to the break even point and the level of profit in each of the following scenarios:

a Rock Around the Clock is selling very successfully and it is really not necessary to advertise. Word of mouth will do the job. This means that fixed costs fall by £100 per month.

b Jane decides to retain her advertising programme but puts the price of the clocks up to £26. Can she be sure that her profit will increase?

c The cost of the clock mechanism increases, adding £2 to variable costs.

2 Will a cut price make a contribution?

A room for the night

It was a foul, wet night. Jim Crossley sat down wearily and began to check the bookings. As owner of the Lamb Hotel, he would normally be serving in the bar and chatting with guests. Brenda looked after the office and reception, but it was her weekly night off and no one else was free. There was another gust of wind as the front door opened and two bedraggled backpackers struggled into the hall.

'Any rooms still free?' asked the young man as he heaved his rucksack to the floor.

Jim scanned the page for 17 February.

'I can manage a twin room. £40 for bed and breakfast.'

At once the young man looked doubtful. 'Anything cheaper?'

''Fraid not.'

'Thanks.' The two hikers began to pick up their belongings. Jim thought quickly. It was a quiet time of the year and he was largely empty.

'What can you afford?' he called after them. They paused.

'Only about £15 each really,' answered the second hiker. 'We just need a room and breakfast.'

'I'll tell you what,' said Jim. 'I can't make a habit of this but I'll do the room at £15 each as a special offer for the tired and wet.'

'Done. Thanks.' The young men put down their packs again.

Your agenda

1 From this evidence, what do we know about variable costs at the Lamb Hotel?

2 How much better off is Jim as a result of his bargain?

3 Is Jim being honest when he says 'I can't make a habit of this'?

We have seen that sales revenue 'chases' total cost provided that the price of each unit sold is greater than its variable cost. The speed with which it overtakes total cost depends on the size of this differential. However, each unit sold at any price above variable cost makes a **contribution** towards fixed costs and ultimate profit.

Suppose that there are ten rooms at the Lamb Hotel, each with an approximate variable cost (laundry, cleaning, heating and food) of £10 each. Fixed costs are heavy at £600 per week. This means that every room booked at the normal price of £40 per night makes a contribution of £30 towards fixed costs and profit. It therefore follows that the hotel must achieve £600/£30 = 20 room bookings each week to cover exactly the fixed costs and to break even. The twenty-first and each subsequent room booking contributes £30 to profit.

At output/sales levels below break-even point, contributions are paying for fixed costs. Above break-even, the contributions go towards profit.

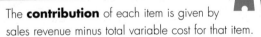

Essentials

The **contribution** of each item is given by sales revenue minus total variable cost for that item.

Notice that once we know the level of fixed costs and the contribution of each unit sold, then the calculation of the break-even point is possible:

$$\text{Break-even output} = \frac{\text{Fixed costs}}{\text{Contribution per unit}}$$

The concept of contribution also opens the possibility of carefully controlled price cutting. So long as reducing the price for one customer does not mean making the same reduction for others, then specific units of output can be sold at a price below average cost but above variable cost, that still adds to profit.

Work in progress

Q Assume that on average 50 per cent of the rooms are booked.

1   What is the actual average total cost of a room at the Lamb Hotel?

2   What is the weekly profit?

In the case of the Lamb Hotel, the £30 rate offered to the two hikers is only slightly above true average cost, but it is above variable cost, and the booking of a room otherwise unoccupied adds a contribution of £20 towards fixed costs – and profit. As a transaction separate from others in the hotel, it represents a straight gain of £20. If the two hikers had been allowed to go elsewhere, the hotel would have been £20 worse off.

This principle lies behind all kinds of special rates offered by hotels for 'weekend breaks', by airline and railway operators for cheap tickets and by clubs for entry on less popular nights. For travel companies, cinemas, theatres and so on the variable cost of extra customers when seats are available is zero or very little. So long as variable costs are covered there is a gain. To the extent that the payment is above variable cost there is a contribution to fixed costs.

Point of view

But is it always profit?

Jim Crossley has constructed a break-even chart for the Lamb Hotel. It seems possible that his break-even point could be reduced and profits increased with a higher price for rooms. He therefore raises the price of a room to £60. The result is that in an average week only 16 room bookings are taken

Your agenda

These questions could be answered using a spreadsheet.

1   What is the hotel's new break-even point?

2   Calculate the new profit or loss.

3   Does this example show any limitations to a break-even chart?

Break-even charts provide a useful way of analysing costs and revenue at different levels of output. However, they cannot explain how people will react to price changes.

Competitive advantage depends on a complex relationship between price and product. The price which can be charged is determined by the market. It is not always the case that a price cut leads to a fall in sales revenue, but if the sales revenue falls below the costs of production, the business will not continue to produce for very long.

Break-even analysis tells us about profit and loss for various levels of cost, prices and sales. Buyers'

decisions will change with price and the effect on sales may be significant. Increased added value may allow the business to charge more. Similarly, cost cuts may be possible. All such changes will affect the break-even level of output.

3 Balancing cost and value

No fudging added value?

Rob Taggart and Liz Diamond own Roly's Fudge, a small company using a traditional Devon recipe to make five different flavours of quality butter fudge. Their town centre premises offer limited space which led Liz to hit on the idea of moving the main production process into the shop where it can be watched by customers and passers-by.

Sugar, butter, flavouring and other ingredients are boiled in an open copper vat and poured out on to a large marble table. Once cooled, the fudge is rolled, cut and packaged on the spot. Rob designed the firm's own brightly coloured boxes that make appealing presents. Although tourists are the main market, local people are significant customers. Fudge sent as a present by post and sales by mail order are turning out to be useful markets.

Your agenda

1 In what ways is Roly's Fudge maximising added value?

2 Give some examples of ways in which the business could potentially cut its costs.

3 Do you see any drawbacks in your suggestions for question 2?

We have seen that market research involves identifying, analysing and tracking demand. The starting point for any business is to match the expertise of the enterprise with a viable customer base or segment of the market. The market-orientated firm gets as close as it can to the heart of that principle in what the US business writer Tom Peters calls 'an embrace'. Simply knowing what kind of product the intended market wants is not enough. A marketing manager needs to understand the typical customer within the target segment in as much detail as possible. The objective is to achieve a full appreciation of the benefits sought by customers.

Good market research will link qualitative and quantitative data to build a detailed picture of the customer's preferences:

■ Qualitative information could cover subjects such as customers' feelings, perceptions and anxieties.

■ Quantitative data might include preferred shopping

habits and times or the size, colours, features and qualities of an ideal product.

For profitable production, the goal is to shape the product as closely as possible to the exact 'contours' of customer demand.

Some products – a Mars bar for example – are aimed at a very wide segment of their market. Others – such as Nestlé's Jelly Tots – are aimed at a very specific segment of the total confectionery market. Whether targeted on a wide or a narrow segment, a product should correspond as closely as possible with the needs and wants of its typical consumer. The art of adding value thus lies in matching scarce resources with these sources of consumer satisfaction.

Throughout the production process, a firm aims to maximise added value and to minimise the corresponding costs. The relationship between increasing costs and adding value is not straightforward. The business must identify the key benefits of the product and then carefully brand and package it so that value is lifted above the additional costs incurred.

Analysis of the market mechanism shows that producers stay in business by generating a profit on all or most of the products they sell. The secret of this ability usually lies in an extremely close understanding of demand as represented by customers and in effective control over costs.

Keeping in touch

Richer sounds

This specialist hi-fi retailer keeps costs low by locating its shops in the low rental areas of selected towns and cities, but the firm spares no effort when it comes to satisfying the customer. For example, when a customer gets home with a purchase he or she will receive a phone call checking that the unit is free of faults and working to his or her satisfaction.

Julian Richer, the chairman, went into business at the age of 18 and made a fortune of over £1 million by the time he was 30. He believes that much of his success stems from studying the customer.

Prêt-à-Manger

'Pret', as it is often known, is a fast-expanding chain of sandwich and coffee shops. Their environments are clean, modern and stylish, but the real distinction is quality. For example, all the eggs used in sandwich making are free-range – a fact made prominent on their wrapping. The founder, Julian Metcalf, believes that his sandwiches are worth their premium price.

Your agenda

1 What are the important benefits which will draw customers to buy from these two companies?

2 Thinking of a business which you know from your own experience, explain in your own words the basis of its competitive advantage.

Tom Peters draws attention to the 'thousand times' principle. Put simply, this refers to the many but often hidden opportunities in a firm for making small improvements in the product that add 'a thousand times' more value than their cost. Of course, this is an exaggeration, but the principle provides a useful way of thinking.

Yet costs remain very important. Small firms are often highly cost-conscious, but as the business grows and prospers it is easy for managers to become complacent about rising costs. However, productive efficiency is not just a matter of 'doing things more cheaply' by chiselling at any cost. The effect of this may only be to slide back down the cost/quality trade-off spectrum – reducing costs at the expense of a greater reduction in added value. Real moves for efficiency are about 'getting more from less'. This highlights the difference between cost cutting and cost-consciousness. A highly inefficient organisation may need a period of deliberate cost cutting, but all firms need a climate or culture of cost-consciousness where managers and staff are vigilant in spotting and eliminating those costs that add little or no value.

Roly's Fudge

A junior accountant observed that the firm could save money if it:

- used margarine instead of butter in the fudge
- told staff not to waste time chatting with customers
- made and pre-packed the fudge in cheaper premises on the town's industrial estate
- discontinued the coloured boxes for packaging and sold the fudge in plain plastic bags.

Your agenda

1 Criticise these proposals one by one. Give your reasons.

2 Instead of adopting the accountant's suggestions, Roly's Fudge incurred further costs by:

- buying specially designed 'fun' uniforms for production and retail staff
- commissioning its own customised 'fudge' font for letter headings, labelling and publicity
- introducing a special previously unknown flavour of the month – these included 'strawberries and cream' and 'lemon meringue pie'
- using superior quality cocoa in the popular chocolate fudge.

Justify each of these additions to costs.

1 How much is profit?

Kingfisher plc

The Kingfisher group includes Woolworths, B & Q, Superdrug and Comet. Kingfisher also owns a property company, Chartwell Land, and the leading French electrical group, Darty.

Kingfisher has its business focus on mass-market retailing. The company's objective 'is to deliver consistent and superior returns to shareholders by being one of Europe's most profitable volume retailers' (Sir John Banham, chairman).

£ millions	1995	1996	1997	1998	1999
Turnover	4 888	5 281	5 815	6 409	7 458
Operating profit	305	317	415	519	637

Figure M1.40 Kingfisher's profits   Source: Kingfisher plc, *Annual Report and Accounts*, 1999

Your agenda

1 How far does the financial record over five years support the view that Kingfisher has been successful in pursuing its objective?

2 'I am pleased to report … a record set of results' (Sir John Banham, commenting on Kingfisher's 1998 accounts). Yet the fashion retailer Next achieved a profit margin in 1998 of 14.7 per cent on sales of £947 million. Does this undermine Kingfisher's claim?

Making a profit is an essential objective for all business activity. Profit must therefore be accurately measured. This enables managers and all other stakeholders to evaluate the firm's performance. Perhaps the most basic identity in business is:

Revenue minus Costs equals Profit

The profit and loss account

Companies are legally obliged to keep account of their profit or loss making activities in the **profit and loss account**. This document itemises revenues and costs over a period of a year. It makes possible an assessment of the company's position.

The profit and loss account starts with a statement of turnover (sales revenue), followed by the subtraction of costs to show the profit made over a given period. Deductions are then made for interest and tax. Finally, **dividends** payable to shareholders are taken away, leaving **retained profit** within the firm.

Revenue minus Costs equals Profit

Deduct interest and tax

Divide what remains between dividends for shareholders and retained profits

It is important to be aware that the presentation of accounting data can vary between firms and that care is needed in making comparisons.

Essentials

The **profit and loss account** shows turnover (sales revenue) together with all the costs involved in earning that revenue.

Essentials

Dividends are the share of profits which is distributed to the shareholders.

Essentials

Retained profit is kept by the firm to finance future investments.

Gross profit

For businesses, profit is not a single figure but a whole range of different measurements. **Gross profit** is always the highest figure for profit. It is calculated by starting with turnover, the sum total of all sales revenue within the accounting period, and subtracting the **cost of sales**. This is the total for variable costs such as labour, materials and bought-in goods or components. For firms in manufacturing and retailing, this value is often called cost of goods sold. What remains is gross profit. Figure M1.41 shows this part of the profit and loss account for Kingfisher.

The cost of sales figure does not include any of the fixed or overhead costs of running the business. It does not include rent, administration, insurance or sales spending. Gross profit has to be large enough to cover these overheads in the long run.

Essentials

Gross profit is sales revenue less the immediate cost of producing the goods sold.

Essentials

Cost of sales means the cost of inputs to the actual production process such as labour, components and materials needed. It excludes all overheads.

	£ million
Turnover	7 458
Cost of sales	(4 961)
Gross profit	2 497
Selling expenses	(1 617)
Administrative expenses	(243)
Operating profit	637

Figure M1.41 Gross and operating profit for Kingfisher, 1999

Source: Kingfisher plc, *Annual Report and Accounts* 1999

Notice that many published accounts, including Kingfisher, as in Figure M1.40, make a single jump from turnover to operating profit with all other details to be found in Notes to the Accounts.

One way to measure profit is to look at the profit margin. The **gross profit margin** is gross profit as a percentage of turnover. The formula is:

$$\text{Gross profit margin} = \frac{\text{gross profit}}{\text{turnover}} \times 100$$

Essentials

Gross profit margin is gross profit as a percentage of total turnover (sales revenue).

Work in progress

Q Petersons Autos is a flourishing car-repair business. It employs three mechanics. John Peterson himself takes care of the more difficult jobs – the ordering of supplies, book-keeping and sales. He has calculated last year's figures as follows:

Turnover:	£168000
Cost of sales:	
Oil, spares, other supplies:	£47000
Wages:	£62000

1 Calculate John's gross profit and his gross profit margin.

2 What outgoings will the gross profit have to cover?

3 What other information would you need in order to decide whether John is happy with the performance of the business?

Arriving at operating profit

Figure M1.40 shows how profit is broken down to arrive at the **operating profit** figure used in the case study at the start of this enquiry.

■ The starting point is always turnover. The first deduction from turnover is the cost of sales. This gives gross profit.

■ Next the overheads are subtracted. In practice firms classify these in different ways according to how particular costs affect them. However, a common distinction is made between administrative expenses (such as rents, management salaries and general office costs) and selling expenses (such as advertising and distribution).

■ We are now left with operating profit which is the key outcome for the company's trading activity. Operating profit is usually referred to as 'net profit' by smaller firms.

Operating profit margin can be calculated in the same way as gross profit margin. It is operating profit as a percentage of sales revenue. The formula is:

$$\text{Operating profit margin} = \frac{\text{Operating profit}}{\text{turnover}} \times 100.$$

Essentials

Operating profit is what remains from sales revenue after the deduction of all operating costs, including overheads. It is one of the most useful measures of profit and can be used to make comparisons over a period of years.

Essentials

Operating profit margin is operating profit over sales revenue or turnover, multiplied by 100.

Work in progress

Q 1 Calculate gross and operating profit margins for Kingfisher (Figure M1.41).

2 What costs would you expect to find under the headings 'selling expenses' and 'administrative expenses'?

3 Will the company be satisfied with operating profit so long as it is greater than zero?

2 From operating profit to retained profit

Extract from profit and loss account, year ended 30 January 1999	£ million
Operating profit	637
Exceptional items	2
Profit before interest	639
Interest payable	(10)
Profit before tax	629
Tax payable	(183)
Profit after tax	446
Dividends payable	(184)
Retained profit	262

Figure M1.42 Kingfisher's profit and loss

Source: Kingfisher plc, *Annual Report and Accounts*, 1999

After operating profit any necessary allowance is made for **exceptional items**. These are profits or losses that are not normally a part of the trading activity. For example, when a firm decides to close a branch or unit of its business, there might be a loss on the sale and some redundancy payments to staff; or there might be a fire in the firm's warehouse; or a major customer could go into receivership while still owing money. These are all real and possible financial events but they are not part of the normal process of producing and selling. They are exceptionals in this sense.

In the example in Figure M1.42, Kingfisher has disposed of some property and made a profit. But exceptionals can often represent a loss. For example, in 1995 the company recorded an exceptional loss of £38.0 million on the sale of a car showroom chain. This made a real dent in the final profit after tax.

After exceptionals the firm declares its profit before interest. Interest is like an overhead expense but is not included before operating profit since it relates to the cost of money in the company and not business activity as such. In practice, the firm may also receive some interest payments from its own investments, so any deduction is the net interest payable.

Next comes the deduction of **corporation tax**. Firms are taxed on their profit after interest. In 1999 large firms paid at a rate of 30 per cent and smaller firms on a scale between 20 per cent and 30 per cent. However, the actual amount payable in any year depends on a variety of rather complex calculations.

Essentials

Exceptional items are part of the profit and loss account but so unusual that the accounts would present an unrealistic picture unless they were listed separately.

The directors of the company will decide how to allocate the profit after tax. Usually, 25–50 per cent of the profit available is used to pay dividends on the shares that have been issued (Figure M1.44). Occasionally, firms in difficulties maintain dividend levels even when it means using all their profit and dipping into past **retained profits**.

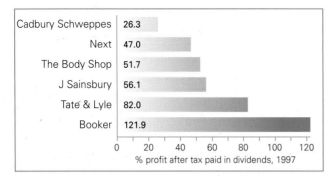

Figure M1.43 Profit and dividends

Source: *Company Annual Report and Accounts*, 1998

Dividends are the shareholders' immediate reward for the success of their investment in generating profits. The remainder of the profit is retained within the business. It will be used (or 'ploughed back') by the directors, typically to finance new equipment, buildings and land. This is also in the shareholders' interest. As their company's assets increase in quantity and quality, so the value of their shares is likely also to rise.

Figure M1.44 provides a summary of the elements in the profit and loss account.

Summarising profit and loss accounts

- Profit is calculated by subtracting the cost of goods sold from total turnover. What remains is the gross profit.
- The overhead expenses are taken away leaving operating profit.
- Allowance is then made for exceptional gains and losses that are not part of the normal trading pattern.
- The value remaining is profit before interest and tax.
- The deduction of interest costs leaves profit before tax. Then the further deduction of tax payable leaves profit after tax.
- Finally the distribution of dividends leaves retained profit.

When looking at company accounts you will find many minor variations in the way they are presented. Nevertheless, with practice you should be able to recognise and identify the important elements in their construction and get a sense of their message.

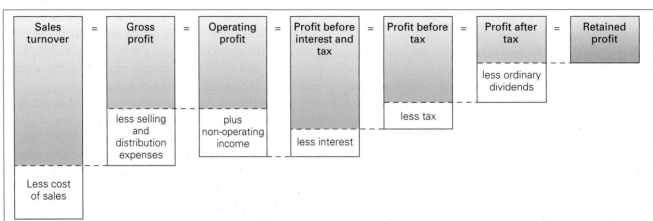

Figure M1.44

3 Profit or cash?

Dart developments

When Roy Green bought an old lifeboat station at an auction, he didn't know he was also starting a business. Back in the 1970s the £15 000 he paid had seemed a lot of money. Yet after two years' part-time work on conversion, his unusual home was valued at over £40 000. With an old friend, Bill Drummond, he now formed Dart Developments and bought a derelict warehouse overlooking the River Dart in Devon. Converted and sold as holiday flats, it was the making of a new business.

A few years later the property market was booming and the demand for apartments in converted buildings was growing rapidly. By now Roy organised the subcontracting of building work while Bill scoured the south of England for sites with potential. The company was highly profitable but, as Bill observed, the money scarcely seemed to reach the bank before being committed to the next purchase or the costs of another conversion. Somehow their account was always 'in the red'. What had started as an overdraft for convenience had become an overdraft for necessity.

It was the day after the company's annual accounts showed record profits. Bill Drummond was looking round another warehouse ripe for conversion. 'Ceiling's a bit low,' he observed.

'Same as our overdraft,' remarked Roy grimly.

Two weeks later the bank bounced a Dart Developments cheque.

Your agenda

1 Why would you think that Dart Developments needed a bank overdraft?

2 How can a firm making record profits run so short of money?

There is a saying in business that 'cash is king'. What does this actually mean? Everyone needs cash to buy what is needed and to pay back debts. Cash is powerful stuff because it is universally acceptable in settlement of what is owing. Every business needs sufficient cash. Yet the normal objective of being in business is not to hold cash but to make a profit. Is there a paradox?

We have seen that all firms incur both variable and fixed costs. From day to day these take the form of bank credit transfers and bills for payment. Clearly, a business must have enough money in the bank to meet these demands. On the other hand, it will not want large deposits of cash lying idle in the bank and earning little interest. The whole purpose of a business is to generate returns on capital that exceed the rates of interest available. So it is a matter of balance. Managers will aim to ensure that the firm has sufficient cash, but not much more than is likely to be required.

In the management of cash, a bank overdraft is useful. This allows the firm to run up a negative balance to the extent of its overdraft limit (also called a 'ceiling'). Interest is only payable on the average amount outstanding over time. If the overdraft ceiling is exceeded or 'broken through', then the firm's borrowing is unauthorised. The bank may then agree to a higher limit, but equally if it has doubts that the debt will ever be settled, then it may 'pull the plug', demanding full and immediate repayment. The firm's survival is then often at risk.

The difference between profit and cash

Although profit is measured in terms of money, profit and cash are different concepts. Profit is a surplus of sales value over costs. Often the cash to represent the profit is not received until a month or more after the sale, but the corresponding costs may need to be paid at once. Thus the flow of cash through the firm needs planning and monitoring carefully.

Particular problems can occur when a business has found a profitable market and wants to expand rapidly. In the short term more money is needed for buying stock and paying for extra labour. For a time the business may be able to use credit from suppliers and its overdraft facility, but if the pace of expansion moves beyond the limits to credit, then the firm is **overtrading** and may become insolvent (unable to raise cash to pay its debts). Creditors – people or other companies to whom the firm owes money – may then force the business into **receivership**, meaning that an official appointed by the courts will sell the firm's property in order to settle its debts.

Essentials

Overtrading occurs when the business expands without having enough funds to pay its bills.

Essentials

Going into **receivership** happens because the business is not able to pay all its debts even if all of its assets are sold for cash.

Building a bigger business in the longer term means spending money now for returns in the future. The likelihood that this investment will prove profitable eventually does not provide the necessary cash at the time when it is needed. Most firms grow by using their retained profit to finance investment.

Sometimes this process is too slow. Attractive market opportunities do not usually last long and the firm may want a fast-track strategy for expansion. There are two possible ways forward:

- The owners or shareholders can supply additional capital.
- The business can borrow money in the belief that the profits earned will easily pay the interest.

Problems arise when a firm gets itself committed to spending more cash on expansion than can be raised in any of these ways. Again the risk is insolvency and entry into receivership.

Two important points should emerge from this:

■ It should be clear that a business can be highly profitable yet endanger its very existence by running out of cash. The reverse picture is also possible. A business that is cash rich may have exhausted its profitable opportunities and be facing decline, takeover or even collapse.

■ Profit is distinct from cash. Profit is a surplus of revenue over corresponding costs that may not be received until well after it is recorded. Cash is simply resources held in the form of money which can be used to settle debt. Firms must always have access to sufficient cash.

Point of view

But is it always profit?

Back in 1996, Sears plc was a huge retail group that owned Selfridges, Miss Selfridge, Warehouse, Wallis, Richards, Adams (childrenswear), Dolcis, Saxone, Curtess, Shoe Express, Shoe City and Freemans Mail Order. The brands made an impressive list but the company was in serious difficulty.

> **Extracts from Sears plc, *Annual Report and Accounts* 1995/96**
>
> Operating profit was £75.7 million and the operating profit margin was 3.2%.
>
> Sir Bob Reid, chairman:
>
> 'For Sears, 1995 was a year of immense change as we met the challenge of focusing our activities on key businesses, condensing our portfolio of brands from 24 to 11.'
>
> 'Total sales moved up by 8.9% from £2.1 billion to £2.3 billion … After exceptional charges, due to disposals and provisions for restructuring, we reported a loss before tax of £119.7 million.'
>
> 'However, Sears remains fundamentally robust …'

What does all this mean? Is the company doing well or not? Actually, Sears was in serious trouble. Margins were feeble, operating profit was down by 48 per cent in one year and anyway masked massive losses in the sale of failing businesses. The loss before interest and tax was equivalent to over £2 for every person in Britain. Unsurprisingly, the chief executive resigned early in 1997. Mail order and shoe retailing operations were sold as the remains of the company was broken into two parts (Selfridges and the clothing stores).

Your agenda

The point of this case study is that it is usually possible to interpret accounts in at least two different ways. Watch out for this in the future.

Module 2 Efficiency

The first module examined the objectives of people, businesses and governments. It is now important to consider how those objectives may best be achieved. Business efficiency is an essential part of the process of improving standards of living. The efficiency with which markets function determines whether everyone benefits from possible improvements.

2.1 What makes firms effective?

Most businesses need to be able to respond to the changes around them. The way they are organised, their motivation and their production decisions all have an impact on their efficiency and effectiveness. All these aspects of business performance are analysed here.

2.2 Do markets work?

Markets are the driving force of the economy. They are responsible for deciding what people can have and therefore need close inspection because the outcomes may not always be equitable or efficient. When markets fail to provide what society wants, there is a need for control or intervention.

What makes firms effective?

Enquiry 1   What is culture?

1 How do corporate cultures work?

A cooperative approach

Edinburgh Bicycle is one of the biggest independent bicycle retailers in the UK. It has a large shop in Edinburgh, a thick catalogue and a web site; 20 per cent of its business comes from outside central Scotland. It designs its own bikes and gets them manufactured under contract. Some models are specially designed for the hilly and cobbled streets of the city.

The cooperative has 23 members. They elect the six-person executive team which runs the business. Strategy is usually worked out in informal discussions before being built into an overall five-year plan. The cooperative may hold a particular department to account if sales figures are disappointing.

'We probably spend more time talking in meetings than people in other companies, but we believe the cooperative structure is a source of strength,' says promotions manager Lindsay McDermid. 'One advantage is that people who work here feel fully involved in the business, and that makes them committed to doing their best for the customers.'

'Edinburgh Bicycle has survived as a cooperative because members are expected to trust the different management teams to take detailed decisions although they can have access to all the information they want. You have to be a particular sort of person to work here. If you're stubborn or self-centred or have grandiose ideas, you probably won't fit in. The general manager has to have the full consent of staff for everything he does.'

Your agenda

1 List the distinctive features of Edinburgh Bicycle.

2 Is sitting in meetings always an inefficient way of taking decisions?

3 What aspects of Edinburgh Bicycle's approach could be appropriate for larger organisations?

Some businesses thrive on their own traditions. Others are constantly looking for new ways of doing things. These differing approaches are part of the culture of the organisation.

Corporate culture is not very easy to define. Sometimes it is described as meaning 'the way we do things round here'. More formally, it has often been defined as the set of important assumptions (often unstated) that members of a community share in common.

When people work together they all bring to the workplace their own beliefs and **values**. Values reflect the underlying principles by which people live their lives. As time goes by, these values assume a life of their own, becoming integrated into the organisation itself. The resulting culture can be an important element in the organisation's performance. Many successful businesses aim to increase their effectiveness by developing a distinctive corporate culture.

Each business has its own priorities reflecting its values and culture:

■ Some businesses have values which centre on profit and shareholders' interests.

■ Others see ethical issues as important, for example the Co-op Bank and the Body Shop. These types of business will give a high priority to suppliers' and employees' interests and perhaps also to the environment.

Essentials

Corporate culture covers all those attitudes, customs and expectations which influence the way decisions are made in a particular business.

Essentials

Values are the principles which guide people in their relations with each other.

Different cultures

Culture may be embodied in a set of strategies or policies, or it may simply be an atmosphere which encourages everyone to behave in particular ways. It is created as much by the workforce as by the management. Even the business which does not think it has a particular culture does, in reality, have one.

However, the business with attitudes and values which persist without being periodically thought over may lack both drive and flexibility.

● Sometimes a culture is embodied in the stories told about past company events.

● Small companies which have not long been in business may have a culture which is not very clear to employees because most decisions have been taken with survival as the most important objective.

● Other small companies have a culture which deliberately encourages creativity and the sharing of ideas.

● Others may have a culture in which willingness to adapt to change is the key feature.

Work in progress

Q **1** What was the crucial underlying value which determined the culture of Edinburgh Bicycle?

2 During 1998, Marks & Spencer found that its profits were falling. How would you expect this to affect the prevailing culture within the company?

3 Think about a business you already know. Answer the following questions about it:

   a Is it organised along lines dictated by a strict set of rules?

   b Does it react quickly to changes in its market?

   c Does it seem to be caring and genuinely interested in the welfare of its employees?

   d Does it encourage employees to suggest new ways of working?

   e What is its attitude to its customers?

4 What conclusions can you draw about the culture of the company?

A carefully defined culture can give everyone in the company a view about how decisions should be taken. It can be used to foster consensus among employees and managers. It provides direction and a sense of purpose. However, there is no single successful culture. Different approaches will be appropriate in different businesses.

Culture and effectiveness

The effective business is one which keeps its costs of production to a minimum while studying carefully its customers' requirements. It makes the best possible use of the resources available to it by adding value in efficient ways.

A positive corporate culture can do much to promote efficient use of resources. Attitudes and values which help people to work effectively together and to adapt to changing circumstances can have a very positive effect on sales, costs of production, design, quality and customer service. Teamwork can be conducted in a highly collaborative way. It follows that the creation of a strong corporate culture can increase effectiveness and profitability.

What makes a culture?

Virgin Atlantic

The airline company Virgin Atlantic sees itself as a company which is quite different from the 'big business' norm. It defines its business goals as follows:

- To develop further a market-leading 'fun' product through innovation.
- To provide top-quality service and customer care.
- To offer good value for money to all its customers.
- To remain committed to providing safe, reliable and comfortable travel services.
- To recognise, develop and motivate employees so that they reach their full potential.
- To enlarge the business while retaining the feeling and culture of a small company.
- To be profitable and retain a good cash flow with a bright future.
- To be a good business partner.
- To be efficient, professional and ethical in all its business practices and dealings.

Your agenda

1 Which of Virgin's business goals are a little different from the 'big business norm'?

2 Which business goals apply particularly to the working environment of its employees?

3 Use the statement of business goals to outline your own view of Virgin's corporate culture.

The ways in which an organisational culture is created are many and various. The business may have statements which actually explain its philosophy. Other aspects of culture are captured in the implicit values which prevail within the organisation.

In order to evaluate the nature of an organisational culture, quite a range of aspects of the business could be considered, as follows:

- The management structure. How many layers of management are there?
- The degree of flexibility in the system. How quickly can the organisation adapt to changing circumstances?
- The working atmosphere. This is important in determining how people feel about their work. Are employees encouraged to share ideas for improving efficiency?
- Motivation. Do employees approach their jobs with vigour and enthusiasm?
- Management style. Do managers delegate effectively?
- Attitudes to status and power. Are there easy communications between different levels within the organisation?
- Attitude to customers. Is the business market orientated?
- Communications. Are lines of communication direct and clear?

Some aspects of culture are embodied not in the statements made or the conventions of the company but in its symbols and stories of past successes. Sometimes a strong culture is linked to a brand which has enjoyed success. Cadbury's Dairy Milk chocolate, launched in 1905, and selling strongly ever since, had this effect.

2 Culture and change

Businesses face a range of pressures for change, both internal and external. An internal pressure might result from a change of ownership after a take-over. External pressures can result from changes in the market place or in technologies. Once these pressures are in place it becomes important for the business to find ways of adapting. The level of flexibility which the business can achieve may be deeply affected by the prevailing culture.

Resistance to change can come from a number of sources. Fear of the unknown may be deeply ingrained in some employees. In particular, they may perceive a change in the extent to which their skills are valued, and this may engender expectations of possible redundancy. Morale will then sink and the creation of a positive attitude which accepts the challenge of change may become very difficult.

Businesses which include an acceptance of change in their overall culture stand a better chance of producing a flexible response to change. They are able to swim with the tide, exploiting new opportunities rather than remaining set in their ways.

Essentials

Resistance to change arises when employees feel threatened by it. They may fear loss of status or responsibility, or redundancy.

Work in progress

Confectionery and soft drinks manufacturer Cadbury Schweppes believes in a 'culture of innovation'. This approach helps companies to compete in markets where new products have an important edge.

Q
1   How would a culture of innovation help Cadbury Schweppes to maintain a competitive advantage?

2   What does the company have to do in order to bring a successful new product to the market? Outline each stage in the process.

Cultures vary greatly:

- Some cultures revolve around the personality of the founder of the business. The very distinctive approach used by Richard Branson at Virgin is an example of this.
- Other cultures particularly value the individual as a member of a group. Decisions are taken collectively: a consensus must be achieved. This is part of the culture at Edinburgh Bicycle. Each member of the group must listen to the others and be prepared to defend his or her own point of view. This increases the likelihood that all relevant considerations will be examined before a decision is taken.

Collective decisions sometimes take longer than individual ones. However, they can sometimes be more effective in producing positive responses to market change. Collective decision-taking implies that large numbers of employees will be involved. This means that they are more likely to be committed to a culture which sees change as presenting opportunities.

Changing the culture

The business which creates a distinctive attitude among its employees is using its corporate culture to motivate and energise its workforce. A strong, carefully thought out and clear corporate culture can give employees a sense of identity. They will feel that they are part of a going concern with objectives they can relate to. If adapting to change is an important element in the culture, they will embrace, rather than resist, change. They will be prepared to perform a range of roles within the business according to need.

Of course, doing this is not always easy. When the business is successful the benefits of a culture of flexibility are clear to all. There may be few, if any, losers and people can see the purpose of the changes they make. If the business is struggling, it is a different matter. People will feel threatened and defensive and the culture may be found to have divisive aspects.

When bicycle and motor parts retailer Halfords wanted to change its culture in the 1980s, it dismissed a large group of employees overnight. This was an expensive strategy but it made it possible to recruit new people who would welcome a culture of flexibility and change.

3 Culture and organisation

British Petroleum

In 1990 Robert Horton took over as chairman of BP, the multi-national oil company. He set to work to make major changes in its management structure. He aimed to bring about a complete change in its corporate culture.

An important part of the programme was to raise employee morale. Linked to this was a series of initiatives in the field of human resource management. These included workshops and communications training. One objective was to enable employees themselves to take the initiative in planning improvements in the way they worked, rather than merely waiting to be handed instructions from above.

Another important element in the culture change involved adopting a much 'flatter', less hierarchical, management structure. This means that there are fewer layers of management; it makes communication easier. BP called it 'cutting the cost of complexity'. It led to decisions being taken mainly by those most directly involved. By early 1992 it seemed that good progress was being made.

All this was very healthy, and should have helped to make BP both more efficient and more profitable. Unfortunately, other things were happening to BP – things which management could do nothing about. The recession in the world economy as a whole meant that demand for petrochemicals and plastics fell sharply, and the world price of oil was falling, again partly because of lack of demand. This made it harder for all the oil companies to make profits.

With cash flow falling, it became imperative to slim down the management team, making large numbers of people redundant. This certainly did not make people at BP feel good: it destroyed the beneficial effects on morale brought about by the earlier changes.

In the summer of 1992, the rows got worse, and Horton had to resign.

Your agenda

1   Make a list of all the changes described here.

2   How might a flatter management structure help to keep costs down?

3   Why might giving people more responsibility increase efficiency?

4   Did the BP reorganisation increase people's job satisfaction?

One important element in corporate culture concerns the management structure. The most efficient enterprises are constantly searching for better ways of managing. The changes they make to their organisational structure can have a major impact on the prevailing culture. Sometimes this is one reason for making changes.

The commonest structure for a business organisation is shown in Figure M2.1. Businesses organise their management effort around certain key functions. In analysing the nature of organisational cultures, the role of the human resources manager has particular importance. This person will regard employees as a valuable resource, to be nurtured and built into a productive team.

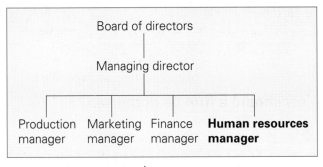

Figure M2.1 An organisation chart

Each functional manager is responsible for a specialist department, while reporting to the managing director (MD) who ensures overall coordination. Not all firms have a human resources manager but those with over 150 employees usually establish some specialist responsibility for people management.

Traditionally, this function has been called the personnel department, which provided a service to the mainstream activities of the business. It would take care of recruitment, training, employee welfare and disciplinary procedures.

The emerging concept of human resource management represents a shift away from personnel management as a specialist department, in favour of regarding the supply of human resources as a fundamental part of the firm's existence and profit-driven activity. An increasing number of human resources managers are seen not as peripheral specialists but as core members of the senior management team. The more central and complex the contribution of people to the business, the more important the human resources function becomes.

Human resource managers are closely involved in the creation and explanation of organisational cultures within the business. The main functions of human resource management are as follows:

- Organisational development – maintaining an organisational and job structure that promotes optimal managerial and operational performance; enabling the organisation to adapt effectively to change.
- Employee resourcing – anticipating future demand and supply for all types of staff; recruitment.
- Appraisal – assessing the effectiveness of an employee, usually through a process of discussion.
- Training and management development: improving employee productivity.
- Pay and benefits – ensuring appropriate levels and types of reward for employees to meet staffing needs and achieve optimum performance.

How should a firm be organised?

Although people are individuals, they do not work in isolation. Each person has a network of responsibilities to other people and these networks form an organisational structure. The corresponding organisational chart illustrates all the pathways of responsibility that connect people in their roles as employees within a firm. The best known method of organising people is in a **hierarchy**, such as that shown in Figure M2.2.

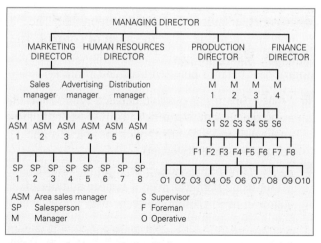

Figure M2.2 **The organisation in depth**

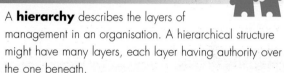

Essentials

A **hierarchy** describes the layers of management in an organisation. A hierarchical structure might have many layers, each layer having authority over the one beneath.

The line of authority or chain of command carries orders from the top towards the bottom of the pyramid. For example, a command might follow the route: managing director → marketing director → sales manager → area sales manager 4 → sales person 2. This order has passed through all five levels in the hierarchy. The same route would be followed in reverse if sales person 2 wanted to communicate with the managing director. These pathways of vertical communication are well defined. It might be more difficult for messages to travel efficiently between sales person 2 and manager 4. Unless there was a special line of lateral communication between the sales persons and the managers, then the formal routing for communication would be through the marketing and production directors. This is clearly likely to be slow and clumsy, opening the possibility of informal links which cut across the formal structure.

In large organisations it becomes impossible for one manager in a leadership role to take direct responsibility for all employees. The organisation chart explains how responsibility is delegated, so that each individual is responsible for other individuals at a lower level in the hierarchy, while being themselves responsible to another individual at a higher level.

There is always a limit to the number of people for

whom one person can be directly responsible. The number in practice is called the **span of control**. The optimum value for a span of control depends on the appropriate balance between trust and control:

- Small spans make possible detailed supervision of subordinate staff, but require correspondingly more managers and a hierarchy with more levels and longer chains of command.
- Wide spans require higher degrees of trust in subordinate staff, but need a smaller number of managers and allow a hierarchy with fewer levels.

Traditionally, spans have been largest where the work of subordinates has either been relatively simple and repetitive or where subordinates are experienced, competent and fully trained.

Work in progress

The managing director at Midland Machines Ltd has organised her 120 staff in a hierarchical structure.

Q
1   How many levels in the hierarchy would be necessary to accommodate these staff given a constant span of control of three?

2   What constant span of control would it be necessary to adopt if there was one less level in the hierarchy?

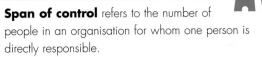

Essentials

Span of control refers to the number of people in an organisation for whom one person is directly responsible.

4 De-layering

Leadership is necessary for efficiency in any organisation, so some element of hierarchy is inevitable. But how efficient is the traditional 'tall pyramid' hierarchy? Looking at Figure M2.2, it is clear that where there are many layers in the hierarchy, there can be communication problems. The organisation may behave in a rather inflexible manner as a consequence.

Significantly, in recent years there has been a powerful trend towards much **flatter** organisational structures with larger spans and fewer levels in the hierarchy. This process is called **de-layering** and often involves removing much of the middle management structure inside an organisation.

Essentials

De-layering occurs when organisational hierarchies are flattened out and given fewer layers. It is then more likely that decisions are taken by the people who are most likely to have to carry them out.

Essentials

Flatter organisations have fewer layers in the hierarchy.

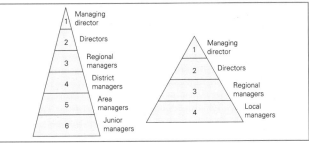

Figure M2.3: De-layering.

The accelerating pace of change in the business world is demanding more adaptable, flexible organisations that can respond promptly and creatively to opportunities in the market place. This need is reinforced by the market orientation of many firms. These are all important aspects of the creation of a culture which responds to change.

With these objectives, decisions need to be taken as close as possible to the interface of customer demand. This means that communications and command pathways should be short and highly efficient. Increasingly, a senior manager feels the need to be known personally by employees and to understand at first hand the business and its workforce. These pressures fit in with the implications of motivation theory, which suggest that people work best when feeling some considerable responsibility and empowerment in their own job.

With fewer, more highly skilled employees, firms are tending to give people more freedom with which to pursue their agreed targets. Removing levels in the hierarchy also reduces administrative overheads relative to sales, thus helping to raise profits. The use of computers to process information eliminated many middle managers' jobs.

Flatter management structures imply a wide span of control. Managers are forced to trust their subordinates and delegate more. This gives employees more responsibility and brings them closer to the customer. It implies that whatever level they are working on they are likely to be more involved in decision-taking.

Point of view

Flexibility and motivation

Andrew Lonsdale had enjoyed considerable success as a property specialist working for a large retail group. He was promoted swiftly and his future looked very bright. On the strength of his high pay, he went ahead and bought a family-sized house in a pleasant suburb of London.

Then the management decided that all new business would be organised using a franchise system. This meant that the company would license independent operators to sell its products, rather than buy and set up its own shops.

One day, a colleague with whom Andrew was friendly, took him aside and told him that he would be made redundant within a month. He gave him a confidential warning, so he would have time to think out his strategy before the blow fell officially. It was made clear to him that he had not done anything wrong; his work had been competently carried out. It was just that a structural reorganisation had left him without a job.

Your agenda

1 Changes in management strategies may be quite stressful for people. Think of three examples of changes which are stressful and explain why.

2 Is it justifiable to create these stresses?

3 Could there be hidden costs for the company which reorganises in ways which involve large numbers of redundancies?

Adapting to change

Change can be very threatening to people. Sometimes the change is coming from outside the business; it may threaten the viability and profitability of the company. Everyone in the company will feel anxious about their future employment.

Other changes may originate within the company. In practice, a flatter management structure means that there are fewer rungs on the management ladder, fewer layers in the organisation. Often this means that the company needs fewer managers, thus making considerable savings in the salary bill. This makes for more effective organisation, but may also cause a lot of redundancies. It may have a significant impact on motivation and on the efficiency with which managers at different levels do their jobs. Promotion may be less likely.

Many business strategies which are expected to have a positive outcome may also have costs. Teamwork and collaboration can help businesses to devise imaginative and profitable strategies. But if reorganisations and redundancies make employees feel insecure, they may compete with one another in ways which damage the quality of their teamwork.

Flexible organisations quite often make their employees feel insecure. The very fact of their flexibility makes them likely to undergo continuous changes. So there are some important trade-offs in the ways businesses choose to organise themselves. Managers must be aware of these when making organisational decisions. The effect on the culture of the business can have very negative elements.

1 How are people motivated?

Motivators?

The Body Shop

At The Body Shop head office we take the lead in our drive to be a model employer with child care, fair pay, participative management, a good work place and health care as basic components of our policy. Staff are motivated by being given the opportunity to have ownership of the goals and values of the company.

Over the past year, The Body Shop has added a number of initiatives to support our commitment to employee care:

- We now have a full-time occupational health adviser and a counsellor providing 24-hour confidential counselling service for employees and their families.

- We have extended our support for child care to our UK company shops by making available a subsidy paid direct to carers across the country.

- We have paid more attention to the way in which people are introduced to the company through our induction process.

- The Body Shop is also committed to the learning and development of our employees. The learning and development department aims to ensure that training and development takes place to enable individuals to perform to their full potential and thus make a valuable contribution to the success of the company.

The Inland Revenue

The Inland Revenue is part way through a major change programme. It is designed to be better for our people with less routine and more interesting jobs; more responsibility and delegation; more opportunities to move between jobs; better performance assessment and better training and personal development.

Caring for staff is a key driver for change. People are recognised as the Inland Revenue's most important asset. Our success depends on all of our people sharing common values in our relations with others. The Department's aim is to treat individuals with openness and honesty. We aim to make the Revenue an organisation which people want to join, enjoy and, more importantly, do well in. We match our business requirements with the need to be a responsible employer. This includes providing equality of opportunity for our people.

Our performance management scheme links pay directly with performance. People agree at the beginning of each year what they will achieve. The emphasis is on results not activities, people are judged on how well they achieve what they set out to do. There are better rewards for those who make a greater contribution to the Inland Revenue's success. We have a competence-based approach to enable recruitment, training and development and selection procedures to address changing business needs and ensure that we have the right people with the right skills in the right job. (Competencies are the knowledge, skills and attributes needed by individuals to do their jobs effectively.)

The Revenue has reduced the number of management layers to improve accountability and communication. The role of the manager focuses more on leading, motivating and developing people rather than the old style of monitoring, checking and correcting work.

Source: Bized, *Company Facts*

Your agenda

1 Using the above case studies, what can you tell about the priorities of human resource management at The Body Shop and the Inland Revenue? Working in pairs, take one organisation each and then compare your conclusions for the two.

2 In general, what sorts of measures do you think might improve employee motivation and benefit the business concerned?

3 Which of the two approaches described above do you think will be more effective in motivating employees? Why?

4 Many Body Shops are franchises: the company allows acceptable people to set up their own independent Body Shop outlets, for a fee. If you work for a Body Shop franchise, you may not get the benefits outlined above. What difference does this make to your view of the Body Shop's policies?

Organising employees

Businesses want to encourage their employees to produce as much as possible. The firm which can maximise its output with given resources will be able to keep costs down and make more profit. Equally, businesses want good-quality products. Motivating their employees and managers effectively plays a large part in the achievement of both objectives.

A number of thinkers have come up with theories that can be used to help find new approaches to business organisation. (This is one area of business management where fashions change very noticeably.) Very broadly, the issues can be approached in two ways:

- The way in which people are organised can be examined and adapted so as to increase the value of output per person.
- New ways can be found to motivate employees so that they work as vigorously as possible.

In the late nineteenth century, business thinkers adopted what has become known as the **scientific approach** to decision-making. The basic logic underlying this originated from the view that careful study of what happens under different conditions can tell us how best to organise people. The assumption was that people are rational and respond to incentives.

The principal exponent of the scientific approach was Frederick Taylor, whose book, *Principles of Scientific Management*, appeared in 1911. Like many of his contemporaries, he believed that people were motivated by money. It follows from this that if pay can be linked to output, then output will rise. This view had led to the widespread use of piece rates. (This involves paying people according to the quantities they produce.)

However, at that time, in many businesses the employees themselves were organising production. It had gradually become clear that they often worked in inefficient ways in order to spin out the job in hand. They wanted to be sure that they would not work themselves out of a job. In this situation piece rates do not effectively help to increase output per person.

Addressing this situation, Taylor recommended that managers should be in full control of the workforce. They should decide who does which job, and how. The order in which things are done, and the nature of

the tools used, should all be determined by careful consideration of scientific principles. Taylor had a very considerable influence on business management. However, he was criticised for being too mechanistic in his approach to management and later thinkers provided a very different approach.

Essentials

The **scientific approach** uses technical investigations to find improved production methods. The approach which yields the highest output per employee will be the one adopted.

Motivating employees

Well-motivated employees achieve more. They are committed, vigorous and productive. Over the years various strategies for motivating employees have been developed.

In reaction to Taylor's approach, a number of thinkers sought to develop a view which took account of the psychological and social aspects of work. This became known as the **human relations approach**. An important writer in this field was Abraham Maslow (see page 17).

Following on from Maslow's work, in 1959 a very important book was published in the USA which has influenced thinking about motivation ever since. It was called *The Motivation to Work* and one of its key authors was **Frederick Herzberg**. Two hundred engineers and accountants in Pittsburgh had been interviewed and asked to name factors that were sources of increased or decreased job satisfaction. The results, shown in Figure M2.4, were rather surprising.

Essentials

The **human relations approach** involves a way of motivating employees which emphasises the psychological and social aspects of the working environment.

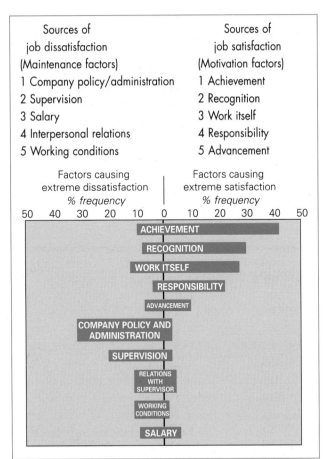

Figure M2.4 **Satisfaction and dissatisfaction**

Essentials

Frederick Herzberg coined the terms 'motivation factor' and 'maintenance factor', and showed that they are, respectively, sources of job satisfaction and dissatisfaction.

Essentials

A **hypothesis** is a supposition, the truth of which is uncertain but which can form the basis for further investigation starting from known facts.

What are the implications of Herzberg's ideas about managing people? There are a number of possible answers. First, managers must recognise that attention to maintenance factors can only help to eliminate job dissatisfaction. To increase job satisfaction it may be necessary to redesign jobs so that they provide access to the motivation factors identified. People need to feel that they are trusted to do the job well. They may need opportunities to use their initiative, so that the job becomes more personally fulfilling.

The motivation factors were sources of job satisfaction but were not generally sources of job dissatisfaction. Conversely, the maintenance factors were sources of job dissatisfaction but were not generally sources of job satisfaction.

This has an important meaning for managers. Maintenance factors, such as working conditions, do matter in preventing dissatisfaction, but having met the need, additional provision of these factors will not create extra satisfaction. Likewise, motivation factors are the real sources of satisfaction, but their absence will not normally cause dissatisfaction.

Herzberg's findings did not represent a proven theory. They were a **hypothesis** about human needs and motivation.

Work in progress

Q 1 Analyse the likely sources of job satisfaction and dissatisfaction for:
   a a teacher
   b someone who assembles televisions
   c a sales assistant in a department store
   d a departmental manager in a food-processing business.

2 Think again about the approaches to motivating employees used by The Body Shop and the Inland Revenue. Which come closest to the scientific, and which to the human relations approach? Give reasons for your conclusions.

This raises an important question: does leadership arise from the qualities of the person or the demands of the situation? According to the scientific approach to management, business managers must be tough and determined in making their own decisions and enforcing them among the workforce. Certain people were thought to be born with leadership qualities, making them able to use power effectively. 'Great men' were born and not made.

During the twentieth century the human relations approach rejected this view, and argued that each situation demanded a different style of leadership. The right style of leadership depends upon the situation. Some leaders concentrate on completing the job in hand, and this may work well if there is a single easily identified business objective. (These are known as task-orientated leaders.) In more complex situations, where a creative approach is desirable, the leader who manages through attention to working relationships may be able to achieve more. (These are relationship-orientated leaders.)

How do leaders perform their role?

Three key leadership styles can be distinguished:

- **Autocratic leaders** impose their decisions on a group. Commands are tightly specified with little or no allowance for discussion or individual choice. Rewards are unpredictable, while the leader's personal identity and underlying plans remain obscure.
- **Democratic leaders** encourage the group to participate in discussion and to feel that they have contributed towards any final decision. The leader mixes informally with the group and is usually well known at a personal level. Methods of work are left to individual choice, while rewards are open and fair in their distribution.
- **Laissez-faire leaders** largely leave the group to make its own decisions. Apart from setting some general objectives, the leader makes few demands. Communications follow no formal pattern, while rewards are highly unpredictable.

Work in progress

Q **1** Go back to the case study, Leaders, at the beginning of this section. To what extent do the labels, autocratic, democratic and *laissez-faire*, fit each one?

Essentials

Autocratic leaders take decisions without consulting colleagues who are lower down the hierarchy.

Essentials

Democratic leaders guide rather than dictate, consulting widely and encouraging everyone to participate in the decision-making process.

Essentials

Laissez-faire leaders leave decision-taking to subordinates, allowing them to be creative, but also providing few guidelines.

3 Communication

Clotted cream or televisions?

Most people know that clotted cream is made in Devon. Far fewer people know that 600 000 television sets are made in Devon every year. Built as the Bush radio factory in 1947, the Rank Organisation's television production plant in Plymouth lost £22 million in 1978. The easy mass market for televisions had become much more competitive with rapidly increasing foreign competition. Rank was falling behind in the technology race, its management structure was top-heavy while costs were racing ahead. Despite some modest improvement, the end came in 1981 with the announcement that the business was to close making a total of 3000 people redundant. This was at the worst point in the recession of the early 1980s.

However, the closure was an opportunity for the Japanese consumer electronics manufacturer, Toshiba which had already unsuccessfully attempted a joint venture with Rank. Toshiba's goal was to overcome the problem of European Union (EU) trade restrictions that severely restricted the import of Japanese-made televisions. Production within the EU would allow open access to key European markets.

Only 300 of Rank's 3000 staff were recruited by Toshiba. Most applicants hoping to regain a job were ready to accept almost any terms of employment. Significantly, the business reopened on a May bank holiday – with no extra pay. The new owners believed that radical changes would launch the factory towards a profitable future. The British managing director, Geoffrey Deith, was a firm advocate of many Japanese-style management methods. The first real shock was the introduction of single status for all staff. This involved demolishing the traditional barriers between workforce and management. Everyone – from the boardroom to the factory floor – was to wear a company blue jacket. Offices for management were deliberately open plan. The old system of four canteens for the different grades of staff was scrapped in favour of one self-service restaurant.

'You could be in the queue for dinner and you'd turn round and the managing director was behind you. It felt odd.' (Ron Pemberton, senior shop steward.)

All staff were actively encouraged to address one another by first names, regardless of differences in seniority.

'You get a much closer relationship with someone if you call them by their first name. It sounds a trifle, but it isn't.'

Another vital change that broke with the Rank era was the signing of a single union agreement with EETPU (Electrical, Electronic, Telecommunications and Plumbing Union). A multiplicity of unions had meant that workforce/management negotiations were complicated, slow and inefficient.

'There were so many unions, you could argue as much between unions as with management.'

A 'no-strikes' agreement provided for 'pendulum arbitration' if deadlock occurred in negotiations. This means that an impartial third party would be asked to make a simple choice between the final positions of management and union. Clearly, this would provide a strong incentive for both sides to be as reasonable as possible or they were bound to lose their case. In the event, this procedure has never been necessary and no strike has ever taken place.

Toshiba quickly made communications with employees as direct and open as possible. Short morning briefing sessions were introduced for all parts of the factory. The previous day's work would be reviewed, plans would be explained and comments taken. Most important of all is COAB, the Company Advisory Board. This includes representatives from all major groups of staff in the factory. Monthly meetings always include a full statement of business information with a profit and loss report. In this way staff become involved in the business realities of the firm while having the opportunity for direct discussion with senior management.

In the period since the Toshiba take-over, annual output has risen fourteenfold while employment has increased threefold. There has been a major investment programme in new technology and a large expansion of capacity. Devon still makes televisions, clotted cream and much more besides.

Sources: Toshiba Consumer Products, and Annabella Gabb,
'A vision of the future', Management Today, April 1991
With permission of the copyright owner Haymarket Business Publications Ltd.

Your agenda

1 What were the main reasons that Rank failed?

2 What other British industries have experienced similar problems?

3 Explain briefly what you consider to be the most important single reason for Toshiba's success. Does this case raise any doubts in your mind about the merits of 'Japanese management'?

4 Could Rank have made the changes adopted by Toshiba? Why?

Changes in organisational structures which improve communications between the layers of the hierarchy can obviously help to cut costs and increase efficiency. If they also lead to improved levels of cooperation and better teamwork, this effect will be even more marked. However, simply changing the structure may not be very helpful if the informal culture which underlies it remains the same. It is important for the business to see changes in the management structure and changes in the way people collaborate with one another as going hand in hand. So attention to the ways in which people communicate within the business can be very worthwhile.

Communication actually means the process of conceiving, sending, receiving and interpreting messages. These messages carry the language of both information and persuasion and on them depend the direction, coordination and motivation of the organisation.

Within a business, the flows of communication may relate to the internal organisation (i.e. employees, directors, shareholders). These include vertical communication – up and down the hierarchy – and lateral communication – across the hierarchy at the same level. They may also relate to the external environment (i.e. consumers, suppliers, creditors, the community, media and government).

The organisational structures within which leaders are meshed are like maps in terms of communications:

- The lines on the organisational chart that connect staff are the lines of official or **formal communication**. They operate through the chain of command laid down in the management structure.
- In reality, an invisible subsystem of **informal communications** exists alongside the formal communications network within any organisation. It includes the 'grapevine' that grows rapidly in any human situation where official information is lacking.

Both formal and informal communication are essential to the efficient running of a business.

Essentials

Formal communication involves passing information along the official chains of command within the organisation.

Essentials

Informal communications means passing information through unofficial channels.

Informal communications assume more importance in a democratically led business. There, all kinds of communication will help to foster effective decision-making. In a business run on authoritarian lines, informal communications may undermine the power of the leader. Equally, if there are problems within the organisation, informal communications may provide the only possible way of uncovering them.

Informal communications can have the appearance of simple gossip, but they should not be thought of as being purely oral. Written messages passing along unofficial channels can be an important means of communication.

Electronic communications of all kinds have brought considerable changes to the way people communicate within businesses. Many businesses are using fewer telephone calls and more electronic mail (e-mails) for internal communications. Intranets (internal websites) can make for very easy communications within the company itself.

People: the greatest asset

Suppose that a manufacturer decides to introduce the most up-to-date technology, properly installed and integrated into its production process. Suppose, too, that it becomes highly market-orientated with systems for responding rapidly to change using a minimum level of working capital. Is this a firm with improved efficiency? Clearly, the business has potential, but what actually happens depends on the people who work there.

Work in progress

Look back at the case study on Rank and Toshiba (page 92).

Q **1** How would the changes at Toshiba improve communications?

2 How were the Rank employees affected by the Toshiba take-over?

Like other factors of production, labour is employed to add value to a firm's product. Indeed, the addition in value generated by an employee must be greater than the total cost of his or her employment. How does labour add value? Clearly, through some kind of output. This could imply a stream of manufactured products, or visits to customers or sending out letters or moving stock. These and many other tasks contribute to the value of the product purchased by the final customer. But a firm does not seek quantity alone in any given flow of output: it will also be concerned with quality. The achievement of quality in each process is a key determinant of a product's market value or price. Thus efficiency is concerned not only with 'how much?' but also with 'how good?'.

The actual level of efficiency achieved by people in an organisation depends on a range of key factors. Skill is vital to the efficient performance of any job. It depends on aptitude, experience and training.

Motivation means the strength of commitment within the individual towards carrying out the work in question. Direction is the effective relationship between work and its agreed goals. Work in itself has no value unless applied in the right direction.

In practice, businesses strive for efficiency against a background of constantly changing conditions. In order to achieve efficiency there must be an effective organisation and leadership and good communications. Indeed, all aspects of human resource management are vital in the creation of a successful culture which makes the most of the resources the business has available to it. This culture can create the flexibility needed to adapt to changes swiftly and effectively.

People are a key source of competitive advantage. They get to know the business and develop firm-specific skills. Their motivation and sense of direction can make them extremely valuable to the business. These qualities are hard for competitors to replicate.

Enquiry 3   Can costs be cut?

1 Does teamwork cut costs?

Making things well

Robert Bracken was a keen mountaineer with lots of experience of ice climbing in tough conditions. He was also trained and experienced in the engineering industry. As an individualist, he found he was not happy working in large organisations and he determined to start his own business making mountaineering safety equipment. He had a good idea for a new style of ice screw which he could make on a small scale. Ice screws enable the climber to tie their ropes on to the ice, giving substantial protection against accidental falls.

In time his product developed a reputation for giving quality protection at a reasonable price. He added a number of products to his range, including chocks and bolts, which are used in rock climbing. Other more sophisticated devices for a variety of adventure sports followed. The company's competitive edge came from understanding customer needs. As an enthusiast, Robert knew the importance of quality and reliability. He understood how to design quality into the product. 'If we try a product we don't understand, it doesn't work,' he says.

By the late 1980s the company had 200 employees at its factory in Sheffield. But they were facing very strong competition from suppliers in Switzerland and Korea. Robert decided to go to the US to study new manufacturing strategies. He learned that he could cut costs dramatically. Three US trips later the company is now super-efficient. The workforce was divided into cells – groups of employees who are responsible for all the tasks which go into making the finished product. This gives them a strong sense of responsibility for producing efficiently.

Careful control of production makes it possible to make all products to order. Employees are trained so that they can make everything in the product range. This means that the company can be highly sensitive and respond quickly to changes in demand. Exports to Canada are growing strongly.

The cost savings came from the reduction in supervisory staff needed when teams are working well. Added savings come from improved quality. Each team has a number which appears on the product label. Customer complaints come back to the team. This creates a powerful incentive to get every product just right. Effectively, the teams are self-managing.

Your agenda

1 List the sources of Bracken's current competitive advantage.

2 How did the changes affect the relationship between the quantities of resources used and the level of output?

3 What lessons does the above experience have for other businesses?

When businesses improve their organisation they generally succeed in cutting costs. This means that they can produce the same amount of output using fewer resources. The resources they save may be labour, or raw materials, or energy, or the finance needed to keep production going. Savings on all these fronts can mean higher profits. Alternatively, they may mean that the business can price its product more competitively and expand its market share. In other words, the outcome may be an improvement in competitive advantage, based on a strategy of cost leadership.

Organising people

In the case study above, the desperate need to cut costs led to the introduction of **cell production**. This involves groups of staff forming physical and organisational clusters where a whole series of tasks can be carried out. These tasks together represent a major stage or even the whole of the production process. Teams take responsibility for the quality of their own output and the efficiency with which it is produced. The approach was pioneered by Volvo in Sweden and has been widely adapted and applied since.

What cell production means in practice is this:

- Instead of each employee standing on an assembly line performing a single repetitive task all day long, people are organised into teams which are collectively responsible for all or part of the production process. This means that people will be moved around from one task to another, and will gain experience of different parts of the production process.
- Employees often need to develop new skills. In fact, **multi-skilling** is one of the advantages of cell production because the people involved become more versatile. Their talents are more likely to be fully utilised.
- In particular, cell production requires that at least some of the members of the team are able to trouble-shoot when something goes wrong. If they have been trained to do this, they have no need to send for a specialist engineer and faults in the production process can be rectified quickly.

> ### Essentials
>
> **Cell production** involves teams of employees taking responsibility for a significant part of the total production process. This allows them to carry out a range of different tasks and ensure themselves that quality is maintained.

> ### Essentials
>
> **Multi-skilling** involves individuals in being trained to undertake a range of processes.

Organising flexible teams

The original logic behind cell production was motivational rather than technical. (See the case study on page 20.) Greater job satisfaction is possible if people feel involved in a clearly meaningful process rather than a repetitive and apparently meaningless task. However, multi-skilling has tended to make it possible to use employees in more flexible ways. Both benefits lead businesses to produce more effectively and economically.

Cell production involves teamwork in manufacturing. However, the idea of teamwork is much more widely applicable. In management and in the service sector, organising people into tightly focused teams means that people pool skills and knowledge. They communicate more easily. If they feel involved in decisions about the way the job is done, they will work in a cooperative way to produce the best possible outcome.

It should be kept in mind that introducing cell production will usually entail a culture change. Much of what you have already learned about corporate culture applies if the business is making this type of change.

> ### Work in progress
>
> Look back at the case study on Robert Bracken's mountaineering equipment company at the start of this enquiry.
>
> **Q** 1 How did cell production increase efficiency at Bracken's?
>
> 2 In what ways can multi-skilling lead to improved motivation?
>
> 3 Can you suggest circumstances in which teamwork might increase rather than decrease costs?

2 Can production become leaner?

Stocks

> …well I said to the manager, fancy Tesco not having any Jersey potatoes left on a Friday morning in mid-May. What am I supposed to do? Find an old-fashioned greengrocer? The only convenient one closed down last week. To be fair, they did find some more round the back, but I had to wait ten minutes…

> Following the trend towards adopting Japanese production methods, employees at Boeing receive all the parts they need in colour-coded boxes which are packed, counted and ready for assembly. No longer do they need to go and fetch the parts from the store when they need them.

Your agenda

1 How would reorganising the way employees get their stocks of inputs cut costs for aircraft manufacturer Boeing?

2 How does running out of stocks affect a business?

3 How can a business make sure it gets stock levels right?

4 What is the opportunity cost of carrying high stocks?

One way of measuring efficiency is to look at **productivity**. You can assess how effectively labour is being used by looking at labour productivity, i.e. output per person employed. During the 1980s it became very clear that productivity in many countries was lagging well behind that of Japan. Experts at the Massachusetts Institute of Technology set up a major research programme to look into the reasons. They termed the Japanese approach which they studied **lean production**.

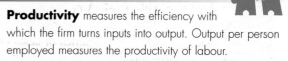

Essentials

Productivity measures the efficiency with which the firm turns inputs into output. Output per person employed measures the productivity of labour.

Essentials

Lean production refers to the way Japanese manufacturing firms used streamlined production methods which cut costs by reducing waste and improving quality.

Lean production involves a whole range of waste-saving measures which have the potential to raise productivity. The term comes from the idea that lean production looks for ways of 'using less of everything', i.e. fewer resources for every process. So it includes organising people effectively, cutting down on stocks, improving quality through a market-orientated approach, an integrated approach to design and technology and a search for ways of making manufacturing systems more flexible. The issues involved in lean production play a big part in the rest of this enquiry.

Lean production is a culture or philosophy for the whole firm. Overall, it requires a collaborative approach on the part of employees and management. Increasingly, western companies have adopted lean production strategies, often with impressive results.

Can stocks be cut?

Stocks are essential in every business. In manufacturing, stocks provide an adequate flow of raw materials and **work-in-progress**. Yet stocks carry an opportunity cost. These costs include warehouse space, handling, deterioration, insurance and administration, as well as the cost of finance to pay for all these. The value of having stocks of inputs must be set against the costs.

Figure M2.6 shows a simple graphical model of **stock control**. Stocks ensure that the customer has a visible choice and immediate delivery. The firm must strike a balance between the achievement of customer satisfaction and the cost of holding stocks.

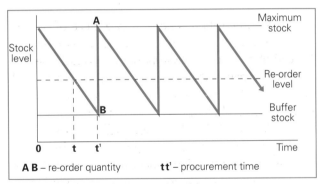

Figure M2.6 The classic stock control model

In setting a maximum stock level the firm will compare any discounts available for larger purchases against the opportunity cost of holding stock. The buffer stock is a minimum reserve level. It depends on flexibility and reliability of supplies and the potential damage to production caused by a stock-out (running out of stock). The downward slopes on the graph represent stock use. The vertical upstrokes reflect stock deliveries. The level of stock to trigger reorder (the reorder level) depends on the time taken between order and delivery. Real models are more complex and less regular, but do help the firm to find an optimal policy.

After delivery, materials are processed and become work-in-progress. Progressively more finished goods move through the production process until the final product is packed and stored to await delivery.

> **Essentials**
>
> **Stock control** is the process by which the business ensures that stocks of inputs are adequate to meet production requirements, and that stocks of the finished product are readily available to meet customer needs.

> **Essentials**
>
> **Work-in-progress** is the value of all stock that is held in a firm as partly finished goods.

■ Just in time

Every time there is a delay between the delivery of stocks and their use in the production process, resources are lying idle and there is a real cost. It follows that efficiency could be improved by reducing these 'gaps' to a minimum. **Just-in-time** systems, an

important element in lean production, use this approach. Replacement stock arrives at the production point just before its time of use.

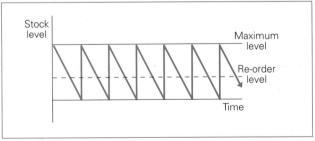

Figure M2.7 Just-in-time stock control

In Figure M2.7 the buffer stock is virtually eliminated. The reorder quantity is small and the procurement time is short. The effect is to reduce – often by more than 50 per cent – the value of stock held by a firm with a corresponding release of resources, so improving efficiency.

Needless stockholding and production bottlenecks are avoided and the movement of resources is kept to the most efficient minimum. The funds needed to cover the cost of stockholding can be used elsewhere in the business or simply to reduce costly borrowing.

Materials and components from suppliers arrive at the factory only when they are needed and in quantities that can be used immediately, i.e. just in time. However, prompt and accurate ordering from suppliers is essential if costly errors and delays are to be avoided. The firm needs to know that supplies will arrive at exactly the right time, in precisely the right quantity and be of exactly the right quality. This requires continuous, open and honest communications with supplier firms. Often cooperation will include inspection of the supplier factories and joint projects for their development and improvement. This makes it vitally important that businesses maintain good close relationships with supplier companies.

> **Essentials**
>
> **Just-in-time** systems involve scheduling the delivery of stocks in a precisely coordinated way, minimising the quantity which needs to be held.

Stock control is especially important for supermarkets. They carry a vast range of merchandise, yet each individual product has a different unit value (and hence opportunity cost) and a different speed of turnover. Sainsbury's was one of the first chains to adopt laser scanning and computerised stock control. This meant that stock levels could be electronically monitored with every sale. Automatic reorder levels could be set to trigger fresh supplies, thus immediately reflecting any shift in consumer preferences. These orders directly affect the pattern of output at the firm's suppliers, and thus their orders for materials and so on, back down the chain.

Work in progress

Q **1** What types of business are likely to gain most from just-in-time stock control?

2 Think of two examples of businesses where just-in-time is really irrelevant.

3 High stock levels can be a good thing, for example when demand fluctuates and the cost of a stock-out is high. What kind of business might this apply to?

Kanban systems

Just-in-time tactics were developed in Japan soon after the Second World War ended. The idea was to make only the quantity of components needed at the next stage of production. The original **Kanban** system was developed using cards which were attached to batches of components whose progress through the factory was tightly monitored to avoid any delay on the production line. The term 'Kanban' is the Japanese word for these cards.

A market-orientated firm regards its business activity as beginning and not ending with the market. All production is directly driven by the pattern of customer demand. The sooner a change in demand is translated into a change in production, the more efficiently the firm is able to match its output to the market, and so gain sales and profit.

Market orientation is not simply a piece of jargon but an attitude that can pervade a whole organisation. Instead of production *pushing* output towards the market, the market *pulls* output through production. A customer order brings together the necessary materials, components and activities, all the way back through the production chain. This is very different from producing a set amount of the product and then hoping that the sales department has got the orders. A pull-system means a move away from guesswork and hope, towards a system that produces the goods when demanded. Kanban is all about pull-systems. Waste at every stage is greatly reduced.

Work in progress

Q **1** Look for examples of businesses adopting lean production strategies in your own locality. Remember that lean production is equally applicable to firms whose output is consumer or producer services. A holiday company producing 'package tours' attempts to match market demand with its own flight and hotel bookings as closely as possible. A strong relationship with 'suppliers', for example foreign hoteliers is essential.

Essentials

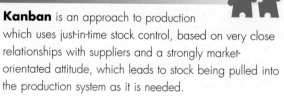

Kanban is an approach to production which uses just-in-time stock control, based on very close relationships with suppliers and a strongly market-orientated attitude, which leads to stock being pulled into the production system as it is needed.

3 Can quality rise while costs fall?

Bonas machines

When Tony Gosling decided a change of emphasis was required at his Tyneside engineering company, he changed his workforce.

Concerned at growing overseas competition and skills shortages at home, the managing director of Bonas Machines opted for a complete overhaul of training and workplace attitudes at the Gateshead-based components manufacturer.

The company, which makes patterning control equipment for the textiles industry, drew up a seven-point action plan to re-educate its 360 employees about quality standards, relationships with customers and suppliers, and the need for continuous improvement.

Two years into surgery, some workers have not survived the treatment. Perhaps that is not surprising, given that everyone at Bonas Machines suddenly found themselves having to abandon old working practices, reapply for their own jobs and submit themselves to a 24-page questionnaire on workplace philosophy. Employees who found themselves in difficulty were given extra training.

This 'Philosophy of Work' programme has paid rich dividends rather than sown discord. Productivity is up by more than 60 per cent; lead times have been halved and inventory times (the length of time stock stands unused) cut from 50 to 12 days.

Your agenda

1 How do low quality standards waste resources?
2 How can quality control increase efficiency?
3 How is quality linked to customer service?
4 Why does improved quality require better training?

Ensuring that quality is being maintained has come to be seen in recent years as having paramount importance. It is directly related to the quest for improved efficiency. It is also an important element in the total picture represented by lean production.

In manufacturing, if substandard goods are being produced, rectifying the matter can be very costly. Either some production is wasted and cannot be sold, or it is sold but returned. Quality is also an important consideration in the service sector. Complaints about poor service will be reflected in lower sales, and in the time taken to investigate. Resources will be being used wastefully, either way. So tightening up on quality economises on resources used in production and leads to greater efficiency.

In the past, many manufacturers had a quality control department. This might test a sample drawn from the output of the final product. Quality targets would be set, and the number of imperfect items would have to be kept below a certain percentage. This type of arrangement was particularly suitable for assembly-line production, where each person performs a single task. Employees might have relatively few skills and little insight into the production process. The underlying philosophy perceived quality as raising costs and threatening profits.

On the whole, the use of this approach was not associated with high quality. A search began to find the reasons why UK products were not competing well either in foreign markets or with imports in domestic markets. During this search, many managers discovered lean production. One element in this was an expectation of very high levels of quality control. It was seen as wasteful to persist in producing faulty products.

Most businesses now make quality control a high priority. If they do not, then their customers will simply go elsewhere. Many customers have access to information about the quality, effectiveness and reliability of the product. Quality is important in determining overall competitiveness.

Improving quality

One way to improve is to make all employees responsible for quality. This entails extra training, but it has also fitted in with the cell production approach, where the team is responsible for maintaining high quality output.

High quality is now seen as an important component of the added value which gives the product its competitive advantage. It is easy to see that quality is an important element in value for money. Also, competition has driven up customer expectations.

To meet these expectations, quality improving strategies have been developed. These may be implemented individually or as a package. The emphasis is upon getting the product right first time, rather than having to correct it later (a *zero defects* strategy).

- *Quality assurance* (QA) implies a commitment to collaboration between the people responsible for design, production and marketing. They will work together towards increased quality and reliability. An important aspect of this approach is that everyone in the business has to become more aware of the need for quality. Instead of monitoring output, as the old quality control departments did, a QA department will be drawn into the design process and the setting up of the production system. Quality becomes central to the basic organisation of production and is checked at every stage.
- *Quality circles* are small groups of employees who meet from time to time to discuss ways of improving quality. This brings the issue right to the very people who are responsible for avoiding mistakes. Where production is carried out by teams, quality circle activities can occur regularly.
- *Total quality management* (TQM) is a philosophy which tries to generate both an individual and a collective responsibility for quality at every level. Each department is seen as having responsibility for quality in both products and services. It is expected to regard the department handling the next stage of production as its customer, whose needs must be satisfied. The term TQM has gone somewhat out of fashion during the 1990s, but the overall approach of making quality a high priority has proved fairly durable.

Work in progress

Q 1 How does quality affect competitive advantage?

2 How did Bracken's address the need for higher quality in production (see case study on page 95)?

Any change in culture involves an element of training. A change in attitudes to quality and the involvement of the whole workforce requires a substantial investment in training and reorientation. This is investment in human capital, a vital element in the production process. In spite of the costs, few businesses have not made changes in the way they approach quality. Increasing competition from abroad and better informed customers have made it essential for the market orientated business to address quality issues directly.

4 Investment, new technology and productivity

Robots and fish

The 'Robofish' looks nothing like most people's idea of a robot. But it can detect, grasp and sort a trawler-load of raw fish faster and more efficiently than any human operator.

Robofish, equipped with sensors, machine vision and a gripper, has received enthusiastic reviews from the fish-processing sector. It was designed by Oxford Intelligent Machines, one of an emerging cluster of UK robotics companies. It employs 17 people and has sales of £1 million a year.

Your agenda

1 How would you expect the Robofish to affect productivity in the fishing industry?

2 What would you expect to happen to the price of fish if Robofishes are installed on many trawlers?

Capital **investment** means spending now on new plant, machinery and buildings which can help to generate more income in the future. Investment has enormous potential for increasing the efficiency of production. The employee who has more capital to work with will almost always have higher productivity.

New equipment is often also better equipment because technological change brings a whole range of developments. Machines may be larger, more efficient, more reliable and require less labour. Similarly, new machines often require people to be trained in their use, so investment in physical capital and human capital go together. Technological improvements require research and development (R & D) and that too involves costly programmes which are themselves investments in future income possibilities.

Essentials

Investment involves spending now which generates income in the future. It may involve buying capital equipment or spending on research or training.

It is often the case that the kind of cultural changes described earlier in this enquiry are implemented together with re-equipment programmes. Approaches which make employees more flexible, such as cell production, can be helpful when new equipment and new technologies are being installed.

Point of view

Is performance improving?

Britain may have one of the lowest unemployment levels in the European Union, but productivity is still low in the UK compared to other countries. Even the largest, most successful companies have lower productivity than competitors elsewhere in Europe. British star performers tend to be small and few in number.

It has been suggested that the UK is inward-looking and that its workers are low-skilled and poorly paid. British companies fail to invest enough in research and development, and export efforts are weak, especially by small businesses. Overall, productivity is a quarter to a third lower than in France and Italy.

The government recommends that businesses study the best practices of companies abroad to increase productivity and profitability instead of comparing themselves to domestic rivals.

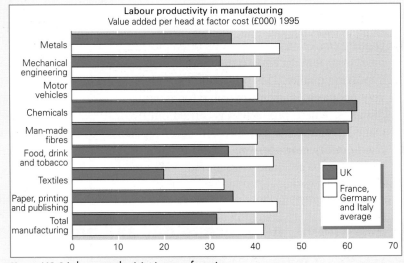

Figure M2.8 Labour productivity in manufacturing

Source: *Independent on Sunday*, 16 November 1997 NOT Independent ©

Your agenda

1 Chemicals, the largest UK manufacturing sector, increased productivity by 44 per cent between 1990 and 1996; the overall average for UK manufacturing is 21 per cent. How does performance in this sector compare with the others?

2 In what ways does this evidence contrast with the case studies from earlier on in the enquiry?

3 Given that most managers have now heard of lean production, what might now be stopping them from making progress in increasing productivity? Is there a solution to the problem?

One way of measuring improvement is to compare productivity levels. People will become more productive if managers are able to increase the level of personal motivation and commitment among their staff. Similarly, productivity increases if work is coordinated so that people are not standing idle too often. This requires careful operations management.

Productivity can be used to compare efficiency between firms, or whole industries, or countries. It is also possible to measure the productivity of capital. UK productivity has improved in recent years but not always by as much as that of competing countries.

5 How does scale affect costs?

Big product, big company

People like to travel. Incomes grow, people go further. Aircraft manufacturers have developed new, bigger, cheaper planes. But the development costs of a new model are huge. For a time, it appeared that of the big manufacturers, only Boeing might be big enough and strong enough to survive.

European governments didn't want to lose their aircraft manufacturing industries. France had Aerospatiale. Germany had Daimler-Benz Aerospace. The UK had British Aerospace. Yet none of these three could afford to develop new planes which could compete with 747s and Boeing's other big jets.

The European governments created Airbus Industrie, a consortium of companies which collaborate. They produced the European airbus, very successfully. As time goes by the member companies are drawing closer together. Collaboration on this scale isn't easy, but it has created a commercial organisation which is big enough to compete with Boeing.

Your agenda

1 Why do companies need to be big to develop new airliners?

2 What are the advantages for European aircraft manufacturers which are prepared to work together?

3 In which other industries is production usually carried out on a very large scale?

4 Is there any room for small-scale production in these industries? Give examples.

The aircraft industry is one in which there are **internal economies of scale**. The businesses which are able to compete effectively have to be able to make costly investments in research and development and in plant and machinery. Once they have done this, they need long production runs and high sales levels which can help them to recoup the development costs.

Essentials

Internal economies of scale occur if a firm which is increasing output is also managing to cut its unit costs.

Many manufactured products simply cannot be produced cheaply on a small scale. Economies of scale can arise from a number of different sources:

- *Technical economies* become possible when the firm grows large enough to employ bigger, better and more expensive machines. Bigger machines can produce more cheaply but will also produce much more, so the firm must have a large enough market to take all the extra output. This is the familiar story of mass production, leading to a fall in costs and in prices, thus creating a mass market. Usually, for this to work, the product must be to a great extent standardised so that long production runs are possible. Then the business will enhance its competitive advantage.
- *Managerial economies* occur when a growing firm is able to hire specialists who are highly skilled at what they do. Using the principle of division of labour, the management team can include marketing and personnel managers, accountants, and so on. Using their skills, these specialists aim to reduce costs by organising production more efficiently.

■ *Marketing economies* can be achieved if the firm is large enough to employ mass marketing strategies, for example TV advertising.

■ *Financial economies* arise because larger firms find it easier to borrow from banks, and will often be able to do so at lower rates of interest. They are regarded as being more secure.

■ *Risk-bearing economies* are to be had when the company is big enough to try a number of possibilities, i.e. diversify. It can afford to take risks because it can be sure that not all of its activities will fail.

We can use **average total cost** (ATC) to analyse economies of scale. Average total cost is defined as cost per unit of output, and applies to the long run. If there are economies of scale to be reaped, average total cost will fall as output rises. Figure M2.9 shows the minimum efficient scale of output at the point where average total cost is first at the minimum. If output carries on rising, costs may begin to rise again. However, for many firms there is a range of outputs at which costs are minimised, so the ATC curve has a flat bottom.

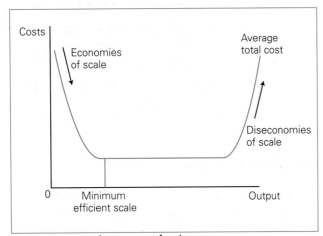

Figure M2.9 Internal economies of scale

Work in progress

Q 1 Think about the economies of scale outlined above. Which of them apply to Airbus Industrie and Boeing, why and how?

2 Which of them might apply to a maker of hair shampoo?

3 What economies of scale might a growing supermarket chain expect to experience?

Obviously, internal economies of scale can all contribute to competitive advantage. Sometimes this fact leads to a good deal of merger activity and rationalisation of production. Companies seek out potential economies by joining forces and concentrating production at fewer factory sites.

Essentials

Average total cost is total cost divided by quantity of output.

A favourable climate for growth

The oil company BP needs to recruit graduates. The steady supply of suitably trained geologists and mining engineers from universities means that it can easily recruit the kind of people it needs for oil exploration and for management. Similarly, when there are facilities for training the workforce available locally, businesses will be able to train their employees more easily. A research establishment which makes available new knowledge, which is relevant to the production process or the product, may be helpful too.

Essentials

External economies of scale occur when costs fall because the industry is growing, and include economies coming from outside the individual firm.

All these things increase efficiency in obvious ways. They are called **external economies of scale**, because they come from sources external to the firm. They are available to all firms in the industry, equally.

External economies can be important wherever there is a concentration of firms within a specific area. Training provided by local colleges, or a local pool of skilled labour, both create external economies, or specialised suppliers of inputs may set up in business and be capable of supplying a number of firms at a lower cost than they themselves can achieve. Component suppliers to the car industry are an example of this.

External economies of scale make average total costs fall at all levels of output for the individual firm. This is shown in Figure M2.10. The whole ATC curve shifts downwards.

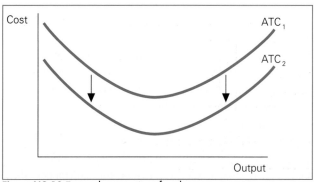

Figure M2.10 External economies of scale

Growth which creates problems

Very large firms sometimes develop communication problems. They may not be at all easy to manage effectively. It may become difficult to motivate the workforce. Contact between the management and employees on the shopfloor may become less personal, and industrial relations problems may develop. Coordinating the work of different departments or divisions may be difficult. Many people may need to be involved in the decision-taking process, and the necessary meetings may become very time consuming. All this will raise costs. We call these problems **diseconomies of scale**.

Essentials

Diseconomies of scale occur if a firm grows beyond its optimum size and average total costs begin to rise.

The optimum size for a firm is that at which average total cost is kept to a minimum. This will vary greatly from one firm to another. The rise in its costs is likely to be due to communication problems within the management structure, or to loss of flexibility in response to changes in the market place, or the firm may have become unable to offer the customer a personal service in an industry where this is important.

If, in order to keep costs down, mass production is necessary, then it is likely that the firm can become very large before diseconomies of scale begin to outweigh the benefits of a large output of a standardised product. If, on the other hand, the product needs to fit precisely the customers' individual needs, then a small-scale operation may have lower costs.

Large *and* small

In some industries small- and large-scale businesses coexist. Sometimes the larger ones seek a mass market; the smaller ones, niche markets. Some businesses are **conglomerates**: they own a lot of different businesses with no particular connection. Virgin is tending in that direction. Having started out in the music business, it moved on to air travel, rail travel… and cola. The component businesses in a conglomerate may gain competitive advantage through the marketing and financial economies enjoyed by the parent company.

Essentials

Conglomerates are groups of very different businesses which are all owned by one parent company. The parent company benefits from being diversified but may lack expertise in the industries concerned.

Work in progress

Q 1   What kinds of business seem to work equally well on either a small or a large scale? Why?

2   What kinds of business are almost always run on a small scale? What particular advantages are small businesses likely to have?

3   What economies of scale do conglomerates have? Explain your reasons.

Scale and efficiency

All the strategies described in this enquiry can be used to improve both efficiency and effectiveness. However, increasing productivity often requires considerable effort. In particular, because market orientation is so important in ensuring that customer requirements are met, there must be close collaboration between the departments responsible for marketing and the management of production. This kind of teamwork takes skill and training. Above all, people have to be able to contemplate change. If they cannot, then the business must first think about how its corporate culture might be altered to encourage a positive attitude to change.

1 Meeting consumer demand

Giving customers what they want

Hennes and Mauritz

Hennes and Mauritz is Sweden's fifth largest company. It sells inexpensive, fashionable clothes all over Europe. It is still largely family-owned and controlled. It has been brilliantly successful. Sales and profits have grown faster over the past decade than those of any other clothes retailer in the world. It sells the same clothes in all its shops. The company believes that the MTV generation's fashion sense is formed by the same diet of satellite television, films and music, wherever they are, and all its stores have the same look.

The management of Hennes is obsessed with keeping costs low. The company has a tiny head office. But being big, Hennes can buy cheaply. It isn't interested in high profit margins. Instead it passes the cost savings on to the consumer. It can buy in bulk and offer a wide choice at low prices. It has turned out to be a winning formula.

Trendy cookers

You can buy a satisfactory cooker for about £300 if you need to. Then again, if you want a large, rather old-fashioned looking cooker with stainless steel surfaces and brass trimmings, you could pay between £1 000 and £5 000. To start with, these particular fashion items were only to be found in specialist shops. Now they can be found in electrical goods chains and department stores.

Your agenda

1   What are the qualities which have enabled Hennes to expand so fast?

2   Why is demand for expensive cookers rising?

3   If you demand more of a product, will you be able to get it? If you are sure about the answer to this question, what are your reasons?

Businesses grow when they have a winning strategy. Hennes does well because it competes successfully on both price and style. The business has expanded and taken on more labour. Although the company keeps profit margins low, profits rise because of the expansion of sales and revenue.

When people begin to want more of a product such as a particular type of cooker, the satisfaction they are getting from it has increased. Their demand rises and they are prepared to pay more. Sellers are able to raise their prices. This increases their sales revenue and their profits. These profits attract additional resources to the industry. Some new firms will enter the industry. Some existing producers will expand. Easy **entry** into the market means that businesses can set up and expand to meet consumer demand.

The process at work here is called the **profit-signalling mechanism**. The possibility of increased profit induces producers to expand. The profit comes from being able to satisfy consumer demand effectively. It can come from a whole range of different kinds of competitive advantage. These will generally involve either added value or cost leadership.

Of course, the reverse is true too. When demand for a product falls, prices will fall. The product will be produced at a loss, but not for long. The firm may discontinue production. Sometimes the producer will be making losses overall, and may therefore go out of business altogether. Either way, this is referred to as **exit** from the market.

Profits and losses reflect market forces, transmitting to producers the messages about what consumers want. They also transmit a message about the efficiency with which demand is being satisfied. A business may exit from the market not because demand for the product has gone down overall, but because some other producer can keep costs down more effectively, satisfying demand more competitively.

Essentials

Entry is a term referring to the way businesses can move into a particular market when the product looks potentially profitable.

Essentials

Exit from the market for a particular product means production stops and resources are released for use in other lines of production and other businesses.

Essentials

The **profit-signalling mechanism** is the process by which increases in profitability can indicate to businesses that an opportunity may exist to produce and sell more. Equally, falling profit can indicate lack of demand and a need to cut production.

■ Finding the most profitable opportunities

Market-orientated companies are constantly looking out for changes in their markets. They look for ways of being flexible enough to adapt quickly.

Changes in the market place create the potential for increased profits. When customers flock to buy a product, stocks may not be sufficient to meet the demand. That makes it possible to put the price up and still sell all that can be obtained. The resulting increase in profits gives businesses an incentive to produce more, so supply expands to meet demand. This is what happened with the fashion-conscious cookers.

When a business finds a way of cutting costs, profits increase. If the business is able to pass some of the cost savings on to the customer in the form of lower prices, sales may rise. This can bring further increases in profits. In this way, the profit-signalling mechanism leads buyers towards the most efficient producers. Hennes provides a good example of this process.

While one industry gains customers, another is probably losing them. Its business will be shrinking, making employees redundant, allowing its capital equipment to wear out and not replacing it. This means that resources move from one line of production to another in response to changes in consumer demand. This process is known as **reallocation of resources**. The resources are moving from shrinking to growing markets.

When this type of process occurs on a large scale, affecting whole industries, there is a change in the structure of production across the economy. **Structural change** refers to the way some industries grow while some decline. When industries are concentrated in particular areas, this process can seriously affect employment opportunities.

Work in progress

Q

1   Think of a product which recently became fashionable. What happened to the price? Think about the time period immediately following the rise in sales, and what happened later on, when producers had had a chance to adjust to the change.

2   Draw a supply and demand diagram for your product, showing what happened to the demand curve when the product became fashionable. What prediction does your diagram give as to the price of the product and the quantity sold?

Many developed countries have found in the past two decades that increasingly their resources are moving out of manufacturing businesses and moving into the service sector. Figure M2.11 shows the scope of this change for the UK in terms of employment.

	1979	1998
Primary	1537	1497
Secondary	8065	4076
Tertiary	13 556	17 664
Total employment	23 158	23 237

Figure M2.11 Employment by sector (000s)

Source: ONS, *Annual Abstract*, 1986 and 1999

Essentials

Reallocation of resources is the process by which the resources needed in the production process move out of less profitable uses and into more profitable uses.

Essentials

Structural change is the process by which whole industries experience falling demand, so that resources become redundant and move into production of goods and services with growing demand.

2 Getting technically better?

Are machines better and cheaper?

During the 1980s banks started to install 'hole-in-the-wall' cash machines. People with bank accounts could withdraw cash at any time of day and without going into the bank. By then, all customers' accounts were computerised and technological developments made it possible to design machines which could read plastic cards, get information from a central computer and count out banknotes. During the 1990s the system changed further with the introduction of cash machines in supermarkets.

Each cash machine involved an investment of several thousand pounds, but it gave customers considerably greater convenience in withdrawing money. Going to the bank before cash machines meant turning up between 10.00 am and 3.00 pm, queuing (usually), writing a cheque, waiting while the teller processed the cheque and counted out the money.

Furthermore, cash machines saved paying the wages of bank tellers. About 20 000 bank employees were made redundant as a result of the computerisation of bank business. Investment in machines cuts costs.

Your agenda

1 Would you want to have an account at a bank which had decided not to install cash machines?

2 What would have happened to a bank which did not install cash machines?

3 What happens to fixed and variable costs when businesses install new equipment? What happens to total costs? Will this affect prices?

The basic building blocks of production are: **labour**, **capital** and land. Together they are known as the factors of production. Of course, some businesses need raw materials. But where do they come from? Iron ore is a raw material. It comes from people digging the ore out of what is usually a large area of land, with a variety of digging implements or machines. The people provide the labour. The implements or machines are capital equipment. The land is the space in which the mining takes place. Ultimately, all goods and services, all products, come from those basic resources.

The ways in which resources are used are determined by the decisions of entrepreneurs. In a competitive market these decisions are made on the basis of market demand and knowledge of how to produce most efficiently.

- *Labour intensive production* takes place when large numbers of people are required. Computer software provides one example. The disks and handbook which need to be reproduced will require capital equipment. However, the cost of these items is small. The cost of the brains needed to develop the software is high. The training of those brains is done mainly by teachers and managers: it is another labour intensive process. So overall, software is a labour intensive product.

- *Capital intensive production* requires much capital and little labour. Electricity producion provides an example. The power station is a major capital investment. Relatively few people are needed to keep it going. In developed countries, most manufactured products are now produced by capital intensive methods. Most farm products are capital and land intensive. Wheat needs a lot of land and big tractors, at least in the developed world. One farmer can work a big land area.

- In some industries both *labour and capital intensive production* techniques can be used. There is a choice: there are alternative technologies. It is up to the entrepreneur to decide which will be the cheapest technology, and therefore the most efficient and profitable. Deciding this will depend very much on the relative prices of labour and capital. If wages are high, it makes sense to invest in labour-saving capital. If sophisticated capital is expensive and wages are low, then a labour intensive approach will probably be more sensible.

Work in progress

Q **1** For each of the following products, say whether production will be labour or capital intensive and why: newspapers, street cleaning, asparagus, water supplies.

2 Which products allow a flexible mix of capital and labour inputs? How would the entrepreneur decide what mix would be best?

Essentials

Capital consists of machinery, equipment and buildings which can be used in the production process.

Essentials

Human capital refers to the skills and training embodied in individual people.

Essentials

Labour consists of the people employed in the production process.

These ideas are straightforward except for one complicating factor. We describe the skills and training people have had which make them more productive as **human capital**. This reflects the fact that education and training require a substantial investment of both time and money.

3 Improving efficiency

Virtual assembly lines

Ford Motor Company, the second biggest US car manufacturer, is using advanced computer technology to test production layouts on screen. It can see virtual workers stretching, leaning and using tools. It can test new assembly line arrangements to see if they are practical and efficient.

Ford expects the new system to allow it to cut £123 million a year from the company's development costs for new models. It will end the process of trial and error in setting up production. The time taken to get a car from the initial design stage to commercial production should be cut by a third.

The technology can be used to create the component parts of the car in three-dimensional form. Then the prototype car can be manipulated and built on screen. Component suppliers will be expected to use the same technology so that their systems are compatible with Ford's. The technology played a major role in the development of the new 'world' Escort for its launch in 1999.

Your agenda

1 What changes were involved in the use of labour and capital in the above example?

2 What advantages do such changes have from the point of view of the consumer?

3 How can competition encourage the adoption of new production technologies?

Cutting costs and improving efficiency often means moving towards more capital intensive production methods. In the Ford case study another important factor comes into play: **process innovation**. Better technology in the production process goes hand in hand with investment in more capital to reduce development time and production costs. Reducing development time is yet another aspect of lean production.

Substituting labour for capital in this way can increase labour productivity: production levels are maintained or increased using fewer people. This means that **unit costs** fall. Businesses which are striving for competitive advantage through cost leadership are involved in a continuous search for cost savings of this kind.

As businesses strive to cut costs, they are working towards a state of **technical efficiency**. This is achieved when unit costs are brought down to the minimum which is technically possible. They must select the production methods which minimise use of the most expensive resource, usually labour, and use the cheapest technology.

Essentials

Process innovation involves the use of new technologies in the production process; it is an extremely important aspect of the satisfaction of consumer demand in the most efficient way.

Essentials

Unit costs are the total costs of each individual item produced.

Essentials

Technical efficiency involves using the production methods which keep unit costs to a minimum for a given quantity of output.

The benefits of increased efficiency

Depending on the pricing strategy the business adopts one of two things may happen subsequently:

- falling costs with constant prices will create higher profit margins
- cost savings can be passed on to the consumer in the form of price cuts or improved value for money, so increasing spending power and real incomes; output may then rise as consumers buy more.

Competition is important in determining what happens. Strongly competitive markets encourage businesses to pass on cost savings to the consumer. Prices will be kept close to the minimum unit cost, forcing all businesses to be technically efficient. If a company tries to charge a price above the lowest possible cost, consumers will buy from a competitor and the firm will go out of business. If, on the other hand, the industry does not have strong competition, there is much less incentive to be efficient. The business which does adopt efficient production strategies may simply pile up profits rather than cut prices.

This is another aspect of resource reallocation. It often starts with a shift to more capital intensive production methods, which involves using less labour. However, without this change the business facing competition may fail completely, creating even more job losses.

The whole process can be very beneficial to consumers. If prices fall for many products because efficiency is improving, their incomes will buy a larger quantity of goods and services. Their standard of living will rise. Sometimes they will buy more of the goods which have become cheaper: this might happen with video games or telephone handsets, for example. On the other hand, they probably will not buy more washing machines or vacuum cleaners. Savings there will leave them with more money to spend on other things, like meals out. Here lies the key to the improvements which structural change makes possible. The production of meals out and fast food is very labour intensive. Many jobs can be created as demand increases.

While many manufacturers have had to exit from the market in recent years, there have been massive numbers of new entrants in the service sector generally and in the restaurant and fast food businesses in particular. This illustrates the overall pattern of structural change which is an essential component of a modern economy.

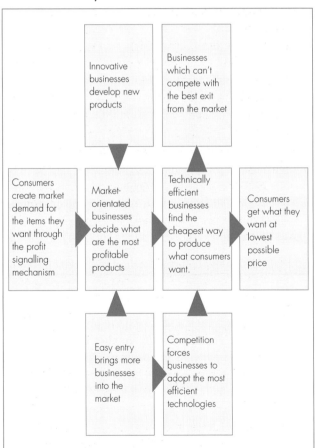

Figure M2.12 Essential conditions for efficiency

Figure M2.12 shows how increased efficiency results from responsiveness to market forces. However, this process works well only when competition is strong and when businesses can easily enter the market place and behave in innovative ways.

Point of view

Competition in sandwiches and software

It is quite easy to buy a sandwich in the business districts of most cities. Sandwich bars, Marks & Spencer, Boots and other chain stores, delicatessens and small cafés all provide products to suit a range of tastes. It is relatively easy to get started in sandwich making and quite a number of new outlets have set up in recent years. There is strong competition in the field and much effort must be made to ensure that the sandwiches are tempting. Prices vary, reflecting the cost of the filling and sometimes the location, but only the most exotic fillings or the best locations can command a price of £2.50 or more. Competition generally ensures that the sandwiches are produced in efficient ways and sold at acceptable prices.

What happens if there isn't much competition in a particular industry? Microsoft provides an obvious example. Its objective is to be the market leader in software. It faces quite limited competition. It can influence the rate at which computer users upgrade their software and the price they pay. In recent years there has been a growing conviction among business observers and others that the company was misusing its market power.

Your agenda

1 What would be the experience of a sandwich outlet that tried to sell cheese sandwiches at a price 20 per cent above that of the nearest competitor?

2 Sandwich making is an easy business activity to enter. Think of three examples of retail products which it is not easy to start producing.

3 Why is it difficult to create genuine competition in computer software? What problems does this raise?

So far in this enquiry, we have looked at a number of ways in which firms can become more efficient. We have also looked at how they make their production decisions.

What benefits will firms get if they improve efficiency? Think back to Module 1 which covered costs, revenue and profit, and showed that if costs could be reduced, profit would rise. The possibility of profit provides a substantial incentive for firms to cut costs and become more efficient.

However, many people would not be optimistic about firms being efficient unless it is clear that the firm does face stiff competition. If it does not, the firm will be able to get away with wasting resources, and still stay in business.

Easy entry is extremely important. There is competition among sandwich bars because entry is so easy that it can be described as totally free. Entry is not at all easy in computer software. There are compatibility problems and Microsoft has enormous advantages. The company has a vast advertising budget and employs large numbers of talented programmers which it pays highly. With those advantages it can attract customers and make huge profits. (Keep in mind the discussion of economies of scale, page 103.)

For consumers, competition is essential; only through competition will businesses be forced to make customer satisfaction a high priority. For businesses, competition provides a constant challenge. One way businesses try to get around the problems of competition is to create new products. This can mean that at least for a little while there is a market which only they can satisfy. New products can increase consumer choice. Provided entry is easy, competition will follow and prices will again be driven down to the minimum needed to provide firms with the incentive to stay in business.

Point of view

Tastes change

Figure M2.13 Household food consumption

	Grams per person per week	
	1987	**1997**
Milk (ml)	2313	2096
Cheese	116	109
Butter	61	38
Pork, bacon and ham	222	188
Chicken	221	254
Fresh vegetables	759	748
Cakes and pastries	75	93
Pickles and sauces	60	92

Source: ONS, *Annual Abstract*, 1999

Your agenda

1 Outline the main trends apparent in the above figures.

2 Explain the implications of these trends for the following businesses and suggest a strategy for each business which might lead to future success:

   a a dairy farmer in Devon

   b a major producer of dairy products such as Dairy Crest

   c a pig farmer in the West Midlands

   d a family-run local chain of cake shops.

The forces described in this enquiry are powerful. They help consumers to get what they want, but they also force businesses to respond. The picture we observe is one of constant change. Patterns of consumer demand change. New technologies become available. Firms develop new sources of competitive advantage. So businesses are seldom static. Their normal mode is one in which new decisions are taken all the time.

What happens to people?

The reallocation of resources which is a constant aspect of market forces is accomplished relatively easily in the case of capital. It wears out and is not replaced. With labour the story is very different. Anyone who has at some time been made redundant will tell you of the trauma involved in shifting to another job. Most people perceive job losses as a terrible event with untold human cost. This means that structural change does have a price tag, which reflects the difficulty people have in changing jobs, and the loss of earnings they experience in the process.

Against that, market forces operating in competitive conditions allow consumers to get the products they want at the lowest possible prices. When prices are cut or, as happens more often, decline relative to incomes, people have more spending power. That means a higher standard of living.

An obvious answer to this is to try to ensure that people are flexible, able to take on new challenges and to move to where opportunities are greater. Education and training both help. Attitudes can be important. Opportunities can still be limited for some people, and governments have to consider the implications in terms of people's needs.

Work in progress

Q 1 How much extra would you be prepared to pay for your clothes in order to preserve the jobs of employees in the textiles businesses of the UK?

2 If you had to pay more for your clothes, what product would you cut back on in order to pay the higher clothing prices?

3 Can employees in the textiles industry do anything to protect themselves from job insecurity?

1 What does profit measure?

Kingfisher plc

Kingfisher is a major force in retailing. It includes B&Q, Darty (which owns several electrical store chains in Europe), Comet, Superdrug and Woolworths. Its Annual Report and Accounts for 1998 made the following points:

'One of Kingfisher's objectives is to produce above average returns for our shareholders on a consistent long-term basis. Our record over the past fifteen years shows that we have achieved this.

At the very heart of our endeavours and values must be a total dedication to the consumer. Only this, allied to insightful and far-seeing corporate strategies, will produce the levels of growth that will make us an even greater success in the decade ahead.'

In the same Annual Report, Sir John Banham, chairman of Kingfisher said:

'Our strategy [is] to focus on mass market goods for the home and family and develop strong retail brands with leading positions in markets expected to enjoy above average rates of growth.

I am pleased to report that this strategy… has produced a record set of results. In the year to 31 January 1998, our sales increased by 10.2% to £6.4 billion. [Operating] profit rose by 29.5% to £519 million.

All our brands contributed to this success … with the opening of two more B&Q stores in Taiwan and the expansion of our presence in Hong Kong, we have continued to build our international position – with all the associated benefits of greater volumes and more competitive sourcing.'

Your agenda

1 What is Kingfisher's main objective?

2 From the evidence above, how successful has Kingfisher been in achieving this objective?

3 If you were a Kingfisher shareholder, what other information would you like to have in order to judge whether the objective has been achieved satisfactorily?

4 What might be the views of stakeholders *other than* customers and shareholders on Kingfisher's performance?

In 1998 Kingfisher was feeling pleased with itself. But how effective had it been? How can its effectiveness be measured? One certainty is that the organisation is expected to add value. As a user of scarce resources with an opportunity cost, the firm must ensure that the value of its output exceeds the cost of the corresponding inputs.

Did the value of its output exceed its costs? Figure M1.40 on page 71 shows sales revenue and operating profit for five years up to and including 1999. Operating profit is found by deducting labour and other input costs and overheads from sales revenue.

Work in progress

Q 1 Using the data on page 71 calculate operating profit margins for Kingfisher for the years 1994–99.

2 What can be deduced from the changes in profit margins?

3 To what extent do these figures indicate increased effectiveness?

■ Is this good enough?

On its own, total profit is never a satisfactory measure. A profit of £1 million might be miraculous for a small business but would be a disaster for Kingfisher. Taken over a sequence of years, the *change* in total profit could be more significant but still needs relating to changes in the firm's *size*.

Operating profit margin measures the proportion of sales revenue that is profit, so it is very useful for measuring profitability from year to year. It allows comparisons to be made between companies of different sizes. Yet on its own it proves nothing:

- Some companies achieve high profit margins because their policy is to charge a high price within a relatively small market.
- Others charge a low price in order to gain a high market share.

Small margins on high sales could be seen as leading to excellent performance. The Kingfisher portfolio includes Woolworths and several other retailers which aim to give their customers very good value. Prices are generally lower than those of competitors, encouraging large numbers to purchase. We could therefore expect Kingfisher to have relatively low margins on a fairly high turnover.

What had actually happened at Kingfisher was that the company had been on a spending spree. Having taken over Darty, the leading French electrical retailer, it had begun to feel confident about running retail chains overseas. It went on to expand in Belgium and the Netherlands. Meantime, B&Q was expanding in Taiwan. Some of the growth in Kingfisher's sales revenue came from these acquisitions.

The implications of this are clear. If you really want to see how effective the company is, you must examine the relationship between profit and the resources which are employed in the company. That means looking at the balance sheet and in particular at capital invested.

2 Balance sheets

A fuller picture

	£ million	£ million
1 **Fixed assets**		3219
2 **Current assets**		2914
3 Stocks	1534	
4 Debtors	753	
5 Investments	312	
6 Cash	315	
less		
7 Current liabilities (creditors)		2726
8 Net current assets (net working capital)		188
9 Total assets *less* Current liabilities		3407
less		
10 Long-term liabilities (loans due in after one year)		791
11 Net assets		2616
12 Share capital	774	
13 Retained profits (reserves)	1842	
14 Shareholders funds		2616

Figure M2.14 Kingfisher's balance sheet as at 31 January 1999

Source: Kingfisher plc, *Annual Report and Accounts*, 1999

Your agenda

1 What is retained profit? What will it normally be used for?

2 Why are stocks an asset?

3 What do you think fixed assets are?

Every company must by law produce a balance sheet each year. It is designed to show the company's assets and liabilities. Assets include anything which brings a flow of benefits to the company. Liabilities are all the debts which might have to be paid back sooner or later.

The balance sheet can show us how capital is being employed. Companies use their capital and their loans (liabilities) to buy assets. Assets are items of long-term value. These two sides of the picture show the meaning of the word 'balance' in the balance sheet. The figures themselves are made into a series of totals which show how the money coming in and the money going out balance with each other.

Assets

In practice, assets are divided into two groups as follows:

- those that deliver the production process and remain in the firm over the longer term. Called **fixed assets**, these include land, buildings, equipment and vehicles.
- those that represent the day-to-day operation of the business. Called **current assets**, these include stock, amounts owed to the firm (debtors), investments and cash.

> **Essentials**
>
> **Fixed assets** include all the buildings and equipment owned by the business.

> **Essentials**
>
> **Current assets** include stock, debtors and cash. Stocks are supplies of inputs or of output, all of which can be turned into saleable items. Debtors are the amounts owed to the company which will be repaid in the future. Cash is cash in the bank. Current assets can also include some investments held outside the company, which will bring in income in the future.

> **Essentials**
>
> **Working capital** means the finance needed to keep the company's day-to-day business going. It includes all current assets but can be covered partly or wholly by short-term loans (current liabilities).

> **Essentials**
>
> **Trade credit** is a loan to the business from suppliers, known as creditors. There is often a time lapse between receiving goods and services and settling the bills. Creditors are in effect providing an interest free loan.

> **Essentials**
>
> **Current liabilities** are short-term loans which must be repaid within a year or less. They will include a bank overdraft and any trade credit offered by suppliers.

> **Essentials**
>
> **Net current assets** is the total of current assets less the total current liabilities (what the firm owes in the short run). This is the amount of working capital which the business needs to fund for itself.

Adding up

Look at Figure M2.14, and at the top part of Kingfisher's balance sheet for 1999. We can now work our way through the lines and see where the totals come from.

- Start with the fixed assets (line 1) as a total figure. It includes buildings and all kinds of equipment – the capital assets which make production possible.
- Now focus on the relationship between current assets and current liabilities. Current assets – stock, debtors and cash – circulate through the firm making it 'work' from day to day (lines 2–6). These resources are therefore called **working capital**. Fortunately for most firms, at least half of their working capital needs are supplied by bank overdrafts and **trade credit** – the **current liabilities** (line 7). These are the loans which must be repaid within one year. They reduce the amount of net working capital that the firm must finance on a long-term basis. Net working capital is also known as **net current assets** (line 8), i.e. all current assets minus current liabilities.

Moving down the balance sheet

- We can now add fixed assets to net current assets which gives **total assets less current liabilities** (line 9 – the total is literally all assets with the value of current liabilities stripped out, i.e. lines 1 + 2 – 7).
- We subtract the **long-term liabilities** (line 10) so that the value of assets now remaining is net of all money owing. This total, **net assets** (line 11), therefore represents those assets which the shareholders really own outright.

> **Essentials**
>
> **Total assets less current liabilities** includes all the assets the business has net of its short-term loans.

> **Essentials**
>
> **Net assets** are fixed assets plus net current assets less long-term liabilities.

Capital and reserves

■ All companies issue **share capital** (line 12). The equivalent for a sole trader is the owner's capital. Share capital is based on the amount initially contributed by shareholders and has no relation to the current price of the shares on the Stock Exchange.

Over time a firm ploughs back a part of its profit after tax into the business: this is the retained profit which appears as the last entry on the profit and loss account. In some company accounts this is referred to as **reserves** (line 13). Share capital and retained profit together are called shareholders funds (line 14).

This total is the value on which a balance sheet balances. So, in effect, we are simply saying 'this is the total amount of money put into the business by the shareholders (line 14) and it is balanced by the total assets that actually belong to the shareholders (line 11), i.e. the net assets.

Capital employed

Together, long-term liabilities (loans), share capital and reserves make up **capital employed** by the business. Shares, retained profit and long-term loans are the three major sources of finance for any company.

Looking again at the Kingfisher case study, we can see what happened. Figure M2.15 shows how shareholders funds and loans (long term liabilities) increased. These increased capital resources financed the company's expansion both in the UK and overseas.

	1994	1995	1996	1997	1998	1999
Shareholders' funds	1091	1219	1289	1433	1770	2616
Loans	355	458	528	399	204	694
Capital employed	1446	1677	1817	1832	1974	3310

Figure M2.15 Capital employed, 1994–9

Source: Kingfisher plc, *Annual Report and Accounts*, 1999

Working capital and liquidity

Liquidity is of vital importance to businesses. It is defined as the ability of the business to meet its debts. In the short term, this can only be achieved if the business has enough working capital in the form of cash to cover its requirements. However some assets can be turned into cash relatively easily. Debts can be collected and stocks can be sold.

A shortage of cash can be very damaging for a company, even one with long-term prospects of profit. This underlines the importance of watching the cash flow position. The business does not want to keep cash in excess of its requirements as this would tie up resources in an unprofitable way, probably requiring more interest to be paid on outstanding loans. Equally, it must have enough cash to meet its obligations, or its creditors may well try to force it to close down. Balance sheets provide vital information as to how safe the company's liquidity position is.

3 What was Kingfisher actually doing?

Growth plans

Kingfisher in the mid -1990s presented a mixed picture. Woolworths and Comet were in the middle of their recovery plans. The Annual Report described these as 'correcting operational deficiencies and developing longer-term growth plans'. B&Q was in some difficulty. Sales increases were achieved through improvements in product ranges and their display, better customer service and competitive pricing.

By the following year, the company was much more secure, with operating profit increasing in all businesses. B&Q was particularly successful – in the Annual Report this was put down to greater efficiency, particularly in its supply chain and stock management. By 1998, the chief executive said, 'All our companies have deepened their understanding of their brand values and developed across the business the ability to deliver the values perceived as most desirable by their customers'.

Kingfisher went on from there. During 1999 the company went into negotiation with Asda, offering its own shares in exchange for Asda shares. Just when Kingfisher thought it had sewn up the deal, Asda announced that it had accepted an offer from Wal-Mart, the biggest US retailer. Watch this space. Will Kingfisher find another partner, once it has got over losing that particular beauty contest?

Your agenda

1 Explain the pros and cons of competitive pricing as a strategy for Kingfisher.

2 How would better customer service help Kingfisher?

3 What changes of ownership have there been among the big retailers in recent years?

Balance sheets give a completely static picture of the company's finances at a specific time. They tell you nothing about what has changed. However, by comparing two balance sheets, you can consider how the changes which took place are reflected in the figures. Keep in mind that balance sheets use data expressed in current prices. They make no allowance for any inflation. This was not a problem from 1996 to 1999 but has been sometimes in the past.

Work in progress

	£ million	£ million
1 Fixed assets		1579
2 Current assets		1704
3 Stocks	873	
4 Debtors	513	
5 Investments	187	
6 Cash	130	
less		
7 Current liabilities (creditors)		1419
8 Net current assets (working capital)		285
9 Total assets *less* Current liabilities		1865
less		
10 Long-term liabilities (loans for more than one year)		578
11 Net assets		1286
12 Share capital	363	
13 Retained profits (reserves)	923	
14 Shareholders funds		1286

Figure M2.16 Kingfisher's balance sheet as at 31 January 1996

Source: Kingfisher plc, *Annual Report and Accounts*, 1996

Note: There are some rounding errors in the figures

Questions overleaf.

Q 1 Identify the main changes in the 1999 balance sheet (Figure M2.14), compared to the 1996 balance sheet.

2 How was the expansion of Kingfisher funded?

3 Improved stock management was identified in one Annual Report as a source of increased efficiency. Do the figures here support this view?

4 Explain in your own words why the balance sheet always balances.

4 How can performance be assessed?

We now have a classification and breakdown of:

- the financial resources available to a firm
- the uses to which these funds are put.

How will this help in evaluating effectiveness? Making a profit reflects the sale of output at a price above the corresponding cost of inputs. In this way the *flow* of added value is measured. But what about the size of investment necessary to produce this flow? To measure efficiency, we must relate profit over a period to the financial capital in use – or capital employed. The resulting measure is called **return on capital employed (ROCE)**.

ROCE is defined as:

$$\frac{\text{Operating profit}}{\text{Capital employed}} \times 100.$$

Operating profit is easily identified from the profit and loss account. Capital employed is shareholders funds plus long term liabilities (loans).
For Kingfisher in 1999, the relevant data were:

    Operating profit = £637 million
    Shareholders' funds = £2616 million
    Long-term loans = £791 million

So ROCE = $\frac{£637m}{£2616m + £791m} \times 100 = 18.7\%.$

Essentials

Return on capital employed (ROCE)

is a measure of the money which can be earned by investing in physical capital. It reflects the effectiveness with which the business uses its capital equipment.

How can we judge a firm's performance using ROCE? One test is to consider the opportunity cost of money invested in the firm. At the barest minimum this must be the rate of interest obtainable from the banks. In 1999 the rate paid on very large sums was around 8.5 per cent. This suggests that money in Kingfisher was well invested. A more telling indication is provided by the ROCE values for other major firms.

Work in progress

Q

			£ millions
Body Shop	Tesco	Sears	Marks & Spencer
Operating profit			
31.9	774	70.9	940
Shareholders' funds			
130.1	3890	1020	4142
Long-term loans			
13.0	631	203	533

Figure M2.17 Comparing ROCE

1 Calculate the ROCE for the firms above.

2 Why do you think ROCE rates vary between:

   a firms

   b industries?

3 What would you expect to happen to a firm that over a period of years earned:

   a a very low ROCE

   b a very high ROCE?

What does ROCE signify?

Two companies

Kingfisher plc

Figure M2.18

	1996	1997	1998
Turnover (£ million)	5281	5815	6409
Operating profit (£ million)	317	415	519
ROCE (%)	17.0	23.9	24.6

Source: Kingfisher plc, *Annual Report and Accounts*, 1998

Kingfisher's objective is to deliver consistent and superior returns to shareholders by being one of Europe's most profitable volume retailers.

Sears plc

Figure M2.19

	1996	1997	1998
Turnover (£ million)	2016	1952	1819
Operating profit (£ million)	106	89	59
ROCE (%)	10.5	8.7	5.6

Source: Sears plc, *Annual Report and Accounts*, 1998

Sears is a major retail group that has included Selfridges, Freemans (mail order), Miss Selfridge, Richards, Wallis, Warehouse, Adams, Shoe Express, Shoe City and Dolcis.

Deteriorating results led the company to sell its shoe businesses and to demerge itself to form three independent firms: Selfridges, Freemans and the combined clothing brands. The chief executive resigned.

Your agenda

1 Why exactly was Kingfisher able to expand?
2 What forces do you think led to the break up of Sears?

We have already seen that profitability attracts resources. Understandably, the owners of scarce resources want them to be used as effectively as possible in the process of adding value. Broadly, the task of business managers is to obtain the best possible return on the capital for which they are responsible.

Interpretation of the 'best return' is not always straightforward. Stakeholder priorities may act as a constraint on profit maximisation. For example, one firm may insist on paying wages above the market rate when operating in a very poor country. Another might refuse to adopt a legal but environmentally damaging method of production.

However, it remains true that in the long run a business enterprise must achieve a competitive rate of return on capital. If resources are to stay in their current use, then that rate needs – at the very least – to keep ahead of the opportunity cost of capital. This is the rate that the resources might earn in the hands of a competitor or even within a different industry.

What happens when a firm fails to meet this condition? Usually, the directors have a year or so to improve performance. The firm may be passing through a difficult period and promise better returns in the years ahead, but continued underperformance or outright decline will eventually trigger change. This may mean that:

- the chief executive and other key directors will be replaced
- part or all of the business is intentionally sold or becomes subject to a take-over bid
- business units with no prospect of recovery close down.

The essential message is that if rates of return on resources are inadequate, other users and other uses stand ready to take over. Low or declining ROCE values signal the need for resources to exit from the existing market. Sometimes this is the experience of one firm, as in the case of Sears, but equally it may be that a whole industry is in decline as the market shrinks and demand curves shift to the left.

Similarly, high and rising rates of return have a 'honeypot' effect as resources are drawn towards a more profitable use. Rising ROCE values in one firm or industry raise the opportunity cost of capital in other firms and other industries. Inexorably scarce resources are attracted by the market force of profitability with ROCE values acting like directional beacons. For the time being at least, Kingfisher would appear from the figures to be attracting resources quite successfully.

Point of view

Some accountants now argue that traditional balance sheets are outmoded. By focusing on the value of tangible assets – the capital invested in plant, machinery, buildings and other equipment – they overlook a whole range of investments which are in many ways more important. The newer, more knowledge-intensive, industries may invest more in intangible assets, the research and development (R & D) and training expenditures which are crucial to their competitiveness. Think about Microsoft. Its balance sheet reports assets worth just 6 per cent of its stock market value, so 94 per cent of its assets are of the intangible sort that accountants find hard to measure, consisting primarily of human capital.

Then there are the brand names. They have the capacity to earn profits in the future simply because they are recognised by customers. Another intangible is 'goodwill'. This is reflected in the existence of a strong customer base which can be expected to have some loyalty to the business. Accountants do sometimes estimate the value of these intangible assets and you will see them from time to time in Annual Reports.

Even more elusive is the value of a culture. Companies have to respond much more rapidly to change than they ever did in the past. This requires a culture which places a high priority on investment in R & D and in marketing, and encourages its employees to adapt. Putting a money value on this is difficult.

Your agenda

1   Why is R & D spending such an important aspect of company performance?

2   Before buying shares in a company you might well examine its published accounts. What other information might you want to obtain?

Taken overall, it can be argued that allocation of resources to their most profitable use is in the long-term interests of society. However, it must be remembered that serious social costs are experienced in the process of reallocation. Thousands of people may lose their jobs and be left with skills that are no longer a basis for employment. Meanwhile, whole communities may find themselves caught in a downward spiral of decline as spending falls and other previously viable firms are sucked into sale or liquidation. There is clearly a price to pay for a flexible and market-driven economy. A major political question is the extent to which government intervention and financial assistance should be used to protect the interests of those most affected. These are matters for another enquiry.

Do markets work?

Enquiry 1   How do markets work?

1 Moving markets

Trends

Paintball battles die a death

The woods were full of business executives clad in fatigues, clutching weapons. They had been set an objective – to take the barn at the other end of the wood from the opposition. Within an hour, half of them were dead – not mortally wounded but covered in blotches of brightly coloured paint fired by their opponents!

You may well ask why. Corporate bonding was the answer. Setting a challenge like this was intended to raise the productivity of managers in all fields of business. Some had fun, but for many it was just a muddy bore. Employers and their staff started to ask questions about the value of such activities.

Team-building on task

An elegant country house, lectures, seminars, a good dinner and bonding in the bar is the new scene. The opportunity to take some outside advice, to listen and exchange ideas gives organisations time to escape the daily routine and look at the bigger picture.

In the workplace people may feel intimidated about offering new ideas. In this relaxed environment work takes on a different feel. It allows open discussion and removes the pressures of the hierarchy that is present even in the flattest organisation. Everyone feels that their input is valued.

Management training has shifted a gear. Such sessions are now offered by training companies throughout the country.

Your agenda

1 Why do businesses want to hold such events?
2 What has happened to the demand for paintball wars?
3 What has happened to the demand for corporate training courses?
4 Draw demand and supply diagrams to represent the changes that are taking place.
5 What will happen to businesses which run paintball wars if the trend continues?

Markets never stay still. The world is a **dynamic** place and the working of demand and supply reflect this. How often have you been shopping in search of the latest trend in clothes, music or anything else, only to find that all the shops have sold out? What has gone wrong? Trends and fashions often take business by surprise and the result depends on how quickly things can change.

■ When demand exceeds supply businesses may:

■ put the price up
■ race to produce more.

The first solution is almost always possible. When there are no more tickets for the football match, they start to be traded at ludicrous prices because there is always someone who values them enough. When the latest Christmas craze runs out, parents will pay any price to have the right present under the tree. Increased demand usually leads to a rise in price.

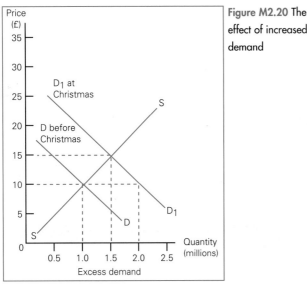

Figure M2.20 The effect of increased demand

Figure M2.20 shows a shift in demand as Christmas approaches. If the price were to stay at £10, people would only be able to buy the one million supplied, so there is one million excess demand. When the price goes up, quantity supplied rises and the market settles at a new equilibrium of £15. There is no excess demand at that price. It therefore shows how the price rises when the demand curve shifts as people are prepared to pay a higher price to have what they want.

Figure M2.21 shows what happens when a football match is sold out. No more seats are available, but people start to trade tickets they have already bought at very high prices.

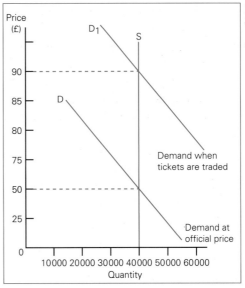

Figure M2.21 When all the seats are sold

When the power of the Teletubbies took the world by surprise, every little girl and boy just had to have one. There were fights in shops when desperate parents battled for newly arrived stock. The business that produced them went into overdrive. The factory worked night and day to meet market demand. Excess demand meant that output was increased so the quantity supplied increased as the business was prepared to sell more at the same price. This can only happen if the business has spare capacity or can easily buy in more of the product without increasing costs. Figure M2.22 shows how this happens.

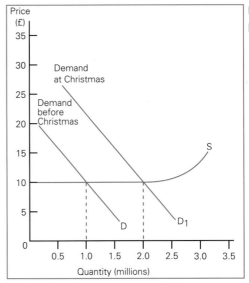

Figure M2.22 Producing more

Drawing conclusions

The examples shown here demonstrate how swiftly the market moves. There are occasions when more than one change is taking place at a time. If this happens, it makes it very difficult to decide which cause is most relevant. So if we are using theory to help us to think through the implications of a change, we may use the assumption **other things being equal**. This means that we examine one change at a time, and assume that nothing else is changing. (Sometimes this assumption goes by its Latin name, *ceteris paribus*.) Saying 'other things being equal' is rather like holding the temperature constant in a scientific experiment so you can investigate what is going on more accurately. In practice, we must recognise that in the real world it is quite possible for everything to be changing at once.

Essentials

Markets are **dynamic** because they are constantly changing. Pressures from consumers and producers cause changes in demand and supply, so output and price change to reflect these pressures.

Essentials

Other things being equal is a strategy used to allow the effect of one change to be studied. It means imagining that other things stay the same so the cause and effects of one change can be identified.

Work in progress

Q **What happens when …**
Explain the dynamics of each of the markets below in words and diagrams. Show excess demand or supply on each diagram. What happens to the price and quantity supplied?

a A record hits Number 1.

b There is a very large harvest of apples.

c Fashion changes. No one wants to buy 'it' anymore.

d The cost of aviation fuel goes up, so air travel becomes more expensive.

Ceteris paribus but one must be aware that although this is all well in theory, in the practical world it is quite possible for everything to be changing at once.

2 How does the consumer respond to change?

A mobile market

Car manufacturers have a clear idea of how a change in income will affect the purchase of different models. They have found that the demand for small cars is more sensitive to change than large cars. This may be because many larger cars are bought by companies which may delay purchases when the economy is doing badly but will buy eventually as they cannot afford to have their employees driving round in elderly vehicles. Individuals will probably delay purchase much longer if their income has fallen or if they feel uncertain about the future.

Your agenda

1 If income falls for both companies and individuals, whose purchasing habits respond most strongly to the change?

2 Sketch a diagram which shows the relationship between income and purchases of cars by both firms and individuals.

3 Does a change in income affect everything we buy in the same way? Use some examples to explain your answer.

A change in income

When income changes people will change their purchasing patterns. They will buy more of some things and less of others. Demand for certain products will stay the same whatever happens to income. Car sales are very responsive to a rise in income but sugar sales are less so. The relationship can be shown using the following formula:

$$\frac{\text{\% change in quantity demanded}}{\text{\% change in income}}$$

If average incomes rise from £20 000 to £22 000 and the demand for cars rises from 2 million to 2.4 million, we can work out the **income elasticity of demand**. The first stage is to work out the percentage change. Multiplying by 100/1 does this.

$$\frac{\dfrac{400\,000}{2\,000\,000} \times \dfrac{100}{1}}{\dfrac{2\,000}{20\,000} \times \dfrac{100}{1}}$$

It is important to use the original income and original quantity in the calculation.
After cancelling the figures, the answer is:

$$\frac{20\%}{10\%} = 2.$$

The fact that the 2 is positive is important. It tells you that as income rises, demand rises. Both the number which results and the fact that it is positive or negative tells us much about the nature of the product concerned (Figure M2.23).

If the result is:	What happens:	It is known as:
Negative	Demand will fall as income rises	Negative income elasticity
0	Demand does not change when income changes	Zero income elasticity
Between 0 and 1	Demand rises by a smaller proportion than income	Income inelastic
1	Demand changes proportionately with income	Unit income elasticity
1+	Demand changes by a greater proportion than income	Income elastic

Figure M2.23 Income elasticity of demand

When income elasticity is negative, there is a rather special situation. A decrease in income actually leads to more of the product being bought. This means that it is an **inferior good**. When incomes are falling, many people will eat more potatoes and cabbage, because they are inexpensive sources of nourishment. Taxis can be an inferior good – if you cannot afford a car, you may take a taxi home from the supermarket if you have a lot of very heavy items. The term 'inferior' has nothing to do with the quality but states clearly that more is bought if incomes fall.

Essentials

When income changes people adjust their spending patterns. **Income elasticity of demand** measures how demand changes when income rises or falls.

Essentials

Inferior goods have negative income elasticity of demand; more is bought when incomes fall and vice versa.

Work in progress

Q 1 If your income rose by 20 per cent, what would you buy more of, less of and about the same amount of? Explain the changes.

2 If your family's income rose by 20 per cent, how would the family expenditure pattern be affected? Explain the changes.

3 Think of two examples of products with zero income elasticity and two examples of items with a negative income elasticity. Explain why demand responds as it does for each item.

4 Why are businesses interested in income elasticity of demand?

5 Think of two examples of inferior goods.

A change in price

A varied response...

Almost every year the tax on petrol is increased in the Budget and the price rises as a result. People throw up their hands in horror and vow that they will use the bus instead. They cut out some of their outings. It does not take long, however, for them to slip back into their old habits and to revert to buying the same amount of petrol as before. Over a period of time, therefore, petrol prices have little effect on demand.

Coach travel is usually very competitively priced. Although the level of comfort has increased, people still regard the coach as a second-class mode of transport when compared with the train. If coach fares rose to approach train fares, many passengers would be lost.

Your agenda

1 Why do people continue to buy petrol when the price goes up?

2 Look back to the formula which is used to calculate income elasticity of demand. Adapt it to produce a formula to calculate price elasticity of demand.

3 Make a list of things which will determine the responsiveness to demand of a change in price.

4 How is this difference going to affect the pricing decisions of coach companies and petrol companies?

The differing response to a change in price is measured using **price elasticity of demand**, which relates the level of demand to the change in price. There are some things which we continue to buy almost irrespective of price increases. These are usually things which we cannot do without, those for which there is no substitute or which take up only a small proportion of income. They are said to have inelastic demand. If the price rises by 10 per cent, the demand for these items will fall by less than 10 per cent.

Items which we feel we can do without when the price rises have an elastic demand. This means that the resulting fall in demand will be more than proportional. In other words, a 10 per cent rise in price will cause demand to fall by more that 10 per cent.

The third category of response has unitary elasticity. In this case, the relationship is proportional. If the price goes up by 10 per cent, demand will fall by 10 per cent. Price elasticity can be shown numerically by using:

$$\frac{\% \text{ change in quantity demanded}}{\% \text{ change in price}}$$

Price elasticity of demand can be calculated for chocolate biscuits when the price rises from 80p a packet to £1 and sales fall from 10 000 to 6 000. The percentage change is first calculated by multiplying by 100/1.

$$\frac{\frac{-4\,000}{10\,000} \times \frac{100}{1}}{\frac{20}{80} \times \frac{100}{1}}$$

It is important to use the original price and the original quantity in the calculation. After cancelling, the answer is:

$$\frac{-40\%}{25\%} = -1.6.$$

Demand for any product rises when the price falls or vice versa. The relationship between them is, therefore, inverse. In the case of chocolate biscuits, demand falls when the price rises, so the top of the formula will be negative. As a result, the answer will also be negative. Either the top or the bottom will be negative, so the answer must be too. The minus sign is sometimes ignored.

The number 1.6 shows the degree of elasticity. As the figure is above 1, it means that demand is elastic. Chocolate biscuits are not, after all, essential to our existence. If the price goes up, we might forego them. If the number were below 1, demand would be inelastic and if it were 1, demand would be unitary.

A crucial factor in determining how elastic demand will be is the availability of substitutes. If the price of chocolate biscuits has gone up, you can eat plainer ones instead. Many branded products are good substitutes for each other; each individual one will have high price elasticity. Alternatively, demand may be price elastic because you can do without the product altogether. Package holidays would fall into this category.

Price elasticity is concerned with changes in price and therefore with movements along the demand curve. Income elasticity involves a shift in the demand curve, brought about by the change in income which causes people to buy more or less.

Essentials

When price changes people adjust their spending patterns. **Price elasticity of demand** measures how the quantity demanded changes when price rises or falls.

Work in progress

Q

1 Would you buy more CDs if they were cheaper? Why?

2 If the price of something that you buy regularly fell, would you buy more of it? How much more? Estimate your price elasticity of demand for it.

3 If the price elasticity of demand for CDs is 1.3, and the average price falls by 18 per cent, what will be the change in quantity?

4 What would you expect the price elasticity of demand to be for Rolls-Royce cars? Why?

3 Who gets what?

King coal sheds its crown

Trains, factories and the fires that kept us warm at home all depended on coal from beneath the hills and valleys of Britain. Without it, we would never have been the leader of the industrialised world.

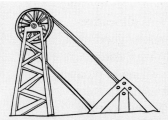

Coal underpinned not only business but the culture of whole regions. The way of life of towns and villages revolved round the pit. It influenced the writing of many famous authors from Dylan Thomas to D. H. Lawrence.

In the 1970s it all began to change. The demand for British coal was falling. Power stations wanted oil and gas. Coal was criticised for turning our spectacular Victorian buildings black with soot. Imported coal was much cheaper. Many people were installing central heating based on other fuels.

	1975	1985	1990	1995	1996	1997	1998
Production (million tonnes)	125.8	104.5	91.6	53.0	50.2	48.5	41.5
Employees (000s)	301.9	179.6	74.3	14.8	17.3	17.2	17.2
Imports (% of sales)	4.8	12.1	16.9	15.9	17.8	20.3	21.2
Price of UK coal for electricity generation (US $)	–	72.74	96.26	68.75	68.04	68.38	61.89
Price of Australian coal for electricity generation in UK (US $)	–	32.82	35.25	31.05	33.19	33.76	24.54

Figure M2.24 Decline of the UK coal industry, 1975–98

Source: IEA/OECD 1999

Your agenda

1 Why did the demand for coal fall?

2 What was the opportunity cost of continuing to use British coal?

3 What has happened to the allocation of resources in the UK?

4 What do you think has happened to the movement of resources in Australia?

The market allocates resources according to the strength of demand and the availability of supply, through the **price mechanism**. The story of the UK coal industry shows how the fall in demand for the product has led to resources moving from the industry. Mines have closed and miners are unemployed or are now working in other occupations.

Essentials

The **price mechanism** is the interaction of demand and supply which allocates resources according to people's ability to pay.

The pattern of change is continuous in the economy. As demand and supply adjust, resources will move to the most profitable location. This dynamic pattern moves the economy towards **allocative efficiency**. This means that the mix of goods and services produced corresponds to what consumers demand and what producers are willing to produce. In theory, it gives consumers the highest possible value from what they consume. In practice, it is usually not possible to achieve full allocative efficiency, but it is desirable for the allocation of resources to be moving towards it.

Essentials

Allocative efficiency means using resources in such a way that no one can be made better off without making someone else worse off. As it is unlikely to be achieved, it represents an ideal situation, although markets do move in that direction.

4 What about the workers?

Average pay

	£ per week
Financial managers	1070.3
Investment analysts	890.8
Solicitors	779.9
Marketing managers	739.5
Police inspectors	726.1
Production managers	614.2
Teachers	502.4
Car assembly workers	382.2
Ambulance staff	358.4
Waiters	226.7
Check-out operators	226.6
Petrol pump attendants	187.9

Figure M2.25

Source: ONS, *New Earnings Survey*, 1998

Your agenda

1 Plot the pay of the people shown in Figure M2.25 on a bar graph.

2 What is the average wage of this group of people?

3 Find out the level of the national average wage.

4 Use demand and supply analysis to explain why there is such a difference between financial managers and petrol pump attendants.

5 Do these differences lead to efficiency?

6 Are they fair?

The market works on pay just as it works on products and services. The interaction of demand and supply affects the price, so shortages lead to high wages and surpluses reduce the level.

At the turn of the millenium everyone was terrified that their computers would fail because of their inability to cope with 2000. As a result, there was great demand for experts who could deal with such problems, so pay rates grew as they were in short supply.

Questions are often asked about the differences between wages earned by different people. Are ambulance personnel really worth less than car production workers? Why should financial experts earn so much? The fact is that in most cases the market is working and determining the level of wages that are paid.

Some wages are not set by the market but by government. Ambulance workers are a case in point. There is often an attempt to carry out a comparability exercise but the outcomes may be questioned. Any government has to look at the trade-off involved in paying public sector workers more. The money has to be raised by making cuts in other areas or by increasing taxes or borrowing. These may all prove unpopular.

1 A bigger slice of the cake?

The cola challenge

What Pepsi-Cola wanted most in the world was the Number 1 spot. Both Coca-Cola and Pepsi had been created at the end of the nineteenth century and have been battling ever since.

They have fought over prices, copycat advertising and even ended up in court. Coca-cola stole a march on Pepsi when it supplied its product to US troops all over the world during the Second World War. Pepsi has never regained its position.

In 1996 Pepsi decided to have a go at the market. Both businesses were afraid of a price war as that would cut their margins down and down. Instead, Pepsi took a bold step. It went blue! A dramatic move as red is the recognised colour for cola drinks.

The creative minds in the marketing and public relations departments went to work to launch the new image. They painted Concorde blue. Pepsi ads were even displayed by cosmonauts in orbit around the Earth. At a cost of £327 million they let the world know that blue was the colour that mattered.

Your agenda

1 Use a spider diagram to show what Pepsi's objectives might have been in wanting the Number 1 spot.

2 Use a spider diagram to show the strategies that both companies might use in their battle.

3 Why is it important to a business to be seen to be doing new things first?

4 What businesses are thought of as being first in the market?

5 Why does having the largest share of the market give power?

6 How does the size of the share matter to the business or the customer?

The sales of a product are usually sourced by a range of suppliers. Each supplier's proportion of the market is known as its **market share**. A business is generally keen to enlarge its market share because it often represents growth which often leads to increased profits.

Trends in market share are important to a business and need to be watched carefully. A business may be satisfied with a 6 per cent increase in sales, but if the market is growing by 8 per cent, the market share will be shrinking.

Companies will go to great lengths to increase sales, as the case study of Pepsi suggests. The outcomes, however, can be less than satisfactory. Pepsi failed to gain market share as a result of all its activities. The battle may lead to a reduction in profits for one of the following reasons:

- The fight may take the form of a price war which can cut margins to the core. This, of course, will reduce profits.
- Increasing sales may also increase costs. If a business is already at a size which makes it efficient, rapid expansion to meet the increased demand may increase costs disproportionately. In other words, diseconomies of scale may set in (see page 105).

The power of leadership

The desire to be **market leader** is very strong. It may result in the name of a particular product becoming synonymous with the whole market. How often do people say 'I'll have a Coke' when they mean 'I'll have a cola'?

Work in progress

Q Make a list of products which are commonly known by a brand name rather then the generic product name.

Having the biggest share of a market may be self-perpetuating. The business with the highest sales will also have:

- the greatest buying power for purchasing raw materials
- the possibility of using people most effectively
- the ability to borrow money more cheaply.

As a result of these economies of scale, the market leader can produce more cheaply or, if price is not the most important factor, research new developments and keep ahead of the game. It is probably further down the learning curve and therefore more efficient.

Large firms have been known to enter a price war with smaller competitors, knowing that their size will enable them to sustain low margins for longer and therefore put the competitor out of business. *The Times*, for example, was priced at 10p for a period, in the hope of putting one of the other broadsheets out of business. It did not work, but the newspaper succeeded in increasing its share of the market substantially.

Issues of this sort lead to suspicions that the other products of a business are being used to cross-subsidise the loss leader. Doing this poses a greater threat to smaller competitors which have more limited financial resources. Questions were asked when BA set up Go in response to the competition from the cut-price, no-frills airlines.

Too much power can therefore lead to problems for consumers. The greater the concentration of power in the hands of one firm, the greater the risk of the firm behaving in a way that is not in the interest of the customer. If there is no one else to buy from, the customer is at the mercy of the business if it puts up prices.

2 What's the competition?

Microsoft versus Netscape

Microsoft founder Bill Gates could see the day when his company's best-selling computer operating sysytem Windows would be redundant. Netscape, the Internet browser, was perceived as a major threat because eventually it would allow people to download competitors' wares from the Web thus Windows would be free.

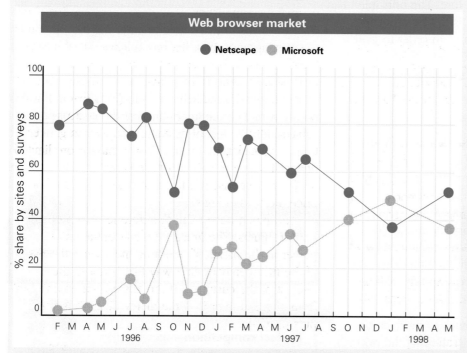

Web browser market

● Netscape   ● Microsoft

By ensuring that every personal computer (PC) had Explorer, the Microsoft browser, as part of the package, the company could guarantee access to all purchasers of new computers. This would discourage the use of Netscape. There were hints that Microsoft bullied PC makers like Compaq and Hewlett Packard into toeing the line by making the inclusion of Explorer a condition for receiving a licence for bundling Windows with their machines. Without the software, of course, no one would want the box.

Figure M2.26 Browser competition
Source: Economist, 23 May 1998

Your agenda

1 Why does Microsoft want to ensure that its Internet browser is the only one to be used?

2 What would happen if Netscape remained the dominant product?

3 What effect would this have on Microsoft's business future?

4 How has the market for browsers shifted?

5 Copy and complete the table right by filling the gaps with an explanation of how both parties would behave or be affected. Use it to weigh up the costs and benefits to the consumer of Microsoft becoming the dominant provider of browsers.

	Microsoft	Netscape
Innovation		
Choice		
Price		
Profit		

6 Draw a line and put an arrow on it to show the spectrum of competition, to demonstrate what has happened in the market for browsers.

Much competition   Little competition

The spectrum of competition

Competition between businesses ranges from situations in which there are many firms with very similar products to the extreme of one business controlling the market.

The extremes of this spectrum are known as **monopoly** and **perfect competition**. Everyone has encountered the term monopoly before. The principle aim in Monopoly, the board game, is to buy up every street, station and electricity company, in order to gain total control of supply in the market and become a monopolist. This is exactly what economists mean by monopoly.

■ **Monopoly** occurs when there is only one firm in a particular industry and the entry of new firms is impossible. As a result, monopolists have considerable power. They may use this power to generate as much profit as the market permits. Some monopolists, however, may find it attractive to opt for a quiet life! This may mean that costs rise or sales are limited by lack of effort on the marketing front. In either case, the firm is less efficient than it might be so profits will be less than the maximum.

Monopolists can decide how much to produce or what price to charge but not both. If they set the price, consumers will decide how many items they want to buy. If they determine output, consumers will decide the price that they are prepared to pay. It is all a question of the interaction of demand and supply. If demand for the product is inelastic, the monopolist can make more profit per unit of output. This is because a consumer's decision will be less responsive to a rise in price. Being able to influence the price or quantity, therefore, gives the firm a great deal of power to charge a high price.

■ **Perfect competition** is at the other end of the spectrum from monopoly. It shows how a market could be completely free and efficient. As one end of the spectrum, it is used as a yardstick to measure the competitiveness of a particular market.

If a market is perfectly competitive, it must have all the following features:-

- The product must be identical, whichever firm makes it, i.e. it must be homogeneous.
- There must be many sellers. None may be large enough to be able to affect the price.
- There must be many buyers. None of them may be large enough to affect the price.
- Perfect information is essential. Everyone must know about products and prices and be able to make comparisons.
- New firms must be able to enter the industry and existing ones must be free to leave.

These conditions mean that perfect competition is almost impossible to achieve in the real world, but this does not reduce the importance of the idea of perfect competition. Perfection is often used as a yardstick. Competitive skaters, for example, all yearn for the perfect 6, but it is very rarely achieved.

Essentials

Monopoly exists when there is only one supplier in a particular industry. This gives the business the power to control price or output.

Essentials

Perfect competition exists when there are many buyers and many sellers all interacting freely with one another. It is unlikely to exist but is an important measure of how much competition there is in a market.

Work in progress

Q   Draw a line showing the spectrum of competition.

Mark the following products on the line according to the degree of competition you think there is in the market:

a Milk	**g** School shirts
b Trainers	**h** Computers
c Cable television services	**i** Petrol
d Cars	**j** Train journeys
e Cola	**k** Potatoes
f Pens	**l** Telephone calls

How much profit?

In a situation of perfect competition, all businesses would have to compete hard. Costs would be kept as low as possible and customers would know all about the prices charged by every company. As a result, profit margins would be very low. In fact, there would be only just enough profit to keep the firm in business. This is known as **normal profit**. It is the amount needed to cover the opportunity cost of the resources which are being used.

> ### Essentials
>
> **Normal profit** is the level of profit needed to keep the resources in the industry in the long run.

By restricting output or controlling price, a monopolist can make much greater profit. This is known as **super-normal profit** (also known as abnormal profit, pure profit or economic profit).

> ### Essentials
>
> **Super-normal profit** is more than enough to keep a business in a particular industry.

The minute that the market becomes imperfect, super-normal profit may begin to appear. Imagine that the market for shirts was perfect. If one producer decides to put buttons on the collars, the product becomes slightly different and people might want to buy these in preference to the standard item. The business would then start to make super-normal profit. However, once the competitors realise what is happening, they may also put buttons on the collars and the advantage will be lost. Competition pushes down profits towards the level of normal profit.

Imperfect markets are the normal state of affairs. Anything that is not 'perfect' is 'imperfect'. Most businesses work in markets that are somewhere in between perfect competition and monopoly.

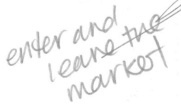

enter and leave the market

> ### Work in progress
>
> **Q**
> 1 Identify two industries which are monopolies and two which are as close to perfect competition as possible.
> 2 Is the car market either a monopoly or perfectly competitive?
> 3 In what ways does it differ from either?
> 4 What effect does imperfect competition have on the allocation of resources?

Competition and efficiency

If all the conditions for perfect competition outlined above are met, the market will be working efficiently, in other words resources will be being used to best effect. There will be a combination of prices being as low as possible, output being at the lowest possible cost and the entrepreneurs making just enough profit to keep themselves in business. This means that the price that people pay for a product is the same as the average total cost – including normal profit – of making it. No firm is making super-normal profit.

Because strong competition keeps prices down to their minimum average total cost, it forces firms to be technically efficient. If firms try to charge a price above the lowest possible cost, people will buy the product elsewhere and they will go out of business.

This process can be very beneficial to consumers. If prices fall because efficiency is improving, their incomes will buy a larger quantity of goods and services. Their standard of living will rise.

Where on the spectrum?

The most crucial of the assumptions underlying perfect competition is that firms and products can enter and leave the market. If this holds good, competition exists because new products can be put on the market and therefore choice is increased. The following example of the launch of a new beer shows how the process works.

Lalune, a Canadian beer, is brewed under licence by one of the major breweries in Britain. On being introduced on to the UK market it faces a downward sloping demand curve as shown in Figure M2.27. Its introduction has an effect on the demand for existing beers. Figure M2.28 shows what happens. Not only will the demand curve shift to the left but it will become more elastic.

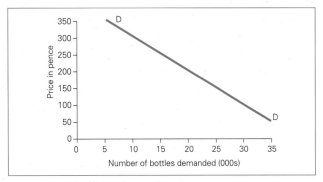

Figure M2.27 The demand curve for Lalune

The shift to the left comes about because the new beer may increase total demand for beer but the majority of its sales will come from people switching allegiance from other brands. The curve becomes more elastic because consumers can switch brands if the price of the original beer rises. They no longer have to pay more or buy less. Competition has given them more choice.

If the producers of the original beer see this happening, they will probably decide to cut their price in order to maintain market share. Their output and price will be lower, so profits will be cut. The consumer will have benefited from the introduction of a new product on to the market even though it is not a perfect copy of the original product. If firms continue to enter the market, both price and profits will continue to fall. Each firm will have a smaller and smaller share of sales until they are making only normal profit. As this happens, the market grows closer and closer to perfect competition.

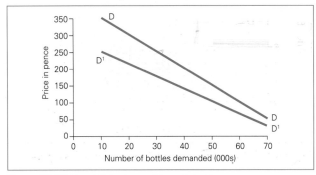

Figure M2.28 The shift in demand for existing beers

Work in progress

Q **1** As new products are introduced to the market, the demand curve becomes more elastic. What effect does this have on the freedom of the individual firm to set the price?

2 Perfect competition assumes that products and prices are identical. Why, in reality do prices vary?

3 If you buy an ice-cream in the corner shop, the supermarket or a local pizzeria, you will pay a different price. Why is this so? What are you really paying for?

4 In what way is a product more than its physical existence?

The conclusion to be drawn from this discussion is that a market which firms can **enter freely** will be closer to perfect competition whereas one which has **barriers to entry** will be closer to monopoly. This creates the variation along the spectrum as barriers will be greater in some industries than in others.

These barriers are often a product of economies of scale. A business that is large has all sorts of cost advantages. These range from buying raw materials to borrowing money. A large company therefore has an immediate cost advantage and it can be difficult for a new company to compete in the same market place.

Essentials

Free entry means that new firms can come into the market without any difficulty.

Essentials

Barriers to entry are all those things which can deter a firm from entering the market and lead to there being less competition.

3 Elasticity: a source of power?

Can the train or plane take the strain?

The line from Springfield to Mancastle is a popular one with commuters, but it is making a loss. The team at Speedrail must decide on a scheme to improve the situation. They could try to attract more customers and spread the cost of running the railway network over more passengers. The problem with this solution is that any increase is likely to come from off-peak passengers who pay reduced rates already and therefore contribute less to total revenue. Attempting to attract more passengers in peak times is going to make existing passengers more unhappy as the trains are already bursting at the seams. Putting up the price seems the only possibility. The commuters, however, have little alternative to the train and therefore have to put up with the increase.

Many airlines are flying on very tight margins. Some of the famous names have already gone out of business. PanAm, for example, once one of the largest airlines in the USA, no longer exists. Its name has even been removed from the famous skyscraper on Park Avenue in New York. If the companies that continue to fly the Atlantic want to make more profit, they will have to devise strategies which enable them to do so without putting up the price. Competition is all in the other direction. Computer reservation systems mean that everyone can see the prices being charged at the touch of a button. No-one can have a price advantage for more than an hour or two. Putting up the price would be disastrous. Customers would rapidly desert the sinking ship in favour of those with lower prices.

Your agenda

1 Which business has more control over its market? Explain why.

2 What effect will raising fares have on revenue for the rail company and for the airline?

3 Both organisations will probably lose customers if they put up the price. Which will find that total revenue has increased despite this loss?

4 Make an estimate of the price elasticity of demand faced by Speedrail and the airline.

5 Explain why price elasticity of demand is crucial to firms which are making decisions about changing the price of a product.

What happens to revenue?

When any firm increases or decreases its prices, it needs to know what the outcome will be in order to make the right adjustment. It is therefore essential to be aware of the price elasticity of demand for the product as the revenue that the firm will receive is directly related to the change in sales resulting from a change in price. Many firms will claim that they know nothing of price or income elasticity of demand. In fact, after some time in a particular market, they will have an instinctive awareness of the relationships, even if they do not work out the formula.

The elasticity of demand helps a firm to predict the effect of a price change. The revenue it can expect will depend on the degree of elasticity of demand for the product it is selling. It can be calculated by multiplying the amount sold by the prevailing price. This is easily assessed by looking at the rectangle formed at the relevant price and quantity demanded. They have been shaded on the diagrams in Figures M2.29 and M2.30 which show two different scenarios.

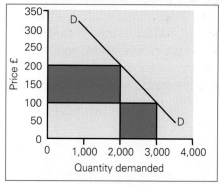

Figure M2.29 An inelastic relationship between demand and price

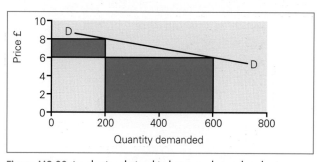

Figure M2.30 An elastic relationship between demand and price

In Figure M2.29, when the price is £100, the firm sells

3 000 items and therefore receives £300 000 in revenue. If the price rises to £200, sales fall to 2 000 but revenue rises to £400 000. If you use the formula to work out price elasticity of demand, you will discover that the elasticity of demand is .333. As this falls in the range between 0 and 1, it is inelastic. The revenue from any product with an inelastic demand will rise when the price is increased. This is obviously very useful information for any firm. Rail companies, for example, are well aware that there is little alternative to the train for many commuters. Demand for rush-hour trains is therefore inelastic, so price rises will provide the company with greater revenue.

In Figure M2.30, at a price of £6, sales are 600, so revenue is £3 600. If the price is increased to £8, sales fall to 200 and revenue is only £1 600. The formula will tell you that the elasticity of demand is 2. This means that demand is elastic as it is in the range between 1 and infinity. In this case, it may not be wise to increase the price as it would lead to a fall in revenue because people would buy something else instead.

This demonstrates the problem that an airline would face if it attempted to increase price. Its customers would go elsewhere.

The final category of demand elasticity is known as unity. In this case, revenue stays the same whatever happens to price and the result of calculating the elasticity is always 1.

Work in progress

 1 If a small car has a price elasticity of 1.2 and a large car's is 0.8, which price should the company increase?

2 At various times in the past the Royal Mail has found itself making a loss. On one occasion it had raised the price of postage, only to find that its losses grew. What mistake had it made?

3 What can a business do to make demand for its products more inelastic?

4 Are we susceptible?

What are we all most afraid of?

Radion was a brand-new washing powder. Its makers were determined that it was going to make instant impact on customers. In a market that was already full of brands, this one needed an angle that would take everyone by storm.

Evil odour was the answer! Radion was advertised as the product that would kill the sorts of smells that we are apparently all most afraid of – body odour! A series of brash, tasteless adverts was created. Everyone saw them and bought the product. The sales record in those early months was quite astonishing. The big question after the product launch was: would those who had swapped to Radion, stay with it?

Your agenda

1 What was the objective of the marketing department for Radion? Use a demand curve to show its objectives.

2 Once customers have bought a product, how does the marketing objective change? Use a demand curve to show what is happening.

3 Why does a business want to increase sales of its products?

Methods of advertising

There are two main techniques which advertisers use. One is to provide information about a product, the other is to persuade us to buy it. It is, of course, possible to combine the two. Often the location of the advert will determine the purpose. On the television a channel ferry company has 30 seconds to convince us that its boats are so well equipped that we will cruise across the Channel in comfort. In the newspaper, it is much more likely to tell us about its special offers and discount fares. In this medium we have time to absorb detailed information and we can preserve the advert if we think it might be useful later. Television is much more ephemeral but leaves us with a strong impression if the advert is effective.

Why do they do it?

- The primary objective of any firm with an advertising budget is to increase sales. A look at the demand curves in Figure M2.31 shows the impact of advertising. At a given price, sales can be increased according to the persuasiveness of the adverts.

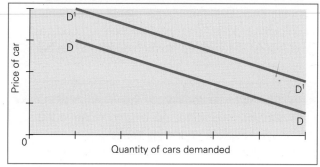

Figure M2.31 The effect of advertising

- The objective may not simply be to sell more but to persuade customers to remain faithful to the product and buy it again and again, in other words, to make demand more inelastic. In Figure M2.32 the effect of this is shown.

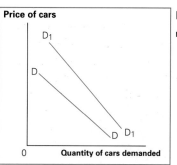

Figure 2.32 Making demand more inelastic

- The third reason for advertising relates to the efficient level of production for the firm. In the Module 2.1 (page 104), the average total cost curve was explained. As a firm produces more, costs tend to fall. This is particularly true of industries which have high expenditure on plant and machinery. The motor industry falls firmly into this category. If a firm can persuade more people to buy its cars, the average cost of production will fall, advertising costs can be covered and hopefully, more profits can be made. Figure M2.33 demonstrates that despite the extra cost of advertising, production may take place at a lower average total cost as sales expand. This allows production to be more technically efficient.

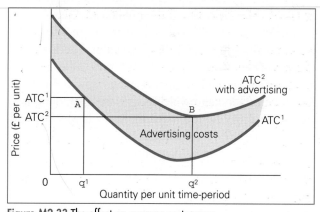

Figure M2.33 The effect on average cost curves

Decent, legal, honest and truthful

Combining the speed and opulence of a BMW with the message that most of the car could be recycled was designed to salve the conscience of the affluent motorist. BMW spent £4.5 million on such an advertising campaign to launch its 3 series. Unfortunately, both Friends of the Earth and Greenpeace objected. These cars were no more likely to be recycled than any other, 75 per cent of all cars have been recycled for 20 years and at the time BMW had no recycling plant in the UK.

The green bandwagon has become very popular and many firms are attempting to take an ethical stand in the way they manufacture their products, but those who attempt to use it as an advertising strategy without genuine cause will find unwelcome attention drawn to the company. The fast food restaurant chain McDonald's fell into the same trap when it claimed that its foam packaging was recyclable but failed to provide any facilities to do so.

These examples might not have survived scrutiny by the agencies which have the task of policing advertising standards. The Independent Broadcasting Authority supervises television and radio and the Advertising Standards Authority controls all other forms of advertising. Members of the public can make complaints if they feel that an advert fails in one of the four categories in the title of this section. The luxury car manufacturer Alfa Romeo was found to be breaking the code with the following copy: "Of course the surge of adrenalin which comes from handling a car like this may be too much for you." It was deemed to be an emotive reference to speed which was capable of encouraging dangerous driving practices.

Point of view

Advertising and the economy

Advertisers argue that they create wealth. The alternative view is that they create wants which, for many, cannot be achieved. Do you remember watching television on Sunday morning and then bombarding your family with demands for the latest novelty?

Many firms have substantial budgets for such spending and their objective is to encourage us to spend more. If by spending more, we are genuinely causing an increase in GDP, which means that more people will be employed, greater economies of scale can be achieved and goods can be produced more efficiently, advertisers have a case.

More often, the outcome is a **zero-sum game** in which the gains made by one company are the losses of another. There is a limit to how many fish fingers can be eaten in the UK, so if Findus's advertising is so appealing that everyone stops buying Birds Eye, there is no overall gain. Such competitive advertising may just push up costs as the market is swapped from company to company.

Your agenda

What contribution does advertising make to the economy? Explain your arguments.

Essentials

A **zero-sum game** occurs when any gain by one player is exactly balanced by losses of other players.

1 Who makes a mess?

Poison that blocks out the sun

In the tiny Cleveland village of Lazenby, people fear the rain because it is black with chemical dust. 'If you look carefully you can sometimes see yellow and orange vapour in the air,' said Jim Maloney, a policeman and Chairman of the residents' association. 'We get dust piling up on car windows and smog clouds sometimes so bad they block out the sun.'

Lazenby, 20 minutes from the North York Moors, is an attractive tangle of narrow streets lined with redbrick cottages. It is also one of the country's worst pollution blackspots. Its villagers are among the forgotten victims of some of Britain's biggest companies, which persistently and illegally emit toxic gases into the atmosphere.

Lazenby residents pay heavily for the irresponsibility of the worst offender – ICI, whose huge chemical and polymers plant at Wilton sometimes overwhelms the village with its fumes and gases.

Maloney never had any respiratory disorder until moving to the village. He now suffers from reactive breathing syndrome and has been in intensive care. John Walker, aged 6, has been dependent on an inhaler since he was 18 months old. His father, Don Walker, who has been diagnosed asthmatic, said: 'No matter what anyone else says, I believe that there is a direct link between what is coming out of those factories and my condition.'

Christine Greenland, 36, became asthmatic five years ago. Her son Carl, now 5, developed the condition at 2½. 'There are a lot of children at primary schools with inhalers,' she said. According to a study by Newcastle University, asthma is not the only health hazard. They found that a sample group of women living in the shadow of the ICI site were four times more likely to contract lung cancer than the national average.

'We concluded that the most plausible explanation was exposure to industrial pollution,' said Dr Suzanne Moffatt, of the university's department of epidemiology and public health. Lazenby GPs believe there could be a link between ill health and local industrial pollution. 'I do think there is a causal relationship between air pollution and lung cancer as the report suggests,' said Dr Dilip Acquilla, who has 9 000 patients on his books.

'There are other factors, of course. An area like this does have many pressing social problems which also do have an impact on health. But I think there is a link between air pollution and lung cancer as well as other respiratory diseases. Last year my drugs bill for respiratory illness was 52 per cent higher than the average for Cleveland.'

Source: *The Sunday Times*, 1 June 1997.
© Times Newspapers Limited, 1999.

Your agenda

1 How does the factory affect the people of Lazenby?

2 Who pays for the damage which is caused?

3 Why do you think ICI does not do something to prevent the emission of fumes and gases?

4 Explain how demand and supply might influence the actions of ICI?

5 How could its activities be controlled?

6 Why might the area suffer from 'pressing social problems'?

7 What effects might these problems have on people and the local economy?

8 Explain how demand and supply might help create these social problems.

Why does it happen?

Businesses want to make a profit and therefore try to keep costs as low as possible. There are some costs which they clearly have to pay for, but there are others which they can avoid. These are known as **private costs** and **external costs**.

■ Private costs are those which are paid by the individual or company when buying goods or services. For a television, for example, the private costs would include the cost of the television, the licence and the electricity to run it. For a business, the private costs are the costs of running the factory, office or shop. They are itemised in the accounts.

■ External costs are the costs which neither the buyer nor the company pay for directly. If the volume on the television is turned up fully, the external cost will be the nuisance to the neighbours.

The same idea can be applied to the factory which emits pollutants into the atmosphere. These are external costs which society as a whole must pay for. They are often described as negative externalities. These costs do not appear on any profit and loss account, unlike the private costs, which do.

Private costs and external costs together are known as **social costs**. These therefore reflect the genuine total cost of production.

Businesses may try to minimise their costs by ignoring the damage they do to the community around them. The decision to minimise impact on the local environment would increase private costs because it would involve installing more efficient filters or monitoring the system more carefully.

Many large businesses have now realised that they need a 'licence to operate', which means ensuring that they are viewed positively by their neighbours. A company which wants to extract oil, for example, will ensure that the stakeholders are not adversely affected. In such circumstances, the company would hold meetings with the local community in order to allay people's fears. As a result, such negative impacts are considered carefully and minimised wherever possible. In other words the external costs are being internalised.

> **Essentials**
>
> **Private costs** are those paid by individuals and firms when buying goods and services

> **Essentials**
>
> **External costs** reflect the side-effects of a firm or individual using goods and services. They are paid for by other people or the government.

> **Essentials**
>
> **Social costs** are the total cost of producing goods and services. They are calculated by adding up private costs and external costs.

Are there any benefits?

Businesses provide goods and services to meet customers' needs and wants. As a result, individuals and society gain benefits from these products. They can be analysed in the same way as the costs discussed above:

■ **Private benefit** is the gain to the individual who buys a product. This can range from the freedom of movement which comes with buying a car to the higher expected earnings which come from investing in higher education. It also applies to firms because they are consumers of products as well. These benefits are less easily quantified than costs and may vary from consumer to consumer.

■ **External benefits** arise when there is a gain for people not directly involved in an activity. A high-speed rail link from the Channel Tunnel means that the residents of Ashford gain because they will be able to travel to London more quickly than before. External benefits are also known as positive externalities.

Private benefits plus external benefits constitute **social benefit**. This is the total gain to society from anything that is produced.

> **Essentials**
>
> **Private Benefit** is received by the firm or individual when goods or services are purchased.

> **Essentials**
>
> **External benefits** reflect the positive side-effects from firms or individuals using goods and services.

Social benefit is the total benefit from producing goods and services. It is calculated by adding up private and external benefits.

■ When do benefits equal costs?

If efficient production is the objective, the aim should be to produce at the point where the extra cost equals the extra benefit from any production or consumption decision. This is demonstrated by Figure M2.34. The **marginal social benefit** (MSB) curve shows how much more benefit society as a whole will gain from one extra unit. The **marginal social cost** (MSC) curve shows the extra cost to society as a whole of this extra unit.

Marginal social benefit is the amount that society gains from the consumption of one more item.

Marginal social cost is the cost to society of the consumption of one more item.

If MSB is above MSC, gains can be made by increasing consumption. If MSC is above MSB, each extra unit is costing society more than the benefit that is being gained, so production should be cut. The efficient point at which to produce and consume is therefore at the intersection of the curves where MSC equals MSB. In practice, it may be difficult to determine where this is.

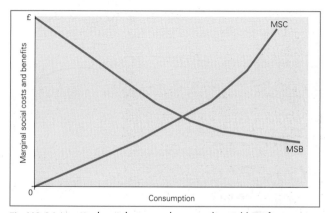

Fig M2.34 Marginal social costs and marginal social benefit

The analysis can be applied to any decision:

■ A company which wants to build a factory in North Wales would be mainly interested in the private costs and benefits. The planners who had to give permission for the scheme would want to look more widely at the implications as there would be external costs and benefits. The costs would be the effects on the environment as large parts of the area are very attractive and need protecting. On the other hand, there is a high level of unemployment and the creation of new jobs would be of considerable benefit.

■ A business wants to install anti-pollution equipment but needs to decide about the sophistication of the filter system. Very small amounts of all sorts of substances do the environment little harm but may be costly to remove completely. The analysis would therefore suggest that the company should take preventive measures to the point where the marginal social cost is equal to the marginal social benefit.

This is the basis on which **cost – benefit analysis** is carried out. The most serious problem in using cost – benefit analysis is trying to evaluate the externalities. Many of the costs and benefits are easy enough to assess, but what is a beautiful valley worth in financial terms? How do you count the disruption to households who have moved to the area because of the peace and quiet? Attempts are made to do this, but it is a very subjective measure.

Cost – benefit analysis counts up the public and private costs and benefits in order to decide whether a project should go ahead. It is a useful exercise, but putting figures on external costs and benefits it not always straight forward.

Does the market work?

The market produces a result which producers and consumers want. It does not always succeed in producing the result which benefits society as a whole because firms and individuals may not take external costs into account when they make decisions. Firms are generally not prepared to risk being the first in the market with a more expensive product which does less damage to the environment, and the majority of customers are unwilling to pay more unless they have to. Legislation is therefore the main method of changing habits.

Work in progress

A by-pass is to be built round a country town on a main road to a popular holiday area. The road is also used by traffic from a major port on its way to the industrial areas of the UK. The planned route passes through an area of outstanding natural beauty but could be put in a tunnel.

Q

1 What are the costs and benefits resulting from each strategy?

2 Which one would you select and why?

3 Why is it difficult to decide?

2 A legal solution

Clearing the air

The air in Paris was sultry. It had been hot, dry and still for weeks. There was no sign of an end to *le canicule* – the dog days. A mixture of car exhaust and industrial fumes smothered the city in a layer of smog which pushed pollution to the highest level. The French government took radical action.

Cars with even numbers were ordered to stay at home. Commuters were offered free public transport and school children were to be kept indoors at break-time.

Checkpoints were set up, manned by paramilitary gendarmes. Cars with more than three passengers, commercial vehicles, taxis, buses and hearses were exempt but motorists who insisted on driving were fined £90.

The dense yellow smog gradually subsided and the famous landmarks of Paris, Sacré-Coeur, the Eiffel Tower and the Arc de Triomphe, emerged from the haze.

Your agenda

1 Why was the solution effective?

2 In what sort of situations does legislation work and why?

3 Is this a short- or long-run solution?

4 What might be done to avoid repetitions of these events?

Most governments have used legislation and regulation as their primary line of attack on environmental problems. The case study here describes a one-off solution, but most environmental legislation relates to setting standards or 'regulatory instruments'.

Throughout Europe such standards are being set for all types of pollution. The newspapers frequently report the UK's standing in measures of drinking water, bathing water and many other indicators. The pollution being generated by ICI is subject to control. There are rules about percentages of emissions, types of filters and other directives for controlling pollution in different circumstances. They are usually enforced by government inspectors.

Although there is evidence that taxation and other ways of using the market are more efficient methods of keeping pollution, for example, in check, administrators prefer to work with targets and standards. There are several reason for this:

- They require less information to work effectively than using the market.
- They can be depended on to achieve the intended target.
- They are readily accepted politically because of the support from administrators and politicians.
- If a total ban is required, they are most effective.

Companies may well favour regulation because they learn to negotiate with the enforcers in order to demonstrate the industry's requirements. A special relationship, known as 'regulatory capture', can develop which enables firms to express their needs in such a way that they become part of the accepted approach of the administrators. This means that business objectives can take higher priority than the objectives of the legislation.

Work in progress

Q   How many different laws can you think of which aim to reduce our impact on the environment?

Point of view

Why does ICI go on polluting?

Six years ago chemicals giant ICI announced a £1 billion environmental improvement programme designed to address growing public criticism over its pollution record. In its latest Annual Report it says that it 'demands full compliance with all … health and environmental laws and regulations'.

According to an analysis of Environmental Agency statistics compiled by *The Sunday Times*, however, ICI was the subject of at least 16 formal legal actions by the government over the last six years. The company confirmed that ten of these incidents involved air pollution. The Environment Agency called in some of ICI's most senior

executives and castigated the company's 'poor environmental performance … and poor management'. The director of the Agency accused the company of widespread environmental failures across all its British operations. 'I want to see a change in attitude across the company,' he said. ICI has been prosecuted three times in three years following alleged air pollution incidents and had to pay a total of £51 540 in fines and costs. Its annual profit last year was £603 million.

Your agenda

1   What are the external costs of ICI's activities?
2   Why does ICI pollute the environment?
3   Why does it continue to break the law?

3 A little give and take

How to change what people buy

Petrol always used to contain some lead. It was designed to make the engines run smoothly. The snag was that lead was getting into the atmosphere and causing some brain damage to children who breathed it in regularly. Then unleaded petrol came on the market.

At first, a few consumers bought it out of community spirit. Then the government announced that the tax on leaded petrol would rise faster than that on unleaded. At that point more cars were built to run on unleaded, and consumers began quickly to switch. They had the incentive in the form of a tax saving. Eventually, leaded petrol was phased out altogether.

Your agenda

1   Explain the effect which the price differential had on demand for the two different types of petrol.
2   What other types of polluting behaviour might be discouraged in this way through the tax system?

The differential tax rates between leaded and unleaded petrol were a simple way of using the tax system to influence the output of pollution. More complex versions of the idea are being used around the world in a variety of ways. Many countries are starting to employ taxes to control environmentally damaging behaviour, from the excess use of plastic bags to city centre traffic congestion. They are one way of using the market to control pollution because, in essence, they increase the private cost of the polluting behaviour.

How do pollution taxes work?

The effectiveness of a pollution tax depends largely on the elasticity of demand for the end product. Figure M2.35 demonstrates the effects on two different products with different elasticities. In the diagram, *t* is the amount of the tax, $P_1 - P_0$ represents the amount of tax paid by the consumer and $P_0 - (P_1 - t)$ represents the amount of the tax that the producer must absorb.

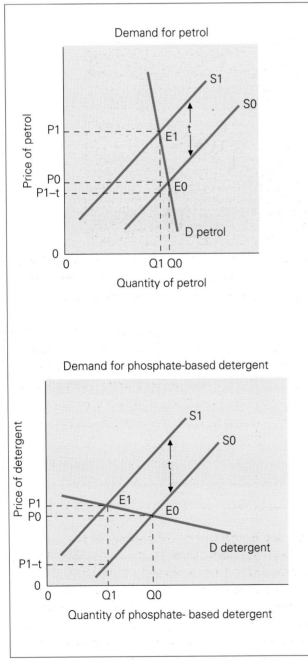

Figure M2.35 Passing on a pollution tax

If demand is inelastic, the cost of the tax can be passed on to the consumer and there may be little change in sales. This occurs with petrol, because if car owners are to use their cars, there is no substitute for it. It will take a large increase in the tax to induce consumers to change their habits and use a different form of transport.

If, however, demand is elastic, consumers may save paying the tax by switching to a substitute. If a tax were imposed on phosphate-based detergents, people would be persuaded to buy a non-phosphate-based detergent instead. The producer will not be able to pass on the tax, which will be highly effective in altering consumption patterns. This will force producers to reduce output of the environmentally unfriendly product.

The trick for the government is to set the tax at a point where it is cheaper to change habits than continue polluting. This is, of course, the most difficult part of the exercise: it is not easy to predict the most effective tax rate.

What are the problems?

■ The problem with green taxes is lack of information. Figure M2.36 shows the range of information required to fix such taxes accurately.

- The firm's output of goods.
- The pollution dose which this output produces.
- Any long-term accumulation of pollution.
- Human exposure to pollution.
- The damage response of this exposure.
- The monetary valuation of the cost of pollution damage.

Figure M2.36 The necessary information
Source: D. Pearce and K. Turner, *Economics of Natural Resources and the Environment*, Harvester Wheatsheaf, 1990

■ Evaluating the damage caused by a particular dose of pollution is hard enough, but the benefit value to society of the product from the factory must be known as well if an equilibrium point is to be found.
■ Difficulties also arise in government because the environment departments have different motives from those of finance ministries. The latter view the prospect of extra revenue with glee, whereas

the former want to see the revenue from the tax used to further environmental improvements. Companies, of course, dislike green taxes because they increase prices and make their products less competitive. Such taxes have also been criticised for being regressive. They add to the costs of production or travel, and hit the poorer sectors of the community hardest.

■ If pollution taxes are not to handicap the companies of any one country they must be universally accepted. Few countries will be willing to set up rigorous pollution control in isolation if it raises production costs and reduces competitiveness. The move towards international standards is therefore a necessary step to achieve significant change on this front.

4 Playing the market

Spreading the jam

There is only one kilometre of road in Singapore for every 220 vehicles. In a country that is very small and very rich, everyone wants to cruise in style. For more than 20 years attempts have been made to keep traffic under control.

There are high import duties on imported cars combined with high taxes to keep them off the road. It can cost up to $50 000 to acquire a permit simply to own a car.

An automated licence system has now been introduced which can carry $150 of credit. Every time the car passes an overhead gantry, a charge is registered which varies according to the time of day. It is even staggered according to the stage of the rush hour. At 6 pm it is $2.00, at 7 pm it is $1.50 and at 8 pm it is $1. Cars with no valid charge card will be photographed and automatically fined.

Your agenda

1 Identify the ways in which Singapore is using the market to control traffic. Draw demand and supply curves to show what is happening.

2 What will determine the effectiveness of their strategies?

3 How equitable is this use of the market for controlling traffic?

As road congestion rises around the world, the willingness of governments to embrace road pricing increases steadily. By setting a price, those who are unwilling to pay will be excluded and therefore congestion will be reduced. The strategy can be used to reduce consumption of any undesirable product.

In many countries, motorists have become accustomed to being charged a price because motorways have been expected to contribute to their costs and have therefore been subject to tolls.

In the UK such mechanisms for revenue raising or limiting demand are in their infancy. Bridges and tunnels are the main example, although roads are beginning to be built on the basis of future funding from tolls. By imposing a price, they help to pay for themselves and congestion will be reduced as the price will reduce the level of demand.

Road pricing raises difficult issues because it results

in usage by people with the greatest ability to pay rather than those with the greatest need. It may also result in local idiosyncrasies as areas are divided by the location of the toll mechanism.

Another strategy: tradeable permits

Whose fish?

In New Zealand **tradeable permits** have been used to overcome the problem of allocating fish to fishermen, a problem which seemed to be insoluble. The initial quotas were decided on the basis of existing catches and then various strategies were introduced to cut the catch to the total amount allowable. The government bought back some of the quota at the full price and offered 80 per cent of the price to anyone else who wanted to sell. The rest of the cuts were made pro-rata across the remaining quotas. The fishing companies had to pay a royalty to the government for their quotas, a figure which was doubled for foreign boats.

The system appears to have worked smoothly and quotas are traded readily both privately and through brokers who act as intermediaries. Initial teething troubles have involved price instability and the perennial problem of any tradeable permit system, the attempt to corner the quota market. With careful monitoring these problems can be solved, so the system provides a model for overcoming many resource allocation difficulties. The fishing industry feels more in control of its own destiny because a business can buy and sell quotas and therefore change the size of its allowable catch.

Your agenda

1 Why were tradeable permits introduced?
2 Explain how the permits market works.
3 How is the size of the total fish catch reduced?
4 What problems crop up in such a market?
5 Why does such a system have low administrative costs compared to legislation?
6 How could tradeable permits be used to encourage businesses to reduce pollution?
7 Why is the market likely to be rather imperfect?

Tradeable permits have been used in various guises both for cutting pollution and for resisting the consumption of products which are 'free'. The two situations are related because they both involve the distinction between private and external costs and benefits.

Pollution is 'free' to a business because it does not have to pick up the bill for the damage – the external costs. Catching fish is 'free' because there is no cost for the product itself. The community, however, can suffer when overfishing occurs as the source of livelihood can be exhausted. There is no incentive for an individual to cease if everyone else continues, so there is no one to take responsibility for the external costs.

The objective is to persuade businesses to cut pollution while allowing them to plan ahead and keep administrative costs low. How can it be done?

The process

1 Decide how much pollution is acceptable.
2 Issue permits to businesses up to this level according to their individual production levels.
3 Allow businesses to buy and sell permits to each other if they have a shortage or surplus.
4 Once the system is working, the total amount can be reduced steadily in order to meet the objectives of cutting pollution.

Does it always work?

The success of tradeable permits comes from putting a 'price' on resources which have no ownership and so creating a market for them. It has been suggested that they might be used on an international basis to deal with whole countries' output of carbon dioxide. If the costs of reducing emissions are low in one country, they would be able to sell their spare permits to countries where costs of reduction were higher. At least an evaluation process would then have to be carried out by each country to decide what could be done.

Although the system has generally been effective where it has been used, it has proved possible to subvert the system and rigidities have set in:

■ A company, or group of companies which buys up all available permits, puts itself in a very strong monopoly position and the government would have to investigate if this started to occur.
■ Much of the trade in pollution permits has taken place between sections within a business because

it has proved difficult for one company to find out enough about other companies' needs and surpluses for a price to be set.

Essentials

Tradeable permits control pollution by putting a price on an external cost which has not previously been measured. They allow firms to decide whether it is more efficient to cut pollution and sell permits or continue current practices.

Point of view

No one can win all the time

High on the top of the Pennines, there are plans to erect wind turbines that will be visible for miles. The site is the protected landscape of Rookhope Common in County Durham. Fifteen turbines will perch on one ridge and 25 will top the next – less than a mile away. The company discovered that this was the best site for these giant machines which are 50 per cent bigger than any operating in Britain at the moment.

Opposition has been loud. Not only is the local community up in arms but conservationists like Jonathan Porritt have opposed the development. He has written to the area's preservation society saying that the scheme would be 'damaging to the overall case for this crucial form of renewable energy'.

Wind power, an endless renewable source of energy, produces none of the pollutants associated with fossil fuels and none of the risk associated with nuclear power. Turbines do, however, have to be sited in windy places. Most windy places, unfortunately, are beautiful, remote and isolated – the sort of places that people want to escape to. The constant swish of giant white turbines disturbs the calm both visually and aurally.

Your agenda

1 What are the social benefits of installing the wind turbines?

2 What are the external costs of installing the turbines?

3 How can planners deal with the trade-offs involved in the decision to go ahead with the wind farm?

Enquiry 4   Are markets equitable?

1 Are there winners and losers?

Forty million Americans have no health care

In the USA health care is provided by the market. There is no National Health Service. Most people in regular employment are looked after through their work as health insurance is part of the package. The old and poor have Medicare and Medicaid which provide a basic service.

But this leaves 40 million people with no care at all.

They may have run out of insurance. There are now tight limits on what is covered and how much can be spent. They may simply be unable to afford the premiums. An average American on US$50 000 a year will receive approximately $4 000 worth of health care insurance from the company. This would cost individuals another $1 000 if they had to pay for it themselves. For many average Americans who are not in a company scheme, the figure is prohibitive. They have to take the risk that they won't fall ill and pay the bills when they do. They have to close their minds to the prospect of serious illness.

Your agenda

1 Why have 40 million Americans got no health care? Use demand and supply to explain your answer.

2 Is it fair? If not, why not?

3 What are the effects of a scheme which leaves people unprotected?

4 Suggest solutions to the problem and consider the issues raised by them.

Is the market equitable?

Competitive markets are regarded as being efficient because they produce the goods and services that people want at a price they are prepared to pay. One of the problems that result is that not everyone can pay the market price, so the system can be inequitable. In some cases inequity of this sort is unavoidable. The fact that people cannot all have everything they want is part of the basic economic problem of scarcity.

The word '**equity**' means fairness and does not mean equality. It is obvious that there is no equality in the amount of money people earn – but is there equity? This is a hotly debated question that is highly political.

- *In support of equality:* It is wrong for a minority to enjoy very high earnings when many people lack equal opportunities and the means for a decent life. Resources are wasted on luxuries for the few when they could be meeting the more urgent needs of many.
- *In defence of inequality:* Inequality is the natural outcome of differing human endowments and the verdict of the market. A free society must allow people to achieve reward for their talents while inequality provides the vital incentive for them to work hard and increase the total well-being of society.

The market therefore simply allocates according to the price that people are prepared to pay. Governments can adjust people's spending power by the decisions made about tax revenue and spending at Budget time. The actions taken will reflect the political standpoint of the government.

Essentials

Equity means fairness, not equality. What is fair is a subjective decision; in other words, it will be viewed differently by different people.

2 What should the state provide?

Before and after

The National Health Service (NHS) was established in 1948.

The average person lived to age 66. Today average life expectancy is 75.

Poor people feared the knock at the door. It might be the 'doctor's man', the one who collected his debts.

BEFORE THEN ONE CHILD IN 15 DIED BEFORE REACHING AGE 11.

Your agenda

1 How has the NHS changed people's lives?

2 What other factors have contributed to these changes?

3 What economic benefits might arise from improved health care?

4 Do you think that the costs or benefits of running the NHS are greater? Why?

5 What are the trade-offs involved in the government spending money in this way?

6 How can the market reduce the financial burden on the state? What issues does this create?

A little more equity?

Although the USA spends a much larger proportion of its GDP on health care than many other developed countries, vast numbers of its people are inadequately covered by the services provided. This may be economically efficient but it does not meet any yardstick of equity.

In 1948 the UK government decided that the market-led system in Britain did not meet the needs of the population and was inequitable. As a result, the National Health Service was set up to provide free coverage for everyone.

The government did this because health care was deemed to be a **merit good**. It could be provided by the market but people who really need the service would be deprived as they would be unable to pay the price charged. Education and housing fall into the same category. All three services exist in both the private and the public sector to ensure that everyone has access.

By doing this the government has demonstrated

Essentials

Merit goods are provided by the state because market provision will deprive people in need of services such as education and health care.

that it considers it desirable to redistribute resources by providing either cash benefits or free or subsidised housing, health care or education.

This redistribution is justified in equity terms, but it may also have efficiency effects. By ensuring that the workforce is both educated and healthy, individuals should be able to make a greater contribution to the economy as a whole. As a result, there will be an efficiency gain. This gain may be partly offset by the need to tax in order to finance the redistribution.

Point of view

In or out?

There is an unlimited demand for health care. The more there is, the more people want. Figure M2.37 shows a close correlation between increased spending since 1948 and growing waiting lists. The NHS must make choices about how it spends its money.

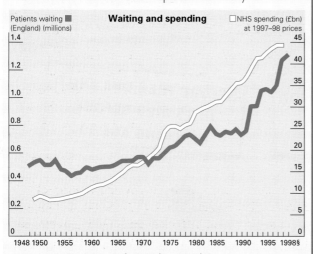

Figure M2.37 NHS spending and waiting lists
Source: Department of Health, Office of Health Economics, HMSO.

Your agenda

1   Put the treatments below into rank order starting with the most essential and explain your decisions.

2   Which treatments should the government pay for?

   a   Mending a broken leg
   b   A liver transplant for an otherwise healthy young person
   c   A liver transplant for an alcoholic
   d   A cosmetic enhancement of the nose
   e   A hip replacement for an elderly person who could then continue to look after themselves
   f   Pinning back the ears for a child who is being teased at school

Making Choices

In the provision of all forms of merit goods, there are trade-offs. Any government has to decide priorities, as we saw in Module 1.1, 'What do people want?' The decisions that the government makes about equity and efficiency will depend on the views of the electorate.

There are always trade-offs on both sides of the equation. The first is between how much can be raised through taxation and the amount to be borrowed. If the government is prepared to do little of either, then there will not be much for the other side of the equation. Equally, greater borrowing or more tax will lead to more expenditure.

The revenue must then be allocated to meet different needs. As the sum of money is finite, the needs must be weighed up and decisions made.

Strangely, when people are asked about government spending, they always want more of it, but at election time they seem to forget this and often vote for a party that promises to keep taxes low.

Point of view

Who should pay?

Student grants and loans have always been a hot issue. The benefits of higher education to the individual and society are extensive. The data below show two ways in which the student gains.

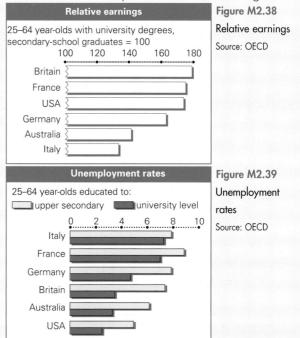

Figure M2.38
Relative earnings
Source: OECD

Figure M2.39
Unemployment rates
Source: OECD

Your agenda

1   Identify the private and external costs and benefits of higher education.

2   Who gains most, the state or the individual?

3   Should the costs be met by the tax payer or the student?

3 What *must* the state provide?

Let's start a business

Suzannah: I'm fed up with working for other people. What could we do instead?

Rahil: We'd need to find something that puts our engineering and business skills together. What is there that everyone needs but no one thinks about?

Suzannah: Is there anything that people complain about but then they can't do much about.

Rahil: Well – everyone wants a zebra crossing on the main road round the corner from me.

Suzannah: The people in our village want streets lights and the council hasn't done anything about it.

Rahil: We could sell these things to people couldn't we? Have we found a gap in the market?

Suzannah: It sounds like it!

Rahil: We'll have to put a business plan together and go to see the bank manager.

Your agenda

1 There is a flaw in Suzannah and Rahil's thinking. Try to imagine the break even position or cash flow. Can you identify the flaw?

2 If a price were possible, how would they collect the revenue?

3 Can you think of other things which have the same problem?

4 How are these things usually provided?

Some things cannot be provided by the market because it is impossible to charge people for their use. These things are called **public goods**. On a larger scale, defence, foreign policy and the legal system fall into this category. Other examples include street lighting and the police. Usually, there is a broad measure of agreement about the need to provide them, though perhaps not about how much to spend on them. If they are there, everyone benefits. You can't charge for them. If someone refuses to pay, they still

benefit. So no one has any incentive to pay. Can you imagine someone standing by the level crossing all day, charging people to cross! This is known as the free-rider problem. Unless there is collective agreement, the service may not be provided. This collective agreement could come from the parish, the town council or central government.

Essentials

Public goods cannot be provided efficiently by the private sector. No one can be excluded from benefiting from them. When one person consumes them, no one else is prevented from consuming them as they will not be used up. So there is no way of compelling people to pay a private sector provider of them.

Governments often intervene because of **market failure**. Markets fail when the allocation of resources is for some reason inefficient and could therefore be improved to make at least some people better off.

* Markets fail to provide public goods.
* Markets fail when there is some degree of monopoly power.
* Markets fail when costs of production do not reflect the true costs to society.

Essentials

Market failure occurs when there is a misallocation of resources which results in people being less well-off than they could be.

4 Making it fair?

This enquiry has so far shown why governments intervene to provide public and merit goods when the market fails to meet society's objectives. There are a variety of ways in which this can be done:

- **State provision** generally means that goods or services are free to those who want or need them. This is certainly the most direct way of ensuring that a need is met. It allows free access to education and health care for everyone. It is, however, expensive as people who could provide for themselves are entitled to claim. The National Health Service is a case in point. Quality issues arise because comparisons are made with the services provided in the private sector. This causes public debate about the nature of such provision.
- **Subsidies** meet some of the cost of provision and therefore reduce the price to the recipient (Figure M2.40). Sometimes there are various classes of customer who receive a product or service free or at a reduced price while others pay something that either contributes to or meets the full price. Prescriptions and eye care fall into this category. By subsidising the product, the price is reduced and therefore consumption can be raised. If the selective measure described above is used, the resources can be targeted at those who need them most.

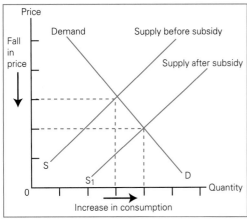

Figure M2.40 The effect of a subsidy

- **Benefits** are usually in the form of financial support for those who have particular needs. They include the unemployed, the low paid and the sick. Most of these benefits are now means tested, so the amount paid out relates to the resources held by

the individual. These are therefore selective which reduces the level of expenditure required from the state. As the opportunity cost is high, this frees limited financial resources so more is available for those in need or for use in other areas.

Essentials

State provision occurs when the market is unable to meet all the needs of society. The government provides health care and education on this basis.

Essentials

Subsidies are payments to producers which will encourage an increase in output and consumption.

Essentials

Benefits are paid when the market fails to meet the needs of society. They are paid to people who are, for example, unemployed, ill or unable to pay the market rate for housing.

The use of subsidies, benefits and state provision is designed to balance the effect of the market. If it is considered important that everyone receives provision, then it is generally provided free at the point of consumption. Hence the provision of education and much health care. The external effects of under-consumption are high because an economy which includes many people who lack education and treatment for illness will be less productive than it could be.

5 Is it all worthwhile?

As the demand for merit goods is unrelated to price, it can exceed supply. The continually growing waiting lists for hospital treatment are a case in point. The question that needs to be answered is: at what point should provision cease?

Marginal social cost and benefit can be used to show this. In Figure M2.41 the consumption of health care is OA and the efficient level of consumption is OB. This means that the country would benefit if more health care were consumed. AB represents the difference.

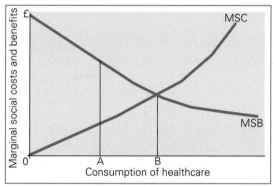

Figure M2.41 Health care and efficiency

The government provides healthcare and education for everyone because the benefits of doing so are recognised to outweigh the costs. Some subsidised housing is also made available. The scale of the provision can be questioned, but as it is difficult to calculate the benefits gained from such services, the decisions will vary according to the value judgements of the political party in power.

Point of view

What price health care?

The British Medical Association proposed that a £10 charge should be introduced for a visit to the doctor in order to reduce waiting time and raise revenue.

Research by the Social Market Foundation, a think tank, and Pfizer, a drugs company, showed that 64 per cent of British adults thought people visit their GP too often because it is free.

Health care consumption by Americans with different levels of insurance cover showed that a 1 per cent rise in the contribution expected from the insured reduced claims by 0.3 per cent.

Your agenda

Should we pay to visit the GP? For or against? Construct an argument to support one view or the other.

1 Keeping the price down

Renting a roof

In the Boston area of Massachusetts rents have been controlled for nearly 30 years. The policy had been introduced to keep rents at a price that people could afford in some areas of the city.

Cambridge, the home of Harvard University, for example, had 16 000 homes which were subject to strict rent control. Recently, all controls have been swept away. Since then rents rose 50 per cent, 40 per cent of tenants have moved out and evictions rose by 33 per cent.

Families who have lived in the area for 50 years have left, many without trace. The buildings are now full of students who share houses or the well-heeled who can afford a whole house at the new rates.

The other side of the picture is that there has been more investment in rented properties so there are more available. Spending on repairs has increased so there has been an improvement in the quality of the housing stock.

To help residents adjust to the new system, Cambridge has allocated US$15 million of local taxes to build affordable housing.

Your agenda

1 What was the objective of the local authority in imposing rent control?

2 At what level were rents fixed in comparison with the market rate? Draw a demand and supply diagram to explain your answer.

3 How may landlords react to rent control? Why?

4 What has happened to the amount and quality of housing since the end of rent control?

5 How have residents been affected?

6 Assess the efficiency and equity of the changes that have taken place.

Governments often intervene in markets in order to modify the outcomes. By offering a higher price, businesses will produce more. By keeping prices low, there will be more customers. Intervention is a powerful tool for adjusting demand and supply and has been used in various sectors, including agriculture and housing.

When governments want to increase consumption, they may establish a price ceiling. This sets a limit on the price which can be charged to the consumer. Figure M2.42 shows the effect when a price ceiling is applied to housing.

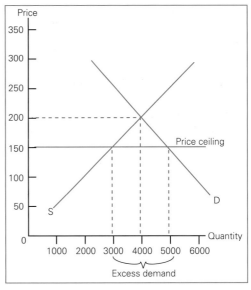

Fig M2.42
A price ceiling for rented housing

Governments set price ceilings with the best of intentions. They want to ensure that everyone has a roof over their heads at a price that they can afford. However, there are always side-effects. Figure M2.42 shows what will happen. In an open market, landlords can expect to receive a rent of £200 per week for a house, but the price ceiling limits the amount to £150. At the equilibrium price, 4 000 houses will be available to rent, but at the controlled price there will only be 3 000. It will also result in excess demand as 5 000 people will want to rent houses at that price.

There are other hazards. Rent-controlled property may fall into disrepair because the landlord is unwilling to invest in buildings for which he or she is not getting a market return. As a result, the occupants may find their living conditions falling below an acceptable level. Once in possession of a property with a controlled rent, a tenant may be unwilling to part with it, despite no longer being in need of the assistance provided. This means that there is little turnover, so houses and flats do not become available for those in need. In Boston, for example, it was rumoured that affluent members of society were living in great style in rent-controlled property!

The solution is not easy. In the UK rents can now be assessed as 'fair', which, as we know, is a difficult term to interpret. Another strategy is to assist people on low earnings to pay their rent. This combination allows help to be provided without distorting the market but can be expensive for governments, especially if market rents are high.

Work in progress

Q The actual outcome of a price ceiling will depend on the elasticity of demand and supply. Try drawing demand and supply curves with differing elasticities and explain the results.

2 Keeping production up

If the CAP fits...

The Common Agricultural Policy (CAP) was set up in 1962. Its objectives were:

- to increase agricultural productivity by promoting technical progress and efficiency
- to ensure a fair standard of living for the agricultural community
- to stabilise markets
- to ensure availability of supplies
- to ensure reasonable prices to consumers.

It provides guaranteed prices to farmers with the objective of making Europe self-sufficient in food. The cost is met by contributions from the member states of the European Union (EU). Just under half of the EU budget is used to support the scheme.

The scheme has been successful as Europe has become largely self-sufficient for non-tropical foods. There have, however, been some costs involved:

- Surpluses have built up.
- Prices in the shops are higher than world prices.
- Tax payers are faced with higher taxes in order to finance the CAP.
- Other countries object because the system 'protects' European farmers from the full impact of world trade.

Despite the fact that changes have been made and the level of support has been reduced, these negative factors combined with the desire to enlarge the EU made the system unsustainable.

The UK government sought major reform:

66The CAP generates significant costs to customers and taxpayers. Estimates made by the Organisation of Economic Co-operation and Development (OECD) suggest that, in 1996, the cost of CAP to UK consumers through higher food prices was around £5 billion, when EU food prices are compared to world prices prevailing at that time.

The cost to UK taxpayers of financing CAP expenditure is estimated at an additional £4 billion. Together these costs are equivalent to £3 per person per week. Since offsetting gains by UK producers from CAP support are smaller than these costs, the CAP reduces national income.99

Source: Ministry of Agriculture, Fisheries and Food/Intervention Board, *Departmental report 1999: Government's Expenditure plans 1999–2000 to 2001–2002.* CM4212, 1999.

Even the National Farmers Union sought changes:

66The NFU wants these changes to end the reliance on price support, to deal with the environment and rural economy issues and to leave EU agriculture better placed to compete on world markets.99
NFU, The Common Agricultural Policy

Your agenda

1 Draw a demand and supply diagram showing the effect of setting the price above the equilibrium. Explain how this encourages farmers to overproduce.

2 Why do food surpluses create a problem?

3 Many potential new members of the EU have largely agricultural economies. Will the current system be 'unsustainable' if they join? Why?

4 Explain why the CAP 'reduces national income'.

5 Why will removing price support make European farmers 'better placed to compete on world markets'?

6 The UK has a highly productive agricultural sector compared to some other European countries where family farms and small holdings play a significant part in both the economic and political community. Why might other governments take a different view from the British government?

When a government wants to ensure a level of production, the simplest technique to use is to set a minimum price that will be paid for all output. This is known as a price floor. Figure M2.43 shows how it works.

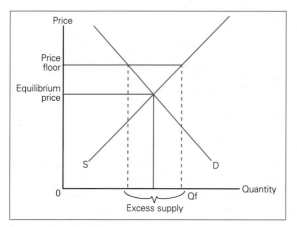

Fig M2.43 A price floor

In figure M2.43 the price floor generates Qf output which is more than the equilibrium price would have done. This may be done if there is a desire to maintain incomes in a particular sector, but as the diagram shows, it will lead to excess supply.

Agricultural products are particularly prone to fluctuations because output will depend on uncertainties such as the weather. The aim should be to set a price as near to the equilibrium as possible in order to avoid shortages or surpluses. This is inevitably difficult and, as a result, the price fixed is likely to be on the high side if shortages are to be avoided. Once the tendency for high prices has been established, it is politically difficult to reverse it as the farming community will have become dependent on the higher income.

The major drawback is that the outcome is likely to be overproduction. Unless limits or quotas are put on products, businesses will simply supply as much as they can in order to pick up the guaranteed price.

Overproduction means a misallocation of resources as the output may well be wasted. The resources devoted to such production would be better used to make other things but are being kept in use by the attraction of the high price. This is not allocatively efficient because the resources are not being used in the way which best fits the pattern of demand.

3 Government failure

There are many circumstances in which governments intervene in the market in order to achieve a different outcome. The actions are generally motivated by the political imperative and will be criticised by people holding different views.

The value of such actions can be measured by evaluating their costs and benefits to society as a whole. The use of marginal social cost and marginal social benefit enables judgements to be made about the efficiency of intervention.

In attempting to solve the problem of pollution, for example, there is no point in enforcing a rule which bans every last unit if this costs society more than it benefits. Figure M2.44 shows how a town in Poland decided whether it was better to spend money on reducing particulate emissions or sulphur dioxide. Research measured the economic benefits in terms of health and mortality of both activities and compared them with the costs of cleaning up. It was then clear that it was much better to go ahead with reducing particulates than sulphur dioxide because the benefits outweighed the costs.

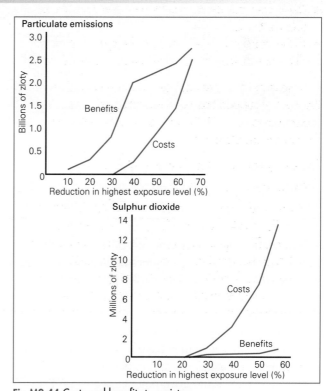

Fig M2.44 Costs and benefits to society

Source: World Bank, WDR 1992.

The same analysis can be used for other forms of intervention. It is, however, not always easy to calculate the effect until a new process or law has been put into practice. The network of cameras which is designed to catch speeding motorists has considerable costs of installation and maintenance. Do the benefits to society outweigh the costs? Until the cameras are in place, their effects are difficult to evaluate.

Any government decision that leads to an outcome at which marginal social cost does not equal marginal social benefit is a form of government failure because resources are not being used efficiently.

Government failure may therefore occur for a variety of reasons.

■ because decisions are made for political reasons as opposed to economic reasons
■ because the outcomes cannot be measured before policy is put into practice
■ because very close monitoring is needed to maintain an equilibrium. This is expensive so governments will use general regulations in the hope of approximating an equilibrium.

Decisions to act otherwise are often made because society has different expectations and objectives. These are perfectly valid, but it is always important for governments to evaluate the decisions that they make.

4 Working together

Whose Post Office?

The Post Office announced another year of healthy profits. At £600 million, its 1998 profit proved a record in seven years of healthy growth. But what of the future? Privatisation has been on the agenda for some time. Other European countries are already some way down the path.

The government is loath to give up such a cash cow as it would lose revenue equalling about four-fifths of the profit. The problem is that the Post Office is losing out through lack of investment and commercial freedom. Unless it changes its status, it can't borrow money for investment as this counts as public sector borrowing.

There are many pressures. The Post Office is popular with the voters. Its management wants more commercial freedom and the main trade union is violently opposed to any sell off. Even the government is divided. The

Chancellor wants a sale, but others want to keep it in the public sector. It seems unlikely that it will be sold, lock, stock and barrel, but some sort of half way house is a likely outcome.

Your agenda

1 Why was the Post Office able to make such healthy profits?
2 What problems did the Post Office face?
3 Who were the stakeholders in the Post Office in 1998? Find out how this has changed.
4 How does the change of status help the Post Office? Has the Post Office's activities changed?
5 What advantages do you think there are in public–private partnerships?

A combination of government and private sector activity has been used in a variety of areas from housing to road building. It enables governments to draw on resources which would not have been available otherwise.

Public sector organisations are very restricted in their activities because they have to be accountable to government. Their income and expenditure is often regarded as part of the government's accounts. They

are unable to borrow money in the same way as a commercial organisation so development and investment may be hampered.

The Post Office was under threat, for example, because eight foreign post offices, which have been liberated from government control, have set up in the UK in order to compete for bulk contracts. As a public limited company it is unable to invest abroad in this way.

Could a public–private partnership work here? The government would keep control over an organisation which it regards as important to the nation. This seems to be one method of having the best of both worlds. The fact that the private sector is looking for a commercial return on its investment also brings a hard edge to the decision-making process.

However, several attempts at public–private partnerships have proved problematic because of the different objectives of the partners. The level of return which is necessary for any commercial organisation may conflict with the need for investments and the targets set by government.

Point of view

More pay – less jobs?

Before the minimum wage was introduced in 1999, a range of anxieties was expressed about its effects. Here are some of them.

> Customers will buy from south-east Asian businesses instead of mine.

> It's not just the lowest paid. Everyone wants to maintain their differentials. It will push wages up right across the scale.

> 250000 jobs lost!

> The regions where pay is lower will suffer more.

> It will cause a surge in the informal economy.

> Wages are negotiated on a local basis and differentials are disappearing so the effect will be negligible.

Your agenda

1 Explain the reasons behind each of these comments.

2 If the majority of these comments are accurate what might happen to inflation and unemployment?

3 What would you need to know about demand and supply for lower-paid personnel before you could make a decision about likely outcomes?

4 Explore past newspapers to track the effect of the minimum wage.

5 Why do you think the minimum wage was initially set at £3.60?

6 Is it more equitable to have a minimum wage?

Can Russia make the market work?

The Russian invasion

The Côte d'Azur, on the Mediterranean coast of France, has long been a playground for the rich and famous. Today a new breed of Russian elite, clad in Moschino and Versace, are conspicuous along the promenades of Nice. They are the wealthy businessmen and Mafia bosses who have grown up with the post-communist economy.

Tales of their expenditure are legion. A Russian rang to book a stay at one of many splendid hotels in the town but wanted to be sure that no other Russians would be there at the same time. On being told that the only way that this could be guaranteed was for him to book all the rooms, he did just that!

Russians are a welcome sight for the estate agents of the Côte. Every year at least 50 properties worth over £5 00 000 each are sold to these new customers. One even bought two properties worth £80 million.

Is it surprising that the Negresco, the smartest hotel in the region, now prints its menus in Russian and has staff specially trained to deal with these big spenders?

A Russian chain

Sir Rocco Forte, who has vast experience of running hotels around the world, now has plans for a chain of 20 across Russia. He summed up the situation as follows:

66 I have a very clear view of how to value a hotel. Throughout Russia, there is now the right kind of opportunity at the right price. The key problem is that we have to contend with the difficulties of operating in the Russian business environment. 99

In poor health

The Russian welfare system has fallen into a state of collapse. Taxes are impossible to collect, so there is no money to keep the hospitals running or to look after the pensioners and unemployed. Under the communist system, there was no such thing as unemployment – everyone had some sort of a job. State employees can now wait months to be paid when the coffers are empty.

Health care is close to catastrophe. Infant mortality has risen to 20 per 1 000 live births, life expectancy for men is 59 and reported cases of TB have doubled.

The Wild West show

Russia's chaotic state is not a novelty. It has all been seen before. The movies tell the story of the USA – one hundred years ago. It was a picture of murder, mayhem and corruption, but as rules were imposed, the dust settled.

What Russia needs is a transparent system in which financial and legal decision making is acceptable to all. Without equitable taxation, people will avoid paying if they can. Russia needs rules and regulations that can and will be enforced so businesses know that the playing field is level for all.

Your agenda

1 In Russia, the market is working after a fashion. What evidence is there of this?

2 How is it failing? Why?

3 What would help to correct some of these failures? How would your suggestions help?

4 What effect might the changes you have suggested have on the future growth of the Russian economy?

Module 3 Change

Organisations with clear objectives and an efficient organisation need to be able to adapt to changes, sometimes rapid and unexpected. The need to adjust affects businesses, individuals and governments. Sometimes the forces of change are international in scope.

3.1 What are the challenges?

The nature of likely changes is examined in detail. Businesses can be affected by change in the market place. This may come from the development of new markets or the shrinking of old ones, or it may come from the activities of other businesses. Overall, everyone in the economy is affected by fluctuations in demand: the business cycle causes demand and output to rise and fall over time. A fourth major influence comes from international trade and the relationships which trade creates.

3.2 Which way forward?

People react to the challenges in a variety of ways. There are strategies which can make for successful responses to different kinds of changes. Businesses can plan carefully and foster an attitude of dynamism in their approaches to marketing and expansion. Governments can develop their understanding of policy so as to react positively and efficiently. They can plan ahead, using macro-economic policies to achieve their objectives despite continuous change.

What are the challenges?

Enquiry 1   How do markets change?

1 What drives demand?

Spending trends

	1987	1998
Housing	16.1	15.7
Fuel and power	5.6	3.9
Food	19.0	17.0
Alcohol	4.6	4.1
Tobacco	2.5	1.9
Clothing and footwear	7.1	6.1
Household goods and services	11.5	13.6
Personal goods and services	3.7	3.8
Motoring	12.6	14.2
Fares and other travel	2.4	2.5
Leisure goods	4.8	5.0
Leisure services	9.6	11.8
Other	0.5	0.6

Figure M3.1 Spending on specific items as percentage of total spending
Source: ONS, *Annual Abstract*, 1999

Your agenda

1 What specific changes in expenditure patterns took place between 1987 and 1999?

2 For each change, what reason(s) can you suggest?

3 The changes you have identified have something in common. What was the general trend?

Is it worth sacrificing a holiday in order to have a car? Or is it better to buy some more shoes or get a camera? Ultimately, the answers to questions like these shape the pattern of demand for goods and services.

Although every individual is different, there are many ways in which people are similar. For example, most people want to eat at midday, be entertained in the evening and take a holiday in the summer. The result is profitable sandwich bars, video hire and package holidays. Wherever and whenever people have needs and wants a market exists and with it the potential for profit.

Over time, people change their minds about what to consume. For all kinds of reasons, they make changes in their purchasing habits. Producers have to adapt. As they do, levels of output adjust. This is known as a change in the structure of production, or **structural change**. It means that businesses must cut back production of the items people want less of, and expand output of the items for which demand is increasing. They have an incentive to do this because they can get a better price for the latter, but the process is not always easy.

Shifts in personal preferences and growing incomes are not the only cause of change. Sometimes the cause stems from an influence on supply:

■ Technologies change – often businesses adopt a new and better technology which is more capital intensive. People are made redundant.
■ Location may also change. It means change in the whole structure of economic activity, for example when a coastline develops a tourist industry or when a region loses its main industries to foreign competitors or a new technology.

Structural change in any economy is inevitable and necessary. It reflects the operation of market forces as the pattern of demand changes or as producers in new locations find ways of meeting demand more efficiently and more cheaply. Ideally, a region that loses an industry will adapt its resources to become competitive in meeting new patterns of demand. In the long run, structural change should benefit everyone.

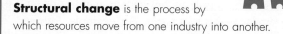

> **Essentials**
>
> **Structural change** is the process by which resources move from one industry into another.

What makes demand change?

Some changes happen solely because of personal preferences. Other changes are brought about by broad economic and social trends which involve all or large parts of society:

■ *Population change* bears directly on demand. Total population is only increasing slowly, but important changes in the age structure and the regional distribution of the population are continuously taking place.

■ *Educational opportunity* has expanded rapidly, especially for women and some minority groups. Culture, taste and lifestyle are all directly affected by education. These, in turn, affect the pattern of demand.

■ *Social change* has been dramatic. House-moving and daily travel have increased, far more women pursue careers and new models for family life have emerged.

■ *Tastes and fashions* cause people to change their choices.

■ *Rising or falling incomes* can have a big impact on the pattern of demand. All consumers have to work within a budget. Given more or less income, they will change their pattern of spending.

■ *New products, new technologies* – competing substitutes may attract customers. Sometimes very similar products become available from a new source at a lower price and cause falling demand for a product which previously sold well. Completely new products also attract customers at the expense of existing products. The impact of these changes is discussed in the next enquiry.

2 Population changes

Does age matter?

Age groups	1971	1981	1991	1997
Under 5	4553	3455	3886	3713
5–14	8916	8147	7175	7665
15–19	3862	4735	3739	3592
20–29	7968	8113	9298	8120
30–44	9197	10 956	12 221	13 165
45–59	10 202	9540	9500	10 702
60–74	7986	8130	7955	7789
75–84	2160	2675	3136	3175
85+	485	602	896	1088
Total	55 928	56 352	57 808	59 009

Figure M3.2 UK population (000s), by totals and age structure
Source: ONS, *Annual Abstract*, 1999

> ### Your agenda
>
> 1 Which age groups in Figure M3.2 were growing in number, and which declining, in 1997?
>
> 2 Analyse carefully the changes in numbers of children and older teenagers, shown in Figure M3.2. How would you expect these changes to affect a UK manufacturer of bicycles?
>
> 3 What changes would you expect to have taken place in the market for residential homes for the elderly?

The total population in most high income economies is now either stable or increasing only slowly. As an influence on demand, therefore, total population is a small factor. By contrast, the 1960s in Britain saw population growth of over 6 per cent – a significant force behind expansion in mass markets at that time.

Changes in the age distribution of population are caused by historical trends and fluctuations in the birth and death rates. Age distribution has a major impact on demand. For example, the number of babies under 12 months fell by nearly 10 per cent in the five years between 1992 and 1996. This was a serious factor at the high street retailers Mothercare, meaning more emphasis on the needs of toddlers and young children. By contrast, the number of people over 84 increased by nearly 20 per cent over the same period. Sharp changes in the birth rate 'ripple' through the age structure of the population creating a quite uneven age structure and steady changes over time.

Age provides a natural criterion for market segmentation. People within certain age groups tend to have similar needs and tastes. For example, Barretts Sherbet Fountain sells mainly to people under 15, while Wallace Arnold coach tours appeal to those over 65.

3 Educational, cultural and social changes

Education changes people. It opens up new possibilities for them: magazines written for people with particular hobbies have been a huge growth area in recent years. At the time of writing, the circulation figures for tabloid newspapers are falling. Broadsheets, on the other hand, are selling well. It is too early to be sure but these changes probably reflect the huge increase in the numbers of young people in education in the 16–25 age group which took place in the 1990s.

The pattern of demand, changes in education and the social structure are all linked. Marketing specialists make extensive use of social data because market segmentation involves identifying and grouping together people who have some key features in common.

Social grade	Occupation type	% of adult population over 15 years
A	Higher professional, managerial or administrative	3.0
B	Intermediate professional, managerial or administrative	17.8
C1	Supervisory or clerical, junior administrative	27.5
C2	Skilled manual	23.8
D	Semi or unskilled manual	18.2
E	State pensioners or unwaged, casual work	8.9

Figure M3.3 Socio–economic groups
Source: *Marketing Pocket Book*, 1999

The data in Figure M3.3 are often equated with social class, but they are really a breakdown of occupational types with well-known links to ways of life and patterns of demand. Striking correlations can be found between socio-economic grade and consumption of product types – see Figure M3.4.

Socio-economic grade	% of socio-economic group who: smoke cigarettes	visit the theatre
A	12	60 (A & B)
B	20	
C1	26	44
C2	31	30
D	38	22
E	40	19

Figure M3.4 Demand and social class
Source: *Marketing Pocket Book*, 1999

The impact of culture on tastes

Carnivores and herbivores

	percentages	
	1984	**1997**
Non–meat eater	4	14
Eat meat occasionally	21	32
Eat meat regularly	61	46
'Eat as much meat as I can'	14	7

Figure M3.5 Vegetarians
Source: Carel Press Carlisle (Factfile 98) Realeat Survey 1997

Your agenda

1 What kinds of changes do these data suggest?

2 How might these changes affect the demand for goods and services?

In recent years marketing experts have been keen to analyse cultural trends. Culture means the patterns of behaviour and values among a population. Values in this sense refer to the levels of approval or disapproval attached to particular beliefs and practices within a culture.

Cultural changes and shifts in taste and lifestyle are not easy to measure, although many pointers exist:

■ Short-term changes in fashion (for example colour or style gaining or losing popularity) are different from long-term changes in culture and values (for example a rise in concern for animal rights).

■ Fashion is difficult to track or predict, but changes lead abruptly to huge increases or decreases in demand.

Changes in culture and value usually happen rather slowly but can be quite fundamental. One example of a cultural change is the rise in environmental awareness, especially among younger people. This has increased demand for all kinds of 'green' products and altered the supply policy of many firms. But sometimes culture changes more quickly for economic reasons. For example, reduced employment in manufacturing industries in many parts of northern England, the Midlands and South Wales has altered ways of life and patterns of demand.

Changes in tastes and fashions can be rooted in wider social change. Quite often, though, they are a matter of simple preference. Or are they? You might argue that they are created by businesses, deliberately.

Point of view

Chicken or egg?

Do firms follow the market or is the market shaped by firms? Out-of-town supermarkets claim that they have responded to consumer demand in their location. Town centres are congested while much housing development has been on the fringe of urban areas. Out-of-town sites have much lower land costs, easy access by road and plentiful parking.

But a new survey commissioned by the government* shows that out–of–town superstores cause a sharp fall in town-centre trade leading to the closure of smaller stores and a reduction in consumer choice. The findings also indicate that the net effect of a superstore on local employment is negative rather than positive.

*Survey by CB Hillier Parker of nine market towns

Source: *Daily Telegraph*, 26 September 1998

Your agenda

1 How could it be argued that a new superstore actually brings – or keeps – trade in a town?

2 Disregarding any legal requirements, on what grounds could council planners decide to refuse planning permission for an out-of-town superstore? How far might these arguments be supported by economic and business concepts?

3 Suppose that a superstore opens on the edge of a country town. Soon after, an established butcher in the town centre is forced by falling sales to close his business. Do you think he is primarily a victim of:

a the changing preferences of consumers, or

b the expansion programme of the superstore?

4 Incomes

Will you want more?

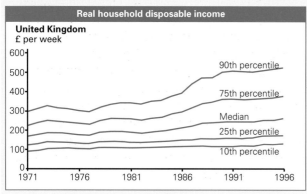

Figure 3.6 Real household disposable income
Source: ONS, Social Trends

Your agenda

1 a Which income groups in the population will be most likely to travel regularly by local bus?

  b How might the demand for bus travel be affected by a 5 per cent increase in real incomes?

2 How might these data be useful to the operator of a luxury cruise ship?

3 Give three examples of products which are likely to face increasing demand when incomes rise?

It has already become clear that rising incomes can lead to rising demand for many products. If income elasticity of demand is greater than 1, then demand will rise proportionately more than the increase in income. The crucial measure of income here is disposable income, since it is that income which consumers can spend as they please.

	Gross income
plus	state benefits
less	taxes
equals	disposable income (i.e. income available to spend)

Since long before the Second World War, there has been an overall upward trend in real **gross and disposable incomes** of around 2 per cent per year. Figure M3.7 shows what this means – constant prices give us the real increase in incomes.

Year	Amount (£)
1960	14038
1970	15878
1980	18424
1990	21838
1995	22374
1997	23386

Figure 3.7 Average disposable income per household, 1997 prices

Source: *Marketing Pocket Book*, 1999 NTC Publications

Essentials

Gross income is the total amount of income paid before any deductions.

Essentials

Disposable income gives the amount paid after deduction of tax and addition of any benefits payable.

Work in progress

Q

1 What impact would you expect the long run rise in real incomes to have on the general pattern of demand?

2 How might businesses find a knowledge of income elasticity of demand for their products useful?

3 If the income elasticity of demand for long-haul holiday destinations is 3.0, what will be the impact on demand of a real economic growth rate of 3.5 per cent?

4 Figure M3.8 gives some indications of sales of consumer durables. Clearly, rising incomes have affected these figures. Are there any other factors which might have been important in determining the growth of sales shown?

Percentage of households owning/renting durable goods			
	1978	**1988**	**1998**
Washing-machine	75	85	91
Video-recorder	–	50	84
Cars	58	66	70

Figure M3.8 Social indicators
Source: ONS, *Annual Abstract*, 1985 and 1999

The changing distribution of incomes

Besides growing overall, gross and disposable incomes in the UK have become increasingly unevenly distributed since 1980. This trend has been caused by a strong rise in earnings among the most highly skilled and a tiny rate of growth in real earnings in the least skilled occupations. Tax changes have also had some impact. The data are shown in Figure M3.6.

There is clear inequality in the **distribution of incomes** and a very significant gap between the highest and lowest levels of income. Increasing inequality has brought additional spending power into the hands of the better-off. This further segments markets and creates demand both for luxury products and for cheap substitutes.

Essentials

The **distribution of incomes** refers to the extent to which incomes vary, with some people receiving very much more income than others.

5 What is the regional pattern of demand?

Where?

Region	Disposable income per head £	£ per person per week spent on eating out	% homes with computer
North East	7420	2.80	17
North West	7971	3.85	21
Yorkshire	7978	3.52	21
East Midlands	8206	3.59	21
West Midlands	8217	3.50	22
Eastern	8376	n/a	27
London	10 513	5.52	24
South East	9589	4.55	28
South West	8192	3.47	23

Figure M3.9 How do UK regions vary?
Source: ONS, *Regional Trends*, 1998

Your agenda

1 How might the data in Figure M3.9 assist:

a the marketing director of a restaurant chain planning to expand outside London?

b an entrepreneur wanting to start a computer software business?

Just as countries vary widely in patterns of performance and levels of income, so do regions within countries. They are affected by geographical, cultural and other differences.

■ Geographical factors place the Highlands of Scotland at a disadvantage in distance from major population centres; south-east England has an advantage in its proximity to markets in London and continental Europe.

■ Natural resources may give special advantages to a region. For example, eastern Scotland has benefited from the North Sea oilfields.

■ Human resources vary by region. A pool of skilled labour is a real asset provided that the skills are appropriate to new business activities.

■ Cultural factors influence the relative attractiveness of regions. To some extent, success breeds success. A reputation for a cooperative workforce, an attractive lifestyle and cultural excellence draws successful firms. Lack of these qualities is a negative influence.

When structural changes take place, some businesses close down and jobs are lost. This can mean that incomes fall locally. Other businesses in turn are affected by falling sales and a general loss of prosperity is experienced. In some regions this has become a vicious circle because a depressed area is often not an attractive business location. These factors interact with those described above. Changes in the pattern of demand affect regional incomes. This process is shown in Figure M3.10.

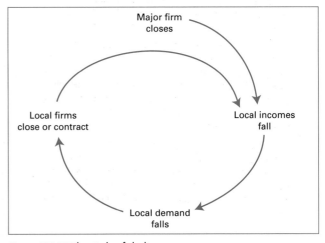

Figure M3.10 The circle of decline

Expanding firms create new jobs and incomes. They often pay higher wages and salaries. Their investment in new buildings and machinery creates orders for other firms, attracting more business to the area. As incomes rise, so households spend more and many local firms see demand rise again.

This process affects the pattern of demand. This upward 'spiral' of economic activity is self–reinforcing. A strengthening economy develops a better infrastructure that then encourages further investment. Expanding regions are also likely to attract and build a skilled workforce. In addition, the culture of a region tends to reflect business confidence and the rising aspirations of local people.

Inevitably, all the same arguments and reasoning can work in the opposite direction. If major industries and key employees leave a region, it becomes very vulnerable to a downward economic spiral. As incomes fall, so demand contracts and more local firms face difficulties. Often the younger and best educated people migrate to more prosperous areas while the region concerned develops a poor 'image' as a place to live and work.

It is to counteract problems of this kind that the government and the European Union have a regional policy to attract new industries in areas with low incomes and business decline.

6 Public or private?

Who supplies the power?

17 September

Dear Consumer

Over the next few months you may well receive offers from a number of different companies to supply energy for your home.

After reading them, you may well wonder which energy supplier really offers the best value for money.

Clearly we think SWEB does, and we're prepared to back that up with a very simple promise. If you're a typical gas or electricity consumer, SWEB offers a better price for your home energy than British Gas. And that's a fact!

We appreciate your custom, and we hope you'll choose to remain with The Home Team. You'll have the peace of mind of staying with a supplier you know, at a competitive price you can count on.

Yours sincerely

John Davies

John Davies
Customer Service Manager

SWEB used to stand for South Western Electricity Board and until 1992 was part of the nationalised electricity supply industry. Deregulation in the late 1990s meant that other companies were free to use the supply grid and enter the industry to compete with regional firms such as SWEB.

Your agenda

1 How might a company such as SWEB gain a competitive advantage in the market for electricity supply?

2 In what ways might marketing strategies at SWEB be affected by the arrival of direct competitors?

3 How do you think the attitude of consumers might be influenced by this letter and any future offers to supply electricity?

Everyone needs business enterprise, but who should be its owners? In the classic view of a free market economy, these should be entrepreneurs and shareholders: those who have chosen to risk their capital in the business venture. In Britain this view was dominant until the 1930s. Then the business cycle became stuck in a worldwide depression or slump.

Key industries slashed output and employment and failed to invest. As the Second World War brought a kind of recovery, plans were laid for the **nationalisation** of such essential industries as gas, water, electricity, coal, steel and the railways. The Labour government elected in 1945 carried out this programme arguing that only the **public sector** could ensure adequate investment and take proper account of the social consequences of business decisions.

In practice, the experience of nationalisation was mixed at best. The heavy industries nationalised were in structural decline and lost large amounts of public money. Levels of investment did not increase significantly. State-owned firms were often immense in scale and unwieldy to manage. Lack of responsiveness to markets appeared to be the main consequence of government monopoly. Without competition, managers lacked any incentive to serve customers well.

The Conservative government elected in 1979 began a long process of **privatisation**, transferring these industries back to the private sector. In most instances shares were sold direct to the general public. The aim was to achieve increased efficiency, better performance and wider share ownership. To help ensure fair play and some continuing public accountability, 'watchdog' bodies were set up for those industries which would continue for a time to have a monopoly, for example Ofgas and Oftel.

The **regulators** of privatised industries have to strike a balance between the interests of producers and consumers. In general, they try to simulate the action of a real competitive market which would keep an upward pressure on quality and a restraining influence on price. So appropriate standards of service are specified and increases in price are limited by some agreed formula. Meanwhile, privatisation itself may be only the first step towards creating a fully competitive market. Where government regulations actually impede competition, further **deregulation** may be needed so that more firms can enter the market and compete on equal terms.

Essentials

Nationalisation means that the government takes an enterprise into public ownership. Then its investment finance comes from government sources and its profits become government revenue. The government (or taxpayer) is also liable to have to cover its losses.

Essentials

The **public sector** includes all activities undertaken directly or indirectly by local or national government.

Essentials

Privatisation returns public sector enterprise to private ownership. Usually, the shares in the enterprise have been offered for sale to the general public.

Essentials

Regulators require the privatised industries to comply with their controls on prices charged and services provided.

Essentials

Deregulation involves reducing the number and range of controls over individual businesses by the government.

What has been the effect of privatisation?

The effects of privatisation are still hotly debated. Most of the industries have seen large gains in productivity and improvements in their return on capital, but these appear just as likely to have occurred in the years immediately before privatisation as in the years that followed. It is possible that a changing business culture in the industries and the expectation of privatisation had an effect.

Privatisation has generally increased competition and led to a rapid growth in market opportunity. In some cases, such as telecommunications, rapid technological advance has triggered a huge expansion in the range of services offered.

All political parties now agree that privatisation provided the way forward. In fact, it has become the accepted way all over the world.

Ways of increasing competition

Deregulating opportunity?

Although first privatisation and then deregulation of Britain's telecommunications market has led to competition for BT, only large companies have been able to enter the market.

Now a small company aims to shake up the market. Redstone Telecom admits that it lacks the capital to build its own fully-fledged network. Instead it is using an innovative strategy. In a £1.8 million agreement, Redstone has gained rights to 'piggy-back' on the Fibernet data communications network. This gives the firm national coverage enabling it – in business markets – to compete directly with such giants as BT and Cable & Wireless.

Managing director, Graham Cove says: 'We aim to open up the market place, offering more choice and real value to businesses. Our return on invest-ment cycle is also much shorter than that of other network-owning telecos. I wouldn't be surprised to see others follow-ing in our wake.'

Redstone was first given a licence to operate a public phone network in 1995 and Graham Cove was its first employee. Based on selling a single number to customers for all their phone links, sales have risen from just under £2 mil-lion in 1996 to over £8 million in 1997 and an expected £30 million for 1998.

But Redstone wants to be more than a successful piece of niche marketing. Given its plans for expansion, the com-pany is considering a flotation on the London Stock Exchange. This would obtain the necessary finance and help establish the required credibil-ity with potential customers.

Source: Adapted from *The Independent on Sunday*, 6 September 1998

Your agenda

1 How might business telecoms consumers benefit from the consequences of deregulation?

2 What are the likely sources of competitive advantage enjoyed by Redstone?

Deregulation involves removing legal regulations that:

■ add to business costs without sufficient reason
■ prevent firms entering certain markets.

The aim has been to reduce business costs – especially for small and medium-sized enterprise – and to increase competition. Since 1985 a long series of government initiatives has tried to cut out any source of excessive regulation that adds to business costs. For small firms, for example, employment regulations have been relaxed, tax procedures simplified and accounting requirements made less expensive.

Meanwhile, legal entry barriers to a number of industries, including telecoms, transport and financial services, have been scrapped. In an increasing range of cases this has led to new firms entering the market, an improvement in the variety and quality of products offered and a fall in real prices.

Another means by which markets have been created and then made competitive has been through **contracting out**. This involves organisations in the public sector identifying various non-core services which are then offered for contract to outside firms. Often the relevant operating unit within the organisation can also tender. The aim is to harness the benefits of competition.

Essentials

Contracting out means that the national or local government pays a private sector enterprise to provide services to the public. Street cleaning has been contracted out in many areas.

How have the markets of the public sector changed?

There have not only been huge changes in the ownership and structure of the pre-1980 public sector, major shifts of attitude and culture have also occurred. It was sometimes said of the old British Rail that 'it could run trains if only it wasn't for the passengers'. Users of the public sector sometimes felt that they were fortunate to be served at all or that the organisation existed to meet the demands of its employees before the needs of its customers. These impressions could also be unfair – the public sector was often underfunded and asked to pursue economic and social goals that could not be reconciled.

Certainly, there was a tendency towards product orientation in the public sector that has given way to a much more market-orientated style of management. Whereas the onus was once on the consumer to follow the required procedures, there is now more flexibility and greater efforts to meet the needs of the consumer. While once the products of the public sector were slow to change, they are now more likely to be respecified as change takes place in the market. The NHS, for example, has changed greatly for the better in terms of its willingness to accommodate individuals' needs.

Consumers, too, have changed in attitude towards the public sector. People have tended to become more demanding and more aware that consumers have legal and market power. They are less likely to behave as mere 'recipients' of services and more likely to assume the status enjoyed by 'consumers' in the private sector.

1 Fair or unfair?

Easyjet cuts the cost

In 1995 Stelios Haji–Ioannou set up Easyjet, a no–frills airline. Its unique selling point is its low fares. It is able to keep prices low because its customers book direct – so avoiding the 25 per cent commissions commonly paid to travel agents.

Its competitors reacted in different ways. British Airways set up its own cut-price subsidiary called Go. Other airlines did their best to compete. The travel agents, increasingly cut out of a lucrative market, tightened their belts and tried to add value in other ways.

The Federation of Greek Travel Agents tried something different. Its members were mad at their countryman. He had advertised his new London–Athens route with the slogan 'Forget your travel agent'. In an Athens courtroom the Federation accused him of 'commercial hooliganism' and destroying jobs when unemployment was rising. It said: 'The airline is deceiving customers with its unfair and provocative advertisement and is leading a whole sector of over 5000 professionals to unemployment'. The Federation wanted his flights banned in Greece.

While he waited for the verdict, Mr Haji–Ioannou ordered 15 more Boeing 737s.

Your agenda

1 Make a list of the courses of action open to businesses which suddenly find themselves facing stiff competition.

2 What impact do price cuts have on consumers? Explain your point of view.

3 Would you recommend a business to retaliate with price cuts of its own?

4 Do you think the Greek travel agents are likely to succeed in reducing their opponent's activities?

Most producers face some kind of competition. If they do not, they have little incentive to keep costs down and strive for efficiency, or to find out what customers really want. The customer ends up paying more than is really necessary for goods and services that may not be of high quality.

Competition forces businesses to change the way they work. If they have allowed inefficiencies to creep in, and prices are higher than they really need to be, improved decision-taking will bring cost cuts. Once they start cutting costs and trying harder, they may even become more profitable.

If costs have already been cut in every way possible, what does the beleaguered business do next? A good deal depends on the nature of the industry.

- If the market is close to being perfectly competitive, there is no option but to compete on price. However, the prevailing price may have dropped below the level of costs for some businesses. Then, in time, the business will have to exit from the market place, admitting that other suppliers are more competitive.
- It may be possible to survive as a business by switching to more profitable products.
- For many businesses, competition comes partly from abroad. As countries develop new industries, they become able to manufacture a wide range of products more cheaply. Their technical knowledge increases and capital investment raises productivity. They seek out export markets. Existing businesses in those markets experience increased competition as economies of scale are exploited.

The fight to cut costs when competition warms up is good for customers. They usually end in getting what they want at a better price. For producers, it means a constant battle to stay in business.

Work in progress

Q 1 What strategies could businesses which face strong competition employ in order to cut costs?

2 Under what circumstances might it be advisable for a business to diversify into some other line of production?

3 Give two examples drawn from your own knowledge of business, showing how the firms concerned coped with competition.

Competition among the few

In some industries there is a small number of producers, each with easily recognisable brands. Competition is often very fierce and may take a variety of forms. Each business will have as its objective to maintain, and if possible increase, market share. The players in the market will be watching each other. They will behave interdependently, each trying to outdo the other in an effort to get the better of the competition. Easyjet is in a market which is just like this. Sometimes the focus will be upon price cutting, sometimes on other competitive strategies.

2 Compete on price?

Eurotunnel at war

In 1996 the Channel Tunnel and the ferries were locked in mortal combat. About 35 million passengers were making the crossing each year.

- Eurotunnel had 35 per cent of the market
- P&O had 32 per cent. It had a policy to match any rival's discount.
- Stena Line had 20 per cent.

Between 1993 and 1996, peak season fares fell by 60 per cent as the ferries tried to stop large-scale defections to the tunnel. They laid on extra boats. Then Seafrance and Brittany Ferries joined in the price cuts, backed up by extra subsidies from the French local authorities which owned them.

At those prices, Eurotunnel might have had difficulty covering its costs. But in late 1996 there was a serious fire in the tunnel. There were no casualties, but for a time fewer trains were running. It looked like a good moment for Eurotunnel to put up prices. The war wasn't over, but it became less intense.

Your agenda

1. How might the ferries have benefited from cutting prices?
2. Could Eurotunnel drive a ferry company out of business?
3. What impact did these events have on consumers?

Price wars can easily develop in a market with relatively few players. They occur when one competitor cuts prices, then another follows suit. To maintain its advantage the first competitor cuts prices again and so it goes on. After a while, all sellers have cut prices. However, none has gained a decisive advantage in terms of market share, so all will find that their profit margins are lower.

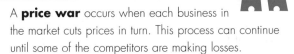

Essentials

A **price war** occurs when each business in the market cuts prices in turn. This process can continue until some of the competitors are making losses.

Some businesses are able to reduce prices to a loss-making level for long enough to drive a competitor out of business. This is known as **predatory pricing**. Once the competitor has made an exit from the market place, the business may be able to pick up at least some of its competitor's market share. It may even be able to raise prices above their original level and make super-normal profit. These may or may not attract new competitors into the market.

Price wars do not necessarily involve predatory pricing. They may start at a time when in fact all the players in the market can afford to cut prices and still stay in business. The price competition which can sometimes be seen in the petrol market can be like this. Oil companies do not as a rule go out of business, although some have merged.

However, once one firm cuts the price below its long-run production costs, weaker competitors are in great danger. So predatory pricing is generally seen as being anti-competitive behaviour.

Essentials

Predatory pricing means setting the price at a level below long-run average cost, with the deliberate intention of driving weaker competitors out of business. In the long run this may reduce the competitive pressure on the business which was able to afford a period of predatory pricing.

3 Non–price competition

The Andrex puppy

The Andrex marketing strategy is based on premium pricing. When Andrex was originally launched, it sold only in Harrods. Even now, its price is usually about 40 per cent above the average for the industry. Yet it has roughly 30 per cent of the market.

How is it done? It has seen off competition from own brands as well as from quality competitors. Is it really the softness or is it the puppy?

The first puppy made its appearance in 1972. At that time, Andrex had 5 per cent of the market. The advertising agency wanted a little girl for the ad. The Independent Television Commission ruled against this idea, believing that it might encourage children to waste paper. So they resorted to the puppy, unravelling the paper and suggesting softness, length and strength.

The visibility of the puppy waxes and wanes. Andrex parted company long since from its original makers, having been taken over several times. It now belongs to Kimberly–Clark. But the puppy still appears on the packet and on TV screens all over Europe.

Your agenda

1 Explain the component parts of Andrex's marketing strategy.

2 Does price play a part in the overall strategy?

3 Are there barriers to entry in the market for premium toilet tissue?

Non-price competition is an alternative to competition on price. You can see it everywhere. It can involve all kinds of promotion, including advertising, packaging, branding, special offers and so on. It can also exploit possibilities which open up through new technologies becoming available to improve the quality of products. Quality, reliability and reputation all figure large in the strategies.

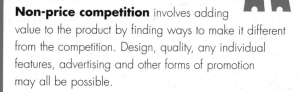

Essentials

Non-price competition involves adding value to the product by finding ways to make it different from the competition. Design, quality, any individual features, advertising and other forms of promotion may all be possible.

Competing on design often goes hand in hand with branding. Good design can create strong brand loyalties. Buyers may be enthusiasts, for whom the product has an impact on lifestyle. Some car buyers behave like this, enthusing over the new features developed by the company and buying new models as they become available.

Some big companies build a reputation for the reliability of their products. Others compete by advertising in amusing or outrageous ways. Advertising can shift the demand curve to the right and allow the business to charge a higher price without losing customers. In some industries, extensive advertising is essential, just for survival. It can create a significant barrier to entry.

All of the strategies mentioned here are really ways of adding more value. They allow businesses to differentiate their products more effectively. In some cases, they rest on the creation of a new and better product. In others, they depend on people's perceptions – the image of the product.

Work in progress

Q 1 Analyse the way each of the following companies or products compete: Persil, Jaguar, Coca-Cola, MacDonald's, Hoover, Microsoft, Nintendo, British American Tobacco.

2 Select one company which you think has been extraordinarily successful, and describe its strategy for competing.

Compete or collaborate?

Psion scares Microsoft

Generally speaking, Microsoft doesn't worry too much about competition. Having invented its Windows operating system, and made sure that it is installed automatically on almost all PCs before they are sold, it doesn't have to.

Competing with Microsoft on price is not easy. It has enormous economies of scale. But some companies have managed to compete on design and product development.

Take Psion, the UK manufacturer of hand–held personal organisers. They are small and light; they fit into a pocket. In case you lose them, you can back up your data on a spare disk and keep it in a safe place. No great threat, you might think, to Microsoft. The stock market value of Psion is £260 million, compared to Microsoft's £136 billion.

In late 1998 Psion embarked on a new venture. The company signed an agreement with the world's three biggest mobile phone companies, Ericsson, Motorola and Nokia. They are to develop software for a new generation of 'smart' phones. The idea is to combine the facilities of PCs and traditional phones.

Microsoft expressed its worries about Psion in a memo, leaked to the press soon after the agreement was signed. At the time, Microsoft was under investigation in the US, because of charges that it had intimidated its rivals in the market place.

Your agenda

1 Identify all the ways in which electronics businesses compete.

2 How did Psion create a competitive advantage?

3 How would collaboration with the mobile phone companies help Psion?

4 What other types of business try to compete in the same kind of way?

The Psion example shows how companies can collaborate to their mutual advantage. Collaboration can take the form of agreeing to develop products jointly. Each can contribute particular kinds of expertise. This can be especially useful when the development costs of a new product or design are very high.

The aircraft industry provides an interesting example. Boeing is big enough to develop new aircraft successfully, but British Aerospace and the French aircraft makers were struggling. By collaborating within Airbus Industrie, together and with their other European partners, they have created well–designed aircraft which can compete with Boeing on world markets.

Collaboration can be carried as far as merger, when two firms combine. The next section looks at the reasons for and the outcomes of mergers.

4 Compete or merge?

Rank-Hovis-McDougall

Itself formed through a series of mergers in the 1960s, Rank-Hovis-McDougall (RHM) was a leader in the production of bread and cakes and a significant force in branded groceries. Its flour milling and baking operations – spearheaded by Mothers Pride and Hovis – commanded 34 per cent of the £2 billion per year UK bread market. The long list of major names owned by the company included Golden Shred marmalade, Mr Kipling cakes, McDougalls flour, Paxo stuffings, Saxa salt, Bisto gravies and Just Juice.

	1989	**1990**	£ million **1991**
RHM total			
Sales	1786	1771	1531
Operating profit	203	180	146
Capital employed	1438	1174	1242
Employees	39189	36155	30340
Milling and baking			
Sales	645	649	667
Pre–tax profit*	69	62	59

Figure M3.11

Note: Pre–tax profit is distinct from operating profit and comparisons should be treated with caution.

Sorce: Rank-Hovis-McDougall, *Annual Report*, 1991

Profits at RHM had been falling – from £203 million in 1989 to £146 million in 1991 with around £100 million expected at the time for 1992. Its return on equity was below the level of its competitors. Its share price was underperforming relative to the stock market as a whole. However, the company remained optimistic:

'The creation and development of strong, profitable brands and brand families requires deep understanding of the market, careful research, innovative flair and substantial continuing investment. We believe we meet all these requirements.'

'Our aim is to continue our successful and profitable progress through innovation, new product development and advertising to ensure that we strengthen our position in the branded grocery markets wherever we operate.'

Rank-Hovis-McDougall, *Annual Report*, 1991

Your agenda

1   What evidence can you find here to suggest failing performance at RHM?

2   Given this evidence, why might another firm be interested in acquiring Rank-Hovis-McDougall?

Companies want to grow in order to improve their market position. This can happen in one of two ways.

● **Organic growth** which occurs as the firm, expands, building new factories or offices and expanding output and employment

● **Inorganic growth** involves expansion through integration with another firm, i.e. a merger or a take-over.

A **merger** is the amalgamation of two or more firms into a single business with the approval of the shareholders and management concerned.

A **take-over** occurs when one firm makes a bid for another and secures over 50 per cent of the equity regardless of approval from the target firm's management. Such a bid may be strongly resisted and a major battle can ensue with bidding and target companies locked in conflict. The outcome will depend on shareholders deciding whether or not to accept the bidder's terms.

Essentials

Organic growth occurs when the business expands through increasing output and sales itself and without taking over other businesses.

Essentials

Inorganic growth involves taking over another company so that the combined output and sales are higher.

Essentials

A **merger** brings together two companies which agree to integrate production under a single board of directors.

Essentials

A **take-over** occurs when one firm succeeds in buying more than 50% of the shares of another.

Mergers and take-overs generally happen because the companies involved believe that the resources of the separate entities could be managed more efficiently as a combined enterprise. The motive may lead to businesses joining up in different ways:

- through **horizontal integration**, where the firms being combined are in similar types of business such as two holiday companies
- through **vertical integration**, where the firms being combined are in the same industry but operating at different stages in the production chain such as a tour operator and a travel agent
- through the integration of firms in unrelated industries such as a tour operator and a car manufacturer to form a **conglomerate**.

Essentials

Horizontal integration occurs where two or more firms operating at the same production stage in the same industry combine to form a single entity.

Essentials

Vertical integration occurs where two or more firms operating at different production stages in the same industry combine to form a single entity.

Essentials

Conglomerates are formed from the amalgamation of firms with differing products sold in different markets.

Any private company is free to buy or merge with another subject to the laws that control monopoly. For public companies, there are precise rules governing take-over activity. The whole process of bids and negotiations must occur within a specified timetable and a period is set aside for a target company's management to make the case for rejecting the bid. The bidder will offer shareholders in the target firm its own shares, fixed interest loan stock or cash. This choice is significant since it will affect the capital structure of the new enterprise.

Work in progress

Q
1 What factors might make a firm the likely target for a take-over?
2 Why might the directors of a target company actively oppose a bid that is later accepted by a majority of the shareholders?
3 How would you expect the trade union representing the workforce to respond in the face of a take-over bid?

Why do mergers and take-overs happen?

Mergers have generally been concentrated in 'booms' that roughly coincide with periods of economic expansion. Two such periods of intense merger activity occurred in the late 1990s and between 1984 and 1989. Many different arguments for integration are advanced by managers at the time of a merger or bid:

- Economies of scale are a straightforward motive. They reduce overhead costs and make the business more efficient.
- The elimination of inefficient capacity which may have been duplicated in the past.
- Sharing administration and other overheads will reduce costs for both companies.
- Complementary strengths may be united. One company may, for example, have excellence in its technology and product quality while the other has a better distribution network and greater expertise in marketing.
- Diversification in products and markets will lead to greater protection from market downturns and wider opportunities for growth.
- Instant acquisition of the brands, technologies, patents and markets of a competitor. Such assets can take many years to accumulate internally and a bid may give immediate access to important future sources of cash flow and profit.

What is the likely outcome of mergers and take-overs?

Any period of declining sales or return on capital is liable to highlight opportunity cost: in other words, could another firm and a different management do better with the same resources? The directors of Rank-Hovis-McDougall expressed confidence in their expertise but the shareholders saw failing performance and the firm became subject to a take-over bid.

Sometimes it is mutually advantageous for two firms to merge and create a new entity. Glaxo and Wellcome, the pharmaceutical companies, joined forces in 1992 and have prospered strongly ever since. Similarly, Royal Insurance and the Sun Alliance group merged in 1996. In other cases, the merger is from a position of weakness as when the ailing Kwik–Save group merged with Somerfield supermarkets in 1998. On occasions a relatively successful firm may fall victim to a larger rival that is willing to pay a premium price for its assets, performance or prospects. The purchase of the Hard Rock Café by Diageo (formerly Grand Metropolitan) is an example. (Diageo later sold it again… Ownership can change quite often when mergers are in full spate.)

These changes of ownership and management are an inevitable, even essential, feature of a free market economy. Markets are dynamic and so are the competitive advantages and sources of market strength enjoyed by firms. Without fluidity in ownership, firms could stagnate in patterns of low performance while expanding companies and talented management teams would be unable to advance. However, there is always a risk that the integration of firms leads to an abuse of market power.

We have seen that firms develop a culture of their own. This usually changes quite quickly or disappears altogether when a merger or take-over takes place. It is understandable that employees and even customers experience regrets.

Does integration deliver?

Some 50 per cent of all mergers and take-overs are reckoned to fail when it comes to delivering the promised benefits. The ones that succeed are often those in which the companies concerned have a clear understanding of the nature of the business and strong possibilities for rationalising production.

Sometimes the motivation for merger is presented in terms of benefits to the companies but in fact the real reason behind it is that the managers concerned perceive a possible increase in their power and influence. Then it may be more difficult to make a success of the change.

The reduced risks associated with diversification are often attractive, but many textbooks, articles and researchers have concluded that diversification is to be treated with caution. The danger is that managers get into businesses that they do not properly understand, and if shareholders want to reduce risk, they can always hold shares in a range of different companies.

1 The ups and downs of the economy

Making the restaurant pay

During the late 1980s Michael and Glynis Jones bought a large house in a beautiful valley in North Wales and created a flourishing hotel and restaurant business. They put all their savings into the business and also took out a substantial bank loan. Michael was a talented chef and the hotel provided the facilities for gourmets to stay overnight. The economy was growing strongly and customers were plentiful. Every indication suggested that this was a business with long-term prospects of profitability.

In 1989 the UK economy started to falter after a period in which it had been growing strongly. By 1990 output was falling generally: recession had set in. Redundancies and rising unemployment meant that many people were experiencing falling incomes. This kind of trend is not good news for restaurateurs. People who are worried about their job security can easily cut back on meals out.

By 1991 sales revenue from Michael and Glynis's business was down by 18 per cent. Meantime interest rates had risen, increasing their monthly payments to the bank. Within a short space of time, cash flow had become negative.

The Joneses were still optimistic. The recession would not last for ever and if the bank would be prepared to allow them to pay just the interest outstanding each month, they could get by. There was no possibility of their repaying the loan without increased business, but they reckoned they could survive if the bank could be patient.

The bank was not. The bank manager wrote to the Joneses saying they would have to continue repaying the loan at the agreed rate, despite the increase in interest rates. This was impossible. The business closed almost immediately, even though the Joneses thought the long-term outlook was excellent. Yet within 18 months, other restaurants in the area were reporting increasing numbers of customers.

Your agenda

1 Use supply and demand analysis to show what happened to the Jones' business.

2 What consequences would follow upon the closing of the restaurant?

3 What other types of business might be particularly vulnerable to a period of recession in which personal incomes were tending to fall?

Economies do not usually grow at a steady rate for more than a few years at a time. The tendency is for there to be a repeating cycle of **recovery**, **boom**, **recession** and sometimes **slump** or depression. This **business cycle** afflicts all developed countries to some degree. Governments have often promised to end the cycle of 'boom and bust'. Mostly, to date, they have not been very successful in this, although there have been times when the seriousness of the problem has been somewhat reduced.

Figure M3.12 shows how economies move through the cycle. A period when output grows rapidly is followed by a period of slower growth, or recession. Sometimes slow growth develops into a slump. This can be defined as a time when output actually falls. Slumps may last for several years, but in time, demand increases, bringing recovery. If and when output begins to grow faster, the economy enters a new boom phase.

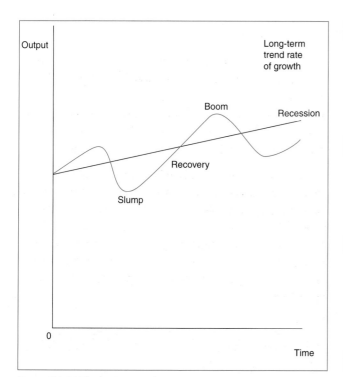

Figure M3.12 The business cycle

Essentials

The **recovery phase** of the business cycle occurs when demand and output begin to grow again after a period of decline or stagnation.

Essentials

The **boom phase** of the business cycle occurs when output is growing fast.

Essentials

The **recession phase** of the business cycle begins when output grows more slowly after a period of rapid output growth.

Essentials

A **slump** occurs when output actually falls for two quarters in a row because of lack of demand in the economy.

Essentials

The **business cycle** is the sequence of recovery, boom, recession and slump which creates significant fluctuations in the demand for many products.

Underlying these short-term fluctuations, there is always a long-term trend rate of growth. In the UK, this is usually assumed to be about a 2 per cent increase in total output each year. It results from increasing productivity brought about either by investing in improved plant and machinery, or by developing better management strategies, or by increasing use of education and training. Figure M3.12 shows how, over the course of the business cycle, total output growth fluctuates around this trend. Long-term growth is looked at in more detail on pages 232.

Very often the time when a failing business finds it must make an exit from the market place is during recession. Similarly, the conditions for entry into new markets are most favourable when the economy is booming. The impact of the business cycle on the business depends on the nature of the product. Those with high income elasticity of demand are likely to encounter larger fluctuations in demand over the course of the business cycle.

During a boom, output grows rapidly. Most businesses will experience increasing demand for their products.

2 The effects of recession and slump

Laura Ashley survives

During the 1980s fashion and home furnishings chain Laura Ashley grew fast and invested heavily in retail outlets. When interest rates rose and the recession came, the company found itself with excess capacity. People whose incomes fell spent less on clothes. The fall-off in house purchases meant less spending on furnishings. Put simply, the company was producing more than it could sell.

Having invested heavily in shops and factories, the company found itself with very heavy interest payments. In a major restructuring operation it closed down some of its factories.

It kept most of its shops but slashed its workforce by almost half from its 1990 peak. This enabled Laura Ashley to survive the recession albeit with profits far below what they had been in the late 1980s.

The recession was not the only problem for Laura Ashley. All the company's interests are in fields where fashion is a major factor in the market, so it must adapt to market change as well as the business cycle. As with so many businesses, the recession brought problems to a head.

Your agenda

1 How did Laura Ashley survive the recession?

2 How were the employees affected by the survival strategy?

3 What impact would factory closures at Laura Ashley have on the local and national economy generally?

The initial experience of recession is of demand for many products growing more slowly. This will affect most businesses, but some more seriously than others.

Depending on its individual circumstances, each business will react to recession in a slightly different way. Module 2.1 explored a number of ways in which firms can cut costs. For some firms these may spell survival. Others may be unable to adopt such strategies. They may have no alternative but to close

down or they may be able to discontinue just some sides of their business while developing others.

The worst-case scenario arises where the attempt to keep going has led to substantial borrowing. The business may become insolvent. If the firm's creditors no longer believe that it will eventually pay off its debts, then they may force it into bankruptcy. This means that the owners of the business are no longer in control; the Official Receiver's office takes over. The receiver will be an accountant whose objective will be to pay back creditors as much of the debt as is possible. The business may or may not continue, depending on its viability. If it has been badly managed, the receiver may find a buyer who will reorganise it.

In general, recession produces changes in levels of investment, liquidity and stocks. Each of these has knock-on effects:

- **Investment.** When future sales are uncertain, many firms will question their investment plans. If demand is falling, they may decide that they do not need new capacity. Their estimates of future sales and profitability may cause them to postpone their expansion plans or cancel them altogether. Firms which sell capital goods may then experience very sharp falls in demand: the construction and engineering industries are especially vulnerable. Sometimes firms may react to recession by investing in labour-saving machinery, as a way of cutting costs, but, in general, low expected profits and a gloomy outlook will make the decision to invest less likely. The low level of profitability will usually imply that there is less retained profit available to finance the investment.

- **Liquidity.** Clearly, a fall in demand will reduce cash flow and may make firms very reliant on bank loans. If interest rates rise, whatever loans firms already have will cost more to service. This increases costs and reduces liquidity further. In some cases it means that firms have to increase their borrowing just to pay the interest charges.

- **Stocks.** When sales are falling, or growing more slowly than expected, stocks of finished goods will rise. When firms cut production in response, stocks of inputs will rise. Stocks cost money: they have to be paid for, and storage may be expensive. One way of cutting borrowing needs is to run the stocks down, sometimes called de-stocking. This means that suppliers may face a period of very low orders while stocks are run down.

■ *Human resources.* In the search for cost-cutting strategies, employees are deeply affected. Redundancies are likely. Who should go if redundancies are inevitable? Obviously, firms will tend to make redundant those people they can best do without. These are often the people who will find it hardest to find alternative jobs. Key workers will be kept on as long as possible. Nevertheless, it is common to observe large numbers of skilled employees being made redundant in a recession. There may be cuts in overtime working too.

Another possibility has been to aim for the adoption of more flexible working practices. Often people will accept new ways of working because they are afraid for their jobs. This can lead to increased productivity, but that, in turn, can entail more job losses.

Trade union bargaining power is much reduced in a recession; the strike threat is worthless if the effect of the strike would be to bring about the firm's closure. People may be forced to accept working conditions which are unfavourable in order to have a job at all. The effects of this can be seen in the increased numbers of people working without contracts which would give them some protection and an element of job security.

■ *Pricing Policy.* Poor trading conditions can give a business the spur it needs to strengthen and develop its marketing strategies. Hotels can be badly hit by recessions. They may create all sorts of special offers, mini-breaks and activity weekends. Some will negotiate their prices. People may bargain, striking a deal much as they might in an oriental market place. (This links to contribution costing, page 68.) In a boom hotels will often be fully booked and no such opportunity arises.

Work in progress

Q

1 Divide the following list of products into those which are vulnerable to recession and those which are not, giving reasons in each case: cauliflowers, yachts, hair-cuts, cars, restaurant meals, factory buildings, winter coats, cat food, pension plans, lorries, and kitchen units.

2 Are there things which the recession-vulnerable products which you have identified have in common?

3 If a manufacturer responds to falling demand by reducing stocks of finished goods, what will the effect be on the firm? If the same firm reduces stocks of inputs, what will happen to their suppliers? Identify all the effects you can think of. What will the end result be?

4 What other cost-cutting measures may help businesses facing falling demand for their products?

3 The effects of recovery and boom

Making comparisons

	1991	1997
Consumer spending	340	395
Gross fixed investment	97	109
Exports	132	194
Total output (GDP)	469	538

Figure M3.13 Spending and output, £ billion, 1990 prices
Source: National Institute Economic Review, 1998 (NIER)

Your agenda

1 Using M3.13, what happened between 1991 and 1997?

2 What can you say about the long-term trend rate of growth of output for the period?

3 On the basis of the figures, what do you think might have happened since 1997? Does your prediction fit what you know actually did happen?

In times of expansion, companies are encouraged to increase their output. High levels of profitability encourage firms to employ more resources of all kinds. This leads to extra people being employed, more overtime on offer to the workforce, unsold stocks being run down and investment in new machinery and productive capacity.

Investment and finance

As confidence in the economy increases, firms think it is the ideal time for expansion. They will invest in new equipment and perhaps also introduce new technologies. High levels of profitability help to generate internal finance from retained profits, and make it easy to get bank loans. Productivity may rise as output rises.

There may be areas of less good news. Financial markets may be imbued with confidence and may willingly finance an amount of investment which really goes beyond what is needed to meet long-term demand. Because banks are confident about future profitability, they may lend to firms whose capacity to manage efficiently in the long run is really suspect. Because firms are not worried about cash flow, accounting procedures may be less stringent. Haphazard management approaches may become a feature of some firms. They do not have to try very hard to make a profit.

Easily obtainable bank loans encourage firms to borrow and, at first, there will probably be no problem with this. However, if interest rates rise, the effect is to increase debt service charges, and if demand for the product then begins to fall, cash flow will be subjected to a swift and serious squeeze.

People, skills and trade unions

As firms expand they need more people. They may be hard to find. (This situation is sometimes described as a bottleneck.) Although in recent years there has usually been a large pool of unemployed people, many of them have reasons why they cannot move to another area or another type of job. So boom years are likely to be characterised by skill shortages, as firms compete for the available people. Employee power will increase, as will trade union bargaining power, particularly for those unions representing skilled workers.

Maintaining motivation in the workforce may require special efforts. The threat of redundancy is absent. Employees may be offered higher wages by competing firms. Indeed, negotiating higher wages may be quite easy: if the profits are good, paying more may seem like simple good sense.

Work in progress

 1 When a skill shortage develops, how will firms seek to recruit? What is the likely effect on wage rates?

2 If wage rates rise, what will happen to costs? What will happen to prices?

3 How might firms tackle the need for measures to improve motivation?

4 Analysing economic change

What next?

Government spending cuts bite

Investment falls by 9 per cent

Output grows by 3 per cent this year.

Consumer spending flat for second quarter.

EXPORTS UP BY 9 PER CENT.

Savings rates fall

Imports at all time high

Chancellor promises not to increase UK taxes

Your agenda

1   Some of the items mentioned in the headlines above involve figures for different types of spending. Which of these will directly affect the demand for UK-produced goods and services?

2   Which items will have an indirect effect on demand for UK products?

3   Trace the effect of an increase in exports on:

   a   businesses producing for export;

   b   their employees

   c   other businesses in the same area.

Nothing succeeds like success – or fails like failure:

● An increase in demand in one part of the economy can lead to increasing demand in other sectors elsewhere.

● Falling demand for the products of one business tends to lead to falling demand for others. These individual changes can add up to a trend which affects the whole economy, i.e. a macro-economic change.

● Changes in demand soon become changes in income. Falling demand means falling sales, then falling output and falling incomes. Equally, rising demand will translate into rising output and rising incomes.

In order to analyse the way spending in one part of the economy affects other parts, we use the idea of the circular flow of money. This is shown in Figure M3.14. Every time we buy a product, we make a payment to the producer. So money flows from households to firms, in return for the goods and services bought by the households. This is **consumption** spending.

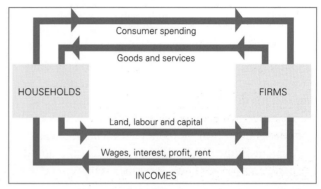

Figure M3.14 The circular flow of money

Essentials

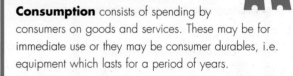

Consumption consists of spending by consumers on goods and services. These may be for immediate use or they may be consumer durables, i.e. equipment which lasts for a period of years.

Meanwhile, firms are using factors of production to make the products consumers want. They pay for the services provided by these factors of production. Wages are paid in return for labour. Interest is paid on borrowed money (capital). Profits go to the owners of the business. Rent is paid to owners of property. All these together make up the flow of income which goes from firms to households.

Work in progress

Q 1   Supposing consumers decide to cut back their spending for a while. What will happen next? Use the sequence of events in the circular flow of money to explain the consequences of this fall in consumption.

2   Now think about what happens if businesses generally decide to spend more money on equipment, i.e. they invest more. Trace the sequence of events through the circular flow of money.

Changes in spending

Consumers who decide to spend less may be **saving** more. An increase in saving reduces the amount of money moving through the circular flow via consumption spending. If tax rates are raised the same thing happens: a likely consequence is that consumption falls. Or consumers may decide to buy more imports. This usually means they are going to buy fewer domestically produced goods.

All three changes – in savings, tax and spending on imports – have the same effect. They reduce demand for domestically produced goods. They are therefore termed **leakages** (or sometimes withdrawals) from the circular flow of money. You can see what happens in Figure M3.15. Leakages reduce the amount of spending on goods and services. Firms receive less from households than they did previously.

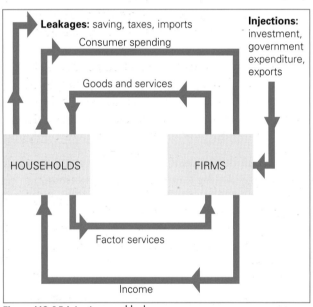

Figure M3.15 Injections and leakages

This would seem like a gloomy picture for businesses but, in fact, leakages are balanced by **injections** into the circular flow. What will happen if firms increase **investment**? Or if the government increases its expenditure? Or if demand for exports increases? As far as businesses are concerned, these are sources of demand for their products. They increase the amount of money they can earn by satisfying that demand. More money will then be paid out in wages and profits. The extra demand adds to the circular flow of money.

Work in progress

Q   **1**   Show what happens to the circular flow of money if the Chancellor of the Exchequer cuts taxes on Budget day. What happens next? Show how businesses and individuals will be affected, tracing any secondary effects through the circular flow of money.

2   In the same way, show the effects of an increase in demand for imports.

Essentials

Saving means keeping back some income, rather than spending all of it, so that the money is available to spend later.

Essentials

Leakages reduce the demand for domestically produced goods and services, by diverting part of people's incomes into savings, taxes and spending on imports.

Essentials

Injections – investment, government spending and exports – increase demand for domestically produced goods.

Essentials

Investment consists of spending now which generates income in the future. So it could be spending on buildings to be used for production purposes or on plant and machinery which will be used in manufacturing.

5 What actually happened?

The business cycle in the UK

1979:   Conservative government elected, making strong promises to control inflation. Immediately raises interest rates. Unemployment rises from 4.7 per cent in 1979 to 11.8 per cent in 1983. Inflation peaked at 17 per cent in 1980.

1980–1:   Slump. 14 per cent fall in manufacturing output. Inflation falls.

1982–6:   Recovery. Steady growth of output. Inflation stable at around 5 per cent.

1987–9:   Boom. Output grows unsustainably fast, by nearly 5 per cent in 1988. Unemployment falls to 6.3 per cent in 1989. Severe skill shortages.

1989–90:   Recession. Output grows much less fast. Inflation peaks at 9.5 per cent in 1990.

1991–2:   Slump. Output falls, unemployment rises to 10.4 per cent in 1993.

1993–6:   Recovery. Steady growth. Inflation stable at around or below 3 per cent.

1997:   Boom. Output growing at around 3 per cent. Unemployment falls to 5.1 per cent. Evidence of skill shortages developing. New Labour government pledges to end cycle of boom and bust.

1998–9:   Recession in manufacturing sector. Services still growing strongly. Inflation edging up from 3.5 per cent to 4.0 per cent but fell back to 1.1 per cent. Gradual recovery in manufacturing.

Your agenda

1   Complete the above sequence for the years following 1999, giving details of output growth, inflation and unemployment.

2   Do the peaks in inflation correspond with the years of fastest output growth?

3   Which years show highest unemployment?

■ *During a period of slump*, people lack confidence in their future because of the threat of unemployment. They may start to cut down on their spending, saving as much money as possible in case they are next to be made unemployed. This fall in spending causes the situation to get worse as **aggregate demand**, the sum total of all demand for consumer and investment goods, falls.

■ *During the recovery period*, industries and services that have survived the slump begin to increase their output. Not everyone has been made unemployed in the slump and these people will wish to purchase goods to make up for the period when they were saving more. One reason for the change in consumers' attitudes is confidence.

■ *During the boom*, the sum total of what companies can produce, **aggregate supply**, will not be enough to satisfy the growing aggregate demand. Companies try to take on more employees in order to expand output but skill shortages develop. This causes companies to offer higher wages, trying to attract the people they need. This begins to fuel inflationary expectations and other employees seek further pay rises. There may be large increases in imports.

Essentials

Aggregate demand is the sum total of demand from all sources in the economy. It includes consumption, investment, government spending and export demand.

Essentials

Aggregate supply is the total output from all sources in the economy.

The boom situation is not sustainable in the long run because aggregate supply is reaching **full capacity output**, the most that can be supplied with all suitable resources working flat out. Pay rises lead to accelerating inflation and this will provoke increases in interest rates. Firms will revise their investment plans. This fall in injections will cause both demand and income to grow more slowly. The process is cumulative and recession occurs as companies readjust their output levels to the new lower levels of demand. Falling output means rising unemployment, which in turn means falling income and further falls in demand, leading into the next slump. Figure M3.16 summarises the phases of the business cycle.

	Slump	Recovery	Boom	Recession
Employment	Low	Low, rising	High	High, falling
Skill shortages	None	Beginning	Frequent	Diminishing
Inflation	Reduced	Stable	Accelerating	Falling
Confidence	None	Low, rising	High	Low, falling
Investment	Very little	Slow growth	Growing faster	Little

Figure M3.16 The four phases of the business cycle

Essentials

Full capacity output is the maximum level to which aggregate supply can increase, given the available resources and levels of productivity.

Expectations and confidence

Expectations are an important factor in the business cycle. If firms expect demand to rise, they will feel more confident about expanding. Often business confidence is based on an accurate assessment of the data and events, but there can be a strong psychological element in confidence – if some people are feeling optimistic, so will others, and vice versa. You may be able to see this working on the Stock Exchange, where a bull market (i.e. one with growing share prices) may persist for some time because the mood of optimism is infectious, rather than because long-term prospects of profit are really good.

Business confidence can change quite fast and have important implications for the fortunes of both businesses and people. Individuals also may vary in confidence over time. If they feel their employment is insecure, they may postpone some consumption plans and save more.

Work in progress

 1 Why does output tend to grow more slowly after a period of boom conditions?

2 Consider how well the UK economy has performed over the past few years. Make a list of the evidence you would need to research before you could comment objectively on the success/failure of the economy.

3 Think about how the UK economy has been influenced by external events. Have these had some impact on the business cycle?

4 How confident are people in business at the present time?

1 Unemployment

People

Fred spent most of his working life as a coal miner in Nottinghamshire. During the late 1980s his pit closed, but he was redeployed to another pit not too far from his home. Three years later in 1991 he was made redundant. Although the pit was to remain open for a time, massive investment in new and bigger machinery was reducing the need for labour.

The village where Fred lived had developed around the pit. There were few other jobs available, and as he had had no training other than his mining experience, there was very little he could do.

Fred's colleague, Brian, was made redundant at the same time. However, he was much younger than Fred and was able to get on to a training course. Within two years he got a job doing washing-machine repairs in Nottingham. The pay was less than he had received as a miner and the journey into Nottingham took an hour each way.

At about the same time that Fred and Brian were made redundant, Graham lost his job in London. He had been working for a business making industrial training videos. The recession was in full swing and most businesses were able to hire any number of skilled people from the ranks of the unemployed. They did not need training programmes. Graham stayed unemployed for nearly a year. Then he got a slightly different job in a small radio production company. After a short time he was promoted.

Your agenda

1 Why were Brian's and Graham's chances of finding work much better than Fred's?

2 What conclusions would you draw about career decisions?

3 Why was Graham unemployed for so long, despite his obvious skills?

4 What were the changes which were taking place in the economy and resulted in these job losses?

The costs of unemployment are obvious:

- The economy is losing the output which unemployed people might have been producing.
- The unemployed are losing the difference between their income in work and the benefits they receive.
- The government is losing the tax revenue which the unemployed would have paid had they been in work, plus the costs of whatever benefits are paid. There may be further costs resulting from the poor health which is often associated with unemployment.

In looking at unemployment it is worth remembering that the labour force grew by nearly 2 million people during the 1980s. This did increase unemployment somewhat. The main reason was the increase in the number of married women working. During the 1990s the labour force has grown more slowly to around 29 million.

The causes of unemployment

There are two main reasons for unemployment: structural change and demand deficiency. Other, more minor, types include frictional unemployment which occurs when people are between jobs and seasonal unemployment which can be significant in some areas or occupations.

- **Structural unemployment.** Changes in the *structure* of industry, such as the use of gas rather than coal in the production of electricity, result in a changing pattern of employment and people are made redundant. Changes like this have happened throughout UK history: the textiles industry, shipbuilding and motorcycle production have all declined and now employ relatively few people. Sometimes the problem is not declining demand as such but the introduction of new technologies which are more capital and less labour intensive. The decline in demand may come from increasing imports. These changes cause structural unemployment.

- **Demand deficiency unemployment.** The other main reason for unemployment is a fall in demand. This occurs during a recession or slump, when demand is less than the level of full capacity output. It can cause problems for people throughout the whole economy as all sectors are likely to be affected in one way or another. It is sometimes called cyclical unemployment because it is associated with the business cycle, or demand deficiency unemployment.

Essentials

Structural unemployment is caused by changes in demand for particular products or by changes in production methods which reduce the need for labour. It may persist even when demand is growing strongly and the economy is approaching full capacity output.

Essentials

Demand deficiency unemployment is caused by a low level of aggregate demand which is less than the value of full capacity output.

In practice it is often difficult to tell whether an individual is unemployed for structural or for cyclical reasons. Both factors may be involved in an individual story. Figure M3.17 shows unemployment from all causes.

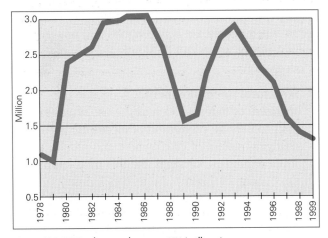

Figure M3.17 Total unemployment, UK (millions)
Source: Department of Employment

Structural unemployment is usually of a very long-term nature. It reflects the difficulty with which economies adjust to change. In the long run, jobs lost through business closures and contraction are replaced, but it can take many years for the redundant people to be reabsorbed. During that time the unemployment can cause serious social as well as economic problems.

Quite often, newly created jobs have skill requirements which are not likely to be satisfied by someone who has been made redundant from a traditional production process.

Demand deficiency unemployment, in contrast, will usually be greatly reduced by recovery. However, even then there are time lags. In the past, changes in employment were observed to be about 12–18 months behind changes in output. Now, with rather more flexible labour markets becoming the norm, that time lag may be reduced. The easier it is for employers to hire and fire, the sooner they will react to changes in demand.

Some people are more likely to be affected by unemployment than others. Skills and qualifications protect people from unemployment because they make them more flexible and more productive. Sometimes people are unemployed because of prejudice on the part of employers.

People lose their jobs for all sorts of reasons, but when they remain unable to find another job the reason may be either **geographical immobility** or **occupational immobility**. Geographical immobility becomes a problem if there are jobs in other areas but the unemployed person is unable to move to that area. This is often the case in the UK for people living in council houses, because they are tied to the local authority in which their house is located. Also, home owners who would have to move to another area to find work may be unable to afford the houses in that area. House prices are often low in areas of high unemployment and high where jobs are available, so this can be a real problem.

Occupational immobility occurs when people have skills which are very specific to a declining industry. If they are unable to retrain, they may remain unemployed for a long time.

Essentials

Geographical immobility occurs when unemployed people are unable to move to areas where jobs are available.

Essentials

Occupational immobility refers to the situation in which an unemployed person is unable to take a job which is available because of a lack of the necessary skills.

Q 1 Which industries are least likely to suffer from unemployment in times of recession?

2 Would you describe unemployment in the mid-1990s as predominantly structural or demand deficiency in nature?

3 Look back at the case study, People, at the start of this enquiry. Say whether structural change or demand deficiency was the main problem in each case, and explain your answer.

4 How much of the unemployment which existed in 1992 might have been caused by demand deficiency?

5 Figure M 3.17 shows that in 1997 unemployment was around 1.6 million. Yet at that time skill shortages were reported by 17 per cent of companies. How could this be?

The impact of unemployment

Unemployment is a significant cause of poverty. In a recession, most of the fall in incomes which occurs will be experienced by the people who actually lose their jobs. Structural unemployment can impoverish whole communities. Redundancies reduce spending power which, in turn, reduces demand in the area. Other people – shopkeepers and other suppliers of local services – will find their incomes falling too.

The costs of long-term unemployment are particularly insidious. People who have been unemployed for more than a year are likely to lose the skills they had. Their work habit may suffer and their health can be affected. As time goes by it will become harder for them to get jobs and they may become 'discouraged workers'. These are people who have given up the struggle to find work after a long period of searching and therefore drop out of the official figures.

Young people who have had very little in the way of opportunities to work have a particular problem. Unskilled people living in areas where traditional industries have closed down are particularly vulnerable to unemployment and poverty. Figure M3.18 shows that about half the unemployed total will have been so for more than six months. This problem worsens during and in the aftermath of a slump.

year	% of total who have been unemployed for over 26 weeks
1990	49.6
1991	46.8
1992	52.8
1993	55.4
1994	56.2
1995	55.0
1996	54.0
1997	48.7
1998	43.4
1999	42.0

Figure M3.18 Duration of unemployment
Source: *National Institute Economic Review*, 1998

Unemployment as measured in the UK

The standard measure of unemployment in the past has been the claimant count. This counts those who are out of work, seeking employment and claiming benefit. However, this figure is less than the actual numbers who are unemployed. Categories of people who would like to work but are not recorded within the unemployment figures include married women, men over the age of 60 and disabled people. Married women are by far the largest group. Often they are not *actively* seeking work and their husbands' incomes make them ineligible for income support so they do not claim benefits.

Men over 60 no longer need to register as unemployed to get their benefit and receive long-term income support. Many disabled people who used to be registered as unemployed now get invalidity benefit. Both groups are treated as if they have left the labour force. These changes have all tended to make the claimant count an underestimate of true unemployment.

Increasingly, the Labour Force Survey is being used to provide a truer estimate of unemployment. This is used to derive the ILO unemployment rate. (The ILO is the International Labour Organisation, an arm of the United Nations, which has a standard definition of unemployment which can be used for international comparisons.) Figure M3.19 gives a rough idea of how the measures differ.

	Claimant Count	ILO unemployment
1996	7.6	8.2
1997	5.8	7.2
1998	4.8	6.4

Figure M3.19 Unemployment measures
Source: ONS, *Economic Trends*, July 1998

Work in progress

Q

1 What sorts of people are most likely to be occupationally immobile?

2 How does prolonged unemployment affect people's capacity to work?

3 Does it matter how we measure unemployment? Explain your answer.

2 Inflation

Dealing with uncertainty

The view from the owner of a small business doing landscape work:

'I see from the papers that inflation is expected to increase. I don't know how this will affect my business. If my costs rise, I shall have to increase prices because my margins are low already. But will sales stay the same if prices rise? I was thinking of investing in a new truck but now I'm not sure that my sales revenue will be sufficient to cover the costs.'

The view from a well-known economist, writing in 1996:

'Inflation is no longer a threat. There is a new business ethos of intense competition. The net effect of increased international trade possibilities and reduced monopoly power is that businesses simply cannot put up prices in the way that they used to.'

The view from the Conservative Party Manifesto in the 1997 election campaign:

'Inflation has to be kept firmly under control for an economy to thrive. Britain is now enjoying the longest period of stable inflation for almost fifty years … low inflation has delivered lower interest rates while preserving the value of people's savings.'

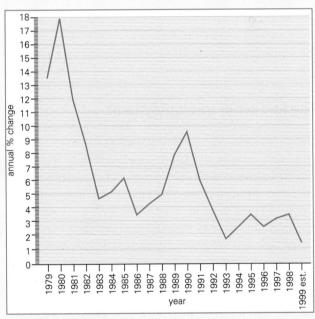

Figure M3.20 UK inflation
Source: *National Institute Economic Review*, 1998

Your agenda

1 How do consumers tend to feel about rising prices? Do they threaten their standard of living?

2 Why have governments put so much emphasis on maintaining stability?

3 Do you think inflation has ceased to be a serious problem?

Why is inflation so widely regarded as being highly undesirable? There are three major reasons.

■ **Uncertainty.** The higher the rate of inflation, the more likely it is to be fluctuating rather than predictable. Firms will therefore find that inflation makes it harder for them to predict both their costs and their revenues. This may mean that when they are estimating the expected future income stream from a possible investment, they simply cannot be sure enough to undertake the investment. Less investment across the economy means less growth of productive capacity: it can harm our standard of living in the long run.

■ **Income redistribution.** Everyone with assets denominated in money terms – bank balances, savings accounts, etc. – will be made worse off by inflation. That includes a lot of young and old people. However, people who have borrowed money will be made better off: the value of their debt will be less after inflation. It will be easier to pay back. So inflation makes people with mortgages or firms with large bank loans better off. It can reduce the size of the government's debts too. People who have lent to the government, for example through National Savings, will be worse off.

■ **Competitiveness.** Firms which are competing with other firms in countries with a lower inflation rate may find that their prices rise relative to those of their competitors. So inflation may cause their sales to fall as customers turn to the cheaper imports. The outcome could be a trade deficit, followed by a fall in aggregate demand and then in output.

Part of the problem with inflation is that because it is perceived to have a lot of disadvantages, governments want it to be carefully controlled. This usually means an increase in interest rates which will cure the inflation by depressing the economy. This in turn leads to higher unemployment and lower levels of income. The costs of curing inflation may be higher than the losses resulting from putting up with it.

Work in progress

 1 If you have £100 in the bank and the inflation rate is 10 per cent, what is the purchasing power of your money at the end of the year?

2 If you have bought a house for £50 000, by taking out a mortgage for that amount, and inflation is 10 per cent, what will happen to your real income in subsequent years?

3 Inflation redistributes income and wealth in arbitrary ways. Is this desirable?

The measurement of inflation

The average rate of change of prices is measured by the Retail Prices Index. This is a data series measured from a base year of 100. The Family Expenditure Survey is used to generate sample data on a wide range of prices collected from different areas and different types of retail outlet. Figure M3.21 shows how it has moved.

Year	Index
1994	144.1
1995	149.1
1996	152.7
1997	157.5
1998	163.5
1999 est.	166

Figure M3.21 The Retail Price Index (1990 = 100)

Source: ONS, *Economic Trends*, 1998

Each month new inflation figures are made available. Where inflation is quoted as a percentage, it is almost always the year-on-year rate. This means that the percentage refers to the change in the price level over the previous year.

It is important to remember that the rate of inflation is not the difference between this year's and last year's index numbers. (That is called a points increase.) It is actually the increase in the index divided by the index number for the start of the year in question. So the rate of inflation for 1998 on the figures given in Figure M3.21 is:

$$\frac{163.5 - 157.5}{157.5} \times 100 = 3.8\%.$$

Inflation and unemployment

Inflation tends to rise when the economy is booming and unemployment is falling. Similarly, during recession, inflation is often falling and unemployment rising. Experience of the business cycle tells us that there is an inverse relationship between inflation and unemployment.

If we look at the data for inflation and unemployment in Figures M3.17 and M3.20, we can see that although this inverse relationship is sometimes quite obvious, at other times it does not seem to hold. One possible explanation for this is that there are time lags.

When the economist A.W. Phillips looked at the data for inflation and unemployment over a long period, he found that the inverse relationship was clear. He analysed the figures for 1913–1948 and found that the relationship could be defined as shown in Figure M3.22. With very high unemployment in the 1930s, prices actually fell on average so inflation became negative. This trade-off between inflation and unemployment became known as the Phillips curve.

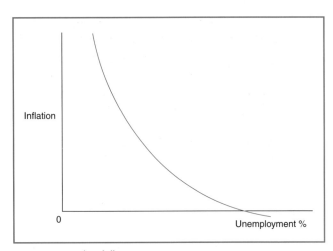

Figure M3.22 The Phillips curve

There were times during the 1970s when inflation was very high and unemployment was rising too. The explanation for this is complex and relates to the way expectations of inflation cause it to become built in to the economy. By the 1980s and even more in the 90s, the trade-off between inflation and unemployment had again become clearer.

3 Analysing the relationships

Ups and downs

	Output, 1990 = 100	Inflation, % per annum	Unemployment, %	Vacancies, 000's
1987	92.7	4.1	10.0	235
1988	97.3	4.9	8.1	248
1989	99.4	7.8	6.3	220
1990	100.0	9.5	5.8	174
1991	97.9	5.9	8.1	118
1992	97.4	3.7	9.8	117
1993	99.6	1.6	10.4	128
1994	104.0	2.5	9.4	158
1995	106.9	3.4	8.3	183
1996	109.5	2.5	7.5	235
1997	112.9	3.1	5.7	285
1998	115.4	3.4	5.5	297
1999 est.	116.6	1.3	5.3	301

Figure M3.23 Output, unemployment and inflation, 1987–99
Source: *National Institute Economic Review*, 1998

Your agenda

1 In which phases of the business cycle was the economy in the following years:
   a 1988
   b 1991
   c 1993
   d 1997.

   Work out the percentage growth of output for each year.

2 Can you see evidence of time lags in the data? Which variables appear to be lagged in relation to output?

3 When vacancies are rising sharply, what is actually happening in the economy?

The circular flow of money is a useful tool for analysing flows of money through the macro-economic system, but it does not tell us anything about the relationships between output, income, employment and prices. These change markedly over the course of the business cycle and it is important to be able to look at the data in any given year and understand the links between the variables. To do this we look at aggregate demand and aggregate supply.

Aggregate demand

By adding up demand from all sources we can arrive at the total level of demand in the economy as a whole, or aggregate demand. Aggregate demand consists of consumption, investment, government spending and the balance between exports and imports – all the sources of demand for the products of business.

Aggregate demand can be very simply expressed in the following formula:

$$AD = C + I + G + (X - M)$$

The idea of aggregate demand relates output to price levels. Other things being equal, aggregate demand will fall when the price level rises and vice versa, so that the AD line slopes downward to the right. This is shown graphically in Figure M3.24. However, a tax cut will almost certainly cause people to consume more, whatever the price level. So it will shift the aggregate demand curve to the right, as shown in Figure M3.25. A change in any of the component parts of aggregate demand will cause the curve to shift.

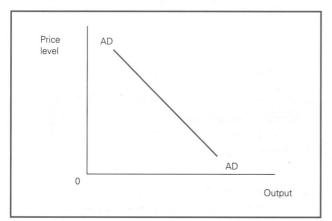

Figure M3.24 Aggregate demand

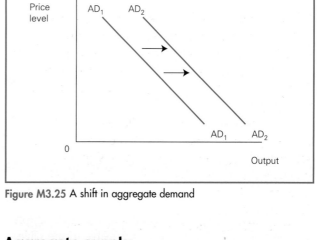

Figure M3.25 A shift in aggregate demand

Aggregate supply

Aggregate supply expresses the total of all output produced throughout the economy. It includes all goods and services whether they are intended for consumption or for use by businesses.

Aggregate supply is related to the price level in an interesting way. Most of the curve shows a situation in which it is possible to increase output without price levels rising. This is the horizontal part of the curve in Figure M3.26, where there is spare productive capacity in many businesses. Then there comes a point where increasing output is possible but raises costs because businesses find it difficult to recruit skilled employees. In order to do so they find they must increase wages. The higher costs will be passed on to the consumer in the form of higher prices.

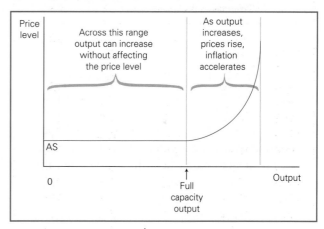

Figure M3.26 Aggregate supply

I = Investment
G = gvnt spending.

Eventually, further increases in output become impossible because the necessary resources are all fully employed. This is the outer limit to aggregate supply and so the curve ends in a vertical line. This line marks the point of full capacity output – the most the economy can produce when working flat out. It follows that as full capacity output is approached, the inflation rate will tend to accelerate as employers bid up wages in an attempt to recruit from a tight labour market.

Putting aggregate demand and aggregate supply together

■ By putting aggregate demand and aggregate supply together on one diagram, it is possible to see what the outcome of different changes may be. Figure M3.27 shows how the intersection of the AD and the AS curves predicts a certain level of output and the price level at which that output will be produced.

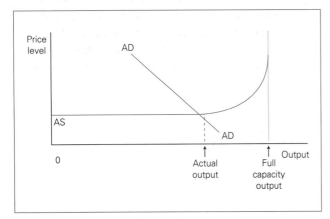

Figure M3.27 Determining the level of output

■ Using this analysis, we can examine what happens when there is an increase in investment. Figure M3.28 shows what happens: the increase in aggregate demand which results from the extra investment shifts the AD curve to the right. If the economy is rather depressed and there is some demand deficiency unemployment, the demand simply induces businesses which produce investment goods to hire more employees and expand their output. There is an injection into the circular flow of money. Because there is plenty of slack in the labour market, with skilled people looking for work, the increased demand has no impact on prices. There is no need for wages to rise to attract the necessary labour and therefore no cause for prices to rise.

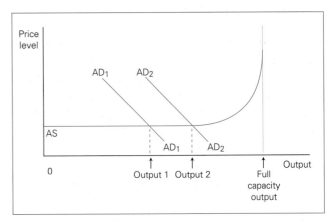

Figure M3.28 Increasing investment

■ Contrast this with Figure M3.29. There the increase in investment comes when the economy is approaching full capacity output. The increase in demand induces businesses to take on more labour and increase output. But there the similarity ends. There are few people with the necessary skills who are unemployed and businesses will try to poach the people they want from competing firms. The effect will be to drive up wage rates. Costs will rise and then prices, as businesses try to pass the costs on to consumers. Inflation will accelerate.

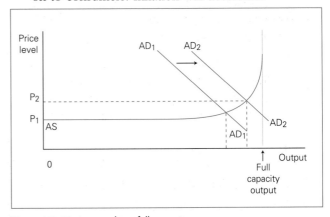

Figure M3.29 Approaching full capacity

Work in progress

Q 1 Using what you have learnt so far, draw AD/AS diagrams for each of the four phases of the business cycle. Explain how each diagram relates to the characteristics of each phase by showing how the diagram links output, unemployment and inflation.

A theory of inflation

The analysis used here gives us a useful theory about how inflation develops. The economy grows fast, approaching full capacity output. Supply constraints, particularly in the form of skill shortages, become a problem. Wages are bid up by employers competing for people with scarce skills. The economy is said to be overheating as excess demand for resources leads to rising costs and rising prices.

Unfortunately, it is quite possible for an economy to experience these kinds of boom conditions, yet still to have much structural unemployment. This occurs when the people who remain unemployed do not have the skills, or are not in a location, that employers want. In other words they are immobile. Increased spending does not help to relieve this structural unemployment.

Point of View

1988

The Conservative government in 1988 honoured a long-standing promise to the electorate to cut taxes. This increased consumption and aggregate demand, as expected. The economy was already approaching full capacity output and the effect was to push it faster in that direction.

The Chancellor was assuming in doing this that productivity was increasing so fast that full capacity output would grow to accommodate the extra demand. Unfortunately, this was a mistake.

Your agenda

1 What were the consequences of the 1988 tax cut?

2 Draw a diagram showing the impact of the change in demand.

3 To what extent are the predictions in your diagram supported by the data in Figure M3.23 (page 194)?

There are still many difficulties in the way of governments that want to promote economic stability. There are many uncertainties and economic forecasting techniques are still far from perfect. Problems can also arise when governments are trying to make themselves electorally popular.

Work in progress

Q 1 Find some suitable figures which show the macro-economic changes from 1999 onwards.

2 Try comparing the 1988 boom with the 1997 boom.

3 What similarities are there? In what ways did the two booms turn out differently?

4 When do you think there could be another boom? Make a note of the date in a place where you won't lose it and see if you were right when the time comes. The economy is a serial. Watch for the next episode.

4 International comparisons

In harmony?

GERMANY	GDP growth %	Consumer prices %	Unemployment %
1990	5.7	2.7	4.8
1991	−0.9	3.7	4.2
1992	1.8	5.0	4.6
1993	−1.2	4.4	7.9
1994	2.8	2.7	8.4
1995	1.9	1.9	8.2
1996	1.4	1.5	8.9
1997	2.3	1.7	10.0

FRANCE	GDP growth %	Consumer prices %	Unemployment %
1990	2.5	3.5	9.0
1991	0.8	3.2	9.5
1992	1.2	2.4	10.4
1993	−1.3	2.1	11.7
1994	2.8	1.7	12.3
1995	2.1	1.7	11.7
1996	1.6	2.1	12.4
1997	2.3	1.1	12.4

UK	GDP growth %	Consumer prices %	Unemployment %
1990	0.4	9.5	5.8
1991	−2.0	5.9	8.1
1992	−0.5	3.7	9.8
1993	2.1	1.6	10.4
1994	4.3	2.5	9.4
1995	1.8	3.4	8.3
1996	2.3	2.5	7.5
1997	3.2	3.1	5.7

JAPAN	GDP growth %	Consumer prices %	Unemployment %
1990	5.1	3.1	2.1
1991	3.8	3.2	2.1
1992	1.0	1.7	2.2
1993	0.3	1.2	2.5
1994	0.7	0.8	2.9
1995	1.4	−0.1	3.1
1996	4.1	0.1	3.3
1997	0.9	1.8	3.4

USA	GDP growth %	Consumer prices %	Unemployment %
1990	1.2	5.4	5.6
1991	−0.9	4.2	6.9
1992	2.7	3.1	7.5
1993	2.3	3.0	6.9
1994	3.5	2.5	6.1
1995	2.0	2.8	5.6
1996	2.8	3.0	5.4
1997	3.8	2.3	5.0

Figure M3.30 Macro–economic change in five countries, 1990–97
Source: OECD, Main Economic Indicators

Your agenda

1   To what extent have the five countries had a similar experience?

2   Do these countries' business cycles move together?

3   How far have the five countries succeeded in creating stable economic conditions?

Reading the newspapers you may think that national governments are responsible for making a good many mistakes. Looking at some international data you might question this. Are they all making the same mistakes? Or are they all facing the same problems and struggling in various ways to overcome them? Certainly, increasing international trade means that nation states are no longer economically independent of one another.

Economic policy is examined in detail later on in this Module, page 241.

Enquiry 5   Why trade?

1 Where is the best choice?

Goods and services

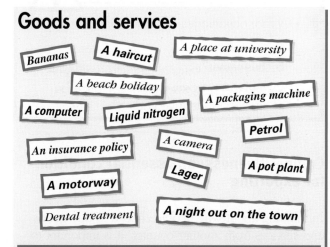

Bananas

A haircut

A place at university

A beach holiday

A computer

Liquid nitrogen

A packaging machine

Petrol

An insurance policy

A camera

A pot plant

Lager

A motorway

Dental treatment

A night out on the town

Your agenda

1 Decide which of the above products are goods and which are services.

2 Which ones do you think might be imported?

3 Are there any items which were not on your imported list, but which you think you might be able to sell to someone who lives abroad?

4 Is there anything on the list which would have to be imported, if you were to consume it at all?

5 Do you ever pay more to get a UK-made product? If so, how much more? Why?

Consumers import to get choice. With imports there are always more alternatives. Different products and different combinations of price and quality become possible. Consumers are made better off when they can choose freely the product which fits their needs most closely.

There is an important link between product price and standard of living. At any one time most people have an amount of income which they cannot easily increase. Maximising purchasing power, and thus the enjoyment which can be had from consuming, means buying the widest variety at the lowest prices possible. When people find a cheaper imported substitute for a domestic product which they have been buying, again they are better off. They have some money left over, to pay for other things. So imports have potential to increase real incomes by giving people more purchasing power. They can help to improve efficiency, world-wide.

Why businesses trade

Cussons Technology

Cussons is a Manchester-based engineering equipment manufacturer which employs just over 100 people and has an annual turnover of around £10 million. About 80 per cent of its production is for export. Its important markets are in Asia and Europe.

Recently, the company was involved in a bid for an Indian government engineering project. It didn't win – a Russian company got the job. Cussons was sure it had the best technical proposal, but India is a poor country and the Russians scored on price. India is a democracy and government officials have to justify their spending decisions.

'When the budget isn't there it's a question of needs must,' says Mr. Cussons. 'India is an area where if a proposal is made for a high-tech facility, there will probably be a local competitor and it is necessary to bring in additional technology or a unique solution to stand a chance of winning a contract.'

In the past, India tried hard to be self-sufficient and to import as little as possible. Now, the government is committed to opening up the economy to competition from imports. This has created considerable opportunities for businesses such as Cussons. But India has a good education system with many businesses capable of producing high technology products. So the competition is stiff.

Your agenda

1 Competition on world markets is often stiffer than it is in the area in which the business is located. Why is this?

2 What advantages does exporting have for Cussons?

3 What advantages are there in exporting for a manufacturing business?

Trade is absolutely crucial to huge numbers of businesses. At the simplest possible level, they export in order to access larger markets. They import to get their inputs at the lowest possible cost.

When firms find cheaper input sources, their costs fall and they may be able to reduce prices. People may buy more of the product, or they may use the increase in their real income to buy other things. Either way, they will be better off.

Trading offensively and defensively

It is useful to think of exporting as happening for two different reasons. When a firm has a product which is doing well, production and sales can be expanded if a wider market can be found. The larger the market, the more the firm can expand. Jobs will be protected and profits will rise. This is called offensive trading.

Alternatively, consider a firm which has been selling shoes successfully within the UK market, and in export markets, for some time, but it is finding it increasingly difficult to compete with imports in the UK, as **import penetration** deepens. Church's Shoes, a well-established maker of high quality, traditionally styled shoes, has been in this position. Part of Church's response has been to expand its export marketing efforts. The company's US marketing is now carried out by its own network of 17 stores. This is defensive trading, a reaction to the loss of one market by developing another.

Taking another example, whisky producers in the UK face competition from white spirits, such as vodka, and wine which some people think is healthier. So the distilleries, located in parts of Scotland where alternative jobs are rather few, are always trying to widen their markets.

Should they seek markets in Europe? On the face of it, competing with brandy in France would seem unpromising. But the French do drink whisky, as an aperitif, before meals. An appropriate advertising campaign, taking into account the French view of the product, may make sense.

Essentials

Import penetration is the extent to which imports have met the needs of the market as a % of the total sales.

Competitiveness: an essential condition for exporting

In thinking about why people choose to buy goods and services from another country, it is important to consider the idea of **competitiveness**. This is the quality which determines how well firms cope with competition from other producers. Competition arises when there are a number of producers, all aiming at the same market. In order to sell their goods, all producers will have to ensure that their products are attractive; if they do not, they may fail to make a profit and perhaps go out of business. However, some markets are much more competitive than others. The computer industry is one where competition is very stiff internationally. Firms strive to offer the most advanced technologies to their customers.

Competitiveness has many aspects. The first is price. If another firm can produce a product more cheaply, then people will buy it. However, price is not everything, because sometimes a dearer product will be better value. Quality, durability, reliability, appearance, after-sales service, may all be more important than price alone. These elements of non-price competitiveness are all part of the marketing mix. Their importance is obvious if you consider cars, hi-fi, clothing, footwear and many other products.

Underlying this there are other factors.

- Price depends partly on production costs, which include the costs of all inputs.
- Low labour costs may be crucial in creating a product with a competitive price.

But low labour costs aren't the whole story. A producer with high labour costs may still be very competitive, through using sophisticated, capital intensive production strategies, aiming to raise productivity (output per person) as much as possible. Thus, although the UK imports large quantities of textiles from countries with lower labour costs, some firms can still compete well enough to export speciality fabrics woven in capital intensive mills. Producers may aim at a niche market and produce a very high quality product, for which they can charge a correspondingly high price.

Essentials

Competitiveness is the ability to offer a product at a price which compares well with the alternatives available.

Work in progress

Q

1   What marketing issues will businesses need to address in order to compete successfully on world markets?

2   What production strategies may be needed to ensure that competitiveness is maintained and improved?

3   In what ways is trading between London and Paris different from trading between London and Manchester?

2 How trade works

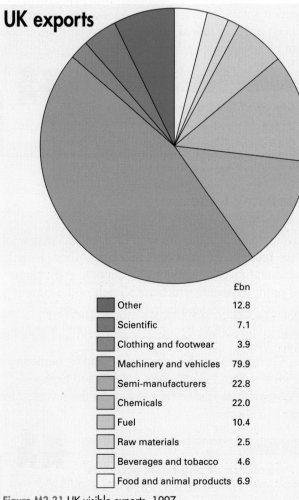

UK exports

	£bn
Other	12.8
Scientific	7.1
Clothing and footwear	3.9
Machinery and vehicles	79.9
Semi-manufacturers	22.8
Chemicals	22.0
Fuel	10.4
Raw materials	2.5
Beverages and tobacco	4.6
Food and animal products	6.9

Figure M3.31 UK visible exports, 1997

Source: ONS, *Annual Abstract*, 1999; Monthly Digest of Statistics via SECOS 4

Figure M3.30 shows how UK exports of manufactures and primary products break down.

One of the UK's most successful areas for export growth is in services. The important ones include:

● banking and insurance
● legal services
● travel and tourism
● communications

In 1997 total **visible exports** were £172 billion. **Invisible exports**, i.e. exports of services, came to £62 billion. (This does not include interest and profit from overseas investments.) These are additional to the visible exports shown in figure M3.31. So exports of services are important earners of foreign exchange, and do have growth potential. Some services are very labour intensive and increased demand can lead to many jobs being created.

Your agenda

1   Which are the UK's most important categories of exports?

2   What sorts of services will figure importantly in international trade?

3   What services will not be traded? Why?

Traditionally, the UK imported food and raw materials, paying for these imports with the revenue from exports of manufactures. Things are no longer so simple. Raw materials now account for just 5 per cent of the UK's total imports. Services are increasingly important in trade.

Like many other countries in recent years, the UK economy is becoming more of an **open economy**. Foreign trade is a large and still growing component part of total national income. This is part of the process of globalisation. It is occurring despite the UK having become almost self-sufficient in food products, and supplying a large part of its oil needs from the North Sea. Being 'open' does not simply mean trading vigorously in primary products and manufactures (visible trade). It also means being open to trade in services, bringing in new technologies developed in other countries, and allowing foreign investment flows both into and out of the country.

> ### Essentials
> **Invisible exports** are exports of services.

> ### Essentials
> **Visible exports** are exports of tangible goods.

> ### Essentials
> An **open economy** is one in which trade is encouraged, exports account for a significant part of total output, and imports for a significant part of consumption.

Much international trade consists of swaps, rather than countries sending to each other things which the other is unable to produce. For example, there is a brisk trade in chemicals between the UK and Germany. This type of trade is the result of individual business decisions based on each choosing the best buy without regard to origin. Similarly, the UK both exports and imports large quantities of office machinery.

Some of the goods which are traded internationally are known as **commodities**. They are:

- normally traded in large quantities
- often, but not always, raw materials

- their distinguishing characteristic is that they are very uniform in nature; for example one tonne of iron ore is much like another, provided it is of a similar grade.

Oil and other minerals, wheat and many other agricultural products are all primary commodities. Some partly processed goods are still regarded as commodities, provided they have not been given a distinctive feature or a brand name which might give them a competitive edge. The microchip is sometimes regarded as a commodity.

Commodity trade is all about large quantities of products which are indistinguishable from one another. This is one area where competition is unlikely to be perfect, but it may not be too far off. In commodity markets there are usually many producers, all producing similar products. People will choose to buy from the cheapest source. Strong competition induces the exporter to keep prices as low as possible. Competitive advantage must be based on costs.

> ### Essentials
> **Commodities** are mainly agricultural or mineral products, or partly processed products, which are traded in bulk.

Measuring trade

Governments measure the level of trade and payments in the **balance of payments accounts**. These record visible and invisible exports and imports, and interest and profit payments which are all part of the current account. Also recorded in the capital account are direct investment in productive capacity and financial capital flows.

When payments for imports and capital outflows are greater than receipts from exports and capital inflows, there is said to be a deficit. In the reverse case there is a surplus.

> ### Essentials
> The **balance of payments accounts** record all international transactions. There may be a surplus or a deficit.

3 Going global

ICI

ICI is one of the UK's largest manufacturing companies. It operates in 40 countries, spread all over the world, and has a combined workforce of 74 000. As such it is a **multi-national** enterprise. It specialises in producing industrial chemicals, paints, plastics and explosives.

The company took shape in the 1920s, investing in the UK and in Canada, Australia, India and other Commonwealth countries. More recently, its activities have also become concentrated in western European countries, the US and south-east Asia. Roughly half of its manufacturing capacity is located in the UK and contributes substantially to exports. So ICI is both exporting directly and selling through its subsidiaries located abroad.

Some multi-national enterprises are **conglomerates** with business interests in many fields. In contrast, ICI has what is known as 'focus'. Its activities are concentrated in particular industrial fields. Within its specialist areas though, it produces many products.

Your agenda

1 What other multi-national enterprises can you think of?

2 What advantages do very large companies have for:

   a the company

   b the consumer?

   What are their disadvantages?

Exploiting competitive advantage: multi-nationals

What are the objectives for companies investing abroad? Some multi-nationals are locating in a particular target market. Others are simply identifying profitable opportunities. They may be seeking the lowest cost location for their production facilities, and may be attracted by the availability of skilled labour or large areas of cheap flat land.

● Some companies invest in another country in order to produce where labour costs are lower, for example Hoover moving production from France to Scotland in 1993.

● Others will locate production in an important foreign market, for example Nissan in Sunderland, benefiting from lower wages than those in Japan, but also avoiding European Union (EU) controls on imported cars.

● Retailers want to invest in their own sales outlets so as to reach their foreign markets more effectively. The Body Shop, Marks & Spencer, Laura Ashley and Church's Shoes all do this.

● Some large firms, such as ICI, Siemens, Ford, Hitachi and Phillips, produce goods with a worldwide market and are large enough to exploit its potential.

Looking closely at multi-national enterprises, one thing is clear. Transport costs are often not very important in the modern world. Only very heavy or bulky items, relative to their value, such as bricks, must be produced close to their market. Avoiding transport costs is not usually a major motive for foreign direct investment, although it can be one of a number of motives.

Essentials

Multi-nationals are businesses with activities in several different countries.

Essentials

Conglomerates are businesses with a very diversified range of products.

A multi-national may acquire a green-field site and build its factory from scratch. This is what happened when Henry Ford built the Dagenham car plant in the 1930s. Alternatively, firms may invest abroad by buying foreign companies: they acquire control by buying the shares. For example, in 1988 the UK company BAT acquired the US insurance company, Farmers. In the same year, the Swiss company Nestlé acquired Rowntree. These sorts of acquisitions can lead to restructuring on a worldwide basis, which can cause people to feel that the activities of multi-nationals are both unpredictable and destabilising for their employees. In fact, in the UK it has been found that job losses are as likely to come from UK-owned as from foreign-owned employers.

Exploiting competitive advantage: the EU

The idea behind the EU is to promote free trade within the Community. That way, member countries can buy from the most efficient supplier within the area. Consumers have easy access to the goods which are produced most cheaply within the EU. It is generally believed that real incomes will grow as a result.

Since the UK joined the EU, trade with member countries has grown enormously. Before membership in 1973, about 30 per cent of UK trade was with EU countries. By 1997 this had grown to 56 per cent of trade. Many more UK businesses have got involved in both importing and exporting. This change represents a real shift in the UK trade pattern. Traditionally, the US was the UK's most important trade partner, and trade generally was biased towards the former colonies. This is no longer the case as Germany has increased its share of UK trade.

On a very simple level the EU has increased consumer choice. It has increased competition and brought some prices down, relatively, thus raising real incomes. It has also enabled some firms to exploit greater potential economies of scale because they have a larger market.

Coping with change

One country's exports are another country's imports. Increasing, and changing, trade means that over time, economies change their character. They become more competitive in some products, and less so in others. This means that trade patterns change too. Imports change because what is available changes, and prices change, relative to each other. We import when there is a price or quality advantage, in order to get what we need from the cheapest sources, and to maximise real income.

The outcome of these trends is structural change. Some industries decline while others grow. Inevitably, the pattern of employment changes and some jobs are lost.

On balance, most experts think that trade in the end creates rather than destroys jobs. However, the process of adjustment can be slow and painful. People are better equipped to cope if they are occupationally and geographically mobile and adaptable. That way they are more flexible and can change jobs if the need arises.

Work in progress

 1 What motivates the decisions of multi-nationals?

2 How can the EU help businesses to exploit their own competitive advantages?

3 How can this process raise real incomes?

4 Trade brings change. How are individuals affected by this?

4 The importance of the exchange rate

What happens when the exchange rate changes?

UK tractor makers had a hard time when the pound rose in 1997. More than half their production is for export and the high rate of exchange with the US dollar meant that they lost competitiveness. Sales fell sharply. On average their tractors sell for around £20000. Figure M3.32 shows how the pound changed against the US dollar and the Deutschmark – the currencies of the UK's two biggest trading partners at the time.

	£ in US$	£ in DM
1996 Quarter 1	1.53	2.25
1997 Quarter 4	1.66	2.91

Figure M3.32 Exchange rates
Source: ONS, *Economic Trends*, July 1998

Your agenda

1 What was the percentage increase in the exchange rates given in Figure M3.32 over the period covered?

2 What would be the average price of a tractor
  a at the old exchange rate
  b at the new one?

3 To what extent do you think a price change of this size would deter buyers in the US and Germany? How sensitive will demand be to price?

Firms need to be able to price their products at competitive levels. Broadly, there are two ways of doing this. First, costs must be kept down. Secondly, firms may be much affected by the **exchange rate**. A low exchange rate means that the price of their product in foreign currency will be relatively low.

A rise in the exchange rate – **appreciation** – means that the pound is worth more; it takes more foreign currency to buy each pound. This means that the price of exports to the customer will rise. Also it means that imports will be cheaper; it will take fewer pounds to buy the necessary foreign currency. The consequence of both these changes will be a loss of competitiveness. Exporters will find it harder to compete on foreign markets. Just as important, firms producing for the domestic market will find it harder to compete with imports.

A fall in the exchange rate – **depreciation** – has the opposite effect. It will make exports cheaper, and imports dearer. Generally, there will be a gain in competitiveness.

Work in progress

Q 1 If you are about to go on holiday in France, and the French franc goes down against the pound, how will this affect your spending power?

2 Would an exporter of Scotch whisky want the pound to be high or low?

3 How will UK importers of French wine feel about an appreciation of the pound?

Essentials

The **exchange rate** is the rate at which one currency is exchanged for another.

Essentials

Appreciation occurs when the exchange rate rises.

Essentials

Depreciation occurs when the exchange rate falls.

Competitiveness has two angles. It affects how much we can export. It also affects firms producing for the domestic market. Can they compete with imports?

Exchange rates and market forces

If exchange rates float freely, they will be determined purely by market forces (supply and demand). Alternatively, they may be fixed in relation to each other, by international agreement. In this case, market forces will still be important, but central banks will need to intervene in the market to stabilise the exchange rate. It makes sense therefore to start work on exchange rates by looking at demand and supply in the market for foreign exchange:

- ■ *Demand for currency* is generated by foreigners who want to buy exports. The cheaper the currency (i.e. the lower the exchange rate), the cheaper exports will be, and the more currency will be demanded. So the demand curve for currency will slope downwards in the usual way.
- ■ People wanting to buy imports *supply currency* when they buy foreign exchange. The higher the exchange rate, the more foreign exchange their funds will buy, the more imports they can get and the more currency will be supplied. So the supply curve slopes upwards, again in the usual way (see Figure M3.33).

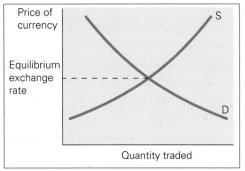

Figure M3.33
Supply and demand in the foreign exchange market

The intersection of the supply and demand curves gives the equilibrium exchange rate. At that rate the amount of currency which exporters demand is exactly equal to the amount which importers wish to supply.

Supposing that many exporters succeed in improving their non-price competitiveness. They improve quality, reliability and design. Naturally, more foreigners want to buy their products. The demand for currency with which to buy them will rise, (i.e. shift to the right). Figure M3.34 shows what will happen: the exchange rate will rise.

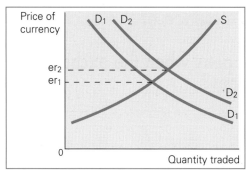

Figure M3.34
The impact of rising exports

But things could go the other way. If exports are not selling well, because too many of the relevant products fail to compete with other countries' products, the demand for sterling (pounds) to pay for exports will fall (i.e. shift to the left). It is likely that at the same time there is a high level of demand for imports. Products which are not selling well on export markets will probably not sell well on the domestic market either. People will buy imports instead, for which they will need foreign currency. They will use pounds to buy the currency. The supply of pounds coming from this source will therefore be large.

Work in progress

Q **1** Draw a supply and demand diagram which shows the demand for sterling from buyers of UK exports, and the supply of pounds coming from UK importers. Put the exchange rate, or price of the pound, on the vertical axis, and the quantity of currency on the horizontal. Draw in the equilibrium exchange rate and label the diagram appropriately.

2 Supposing there is an increase in demand for imports in the UK. On your diagram, show what will happen to the exchange rate. Is the change going the way you would expect?

3 If the exchange rate is unstable, how will an individual exporting firm be affected?

4 What choices do exporters have about their prices when the exchange rate goes down?

5 What would you expect to happen to firms specialising in importing, after depreciation? Explain your answer.

The exchange rate provides an adjustment mechanism which reacts to trade flows and at the same time affects them. Changes in the levels of imports and exports change the demand for, and supply of, currency, and therefore its value (the exchange rate). But there are feedback effects. Changes in the exchange rate make exports and imports more or less competitive. So the effects are complex and circular.

Changing exchange rates

Although trade has an important effect on exchange rates, it is important to remember that the demand for and supply of a currency can be greatly affected by capital movements. In the UK, capital movements can actually dwarf the influence of trade. So an abrupt capital outflow will lead to a sharp depreciation if the exchange rate is floating freely. Similarly, the pound has often been kept higher than exporters would like by capital inflows.

Politicians often resist depreciation, feeling that if they choose this strategy they are somehow losing face. However, it can help exporters to maintain competitiveness.

The exchange rate index: measuring competitiveness

Exchange rates for individual currencies are easily available, but to get an overview of current trends the sterling exchange rate index is needed. This is a weighted average of the value of the pound against currencies of the UK's trading partners. Those currencies with which the UK does the most trade have the largest weight.

Year	Index
1989	114.7
1990	112.0
1991	113.0
1992	108.7
1993	99.7
1994	100
1995	95.1
1996	96.7
1997	112.7
1998	116.5
1999 est.	113.3

Figure M3.35 The sterling exchange rate index (1994 = 100)
Source: *National Institute Economic Review*, 1999

Work in progress

Look at Figure M3.35

Q

1 What happened to the pound during the 1990s?

2 What do the figures imply about competitiveness?

3 Look for data on the level of imports and exports during the 1990s. Did exchange rate changes have a noticeable impact on UK trade?

5 More stability, less risk?

UK exchange rates

From 1972 until 1990, the UK had a floating exchange rate, subject to day-to-day management by the Bank of England. This meant that over the long run, the exchange rate was determined by market forces. It made sense because there were some sharp fluctuations in the rate of inflation during that time. A rapid rise in prices makes it very difficult for firms to compete abroad, unless the inflation is accompanied by matching depreciation. Equally, if market forces are pushing the currency sharply down, it becomes very difficult for the central bank to maintain a fixed rate.

Meantime, in 1979 the EU member countries set up the European Exchange Rate Mechanism (ERM). The ERM was a system whereby some EU currencies were fixed in relation to each other, while floating against the rest of the world. Central bank intervention was needed to keep the EU currencies in line with each other. The ERM prepared the way for full Economic and Monetary Union (EMU)*. The advantage of the ERM was that businesses could be sure that exchange rates in member countries would be stable.

In 1990 the UK joined the ERM, partly in the interests of European unity, partly to create greater stability for trade between the UK and the rest of the EU, and partly with a view to sharing in a European counter-inflationary policy.

The UK joined the ERM at a fairly high exchange rate. It withdrew again in September 1992, because of intense speculation on the foreign exchange markets. The dealers did not believe that the Bank of England could maintain the fixed rate. Once the pound was floating again, it depreciated by about 15 per cent. This improved competitiveness and brought some relief to businesses, many of which were able to increase output quickly. They had spare capacity because of the recession. Many benefited considerably from the sudden growth in demand for their exports. But the government had reversed its policy and this caused much concern to its EU partners.

The British Ski Club organises skiing holidays, and sells ski clothing and equipment, most of it imported. After the 1992 depreciation it immediately raised the cost of its holidays. It was able to keep clothing and equipment prices the same 'while stocks last', but had to reorder at new higher prices, and then pass these on to the consumer.

Your agenda

1 How would exporters' profits be affected by the 1992 change in the exchange rate?

2 What sort of response would you expect to the price changes for skiers? What other imports might show a similar story?

3 What conclusion would you draw about the likely effect of the depreciation?

4 What disadvantages do floating exchange rates have for businesses?

The major advantage of floating exchange rates is that they can, at least in theory, bring automatic adjustment to a large trade deficit. (A deficit occurs when imports persistently exceed exports, so that the country begins to have serious difficulty in paying for all its imports.) As imports grow and exports fall, the exchange rate falls. This makes exports cheaper, so that they increase. Imports become dearer and decrease. So the trade deficit decreases overall. The gain in competitiveness can increase profits and the deficit should diminish. Figure M3.36 shows the sequence of events.

*EMU stands for Economic and Monetary Union, not European Monetary Union.

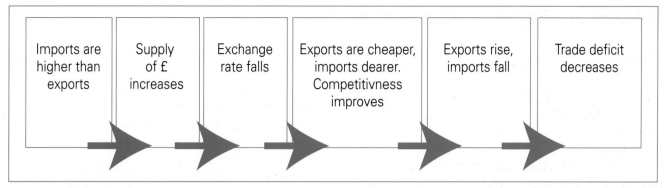

Figure M3.36 Depreciation restores balance

Floating exchange rates have two serious problems:

■ They do tend to fluctuate. Further, they sometimes do so in an unpredictable way. A firm which imports trainers will find, if the exchange rate depreciates, that it is having to pay more for them. It will try to pass the increased costs on to the consumer by raising prices, but this will cause sales to fall somewhat and profits will be affected. This means that the firm will be subject to exchange rate risk. It will be difficult to make firm plans for the future because of the uncertainty.

■ The benefits of depreciation to exporters often do not last very long. Within a few years, they may find that they are losing competitiveness again.

Businesses can take some of the risk out of an uncertain exchange rate situation by using **forward markets**, for a fee. These allow businesses to buy foreign exchange for 'delivery' later, say in three or six months time, at an exchange rate which is decided now. So an importer can buy foreign exchange on the forward market, to pay for a consignment of trainers which must be paid for in three months' time. Because the exchange rate is already decided, the importers know what they have to pay and risk is eliminated from the transaction. But not all risks can be reduced in this way. In the end, floating rates tend to be unpredictable.

Essentials

Forward markets allow traders to avoid exchange rate risk: they buy their currencies at a rate fixed in advance.

Work in progress

Q **1** A manufacturer of high-quality marmalade is considering a new investment project. In order to make an informed decision, the expected future income from the investment must be estimated. This means estimating both price and sales levels. Part of the sales are expected to be in the USA. The pound is floating and rather unstable. If it goes up against the dollar, what will happen to the expected revenue from export sales? Does this make the project riskier?

2 Consider a shoe manufacturer with a niche market, who imports leather and also exports some high-quality shoes. If the exchange rate is floating and depreciates, what happens? (Explain this carefully.)

3 If the exchange rate is fixed, at least for the manufacturer's main markets, and there is inflation, wage costs will rise and so will prices. What happens to the shoe manufacturer this time? What happens to the marmalade manufacturer?

4 What conclusions can you draw as to whether businesses would prefer fixed or floating rates?

Point of View

EMU: now or later?

EMU (Economic and Monetary Union) came into being in January 1999. Eleven EU countries joined from the outset. The UK, Sweden, Denmark and Greece stayed out. Here are two different views as to what the UK should be doing.

Janet Bush, director of the New Europe campaign, which is pro-Europe but against UK membership of the euro:

'The UK would have been mad to join in 1999. In the short term, it is at a different stage in the economic cycle from most of the eurozone. At euro interest rates, the UK would soon face an inflationary boom. There are, however, many far more fundamental and long-term reasons.

The eurozone economies are far too different to make monetary union work and the dangers of a 'one size fits all' interest rate is already evident in the cases of Germany and Ireland. The institutional structure of EMU enshrined in the Maastricht Treaty compounds this imbalance. The European Central Bank (ECB) was conceived in an era when inflation was public enemy number one and its remit is simply to achieve price stability. At a time when the major threat is deflation, the ECB's task is too narrowly defined. The strict budget deficit limits mean that fiscal policy is not available as a counterweight to monetary policy.'

Christopher Johnson, a leading figure in the Association for Monetary Union in Europe:

'By not joining at the outset, the UK has missed the chance of taking part in the euro–11 Council of Finance Ministers, and influencing the running of the ECB.

All the economic variables will be improved by the UK's entry into the euro. Economic growth will be faster, thanks to lower interest rates, higher business investment, and the scale advantages of buying and selling in a bigger market. Inflation will be reduced, because the ECB will have greater credibility than the Bank of England. Transactions costs for eurozone trade will be cut. The elimination of different exchange rates will benefit trade and investment.'

Source: *Centrepiece*, published by the Centre for Economic Performance, Volume 4, Issue 2 (Tel: 0171 955 7673).

Your agenda

1 What would be the views of a UK wine importer on the subject of the euro? Is uncertainty a problem for the business?

2 Would someone who ran a hotel be equally concerned? How might his or her views differ?

3 Would a hairdresser hold a similar view?

4 What has happened since the above views were set out?

5 To what extent do you agree with either of the views above?

6 From January 1999, when EMU came into being, the Euro floated steadily down against the dollar and the pound for the rest of that year. If the UK had joined at the start, how would the UK economy have been affected by this depreciation?

Which way forward?

Enquiry 1   Why are business plans important?

1 The business plan

Manicmixers

When Gina and Steve set up their mobile disco, Manicmixers, they had no intention of making a living from it. They enjoyed the music and creating a party atmosphere. Getting paid for the evening was almost a bonus. Then, one Friday night near the end of one of their regular party bookings at a local hotel, Chris Dixon approached Steve and started chatting about how impressed he was with their work. It was always nice to receive praise, but this situation was different. Chris ran a local nightclub and was looking for talented DJs to compare two evenings each week (Tuesday and Thursday). A key point in the life of Manicmixers had been reached. Could Gina and Steve really turn a hobby that had made a little money into a successful business?

Manicmixers was established with a loan from Steve's mum of £960 and a further bank loan of £750. That was more than two years before the evening they met Chris and they had now paid back what they owed. The equipment they had purchased when first starting was getting a bit old, particularly the speakers which had never worked well anyway, but they had built up a good selection of CDs and records which helped to provide a sound which was unique in the local area.

Gina had visited the club Chris owned a few times and they both knew that its reputation was growing rapidly. The offer being made was £200 a night, £100 more than they had been charging recently. They would not need to set up their own gear either, because the club had permanent CD players, turntables and lights in place. In fact, Gina couldn't wait to use the more sophisticated equipment. The choice was not that simple, however. They both knew that if they decided to run the disco full time Gina could not continue the Art course she had started at the local Further Education college last year and that would mean giving up her ambition of pursuing a career in fashion design. Steve would also have to sacrifice his job as a trainee manager with a local department store. They had to do some careful thinking.

The £400 a week from the nightclub work would not really be enough to justify running the business full time. It would mean a payment of only £10400 each before tax every year and there would be additional expenses like travel. They decided that they would have to build up other regular bookings if Manicmixers was to become a successful business in the long term.

Steve pointed out that they would still have Friday and Saturday nights free to take bookings and this was obviously their busiest time of the week. On the other hand, they had not been getting more than eight bookings a month over the past couple of years. In the summer it could fall to two. They were not sure this level of demand would be sufficient to make a success of Manicmixers.

After a lot of discussion they both felt it would be worth investigating further the possibility of setting up the business on a full time basis. As a result, they arranged a meeting with Graham Wharton, the small enterprise adviser at the local branch of the bank which had previously loaned them their starting capital. Acting on his advice they decided to prepare a business plan.

Your agenda

1 What do you think is the most essential single factor in making a business plan? Why?

2 Why is a formal business plan needed when Gina and Steve have all the ideas in their heads?

When banks are approached by new or small businesses about loans, they recommend their customers to use their advice booklets. These provide a format for the information they are going to require.

The answers to the questions below contain Manicmixers business plan.

What product or service will your business offer to customers?

Manicmixers will offer high-quality dance music and a club atmosphere – 'party nights to remember!'. We have already operated for two years, partly as a hobby but also making a little money. The plan now is to establish a full time business. We hope to do this by increasing the number of private bookings in local hotels and pubs we undertake using our own equipment. Residencies at nightclubs will complement this work. In the long term our aim is to play the big club venues around the country like 'The Ministry of Sound', but at first we will stick to opportunities offered in the local area and build up a strong reputation.

How many units of the product do you hope to sell, and at what price?

Initially, the target is to do 12 private bookings and eight nights as resident DJs at Bo-jangles each month. The charge for private parties in the last few months has been £100. We increased our price from £80 and demand really didn't seem to fall. It might be possible to try £120 once we are better known in the local area because of our nightclub work, but we will stick with our existing price for the moment. We might also be able to vary this to suit different nights of the week, or times of the year, in order to keep us busy. We have been offered £200 a night for the club residency.

Why do you think people will buy your product or service?

We have learnt a lot over the past two years running Manicmixers. At first, we tended to play just the club music we liked, but now we are good at judging the audience. The atmosphere that we can create is really something special. Gina is very creative with the light show and our music collection has really grown. We are also good at mixing sounds in a way that you can only appreciate if you see us live. People have always said to us that we should look for nightclub work. Now that

Chris Dixon, the owner of Bo-jangles has offered us the chance of a residency, we are sure other possibilities will open up quickly.

The opportunity for private bookings has also clearly grown since we started. Lots of students now do a good deal of part-time work and so have quite a bit more spending money. This is bound to mean increased demand for Manicmixers.

How much competition do you expect your business to face?

In this region there are quite a few mobile discos of various types. The big difference is that Manicmixers is targeted at a particular audience. We don't do wedding anniversaries or sixties parties and that kind of stuff. Our work is based on mixing the dance music you hear in the big clubs, not pop, and ours is a creative lights show, not a dozen coloured lamp-bulbs attached to the turntable console! The Yellow Pages does not have one mobile disco focused on the club market in the way we would be doing. Having talked to quite a few people, nobody can think of a disco in the area anything quite like the Manicmixers idea.

How will you make potential customers aware of your product or service?

The intention would be to advertise in the local paper at first. We have never tried to build our business up in this way before because it was really only a hobby. We could use our residency at Bo-jangles as a feature and encourage potential customers to visit and see us at work. As we make a success of things, our reputation should grow quite rapidly. If people enjoy the show, then they might book us for their private parties. Recommendation from past customers has always been a very effective form of promotion in the past.

We could circulate the local student area with handbills. Later on, we might try advertising in the specialist music magazines, but this would be too expensive to start with. We may also contact other local nightclubs about possible residencies.

Who will work in the business?

There are two of us:

Gina Stevens: aged 19 and currently studying Fashion and Textiles Design. I set up and run the lights show and do some microphone work. I also keep some basic accounts for the business.

Steve Harman: aged 20 and currently a trainee store manager. I am the main DJ and driver. I also deal with administrative work like taking bookings.

What premises and equipment will be needed?

Obviously, we don't need any premises, but equipment is a different matter. Our existing gear is getting a bit dated, although we have no intention of throwing it away. As we will now be full time we would like to re-equip. New lights are vital because these are a key part of what makes us different from other mobile discos. A better effects unit and new speakers are also necessary. The existing turntables and CD player are fine and our music collection is no problem. To get the right kind of quality a minimum of £2000 is going to be needed.

The most urgent issue is our transport. At present, the van we use is so old that our equipment is damaged on the way to bookings because of its poor suspension. If we are going to be full time we cannot go on as we are. It gives a terrible impression if we turn up at bookings in a wreck! Equally, we know a brand new van is unrealistic, but a friend at a local garage thinks she can get us a good deal on a second-hand one for about £5000.

What is the likely profit in the first six months of operation?

We have set out the details in Figure M3.37, but obviously these are rough estimates. Demand depends upon which six months of the year we are looking at. Rather than show each month in turn we have worked on an average over the time period.

SALES REVENUE

Twelve private bookings per month:
12 × £100 = £1200   6 months @ £1200 = £7200
Eight night club bookings per month:
8 × £200 = £1600   6 months @ £1600 = £9600
Total revenue = £16800

COSTS OF PRODUCTION

Total variable costs:

Private bookings:
The cost of each private booking is approximately £20.
This covers petrol, wear and tear on the van and breakages (light bulbs, etc.).
12 × £20 = £240   6 months @ £240 = £1440

Nightclub bookings:
It is not necessary to transport equipment on these evenings and Bo-jangles is not far to travel; £5 should cover the cost easily.
8 × £5 = £40   6 months @ £40 = £240

Total variable cost: = £1680 (£1440 + £240)

Total fixed costs:

Wages:
In the past we have each received £50 a month from Manicmixers, but this is clearly not a high enough wage if we are going to work full time. We would hope to pay ourselves £800 a month each in the future.
£1600 a month   6 months @ £1600 = £9600

Equipment:
We estimate the life of the equipment will be approximately five years.
If the cost is spread out evenly over this period:
£2000 ÷ 5 years = £400 each year   In six months the cost will therefore = £200.

Van:
We estimate the life of the van will be approximately 5 years.
If the cost is spread out evenly over this period:
£5000 ÷ 5 years = £1000 each year   In six months the cost will therefore = £500.

Local newspaper advertising:
4 advertisements each month @ £50 = £200 6 months @ £200 = £1200

Total fixed costs = £11500 (9600 + 200 + 500 + 1200)

Total costs of production = £13180 (1680 + 11500)

PROFIT

Total revenue (£16800) − Total cost (£13180) = £3620

Net (or operating) profit = £3620

If your bank was to offer us a £8000 loan and asked for 15% interest to be paid on this sum each year, a £600 payment would be required in the first six months.

Profit before tax = £3020

Given the above calculations our profit and loss account for the first twelve months of trading would be:

	£	£
Sales		33600
less		
Cost of goods sold	3360	
Gross profit		30240
less		
Overheads	20600	
Selling costs	2400	23000
Net (operating) profit		7240
less		
Interest charges		1200
Profit before tax		6040

Figure M3.37 Estimated profit

What is the likely cash flow position in the first six months of operation?

Again these are estimates, but because we are looking at cash flow we have tried to predict the number of private bookings each month. The average is still 12, but we have adjusted demand to reflect the pattern we expect over the first six months of our full time operations. See Figure M3.38.

	Sept.	Oct.	Nov.	Dec.	Jan.	Feb.
Opening balance	8000	1620	2240	3180	4440	4580
Money in:						
Nightclub bookings	1600	1600	1600	1600	1600	1600
Private bookings	1200	1200	1600	2000	600	600
Total in:	2800	2800	3200	3600	2200	2200
Money out:						
Nightclub bookings: variable cost	40	40	40	40	40	40
Private bookings: variable cost	240	240	320	400	120	120
Wages	1600	1600	1600	1600	1600	1600
Advertising	200	200	200	200	200	200
Equipment	2000	0	0	0	0	0
Van	5000	0	0	0	0	0
Interest	100	100	100	100	100	100
Total out:	9180	2180	2260	2340	2060	2060
Difference	(6380)	620	940	1260	140	140
Closing balance	1620	2240	3180	4440	4580	4720

Figure M3.38 Estimated cash flow

What are your objectives for the business in the short and long term?

The basic goal of our business is to provide a memorable evening for our customers by creating an exciting party atmosphere, using a unique mix of different types of club music and an inventive lighting show. In doing so, we both hope to make a reasonable living. The short-term objective is to build up a viable business in accordance with this aim. The long-term objective is to establish a reputation in order to become nationally known DJs on the club scene.

How much money do you propose to put into the business yourself?

When Manicmixers was first set up we put £1710 into the business to get it going. In a sense, this money is our contribution to the business going full time because we will still be using quite a lot of the gear it helped to buy.

How much do you wish to borrow from the Bank?

We are applying for a £8000 loan over five years at an interest rate of 15%, with the lump sum repaid at the end of this time period.

The questions in this case study are adapted from the National Westminster Bank business setup guide.

Your agenda

1 What is the real value of a written business plan such as the one drawn up by Gina and Steve?

2 If you were Graham Wharton, the small enterprise adviser at the local bank considering this loan application, what would be your comments on the plan?

2 Why plan?

The early days

'When we first started running the business part time I suppose our discos were largely based on the music we wanted to play. We enjoyed ourselves and so we thought the product would sell itself. Of course the market wasn't there. We didn't get the bookings because people did not just want to hear the tracks we liked. As a result, very little money came in. Then when we got to know our audience and our unique style finally took off we were short of cash and needed to make the decision about going full time. Marketing opportunities were lost because we were too busy at that time to take all the potential bookings. We did not really know where we were going and that definitely held back the development of the business.' (Gina commenting on her early experience of running Manicmixers.)

Your agenda
1 What kind of planning might have helped Manicmixers when Gina and Steve first set up the business as a part-time undertaking?   **2** In practice, many small firms fail to plan. Why might this be?

We all face an uncertain world. As the pace of change quickens in many areas of life, so the sense of uncertainty increases. Some people feel helpless; others feel safest in the present and dismiss looking to the future as 'mere speculation'. Others again make active plans – analysing the past, evaluating the present, making forecasts and setting targets for the future.

Change is inevitable and always releases opportunities. If it is not seen as a threat, it can become a creative force, allowing firms to see new possibilities, to shape new goals and to see new ways of moving forward.

The uncertainty of the future need not be disabling. Events occur as parts of chains of cause and effect. Many future events can be predicted with reasonable accuracy if the factors causing change are properly studied. The extent to which events may be anticipated depends on how complex the situation is and how far into the future the organisation wishes to look.

Predicting the approximate takings of a shop from one day to the next may be relatively straightforward – the factors causing change are fairly simple and the time period is short. To predict the profits for a year ahead is much more difficult. The range of issues which might influence the situation are complex and the time scale is long enough for any amount of unexpected change. This kind of forecast would depend on how valid the assumptions that have been made are and, as a result, it may be subject to much wider margins of error.

A basic requirement for a new or young business enterprise is therefore to prepare a business plan. This is a written statement that describes how the business might expect to develop in the future. It should act as a series of signposts showing the direction the business intends to move in. Over time it must be updated in response to events so that it remains a relevant document which guides decision-making in the organisation long after it was first written.

Work in progress
1 What assumptions have Gina and Steve made in drawing up the business plan for Manicmixers? What uncertainties do they face?   **2** What are the advantages and disadvantages of planning for a short time period, such as the first six months of operation, as Manicmixers have done?   **3** How would you expect the business plan prepared by Gina and Steve to be updated as the business develops?

How does planning begin?

Every business is offering a 'proposition' to its customers. Specialist skills and other resources are combined to form a product that is then projected into a target market. The relationship between cost, price and value is intended to be profitable for the firm yet also rewarding for the customer. Effective planning starts by exploring and analysing this relationship.

What do customers want that the firm can profitably provide? This apparently simple question should release related and vital lines of enquiry:

- What is the target market?
- What distinctive competencies does the firm have to offer?
- What is their unique selling point?

Some firms believe that they already know their product and their market. It is not a safe assumption. Should the product be modified? Might the range be extended? Are there other products that the firm might successfully introduce? Could other market segments be entered?

It is not surprising that careful and extensive market research is the beginning of a good business plan. Too many new business ideas are launched because they are thought to be good ideas. This is a classically product-orientated and inadequate basis for committing resources. The really important questions to be asked are:

- Exactly which customers might buy the product?
- What price will they be willing to pay?
- Does this price allow for adequate profitability?

Work in progress

Q 1 Does the business plan prepared by Gina and Steve make clear what the target market of Manicmixers is?

2 What are the strengths, or distinctive competencies, which Manicmixers has to offer? Are these clearly identified in the business plan?

3 Do you think Gina and Steve have conducted sufficient market research to back up their plan for Manicmixers? What further research might be useful?

3 How is planning carried out?

So far, this analysis has suggested quite a formal background to planning. However, in the real world firms interpret these basic ideas in very different ways. Much depends on size. Large public companies often have an elaborate planning process based on stated aims and objectives. They may also publish the aspects of their strategy that are not confidential. Hidden inside the firm will be consultation channels, key committees and, most important, directors' board meetings that will form and shape the planning process.

The way in which planning takes place in any organisation depends upon its culture and the style of leadership (see pages 78 and 89). In smaller firms the process is often more informal and may be confined to a few key directors. Very small enterprises may scarcely plan at all. Some owners claim that they are too busy coping with the present, while others argue that the future is too uncertain and that detailed planning is not worth the time and resources.

But the arguments for planning in larger organisations are just as valid for the small firm. It may be implicit rather than stated but the entrepreneur does have an underlying aim or direction. Even if it is informal and under constant review, there does need to be a long-term strategy, including definite objectives. Operational targets and short-range planning increase efficiency and provide a control system for the business.

Work in progress

Q 1 How do you think Gina and Steve went about writing their business plan? What features might they have added if they had had more advice?

2 How do you think Manicmixers should organise updating the plan in the future if the business grows in size?

How can a plan be used to control operations?

An effective business plan lays out the future direction an organisation intends to take. The long-term aim of operations is established. This means that the plan provides a framework around which the organisation can build a system that can be used to control all of its activities.

If each area within a firm is given a series of short-term targets that are consistent with the aim outlined within the business plan, then all the actions which employees take will be focused on achieving the same long-term outcome for the organisation. A hierarchy of objectives is created providing a means by which to control the business.

Budgets

Financial control employing a system of **budgets** can be used to further ensure that actions at every level of the business are consistent with the plan. A budget establishes target levels of revenue and costs for specific areas of operation within the business. For example:

- A sales department might be expected to sell at least a certain value of goods within a defined time period, while keeping expenses below a given sum.
- A production department might have a target cost level.

The aim of the business presented in its plan should be consistent with the financial forecasts for profit and cash flow that are also outlined in the document. These figures can be carefully built into the budgets established for each section of the organisation. In this way, the financial implications of operating activities can be monitored to ensure they are in keeping with the overall direction the plan establishes for the business.

If an area of the business fails to meet the budget figure established for its revenues or costs, then the controlling manager must investigate why this has happened and take appropriate action if the situation requires it. This will be necessary if:

- revenues are too low or costs too high, leading to reduced profits
- a section of the business has performed in a way that adds to profit by keeping costs below budget or exceeding the revenue target, in which case good practice may be identified and spread to other areas of operations.

Essentials

A **budget** is a financial plan which forecasts costs and revenues and maps projected changes. It can be used to help the management keep control of the business.

Working capital

One area where financial planning is vital is the management of working capital. This is the day-to-day finance available for running the business. The organisation has at its disposal three current assets that can be used to meet immediate bills if necessary:

- *Stock* is the most difficult current asset to turn into cash. This is particularly true if it has not yet been processed (raw material stock), or if it is partly processed (work-in-progress). Finished goods may be more readily sold to generate cash.
- *Debtors* are customers who have received delivery of the product but not yet paid. The firm can reasonably expect to receive this money at some point in the near future, but it is not at the immediate disposal of the business.
- *Cash* is available in the organisation's bank account and is available to make payment at any time.

Managing working capital in a way consistent with the cash flow forecast presented in the business plan may involve careful judgement when dealing with each of these three items. The firm will wish to keep stock to a minimum in order not to tie up cash that could be working elsewhere in the business (see pages 00). At the same time it must ensure that enough raw materials are present to sustain production and the final product is available to meet customer demand.

The business may find it attractive to ask its debtors to pay for products as quickly as possible, but this must not be done at the expense of forcing customers to buy from competitors offering terms which allow delayed payment. The temptation may be to hold a large amount of cash in the firm's bank account in order to act as a buffer against the unexpected. However, this action has an opportunity cost for the business in that the money could be put to more productive use if employed actively in other areas of the firm.

An alternative tactic available to the business when managing its working capital is to delay payment of money to creditors in order to retain cash within the firm for as long as possible. Once more, although this approach is tempting, it must be pursued with caution because a supplier may choose not to sell raw materials to the organisation any more, or may even be forced out of business because of its own working capital crisis. These issues can become troublesome when trading conditions are difficult.

The secret to managing working capital is good planning. By anticipating the impact of the firm's operations on its working capital position in advance, the organisation can take appropriate action to avoid a potential crisis. Sometimes a short-term cash flow problem can be solved with a bank overdraft facility.

4 How can finance be obtained?

Making finance work

You form a company with nine other people and each contribute £1000 in return for 1000 ordinary shares. The resulting £10000 in share capital is now used to establish a business. After one year, sales amounting to £20000 have been achieved at a cost of £16000. The tax bill is £1000, dividends worth £1000 are distributed (£100 per person or 10p per share) and £2000 is reinvested in the company.

Your agenda

1 What is now likely to be the minimum value of a £1.00 ordinary share in the company?

2 Why might an outsider be willing to pay a price above this figure?

Every business needs finance in order to make a start. Easily the most important source of new finance is profit retained within the firm. This has the great advantage of being unconditional, with no external parties to satisfy and no interest to pay. However, it is not 'free' of any cost. As a use of scarce resources, it carries an opportunity cost which, at the barest minimum, is the current rate of interest available. Any addition to the net resources controlled by a firm places an obligation on management that their use generates an adequate minimum return.

Retained profit accumulates within a firm relatively quickly. Say a business achieves an average 20 per cent return on capital employed: if 7.5 per cent is distributed in dividends, then a 12.5 per cent retention rate will double the firm's capital in six years without any borrowing.

Retained profits are known as internal finance: the resources are coming from within the business. They provide an indirect means for shareholders to invest in their own firm.

External sources: share issues

The directors can sell additional shares to existing or new shareholders. In a private company the shareholders are usually members of the family or close business associates. Some of them may well be willing to increase their stake, especially if the company's prospects appear favourable.

When the scale of proposed investment exceeds the funds available from existing shareholders, the company may decide to 'go public'. This means taking on the legal status of a public limited company (plc) with an issue of shares to investors and the general public who can then buy and sell them on the London Stock Exchange. An issuing house (usually a merchant bank) is appointed, which will publish a detailed prospectus explaining the nature of the firm's business with a record of its financial performance.

Although a public company has easier access to sources of new finance, there are pressures and responsibilities. Shareholders and 'City opinion' (the views of investors, brokers and commentators in the City of London) must be satisfied with the firm's performance in terms of profitability, dividends and share price. This can drive management to seek short-term results rather than strategies for long-term investment. Indeed, the City has often been accused of causing 'short termism' in business management.

Yet investors must have confidence in the company if future share issues are to succeed. Institutions such as insurance companies and pension funds may take major stakes in the firm. Then their investment managers will be significant players in the delicate calculations of decision-making.

External sources: loan finance

In practice, the great majority of firms make use of external finance through raising loans. The terms, conditions and rates of interest attached to loan finance vary widely.

Very large firms (especially multi-nationals) may borrow in the foreign currency markets: international banks lend on their foreign currency deposits. For most firms, loans are obtained from local banks. Interest rates can be fixed, variable or renegotiable at agreed dates. The scheduling of repayments may also be flexible and related to the expected stream of additional income to be generated by the business.

In general, a longer term and a higher element of risk will carry a higher rate of interest and a greater demand for **security** by the bank. The need to provide a bank with adequate security is a major issue for many small firms. There can be a lack of readily marketable assets within the firm and the owners may need to use their homes as security.

Essentials

Security is provided by an item of value that becomes the property of the lender in the event of the borrower being unable to repay.

Work in progress

Q

1 Gina and Steve have applied for a bank loan of £8000. Do you think they have placed a sufficient amount of their own money in Manicmixers to make the bank confident about the safety of its investment?

2 If the bank refused Manicmixers a start-up loan, what alternative sources of finance might Steve and Gina consider?

1 Why innovate?

Amstrad hits the spot

Alan Sugar – founder and chairman of Amstrad – was on a plane over Japan when he conceived one of the really classic new products of the 1980s.

It was July 1984 and Amstrad, a fast-growing audio, television and video company, had just launched its first home computer. Now on a journey to Hong Kong, Sugar dreamed of an all-in-one wordprocessor at a price that small business and ordinary individuals could afford. Back in the early 1980s wordprocessors could cost thousands of pounds, meaning that they were only used in large corporations. Sugar's plan was to revolutionise the market and to make the electric typewriter effectively obsolete.

On arrival in Hong Kong he immediately sent his designers a confidential fax: this triggered a rapid development process for the new machine. Costs were cut by simplifying electronics and by ordering parts in very large quantities. Advanced or complicated functions were rejected. The essential idea was to offer a machine that ordinary people could use immediately without experience of computers. At £399 + VAT it would not only hugely undercut the competition but also enter the mass market of smaller firms and professional people who were still using typewriters. As well as being a wordprocessor, it would also operate as a personal computer and run a wide range of business software. It was called the PCW 8256 – Personal Computer Word processor with 256k memory.

At the launch in August 1985 Alan Sugar claimed that it 'will blow the lid off the personal computer and wordprocessor market'. Reviews were highly positive: 'Spectacular value for money' (*Personal Computer*).

Later, Stanley Kalms, chairman of Dixons commented:

❛It was one of the great phenomenal take-offs in my experience. Products very rarely take off at the beginning. Usually, they're on the market years before they take off. They're like actors: they can be around for years and one day they become stars. But this was an absolute bombshell. He'd brought a wordprocessor and a computer down to the level of your school-teacher, your local vicar – everybody who was in the business of typing and communicating. Every secretary in every small company went to the boss and said: 'I want one.❜

When the Amstrad's results were published in February 1986, profits had trebled since a year earlier and the share price soared, now 38 times higher than at flotation on the stock market in 1980.

Before 1985 the size of the whole British wordprocessor market was around 65 000 units per year. Amstrad sold 350 000 of its new machines in the first eight months after launch.

Your agenda

1 What factors made this new product so successful? Try to assess their relative importance.

2 How might the success of this product have assisted the firm in future expansion?

The pattern of demand changes continuously. Change can be random or seasonal. Yet just a very few key consumers deciding to switch brands may be the start of a trend that will eventually open and close factories, create and destroy jobs and redirect huge sums of money.

What makes a new product?

The market-orientated firm responds to change with new products and **innovations** that aim to keep the best fit between its own capabilities and market demand. Only through prompt and sensitive responses to the market can a firm maintain its expansion with a return on capital that will attract the necessary scarce resources.

The term 'new product' includes:

- *major innovations*, which are entirely new products not previously sold by any firm, for example the first UK minidisc players in 1996
- *minor innovations*, which are products new to the firm concerned but previously sold by other firms, for example Starburst ice lollies as a brand extension from the sweets
- *modifications*, which are alterations to an existing product, for example successive designs for the Ford Escort. **Variants** include new features, sizes, colours, flavours, etc. that widen a product's consumer appeal such as Coca-Cola in 150 ml cans.

In small firms, formal planning for new products is often limited or non-existent. Ideas may 'emerge' from existing products or through feedback from customers or trade contacts. Sometimes the firm's creative energy may be concentrated in one member of staff or the business owner.

Larger firms cannot afford to leave new products to chance. They are likely to have a programme for new product development (NPD) and may have a special department for **research and development (R & D)**. In technology-based industries there are often long lead times for R & D, linking the first germ of an idea and the moment of commercial launch. (For a new aircraft this lead time may be ten years; for a new drug it can be 20 years or longer.) Some firms have high-level new product development groups and may appoint special project teams whose work cuts across traditional chains of command.

There used to be a tendency for R & D to occupy a world of its own within the firm and to put forward product ideas for which a market then needed to be found. Today most firms adopt a market-driven approach where the results of market research fuel R & D.

Essentials

Innovation: the process of bringing a new idea to the marketplace.

Essentials

Research and development (R & D) is the process by which ideas based on new technologies are developed into a saleable product.

Essentials

Variants are new products which are actually different versions of an existing product.

Major new product developments broadly follow the pattern shown in Figure M3.39.

Ideas generation
Stimulating and collecting ideas within an R&D department, or from the production department, the sales team, employees, from customers, competitors and external sources such as research reports and trade associations

Screening
Giving the ideas ratings according to marketing, production and strategic factors

Concept testing
Assessing likely consumer response to a product before serious development

Business analysis
Projecting probable costs and sales: will profits reach the firm's targets?

Product development
Translating the idea into reality through prototypes or simulations

Test marketing
Releasing the product into a small but representative market where consumer reactions can be assessed and the marketing mix checked and adjusted

Commercialisation
Launching into intended market.

Figure M3.39 New product development

Is innovation risky?

The New Coke disaster

Coca-Cola was introduced to the USA in 1885 and first bottled for mass distribution in 1913. By the 1980s it was still the country's leading soft drink brand but was losing market share to the sweeter-tasting Pepsi. In response, Coca-Cola spent $4 million and two years on a market research programme. The result was New Coke with a smoother, sweeter taste. After conducting over 200 000 taste tests, the company was reassured to find that 60 per cent of consumers preferred the new product.

In 1985 a high profile marketing campaign launched New Coke and sales briefly took off. But the reaction soon began. As the sales curve faltered and fell, complaints poured into company head office and consumer pressure groups formed, demanding the return of the old formula. After three months the company reintroduced the original product. Now named Coke Classic, its sales rapidly overtook those of New Coke and despite every effort to retrieve the situation, the decline of New Coke seemed unstoppable. By the end of the 1980s the original formula was outselling New Coke in a ratio 10:1.

In retrospect, the market research was perfectly correct within its limited terms of reference: 60 per cent of consumers *did* prefer the *taste* of New Coke. But Coca-Cola is about more than taste. As a brand and a drink, it is a powerful symbol of US life and culture. It carries a huge hidden agenda relating to image, style, youth, memories, history and nostalgia. In the words of one of Coca-Cola's own slogans: 'You can't beat the feeling'.

Your agenda

1 How could such an expensive and thorough market research programme lead to such a faulty conclusion?

2 What kind of research might have led the company to a more cautious assessment of the prospects for New Coke?

New Product Development is essential but risky. Even major firms with sophisticated market research can still make disastrous decisions. New Coke is a famous case, but there are many more. Generally, the more innovative the product, the higher are both the potential returns – and the risk. Back in the 1980s, Sinclair Electronics launched a small electric car called the C5. It was innovative but spectacularly unsuccessful. On the other hand, the Sony Walkman, introduced in 1980, was hugely profitable and gave its name to a whole new product range.

By contrast, modification and variant products carry much lower risks but also fairly modest returns. New product ideas have a very high failure rate: for every 20 serious new product ideas, only one is likely to be successful. Clearly, this rate varies widely between firms and industries. Hence some firms imitate, rather than innovate – to reduce their risks.

Innovation as competitive advantage

In a nutshell

Nutshell is a small innovative enterprise based in Salisbury, Wiltshire. Among its products are sugar sachets – the sort of product routinely offered in pubs, cafés and restaurants and on ships, planes and trains. But there is nothing routine about Nutshell. After careful analysis of market demand, it designed sugar sticks – long, stick-like sachets – in vibrant patterns and colours. The result is a product offering that adds value in any setting. It is a simple but clever innovation that has given the company a real competitive edge over its larger rivals.

Unfortunately, such new products are easily copied with the risk of losing that vital distinctiveness in the market. However, Nutshell exploits its creativity, flexibility and rapid reactions to competition. Thus when its competitors move one way, Nutshell moves the other way. Or, as the marketing manager memorably puts it: 'When they zig, we zag...'

Your agenda

1 Why, exactly, can product innovation yield a competitive advantage?

2 What kind of culture in an organisation makes creative innovation likely to happen?

3 Innovation is liable to be a short-lived source of competitive advantage. How might a firm such as Nutshell achieve long-term superior profitability through innovation?

In business, innovation is not an extra. It is a key element in the power of enterprise, the dynamic in the firm that matches the dynamic in the market. In that sense it is a condition for business survival. Yet it is also a major source of competitive advantage.

Major innovations often allow a period of high margins and, in addition, by being first in the market, the firm can gain long-term customer loyalty. Minor innovations and modifications help to differentiate products and for a time at least, are likely to yield a higher level of profit. However, what really gives a competitive advantage is the ability to produce a stream of significant but unpredictable innovations that leave competitors out-manoeuvred and effectively out-classed.

This quality requires either a special creative and entrepreneurial talent (often in a business founder) or – more sustainably – a culture that celebrates change and deliberately encourages creative and original thinking. Such a culture must tolerate mistakes, accept conflict and even encourage deliberate assaults on established ways of thinking. It is not surprising that strongly hierarchical firms with fairly autocratic leadership usually yield fewer ideas than flatter management structures with a climate of open and free debate.

2 What is the life of a product?

Yorkie – still chunky?

Year	Sales by value £m
1976	3.18
1977	18.02
1978	34.93
1979	36.31
1980	39.57
1981	38.28
1982	35.86
1983	30.98
1984	30.85
1985	26.28
1986	29.64
1987	29.77
1988	33.45
1989	35.03
1990	33.22
1991	33.60
1992	33.68
1993	33.88
1994	38.08
1995	34.19
1996	36.06
1997	26.84

Note: the figures are not adjusted for inflation.

Figure M3.40 Yorkie Bar sales figures, 1976–97
Source: Nestlé Rowntree

Your agenda

1 Sketch a graph of the sales data given in Figure M3.40. What factors might have caused the changes in the gradient of the sales curve over the years 1983–5 and 1994–7?

2 How profitable would you expect sales to have been over 1995–7? Explain your conclusions.

3 What realistic options for the marketing of the product do you think existed in 1997?

A product launch is always a time of tension and anticipation. Large amounts of time and money – and some careers – are at stake. The hope is always that the product will achieve a rapid take off. The reality is that certain classic patterns have been identified. Most products have a finite life and their progress fits into a sequence which is called the **product life cycle**. You can see from Figure M3.41 that Yorkie sales were well established within two years of its launch.

The stages of the product life cycle

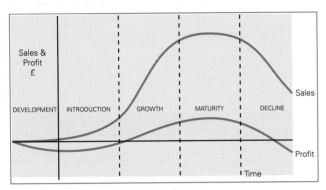

Figure M3.41 The product life cycle

■ **Development stage**
This covers the whole period of new product development. Sales by definition are zero, but costs are increasing as the launch approaches. Thus profit is negative.

■ **Introduction stage**
Initially, sales are slow to build as distributors and customers take time to accept the product. Innovative products take longest to gain acceptance while imitative ('me-too') products are faster in moving through this stage. Promotion informs the consumer of the product's existence and explains its value. The marketing effort at this stage is particularly vital in guiding the product towards the hazardous take-off point and ensuring safe arrival in the target market. Any error in its early market position may be difficult and costly to correct.

Usually, short-run profit maximisation is not the goal. The launch strategy is just the opening shot in a longer-term marketing plan for profitability over the product's life. While sales are low in the introductory stage, costs tend to be high.

Production levels are low relative to fixed costs and many scale economies cannot yet be achieved. Meanwhile, marketing expenses are particularly heavy and profit often remains negative for a time.

■ **Growth stage**
For those products that the market accepts, a growth stage will begin. Sales accelerate rapidly as the core of the target market accepts the product. Distribution is quickly expanded and promotion balances information with persuasion. At this stage an innovative product is likely to start attracting competition. Meanwhile, the first variants on the basic product are offered, stimulating further sales and assisting entry into new segments. Profit can rise steeply: both unit production costs and marketing expenses fall.

■ **Maturity stage**
Growth eventually slows and levels off as the market becomes saturated and competition intensifies. Over-capacity is now a risk. Price cutting becomes likely with strongly persuasive advertising and sales promotion. Profits plateau and then may fall. Weaker firms are often taken over or forced out of the market. It is important, though, to realise that the maturity stage is often the longest in the life cycle and these events may occur over long periods of time.

Late in the maturity stage, the level of sales becomes static or begins to falter. This is a common time to opt for an **extension strategy**. This means modifying or repackaging the product to renew its consumer appeal. Once relaunched, it may re-enter a growth phase and recover its sales and profitability.

■ **Decline stage**
Eventually, sales of most products begin to fall. Producers reduce capacity as profits fall sharply. Sales may drop to near-zero or may stabilise at a low level. The company may decide to reduce or withdraw marketing support and take what remaining profit it can. The other alternative is to cease production altogether. This becomes essential if sales revenue is failing to cover variable cost. It is still likely once profits fall below the opportunity cost of the resources committed and a greater return on capital employed can be obtained in other ways. An exception might be made if the product is part of a range or has a favourable cross-price elasticity with a more profitable product.

The **product life cycle** refers to the phases which most products go through between their first introduction to the market and the eventual decline in sales which may lead to production ceasing.

An **extension strategy** is a way of increasing sales by relaunching the product with a new image, or aimed at a different market segment and promoted in fresh ways.

■ Applying the product life cycle

The concept of the product life cycle applies both to broad generic product types (for example petrol-driven cars) and specific brands (for example Vauxhall Cavalier). Although the traditional cycle outlined above is a useful guide, each product life has a unique profile both in terms of sales changes and duration. For example, the maturity stage of a 'fad' product may last a few weeks while the same stage in the life of a key market leader may extend over several decades.

The life cycle concept is a valuable tool in product planning but must be used with some caution. Given that each product has its own cycle, it is often very difficult to identify the start and finish of each stage in the cycle.

Work in progress

Creative Kitchens Ltd is examining sales data for two styles of fitted kitchen:

Sales record 1996–2000

Number of kitchens completed

	1996	1997	1998	1999	2000
Hi-Tech	–	21	23	25	26
Manor House	99	101	102	96	89

The Manor House kitchen was launched back in 1989 and has been the company's most important product. The Hi-Tech style is a more recent product, launched in 1997.

Q

1 Assess the position of each product on its life cycle.

2 What action might this analysis prompt from the firm's marketing management?

3 Suggest dangers in your answer to question 2.

3 How can sales be increased?

Lucozade

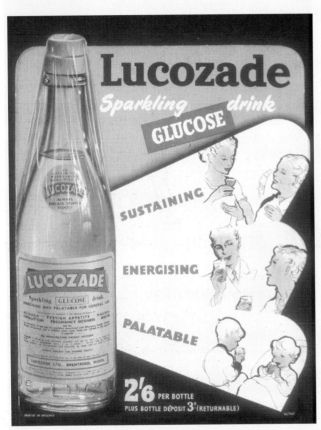

It seems strange today, but until the early 1980s, Lucozade was bought mainly for people who were ill. Introduced in 1927, it had become established as a soothing and energy-giving drink in times of sickness and convalescence.

In life cycle terms, Lucozade was in advanced maturity by 1980. Consumers saw it as old-fashioned, associated with elderly people and hospitals. The brand-owners, SmithKline Beecham, decided to reposition the product as a youthful and fashionable drink strongly linked to athletic and sports pursuits. This was only possible through an imaginative and entirely new marketing mix, which effectively extended the life of the product.

The core product remained unchanged, but its packaging was transformed. Traditionally, Lucozade had been sold in a 750 ml glass bottle with yellow cellophane wrapping and a gold seal. Market research pointed to the growth in sales for 'one-shot' soft drinks consumed outside the home – in the street, in the car, at work or on the sports field. The new packagings were a 330 ml aluminium can and a 250 ml screw-top single-use bottle. The yellow livery – with orange and red – was adapted in a faster, modern design on the can with a related pattern for the bottle. The focus of distribution shifted away from chemists into the mainstream soft drinks channels. In supermarkets, newsagents and service stations, Lucozade began to sell alongside Coke, Pepsi, 7-Up, Tango, Sprite and other top brands.

The advertising campaign – planned by Ogilvy & Mather – made Lucozade the choice of star athletes emphasising its new image of youth, vigour, fashion and success. Compared to its rivals, price was at a premium level – around 25 per cent above 'ordinary' soft drinks.

Despite this price differential, sales of Lucozade soared from £15 million in 1980 to £127 million by 1990. This far exceeded SmithKline Beecham's best expectations and the brand further consolidated its position with the launch of extension products such as Lucozade Light and Orange Barley Water. Meanwhile, the product continues to sell in its original market and is distributed for that purpose in a litre-size plastic bottle.

Your agenda

1 Why might a firm be prompted to consider 'repositioning' a product?

2 How might successful repositioning affect a product's demand curve?

3 Suggest another well-known product which could be repositioned and explain how you would go about this.

Almost every firm hopes for increased sales as a source of profitability and growth. Extraordinary successes such as Lucozade are rare, but ordinary good performers are the building blocks of a business. No matter how well conceived and planned, every product needs professional support from the firm if its full sales and profit potential is to be realised. This is the special task of the marketing department.

Targeting the market

In developing new products, there is always a risk of being driven by wishes rather than markets. This is really a form of product orientation. Many products have been launched that seemed exciting to the firm concerned yet failed to register with the market. It is therefore essential to base new product development on careful market research and proper market analysis. Aiming the right product into the wrong segment or the wrong product into the right segment can be equally disastrous. Would the consumer look to Cadbury's for a box of luxury handmade truffles? It must be unlikely. Cadbury's is an outstandingly successful producer of mainstream chocolate assortments. It does not pretend to have expertise in the specialist niche market for handmade truffles. Equally, the exclusive truffles manufacturer would be seriously misguided in launching a 'family assortment'.

Markets never stand still. Very few firms or products can afford to remain pegged to the spot where they started. Even 'classic' products – such as the Mini car, the Bic Crystal ballpoint or Perrier mineral water – have had to adapt to market change. If the product stays still and the market moves on, then sales will fall, profits will be eroded and resources will be reallocated elsewhere.

Reaching particular target markets involves using a whole range of marketing strategies. Lucozade reorganised all of its marketing effort by switching its focus from one market segment to another.

The marketing mix

There are two basic factors to consider when planning how to sell any product:

- the *price* that the consumer must pay
- the *benefits* offered to the consumer (for example quality, type, colour, service level, etc.).

Product benefits can be delivered or enhanced in various ways. The product itself can be given a combination of features to fit demand in the target segment. Promotion of the product through advertising, sales promotion and the efforts of a sales team can increase demand.

Distribution – in making a product known and available to the consumer – will increase sales at a given price. Taken together, these sources of product benefit and the product price represent the **marketing mix**.

If the marketing mix involves a rise or a fall in price, then, other things being equal, the quantity sold may change. However, if the product benefits are enhanced by other aspects of the marketing mix, the effect may be to shift the demand curve to the right. These two possibilities can be seen in Figure M3.42.

Essentials

The **marketing mix** refers to the combination of price, product benefits, promotional activity and distribution effort which covers all aspects of marketing.

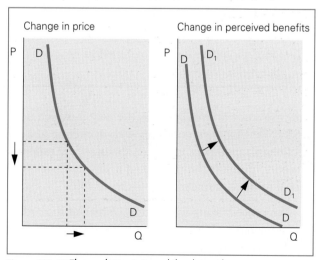

Figure M3.42 The marketing mix and the demand curve.

4 What will the product benefits be?

Go Ahead!

One of United Biscuits' most successful brands is the Linda McCartney range of vegetarian ready-prepared foods. The company was early in recognising a desire among consumers to enjoy cakes, biscuits and other snack foods that are made to more health-conscious recipes, including the reduced use of fat.

Market research showed that a growing proportion of consumers perceived the more traditional McVitie's products as unhealthy or 'not-good-for-you'. This was particularly marked among the higher socio-economic groups.

Healthy cereal and fruit snacks were already established as a successful niche segment. Given the right product range and promotional activity, key features of this segment were ready to transfer into a more mainstream market. As a result of this analysis, the better-for-you or 'BFY' segment was targeted by the launch of the 'Go Ahead!' brand in 1996. In its first full year the brand achieved UK sales of over £33 million.

Your agenda

1 Market change creates market opportunity. How might McVitie's have detected the emergence of the market segment into which Go Ahead! was aimed?

2 What qualities did this new product range need for market success? How far are these expressed by the name Go Ahead!?

3 How might McVitie's have tested its products before launch?

The case study above illustrates the way in which new product development combines with marketing in a carefully planned package. Then the branding process is used to promote the product in a way that will appeal to the target market.

- The process starts with extensive market research, and considerable emphasis on the selection of an identifiable market segment.
- The product is developed to fit the consumer preferences of the target segment.

When making a purchasing decision in the market, a buyer weighs the price against the product. Better materials, extra features or a longer guarantee all increase costs. Thus the firm faces a trade-off between cost and added value.

This raises the question of quality. Product quality does not mean simple reliability or that the product is top of the range. A quality product achieves excellence in performing its intended function and is often pleasing to the senses, for example in appearance or touch. Quality is achieved through product design in technology, engineering and services.

Careful market research may also reveal ways in which value can be added at less than proportional cost. For example, an airline may introduce 'free' champagne for its business-class passengers. Conversely, there may be ways in which a product's cost can be reduced with little or no effect on consumer valuation.

Branding

Brands have become powerful tools for selling that are tightly linked with advertising through the mass media. A brand comes to represent the market position for a product range and pinpoints a cluster of benefits anticipated by the consumer. A firm may expand its sales through using brands to act as 'umbrellas' under which a variety of products can be marketed. For example:

- St Michael (the Marks & Spencer's brand) is perceived as representing quality, value for money and a more subtle psychological power of reassurance.
- The Virgin brand is associated with youth, style and excitement.

Branding is a powerful way of distinguishing the product from its competitors. A successful brand pushes its product demand curves towards the right, and this allows a premium price without proportional loss of sales. A broader application of the branding concept is the development of a distinctive corporate identity for firms. This means that consumers learn to recognise a firm through its 'housestyle', logo or brands and make an association with certain abstract but positive qualities, for example BP with its yellow lettering on a green background, conveying both reputation for technical innovation and environmental concern.

Advertising and sales promotion

The price and quality of a product must be effectively communicated to consumers in the target market. Thus the goal of promotional activity is to achieve consumer awareness of a product and to maximise perception of the gap between its price and its value. Advertising, sales promotion and personal selling are all used in this effort.

Advertising can both inform and persuade. In both ways advertising aims to shift the product's demand curve towards the right.

- *Informative advertising* tells consumers about a product's function, features, performance and availability.
- *Persuasive advertising* urges consumers to believe that the relative benefits of a product are high while its relative price is low.

Strong branding may persuade most consumers to remain loyal to the product despite a rise in price. Similarly, a firm may wish to enter a mass market via price cutting and use advertising to make the product seem generally affordable.

Firms vary widely in the extent to which they use advertising in their mix. Consumer goods are the most intensely advertised with relatively less personal selling. By contrast, personal selling is vital in the market for industrial products while advertising is comparatively little used. But even in fiercely competitive non-durable consumer goods markets, there are interesting variations. Unilever, the producer of numerous lines in household goods and foods, has the UK's highest advertising budget. Yet Marks & Spencer has a very small advertising budget relative to its sales and the Body Shop hardly advertises at all.

Work in progress

 1 How might the balance between information and persuasion differ in advertising consumer goods at the introduction and maturity stages of the product life cycle?

2 How would you account for the wide variations in the relative importance of advertising for firms selling consumer goods?

Large firms carry out in-depth psychological research to design and execute their advertising campaigns for greatest impact on demand. In many cases this work is carried out by a professional marketing agency which will compete to win a good 'account' with a major client. Each campaign requires its own mix of advertising media.

A major product launch might have a budget that was apportioned 70 per cent to television, 10 per cent to cinema and radio, 15 per cent to press and 5 per cent to billboards and posters. Television has the greatest impact and largest audiences, but is very expensive. Press advertising can supply more detail and can be read at leisure, but its lower impact is reflected in its price. Outdoor advertising achieves high national exposure but can only convey a simple message. Increasingly, advertising is likely to utilise fax and e-mail as well as the conventional media.

There is a wide range of techniques for prompting the final decision of consumers to purchase a product. Merchandising is the art of store arrangement and presentation which can be highly influential in determining purchasing behaviour. Point-of-sales displays are often used to generate customer interest and trigger impulse buying. Short-term prices cuts and offers of cheap credit may also stimulate sales. Special offers and associated mail shots are effective in some markets while consumer durables and industrial goods may be sold through exhibitions and special events.

Distribution

All goods and services need outlets through which they can become the subject of consumer purchasing decisions. The goal of distribution is to ensure the right quantity of the right product in the right place at the right time. The complex patterns of ownership, transport and storage that link producers with consumers are called the channels of distribution. There are several well established patterns, shown in Figure M3.43.

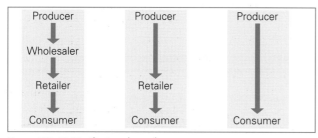

Figure M3.43 Distribution channels

The choice of channels will depend on the nature of the product and the target segments of the market. Some products need specialist distribution services (for example perishable foods) while for others the firm may need a high level of control over the selling process to ensure adequate quality and customer care. Internet shopping and telesales will increase the importance of direct selling.

Quality in the experience of the consumer is often critically linked to the performance of distributors. A high-quality product with real sales potential can still seem uncompetitive with weak merchandising or personal selling. Similarly, any breakdown in after-sales service can start to undo even the most carefully earned reputation for reliability and customer care.

5 How is price decided?

Your agenda

1 For the melons on the market stall, the newspaper and the shades, explain how you think that the price was decided.

2 In which cases was competition important in deciding the price?

3 Give four examples of products which can command a higher price than that of competing products. Explain why.

In the marketing mix, price is important for two reasons:

- It represents the level of expenditure required from the consumer in exchange for the product. Clearly, unless the consumer anticipates benefits from the product that yield value which is greater than its price, no sale is possible. Price determines the opportunity cost of buying the product and this forms a kind of threshold that the benefits of the product must combine to cross.
- The unit revenue received by the firm determines the profit margin achieved.

The effect in terms of revenue – and profit – of any change in price depends on the price elasticity of demand. An inelastic demand curve allows an increase in price with relatively little loss of sales volume and an increase in total sales revenue. An elastic demand curve rewards any reduction in price with a disproportionate increase in sales, and so a rise in revenue. However, it is important to remember that the firm's goal is profitability and not sales revenue for its own sake. (Predicting the nature of the demand curve is always difficult.)

However, elasticity can be affected by a whole range of marketing strategies. For example:

- In the early stages of the product life cycle, demand may well be inelastic because the product has few competitors. The policy may be to set the price high. Later, in the maturity phase, demand will be more elastic because there are more competing substitutes. (see Figure M3.44).
- Advertising and promotion strategies may make customers less price sensitive and promote brand loyalty.

In some markets price is the key factor that determines the level of sales. This is most likely in industries where competing firms and products offer very similar benefits: for example, when selling petrol or basic foods or commodities. Indeed, in conditions of perfect competition, price becomes the only influence on demand. It is imperfections in real markets that make non-price competition so important. The benefit of a product – its capacity to yield consumer satisfaction – can be endlessly manipulated and refined through the other elements in the marketing mix. The product itself may be given special features. Packaging and branding may increase its consumer appeal. New distribution channels may make it attractive to additional segments of the market.

Each mix factor is highly interdependent (changes in one cause or require changes in another) and a successful mix is tightly integrated in representing a carefully calculated total marketing strategy. Furthermore, each factor has a distinctive role in the overall effort to increase profitable sales.

Work in progress

Q 1 How might a firm track movements in the demand curve for its product?

2 Why should it be so important to coordinate each element in the marketing mix?

3 Why might a firm in its marketing mix deliberately not aim for maximised total sales?

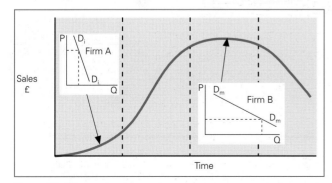

Figure M3.44

Enquiry 3   What makes an economy grow?

1 What is growth?

Talk to me

It is a long time since the telephone was a new product. Alexander Graham Bell, a Scotsman working in Boston, in the USA, discovered in 1874 that sound could be transmitted using electrical impulses. Telephones have been developing ever since and use has increased steadily.

For many years telephones used fixed cables, supplemented by radio for very long distances. Then satellite transmissions improved international calls and made them cheaper. In time, copper cables were replaced by optic fibres which have far greater capacity. Then came wireless … and mobiles.

The companies which operate telephone systems have grown very rapidly. In the early years, many governments kept control of their telephone companies and some still do. But in most developed countries there is now strong competition. This is accelerating the pace of change.

Figure M3.45 shows how fixed line telephone ownership is increasing. Figure M3.46 has some data on mobile phone penetration. The race is on.

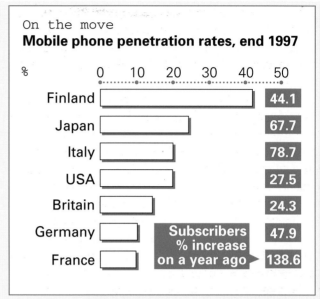

Figure M3.46 Mobile phone penetration rates, end 1997
Source: *The Economist*, 12 September 1998

The development of electronic communications is creating a new picture. Phones used to be used for voice communication. Increasingly, they are used for e-mail and data transmission. This means that the market for telecommunications (or telecoms for short) is growing at an unprecedented rate.

Your agenda

1 What effect has technical change had on the telecoms industry over the years?

2 What has happened to the price of a telephone call?

3 Draw a supply and demand diagram which shows these long-run changes. What has happened to the quantity demanded? Explain the changes you identify.

4 What other products are facing rapidly increasing demand? Why?

5 What other changes can lead to an increase in demand?

6 Describe the developments which can be observed in any growing industry.

7 What effects have these changes had on the economy as a whole?

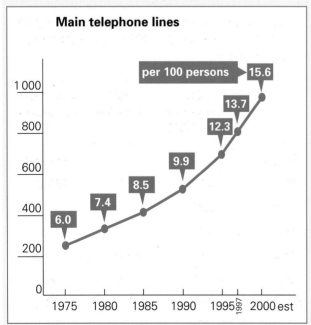

Figure M3.45 Main telephone lines per 100 persons
Source: International Telecommunications Union

Economic growth describes the way the output of an economy increases over time. The easiest way to measure it is to use gross domestic product (GDP), or the sum total of the value of all output for a year. When a number of different sectors and industries are experiencing healthy growth, it is likely that overall the economy will be growing.

We saw in Module 3.1 that there are quite regular fluctuations in GDP which reflect the ups and downs of the business cycle. Economic growth is more long term in nature. It is possible because over time productive capacity grows. Effectively, there is an increase in the quantity and quality of resources available, so that more goods and services can be produced.

Figure M3.47 shows how an aggregate supply diagram can be used to demonstrate this. Full capacity output – the most that the economy can produce when all resources are working flat out – increases, shifting to the right. It is easy to see how changes such as that in the telecoms industry can lead to increasing capacity. When similar changes happen in a number of industries, the growth process is greatly encouraged.

Essentials

Economic growth is the long run trend rate of growth of output in an economy, usually measured by the percentage annual change in real GDP.

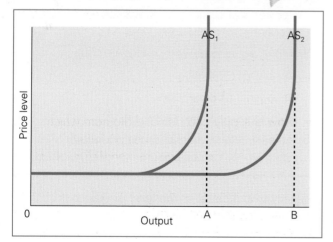

Figure M3.47

The long-term trend rate of growth is the average increase in output which is made possible by the growth of productive capacity. In the UK since 1980, the trend rate of growth has averaged just over 2 per cent

per annum. Figure M3.48 shows annual growth of GDP together with the long-term trend line which underlies the fluctuations associated with the business cycle.

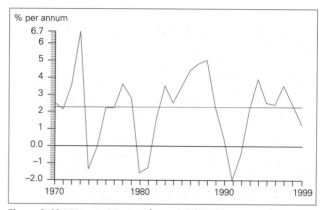

Figure 3.48 UK economic growth rates, 1970–99
Source: ONS, via Secos 4

GDP is not the perfect measure of changes in the standard of living. It includes the costs of cleaning up the environment and excludes all kinds of do-it-yourself activity from child care to decorating and beyond. It does not make allowances for negative externalities. However, it does give us figures which can be compared over time and with other countries. They provide a guide as to current economic performance. The Human Development Index published by the United Nations Development Programme provides a contrasting picture which gives more attention to qualitative aspects of standards of living. Figure M3.49 shows how incomes and the HDI compare for a few selected economies.

	Human Development Index (HDI)	HDI ranking	Real GDP per capita $
Canada	0.96	1	21 916
UK	0.93	14	19 302
Brazil	0.81	62	5928
Russia	0.77	72	4531
China	0.65	106	2935
India	0.45	139	1422
Sierra Leone	0.19	174	625

Figure M3.49 GDP and the Human Development Index, 1995
Source: UN Human Development Report, 1998

2 How is growth achieved?

Productivity

	UK	USA	Japan	Germany
92	94.0	98.1	99.3	96.9
93	96.8	98.9	99.4	97.3
94	100	100	100	100
95	100.8	100.8	101.3	101.9
96	101.2	102.8	106.1	103.5
97	102.7	104.5	106.4	106.2
98	103.5	106.9	104.0	108.0

Figure M3.50 Productivity data for the UK, USA, Japan and Germany: gross product per person employed (1994 = 100)
Source: *National Institute Economic Review*, 1999

Your agenda

1 What is the percentage growth in productivity for each country between 1992 and 1998?

2 Which countries would you expect to have the highest growth rates?

3 How might productivity be increased more in the countries which are trailing?

Very broadly, an increase in the quantity and quality of resources available will usually lead to some economic growth:

- An increase in the working population makes more labour available. Over time, the number of jobs expands to absorb the extra labour and output rises. The USA and Australia have both expanded output as a result of steady flows of immigrants. All developed countries have grown partly through the absorption of large numbers of women into the labour force.
- More capital means more output. When employees have bigger and better machines to work with their output rises.
- Land can be used more effectively and improved in quality.
- Entrepreneurs can identify new, profitable opportunities and take the risks which are often involved in the implementation of new ideas.

These are very generalised points. In practice, managers who want to improve performance need to find practical ways of using resources more efficiently. Also, there must be growing demand. Otherwise it will not be worth increasing output because it will not sell.

In developing countries which have rapidly increasing populations it is usually possible to increase GDP, but it may be more difficult to increase GDP per capita. Simply having more people does not help.

Producing more

Rover

In late 1998 the giant Rover car plant at Longbridge was dogged by low levels of productivity. This meant that its costs were higher than they needed to be, affecting the company's level of competitiveness relative to other car manufacturers. BMW, which owns Rover, gave the trade unions two weeks to agree to new working practices, otherwise the plant would close.

Your agenda

1 What impact would the closure of the Longbridge plant have on the rate of economic growth in the West Midlands?

2 How would improved productivity affect:
   a BMW's profits
   b buyers of Rover cars
   c wages and jobs at the plant?

3 How can lean production help to raise productivity for car manufacturers?

Productivity is defined as the level of output per person employed. There are many ways of increasing productivity, including:

- investing in more capital equipment
- finding better ways of organising production
- investing in human capital through additional training and education
- implementing new technologies.

Making full use of these can help businesses to cut costs and increase profits. It can also make it possible to pay higher wages, which may be important in motivating employees.

Module 2.1 looked at numerous ways of increasing productivity. Culture, flexible organisation, lean production, good communications and leadership were all found to be important in improving business organisation.

When productivity is increasing across a large part of the economy, growth becomes possible. Real incomes will rise.

- Employers may be seeking to motivate employees as part of the move to increase productivity.
- Cutting costs may allow businesses to cut prices, which gives customers more purchasing power.
- If profits are rising, increased investment may be possible.

Investment

Investment is defined as expenditure which will generate income in the future. All investment therefore has some impact on growth, provided it is directed at an objective which can meet a demand.

Investment in plant and machinery may be completely new or it may replace existing equipment. However, in the latter case, it will usually represent an improvement in quality. Investment almost always helps the people who operate the equipment to increase productivity.

Very often human capital increases when new equipment is used. Retraining, enhancing existing skills, will be a part of the investment process. Of course, people who are going to be able to adopt new ways of working need to be educated to be flexible in the first place, so providing good education is also very important to the growth process.

Some countries which achieve consistently high rates of investment have grown impressively. However, the relationship is not always clear from year to year, and the investment does need to be directed towards production for which there is growing demand. Nevertheless, some of the Asian countries both invested and grew impressively before the Asian financial crisis, as shown in Figure M3.51.

	GDP	Investment
Korea	7.2	6.3
Malaysia	8.7	15.1
Thailand	7.5	10.3

Figure M3.51 Growth and investment: average percentage growth rates, 1990–97

Source: World Bank, GDR 1998

3 How can new technologies help?

Talk to me more...

A single pair of optic fibres, each the thickness of a human hair, can carry all of North America's long-distance telephone calls. The 'backbone' of the fibre optic highway, the basic telephone network, can cope with ten times as many calls as networks built just a few years ago. New technologies make it possible for the same cable to carry 16 or 32 times as many calls as it did before.

These developments have made telephone networks much cheaper. They have also made it easy for new telephone companies to enter the market and compete with the established ones. This has helped to ensure that the cost of a phone call fell as the new technologies were developed.

Meantime, BT has forged an alliance with AT & T, the largest US supplier of long-distance call capacity. Their jointly operated system will have huge economies of scale and should make international calls cheaper again.

Your agenda

1 In which products has technology been most important in creating new developments in recent years?

2 Think of five examples of products for which technology is unlikely to bring about change.

New technologies can have their impact in two ways:

- They may lead to **product innovation**. Businesses which can develop new products can tap a new market. They are quite likely, at first, to face relatively little competition, so their profits may be impressive. In time, competitors will be attracted by the profits and will enter the market.

- **Process innovation** involves finding better production methods and can cut costs, sometimes dramatically. The consumer may never know what difference the new process makes, because the product is essentially the same. However, if the market is competitive, the reduced costs may lead to lower prices, at least in real terms.

Essentials

Product innovation involves the development of a new product.

Essentials

Process innovation is defined as the development of new ways of producing an existing product.

It could be argued that a telephone call is much the same as it has always been, although connection may be faster and sound quality clearer. The big difference is in process technologies, which have made phone calls much cheaper. What then happens? People and businesses make more and more calls; they come to depend more heavily on telecommunications generally and the industry grows.

Of course, it could be suggested that many recently developed uses for telephones are really new products. Telephone lines set up for Internet connections and data transmission might be an example. With many products the distinction between product and process innovation becomes blurred. An improved product is manufactured at a lower cost. Value is added more effectively – the product may be more reliable or look better. Perhaps the price actually stays the same, but the consumer gets better value.

New technologies create economic growth in that they provide a variety of industries with ways of growing. They are also of vital importance in creating competitive advantage. It follows that finding ways of

Work in progress

Q **1** Make a list of at least five products for which you know process innovation has been important at some time in the past or present. Describe the impact of the change on:

   a the consumer

   b the economy.

2 Think of some examples of products for which new technologies have provided an improved substitute. What has happened to those products?

3 What are the employment implications of the situations you have been considering?

developing technologies is an important element in the growth process. One way to do this is to have strong research and development programmes (R & D).

Figure M3.52 shows some data for R & D spending over time. This can come from the private sector or from the government. Where the commercial possibilities of research are clear, the private sector can be expected to undertake it. Where they are less so, it is helpful if governments support the work. The impetus towards miniaturisation in electronics came first from the US space programme. The commercial applications of this, at the start, were not obvious at all. It is clearly beneficial to the growth process if governments are prepared to subsidise some research.

% of GDP					
	1981–5			1990–4	
Total	Government	Industry	Total	Government	Industry
UK					
2.30	1.10	1.00	2.19	0.71	1.11
France					
2.12	1.14	0.88	2.42	1.13	1.08
US					
2.70	1.30	1.34	2.73	1.10	1.57
Japan					
2.34	0.52	1.66	2.82	0.49	2.15

Figure M3.52 R&D spending

Source: Annual review of government-funded R & D, 1996 HMSO

Note: Japan spends very little on defence-related R & D. The proportion is decreasing, but the UK government spends roughly 40 per cent of its research funds on defence. Some R & D is supported by charitable funding.

Employment

It is fairly obvious that some kinds of technological development can lead to significant labour-saving investment. This means that there are far fewer jobs in the manufacturing sectors of developed economies than there used to be.

However, that is not the whole story. New product development can lead to significant *labour-using* investment. Telecommunications and computing sectors provide obvious examples. New processes often make the organisation of production more complicated and there have been big increases in the number of people who work as management and training consultants. However, they appear not as employees in manufacturing but as suppliers of services to business. Technology both destroys and creates jobs, although the changes can take time.

4 Growth in the service sector

Burgers: fast forward

During 1998, both McDonald's and Burger King announced expansion plans in the UK. McDonald's planned to open another 100 outlets, making 930 in all. Burger King planned 55, bringing its total to 500. These plans meant 5000 and 2000 more jobs, respectively, in the two companies. All this was despite very strong competition in the fast-food sector generally.

Furthermore, McDonald's made clear that it intended to keep up the expansion. It began to consider diversifying with new products. Director of communications Mike Love said: 'We provide the service and the food that people want. We base what we do on what customers tell us. We are good listeners.' Although not everyone likes burgers, both companies were very optimistic.

Your agenda

1 Why has consumption of meals out grown rapidly in recent years?

2 How have burger outlets managed to take an increasing share of meals out?

3 Is burger production labour or capital intensive?

4 What might the future hold for burger outlets?

A major factor in the growth process for the service sector is the growth of real income. There is a circular relationship here because economic growth usually brings with it income growth.

Most **mature economies** have service sectors which are growing fast enough to absorb an increasing proportion of the labour force. Figure M3.53 shows what has happened. There are limits to the quantities of manufactures which consumers want to own (and store). The demand for services is less limited. You are unlikely to buy two vacuum cleaners in a year, but you might take two holidays, or more... if you can. Figure M3.53 shows how employment is now concentrated in the service sector.

	Agriculture	**Industry**	**Services**	**%**
France	5.2	26.8	67.9	
Germany	3.3	37.0	59.7	
UK	2.1	27.6	69.7	

Figure M3.53 Employment by sector
Source: ONS, *Regional Trends*, 1998

Essentials

Mature economies have well-developed manufacturing sectors and their labour forces are increasingly concentrated in the service sector.

Generally, businesses in the service sector have grown significantly. Services are rather less affected than manufacturing by new technologies. Productivity can be increased by computerising records and accounts, but it is usually not the driving force behind growth.

5 Is trade the engine of growth?

Mexico, exports and GDP

Mexico has been growing well. The estimates of likely growth of exports for 1998 and 1999 suggest a rate of 11 per cent. GDP for the same period is expected to grow by around 5 per cent. The economy is beginning to benefit from the North American Free Trade Agreement. Set up in 1993, this allows free trade between Mexico, the USA and Canada.

Many US and Canadian business are shifting their more labour intensive activities to Mexico. Wages are considerably lower there and this is a good way to cut costs. The inward investment helps Mexico to grow. Equally, with rising incomes, the Mexicans provide a large potential market for US and Canadian exports. The agreement helps all three countries to specialise more effectively. Figure M3.54 shows that in general there is a connection between international trade and economic growth.

Your agenda

1 Trace the impact of growing exports on the circular flow of money, showing how they can affect the growth of GDP.

2 How can free trade agreements lead to increasing levels of exports?

3 What implications does this have for governments' trade policies?

4 What costs might increasing trade involve for the countries concerned?

Much growth takes place because countries find better ways of utilising their resources. They specialise in the items they can produce cheaply. When they do this, they are able to produce efficiently, getting the maximum quantity of output from the minimum quantity of resources.

Rapidly increasing trade has been an important engine of growth for many **developing countries**. A number of Asian countries have done particularly well. The Asian 'tigers' – Taiwan, South Korea, Hong Kong and Singapore – have become, in effect, developed countries. The Asian financial crisis which began in 1997 caused growth to fall off very sharply for the first three, but it began to pick up again in 1999.

Trade has helped other developing countries too. However, there are costs to this path for development. The structural change which accompanies trade can be painful. Not all countries relish those costs, which can involve unemployment in some sectors, environmental degradation and cultural changes. In many cases, the attractions of rising real incomes have overcome the fears of change. Some countries, particularly in Africa, might have liked to trade and grow but have found that success eluded them.

Trade often grows along with **foreign direct investment** (FDI). This occurs when multi-national companies set up production and distribution facilities in a range of countries. Most countries are keen to attract FDI because it brings in valuable funds which can be used to increase the overall level of investment. It creates jobs and sometimes, **technology transfer**. This means that the multi-national brings with it access to technologies which the host country does not currently have. It will train local people, whose knowledge of the technology will be a net gain to the national economy.

Essentials

Developing countries are those countries where standards of living are still low compared to those of western Europe, the manufacturing sector is still relatively small and the majority of the population is engaged in agriculture.

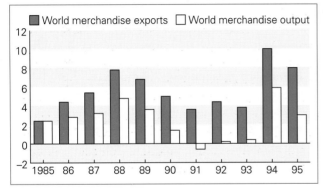

Figure M3.54 Growth in the volume of world merchandise exports and merchandise ouput, 1985–95. (Annual percentage change)
Source: WTO, Annual Report, 1998.

6 Has the European Union created economic growth?

Growing in Europe

Quest Refrigeration makes display refrigerators for pubs, restaurants, shops and anyone else who wants the contents of the refrigerator to be visible as an aid to their marketing. The business is located in the Delyn industrial park in north-east Wales.

Quest's unique selling point is the plastic-type outer casing of the refrigerators, which makes them resistant to impact and rust. They also have to compete on price: there are other manufacturers with an eye on its market. Some 30 per cent of the output is exported, mainly to the EU, the Far East and Australia. The EU markets are crucial to Quest. The advent of the single market has been a help; it has reduced the amount of paperwork involved in exporting within the EU. This has made a useful contribution to the continuous search for ways of cutting costs.

Highland Distillers, maker of Famous Grouse and The Macallan Scotch whiskies, is in a very competitive market. Although it has two well known brand names there are so many other things people might choose to drink. In 1998 the pound was high and the prospects did not look good. Furthermore, the Asian financial crisis looked bound to hit sales. The company took action. It increased its marketing budget by 8 per cent. The result was an increase in sales in Spain, Greece, Sweden and the Netherlands, giving an overall increase in exports of 12 per cent. Thirty per cent of output is for export so this was a good result in a difficult year.

Your agenda

1 How can the EU help potential exporters?

2 Many exporters face strong competition in Europe. Make a list of the ways in which they might seek to compete effectively.

3 How will businesses which already do substantial business in the EU react to EMU?

4 How does trade encourage growth?

When the UK joined the EU in 1973, it was estimated that the increase in trade would add half of 1 per cent per year to the UK growth of GDP. It is impossible to say what would have happened if the UK had stayed outside the EU. However, there has been a big increase in UK trade with the other member countries. The whole direction of UK trade has altered.

Businesses which have expanded into the EU market have been able to exploit economies of scale. Indeed, they may depend on EU markets to allow them to operate at an efficient scale of production.

The **single market**, introduced in 1993, was an important development. It harmonised all trade regulations across the EU. This means that businesses do not have to produce to different specifications for each individual market. A single version of the product will sell in all 15 member countries. The impact of this on export businesses has been considerable. Frontier controls were also greatly reduced by the single market provisions. This reduced time wasted and so also costs.

Some businesses have integrated their operations across all their European markets. The vehicle manufacturer Ford provides an example. Production of each of its models is concentrated in particular locations. When a British consumer buys a Ford it may have been imported from Belgium or Spain. Equally, continental buyers may find that their Fords have come from the UK. This level of specialisation cuts costs and allows increased economies of scale.

Essentials

Foreign direct investment occurs when multi-national companies invest in productive capacity in countries other than the one in which they are based.

Essentials

Technology transfer occurs when multi-national corporations bring new technologies to the countries in which they invest.

Work in progress

Q 1 Think about the major businesses in your area. Which of them are operating in other EU countries besides the UK?

2 What advantages do these businesses get from exporting within the EU?

3 What advantages does exporting within the EU have over exporting beyond the EU?

An interesting aspect of the single market is that it appears to have encouraged foreign direct investment coming into the EU from outside. During the 1990s there was more FDI in the EU than in the USA. A large unified market makes an attractive location for a foreign business with a strong interest in selling within the EU. The UK has been able to pick up a disproportionate share of this investment, perhaps because of the advantages conferred by the English language. It remains to be seen whether this advantage will be lost if the **euro zone** becomes the favoured location and the UK remains outside. It is likely that the Republic of Ireland will benefit from being within the euro zone.

Essentials

The **single market** refers to the changes in the EU which took place in 1993 and ensured that all EU producers were competing on equal terms within the EU.

Essentials

The **euro zone** came into operation in 1999 with the implementation of EMU.

1 What are the tools available?

Objectives and priorities

Here are some excerpts from the Labour party manifesto laying out plans for the future during the 1997 general election campaign.

No risks with inflation
We will match the current target for low and stable inflation of 2.5 per cent or less. We will reform the Bank of England to ensure that decision-making on monetary policy is more effective, open, accountable and free from short-term political manipulation.

Fair taxes
There will be no return to the penal tax rates that existed under past governments.

Labour's welfare-to-work Budget
We will introduce a Budget within two months after the election to begin the task of equipping the British economy and reforming the welfare state to get young people and the long-term unemployed back to work.

Source: Labour Party HQ, Millbank

Your agenda

1 Why do governments try to control inflation?

2 What other high priorities do governments have?

3 Is it possible to have low inflation, with low tax rates and low unemployment, all at the same time?

4 To what extent did the government elected in 1997 succeed in fulfilling its manifesto promises?

Controlling the economy is usually a complex task. First, there are a number of different objectives. A rising standard of living, low unemployment and low inflation are all reasonable expectations. However, it may not be possible to achieve all of them, all the time. We have already seen that the business cycle involves fluctuations in the state of the economy. There can be difficult trade-offs. Furthermore, stabilising the economy can be made harder by unforeseen events. Changes in the world economy can have major effects on the domestic economy.

The policies which are used to control the macro-economy can be divided into four main groups:

- **Monetary policy** involves the use of interest rates as a way of influencing the level of aggregate demand in the economy. Since 1997 it has been the responsibility of the **Monetary Policy Committee (MPC) of the Bank of England**. However, the Chancellor of the Exchequer maintains close contact with the Governor of the Bank of England.

- **Fiscal policy** comprises taxation, expenditure and the level of public borrowing. Changes in these variables can have an important effect on aggregate demand. However, political priorities may affect the use that can be made of these policies. For example, a commitment not to raise taxes may mean that aggregate demand cannot be reduced except by cutting spending.

- **Supply-side policies** are used to help markets to work more efficiently. They are sometimes described as micro-economic policies. They provide a useful complement to macro-economic fiscal and monetary policies. For example, policies which involve retraining help to meet employers' labour needs, reduce the excess supply of labour which is characteristic of unemployment and improve the efficiency of the labour market. Supply-side policies are useful in dealing with structural unemployment and contribute to economic growth.

- **Exchange rate policies** have a major impact on the level of competitiveness. In this way, they can affect aggregate demand. Exchange rate policies are closely tied up with the conduct of monetary policy. This means that they are an important part of the macro-economic policy package.

Macro-economic policy can be expansionary or contractionary. If there is accelerating inflation, a contractionary policy may be called for. Interest rates can be increased and government expenditure cut. If, on the other hand, the economy is running below full capacity output and there is substantial unemployment, expansion will help. Interest rate cuts and increased government expenditure would make sense.

Work in progress

Q **1** Why did the Labour government promise in 1997 to make the Bank of England independent of Treasury control?

2 What drawbacks do fiscal policies have as a way of controlling the economy?

3 Why have several governments used supply-side policies as a way of reducing unemployment? (Go back to page 241 if in doubt).

4 If the economy is facing a recession, what policy package might be appropriate?

Essentials

Monetary policy uses interest rates to make borrowing more expensive and so reduce spending and aggregate demand.

Essentials

The **Monetary Policy Committee** is the committee of the Bank of England which decides the level of the Bank's base rate.

Essentials

Fiscal policy involves changes in taxation, government spending and public borrowing.

Essentials

Supply side policies work to expand output by making markets work more efficiently.

Essentials

Exchange rate policies work to influence the exchange rate and affect the relative competitiveness of exports and imports.

Apr. 2007

Inflation at 3.1% above its 2% target.

→ higher monthly bills with variable rates + base rate teacher mortgages

2 How is inflation controlled?

Employers demand rate cuts

In late 1998 employers in the engineering industry were expecting a hard recession in the year ahead. Gordon Scott, regional director of the Sheffield branch of the Engineering Employers Federation, said difficulties in global markets and declining confidence because of interest rate levels had together caused recruitment of young people to decline by 20 per cent. 'The last 0.25 per cent point reduction in interest rates was a good sign, but not enough,' he said. 'When you have had two or three interest rate rises in a few months, that shatters confidence, and the length of time it has taken for rates to start to come down means we cannot rely on things getting better quickly. There has to be at least another half-point cut before manufacturing sees light at the end of the tunnel and starts investing again.'

Your agenda

1 What effect had increased interest rates had on engineering firms?

2 What effects would the firms' decisions have on the economy as a whole?

3 How might wage costs be affected by these events?

4 Why are engineering businesses particularly vulnerable when interest rates rise?

In fact, Gordon Scott was in luck. At the first meeting after he made his press statement, the MPC of the Bank of England decided that the Bank's **base rate** should be cut by half a per cent. Then it went on to cut the rate again, the following month. This brought immediate relief for businesses with large loans. Interest rates on loans are always rather above base rates, but base rate is what the banks have to pay when they need to borrow from the Bank of England. So a change in base rates usually means that the banks will shortly adjust their rates to borrowers. Figure M3.55 shows what was happening at the time.

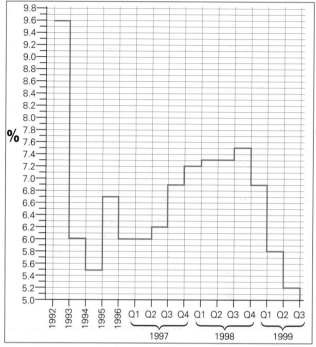

Figure M3.55 Base rate changes.
Source: *National Institute Economic Review*, 1999

The MPC was set up in May 1997. The Chancellor, Gordon Brown, implemented the incoming Labour government's promise to make the Bank of England more independent, just a few weeks after the election. The committee consists of Bank officials and eminent economists with wide experience of business and economic policy. At their monthly meetings, they review the statistical evidence and adjust interest rates. They are charged with ensuring that the inflation rate is kept within 1 per cent of the target rate of 2.5 per cent per annum.

Essentials

Base rate is the interest rate which the Bank of England charges banks when they need to borrow from it. This determines the level of rates generally throughout the financial system. It is set by the MPC.

Not long after the MPC began its monthly meetings, inflation began to accelerate. By the third quarter of 1997, it was well above its target rate. The committee promptly raised interest rates.

The economy in 1997 was growing fast – at more than 3 per cent per annum. This was well above the long-run sustainable rate of growth of approximately 2 per cent. Not surprisingly, there was evidence of skill shortages. This meant that employers were having difficulty filling vacancies with appropriately skilled people. Wage rates were beginning to rise, as employers tried to attract people from other companies.

Once wage rates begin to rise, costs rise and prices start to rise. If the process continues, inflation will accelerate. In order to control inflation, interest rates are raised.

In contrast, by late 1998 there were compelling signs that the UK economy was slowing down. There were quite widespread redundancies in manufacturing businesses. The inflation rate had begun to fall. Business expectations were gloomy. Interest rate cuts were clearly in order.

Work in progress

 1 What is the current level of base rates?

2 When did the MPC last meet?

3 What action did the MPC take then, if any?

4 What reasons did the MPC give for its decision?

5 Why are the decisions of the MPC widely reported in the news media?

3 How interest rates work

What was happening?

		Year-on-year inflation %	Unemployment % of labour force	Base rate %
1996:	Q3	2.1	7.3	5.8
	Q4	2.6	6.8	5.9
1997:	Q1	2.7	6.2	6.0
	Q2	2.7	5.7	6.2
	Q3	3.5	5.3	6.9
	Q4	3.7	5.0	7.2
1998:	Q1	3.4	4.8	7.3
	Q2	4.0	4.8	7.3
	Q3	3.7	4.6	7.5
	Q4	3.0	4.6	6.8
1999:	Q1	2.2	4.5	5.8
	Q2 est.	1.3	4.4	5.2
	Q3 est.	1.5	4.3	5.0

Figure M3.56 Inflation, unemployment and interest rates: quarterly data. (Year-on-year inflation is the rate for the year preceding the date in question.)
Source: *National Institute Economic Review*, 1998

Your agenda

1 Inflation might be expected to be diminished by higher interest rates. To what extent can this be seen in the figures?

2 How much of the unemployment which persisted at the end of 1997 do you think might have been due to demand deficiency?

3 What would you expect to happen to unemployment and inflation in 2000?

4 What actually did happen to inflation and unemployment in late 1999 and 2000?

When interest rates are raised, all borrowers find that they have to make larger interest payments just to continue to borrow the same amount. This has several effects:

- Businesses which are borrowing in order to finance investment will find that they get a lower rate of return on their investment. They may well cut back on their expansion plans, reducing the level of investment.
- Businesses which are making losses will have to contract or close down, as they will be unable to afford the increased interest payments.
- Consumers contemplating borrowing in order to finance purchases of durables may decide to postpone their spending plans.
- Consumers who already have loans (for example for house purchase) will have less money to spend on other things.

It is easy to see that all of the above outcomes involve reduced spending on either investment or consumer goods and services, so an increase in interest rates leads to a fall in aggregate demand. This means falling demand for a wide range of products. Businesses will react by cutting output and job losses will follow.

When people find themselves out of work, they will cut back their consumption: they will have to because their incomes will have fallen. This leads to a further fall in aggregate demand. The circular flow of money diminishes. This process will become cumulative as first one and then another business experiences falling sales.

Once unemployment starts to rise, skill shortages will become less of a problem. Those employers who are recruiting will find good candidates easily. There will be no need for them to pay higher rates to attract people from other employers. Indeed, unemployment means that people accept lower wage rates in order to have a job at all. Costs will stabilise and stiffer competition will occur between producers as markets shrink. Prices will be much less likely to rise.

Work in progress

Q
1. Draw a diagram showing how aggregate demand and aggregate supply are affected by rising interest rates. Show what happens to the price level.
2. What types of business are most likely to be affected by a contractionary monetary policy? Give three examples.
3. How will consumers who do not lose their jobs react to a contractionary monetary policy?

The long-term goal

What governments really want is low inflation, low interest rates, rising standards of living and low unemployment. In a period of rapid growth (above the rate which is sustainable), the economy has to be made to contract or at least slow down in order to stop inflation from accelerating. This process is usually painful. It brings redundancies, reduced profits and falling incomes generally. It is not something politicians want to have to do shortly before an election.

If monetary policy is the responsibility of the central bank, rather than the Chancellor of the Exchequer, a period of contraction will be brought about when it is needed to control inflation. Elections will not affect the timing. This is why some countries make their central banks responsible for the implementation of monetary policy. The *Bundesbank*, the central bank of Germany, was set up in this way after the great German hyperinflation of 1923. This was the forerunner of the European Central Bank, which controls monetary policy for the euro zone in the same kind of way. The Federal Reserve Bank of the USA is also independent of the US government.

4 How have attitudes changed?

Past experience

1930s' depression: the government reacted to prolonged and very serious unemployment by cutting spending. It considered this prudent. The great economist J. M. Keynes showed that depressions like this could be avoided if governments would borrow and spend more when unemployment was high.

1950s: the work of Keynes was accepted as a basis for government policy although Keynes himself was dead by then. For a while it worked well.

1960s and 1970s: governments tried to stabilise the economy by spending in recession and cutting back in the boom phase. But they were not very good at predicting what would happen. Efforts to obtain big pay increases and oil price rises led to rapid inflation. The Keynesian approach was discredited. The term 'stop-go' was used to describe the way policies tended to be implemented too late, and too strongly.

1980s: Thatcherism. The reaction to the 1970s brought very tight monetary policies and a big increase in the level of unemployment.

1990s: Conservative inflation targets were continued by New Labour. The independence of the Bank of England was gradually increased, so that inflation control might become less political.

Your agenda

1   What happened to standards of living while the above changes of approach were tried? (If you don't have numerical data to hand try asking someone who remembers. Pool your information.)

2   Were politicians perceived as being successful in their efforts to stabilise the economy during the 1980s and 1990s?

3   What is the main drawback to a strict inflation target achieved through monetary policy?

4   What do you think a thumb-nail characterisation (like those above) of the decade after 2000 might say?

Governments like to present themselves as acting responsibly. However, a threat to their survival often causes them to do something which will attract short-term support. A tax cut perhaps – it could be just the thing if an election is looming. It should not be assumed that UK politicians have been particularly irresponsible. Careful study of other countries will show that electoral popularity is a common objective in democracies.

A feature of the period in which the Keynesian approach was important in the formulation of macro-economic policy was the use of fiscal and monetary policy in combination. In particular, governments would cut taxes and increase expenditure in order to reduce unemployment.

- Tax cuts increase disposable income and consumption, and so aggregate demand.
- Increased government expenditure adds directly to aggregate demand.

This approach can be very successful if the unemployment is caused by lack of demand, as in recession. Indeed, there was an element of fiscal expansion in the government response to the 1990–92 slump. Fiscal policy could be used in this way in the future. It makes sense to invest in infrastructure projects during recession because that creates jobs and provides improvements which can increase productivity when the economy recovers.

No tax increases, promise!

Fiscal policy has not been used to manage aggregate demand in recent years because that would mean increasing taxes. For both Conservative and Labour governments that has been contrary to their election promises. This means that they have relied on monetary policy to control the rate of inflation. That could change.

Sometimes expenditure cuts have been important in reducing aggregate demand. However, expenditure cuts seldom fall only on items which most people feel they can do without. They can be extremely unpopular, especially if they lead to rising class sizes in schools or cutbacks in the availability of medical care.

Fiscal policy can be very important in helping to bring about micro-economic changes. This will become apparent later in this module. Enquiry 5 deals with fiscal policy in more detail.

Is more change on the way? Joining the euro zone would bring further changes in the way interest rates are decided. Responsibility for monetary policy would move from the UK government to the European Central Bank. In these circumstances, fiscal policy might be an important area of flexibility for national governments.

5 What can be done about unemployment?

The New Deal: a way into work

Steve has been out of work for two years since losing his job as a labourer. 'I'd like a job, but there's not much about,' he said. 'As long as it gave me a chance to get some experience, I'd take something basic – so I could get used to getting up; getting to work on time and getting on with my workmates.'

Under the New Deal, after six months of unemployment, all young people in the UK under the age of 25 are offered a period of intensive counselling. At the end of this, their benefits stop and they either get a job which is not subsidised, or are offered a choice:

- a subsidised job with a regular employer

- work on an environmental project

- voluntary work, or

- full-time vocational education.

Employers receive £60 per week for each subsidised employee. Strict rules prevent them from sacking existing employees to make room for New Deal employees.

Your agenda

1 Why is unemployment costly to society?

2 Why is training important as a means of reducing unemployment?

3 What are the costs and the benefits of the New Deal?

Increasing aggregate demand can be helpful in reducing unemployment when demand is low because of recession. However, many people are unemployed for other reasons. These are broadly structural in nature:

- *Geographical immobility* – people who have been made redundant from declining industries such as coal and shipbuilding may be living far away from the places which have vacancies.
- *Occupational immobility* – many people have skills which are no longer in demand and have not had chances to acquire new skills.
- *No skills* – unskilled people are significantly more likely than skilled to be unemployed.
- *Long-term unemployed* – people who have not worked for some time become de-skilled and lose their work habit. Employers have shown themselves to be consistently unenthusiastic about hiring people who have been out of work for over a year.

No amount of increased aggregate demand solves these problems, although it can help. Something else is needed. Many governments have tried a variety of job creation schemes and some retraining has taken place. However, none of these has been sufficiently comprehensive to give unemployed people real improvements in their prospects.

The New Deal is designed to prevent people from becoming long-term unemployed. The combination of stopping benefits and offering meaningful opportunities could help. In early 2000 the scheme was extended to cover unemployed people of all ages.

Supply-side policies

Any policy which helps to increase supply is defined as a supply-side policy. Measures which help to deal with the causes of structural unemployment outlined above have potential to increase supply. Training and retraining make people more attractive to employers and more productive. The effect is to shift the aggregate supply curve outwards. This makes it possible for output to expand without creating inflationary pressures. Figure M3.57 shows how it works.

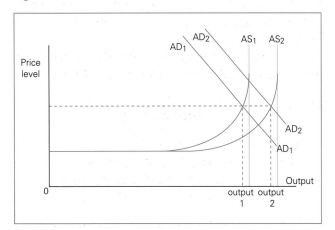

Figure M3.57 Expanding aggregate supply

Supply-side policies are primarily aimed at helping markets to work better. Training makes people more flexible. Labour markets are generally thought to be working well when they respond flexibly to employers' changing needs.

The New Deal provides training, but it also creates incentives. Losing benefits at the end of six months gives people a strong incentive to participate. Incentives are important in ensuring that people are actually available for work. Again this helps the labour market to work by guiding more people into paid employment.

Incentives to work can be reduced when people are caught in the poverty trap. This becomes a problem when the wages they can get in work are not much above benefit levels. The extra costs of working may leave them less well off working than they are on benefits. An integrated tax and benefit system which made sure that they were definitely better off working could solve this. The Working Families Tax Credit has made a start with this approach.

Spending on infrastructure in regions with high unemployment can be helpful in overcoming unemployment which has persisted because of geographical immobilities. It is often cheaper to encourage employers to move to such regions than it is to make moving house easier.

6 Where does the exchange rate fit in?

The Monetary Policy Committee versus the European Central Bank

Since the launch of the euro in 1999, the European Central Bank (ECB) has decided monetary policy for 300 million people. It displaced the *Bundesbank*, the Bank of France and all the rest. Can it think quickly? Can it be flexible?

Could it do a U-turn like the one the Bank of England did in late 1998? Then, the MPC of the Bank of England cut interest rates dramatically as new evidence came in suggesting that inflationary pressures were less of a threat than mounting redundancies. A small group of people, chosen for their expertise and meeting frequently, they were in a good position to make swift changes. The minutes of their meetings are published after two weeks, so everyone knows their reasoning.

In the ECB, interest rate decisions are made by the governing council. There are six executive members who are the most influential people on the staff of the ECB. In addition, the central bank governors of all the euro countries will attend. Some of the latter group may well sometimes want to push policy in the direction of their own national interests. No minutes will be published.

The head of the ECB, Wim Duisenburg says the financial markets will be kept fully informed by press conferences and interviews.

Your agenda

1 What are the main advantages of the euro to member countries of EMU?

2 Why do you think it is important for the financial markets to have good information on negotiations within the governing council of the ECB?

3 How is monetary policy working within the euro area at the present time? Compare this with UK policy (if different).

increasing the demand for it. The exchange rate will then rise; import prices will fall and domestically produced goods will lose some competitiveness on both home and export markets.

This has two important effects. Cheaper imports will help to calm down inflation, but loss of competitiveness will hurt exporters and businesses which compete with imports. If the objective is to reduce aggregate demand, then the policy will be deemed a success. In fact, the interest rate actually takes effect partly through its impact on the exchange rate.

In the euro zone, monetary and exchange rate policy are both controlled by the European Central Bank.

Point of View

'The UK chemical industry is 'world class' because it has to be to survive. My company has to be world class because we face some very good competitors.

Governments can and do survive without having to be competitive. For us, it's different. What we want the government to provide is an environment in which we can grow. Exporting businesses like ours need stable interest rates, so we can set a worldwide pricing policy that lasts for more than five minutes.' (Graham Green, W. Canning plc, in an interview with the *Independent*, 19 August 1998)

Your agenda

1 Why does Mr Green suggest that he can have a long-run pricing policy if interest rates are stable?

2 Why does Canning want a pricing policy which will last?

3 Trace the effects of an interest rate increase on the fortunes of a company such as Canning.

The exchange rate and monetary policy are intimately connected. If the exchange rate is floating, an increase in interest rates will attract a capital inflow. Holders of foreign currency deposits will buy the currency,

What is fiscal policy?

The Budget

'The Budget I bring before the House and country today begins the task of modernising not just taxation but the entire tax and benefits system of our country.

We do this to encourage enterprise; to reward work; to support families; to advance the ambitions not just of the few but of the many.

...inflation is forecast to be at our target of 2.5 per cent next year.

...we reduce corporation tax further by another 1p to 30p ...Small companies tax will be cut again to 20 per cent.

...Employers will now pay no National Insurance on any employee earning less than the starting point of the personal tax allowance, £81 a week.

...road fuel tax will rise by 4.4p a litre for unleaded petrol. And to encourage all diesel users to switch to cleaner fuels, ordinary diesel will rise by 1p more than that.'

– Gordon Brown, Chancellor of the Exchequer, in the House of Commons, 17th March 1998.

Its a wicked budget for me. The 12 per cent increase in diesel fuel tax adds £1.8 million to my costs. I will have to try to pass that on to my customers.

– Eddie Stobart, road haulier

I welcome the cut in corporation tax but the inflation target is still too high.

– Peter Weston, joint managing director of SP Engineering

Your agenda

1 What impact does a cut in corporation tax have on the economy?

2 National Insurance Contributions go into a fund which helps to cover social security payments. Both employers and employees must contribute. What arguments can you think of for the change made in the Budget statement above?

3 Find out the main changes in the last Budget, and the current rates of income tax, corporation tax and VAT.

4 How will each of the recent Budget changes affect both the macro-economy and individual industries and people?

Fiscal policy involves the whole range of taxation and expenditure measures. The public expenditure survey outlines spending plans each autumn. The Budget reveals tax changes, usually in March.

We have already identified a number of government economic objectives. Very broadly, we might divide these into four groups:

● provision of services
● macro–economic stability
● resource reallocation
● income redistribution.

All of these objectives figure large in the Budget, which generally makes a wide range of changes.

Some fiscal policy objectives require expenditure. Others can be achieved by manipulating taxes. This enquiry examines some of the possibilities and illustrates the options available.

Why is expenditure needed?

We saw in module 1 that people have very high expectations of governments. They would like them to provide good healthcare, education, training and many other services, while simultaneously keeping taxes low. Trade-offs are inevitable. Figure M3.58 shows what changes in public spending people would like to see.

| **Great Britain** | | | | | Percentages |
1985	**1990**	**1991**	**1993**	**1994**	**1996**
Health					
87	89	89	87	87	90
Education					
72	78	82	80	74	82
Old age pensions					
73	80	76	78	74	76
Police and law enforcement					
38	50	54	68	72	70
Environment					
34	61	60	54	48	41
Unemployment benefits					
40	36	39	48	36	33
Military and defence					
17	8	14	21	19	17
Culture and arts					
9	12	15	10	12	6

✱ *Percentage who thought spending should be 'much more' or 'more' when asked: 'Please show whether you would like to see more or less government spending in each area'.*

Figure M3.58 Attitudes towards government expenditure.
Source: ONS, *Social Trends*, 1998

In fact, priorities change quite considerably over the years, and not simply because of changes of government. Figure M3.59 shows the totals for each major spending department in real terms. Social security spending reflects both levels of unemployment and the ageing population. With health, similarly, spending rises because of increasing treatment possibilities and the ageing population.

| **Great Britain** | | | £ billion at 1996 prices | | |
1981	**1986**	**1991**	**1994**	**1995**	**1996**
Social security					
64	80	85	104	107	107
Health					
28	31	36	41	42	43
Education					
29	31	34	38	38	39
Defence					
26	30	27	25	24	23
Public order and safety					
9	11	15	16	16	15
General public services					
9	10	13	14	15	13
Housing and community ammenities					
15	13	10	11	11	10
Transport and communication					
9	6	8	7	9	8
Recreational and cultural affairs					
3	4	5	5	5	5
Agriculture, forestry and fishing					
3	3	3	3	4	5
Other expenditure					
46	41	28	38	44	37
All expenditure					
241	259	264	302	314	306

Figure M3.59 General government expenditure (Real terms, 1996 prices)
Source: ONS, *Social Trends*, 1998

Some expenditure increases reflect rising standards of living and increased ability to pay. Nevertheless, the figures show that despite the commitment of Conservative governments to restrict public spending during the period 1979–97, there was a steady rise.

Where's the money coming from?

Generally, there are **direct taxes** (levied directly on incomes) and **indirect taxes** (based on expenditure). Figure M3.60 shows the relative importance of each tax as a revenue raiser.

● Income tax is direct, based on incomes and collected by the Inland Revenue. Corporation tax is levied on company profits and is also direct.

- VAT and the excise taxes are indirect (i.e. expenditure) taxes and are collected by Customs and Excise.
- Excise taxes include taxes on fuels, alcohol and tobacco.

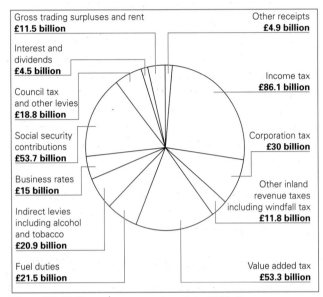

Figure M3.60 General government receipts, 1998–9.
Source: Treasury, HMSO

When government expenditure is greater than tax revenue, the difference is made up by borrowing. The annual amount which needs to be borrowed is called the **public sector net cash requirement (PSNCR)**. Now and then there is a surplus and therefore a debt repayment rather than borrowing.

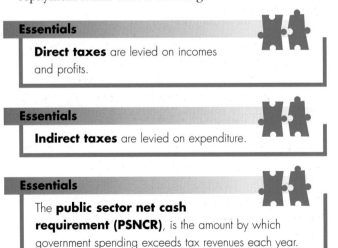

Essentials

Direct taxes are levied on incomes and profits.

Essentials

Indirect taxes are levied on expenditure.

Essentials

The **public sector net cash requirement (PSNCR)**, is the amount by which government spending exceeds tax revenues each year.

In general, taxation is a leakage from the circular flow of money. (Go back to page 186 if you are not sure about this). An overall increase in taxation will reduce aggregate demand, but each tax has a specific effect which can alter the structure of incentives in the economy. So the tax system can be used to change spending patterns in a wide variety of ways. Similarly, increased expenditure is an injection into the circular flow of money and different types of expenditure will have their own individual effects as well. In sum, changes in taxation and government expenditure have both macro-economic and micro-economic effects.

Most of the funds raised are spent by the central government. Some, however, are passed to local authorities. These supplement the amounts raised through council tax and the uniform business rate. They fund local spending, mainly on education, roads, social services and housing. Figure M3.61 outlines the way in which funds are spent.

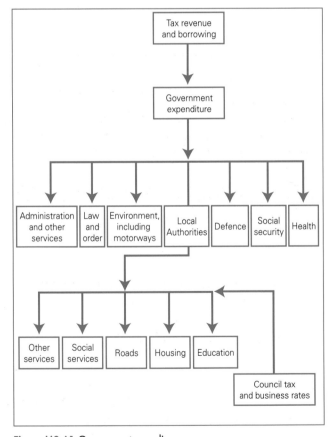

Figure M3.61 Government spending

2 Meeting macro-economic objectives

Dealing with the recession, 1990–92

From the 1979 election onwards, the Conservative governments of Margaret Thatcher and John Major always said that cutting public expenditure was a high priority. Figure M3.62 shows government expenditure as a percentage of GDP, the most usual way of measuring change in public spending. Overall, it doesn't seem to have gone down much.

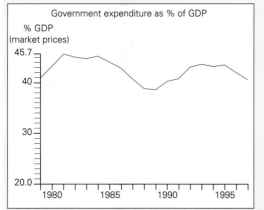

Government expenditure as % of GDP

Figure M3.62 Government expenditure as percentage of GDP
Source: Eurostat, via Secos 4

Now look more closely. In which periods has the total risen? Could it be something to do with the business cycle? Go back to the data on page 187 to check this.

Your agenda

1 In which years was public expenditure rising?

2 When were the recessions during the relevant period?

3 What effect does increased spending have during a recession?

4 What reasons can you give for rising public expenditure during recessions?

Social security spending is a significant proportion of public spending. It follows that when unemployment is rising, social security spending will rise too. Government spending is an injection into the circular flow of money. Wherever it is spent, it adds to aggregate demand. So if expenditure rises, it will have an expansionary effect on the economy.

The government is committed to paying unemployment benefit to all who qualify, so in a recession, spending rises automatically. The reverse will happen during recovery and boom as unemployment falls.

Equally, people who are made redundant face a drop in income. They will therefore be paying less tax. Again the reverse happens as the economy recovers, people go back to work and pay taxes again. So tax revenue rises during recovery and falls during recession. Taxes are a leakage and if tax revenue falls, leakages are reduced and the effect on the economy is expansionary.

The effect of these changes is therefore to limit the depth of a recession and to constrain growth during a boom. Thus taxes and benefits are referred to as **automatic stabilisers**.

Essentials

Automatic stabilisers operate when tax revenues fall and unemployment benefits payments rise as a result of recession. Similarly, taxes rise and benefits fall during the recovery. The fluctuations of the business cycle are made less severe.

Discretionary fiscal policy and the business cycle

The last enquiry touched on the Keynesian approach to monetary and fiscal policy (see page 246). It is perfectly possible for governments deliberately to increase spending and cut taxes during a recession. A strong case can be made. There may be pressing needs for investment projects which improve infrastructure. There may be unemployed construction workers – typically, recession with its gloomy expectations, causes a fall off in construction activity. By increasing aggregate demand generally it may be possible to reduce the income and output lost during the recession.

Decisions to change tax rates or to alter expenditure totals are all part of **discretionary fiscal policy**. The reverse policies can be used if the economy overheats in a boom. Reducing aggregate demand in this way will reduce inflationary pressures. But, as has already been observed, while expenditure cuts have been tried in recent years, tax increases have generally been avoided for political reasons.

PSNCR: the net effect of fiscal policy

The quickest way to assess the impact of fiscal policy on the macro-economy is to look at the public sector net cash requirement – see Figure 3.63. PSNCR is usually measured as a percentage of GDP.

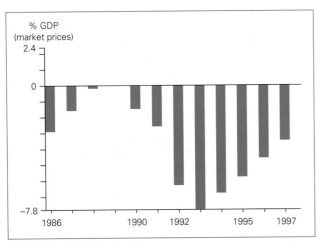

Figure 3.63 The public sector net cash requirement as a percentage of GDP
Source: Eurostat, via Secos 4

It is easy to see how borrowing was higher during the early 1990s recession, shrinking as the economy recovered. This deficit spending reflected the effects of both automatic stabilisers and increased expenditure.

Essentials

Discretionary fiscal policy involves changes in tax rates and expenditure plans which are designed to change aggregate demand. This is sometimes termed counter-cyclical policy because it may reduce the impact of recession and of accelerating inflation during a boom.

Work in progress

Q **1** Draw an AS/AD diagram showing the impact of increased government spending during a period of recession.

2 Why have tax changes contributed very little to stabilisation policies in recent years?

3 To what extent did the most recent Budget change aggregate demand overall?

4 What is the current level of government borrowing? Why?

Encouraging job creation

Employers' social security taxes increase the cost of employing people. National Insurance Contributions (NICs) can act as a disincentive to employers who are thinking of taking on more employees, so there have been efforts to reduce the impact of this tax, especially for low paid and part-time employees. This is a supply-side policy directed towards reducing unemployment, especially of unskilled people. High social security taxes in other EU countries have at times been blamed for high rates of unemployment there.

Encouraging enterprise

Some government expenditure is directed towards regenerating particular areas which have suffered badly from structural change. This too can be a useful policy to reduce unemployment. Again, the objective is macro-economic, but the effect is to increase the incentives for businesses to locate in places where unemployment is high.

3 Can fiscal policy change choices?

Creating incentives

❝... to reduce the amount of waste going into landfill, the landfill tax, £10 per tonne in 1999, will in future rise by £1 per tonne per year.

...last year, to encourage a switch to cleaner fuels, I promised to give an additional tax advantage to ultra–low sulphur diesel. By the end of the year, almost all producers will have switched to this cleaner fuel. This alone will cut emissions by 20 per cent. At a revenue cost of over £400 million a year, I will maintain the favourable tax treatment for cleaner diesel❞

Gordon Brown in the House of Commons, 10 March 1999

Your agenda

1 What do you think the result of increasing the landfill tax might be?

2 What other taxes are used to change consumption or production decisions?

3 Why are taxes particularly useful as a way of implementing environmental policies?

Governments often want to influence the allocation of resources. Sometimes this means changing consumer spending patterns. Taxes can be used to create incentives which induce people to adapt their behaviour in the desired manner.

The impact of expenditure taxes depends on elasticity of demand. Provided demand is price elastic, a tax will deter consumption. The demand for a particular type of petrol can be quite elastic. Often there are alternatives to the products which are taxed.

Figure M3.64 shows two possible scenarios for an expenditure tax. The tax raises the price required by the producer at all levels of sales, so it shifts the supply curve upwards by the amount of the tax.

Diagram A in Figure M3.64 shows what happens if a product with elastic demand is taxed. The tax has the effect of reducing quantity demanded by amount A. A new equilibrium price is established which is higher than before. The main effect of the tax is to reduce consumption. This is just what is required in the case of polluting fuels.

Now think about tobacco. Demand for tobacco is rather inelastic because buyers are addicted. Increasing taxes will not be very effective in reducing quantity demanded. Producers will be able to add most of the tax to the price without losing too many sales. On the other hand, tobacco taxes are very useful revenue raisers!

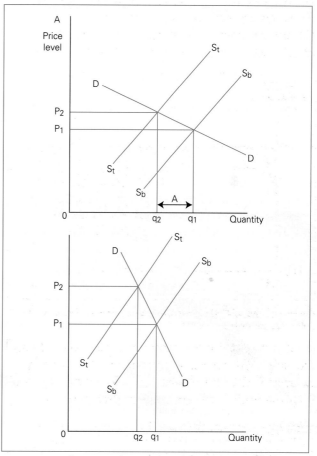

Figure M3.64 Elasticity and taxes

Work in progress

Q 1 Go back to the case study at the start of this enquiry. Explain why the Chancellor was putting an extra penny on diesel. What are the pros and cons of this approach? What effect would you expect it to have?

2 Tobacco sales are in fact falling. Use supply and demand diagrams to explain the reasons for this.

Point of View

In 1998 the Treasury proposed a £2 billion a year energy tax on business. The Treasury thought this would be a cost-effective way of improving energy efficiency. It might help to push the economy closer towards its internationally agreed targets for fossil fuel emissions.

There were immediate protests. Many businesses and the CBI (Confederation of British Industry) said that it could damage UK competitiveness. Unless the tax was set at a very high level it would have little effect. If it were to be high enough to be effective, then it would also increase costs significantly.

Alternative possibilities were put forward by the Institute for Public Policy Research (IPPR): 'Introducing a business energy tax would not be anti-competitive as the CBI claims. Indeed, if, as the IPPR proposes, the revenues are recycled back to business through cuts in employers' National Insurance Contributions and investment incentives for energy efficiency, then the vast majority of companies would see their overall costs fall.' Figure M3.65 shows the share of total taxes taken by energy taxes in EU countries.

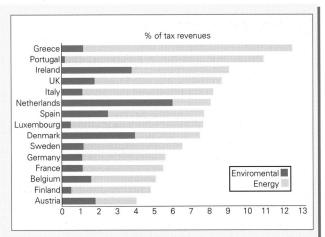

Figure M3.65 Europe's environmental taxes, 1996
Source: European Environment Agency

Your agenda

1   What are the arguments for increasing energy taxes on business?

2   To what extent do you think energy taxes would create disadvantages for businesses?

3   Explain 'the polluter pays' principle which is sometimes applied to issues involving possible energy taxes.

Fiscal policy and incentives

Fiscal policy can alter incentives in a wide variety of ways. It has been claimed that income taxes discourage hard work, but there is very little hard evidence to support this view. It is known however that lower tax rates reduce the incentive to avoid and evade tax. (Tax avoidance is legal, evasion is not.)

It is quite clear that specific taxes can discourage consumption of the product in question, provided there is a satisfactory substitute (i.e. demand is elastic).

Point of View

Paul Zetter is chairman of Zetters, the smallest of the three UK football pools operations. He said after the 1999 Budget:

'I'm delighted that the pools tax was cut to 17.5 per cent from 26.5 per cent. We now have a chance of saving the industry. We're still paying more duty than the National Lottery and more than three times as much as any other form of betting. Still, I'm very pleased. Without a change, the pools wouldn't last much longer.'

Your agenda

1   Why was the future of the football pools threatened by the tax on them?

2   Will people switch back to doing the pools if they are taxed less heavily?

4 Does fiscal policy redistribute income?

Getting and spending

What do you get from the government? What do you pay?

Mrs Jones needs a good deal of help. She receives housing benefit to cover her rent, as well as her pension. She pays no direct taxes, except for a small amount on the interest from her small savings. She has been disabled by a stroke and a nurse comes to help her have a bath each week. Every time her diabetes takes a bad turn she has to go to hospital for a few days. Meantime her daughter, who lives nearby, cooks most of her meals. However, the cost of these services is a lot less than the cost of care in a nursing home would be.

Mr Barker requires little in the way of public and merit goods. He is in good health and has no children. However, he is drinking more than is good for him. He drives a large BMW. What he would like is a better, faster, road system. He feels he pays a lot in tax and gets very little for it. He will always vote for the party which promises to cut taxes.

Your agenda

1 List the public goods and merit goods you have consumed during the past two weeks.

2 Why is Mr Barker paying high taxes?

3 Why are public and merit goods provided by the government?

4 Make the case for increasing spending on public and merit goods. Then make the case for decreasing such spending.

One of the objectives of fiscal policy is income redistribution. Market forces, left alone, tend to distribute income very unevenly. Attitudes to social justice vary very much from one person to another. Nevertheless, a sense that some redistribution should take place persisted throughout the twentieth century. Some governments reinforced the process while others reduced the extent of redistribution. The Labour government of 1945–51 was particularly active in setting up the NHS and extending the provision of free education. No government proposed to end redistribution.

First, we should look at the extent to which different kinds of taxes do actually redistribute money income. Later, we show how the picture changes if welfare is defined as including education, healthcare, housing and personal care services, as well as pensions and benefits. Real income does not simply mean the amount each person is paid. It includes all aspects of welfare.

Do taxes redistribute income?

Taxes come in three groups:

- Progressive taxes take a higher proportion of income, the larger the income is.
- Proportional taxes take the same percentage of income, whatever its level.
- Regressive taxes take a higher proportion of income the lower the level of income.

Figure M3.66 shows how much of people's incomes are taken by direct and indirect taxes. It helps to show the relative impact of the two types of tax on people at different income levels. Within the indirect tax category, VAT generally amounts to less than the other indirect taxes because it does not apply to food, housing, public transport and books and newspapers.

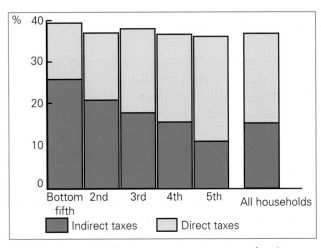

Figure M3.66 Direct and indirect taxes, as percentage of total income
Source: ONS, *Social Trends*, 1998

Redistributing welfare

When the value of welfare spending is included in an assessment of real incomes the picture changes somewhat. Figure M3.67 shows taxes paid and welfare benefits received for each quintile (i.e. fifth) of the population. Keep in mind that Figure M3.67 gives payments in pounds, whereas Figure M3.66 gives tax payments as a percentage of income. The data are not inconsistent, but they do present the information from a different angle.

It is clear that health spending is an important aspect of welfare. However, Figure M3.67 shows that the UK spends relatively little on healthcare compared to similar developed countries. There is scope for more effective redistribution, but political attitudes to this may vary.

Work in progress

Q 1 Are (**a**) income taxes and (**b**) indirect taxes, progressive, proportional or regressive? Explain your conclusions.

2 What happens to total tax paid as income rises? Would you describe the tax system as a whole as being progressive, proportional or regressive?

3 Do taxes redistribute income?

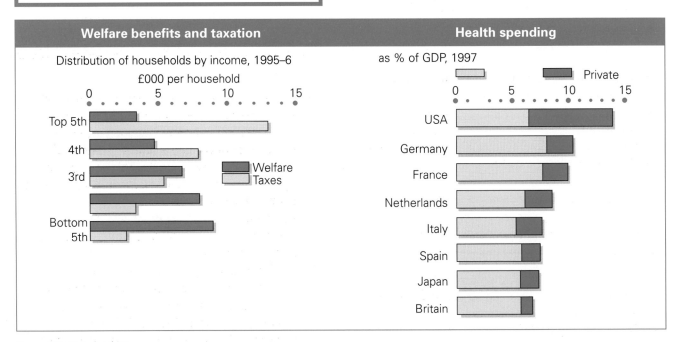

Figure M3.67 Redistribution
Source: ONS, OECD

5 Will the EU change everything?

The birth of the euro

While most people were celebrating New Year at the start of 1999, eleven EU countries were beginning the process of moving to a single currency, the euro. For the first time in history, a group of diverse countries was aiming for economic and monetary union. The euro is the second most traded currency after the dollar.

The financial markets closed on Thursday 31 December 1998 and reopened on Monday 4 January 1999. All over the euro zone and also in London technicians worked on the computers to get them ready for trading in euros. After working flat out to get their conversions ready in time, they finally started partying just as everyone was going back to work on Monday morning.

Your agenda

1 What are the main advantages and disadvantages of monetary union to the participants?

2 Which aspects of economic policy are affected by monetary union?

3 Which aspects of economic policy remain the responsibility of national governments?

4 How has EMU affected UK economic policy?

Within the euro zone, all member countries will have their monetary policy and so their base rate set by the European Central Bank. This will happen regardless of whether that base rate suits the economic situation in an individual country. It will be decided on the basis of statistics covering the whole euro zone.

In order to be part of EMU, each member country has to satisfy a range of convergence criteria. You met these in module 1.1 but here they are again:

- Price inflation should be not more than 1.5 per cent above that of the three lowest inflation rates of other member countries.
- The public sector deficit should be no more than 3 per cent of GDP.

- The member currency should have stayed close to its target exchange rate for at least two years.
- Rates of interest should be close to those of other member countries.

This means that fiscal policy is really the only area of macro-economic policy where national governments remain in full control. However, the 3 per cent rule means that there will be only limited variations in the overall impact of fiscal policies.

Level playing fields

The principle behind the European single market is that of the level playing field. If companies and nations are to compete freely with one another, it follows that they should all be competing on the same terms. So the European Commission works to create harmonised regulations covering safety, health, the environment and consumer protection. National regulations are adapted to fit a EU standard. Member countries can no longer keep out the exports of another member country simply because the product is slightly different from the home-produced version.

However, fiscal policy remains very much within the power of national governments, and does vary from one EU country to another. Several problems can arise:

- People cross national boundaries to buy goods which have lower specific taxes in the country concerned. Crossing the Channel to go to a French supermarket to stock up on tobacco and alcohol is one example. This has seriously upset newsagents and off-licences along the south coast of England.
- Businesses locate in countries with lower taxes. This tends to reduce the level of economic activity in high tax countries.
- On the national level, if one member country pursues an expansionary fiscal policy (cutting taxes and increasing expenditure), its economy may expand and inflation may accelerate This will probably cause its inflation rate to rise. Higher inflation rates within the euro

zone may mean higher interest rates for all and will not be popular.

Difficulties of these kinds have led some politicians to call for harmonisation of fiscal policies. This will entail agreements between national governments and therefore some loss of sovereignty.

Work in progress

Q **1** What would be the advantages for member countries of harmonised fiscal policies?

2 What arguments are likely to be used to resist harmonisation of fiscal policy?

3 To what extent are fiscal policies already being harmonised in the EU?

Module 4 Competitiveness

4.1 What shapes the contest?

This shows the links between business behaviour and the spectrum of competition. It demonstrates ways in which businesses work to increase their power through their products and place in the market. Business strategy, pricing and methods of ensuring that the product meets the needs of the market all contribute to the picture.

4.2 How competitive?

Both countries and businesses strive to be competitive. The strategies that are used to achieve an advantage over others are investigated. Sometimes there is temptation to overstep the mark which results in behaviour that has a negative impact on both people and economies. It is therefore important that these activities are watched and controlled when necessary.

What shapes the contest?

Enquiry 1   What makes a difference?

1 If it's all the same to you?

A chip is a chip–is a chip–is a chip!

If you decided to set up a factory to make laptop computers, you would need to buy chips to go inside them. The microchip was invented about 40 years ago and has grown steadily more powerful as well as smaller and smaller until it is the shape we know today.

It would make little difference who you bought them from as, for most purposes, all chips perform the same functions perfectly effectively. When first invented, chips were relatively expensive so the computers they went into were also expensive. Today, chips are manufactured on a large scale throughout the world and have therefore come

down in price. Competition between producers keeps prices low and puts buyers in the driving seat. As a result of these changes in the market place for chips, they have become what is known as a commodity product.

Your agenda

1 Why can computer producers buy chips from any supplier?
2 Why is price competition so intense?
3 Why does large-scale production reduce the price?
4 What might make the price of chips fall further?
5 What is a commodity product?
6 If you were a chip producer, what might you try to do in order to be able to charge more for your chips?

Perfect competition is one extreme of the spectrum of competition. Its characteristics were described in Module 2, (page 132). It demonstrates how the market would work if there were no impediments to change:

- if there are many buyers and sellers
- if buyers and sellers know all about each other
- if the products are all exactly the same – or homogeneous
- if new developments are common knowledge
- if firms can enter or leave the industry at any time.

This is, of course, impossible to achieve. The microchip comes close, but entering and leaving are not easy because chips have to be made in complex, expensive manufacturing units and therefore require a great deal of investment. This makes the entry and exit rule difficult to achieve.

The term 'commodity' usually refers to mineral ores or

agricultural output, but it has increasingly been used to describe other products and services which demonstrate similar attributes. They are often described as mature products.

Businesses work hard at product development, which they expect to lead to high profit levels. As a product becomes mature and other companies can produce something which is much the same, profit levels fall towards normal profit. This defeats the objectives as most businesses are seeking a greater return on their investment than this. Normal profit is the minimum required to keep a business in the industry and therefore may fall below the expectations of shareholders and other interested parties.

In order to keep ahead of the game, businesses will be constantly seeking strategies which enable them to make more than normal profit. Of course, if they succeed, chips will become less like a commodity product.

Point of view

What's the point of perfect competition?

BECKY: Why do we have to learn all this stuff? It doesn't happen in the real world. It's just a waste of time!

STEVE: D'you know – I'm just beginning to see that it does have a purpose. It's just like deciding which course I want to do next. I know what's perfect for me, but I can't find it anywhere, so I'm looking at what's on offer. Some places at least give me lots of choice so I can select the package I want. I'm certainly not going to do a course where all the choices are made for me.

BECKY: So what's the connection?

STEVE: Well – my perfect course is like perfect competition. It provides a yardstick to compare all the others. I know that I will never find it, but it makes a model to work from.

BECKY: I'll have to think about that. I wonder if there are any other examples?

Your agenda

Can you help Becky? What other examples are there of a perfect model which is used as a yardstick to compare others?

2 What's the difference?

Desperately seeking something different...

As the microchip has become a commodity product, the businesses that produce it are looking for ways to make their products distinctive. The usual gains are cost, speed or a combination of the two. Several companies are working on different strategies:

● IBM is working on several fronts. Copper connections are generally accepted as the next move. Their other two areas of research are more speculative.

● Intel, the market leader, has looked into copper connections but does not feel that they can be produced at a price that the market will bear. The benefits are insufficient. It is convinced that when copper eventually becomes standard, it will be able to put its own products in the place at the right moment.

● Everyone's chips are flat – except at Ball Semiconductor, where they are round! The 1mm ball is quick and cheap to produce. It takes only 5 days instead of 100 days for a flat chip. There are some problems, but if successful, this development could revolutionise the market.

Your agenda

1 Why are these companies working so hard to make a product which is different from everyone else's?

2 In a market where the product is almost a commodity, what does Intel mean when it claims that the benefits of copper connections are insufficient at the moment?

3 When the moment is right, what will happen to the market for chips with copper connections?

4 Ball Semiconductor has taken a completely different line from other developers. What do you think are the risks it is taking and rewards it may get?

A business which is selling a commodity product will probably be seeking ways of increasing its profit margin. One way to do this is to identify strategies for making your product a little different from everyone else's. This is known as **product differentiation**. In the case of the microchip, many companies are spending millions of dollars on that search because a breakthrough will lead to a major shift in the competitiveness stakes.

> ### Essentials
>
> **Product differentiation** is a competitive strategy used by companies. It involves making the product distinctive from its competitors.

There are various ways of doing this:

- *By providing a better service.* Customers increasingly require a higher quality of service when buying goods or services. Take-away restaurants, for example, quickly learnt that a delivery service would increase demand for their food. After all, if you want to stay at home and eat, why should you want to go to the shop to collect the meal? Insurance companies have also identified service as a source of competitive advantage. They now compete on the basis of the simplicity of signing up for such a complex purchase and how quickly and easily they will meet your claim.
- *By looking different.* A slight alteration to the appearance of a product can make all the difference. To achieve this, a company will survey the market and identify the segment at which their product is aimed. Market research and designers will come together to achieve the right image for potential purchasers. Sometimes the result may be radically different as in the case of the Ford Ka. It is just another small car, but it looks very different and fits a particular market segment. Sometimes the differences will be more subtle. A personal stereo has little scope for really radical design but the casing may be of a different colour or the facilities that it provides may vary in sophistication.
- *By branding.* A brand name gives a product a dinstictive characteristic which enhances opportunities for instant customer recognition. Branding has become one of the most significant promotional strategies in recent years.

All the above strategies are devised to give a

> ### Work in progress
>
>
>
> Q Take six products which are readily available and identify the ways in which each make is differentiated from its competitors.

product an edge in the market place. One bar of chocolate in its simplest form is much the same as another. It could almost be described as a commodity product. By creating a separate identity, the business aims to increase its share of the market or charge a higher price than its competitors.

3 What's in a name?

Channel 5: creating a brand

Channel 5 is the first terrestrial television channel to wear its own label on the screen. The C5 logo is there permanently in a box in the corner.

Why?
The whole drive of Channel 5 is to make its mark with its market. That market is the one which seeks out and recognises things by their label. A modern image therefore means a label. The objective for the 'C5' and the colour bars is to become as well known as the Nike swoosh or the cK of Calvin Klein. Brand identity is the marketer's dream. Product recognition is therefore an integral part of building a brand.

The image is 'modern mainstream' – not just modern like 'Red or Dead', not just mainstream like Marks & Spencer. C5 viewers would feel much more at home in Gap or a Virgin Megastore. On television they were identified as viewers of 'Absolutely Fabulous', 'Have I Got News For You?' and 'They Think It's All Over'. The mix of irreverence with acceptability defines the watching habits of the audience.

How did they do?
❝ Channel 5 has shown the importance of marketing in the multi-channel age of TV. Its colourful five-bar symbol emblazoned across posters, football stadium boards and in the TV sections of newspapers and magazines, is instantly – almost subliminally – recognisable.❞
(*Marketing Week*)

Your agenda
1 How did Channel 5 identify its target market?
2 Why is it important to identify the market in this way?
3 Why did *Marketing Week* judge the campaign to have been successful? What do you think?
4 What advantages does such brand recognition give?
5 What is a 'brand'?

Businesses today go to great lengths to promote product names in order to differentiate their product. This ranges across the spectrum of competition. Commodity products work hard to differentiate themselves in order to gain an edge on their competitors. Businesses that are subjected to little competition, such as the rail companies, also go to great lengths to create a brand image.

Companies compete to take over businesses which are in possession of popular trading names. Nestlé, for example, paid £2.5 billion for Rowntree because of the famous brand names such as Smarties, Kit-Kat and Rolo which it owned. This was more than five times their book value on the balance sheet. The prices paid for such companies clearly reflect the value associated with brands. Figure M4.1 shows the percentage of the purchase price that represented this 'goodwill' for four different take-overs.

Acquirer	Target	Goodwill (% of price paid)
GrandMet (now Diageo)	Pillsbury (Burger King etc.)	88
Nestlé	Rowntree	83
Cadbury Schweppes	Dr Pepper	67
United Biscuits	Verkade	66

Source: Greig Middleton and Co Ltd

Figure M4.1 The value of brands

Why?

- The development of a brand encourages customers to ask for a product by its name and therefore reinforces the consumption habit. Some have been so successful that the product, whoever makes it, is now called by the famous name. Hoover, Sellotape, Thermos and Biro are just a few examples. A strong brand builds customer loyalty and gives great competitive advantage.

- Successful brands command a premium price which generally results in higher profit margins.

- As demand rises, average costs may fall. Economies of scale appear in procurement, manufacturing, distribution and research and development. Even marketing becomes relatively cheaper if the response is strong.

- Once the image has been created it forms a powerful barrier to the entry of other firms. When a name has become part of the language, competitors find it very difficult to introduce a new product of their own. The investment required to create and maintain a new brand is substantial.

Building a brand is a long-term activity and cannot be treated lightly. To be successful, a business must be committed to the long term and see beyond the short term.

Branding alone, however, cannot achieve the effects that businesses seek. It is essential that customers feel that they are receiving the product and associated services that they expect if they are to continue to make their purchases.

4 Making a mark

On the fast track

Mars, for the first time in its history, is entering the £600 million chocolate box market. The market, already stuffed full of famous names – from Dairy Milk to Roses – is a major challenge. Celebrations, as the new product is called, is set for a speedy start.

Of the £2 million invested in the campaign, £500 000 has been spent on decking out the Celebrations Express. It will travel from city to city packed full of celebrities. The rest will be spent on adverts in magazines and on television.

Celebrations is a box of famous names. It contains twist-wrapped mini versions of Bounty, Snickers, Mars and Galaxy – all existing Mars products.

The company has set a tough challenge. Its aim is to put Celebrations in the confectionery top ten within two years and achieve sales of £75 million within three years. The plan is to put the new name into everyone's vocabulary. By Christmas, every adult will have seen the Celebrations logo at least 50 times.

Your agenda

1 Explain what Mars were trying to do through the design of the product and the launch strategy for Celebrations.

2 Why did Mars want to make its mark on the market quickly and maintain high sales?

3 Where did the market for boxes of chocolate fit on the spectrum of competition?

4 Why was it a challenge to try to enter this market?

5 What were the barriers to entry?

6 Why do you think Mars wanted to enter this market?

Advertising is the life blood of the media. We buy newspapers and magazines that are full of adverts. We watch television that is kept on air by selling commercial breaks. Companies will pay a fortune to buy space in the right place. A peak time slot, such as the middle of 'Coronation Street', can cost as much as £20 000. Why?

In a very competitive world, businesses need to ensure that they are in the public eye and disseminate their message. Advertising is therefore the lynch pin for such activities. In Module 2.2 the economic rationale behind advertising was explained Figure M4.2 sums this up.

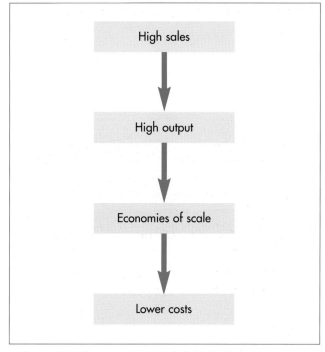

Figure M4.2 The economic rationale behind advertising

Any business must be convinced that high advertising expenditure will earn increased revenue – or prevent loss in bad times. The idea of elasticity can be used to work out the effect of an advertising campaign. The percentage change in sales divided by the percentage change in advertising expenditure will give a figure which measures the impact of the campaign.

A particular objective of advertising is to build brand image. Without a significant advertising budget, creating and maintaining that image is difficult. To change an image is even more costly as Pepsi found when it went blue (see page 129).

Work in progress

Q Look at some adverts in papers and magazines or on the television and identify their objectives.

Polish your Halo

Chocolate bars are often eaten with a touch of guilt. They may rot your teeth, make you fat or divert you from healthier eating. Halo is a small company in Wales which has overcome some of these problems by creating a healthy chocolate bar containing very few calories. Its problem was to get into the market. Shop counters brim over with famous names. Nestlé and Cadbury spend millions on creating an image for their products on television. How can the little firm compete?

Your agenda

1 Why can Halo not compete on this scale?

2 Halo has found a place on the shop counter. How and why do you think it might have achieved this?

3 Can you think of any products which would find it difficult to penetrate the market? Why?

Heavy advertising is a very good way of limiting competition. Wherever the product sits on the spectrum of competition, advertising can be used to prevent others from entering the market. It makes the market more imperfect. If sales need to be high to produce at a competitive price, it will be necessary to capture enough of the market, which probably means advertising. A new entrant will find this a great barrier as advertising costs will be high if expectations are to be met. For example the £2 million that Mars spent on Celebrations may well be out of reach for a smaller company.

Point of view

But Mum...

MUM: Those trainers look just the same. What's wrong with them?

JADE: But Mum ... everyone's got the other ones. I can't be seen in these. I'll just die!

MUM: But they are twice the price. I really can't afford them. It's the beginning of term and there is so much to buy this month.

JADE: Well, let's buy the books later. I'm sure that I can borrow Michelle's. She won't mind.

MUM: But you must have the books, your education is really important. It's hard enough to manage the books anyway when there are so many other things. They just have to come first. Will your old ones last a bit longer?

Your agenda

1 How do you think Jade responded to the final question?
2 Why was she so insistent about the chosen pair of trainers?
3 How did Jade's opportunity cost for trainers differ from her Mum's?
4 What strategies has the trainer manufacturer employed to attract customers?
5 How might the company measure success?
6 What ethical issues does this sort of advertising raise?

5 How competitive?

Out of the frying pan

Prestige is a name that has been on saucepans for generations. The business found itself in deep financial trouble partly because the pressure cooker, which was one of its key products, had fallen out of fashion. Changing technology meant that speedy cooking took place in a microwave instead.

The company was deep in debt and in search of a purchaser who could take over and help it out of its problems. No one was willing to do so because it would involve taking on the heavy debts as well as the responsibility for making the business efficient.

In the end, Meyer, the German saucepan manufacturer, bought the name but not the business. Pots and pans will continue to be for sale under the brand name, but the company left the market place.

Your agenda

1 Identify the causes of this company's ceasing production.
2 Are all businesses liable to encounter this type of difficulty?
3 Are large or small companies more likely to leave the market place? Why?
4 Why might it be difficult for a new business to set up in the pots and pans market?
5 Why was it easy for Pocket Pants and DX Communications, the companies in Module 1.1 (page 4), to set up in business?
6 Draw up a table showing all the factors that you can think of that facilitate entry into and exit from the market place.

The ins and outs of the market

Some businesses function in markets that are much more competitive than others. By looking carefully at what is going on in a market, it is possible to position it on the spectrum of competition. A useful way of assessing the degree of competition is to look at how easy it is for firms to enter and leave the market. This is known as **contestability**. A market which is easy to enter and exit is more contestable. A market which is difficult to enter and exit is less contestable.

Essentials

Contestability is a way of measuring how competitive a market is. A new business can set up in a contestable market because access is easy. It is also easy to leave because overheads are likely to be low. If a market is not contestable, it is very difficult for new businesses to enter and therefore will not be very competitive.

■ What makes entry easy?

⮝ Low start-up costs

One of the prerequisites for many people who want to set up a business is that it is cheap. A window-cleaning business needs little more than a bike, bucket and a ladder and insurance, so it is within the reach of most people with entrepreneurial plans.

⮝ Simple technology

The technology required for window cleaning is an extreme case. There are, however, many small businesses which make use of readily accessible technology which is available on every high street. The local copy shop, for example, will lease photocopiers from a supplier and make a profit on selling its services.

⮝ A personal dimension

Many businesses that are easy to set up depend on personal skills. The aromatherapist, who advertises in the local sports centre or corner shop, may be working from home. He or she will be selling skills in a way that also keeps costs down.

■ What makes entry difficult?

⮟ Economies of scale

No one would ever consider going into the oil production business from scratch. The investment in oil-drilling facilities combined with the cost of refining the raw material to provide a marketable product would defeat the boldest entrepreneur!

As most businesses start small, those which can only function effectively on a large scale are unlikely to be contestable.

⮟ Branding

A strong brand name makes it very difficult for others to compete. Any market in which there are a few strong brands will mean that a small company will have to work very hard to make its name heard.

⮟ High advertising budgets

Any market in which companies are fighting for market share through heavy advertising will be difficult to enter. The level of expenditure required to feature at key times on television or in conspicuous locations elsewhere, will be too great for most entrants.

■ Contestability

The degree of contestability may affect how firms behave. If there is a strong possibility that other firms will enter if they see great profits being made, existing businesses may think twice before trying to raise prices. Many products go through cycles which reflect the maturity of the market.

When double glazing and conservatories became popular, their markets were full of small companies trying to make a fast buck. It was cheap to enter the market because small contractors took deposits, then ordered the materials and finally installed the products. This lead to a positive cash flow and excellent profits for many. The ease of entry encouraged some very fly-by-night characters who were much more interested in profit than quality. When they had left a stream of disgruntled customers, they found it was also easy to exit the market, and the companies were closed down, often leaving a trail of debt.

This market has now settled down to a state in which the big players have a clear idea of the competition, the little players are often specialists and the customer is wary. As a result, despite the fact that the market is contestable, it is much more stable.

At the other end of the scale, markets which are not very contestable may still be competitive. The markets for products like soap powders and petrol are difficult to penetrate, but the companies within will fight hard for their share.

1 Tactics or strategy?

The Ball strategy

The first phase: research and development
From 1997 through 1999 Ball Semiconductor will develop and refine its basic manufacturing technology and equipment for ball-shaped microchips.

- Three years around-the-clock research and development focusing on:
  - new methods for material processing
  - new methods for integrated circuit fabrication
  - new plasma and laser beam technologies.

- Dual source, joint development arrangements to accelerate technology development. Goal for 1998 is to demonstrate basic integrated circuit functions on a ball.

- During the three years, Ball will also begin to define the commercial product and plan production.

- Initial production expected to begin in 2000.

Second phase: commercialisation
After the research and development phase, Ball plans commercial manufacturing of the Ball semiconductor with industry partners.

- Earliest commercial products are expected to be simple devices, primarily oscillators, discrete devices and small-scale integration semiconductor devices.

- Additional products will be developed once commercial feasibility of the Ball semiconductor has been proven.

- The company may also license Ball semiconductor technology to third parties.

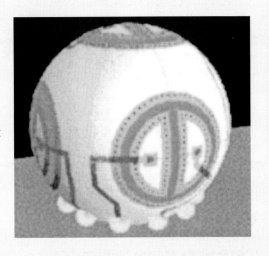

The roadmap

	1996	1997	1998	1999	2000
Company established	October				
Recruitment/construction		April			
Research and development		Start			
Pilot line			Start		
Trial production				Start	
Mass production/sales					Start

Source: Ball Semiconductor web site

Your agenda

Don't worry about the jargon – just consider what Ball Semiconductor is trying to achieve by setting out its strategy in this way.

1 Why does Ball want to penetrate the market for chips?

2 If silicon balls became standard technology, what effect would this have on the business? Why?

3 Where would the business be positioned on the spectrum of competition?

4 Why is it necessary to plan as carefully as this?

5 This is Ball's strategy. What sort of decisions need to be taken at different levels in the organisation to ensure that the strategy works?

6 If a competitor started to market a similar product, the company would have to take some tactical decisions. What is the difference between strategic and tactical decisions?

Any business which wants to stay ahead of the game must plan. Whatever the position on the spectrum of competition, the need to identify objectives and decide how they will be achieved is an essential part of any business's planning process. This planning happens on various time scales and influences either the whole firm or sections of it.

■ Strategic decisions

Strategic decisions are very important and will affect the future of the whole company and are therefore the responsibility of the board of directors. They require considerable expertise and knowledge and carry a high element of risk – the consequences of a wrong decision might be very damaging to the company. Such decisions will range from a long-term strategy to defeat competitors to restructuring and acquisitions.

■ Tactical decisions

Tactical decisions are made to meet shorter-term objectives. They will contribute to the strategic plan of the organisation, either as a stage in the process or by dealing with unforeseen opportunities or threats.

Cutting prices in response to competitors' actions may be a tactical decision. It would be made in the marketing and finance departments and with the objective of reflecting long-run strategy.

■ Operational decisions

Operational decisions are made at many levels within a business. Their objective is to keep the organisation running smoothly. Individually, each decision seems quite small, but cumulative errors will lead to larger scale problems. It is therefore important to ensure that decision-making at all levels is organised efficiently.
- Stock ordering, for example, has a short-term effect. A shortage of paper clips will have no long-run effect on the business and therefore such ordering decisions can be made by an administrative assistant. It is an operating decision concerned with the day-to-day running of the business.
- The preparation of quarterly figures required by head office has longer term effects. If a department's costs seem too high, it will be asked

to account for the extra expenditure. Such activities are periodic – they happen on a regular basis. They are concerned with the control of a business – head office controlling the expenditure of a department. The sums of money and consequences of a wrong decision are greater at this level, so such decisions tend to be made by the management of a particular department.

In the end, the way in which these decisions are made reflects the unique way in which a company is run. One company will make similar decisions but in an entirely different way to another. Both are equally valid, but will depend on the culture and ethos of each company.

Point of view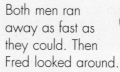

Strategic speed

Fred and Bill were walking in the woods when, suddenly, a bear leaped out from behind a tree and started to chase them.

Both men ran away as fast as they could. Then Fred looked around. Bill was crouched on the ground, putting on a pair of running shoes.

'For heavens sake, Bill, what do you think you're doing,' said Fred. 'You don't think that those shoes will help you to run faster than that bear, do you?'

'No,' said Bill, 'but they'll help me run faster than you.'

Your Agenda

Bill had a rather urgent problem to deal with. Was he thinking strategically or tactically? Explain why.

2 What's at the core?

Whither Mitsubishi?

Once a diamond in the Japanese crown, Mitsubishi has lost its sparkle. Like many of Japan's other top companies, it has a long history of producing a vast range of goods.

The Mitsubishi group contains more than 28 companies which produce almost everything. It includes oil, electricals, beer, capital goods, department stores, a bank and many others. The company's tradition is that companies within the group buy from each other and the bank lends them cheap money when they need it.

This model formed an excellent foundation for Mitsubishi's sustained growth to the position of Japan's most powerful industrial group.

It created strong relationships between suppliers and purchasers. Cheap credit was always available for development in a context in which the pressure to make the most of it was not top of the list.

In a context where growth and power were the focus of attention, the formula was most effective. It may not be so effective today.

The management strategies of the past still reign supreme. The chairman of MHI, the biggest member of the group, was heard to say that he did not consider maximising profit to be appropriate for manufacturing industry.

Once a Mitsubishi business is in place, it stays. Some have dabbled in trendy areas in which they have little expertise. Kirin, which produced beer among other things, moved into biotechnology! MHI makes every capital product that you can think of and has become renowned for being second best. Easy access to capital facilitates development but does not always lead to wise decision-making.

Your agenda

1 What features of the Mitsubishi group have helped it to grow into the mammoth enterprise that it is today?

2 How have these features contributed to growth?

3 Why might they be inappropriate for today?

4 What sort of features might help Mitsubishi to regain its sparkle?

Core competencies

Businesses develop a special place in a market because they have a unique attribute that distinguishes them from the competition. It may be to do with the internal organisation, the way it deals with customers or its products. Often, it is the combination of different **core competences** that really creates the competitive advantage. It is rarely simply a matter of different resources because this would be easy to imitate. It is usually a mix of appropriate resources and the way in which the business works to organise them.

Work in progress

Q 1 What are the core competences of the local supermarket compared with the corner shop?

2 Why do the differences help both to survive?

3 If it is not easy to tell, what do you think that they should be?

4 Is the focus on these competences helping them to move forward or are they in need of review?

Once a business has identified its core competences, it must build a strategy which makes the most of them. Figure M4.3 comes from *Exploring Corporate Strategy* and sums up the terminology and its meaning most effectively.

Essentials

Core competences are the resources, processes or skills which distinguish a business from others in the market and therefore provide competitive advantage.

Term	Definition	A personal example
Mission	Overriding purpose in line with the values or expectations of stakeholders	Be healthy and fit
Vision or strategic intent	Desired future state: the aspirations of the organisation	To run the London Marathon
Goal	General statement of aim or purpose	Lose weight and strengthen muscles
Objective	Quantification (if possible) or more precise statement of the goal	Lose 4.5 Kg by 1 September and run London Marathon next year
Core competences	Resources, processes or skills which provide 'competitive advantage'	Proximity to a fitness centre, supportive family and friends and past experience of successful diet
Strategies	Long-term direction	Associate with a collaborative network (for example join running club), exercise regularly, compete in marathons locally, stick to appropriate diet
Strategic architecture	Combination of resources, processes and competences to put strategy into effect	Specific exercise and diet regime, appropriate training facilities, etc.
Control	The monitoring of action steps to: • assess effectiveness of strategies and actions • modify strategies and/or actions as necessary	Monitor weight, miles run and measure times: if satisfactory progress, do nothing; if not, consider other strategies and actions

Figure M4.3 The vocabulary of strategy

Source: *Exploring Corporate Strategy*, G. Johnson and K. Scholes, Prentice Hall, 1997

Work in progress

Q Use Figure M4.3 to develop your own personal example – getting good A-levels perhaps!

3 How capable?

Will the sparks fly?

The changes being felt at Baker Street, Marks & Spencer's head office, go far deeper than the latest round of job cuts may signify. Having pruned his team of executive directors, Peter Salsbury, the new chief executive, has told those who remain that they are to review the business as if they had just bought it.

They are taking a fresh look at M&S and finding drastic flaws. That's the good news. The bad news is that, having been brave enough to admit that problems go far beyond a bad season's range, they must also know that the solutions will not appear as quickly as a colourful rack of spring merchandise – although that can take a dreadfully long time at M&S.

Peter Salsbury is keen to be seen as the spirit of change. For someone who has held an important position, he seems to have awoken rather late to its shortcomings. The decision to oust Sir Richard Greenbury from the chief executive's chair swiftly showed that all was not well.

The problems go far beyond an outdated, autocratic management style. In a new spirit of openness, M&S will admit that it was slipping up on retail basics. Sizings, for instance, had stopped being properly standardised, so that a size 12 in one line was not necessarily the same as a size 12 in another. A minor discrepancy like this can create some majorly upset customers. Such horrors persisted because buying and selling existed as almost unrelated functions within M&S.

Source: adapted from *The Times*, London, 30 March 1999. © Times Newspapers Limited

Your agenda

1 In 1999 Marks & Spencer found itself in deep trouble. The article gives some clues to the internal problems facing the company. Using this and anything that you know or can find out about the company and its products, draw up a chart showing:
   a its strengths and weaknesses,
   b the opportunities and threats which face the business.

2 Does your analysis suggest a future direction for Marks & Spencer?

SWOT analysis

A business may have identified its core competences and strategies, but it needs to draw them together in the context of the wider environment. **SWOT analysis** is an effective technique for looking at the whole picture. It looks inside the business by surveying its *strengths* and *weaknesses*. *Opportunities* and *threats* paint a picture of the world in which the business is working.

Figure M4.4 SWOT: a formula for the future

■ The internal factors

- Strengths: positive factors of a business when compared with its competitors

- Weaknesses: negative factors of a business when compared with its competitors

■ The external factors

- Opportunities: factors in the market place which can be developed for the benefit of the business

- Threats: factors in the market place which might be a threat to the business

The development of a SWOT analysis takes both care and creativity. People who have worked in a business for a long time may not be able to see the wood for the trees! This happens simply because they have worked in a particular way for a long time and may be unable to see the flaws. Mitsubishi had probably reached this state.

Because of this, consultants may be brought in to carry out a SWOT analysis. They will carry out their research and then look for dynamic ways to interpret the information in order to be of greatest help to the business.

Essentials

SWOT analysis involves the assessment of a product or an organisation in terms of its strengths, weaknesses, opportunities and threats. Strengths and weaknesses reflect the current position, while opportunities and threats may be important in the future.

What next?

Having carried out a SWOT analysis, the business can move forward and make decisions about where it should be going. The information gleaned from this activity must be combined with the business's knowledge of its core competencies as well as the **critical success factors** which are often common to any company in a particular sector of industry. In the fashion industry, for example, getting products into the shops at the right moment and increasing supply rapidly in lines which prove to be successful is vital to the success of any business.

The outcome should be a firm plan or strategy which underpins all the actions of the business. It will be a complex document because it combines the contribution of all departments in the process of moving forward.

The strategy must not be treated as inflexible because all businesses work in a dynamic environment and businesses must expect to change direction as the market changes. The clever part of strategic planning is the ability to forecast these changes accurately. The company's portfolio of products can be adjusted in the light of this work.

Essentials

Critical success factors are activities which a business must get right if it is to succeed.

Work in progress

Q Carry out a SWOT analysis on your school or college.

Use it to develop a strategic plan. You will need to carry out some research into funding and future planning in post-16 education policy. The *Times Educational Supplement* web site might be useful (http://www.tes.co.uk).

A healthy mix

Having identified niches and developed segments, a business which is seeking a secure, powerful position in the market must look at its whole product portfolio. In this, it will need a range of products which are developing their position and others which have less uncertainty about the rewards that they will bring in.

The **Boston Matrix** is a strategy which was developed to identify where products sit in a company's portfolio.

Market share

	High	Low
High	Stars	Question marks
Low	Cash cows	Dogs

Market growth

Figure M4.5 The Boston Matrix

The four quarters of the matrix, shown in Figure M4.5, have very distinctive characteristics which all make their own contribution to the company's profits:

- *Question marks*. Almost all products start in this box. New products have an uncertain future and may become stars or dogs. They have a small market share but high growth. To become stars, they will need a great deal of investment. Even with such support, they might become dogs. They are sometimes called Problem Children!

- *Stars*. These have large market shares and high growth. They produce high cash returns but are expensive to maintain because they require a high level of investment. Net returns may be low, but they hold promise for the future.

- *Cash cows*. These are usually old stars. The product has matured and the market share stabilised at a high level. They require little investment and produce high returns so they can be 'milked' to supply finance for the development of new products.

- *Dogs*. Some question marks turn into dogs. They have low market share and little or no growth. They are no-hopers and investment should not be wasted on them. Usually, a business will delete them from the product range but they might have a niche of their own which means that they can continue to contribute to profits at no cost to the company.

Essentials

The **Boston Matrix** is a method of analysing a company's products in terms of their market share and their growth potential.

The four quarters of the Boston Matrix are linked to the phases of the product life cycle. The combination of the matrix and an analysis of the product life cycle of each of its constituent parts builds a picture of the future prospects for the business. If there are more dogs than stars, the future of the business might be insecure. However, the Boston Matrix is rather more sophisticated than product life cycle theory. The latter suggests that declining brands have little future, whereas the Boston Matrix might reveal them as cash cows which can contribute to the success of the product range as a whole.

The matrix can be used by a company to map its product range in order to identify strengths and weaknesses. From this information, a business can look ahead and plan its future strategy. Every company needs products at different stages of development in order to be secure in the future.

As businesses seek ways of developing market power, they will be looking for products which give them a strong position in various markets. They will look for ways of making their products more distinctive in order to reduce competition and make demand more inelastic. An estimate of the price elasticity of demand is always useful for a business because it helps it to predict the effects of a change in price.

Work in progress

Q Identify the likely position on the product life cycle of each of the four quarters of the Boston Matrix. Explain why a spread of products is important to a business.

Building a portfolio

Having researched the market and looked carefully at the outcomes of the SWOT analysis, the company can use the Boston Matrix to ensure that it has a mix of products that will carry it forward.

Most firms have a range of products in the market at any one time: this is called a **product portfolio**. An important aspect of strategic planning is to ensure a balanced portfolio where the firm's products are reasonably spread across the stages of the product life cycle as shown in Figure M4.6.

Essentials

A **product portfolio** is the range of a firm's products within the market.

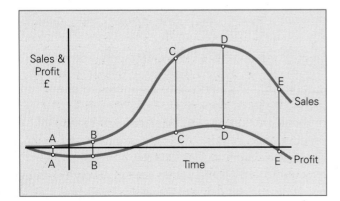

Figure M4.6 Product life cycle and product portfolio

This is a highly simplified model, but it illustrates an important principle. Products C and D are generating profits that can support the costs of developing Product A, introducing Product B and deleting Product E. Balance within a portfolio means that there are sufficient cash cows to fund the necessary investment in stars and question marks. The goal is to ensure that stars mature into large and powerful cash cows, while question marks with promise grow into stars. The remaining question marks and the dogs without profit potential should all be deleted as soon as possible. Meanwhile, the portfolio is *dynamic* due to competitive and other external pressures and to the underlying profile of the product life cycle. Without any action by the firm, the position of products will tend to drift 'downwards' in the matrix, with stars becoming cash cows and problem children becoming dogs. It is most important that a firm has a proactive strategy for the development of its product portfolio.

The Boston Matrix is a useful model, but it has certain limitations. It can be very difficult to define 'high' and 'low' in placing products on the matrix. Market share and market growth are important, but they are not the only criteria in planning a portfolio and do not always define profitability. It is also easy to overlook internal human resistance to scrapping particular product groups or to transferring the profits of one group to support the development of another. Such decisions affect the jobs, ambitions and other vital interests of real people.

Work in progress

Declining ROCE prompts a garden-tools producer to analyse its product portfolio. Its six main product ranges are classified as follows:

Garden shears – cash cow
Patio furniture – question mark
Spades/forks – dog
Saws and pruners – dog
Barbecues – question mark
Rakes, hoes, etc. – dog

Q 1 What are the dangers of 'milking' the cash cow?

2 What strategy might the firm adopt towards its question marks?

3 Suggest *two* different lines of action for dealing with the three dogs. Indicate the potential advantages in each approach.

4 What about the people?

Keeping everyone on board

Do you remember Jim Anderson from DeVilbiss (Module 1, page 20)? He reorganised the paint spray business to give it competitive advantage to keep it ahead of the game. His plans were so effective that the firm produced 20 per cent more with half the staff. When big changes like this take place it is important to keep the staff on side or effort can be wasted.

I phoned Jim to find out how the company went about it.

A: Good morning Jim. Thanks very much for the help you gave me last time I phoned. The information you gave me has thrown up some further questions. Have you got a moment to help me a bit further?

JIM: Yes certainly. Go ahead.

A: When you made all the changes at DeVilbiss, you must have had to work hard at taking people with you and at helping them to be effective in the new environment. I'm wondering how you did it.

JIM: I believe in simplification and focus to create an environment in which people can do a good job. This enables people to empower themselves because they see that they are in control. The cells we created were all small businesses within the firm. Everyone knew their objectives, the systems we set up were simple and people could use their initiative to succeed. The staff developed pride and ownership because we gave them the authority to go with it.

A: So Maslow really works!

JIM: This strategy has worked everywhere I have been. As you know, the parent company IWG has now put me to work at other businesses in the group, so it must be effective.

A: How do you reward the staff?

JIM: I'm much more of a Hertzberg man here! You must reward people fairly but there is no need for it to be excessive. We don't have one flat rate. Rewards are based on the grade which results from individual appraisals. This grade will then determine the personal supplement which tops up the basic pay. This is the tricky bit because you have to be careful to identify the things the firm wants.

A: What sort of things do you have in mind?

JIM: At DeVilbiss we had a list of eight – such as flexibility, time keeping, absence and attitude. I'll get someone to fax you the full list.

A: Did you use any corporate strategies to reward people?

JIM: Oh yes. We celebrate success – but I believe in little and often. We might give them free soft drinks on the factory floor or take a cell out to dinner. We wouldn't go to the most expensive restaurant, but we would look for somewhere congenial. It's important to make people feel good about success.

A: Well, thanks very much Jim. It was good of you to give up your time to help me. I am looking forward to receiving the fax.

JIM: Glad to help. Ring me again if I can be of further assistance.

Managing people

Becoming increasingly competitive means changing. If a business is to change successfully, the staff must be working in harmony with the company. If they are left in the dark and feel that they are not involved, change is likely to fail. Since it is people above all who add value and determine efficiency, the management of expansion in human terms is a crucial priority. Ideas on motivation confirm this.

Change can lead to increased opportunities and, as in the case of DeVilbiss, gives people more responsibility. Potential career pathways become longer and more diverse, long-term job security may improve and levels of pay and other rewards tend to rise. Set against these positive factors are many dangers:

■ Small firms often lack any organisation chart to ensure coherence in their management. Larger firms may have a nominal chart but fail to keep it updated or ignore its implications. As a result, change may make spans of control unworkably large and confuse lines of responsibility. Individuals may find their jobs growing in all directions yet lack the resources, expertise or assistance that are necessary to cope. Some employees may dislike the way in which their job has changed or lack the appropriate skills to meet its new demands. The provision of training is often haphazard in times of rapid change – yet this is often when it is needed most.

■ Communication, too, can become a problem. Smaller firms are often friendly places to work where everyone knows each other and staff feel close to the management. As the firm grows the gaps between people inevitably widen and the managers may become remote from ordinary staff. Formal channels of communication may be late in evolving and then prove inadequate to their task. Growth in scale can also have a serious effect on motivation. Both management and workforce may feel a reduced sense of urgency in their work combined with a perception that waste and inefficiency are affordable. Rules and systems can come to seem more important than the purpose they were designed to serve. Individual staff and whole departments may pursue trivial disputes between one another while performance of the real job suffers.

For these reasons, inefficiency and frustration can be the result of change. The growth of a firm with a good product and strong markets may easily be halted or even reversed by failures of this type. Much depends on the quality of senior management. Sometimes the inspired entrepreneur grows with the size and challenge of his or her job. In other cases, the founder of the firm may prove unequal to the demands of change and become a liability to his or her own firm. The success of strategies for change in large firms often depends on key appointments to the senior management. Sometimes one charismatic, dynamic leader can be worth any number of merely competent middle managers.

Whatever happens, the company must plan. It needs to consider the impact of change on people and look for strategies to develop commitment. The culture of the company will affect the willingness of people to change. As any company must face the prospects of adapting to a dynamic market, managers must look carefully at ways in which people can be encouraged to be flexible.

Rewards are always important. If people are taking on greater responsibility, they will seek extra reward. It is important that the company looks at the relationships between output and reward if change is to be successful.

An appraisal system can help as it allows a business to assess the relationship between the contribution of individuals and the needs of the business. Rewards must be devised in such a way that they encourage activity which enhances the company's success in meeting its objectives. Figure M4.7 shows the criteria that were used for rewarding people at DeVilbiss. The achievement that the company valued shows clearly. It was measured on a scale of one to four.

Attendance	**Attendance** is faithfulness in coming to work daily
Timekeeping	**Timekeeping** is adherence to set working hours
Job suitability	**Dependability** is the ability to do a required job well, with minimum supervision
	Knowledge is the information an individual must know for satisfactory job performance
Co-operation and attitude	**Commitment** is the amount of personal responsibility an individual feels
	Courtesy is a sociable and thoughtful attitude to customers, fellow employees and those supervised
	Stability is the ability to withstand pressure and remain calm in crisis situations
Flexibility/ versatility	**Experience** is relevant experience to the cell and company, products, processes and systems.
	Initiative is the ability to meet changing conditions and to solve novel or problem situations without seeking help
	Creativity is the talent for having new ideas, suggesting better ways of doing things and being imaginative
Skill	**Skill** is the practised ability to do a job in the quickest and most effective way
	Accuracy is the correctness of work done
Work rate	**Self-motivation** is the desire to attain goals and achieve ambitions
	Quantity is the amount of work an individual does in comparison to others in group
	Alertness and energy is the ability to work consistently and remain alert even when tired

Source: Employee assessment form, DeVilbiss

Figure M4.7 Appraisal at DeVilbiss

Work in progress

Q 1 Why can small firms often seize business opportunities that large firms ignore or miss?

2 Managing a firm through functional departments – marketing, production, finances, etc. – seems logical. What drawbacks can you see arising from this approach during a period of rapid change?

3 Why is cell production an increasingly popular way of organising a business?

4 Why may the quality of a firm's internal communications be so important in managing change?

Effective leadership requires a proactive approach to change. There is a constant searching for growth opportunities and a sense of excitement – even celebration – at enacting the changes that these imply. Aims and objectives are readily refocused. The corporate culture is innovative, flexible and vitalised. Staff are made to feel that they matter while commitment to a common purpose is a powerful agent in converting ideas to reality.

Being responsible

The pattern at DeVilbiss is to be found throughout the world. Many businesses have developed much flatter pyramids with larger spans of control and fewer levels in the hierarchy. This process is called de-layering. It usually means that one or more management grades has been removed. Communication between senior management and the people who are actually running the business is then much closer. (This was covered in Module 2.1, page 92.)

De-layering can often save on administrative costs. Employees are likely to be given more responsibility and they may feel more motivated as a result. It may mean that the important decisions are being taken by the people who actually have to carry them out. They should, then, be better informed decisions, which reflect the realities of the business.

The down side of de-layering is that employees may feel stressed and overworked. There may be a sense that the company is looking for an excuse to make some people redundant.

Decentralisation?

When most decisions are made at or close to the 'centre' of an organisation (for example. head office or the largest branch), the organisation is said to be **centralised**. If major decisions are taken away from its centre, then the organisation is **decentralised**. Some firms will centralise certain key functions such as strategic planning and accounts while choosing to decentralise other areas of decision-making such as purchasing and personnel. Although firms are often geographically centralised with major decisions taken at corporate head office, others may be organisationally centralised, with decision-making confined to a small group of senior management. If a centralised firm chooses to push significant areas of decision-making towards its branches or its junior or middle management, then it is following a policy of decentralisation.

Essentials

Centralised decision-taking implies that all decisions are taken at head office.

Essentials

Decentralised decision-taking is carried out at the point where the decision is to be put into effect.

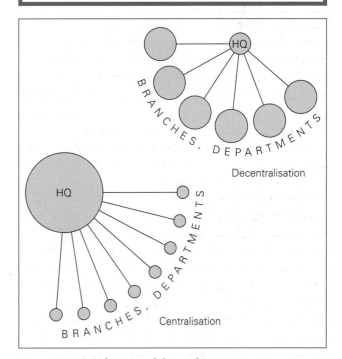

Figure M4.8 Centralisation and decentralisation

There is no perfect degree of decentralisation for optimum efficiency. Much depends on the firm, its business and its human resources. Ideally, centralisation should enable the firm to create the most efficient pattern of resource allocation. Policies can be implemented in a consistent way across the organisation and some resources can be shared. But over-centralisation may drain the firm of initiative and creativity as staff come to feel that their only role is to carry out orders from head office. It may also rob the enterprise of its ability to meet detailed customer preferences and to respond quickly to the stimulus of change and opportunity. For exactly these reasons many firms have been undergoing quite radical decentralisation. Computer manufacturer IBM is one such example:

❛ *Now the market is driving the business, customer satisfaction is all. This means putting decision-making and accountability within IBM at the best level of responsibility - that is, closest to the customer. This is known as empowerment: giving employees the authority, responsibility and power to deliver their best results to the customer.*❜ (IBM report, 1992)

Decentralisation usually goes hand in hand with a culture which encourages **delegation**. This means allowing decisions to be made at a lower level. It entails giving local managers the authority to make certain specific decisions for themselves on the basis of the conditions they themselves face.

Delegation works well when the conditions are appropriate. There must be:

- trust – so that manager and employee feel sure of each other
- good communication – so that there is a full mutual understanding of the objectives of the business
- relinquishing of some control by senior management.

Empowerment goes a stage beyond delegation. The employee is empowered to decide how things will be done. Empowerment applies to a wide range of decisions, giving people a large degree of control over their working situation. This approach fits well with the ideas of cell production and with decentralisation. Some businesses have talked a lot about empowerment but really changed very little. For others, it has become an important part of the culture.

Essentials

Delegation means passing responsibility down the hierarchy so that decisions are, as far as possible, taken by those who have to carry them out.

Essentials

Empowerment involves giving subordinates power over their working lives. It means giving employees some discretion as to how they carry out their tasks.

As the above extract from the IBM report makes clear, these approaches can foster improved market orientation and a flexible response to changes in market demand. They can also motivate staff, making them feel fully involved and therefore more enthusiastic.

Work in progress

Providing good refreshments for jaded rail travellers is not always easy. Quicksnack has a range of products which all branches sell in their outlets on station platforms. On top of that, managers decide what extra products they want to make available. This allows them to study their own local market and provide the items which people particularly want. Customers are invited to comment on their experience.

Q Explain the above approach in terms of delegation and empowerment. What are the conditions needed to make this approach work well?

Decentralisation is closely related to the flatter, looser hierarchies emerging through de-layering. A more highly qualified, highly motivated staff are given more trust to make decisions and learn to accept more responsibility. Information technology is important in assisting the process as communications become both faster and more sensitive, while the information stored at Head Office can easily be transmitted to lower levels of management.

Enquiry 3   Is the price right?

1 Has pricing got a purpose?

McBungle

McDonald's celebrated its 25th birthday in style. It offered Big Macs at two for the price of one, an offer which the public found hard to refuse. In fact, they noshed their way through four million Big Macs in 48 hours! Predictions had suggested that they would sell one million a day for the first two days of the promotion, a figure that was already double normal sales.

Chaos ensued. Restaurants closed through lack of stock, others gave free substitutes and therefore ran short in unexpected areas. Both head office and newspapers were besieged by indignant customers. Sales at Burger King doubled.

Your agenda

1 McDonald's was short of one vital piece of information. What was it?

2 How would it have helped the company not to make such an enormous mistake?

3 In what ways are mistakes like this harmful to a business?

4 How can they be avoided?

Pricing is a very sensitive issue. If the price is set too high, people just will not buy. If it is set too low, demand may exceed supply, as happened to McDonald's. Equally, people may even think that a cheap product cannot be up to standard and look elsewhere.

Getting the price right is therefore not always easy. There are a variety of strategies which can be used to match the product with the appropriate price in the market place. The chosen strategy will inevitably vary according to the:

- nature of the product
- nature of the market
- objectives of the business.

The following categories show how different strategies work in these different circumstances.

■ Demand-based pricing

A star price

The new Astra is a star in the small car firmament. It has all the features a driver might want. Vauxhall has described it as 'a drive to rival anything in the market'.

As a new product, it has to fight for its place in the market. Its price has therefore been set to be super-competitive.

Your agenda

1 What is the market like for cars in the Astra category?

2 What is a super-competitive price?

3 Why was it important for Vauxhall to set a super-competitive price?

When a demand-based pricing strategy is used, decision-takers are considering the nature of the market they face, and using the strength of consumer demand as the main determinant of the decision, rather than costs of production. This means that once a price has been decided, other decisions, involving costs, follow on. The question is not 'How can we cover our costs?', but 'If we can get this price for the product, can we produce it at a cost which allows us to reach our profit target?'

Perceived value pricing involves finding out from potential customers what they would be prepared to pay for a particular product or product concept.

The producers of the Astra worked on this basis. They know that getting the price right is important, but they do have some games that they can play. In selling cars, there are certain strategies that can be used to make the most of the market. The car with the 'super-competitive' price is the bottom of the range. To have all the safety features such as driver and passenger airbags and ABS brakes adds £800 to the price. In this way, they can segment the market and match the product to the price that people are prepared to pay.

Demand-based pricing can be used to effect to deal with the uncertainties of the business cycle. It enables businesses to set a price which works in different parts of the cycle. In a period when sales are falling, a price increase will make matters worse. When the economy recovers it may be possible to raise prices without any loss in sales. Rising incomes may make consumers less liable to 'shop around'.

The motor industry is well known for using such strategies. Individual showrooms will be prepared to discount the list price in order to attract custom during a recession, but when the economy is growing, there is no need to do so. Demand-based pricing strategies show that the market is competitive and demonstrate the way in which demand and supply interact.

■ Skimming

Price skimming entails charging a relatively high price for a product. It may mean lower total sales but higher margins. Designer label companies, for example, sell products at prices which exclude many customers because they have taken the decision to create a product with a particular image. Each company is using the price inelasticity of demand for its brand to increase the level of super-normal profit that can be made. In each case the label is sufficient to differentiate the product.

The product life cycle may dictate pricing strategies. For a product in the early stages of its life cycle it may be that skimming is appropriate. This entails charging a relatively high price because the market will, at this stage, be fairly small, but demand may also be relatively inelastic. A high price will not

£6.00

£21.99

Your agenda

1 Do you think that the production costs of the two items are widely different?

2 Why do you think the prices vary?

3 What would happen if a High Street shop charged prices like a designer label company or vice versa?

4 What does this tell you about the pricing strategies of the companies?

deter the buyers, who will perhaps perceive the product as having high status or interest because of its newness. This will allow the company to earn a quick return on its investment.

The following story shows how it works.

Venue: The hi-fi store, CD player section

AHMED: That's just what I want! That one over there with the stainless steel casing!

LIZ: But have you seen the price? It's twice as much as this one.

AHMED: That doesn't matter. It's got to look good.

LIZ: Well, I'll have to make do with this model. It's got all the right features, and I don't think that one is worth the extra. I wouldn't buy this if it were any more expensive. I'd have to put up with my old tape player.

SALES PERSON: Can I help you?

AHMED: Oh yes, I want one of these. Can you see if it is in stock, please?

SALES PERSON: You're in luck there! We've just heard from head office that model is on special offer, so it's £20 cheaper than marked.

LIZ: You lucky thing! I don't suppose mine is?

SALES PERSON: No, sorry. That's at rock bottom price already. I'll just go and check the stockroom.

Your agenda

1 Describe the reaction of the two friends to the prices they were offered.

2 Which one was only prepared to pay the equilibrium price?

3 Explain why he or she was not prepared to pay more.

4 Why was the other friend prepared to pay more?

5 How did the value he or she put on the CD player compare with the price he or she paid?

Ahmed has shown that he is prepared to pay more than the going rate for the CD player of his choice. Any demand and supply schedule shows that some people are unable to buy a product because they are unwilling to pay the market price. Others, however, are prepared to pay more. The difference between the market price and someone's top offer is known as the **consumer surplus**.

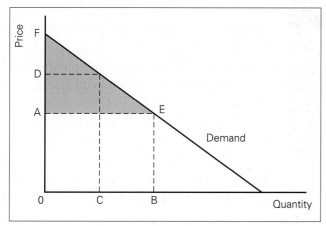

Essentials

Consumer surplus is the amount people are willing to pay less the price they actually do pay.

It works like this. In Figure M4.9, the equilibrium price and quantity are A and B respectively. However, some people would have been prepared to pay a higher price. (The demand curve indicates their willingness to pay for each quantity.) They would have demanded quantity C at price D. Those people are actually getting quantity C of the product for price A, so they are getting satisfaction at a price less than they were actually prepared to pay. This is their consumer surplus. The total of all consumer surplus is shown on the diagram by the shaded triangle EFA.

Figure M4.9 Consumer surplus

■ Penetration pricing

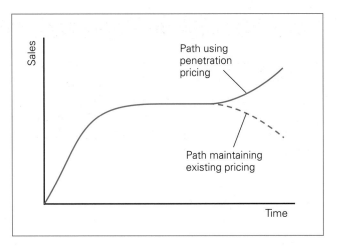

Figure M4.10a Penetration pricing for an existing product

The objective of penetration pricing is to persuade people to buy your product rather than someone else's. In order to do this, the price is set below the competition or below the price that people know that they will have to pay later.

The introductory special offer allows the new product to become established in the market. Simply persuading people to try something new can be quite a challenge and pricing is very often used as a strategy to achieve this end.

If there has been a great deal of investment in a new enterprise, it may be important for the business to recoup this quickly. Although business advice might be to take a skimming approach in this situation, it may be a luxury that a new business cannot afford.

Later on in the product life cycle penetration pricing may be employed to bring about a substantial increase in market share. The business may want to take an aggressive view of the market, and assuming that price elasticity of demand is high, seek both to expand the market and take an increasing share of it. An added advantage might be to reap economies of scale through increased sales. If costs fall, prices can be cut at the same time as profits increase. This strategy may also drive competitors out of the market if they are unable to match the new low prices (Figure M4.10a).

■ Cost-based pricing

Some businesses will decide their prices purely on the basis of production costs: this is known as cost-based or cost-plus pricing. They will work out the direct cost of producing the actual product and then add a percentage mark-up to cover overheads and profit. For example, if the cost is £40, 25 per cent might be added for gross profit, giving a price of £50. This would cover the overheads, and anything remaining would be net profit. This method of pricing can cause problems because the business may not earn enough revenue to cover all the overheads. It depends whether estimates of both sales and overheads are reasonably accurate. A fall in sales may make it impossible to cover overheads, let alone provide a margin for profit.

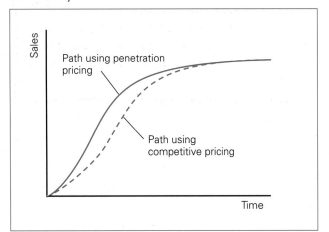

Figure M4.10 Penetration pricing for a new product

2 Playing the pricing game

Some pricing strategies allow businesses to make the most of market behaviour in either the short term or the long term. Customers may have a variety of reasons for their purchasing patterns and if these can be put to use by the business, it may be possible to optimise profits.

■ Price discrimination

Fare's fair?

Time of departure from London	Price
7.05	£109
7.50	£109
8.20	£109
9.10	£51.50
10.10	£51.50
11.10	£51.50
12.10	£51.50
13.10	£51.50
14.10	£51.50
15.10	£61.10
16.10	£61.50
17.02	£61.50
17.33	£61.50
17.50	£61.50
18.03	£61.50
18.50	£51.50
19.30	£51.30
20.30	£51.30
21.30	£51.30

Apex tickets, which are available on some trains, cost £30 and must be booked seven days in advance.

Super-advance tickets, which are also available on some trains, can be booked up to 2 pm on the day before travel and cost £40.

Figure M4.11 Return train fares from London to Leeds

Your agenda

1 How do the fares vary?

2 Why is it possible to vary fares in this way?

3 Why do the train operators want to charge varying prices?

4 Why can the train operators successfully maintain this differential?

If a business looks carefully at its market, it may discover opportunities to increase its profit margin by identifying distinctive features of its market segments. Holiday companies charge different amounts according to when you want to go away. The most expensive times are during the school holidays because families with children have little choice. Their demand is therefore inelastic so they can be charged a higher price. The rest of the year is cheaper because people have more flexibility and demand will probably be lower, so there is more competition between companies.

Price discrimination is a variant of demand-based pricing, based on an assessment of variations in price elasticity of demand in different segments of the market. By charging different prices to different customers, it is possible to increase the company's revenue. The train operators do this, exploiting the fact that commuters have a much lower price elasticity of demand than do, say, leisure travellers.

Price discrimination only works if the business is able to divide its market into segments, and buyers required to pay the higher price can be prevented from buying at a cheaper price. The train operators can do this by charging according to the time of day. Elsewhere, there may be different prices for buying in bulk, or prices may vary between the home and export market, or mail order prices may differ from the price charged by retailers.

Essentials

Price discrimination takes place in markets that can be separated into clear segments with different elasticities. A higher price can be charged when demand is more inelastic enabling a business to increase its revenue.

■ Predatory Pricing

Only 30p!

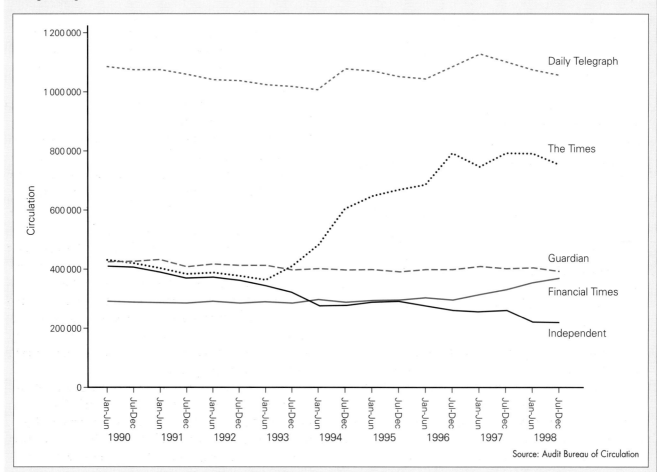

Figure M4.12 National daily quality newspaper circulation, 1990 –98

The Times, after 200 years of being the country's foremost broadsheet, was in deep trouble. Circulation had tumbled to a level that seemed unsustainable, and the prospect of closure was threatening.

In 1993, *The Times* took the plunge and slashed its price to a mere 30p. Circulation started to rise and the other newspapers complained vociferously that *The Times* was charging a price that was below the costs of production. They argued that the price was only possible because it was being subsidised from other activities of its owner, Rupert Murdoch.

The *Independent* pe rceived itself to be the target. It was the most vulnerable of the big dailies because it has never had their grass roots, political allegiance. If it could be put out of business, there would be a greater market share for the rest.

Your agenda

1   What conclusions had Rupert Murdoch drawn about the elasticity of demand for *The Times*?

2   Was he proved right?

3   What effect did the price cut have on the other papers?

4   Where do you think the extra customers came from?

5   Was it considered unfair practice to sell below cost price?

6   Did he achieve his objective.?

7   Why do you think the outcome is as shown?

An application of pricing strategies to the enhancement of market power can be seen when predatory pricing is employed. Supposing there are new entrants to the market. They may undercut the prices of existing suppliers. A possible response is to make even deeper price cuts. Variable costs may still be covered, but if a price war develops, then an absolute loss with price below variable costs may deliberately be accepted. The goal of the larger established firms is to bleed their competitors to death financially. When the new entrant finally leaves the market, the original firms may restore prices close to previous levels.

Predatory pricing may, then, succeed in driving the new entrants out again. Alternatively, over time one business may develop to the point where it can contemplate driving out competitors of long standing.

Essentials

Predatory pricing involves cutting prices in an attempt to put competitors out of the market.

By contrast, the firm which seeks to establish and hold a commanding market position may try to keep its price low enough to ensure its having a substantial market share. If it is operating in a market which is to any extent contestable, any tendency to earn super-normal profit will bring new entrants into the market. Deterrent pricing is an alternative strategy: the price is kept too low for the market to be attractive. Thus a market may be contestable but still have just a few competitors, all behaving in ways which respect the fact that there would be new entrants if the price were higher.

■ Other tricks of the trade

Demand affects most businesses' pricing decisions. The following examples show ways in which our sense of price can be used to encourage us to buy, even though we may be being misled! They are all tactical rather than strategic.

● *Loss leaders* may be priced below cost. Supermarkets often use this technique to persuade customers to come through the door. Once in, they always buy more than the item on special offer.

● *Known price items* (KPI) are those which people buy frequently. A business will price them competitively to attract customers. Products whose prices are not well known can be set to earn higher profits. Often used by small retailers, the KPI formula applies to goods such as milk, sugar, coffee and bread where customers are aware of the supermarket prices and small retailers need to be competitive.

● *Psychological pricing* is commonly used in retailing where prices all end in 99p or 95p. A famous entrepreneur was heard to proclaim to a group of minions who had broken the rule '£10 is not a price!' It seems unlikely that consumers are fooled by this, but it is an important device for reducing the perceived price of a product at minimal cost.

The demand for any product or service is influenced by a large number of factors. If asked, most people would probably answer that price is the single most important factor in deciding what to buy. Business people know that other factors such as brand loyalty, image, quality and the level of customers' incomes are also important. Nevertheless, price remains a very significant consideration in the demand for a company's products.

Very few businesses enjoy the privileged position of a monopoly, either regional or national. The majority of products face an imperfectly competitive market. Some companies rely heavily on price as their main means of competing with rival businesses. The alternative is non-price competition, which you encountered in Module 3. This includes all aspects of product differentiation, branding, advertising and promotion.

3 What about the costs?

Cost cutters

Jobs go at Sainsbury's as competition hots up
Sainsbury's battle to regain the leadership position has driven it to cut costs. Job losses, mainly at the management level, have been scheduled for the near future.

Holiday operators slash prices as take-overs threaten
In a business where a mass market company earns just £24 per holiday maker, competition is rife. Price is the main plank in most companies' marketing strategies. Volume must be the key to success.

BA set to Go
The explosion of low price, no-frills airlines has led BA to do its own thing. Go has been established to capture BA's share of the growing demand for cheap flights.

Your agenda

1 What was Sainsbury's objective in cutting jobs?
2 Why is volume the key to success in the mass-market holiday business?
3 How does BA manage to sell plane tickets at high and low prices?
4 What do all three businesses have in common?
5 Why is price such an important element of the marketing mix?
6 What are the advantages of being a price leader in the market place and what implications does this role usually have for costs?

Many businesses are working in a highly competitive environment and have to work hard to ensure that they are not being left behind in the fight to win market share.

If they are to do this, they must know how costs come about. It is possible to cut costs in some areas without realising that it will have a smaller than expected effect on total costs. The relationship between overhead costs and the costs generated by actually producing things must be understood if a business is to make the correct decision.

A business often wants to reduce average total cost. To do this, the ability to distinguish between different categories of costs is crucial. There are several ways in which the data can be interpreted. Fixed and variable costs were discussed in Module 1.2 (page 65). There are two other perspectives on cost data. The first involves distinguishing between direct and indirect costs and the second is contribution costing.

Direct and indirect costs

What is the cost?

Hi Fi Plastics is a small manufacturer of CD storage racks with a rented factory unit on a South Midlands industrial estate. The firm has four machines with the capacity to produce 100 000 units per year, but at present is operating with production and sales at 80 000 units. It employs three staff who make the product. The two owner-managers share the profits as part of their reward; they also draw salaries which, with that of the secretary, create an overhead cost of £40 000. In addition to labour, money is spent on a wide range of inputs. These include the factory buildings and offices, raw materials, replacement machinery, electricity and insurance.

Hi Fi Plastics' main costs are as follows:

	£ per year
Rent for the factory building and offices	9000
Rates	1600
Wages of production workers	36000
Raw materials, packaging, etc.	10000
Insurance	1500
Electricity*	4000
Depreciation of capital equipment	7500

* 75 per cent of electricity costs can be related to the production process, 25 per cent to general heating, lighting, etc.

Your agenda

1 Calculate:
   a the current total annual profit, if Hi Fi Plastics can sell the CD racks for £1.50
   b the percentage operating or net profit margin.
2 What were the total costs arising directly from the production process? What was this cost per CD rack?
3 What are the total overhead costs?
4 What is this cost per CD rack?
5 How would this cost change if production increased by 25 per cent?

Production decisions often require information on the costs of different items produced. It is not always easy to decide how different costs should be attributed. Direct and indirect costs provide one way of analysing production costs.

Direct costs are those which can be attributed directly to the production of a particular product. They include the cost of direct labour, and direct materials. Sometimes also, direct expenses can be identified. Equipment hire charges might be an example of these. Direct labour cost covers the wages of the people producing the product, and direct material costs cover the raw material and component inputs.

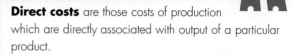

Essentials

Direct costs are those costs of production which are directly associated with output of a particular product.

Indirect costs are all those costs which cannot be directly related to the production process. These too can be split up. Indirect labour covers the wages and salaries of the management and sales teams, the office staff, the cleaners and the maintenance staff. Indirect materials refers to all the consumable items which are not directly attributable to producing a particular product. Often, indirect costs are referred to as **overheads**.

Essentials

Indirect costs, or **overheads**, are those costs which cannot be related solely to the production of one item.

Knowing what the costs are for each product is important. It helps greatly in the control of costs, a vital element in the search for efficiency. It also has a strong effect on pricing decisions, as well as the decision about what and how much should be produced.

■ Contribution costing

Picking a price

The Riviera Hotel in Blackpool has rooms to spare in the wintertime. In summer it charges £48 per double room per night. It needs to: it has a bank loan with heavy interest charges and major expenses in keeping up with customer requirements. But at the summer price most rooms would be empty all winter. However, the direct costs of having each room occupied are £2 per night for heating and £2 for cleaning and laundry.

Your agenda

1 If the proprietor offers winter breaks at £25 per night, what will be the contribution to the hotel's overheads, for each night booked?

2 How does this information help the business?

3 What other information would the hotel need in order to decide on the price to set?

Business decisions are based on a sound understanding of the cost of producing each item, and the sales revenue which that item can generate. **Contribution** costing helps a business to distinguish those products which contribute most effectively to profit. If the Riviera Hotel also has a restaurant, it could work out the contribution of selling rooms compared with that of selling meals. As a result, it might decide where to concentrate its limited resources.

By deducting direct costs from total sales revenue for each product, we can find out the contribution which the product makes to overheads. We can compare that contribution with those generated by other products. This can lead to a decision to discontinue a product which is contributing relatively little, or to expand production and sales of one that contributes more.

Essentials

The **contribution** of a product is its sales revenue minus direct costs. The combined contributions of all products may or may not be sufficient to cover overheads and thus yield a profit.

Another use for the idea of contribution arises when there is spare production capacity. Provided revenue is greater than direct cost, it pays to increase output, because even if the full costs of production cannot be covered, a contribution to overheads can be made. (This was covered in Module 1.2, page 68.)

However, it is not always easy to relate overheads to a particular product. A publisher with, say 50 books on its list, might very much want to know what the costs are for each of its titles. The direct costs will be those for writing, printing, binding and distribution; all are easily identifiable. But how much would the editing, designing and marketing costs be? If all these tasks were performed by in-house departments which work on a wide range of the company's titles, then splitting up the overheads among all the different books will be difficult. The management may have to be satisfied if the revenue from each title covers direct costs and makes a contribution to overheads.

Work in progress

Hi Fi Plastics has expanded successfully and decides to diversify. The two new products are mini disk racks and carrying cases. Two further machines are purchased (one for each product), each with annual depreciation charges of £5000. Most of the overheads remain unchanged, except insurance which rises by £1000 per machine. Two additional production staff are required for each machine at an extra £12 000 in wages per worker, while raw material and packaging costs are £6000 for each new machine. Charges for electricity used in production are £1000 per machine. In the first year 20 000 mini disk racks and 20 000 carrying cases are produced and sold at unit prices of £2.00 and £1.80 respectively.

Q 1 Calculate the contribution of mini disk racks and carrying cases to total overheads.

2 Are both products profitable?

3 In light of your answer to question 2, what might the business do?

Costs and prices

Companies wage a war on costs in order to beat the competition. If average costs can be reduced while quality is maintained, a business will be able to work in a situation of increasing power. Unfortunately for the individual company, this position cannot generally be held for long because of the dynamic nature of the market. Other businesses will be striving to catch up and usurp that leadership position.

When competition is strong in a market with few competitors, one may become the leader. A company which is particularly powerful in the market may decide on a price. All the competing companies will then charge a similar price. If they try to charge more, they will be likely to lose market share.

Charging less may precipitate a price war as all the players in the market attempt to recapture their market shares. A price war can have a detrimental effect on all of them, reducing profits to a serious degree.

The most vulnerable may end by going out of business. A powerful company with ample financial resources may, in fact, deliberately cut prices with this outcome in mind. It will be the one to survive, and with fewer competitors, its market power will be enhanced. This is predatory pricing.

If price cutting becomes competitive, and a price war results, everyone will lose profits with no advantage in increased market share. Some industries are more vulnerable to price wars than others.

Customers may benefit in the short run, but such gains are likely to be ephemeral. Price wars may lead to small firms being swallowed up or going out of business. As the number of competitors is reduced, the desire to compete in ways other than price may become the driving force, especially in a market where margins are very small.

Consumers may benefit from a price war, although this may be temporary. The larger companies will benefit if a smaller company is driven out of the market and its market share divided among them. Prices may then rise.

Point of view

Wars and mergers

One of the industries well known for using price as a basis for competition is the travel industry. Almost every year one of the large package holiday companies introduces a price cut to attract new customers. In 1993 it was Thomas Cook which got the ball rolling. In August 1993 it announced a 10 per cent discount for early booking of a 1994 holiday. This was immediately followed by Pickfords Travel and Hogg Robinson offering a similar discount. Not to be left out, Airtours offered 100 000 free places for children up to the age of 19! Cosmos offered £7 million worth of free places for people booking early. The warning from Thomas Cook was 'blood will be spilt'. To some extent, it appears that this price war was part of the standard marketing strategy of the holiday companies and a very effective way of getting publicity.

Since then, many of these names have disappeared. The holiday business is now in the hands of four major groups which include travel agents, airlines, tour operators, insurance and even car hire. Further mergers are on the cards.

Your agenda

1 Who gained from the price wars of the 1990s?

2 What term is used to describe a company which includes travel agents, airlines, tour operators, insurance and car hire? What benefits does this have for the company? How might it affect the consumer?

3 What are the advantages and disadvantages of the travel business being in the hands of three or four large companies?

4 If their power was considered to be too great, what would you advise as a solution?

1 Quality?

Quality at BP Amoco

Every batch of BP Amoco's oil products is tested at refineries to ensure it meets its manufacturing specifications. After testing, the product is moved to bulk storage terminals by either rail, sea or pipeline. Further key tests are carried out at the terminal and there are procedures to monitor quality at various points during the product's distribution. BP Amoco is governed by its ISO 9002 accreditation, which means that it has processes in place to meet the international standards for quality management.

At service stations, BP Amoco arranges a monthly visit by a 'mystery motorist' who looks at:

- Standards on the forecourt. For example, is it well lit? Are all the signs clean and in good condition? Is the car wash working properly? Are there any obvious health and safety hazards?

- Standards in the stores. For example, are the floors, windows and shelves clean? Are the chillers and food preparation areas clean? Are the shelves fully stocked with clean undamaged products – and are all the products within their sell-by dates? Are relevant promotions on display? Are the toilets clean?

- Standards of service. For example, are staff well presented in uniform? Are they polite? Did customers have to wait excessively long to be served? Does the cashier have the necessary product knowledge?

BP Amoco produces league tables of service stations district by district. The top sites are rewarded and the worst shamed. Trends are tracked over the entire network to monitor levels of service.

Source: BP Amoco's web site on Bized, www.bized.ac.uk

Your agenda

1 Why does BP Amoco spend so much time, and money on ensuring quality?

2 How does quality contribute to customers view of a product?

3 How does quality give competitive advantage?

4 Choose a product and a service and identify ways in which quality contributes to their appeal.

Businesses live on their reputation. A reputation for poor quality sticks with a business and may lead to its downfall. Once formed, a bad reputation is very hard to adjust. This does not mean that there is no market for the cheap and cheerful product, but it does mean that if the business which supplies them is inefficient, its prospects will be gloomy. Quality in management is therefore crucial to the total quality picture of the business. Of course, this includes product performance and consistency of delivery among all the other features that quality involves.

Quality can be worked on effectively by businesses which have embraced the idea of **continuous improvement** or **Kaizen**. With this approach the objective is to look for regular small improvements which can be implemented at low cost and quickly. This can work better than a major reorganisation of quality standards and procedures. It involves developing a culture which encourages everyone to be on the lookout for ways of doing things better.

Measuring quality

Quality has always been a rather subjective concept. It has been difficult to define as different people have different views. Things have changed. The British Standards Institute now administers international quality standards which are recognised worldwide.

ISO 9000 is available to any sort of organisation, whether a manufacturing or service industry, a charity, an educational, professional or public sector body. Any organisation which is seeking a stamp of approval on the quality of its management can apply.

To achieve the standard a company must

- define the work it does
- document it
- do what it says it does
- make sure that it is done effectively
- monitor the system, learn from observation and experience, and be prepared to make improvements and changes.

What's the gain?

The initial process of setting up quality systems can be lengthy but the rewards are considerable both internally and externally. The combination of the two may give a business a head start among its competitors.

■ Internal gains

- greater responsibility, accountability and quality consciousness among staff
- better use of time and resources
- greater consistency and traceability of product or services
- less wastage through product or service failure.
- continual improvements to your quality and efficiency

■ External gains

- wider market opportunities
- increased customer satisfaction
- improved customer loyalty.

A company which finds that quality really works will be in a much more powerful position. The enhanced management systems will increase the appeal of the company to both its trading partners and customers.

As the business world becomes tougher, being able to maintain strong, high quality relationships between suppliers and customers will enable a company to compete more effectively.

Many companies have found that some customers are even more interested in quality features than they are in price. Quality and reliability are both forms of added value. A customer who knows that the supplier will deliver the right quality of product on time, may well consider that a less certain arrangement with a cheaper supplier is less desirable. The combination of internal and external gains should reduce costs and therefore increase profitability.

Essentials

Continuous improvement means constantly looking for new ideas about how to produce more efficiently. Usually, these ideas come from employees who are actually involved in the production process.

Essentials

Kaizen is the Japanese term for continuous improvement.

Point of view

Companies which have gained ISO 9000 have found the changes in the business have led to:

- increased customer satisfaction
- improved profits
- increased competitiveness
- increased efficiency
- less waste
- less duplication of work
- fewer errors
- cost saving
- better use of time and resources

- improved communications
- improved customer confidence
- wider market opportunities
- continuous improvements.

Source: Adapted from British Standards Institute Website

Your agenda

Explain how the above factors make a company more competitive. Use a business you know about if possible in order to consider the practical impact of such changes.

2 Who is ahead of the game?

Works like clockwork

The wind-up radio proved a success after long efforts by its inventor to find someone to put the money up for its development. Once it was in production, it generated much demand because there are many parts of the world in which neither electricity nor batteries are easily or cheaply available.

Freeplay, the Anglo-South African company which was set up to produce the radio, developed a tensator, the sort of spring which is found in seat-belts. More recently, it has created a technique for storing energy from the spring in a rechargeable battery. This technology has been used in its follow-up product, a torch.

Since this latest innovation, the concept of wind-up power has opened up many avenues for development. The spring can be wound several times to fill a battery. This made it possible to develop both land-mine detectors and a global positioning system, which is used to tell sailors where they are. These are both items which need to function in locations where the supply of power is not guaranteed.

Of course, the radio has not stood still. The third-generation model uses the rechargeable battery which allows the radio to run for longer. Technology never stands still.

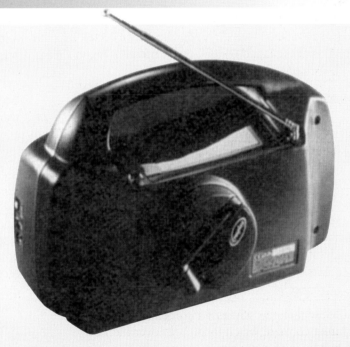

Your agenda

1 Why do you think the inventor of the wind-up radio had trouble finding financial support for his product?

2 How has research added value to the product?

3 What effect do you think research has had on Freeplay's competitive edge?

4 How can research and development help a company to maintain or improve its position in the market?

Finding a niche

Developing the product offers considerable scope for increasing market power. Product positioning is an attempt to find a segment of the market which is poorly catered for. Self-evidently, its being so means that there will be less competition within that market segment. However, doing this successfully means being sure to keep in close touch with the market so that consumers' needs really are effectively met.

In the case of Freeplay, having developed the technology which runs the wind-up radio, the company started to look for other niches which could use the same technology. This meant looking beyond the market for radios and thinking laterally about where electricity is in short supply or difficult to use. No doubt the company will come up with more possibilities in future.

In the short run, Freeplay has a monopoly in this niche, but unless the technology can be protected by patent, other competitors will come up with 'me-too' products.

By definition, the niche market is one which the main competitors in the field have chosen to ignore. It therefore creates a small but less competitive market. Within it the producer may have some market power.

Keeping up

As products and consumer expectations evolve, many businesses feel that far from exploiting their market power, they are having to come up with new ideas just in order to survive. There is sometimes a fine line between achieving a position of some control over the market, and simply staying in business. Survival may require a constant watch to be kept over the new product lines of competitors.

Product development may mean actually searching for new products, as happens in the pharmaceuticals industry where there is constant research for new and more effective drugs. Or it may mean improving an existing product to make it more attractive or more reliable, effectively prolonging the product life cycle in the way shown in Figure M4.13. This is known as an extension strategy (see Module 3, page 224). The curve can be shifted from A to A$_1$ by relaunching the product in a new design, by more advertising, or by increasing product appeal in another way.

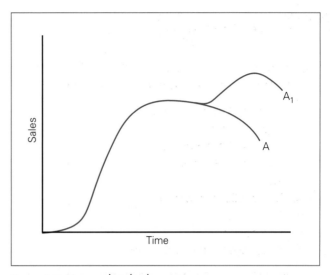

Figure 4.13 New product development

Along the spectrum

A genuinely new product may, for a time, create a degree of monopoly for its producer. Later, 'me-too' products will emerge to compete, but the firm which can keep up a continuous flow of new and different products will have a substantial competitive advantage. Rivals may find it difficult to keep up, particularly if there are legal restraints such as copyrights or patents associated with the new developments.

All research and development involves risks, so the successful company will seek ways of minimising them. One way of doing this is to aim for continuous product modifications, especially if the life cycle of the product is short. Another aspect of new product development involves carefully relating the new product to consumer demand. This may be achieved by skilful analysis of the market. Alternatively, it may involve advertising and promoting the product in such a way that consumer demand is created.

In electronic games manufacturing, all these features are significant in determining the market power of the contestants. The successful company has to have a complex strategy which takes care of all aspects of marketing, but the prizes for a firm which succeeds in dominating the market are enormous.

The end result of new product development in some markets is product proliferation. From time to time, one firm may emerge from the crowd and take a dominating position for a while. Quite quickly though, its competitors will catch up with new products of their own, eroding the position of the market leader. This state of affairs can bring major benefits to the consumer, if the competing firms are making genuine efforts to meet demand in meaningful ways. But many consumer durables now come in so many designs and variants that it is difficult for the consumer to decide which is likely to offer the best buy.

Research and development is an important part of the strategy of any business in a competitive market. There is always a group of consumers who want to be out in front of the rest and therefore lead the way to new products. There are opportunities for research and development in almost all businesses, from making shoes to high-tech electronics. Its use enables companies to gain an advantage over the competition, even if it is only in the short term.

Point of view

Creative instincts

Xerox's life blood is research and development. It's selling products which must be ahead of the game. At Palo Alto Research Centre in California, more commonly known as PARC, Xerox has a band of creative people working on the future.

For every bright idea that is produced, ten are of no immediate relevance to Xerox. In the past, these have had a habit of cropping up in other businesses and making millions of dollars for the entrepreneurs who were prepared to make the investment.

The thing about bright ideas is that the originator needs to carry it forward. This often doesn't happen. No one feels the same sense of ownership as the inventor. Unfortunately, inventors are often not astute at business.

Many businesses have tried to move innovation to the factory floor without taking this into account. The results tend to flop. One person who understands the process is Robert Adams who invented laser imaging which turned into a multi-billion dollar business for Xerox. His idea emerged from PARC but took him with it.

Xerox turned its attention to all the ideas that might have fallen by the wayside. Xerox Technology Ventures has been created to make use of the ideas which often made billions for someone else in Silicon Valley, California, and Robert Adams is in charge.

He understands both sides of the picture. The bright sparks with the ideas which Xerox cannot use are set up in low-cost business premises and are provided with a business manager to keep everything under control. The bright sparks receive a 20 per cent stake in the business.

One of them invented a product which undercut an existing $13 000 Xerox product by $12 600. Xerox moved fast and spent $15 million to buy back control! A competing product at $400 would have been too much …

Your agenda

1 Why has Xerox set up Xerox Technology Ventures?

2 What are the advantages for the inventors?

3 Why are they more likely to be successful than others who have to compete outside the Xerox fold?

4 How does this activity contribute to Xerox's competitive position?

3 Marketing

Divide and rule

The pub business had been in decline for years. The sight of a couple of sleepy old characters lurking in the corner over a pint deterred many potential customers. The fall in the number of pubs has had a strong correlation with this fall in customers. They had simply lost market appeal.

The realisation that the pub market was not full of identical customers led the revival. By identifying the segments and creating brands which met their needs, phoenixes grew from the ashes of the Rose and Crown, Kings Head and Coach and Horses.

Who were these groups? Women for a start had often been made uncomfortable by the macho, smoky environment of the traditional pub. The big windows, airy atmosphere and a decent Chardonnay to be found in All Bar One are designed to welcome them in.

The Firkin chain has a style all of its own. Full of teeming humanity on a Saturday night, the pubs provide just the environment that the student sector is seeking. It even sells its own line in leisurewear to add to the profits. Its branding means that anyone visiting another part of the country knows just what to expect.

Irishness has sprung up across the country. Is there a town in the UK which does not have an Irish pub? A glass of stout and an Irish jig seems to have enduring appeal. They must be raking it in because they are always packed.

Although the licensing laws still keep children out of bars, the family market has much potential. A Big Steak House with a Wacky Warehouse means that the whole family can go out for a meal and the children can play without disrupting life for everyone else.

Such modernisation brings pain to the Real Ale brigade, but even they do not need to feel left out. Some of the breweries have tried to meet their needs – not always successfully, in the eyes of the purists. In Lancashire the Tom Cobleigh chain aims to provide an unspoilt environment for the traditionalist.

Your agenda

1 Why did brewery companies start to look at their product range?

2 What effect does the identification and development of a segment have on the business and the customer?

3 These new outlets require considerable investment. How do owners calculate whether they have been successful?

4 Why is a business interested in developing products in a range of segments?

5 How does the development of a successful segment affect the position of the business on the spectrum of competition?

Positions, segments and niches

Market segmentation is a useful way for a business to increase its ability to have a significant position in the market for a range of products. A single product cannot hope to meet the needs of all consumers, so a carefully chosen range will meet more needs.

Businesses work hard to identify such segments. They are not a stationary phenomenon, so the need for research is constant. The business which wants to maintain its place in the market or improve on it will need to keep a close watch on current patterns of consumption and future desires.

Such research may open up niches which allow the development of new products. Such niches often grow into segments as they are developed. By careful observation of the market and proactive development work a business can secure a stronger position in the market place and may be able to move along the spectrum of competition and increase profitability.

■ What position?

As a basis for the development of a product range, a company needs to be certain about the **position** of its existing products in the market place. Market research will assist in the process by providing information about how consumers view the products. A company will be looking for a range of products with different positions in the market.

Position can be achieved in a variety of ways. In general, it relates to the way in which a product adds value. Is it cheap and cheerful? Is it high quality? Does it have a famous name that people want to be seen with? All these factors will determine the position of a product.

Kwik-Save and other similar 'cheap and cheerful' supermarkets achieve profitability through low margins with high turnover. Firms often wish to shift their market position either to achieve better competitive exploitation of the segment or to escape a negative consumer perception. Woolworth used to suffer from positioning as low quality and old-fashioned until vigorously repositioned by Kingfisher group as a smarter value-for-money family store.

A position might credit a company with offering consumers a high 'margin' of utility over expenditure so its prices represent excellent value for money or its premium prices are amply justified by the quality of its products. A position of this sort would be a valuable source of competitive advantage. Such a reputation can become a major intangible asset and is increasingly likely to appear on a firm's balance sheet through brand valuations. However, it is essential that a firm and its products live up to the claims made in promotions and public statements. Promises kept are often taken for granted: promises broken are remembered.

By keeping an eye on the position of a product, a business can decide whether it is still meeting the needs of the market. If not, decisions can be made about the best way to adjust the product and its marketing. Figure M4.14 shows a matrix for part of the restaurant business. McDonald's would find itself in the extreme bottom left-hand corner. A restaurant with many stars and a vista over lakes and mountains would probably be at the top right.

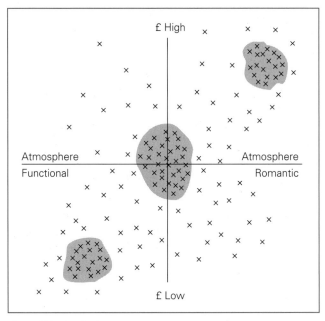

Figure M4.14 Which position?

Module 3 (page 226) includes the case study of how Lucozade repositioned itself. It had been sold for decades as a restorative for people who were ill. The fact that this market is inevitably limited in scope combined with the product's old-fashioned image meant that there was little possibility of development. The product was successfully repositioned as an energy-giving drink for active sporty types, and its sales rocketed.

Essentials

Market position refers to the way the product is perceived in comparison with competing products. Considering the positioning of the product helps the company to make decisions about its product range and promotional activities.

Work in progress

Q Choose a product which you know well and decide its position in the market. Think carefully about the categories that you use on your matrix. Look at the ones for restaurants in Figure M4.14. Complete the matrix by adding products of a similar nature which have different positions.

■ Which segment?

If consumers were all alike in every way, then there would only be one mass market for every product. More products used to be marketed in this way on the assumption that the nature of most people's demand was roughly similar. Supermarkets in the 1960s mostly concentrated on low prices and popular brands without attempting to meet any specialist preferences. Some products still sell most effectively through a mass-marketing approach. A Mars Bar is one example. The fact that someone has bought a Mars tells you virtually nothing about the individual. Yet what about someone who has bought a Porsche? Or a pair of Dr Martin's? Or who shops at Laura Ashley? You may guess something about these people. Indeed, the contents of a supermarket trolley at the checkout are often deeply revealing about the person concerned and the household in which he or she lives. This is the basis for segmentation.

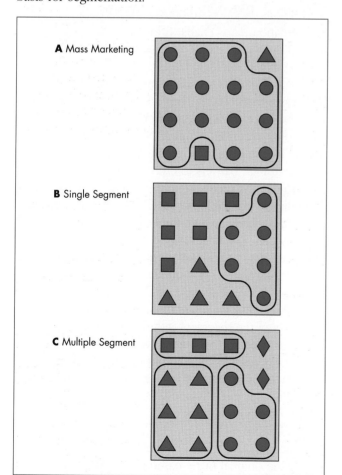

Figure M4.15 Target markets

In Figure M4.15 the symbols represent groups of consumers with different characteristics in terms of their demand. In Market A the firm adopts a mass-marketing strategy aimed at broadly satisfying 14 consumers out of every 16 or 87.5 per cent of the total market. In Market B the firm targets a single segment of the total market with a specialised product and marketing mix. The firm in Market C attempts to satisfy multiple segments by offering a product range that satisfies different consumer groupings.

The market for bicycles

Most products offer a range of features that combine to give the consumer some overall level of satisfaction. The buyer of a bicycle may gain satisfaction from:

- speed
- safety features
- range of gears
- all-terrain capability
- styling
- luggage-carrying capacity
- accessories
- ease of loading in a car, etc.

Suppose that buyers were asked to rate the importance of each feature on the scale below:

5 Very important

4 Fairly important

3 Neither important nor unimportant

2 Fairly unimportant

1 Very unimportant

Your agenda

1 It is at once clear that each consumer would have his or her own individual pattern of preferences. What features would score highest with:

   a a middle-aged buyer wanting a bicycle for shopping in a busy town

   b a teenager at school

   c a cycling club enthusiast?

A bicycle that scored superlative ratings on all of the criteria above would not only be technically impossible or fantastically expensive, but would also be providing most customers with benefits that they did not value. In other words, 'a bicycle is not a bicycle' but a racing bicycle, a touring bicycle, a mountain bicycle, a shopping bicycle, a child's bicycle, etc. As a result, a cycle manufacturer – such as Raleigh – produces a wide range of models, each of which aims to offer the consumer a different mix of benefits for a given price.

The same principle explains why Unilever produces nine different brands of washing powder which appear to compete against each other on the supermarket shelves. In fact, each brand carries its own mix of benefits in terms of image, bleaches, perfumes, suds levels, environmental qualities, etc. Thus Unilever is able to appeal to many different areas or segments within the total market for detergent by 'positioning' a key brand within each.

There are many possible criteria for market segmentation:

- benefit – by sources of satisfaction in consumption
- demographic – by age group, sex, family size and life cycle, income group, occupation, education, etc.
- geographic – by country, by region, by city size, etc.
- psychographic – by social class, lifestyle, personality type
- behaviouristic – by frequency of purchase, by usage rate, by product loyalty, etc.

Any of these criteria may be used to produce a segmentation 'map' of the market for a given product. For example, Gambit Games might undertake a 'benefit' segmentation by relating educational/entertainment value to the age group of game users.

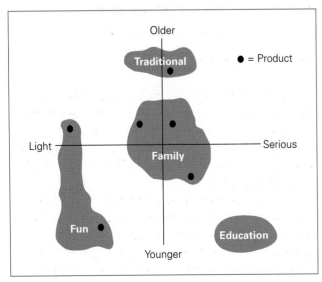

Figure M4.16 Market segmentation: Gambit Games

Figure M4.16 shows that the company has a good range of products in the 'Family' segment and some representation in the 'Traditional' and 'Fun' segments. Notice that it is not represented in the 'Education' segment where there might be some possibility for a new product launch. However, a firm will not necessarily try to enter every segment of the market. Indeed, some firms may prefer to build a reputation as specialists in serving the needs of one particular segment.

The segments revealed by the mapping process obviously depend on the criteria used. Gambit Games might discover other important market segments by applying demographic or psychographic criteria.

Understanding needs

Segmentation models are particularly useful in helping the firm to understand the nature of both the people who buy its products and those who do not. Segmentation maps enable firms to see inside the multi-dimensional nature of markets and to target customers with increased accuracy.

Some segments are much more attractive to businesses than others. They are of different sizes, may be growing or declining at different speeds and may allow different profit margins. New entrants are usually unable to enter the most profitable segments because they have high barriers to entry. They will probably have to confine themselves to segments which are less immediately profitable but may have greater potential if a firm becomes expert at meeting its needs.

This principle is developed further in the concept of a market niche. Because of its small size and special characteristics, it is often overlooked or disregarded by the major firms, allowing a smaller enterprise to exploit its potential. For example, the large mainstream segments of the detergent industry are dominated by brands owned by the industry giants Unilever and Proctor & Gamble. This did not prevent Ecover, a small Sussex-based company, entering an initially tiny but significant niche where greatest emphasis was placed on environmental qualities. The danger with any successful niche marketing operation is that it will become attractive for major producers to enter and engulf the original niche-based firm. Ecover faced this threat from 'green' own-label brands. Similarly, Tie

Rack, in Figure M4.17, found its pioneering developments in fashionable ties imitated by the high street chain-stores.

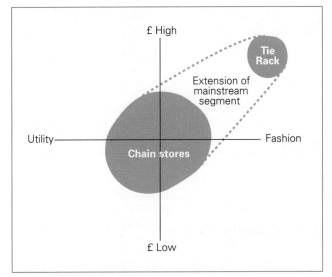

Figure M4.17 Market segmentation: Tie Rack

Segments can now be divided into subsegments. Some customers are looking for a perfect match to their needs and modern technology has made this available to many more people. In the past, the custom-made product has been very expensive and out of reach of most people.

Computer-aided design and manufacture (CAD/CAM), combined with flexible production systems, is making this concept more widely applicable. Triumph motorbikes, for example, rose from the ashes of a historic company on this basis. It produced every bike to order so it could meet the needs of each and every customer. This is known as **micro-marketing**.

Essentials

Micro-marketing is the tailoring of a firm's marketing effort to the particular needs of individuals or small consumer groups.

The marketing process is made up of a series of constituent parts which build up to the development of the marketing mix for a particular product. Figure M4.18 shows the links and connections.

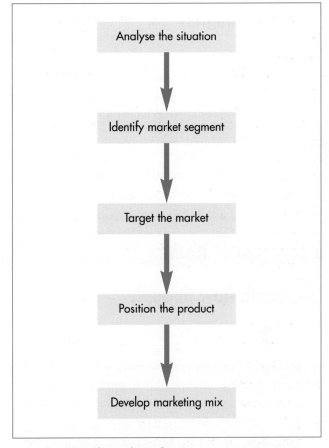

Figure M4.18 Developing the marketing mix

By going through this process effectively, a business will enhance its opportunities for achieving competitive advantage as it will be looking for opportunities to adjust the product and market it in an appropriate way in order to reach the targeted customers.

Where on the spectrum?

The nature of the segment will determine the position of a product market on the spectrum of competition. A firm that is into a market early with a brand new product may have some initial monopoly power. It will probably soon discover that other firms are developing competitive products.

Other segments may be much more competitive from the start. Unilever and Proctor and Gamble fight each other in various domestic cleaning product segments. To some extent, they can decide the focus of competition. Is it price, brand or just how white your washing is?

Work in progress

Where shall I eat?

People are spending more and more on eating out. There is an enormous range, from chains to small individual restaurants, and they all slot into their different segments. You are thinking about opening a restaurant and are considering its style. You haven't got a lot of money, so it needs to be at the cheap and cheerful end on the market.

Q

1 Make a list of segments at this end of the market.

2 Which are already highly competitive? Can you think of other possibilities for a new business?

3 What other information would you need before going ahead?

4 Not just at home

A smooth flow through

Farmers have always had a problem in persuading the grain to flow smoothly from the silo. Just like the salt pot, it gets blocked up as it reaches the funnel. Matcon, a company based in Gloucestershire, produced a cone which pumped up and down to allow the grain to flow smoothly – just like shaking the salt pot.

This innovation sold like hot cakes throughout the UK and proved to be the start of a much bigger business. It had applications to any business which wanted to move powder. These ranged from pharmaceuticals and fertilisers to paint and food. Having established itself successfully in the UK, the market moved overseas.

This was not an easy move for a business in which attention to detail is crucial. Many of the products being moved are toxic, so it is essential that safety is at the forefront of any installation. Selling and service needs were therefore complex.

The company considered a variety of ways of moving into overseas markets. Licensing the product for others to produce was a possibility, but it is difficult to control the intellectual property once it is out of your hands. Joint ventures were an alternative, but they can be administratively burdensome. It considered setting up subsidiaries, but they are expensive to maintain unless turnover is high.

After much consideration, Matcon opted to employ a highly trained workforce who could go out into the field and secure orders, decide specifications which were sent back to Gloucestershire and then supervise the installation and training.

Good engineering skills combined with the ability to explain the installation in Spanish is an infrequent combination of assets. The necessary workforce was therefore hard to find.

The company had to recruit well-qualified engineers and train them for a year before they were ready for the flight to Australia or other far-flung destinations. They had to be steeped in the Matcon culture so that they would not take their training to one of the company's competitors.

Your agenda

1 What factors determined the strategy that Matcon employed for selling overseas?

2 Why was its product more difficult to deal with than many others in overseas markets?

3 What features of Matcon's strategy are important for other companies to consider when setting up their overseas marketing plans. Why?

Shall we go ahead?

Selling overseas is a different game from selling at home. It involves more costs, and a long-term commitment is essential if after-sales service, for example, is to be maintained. The first issue is, however: does the product match the market? Matcon's technology was obviously something that could be put to use in a wide variety of international contexts. Selling fridges to Inuit would have been more difficult! Without market orientation much time and money can be wasted.

There is a series of questions that a company should ask itself before a decision is made to go ahead:
- Is our product acceptable abroad? Does it meet product safety laws? Is it culturally acceptable?
- Are there tariffs or quotas that will keep it out?
- What are the transport costs?
- Can we organise the supply chains?
- Is payment reliable?
- How will exchange rates affect profit margins?
- Is the country stable?

If the answers to these prove positive, further investigations need to take place.

How shall we go ahead?

E-sausages

When the local butcher searches for ways to increase business, not many turn to the web. In fact, Chris Battle was very sceptical when his family suggested a web site but he has had to eat his words. Many others are now eating his sausages.

The prospect of spending money on setting up the site went very much against the grain, but he succumbed to family pressure. They spent £1600 on setting up the web site and now 25 per cent of sales go for export to places as far away as Japan and Peru.

In fact, more than three tonnes a week of Yorkshire delicacies feed people in unexpected places.

The web site is located in the Classic England online shopping mall. It turned a small mail order business, which sold specially smoked bacon, into a business with a turnover of £750 000 a year. The web proved much more effective than word of mouth.

Your agenda

1 Why was Chris Battle unhappy about investing in a web site?
2 Why was it important to locate the site in a virtual shopping mall?
3 Why was Classic England particularly appropriate?
4 What advantages might e-commerce have over other forms of export marketing?
5 Why would it not have worked for Matcon?

Deciding on the right strategy for a particular business is a complex affair. There are many alternatives which are appropriate for different products and different countries.

The first question to ask is whether production should take place at home or abroad. Matcon's research suggested that it should produce in the UK and export, despite the fact that many people were buying one-off products which were specially built for them.

■ The alternatives for home production are as follows:

● Direct from the company.

● Through a trading company.

   The former keeps the business closely involved in the process but requires employees to develop considerable expertise. It may also involve setting up marketing subsidiaries or employing an agent.

   The latter means accepting a lower price because the goods are sold to an intermediary and the responsibility is passed to others.

■ The alternatives for overseas production include:

● Franchising the sale of your products. The Bodyshop, for example, is found around the world.

● Licensing people to produce your goods in other countries.

● Screwdriver assembly which means that kits are exported for local assembly.

● Joint ventures with a local business.

● Setting up a branch factory.

   The decision will depend on the scale of export that is envisaged and the nature of the economy in the country concerned. A small firm will obviously be looking at lower levels of investment and complexity than a multi-national corporation.

Work in progress

Q What factors will affect the decision to enter an export market by a small firm compared with a large firm?

What about promotion?

The promotional strategies that would be used in the home market need to be considered carefully for use in export markets. Many multi-nationals have developed internationally appropriate adverts which use the same visuals and have a different soundtrack. There are obvious economies of scale in such strategies.

Great care has to be taken, however, not to offend local culture. Even product names which seem quite acceptable in the UK can have unfortunate connotations in other English-speaking countries. When translated into other languages, the sensitivities become even greater!

Many multi-nationals have bought other businesses for the brand names that they bring with them. There are both advantages and disadvantages to their use in the international context.

■ The down side

● Cultural – Some countries have banned famous-name western products because they believe that it will have an adverse effect on the population.

● Quality – It is more difficult to ensure quality in products from branch factories.

● Differentiation – There may be a need for a different type of product in some areas.

■ The up side

● Economies of scale in production and packaging.

● Marketing economies.

● Familiar image in old and new markets.

● Prestige.

Does it affect competition?

The increased scale of production leads to economies of scale and therefore lower costs. Assuming that businesses are not going to enter markets where profits are lower than the expected return, apart from in the short run, a company which trades internationally should expect a larger turnover because of the increased size of the market.

Increased scale should therefore make a company more competitive. As a result, it should be able to charge lower prices and attract more customers. If it moves to a position in which it supplies a significant part of the market, it will have achieved a degree of control compared to competitors who are restricted to the home market. In other words, a company involved in trade has an opportunity to slide along the spectrum of competition and join those businesses which have greater control over their markets. (These issues are explored further in option 1.)

Enquiry 5   In search of dominance?

1 To merge or not to merge

Not once – but twice

BP was the world's 3rd largest oil company. Its boss, Sir John Browne, referred to it as being 'at the top of the second division'.

In August 1998 it merged with the USA's Amoco. It was still in 3rd place but much closer to the two market leaders, Exxon and Shell. This moved it into the first division. There were many good reasons. In a depressed oil industry, size matters as it reduces overhead costs and spreads risk around the world.

The two companies had synergy. They fitted together well because BP is good at finding and extracting oil and Amoco has a reputation for refining, distributing and marketing. BP is strong in the UK and Amoco's strength lies in the USA.

Between them, the two companies spanned the world. Exploitation in developing countries, however, often has strings attached. If companies want to exploit the valuable assets, a country is often looking for something in return. Infrastructure deals are often the pay back. Now BP Amoco can bid more adventurously.

Within the year, BP Amoco had found another partner. Mike Bowlin, the boss of Arco, a smaller player in the US industry, rang John Browne and suggested that they got together. The BP Amoco deal had been much more of a merger, but this was really a take-over. All the Arco directors received a golden handshake, leaving just Mike Bowlin on the executive board.

This moved BP Amoco-Arco to number two in terms of market value in the world league.

Company	Market value (£ billion)	Profits (£ billion)	Sales (£ billion)	Staff
Exxon-Mobil	149	12	111	130000
BP Amoco-Arco	119	5	53	115000
Royal Dutch Shell	112	9	88	102000
Chevron	35	3	22	43000
ENI	32	3	31	81000
Total/Petrofina	29	2	32	69100
Elf	23	2	26	85000
Texaco	19	2	28	28000

Fig M4.19 The oil league – at the time of the take-over
Source: company reports

Your agenda

1 How would the merger between BP and Amoco assist the company to develop in the future? Include the effects on overheads, skills and risk.
2 Why can the new company 'bid more adventurously'?
3 What is the difference between a merger and a take-over?
4 Are there any drawbacks to merging or taking over another company?
5 In what other ways might a company grow?

One way of dominating the market is to grow large enough to be able to influence the future or achieve enough security that a challenge in one area cannot threaten the life of the company in other areas. As it can take a long time to grow organically, such change usually comes about inorganically through mergers and take-overs.

Increased size generally gives a company more market power, so it will probably move further along the spectrum of competition. Size gives leverage in all sorts of directions. Not only can a business buy on a larger scale and receive bigger discounts but it can borrow money more easily and cheaply, so it can have bolder strategic plans.

The new organisation can be more efficient because functions do not need to be duplicated. Finance, marketing and other organisational functions are quickly merged in order to made one cohesive company.

Companies want to grow in order to improve their market position. In BP's case, its merger with Amoco made it more efficient and increased its leverage. Arco hoped that joining up with BP Amoco would be beneficial in terms of its future place in the oil industry.

Not all take-overs happen as smoothly. As any company can be taken over if a majority of its shareholders agree, the directors and management may object violently. Newspapers are sometimes full of adverts from companies which are threatened by take-over. Their aim is to persuade shareholders not to sell out. The other side often advertises as well to explain the merits of the bid.

Changing trends

The Hanson decade

Led by Lord Hanson, its executive chairman, the company was a vast industrial conglomerate (turnover in 1992 was £7.6 billion, fourth largest for UK-based firms) built on a long series of mergers and take-over bids. Hanson looked for companies which it considered to be underperforming, acquired them and then pursued policies of 'asset disposal' and more efficient management. Quite often, the assets sold were complete businesses which were previously part of the company Hanson had purchased. Usually, the true worth of such enterprises had been hidden by inefficient management of the 'group' concern to which they used to belong. By isolating each business and selling it 'with no strings attached' (in other words, separated from the previous owning group), its real value could be recovered. This came in the form of cash receipts which could then be used to pay back any loans taken out in the first place to help pay for the total acquisition. Hanson had a reputation for the rapid repayment of debts.

Although large parts of acquired firms were sold off, other parts remained and were then managed by Hanson. Industrial commentators refer to this process as 'Hansonisation'. Usually, this involved rigorous job-cutting (particularly for senior managers) combined with opportunities offered to capable middle managers. At the same time, spending on plant was reviewed and often cut ('we are oriented towards profit centres, not to product'). Once complete, the second stage of 'Hansonisation' was to allow the company to stand on its own feet, run by its new management with very little involvement from corporate head office.

In many cases, both the companies sold off and those retained within the Hanson empire have prospered and expanded subsequently.

By 1996 conglomerates were going out of fashion. There was more interest in businesses which stuck to their core competences. The Hanson Group was broken up. Many of the small US companies were sold off and the rest was broken up into four groups. The one which continues to bear the Hanson name is in bricks and building materials

Your agenda

1 What common characteristics were there in the companies that Hanson took over?

2 What might account for Hanson's success?

3 Why do you think that the companies sold by Hanson might then prove to be successful and begin new growth?

4 What was the attraction of businesses concentrating on their core competences?

Integration in practice

The outcomes for mergers and take-overs have been very mixed. Often it is difficult to judge the success of inorganic expansion since it is not possible to know how the firms would have fared if remaining independent. Research suggests that although there are both successes and failures, integration does not improve overall business performance. In particular, the firms involved may find that their cultures are very different and that their technical and business systems can be difficult and costly to combine. The anticipated **synergy** (the '2+2 = 5' principle) of many mergers is never actually achieved. Managerial diseconomies of scale may cancel out many technical economies, while the human costs of integration can be very high. Uncertainty and resentment among staff may build while motivation and commitment slump. There is also the danger that mergers and bids may be fuelled by an economic boom leaving serious problems with indebtedness and underperformance when the next recession begins.

> **Essentials**
>
> **Synergy** refers to the way in which two companies combined may have greater strength than they did separately. They may reap economies of scale and may be able to reduce the duplication of some of their management resources. However, synergy may be expected but fail to emerge.

Demergers may occur if the new company decides greater efficiency could be achieved by restoring the original firms, as with tyre manufacturers Dunlop and Pirelli in 1982. In other cases, integrated firms opt for **divestment** of smaller business entities within their 'empires', either selling them on the open market or allowing their managers to purchase the enterprise in a **management buy-out**. Significantly, the 1990s have seen a reaction against the idea of diversification and a new desire by firms to achieve **focus** by concentrating on core capabilities and areas of excellence. Sometimes referred to as 'sticking to the knitting', this movement reflects the need for a firm to play to its strengths and concentrate scarce resources on the products and markets it knows best.

> **Essentials**
>
> **Divestment** means selling off businesses which are either not very profitable or peripheral to the core activity which is to be developed by the parent company.

> **Essentials**
>
> A **management buy-out** allows the existing managers to buy the business from the parent company and run it themselves. If they find they have increased incentives, this may be successful.

> **Essentials**
>
> **Focus** means staying within the core competences of the business and selling off peripheral businesses. It is the opposite of diversification. It ensures that the business concentrates on products which it really understands.

The mergers that have taken place have tended to be horizontal in nature. Industries where this has been notable have included motor vehicles, oil and food retailing.

There have been some attempts at mergers which have failed to come to fruition because the culture of the companies involved was too diverse. This reflects the fact that some mergers do not generate the gains anticipated because the fit is not good enough. It is better to recognise this before getting too involved because the process can be expensive and time consuming to take apart.

Point of view

'Til death do us part???

When ICI divided its business into two, it was the strongest evidence yet that big, diversified corporations have had their day. By cutting itself up, ICI was following an increasingly popular path. Racal, Courtaulds and BAT have all adopted the same strategy. All have acknowledged that they were previously overdiversified.

Senior managers can be tempted to diversify for two main reasons:
- to spread risk – in other words, so as not to have too many eggs in one basket
- to drive expansion – when low growth in the core activity causes ambitious managers to seek growth opportunities in less familiar activities.

But the early 1990s were full of examples of the danger for companies in becoming too diversified. British Aerospace plunged into cars, property, construction and munitions – with such poor results that the chairman and finance director both resigned. BP has been reversing its unhappy moves into minerals and nutrition to concentrate on its oil and chemical business. It has since sought opportunities for horizontal inorganic growth in its merger activity.

There have also been a string of near misses when businesses turned out to have very different corporate cultures.

Your agenda

1 Why do you think expansion through diversification is liable to reduce efficiency?
2 Why do you think that firms which have been one unit for a long time may divide into constituent parts?
3 What can lead a well-considered merger to fail to take place?

2 Compete or collude?

Fighting dirt

	Proctor & Gamble	Unilever
Sector: household cleaning products		
Global market share	16.72%	16.02%
	Ariel, Bold, Bounce, Daz, Dreft, Fairy, Lenor, Flash	Persil, Surf, Radion, Jif, Domestos, Frish, Comfort
Sector: shampoo		
Global market share	19.4%	18.9%
	Pantene, Pro-V, Head and Shoulders, Vidal Sassoon	Salon Selectives, Organics, Sunsilk, Timotei
Sector: bath soap		
Global market share	12.59%	32.6%
	Camay, Ivory, Zest, Shield	Dove, Lux, Pears
Sector: deodorant		
Global market share	6.08%	24.4%
	Old Spice, Sure (USA), Safeguard	Sure (UK), Vaseline, Lynx, Impulse

Source: Euromonitor

Figure M4.20 Percentage of worldwide sales in personal and domestic-cleaning products

Proctor and Gamble and Unilever are the two companies which dominate the personal and domestic-cleaning products markets. Figure M4.20 shows some of their ranges. They also produce perfumes, nappies and over-the-counter medications, to name but a few.

Your agenda

1 In which category do the two companies have the greatest market share?
2 In which category is one company dominant in terms of:
   a competition with the other
   b the market in general?
3 Draw a spectrum of competition and place each of these markets on it.
4 How do these companies compete for sales?
5 How important is price in their competition?
6 What barriers to entry are there in this business?
7 To what extent do you think barriers to entry contribute to the power of these companies?

	Raise price 1	Lower price 2	Differentiate products 3	Increase advertising 4	Other non-price competition 5
Raise price 1					
Lower price 2					
Differentiate product 3					
Increase advertising 4					
Other non-price competition 5					

Figure M4.21 Strategies open to Firm A

To understand competitive strategies, the activities of businesses need to be observed. An observation of supermarkets, magazines and television will quickly paint a picture of the way companies like the ones discussed in the above case study compete.

An industry with high barriers, like the market in which Proctor & Gamble and Unilever are major players, will tend to be dominated by a small number of firms and is known as an **oligopoly**. The main competitors share most of the market. As the personal and domestic-cleaning business market is actually dominated by two players, it is a **duopoly**, a more extreme form of oligopoly.

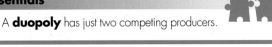

Essentials

An industry which is dominated by a few large firms is known as an **oligopoly**. The decisions which each firm makes depend on the actions of the other firms in the industry, so it is difficult to predict the behaviour of oligopolists.

Essentials

A **duopoly** has just two competing producers.

In this situation, firms will be keen to maintain or increase their market shares. They will look for a strategy which will give them a clear identity and persuade people to buy their products. They will try to differentiate

their products from others by styling or other techniques.

Many oligopolies are very rivalrous. An inspection of advertising will show current strategies very clearly. Each firm will be conscious of the activities of others and will attempt to second guess the next move. This makes them very interdependent. Figure M4.21 shows some of the possibilities.

The table makes it very clear that there is a multitude of alternatives. Two firms give 25 combinations, three firms would make it 625. It could even be more as the strategies are not mutually exclusive, in other words, they may use several at the same time. The interdependent behaviour of oligopolists which can use such a large range of strategies makes the outcome very unpredictable.

Industries with few competitors often use a wide range of methods to persuade us to buy. If you draw up a similar chart which reflects them all and think of the number of firms involved in making cars, you will have an idea of the scale of the problem facing each manufacturer in a market where the actions of others can have a strong influence.

In a perfectly competitive market this degree of competition would lead to producers making normal profit which would be just enough to keep them in business. Such competition would lead to efficiency, but in an industry which new firms find hard to enter, existing companies have more influence over the market. They spend time and money trying to make the market more imperfect, so a market with only a few firms is unlikely to achieve allocative efficiency. Each firm is trying to increase its profit and look for ways of reducing the impact of competition.

Strategies used will normally try to avoid price cutting in the hope of keeping profits above the normal level. Non-price competition is therefore more frequent. This involves advertising and other ways of persuading people to buy products. One of the most successful methods is to give a product a particular identity. Who would have thought that for a time jeans with buttons down the front would become an essential item in every wardrobe! This is known as product differentiation, a common feature of oligopolistic markets.

Game theory

One way to seek understanding of the workings of oligopoly is to use **game theory**. It shows how each firm might think about its choice of strategy in the light of the likely behaviour of the competition. The outcome of such strategic games may or may not be efficient.

Essentials

Game theory likens the behaviour of firms in uncertain situations such as oligopoly to players in a game of strategy. It looks at ways in which they will attempt to deal with the uncertainty.

The one thing that all firms want to avoid is a price war unless they are certain of winning. The only result would be a fall in everyone's profit. The profit-pay-off matrix in Figure M4.22 shows why.

	Electric Audio	
	£1000	**£500**
Supersonic Sound	**A** £6000 / £6000	**B** £9000 / –£2000
	C –£2000 / £6000	**D** £0 / £0

Figure M4.22 Price cutting: a Profit-pay-off matrix

Box A shows the initial situation. Both Electric Audio and Supersonic Sound offer a particular top-of-the-range sound system at £1000. On their total sales they each make a profit of £6000. This is the best each can do as long as they both charge £1000.

If Electric Audio thinks that Supersonic Sound will hold the existing price, it could take advantage by reducing the price to £500. In this situation (Box B), few people would buy from Supersonic Sound who would make a loss of £2000 while Electric Audio increased its profits to £9000. Box C shows what would happen if the decisions were reversed. Neither of these boxes represent a stable situation because the firm making a loss would respond by cutting price. This leads us to Box D which explains why no one wants a price war. In this case, both firms have cut the price to £500 and profits have been completely eroded. They were both better off in Box A.

The situation is, however, stable because, given Electric's strategy, Supersonic can do no better, and given Supersonic's strategy, Electric cannot improve things. Look at the profit figures in the boxes to confirm this. Although this may not be the ideal situation for the firms, it is very efficient for the consumers and the economy as a whole. The shops are just covering their costs and making enough to keep the entrepreneurs in business while customers are buying sound systems at the lowest possible price.

In an oligopoly, firms must always take the expected actions of others into account when making decisions. The profit-pay-off matrix box shows clearly how such firms are interdependent. The decisions of one firm have a major impact on the other firm and this is reflected in the profits of both. With this expectation, each firm must look ahead to devise a strategy to outwit the other.

Competition in oligopolistic industries demonstrates this interaction. When one firm cuts prices, others often follow. When environmental awareness is the main focus, every product becomes 'green'. The whole process is extremely expensive. Every large firm will employ a whole department of people who spend their time predicting economic change and what their competitors are likely to do next. They then must devise ways of coming out on top.

Work in progress

Q 1 Which box represents the best situation for:
    a Electric Audio
    b Supersonic Sound
    c both companies
    d the consumer?

2 If firms wanted to make as much profit as possible, what would be the easy solution?

3 Is the motor industry an oligopoly? Explain the evidence for and against.

3 Is 1 a winner?

Total complaints about train performance

		% change
Punctuality	4014	+38
Reliability	1705	+42
Overcrowding	980	+36
Comfort	963	+34
Journey information	482	+41
Staff conduct	305	+22
Catering	269	+37
Reservations	290	+45
Safety/Security	219	+24
Disabled facilities	58	−11

Source: Central Rail Users Consultative Committee

Figure M4.23 Discontented customers

Your agenda

1 What do the data tell you about customer satisfaction with the train operating companies?

2 If people are so unhappy with the service, why do they not use an alternative? What does this tell you about the elasticity of demand for train journeys?

3 Where do train operators sit on the spectrum of competition?

4 Find out what has happened to the profits of your local train operators.

Monopoly power can bring high profits for those who run a business with influence, providing that people want the product. If demand is inelastic, the owner is on to a winner. It enables the business to increase the price without fear of losing customers.

There are relatively few pure monopolies, although there are sectors of industry in which choice is increasingly restricted. Most monopolies which exist are a product of privatisation. Train operating companies, for example, face little real competition. The data in Figure M4.23 suggest that all is not well.

The combination of a shortage of alternatives, or substitutes, and inelastic demand puts power into the hands of the companies. Despite the fact that each privatised industry has its own regulator, there are still issues in some industries which have not been resolved.

Barriers to entry naturally make a market less contestable. Many of these industries have vast capital investment and duplication would lead to an inefficient allocation of resources. They are therefore highly incontestable.

The economies of scale which result from output being in the hands of one producer or supplier can generate efficiency because fixed costs are spread over many units of output. However, it seems difficult to combine the objective of allocative efficiency and an efficient business organisation.

In some of these industries, strategies have been devised to generate competition and therefore combine the gains from large-scale investment and those from competitive efficiency. Gas and electricity, for example, can be supplied by a variety of companies because it is possible to measure the amount of power that one company has sold and therefore how much it must have put into the system.

Even on the railways, different operators can run trains on the same track. In practice, particularly on local routes, little of this has developed. In these circumstances, most people just want to catch the next train that arrives, so demand tends to be inelastic.

In general, the power of the monopolist will depend on the elasticity of demand. If it is inelastic, the company will be in a very powerful position and will be able to determine either price or the quantity supplied. It will be able to make plenty of super-normal profit.

In such circumstances, some sort of regulation will be essential if the market is to approach efficiency and consumers are not to be subjected to the acquisitive objectives of the business concerned. Offer and Ofgas, the regulators for the electricity and the gas industries, do control prices to a degree and have provided some protection for customers. Other regulators try to do the same for other privatised industries with a degree of monopoly power.

Work in progress

Parents come under great pressure from their children to buy the replica football strip from their favourite club. These only come from one source, the club itself. Clubs have even been known to restrict the supply of strip to shops which undercut the list price.

Q

1 What is demand like for replica football strip? Why?

2 How great is the club's power over:

   a retailers

   b customers?

3 What effect does this have on price?

4 Why are football clubs so keen to sell such products to their fans?

How competitive?

Enquiry 1 An enterprising environment?

1 One up?

What makes a nation competitive?

Can industry innovate and upgrade?

Is there competition, pressure and challenge?

Are there strong domestic rivals?

Are there aggressive homebound suppliers?

Are local customers demanding?

Your agenda

1 Why does the answer to each of these questions have to be 'yes' if a country is to be a successful player in the global economy?

2 What might be done to increase the level of competitiveness in a country?

For a long time competitiveness was simply viewed as having low costs. There are many countries round the world where industrial costs are low but they are not to be found on the competitiveness map. Much of Africa for example, falls into this category.

The questions above cover the key areas which need to be considered if a country is to compete successfully both at home and abroad. These are brought together in Figure M4.24 which shows their interrelationships as well as external influences.

There are many more questions to be asked about an economy to find out if it is competitive. Each of the questions above can be opened up to discover the advantages and disadvantages of a country in the competitiveness stakes.

The four determinants are:

1 **Factor conditions: what resources does the country have?**

- **Human resources.** Are they skilled? What do they cost? How many are there? What is the work ethic?

- **Physical resources.** What raw materials are there? Are they accessible? What is the climate like? Which time zone is the country in?

- **Knowledge resources.** What is known about science and technology? Do people know about the markets that they are competing in?

- **Financial resources.** Is there finance available to businesses that want to develop? What does it cost?

- **Infrastructure.** What is the type, quality and cost of using the country's infrastructure? What is the quality of provision of housing, health care and cultural activity?

2 **Demand conditions: what is home demand like for the country's own products?**

- **The composition of home demand.** Customers who are ahead of the game lead businesses to anticipate international demand.

- **The size and pattern of growth of home demand.** A large home market gives economies of scale, although a small market can give an incentive to export. Fast-growing home demand means that firms invest in the latest technology.

- **Ways of accessing foreign markets.** Buyers who are multi-nationals will take products into foreign markets. Training people from abroad will lead them to want the host countries products. Seeing new products in the movies works well.

3 **Related and supporting industries: are they competitive?**

- A business that can draw on supplies from competitive supplier industries has an advantage.

- The existence of successful related industries is an indicator.

4 **Firm strategy, structure and rivalry: how are businesses created, organised and managed? Is there rivalry?**

- National attitudes to organisations, risk, trade and success can influence the type of products in which a country has competitive advantage.

- A rivalrous home market will stimulate competitive advantage.

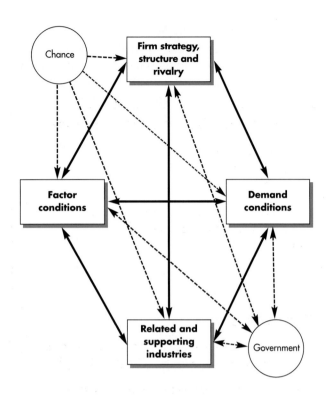

Figure M4.24 The sources of competitive advantage

Source: M. Porter, *The Competitive Advantage of Nations*, Macmillan, 1990

Beyond the market

All the factors in Figure M4.24 are integral parts of the market. There are two other factors which can play a significant role in the competitive advantage of a country.

■ Chance

Chance can change the pattern of competitive advantage almost at random. A new invention, for example, will give one economy a sudden lead in a particular field.

Wars and political events may cause a shift in demand from one economy to another. These and other shocks such as hikes in oil prices, may lead to changes which give or remove competitive advantage.

Changes in financial markets or exchange rates can alter the pattern unexpectedly.

Whatever the source of change, the instincts of the economy will lead to some countries making the most of opportunities. The more positive factors there are in the diamond in Figure M4.24, the greater the chance of success.

A country which combines inventiveness with entrepreneurship has the highest probability of turning chance into competitive advantage.

■ Government

The government can influence each of the four market determinants for good or bad. It cannot create competitive advantage by itself, but it can improve an already encouraging situation.

● Policies towards education, financial markets and subsidies can all affect the market for factors of production.

● The government is a buyer of a wide range of products.

● The government lays down standards for many industries which create confidence in international markets.

If the government merely supports industries which would not be viable otherwise, it will not create competitive advantage. If its actions remove the need to innovate and upgrade, it will not be acting in the best interests of an industry.

Point of view 66 99

Making the UK more competitive?

Human resources

⁶ They must understand that without a broader pool of trained human resources, their competitive advantage will be constrained.⁹

⁶ The rate of social investment must rise substantially.⁹

⁶ Company investment in universities is still minimal.⁹

⁶ Companies need to accept greater responsibility for internal training of all employees.⁹

Research and development

⁶ Government investment should be maintained, but funds should be channelled through universities and specialised research institutes and not into direct subsidies.⁹

⁶ More troubling is the low rate of R & D spending in firms.⁹

Demand conditions

⁶ The challenge is to upgrade British consumer and industrial demand and broaden the areas in which British companies benefit from challenging and well-informed buyers.⁹

Financial markets

⁶ Corporate goals revolve around short-term financial results… A long-term bias is in the interest of national economies. Policies should be adjusted to create one.⁹

Regulation and government ownership

⁶ British industry has been undermined by monopoly companies. Innovation in these fields is stunted.⁹

⁶ Privatisation without effective competition defeats much of the purpose of the policy change.⁹

Competition

⁶ The wave of mergers and take-overs threatens to go too far in consolidating British industry.⁹

⁶ A strong orientation to monopoly control is increasingly necessary.⁹

New business formation

⁶ New business formation depends on skills and ideas, on appropriate motivation and goals, on active competition, and on access to capital. One of the urgent reasons to upgrade education, especially in universities is to contribute to seeding new ventures.⁹

Source: M. Porter, *The Competitive Advantage of Nations*, Macmillan, 1990

Your agenda

1 Create a policy agenda for the UK government to meet these challenges.
2 What should business be doing?
3 Check out current government policy to see if it is rising to the challenge.

2 Why help?

Government assistance

Red tape cut for small businesses

The minimum wage threatened to submerge small businesses in red tape. According to Chris Humphreys, director general of the British Chamber of Commerce, the paperwork involved would have been 'perhaps the most burdensome requirement on firms'.

What is the Small Firms Loan Guarantee Scheme?

Small firms with viable business proposals which have tried and failed to obtain a conventional loan, either because of lack of security or business track record, or both, may be able to obtain finance under the Small Firms Loan Guarantee Scheme. By providing a government guarantee against default by borrowers, the scheme enables high street banks and other financial bodies to lend between £5000 and £100 000 to new and existing businesses.

Source: Loan Guarantee Scheme, DTI

BMW seeks £180 million

The German car producer claims that it will not go ahead with the production of the new Rover model at Longbridge if it does not receive help from the British government... After much negotiation a package was agreed which provided both financial assistance and skills training.

Your agenda

1 Explain how each of these activities assists business.
2 Which example does not live up to the criteria for increasing competitive advantage?
3 Why does the government assist businesses:
   a in ways which aim to increase competitive advantage
   b in ways which do not ?

Governments offer a range of help to businesses. Much of it comes in the form of advice. Any new business has to conform to a wide range of legislation and monitor its activity to ensure that it provides the required information to government agencies at the right time.

Apart from dealing with legislation, there are also services which assist with innovation, design, finance, suppliers, training and exports. Some of these are free and others are subsidised. Much is focused on developing entrepreneurship and competitive practices. By doing so, the attitudes of people in business can become more focussed on product development which meets the needs of the market. The UK does not rank very highly in the enterprise stakes. By providing such services, the objective is clearly to improve this ranking.

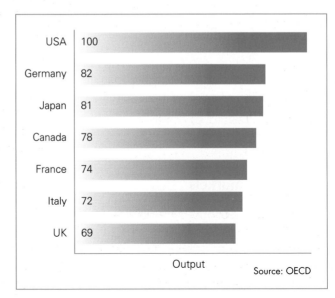

	Output per head
USA	100
Germany	82
Japan	81
Canada	78
France	74
Italy	72
UK	69

Output

Source: OECD

Figure M4.25 Output per head (USA = 100)

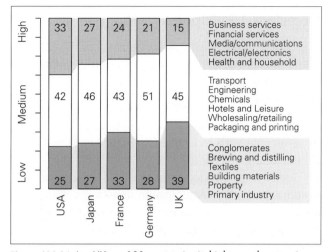

Figure M4.26 Are UK top 100 companies in high-growth sectors?

Source: (*Times* 100; *Die Zeit*; McKinsey)
as reported in *The Sunday Times* 11 October 1998 © Times Newspapers Limited

Figures M4.25 and M4.26 are two indicators of the UK's competitiveness. Although much government support is aimed at small businesses, the development of a more entrepreneurial mentality among people who run their own businesses can alter attitudes in the community.

Other support

Not all assistance provided by government is solely aimed at improving competitiveness. Support for businesses in parts of the country which are suffering from economic decline is available both from the UK government and the European Union. The motive may also be social as high levels of unemployment in such areas have high costs to the economy and to society.

3 Why build bridges?

Going for growth

Liverpool is a city which comes very close to the top of the country's poverty league – but things are changing. Right in the centre of the city, you will find one of the country's largest inner-city regeneration projects.

The Queen's Square development started with the clearance of an enormous site and the construction of a bus station and transport infrastructure. This initial work was paid for by European Union Objective 1 funding.

The impact on Liverpool has been extensive. Once this public sector funding was secured, the private sector came to life. Swallow invested £14 million in a magnificent new hotel and Neptune Developments has built a mix of retail, office and leisure facilities.

The area is turning into a thriving community where people can enjoy their leisure time in the new bars and open spaces of the square. To keep it all pristine, the tenants in the area pay a management fee for the upkeep of the square.

Source: Communications service, Liverpool City Council

Your agenda

1 What effect does the Queen's Square development have on:
   a employment in the area
   b spending power in the area?

2 How does it affect the impression that the city has on:
   a people who are thinking of setting up a business
   b outsiders visiting the area?

3 Why are the tenants prepared to contribute to a system which maintains the new environment ?

4 Why is the initial injection of public sector investment important?

5 Why does such a development increase competitiveness in:
   a Liverpool
   b UK?

Some parts of the country, like Liverpool, are relatively poor when compared with the rest of the UK. To a large extent, this results from industrial decline and leads to unemployment and associated social problems.

It can be difficult to extricate a region from such difficulties because the images of decline are not attractive to new industry and the resident population can become very demotivated if there is no prospect of employment. This not only affects the people in the area but also the overall competitiveness of the economy. Resources are being wasted and resources have to be redirected to support people and therefore potential output is reduced.

There are two sources of government assistance for such areas.

■ Assisted Area status

Grants are available from the government for parts of the country which are classed as Assisted Areas. These grants can provide between 5 per cent and 15 per cent of fixed costs depending on the viability of the investment and the number of jobs created.

Regional Enterprise Grants are available to small firms in manufacturing and some service industries. They provide:

● investment grants of up to 15 per cent of the cost of fixed assets

● innovation grants of up to 50 per cent of agreed projects to develop new products or processes.

■ Objective 1 European Funding

Objective 1 funding is available to areas of the EU where average GDP is less than 75 per cent of the EU average. It is given through the local authority and is available for the following:

● capital investment
● assistance with Industrial Development Plans
● marketing assistance
● developing supplier networks
● advanced telecommunication links
● energy efficiency and environmental best practice
● support for training needs, including Investors in People.

What are the objectives?

The objective of much government support has shifted from propping up industries which are no longer competitive in a national or international context. It is now available for regeneration projects which encourage business activity which has longrun viability. These have the potential to improve permanently the **infrastructure** of whole communities.

Such grants are often available in the context of the broader agenda for the region. Figure M4.27 shows the range of activity in Liverpool which contributes to the overall regeneration agenda. The combination of these plans with the city's Economic Development Plan builds an integrated programme of work for the city and its agencies.

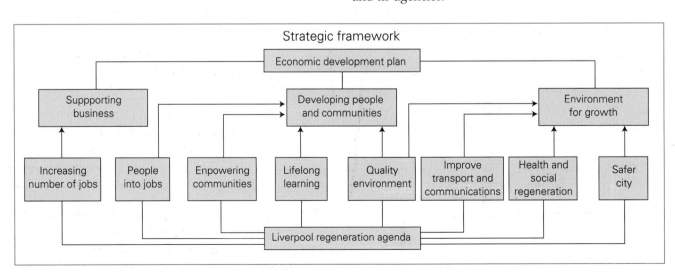

Figure M4.27 Economic development and regeneration

Source: Economic Development Plan, 1998/9, Liverpool City Council

The nature of the schemes involved in the Regeneration Agenda reflects the scope of factors which lead to the creation of a competitive economy. This mix of industrial investment with improved training, environmental and infrastructure is a common factor in all contexts.

What is the effect?

The results of regeneration programmes can be much greater than the sum of the initial investment.

The infrastructure investment creates new jobs which puts money in people's pockets. When they spend this money in shops and facilities within the area, it increases other people's income and they have more to spend. Some of the spending will increase demand for the products of other local businesses. The initial injection therefore goes round the system many times. This is known as the **regional multiplier** effect because the initial investment is multiplied, maybe several times.

The real effect will depend upon how much money stays in the local area and how much leaves it. If many of the employees are only in the area on a temporary basis, the money will leave with them or be sent home to their families. The added profit to businesses which are based outside the area will also leave because they will go back to headquarters. Finally, if people save their extra income instead of spending it, the effect will be reduced.

Developing people

Investing in people

Blackburne House was once a girl's school, the sister to Paul McCartney's old school. It looks very different today.

Since the opening of the Women's Technology and Education Centre, it has become a focus for the community around Hope Street and further afield. The beautiful building has been rejuvenated and is now full of a very different sort of activity. As Liverpool is one of the poorest parts of the country, Blackburne House receives support from Objective 1 funding and the European Social Fund.

The original objective was to raise the skills of women in the area. A range of courses was developed to help people find jobs in the information technology world. The courses range from simple computing skills to NVQ level 3 in Digital Technology. All introductory courses take into account the fact that English isn't everyone's first language.

The centre has gone from strength to strength since it first opened in 1994. It now has a nursery, café-bar, fitness centre and conference and exhibition centre. It also rents space to other organisations.

The initial investment has had many spin-offs within Blackburne House as well as in the local community.

Your agenda

1 How does Blackburne House help the people of Liverpool?

2 How does the development of the facilities help Blackburne House?

3 Why does the EU put funding into such areas?

4 How does Blackburne House contribute to making Liverpool more competitive?

5 How does it contribute to making the UK more competitive?

The European Social Fund goes to depressed areas in which people skills are often at a low level or out of date. By developing skills people are able to move into the labour market instead of being dependent on state aid. There is, as a result, a double gain:

- People are supporting themselves and therefore not in need of support from the state.

- They are also adding value to the community because they are earning and spending.

Because people are earning, they are contributing to the GDP of the region. The multiplier effect comes into play and the net effect of training people is therefore considerably greater than the initial outlay.

The level of skill in the workforce not only helps existing business but it also facilitates the establishment of new business in the area. At Blackburne House courses which train people in Internet skills and setting up web sites are available. New businesses, based on such skills, are easy and cheap to start up. The courses therefore need to identify the needs of business in order to achieve an increase in competitiveness.

Companies from outside the region will look carefully at the skill structure before deciding to move or expand into the area. The focus of training is therefore important in developing an image which will promote competitiveness.

The improvement in the economic environment will help to dispel the region's negative image. As a depressed area with high unemployment and labour market problems, Merseyside has appeared an unattractive location for business. As skills rise and economic vibrancy increases, businesses will think again.

If help of this sort can improve the economic outlook for such parts of the country, the overall income and output figures for the country improves and less has to be spent on support. This increasing productivity will, it is hoped, lead to general improvements in competitiveness.

4 What about the people?

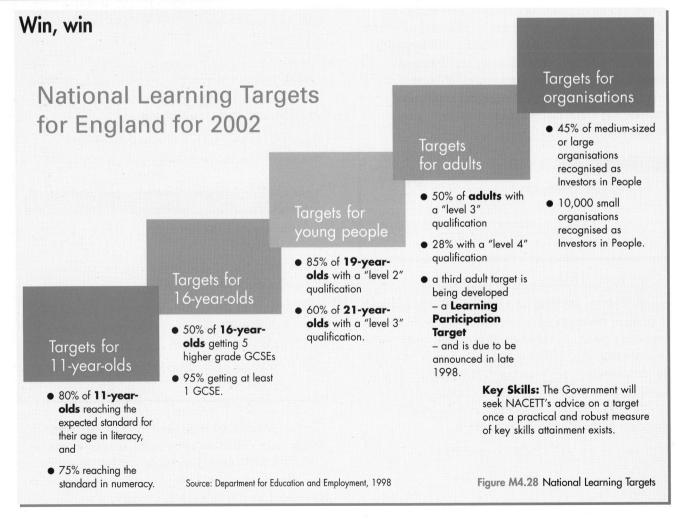

Win, win

National Learning Targets for England for 2002

Targets for 11-year-olds

- 80% of **11-year-olds** reaching the expected standard for their age in literacy, and

- 75% reaching the standard in numeracy.

Targets for 16-year-olds

- 50% of **16-year-olds** getting 5 higher grade GCSEs

- 95% getting at least 1 GCSE.

Targets for young people

- 85% of **19-year-olds** with a "level 2" qualification

- 60% of **21-year-olds** with a "level 3" qualification.

Targets for adults

- 50% of **adults** with a "level 3" qualification

- 28% with a "level 4" qualification

- a third adult target is being developed – a **Learning Participation Target** – and is due to be announced in late 1998.

Key Skills: The Government will seek NACETT's advice on a target once a practical and robust measure of key skills attainment exists.

Targets for organisations

- 45% of medium-sized or large organisations recognised as Investors in People

- 10,000 small organisations recognised as Investors in People.

Source: Department for Education and Employment, 1998

Figure M4.28 National Learning Targets

NEW DEAL has helped 69 000 young people into jobs, training or work experience, according to figures released by the DfEE. More than 38 400 have so far secured jobs, over 27 000 are unsubsidised.

More than 45 000 jobs have also been pledged by 33 000 employers who have signed New Deal Employer Agreements, providing many opportunities for young people in the near future.

Source: *DfEE Employment News, January 1999 HMSO*

Figure M4.28a New Deal

Cash for New Deal skills training

EMPLOYERS OFFERING permanent jobs to young people under New Deal can receive money up front in a bid to help solve skills shortage.

Announcing the new payment, the Upfront Skills Shortage Subsidy, the Employment Minister said: 'The money will address the very real problems some employers encounter when recruiting employees who need precise skills and require a significant amount of upfront training.'

Employers can receive three-quarters of the training and subsidy payments when a New Deal employee starts a job. The remaining quarter will be paid after 26 weeks, when the agreed training objectives have been achieved.

Any employers facing a skill shortage will be able to receive the training and subsidy payment on condition that they provide a person on New Deal with a permanent job lasting at least one year and a minimum of 15 days training in the first eight weeks of employment and 26 days or more during their first six months.

Source: *DfEE Employment News, January 1999 HMSO*

A New Dealer

Joe Warburton had been unemployed for 18 months. He was just 21 and hadn't really had a job since he left school. His personal adviser at the Job Centre noticed that he was really into fitness and helped him to use his enthusiasm to find a job. They discovered that the gym where he worked out had signed up for the New Deal and a match was quickly made.

Your agenda

1 Why has the government set targets for education and training?

2 Why does the government subsidise training?

3 Why is there a special focus on areas of skills shortage?

4 How did finding a job for Joe help both him and the economy?

5 New Deal is an example of the type of strategy which can be used to help young unemployed people into employment and training. How do such policies improve the nation's competitiveness?

Raising the skills level

As the world becomes a more complex place, people need higher and higher levels of skill to play a successful role. Governments have therefore sought to raise the skills levels of the population. This has two effects:

● It makes the workforce more competitive.

● It makes the unemployed more employable.

■ A more competitive workforce

Education and training are carried out by both the government and industry. The National Learning Targets (Figure M4.28) show how the two work together. Governments generally have the objective of raising levels of achievement in schools and colleges as well as encouraging business to increase the amount of training it carries out. The UK is short of people with lower skills levels but has a better record at high levels as Figure M4.29 shows.

	UK	France	Germany
% of population qualified to level 2 and above	45	65	70
% of population qualified to level 3 and above	30	30	62
% of population qualified to level 4 and above	19	16	15

Source: Skills Audit DfEE, HMSO

Figure M4.29 Level of qualifications

The world is a rapidly changing place so skills constantly need to be updated. Few people are in jobs which will remain the same throughout their lives and many will change direction completely at least once. Investment in human resources is a major part of any country's investment programme. Figure M4.30 shows the UK's position in relation to other members of the EU.

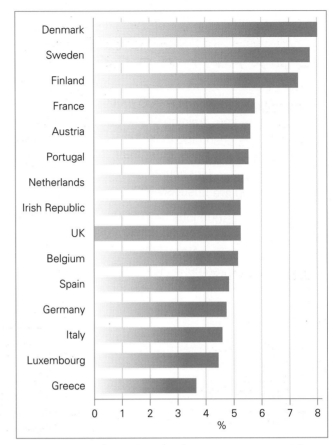

Figure M4.30 Public expenditure on education as a percentage of GDP

Source: ONS, *Social Trends*, 1999

■ Making the unemployed more employable

There is a strong correlation between an individual's level of qualification and his or her employment prospects. Figure M4.31 shows the link. Someone with no qualifications has a much higher risk of unemployment than anyone else. It is therefore in the country's interest as well as the individual's to ensure that everyone has at least a basic standard of education and preferably a marketable skill as well.

% Unemployed	Males	Females	All
Higher education	3	3	3
Level 3	5	5	5
Trade apprenticeships	5	4	4
Level 2	8	5	7
Level 1 and below	11	9	10
No qualifications	16	9	12

Figure M4.31 UK qualifications and unemployment

Source: ONS, *Social Trends*, 1999

Three benefits arise from achieving a well-educated and highly skilled work force and therefore increasing participation:

- Unemployment is a waste of resources. If people are not working, there may be a high opportunity cost. The economy loses the output which might have been created and therefore the GDP is lower than it could have been.

- Unemployment leads to social exclusion which alienates people from the working world and can lead to increased costs in terms of social services and health care. The inevitable additional cost comes from the payment of benefits to people who are without work.

- Unemployment reduces tax revenue. People who are in work pay taxes and therefore enable the government to increase spending or reduce the average tax take.

What sort of training?

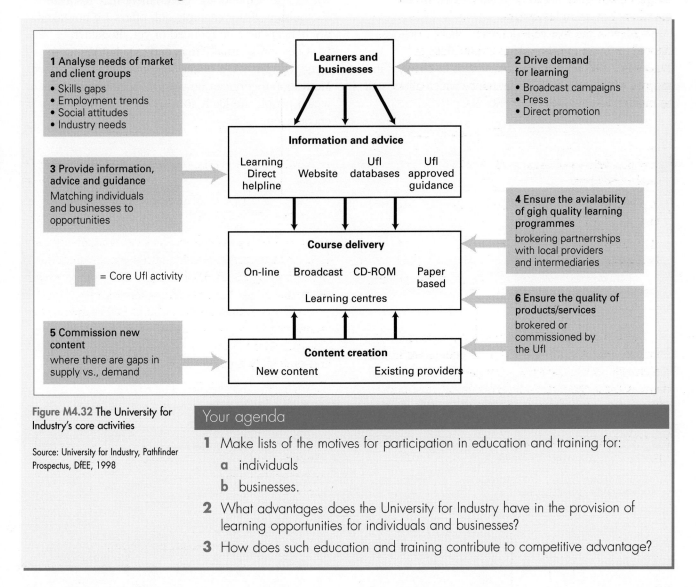

Figure M4.32 The University for Industry's core activities

Source: University for Industry, Pathfinder Prospectus, DfEE, 1998

Your agenda

1 Make lists of the motives for participation in education and training for:

  a individuals

  b businesses.

2 What advantages does the University for Industry have in the provision of learning opportunities for individuals and businesses?

3 How does such education and training contribute to competitive advantage?

Over the years there have been many strategies employed by governments to encourage people and businesses to participate in training. They have had mixed results. The UK's record is not good and targets set by recent governments have not been achieved. It is, of course, true that people may be skilled to a particular level but not have a qualification to reflect the level of attainment. Their skill would therefore not have recognition in national data.

Training must meet the needs of the people or organisations it seeks to serve. It must be in the right place, at the right time and of the right quality. Many people who follow the traditional route through education are prepared to forfeit earnings at the beginning of their career because they expect their lifetime earning stream to be higher. Later on, the trade-offs can seem less clear.

It is often the fear of redundancy that persuades people to investigate broadening their skills. Businesses also react to loss of markets or changes in technology by retraining programmes which allow staff to move into new areas of work.

The University for Industry is a long-run project which aims to meet the needs of both businesses and individuals. It will work both from a physical basis and through electronic systems. Its flexibility should help to meet many of the requirements of its potential users. If people can be attracted to further training by a system that responds to their needs, the skills level in the UK should be increased and the country's level of competitiveness should improve.

If nothing works...

Most policies aim to provide carrots to help people to join the labour market. For sectors of the population who fail to respond, the government may resort to compulsion. If, for example, job offers are not taken up, benefits may be reduced or cut altogether.

Coercion is usually regarded as a last resort as incentives provide a better outcome for all concerned. Motivation theory can be used to demonstrate ways in which people are likely to respond more favourably if encouraged.

5 What will the price be?

Sensitive antennae

Panorama Antennae makes aerials for mobile phones. Christopher Jesman and his brother Andrew have grown used to the sweet smell of success. Last year, sales had grown by 13 per cent.

Exports were rising after doubling investment in export marketing. At one-third of sales, exporting had become a key focus for the business. It had reached this point after a period of phenomenal growth, achieving 85 per cent a year.

Then the pound began to rise. Overseas sales began to slide. Despite the fact that Europe's mobile phone market is growing by 50 per cent a year, Panorama's mainland European sales have fallen by 5 per cent.

Sales to Germany no longer make a profit. Prices had to be cut by 25 per cent in order to stay competitive. The brothers made this decision because they knew that it was much harder to recapture the customers once they lost them. At least, Germany only represented 5 per cent of total sales. Had it been on a larger scale, the strategy would not have been sustainable.

Even life at home is uncomfortable. They have held on to their 75 per cent market share but only by cutting prices. There are many foreign companies seeking new business and the high pound makes the UK a tempting market. Without the 20 per cent price cuts, the Jesman brothers think that they would have lost half the business to cheap imports.

There have been opportunities to cut costs, however. They are now sourcing more cheaply from abroad. Home suppliers have lost out badly: 75 per cent of components used to be bought in the UK, now the proportion has fallen to 25 per cent. As components make up 48 per cent of costs, the change in suppliers has just about made up for the price cut.

They have changed their financial systems for overseas work. Invoicing is always in the local currency and sales personnel and office staff are never paid in pounds. Life is straightforward as long as revenues and costs balance in any one currency. Trouble only arises when conversion takes place.

Your agenda

1   Explain why the change in the value of the pound has affected Panorama.

2   What are the knock-on effects for other UK businesses?

3   What would have happened if the pound had fallen?

4   Why is it hard to regain markets which have been lost?

5   What effect does uncertainty have on the management of a business?

6   How might a single currency help?

7   How can movements in exchange rates affect competitive advantage?

If a country is to be competitive, businesses need to be able to tell potential customers about the price of their products. Changing exchange rates can make this complex.

There are winners and losers in any movement of exchange rates. These occur both within and between countries. Panorama had to fight hard to maintain profitability. It did so by changing to imported sources which had become cheaper as the value of the pound fell.

Any business which is exporting will suffer, while importers will gain when the pound rises. The reverse is, of course, true if the pound falls in value. Few businesses in export markets are as simple as that,

however. As Panorama found, trade often involves staff in the partner country and consideration of the financial complexities of changing currency values. All these activities take time and add costs to the business.

Industry, in general, dislikes uncertainty. Exchange rates are a prime source because even the most reliable economic forecasters can get it wrong!

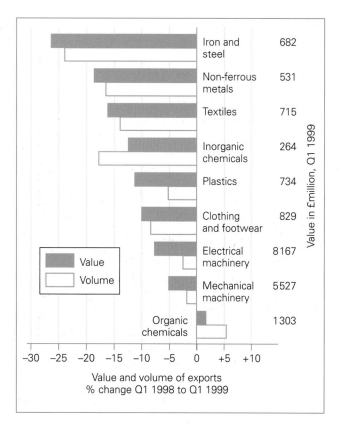

	Value in £million, Q1 1999
Iron and steel	682
Non-ferrous metals	531
Textiles	715
Inorganic chemicals	264
Plastics	734
Clothing and footwear	829
Electrical machinery	8167
Mechanical machinery	5527
Organic chemicals	1303

Value and volume of exports
% change Q1 1998 to Q1 1999

Figure M4.33 The effects of the rising pound   Source: Primark Datastream
(graph from *Economist* 12.6.99)

Figure M4.33 shows the effect of the rising pound in 1998 on various industries. The strong pound had reduced demand for UK output as people in other countries looked for cheaper sources. The impact on the profitability of the businesses in these industries would obviously be severe. Panorama was struggling to reduce costs in order to keep prices down but faced limits to the extent of such cost cutting.

As export business suffers, employment in such sectors is likely to fall. Once export business is lost, it is difficult to regain and therefore some jobs may be gone forever.

The changing value of the pound has the obvious costs of making prices change in another currency, but there are all sorts of hidden costs involved. At the lowest level, it can mean reprinting price lists, for example. Although it sounds a small cost, it will affect budgets and creates uncertainty in the minds of customers if they are not sure that a company's prices will stay the same throughout the next pricing cycle.

Whichever way currencies move, some businesses are likely to complain. Such movements can change the relative importance of products and trading partners.

Business and a single currency

The euro is popular with some businesses because it:

- creates stability, so levels of uncertainty are reduced

- reduces transaction costs because all deals are carried out in one currency, so there are no costs involved in changing currencies

- increases the probability of economic stability.

Other businesses consider it to be a threat because:

- exchange rate flexibility has been the way economies adjusted to meet changing price levels

- a single interest rate is unlikely to suit all countries at one given moment

- Britain is more sensitive to interest rate changes than the rest of Europe as it has more mortgages, for example

- it will increase bureaucracy resulting from European legislation.

Exchange rates obviously have an important role to play in the competitiveness of a country. The euro will assist competitiveness for some businesses in their trade with Europe. With all prices given in one currency across the eurozone, it will be easy to identify the most competitive products. This transparency will remove many uncertainties.

1 How size matters

Market chemistry

The chemist round the corner has been there for ever. It has been run by the same family for the past 50 years. The pharmacist has been a great source of support to members of the community of all ages. He helped worried mums and arranged for prescriptions to be taken to the elderly. He knew what people wanted and kept supplies of products for particular customers. If he didn't stock something you wanted, he would order it for the next day. He knew that this was the way to keep his customers and stop them going into town to shop at Boots or Superdrug.

Just recently, an enormous branch of Boots opened up on a local retail park. It is much closer than the town centre and you can always park your car right outside the door.

It didn't take long for the pharmacist to decide that he could no longer make ends meet. He had always belonged to a purchasing group which made products cheaper but still he could not compete, especially as everyone had a Boots loyalty card. Was there anything else he could do?

He thought long and hard as selling up was a great wrench. At least, there is still a chemist round the corner because it sold out to one of the chains. It's not the same. Although the pharmacists there have all the expertise, they will never be part of the community in the same way. They are always looking for a move to a bigger and better location and will never get to know the customers like the previous owners.

	1991	1992	1993	1994	1995	1996	1997
Total number of registered community pharmacies	11,782	11,783	11,882	11,889	11,954	12,079	12,048
Total number owned by companies with 50 or more	2,087	2,392	2,767	2,949	3,119	3,479	3,621
Total number of independents and small groups	9,695	9,391	9,115	8,933	8,835	8,600	8,427

Source: National Pharmaceutical Association

Figure M4.34 Trends in pharmacy ownership, 1991–7

Your agenda

1 Why did the chemist always have an interest in working closely with the local community?

2 Why could it buy things more cheaply through the purchasing group?

3 Why does a loyalty card affect people's purchasing patterns?

4 Why is it difficult to create the same sort of culture in a chain as in a business run by a sole trader?

5 Is the experience of this chemist repeated nationally?

6 What trends do the data in Figure M4.33 suggest for the future?

7 Why are these changes taking place?

8 Explain the trends in terms of the spectrum of competition.

The up side

Size brings many advantages to a business. Economies of scale reduce costs and therefore make a business more competitive. This influences all parts of the business from production to marketing. Here are a few examples of the practical ways in which economies of scale empower a large company:

- Adverts on the television cost the same whether you are aiming to sell 100 000 items or a million items.

- High street rents are affordable because chains can spread other overhead costs.

- Own brands become possible if sales are high enough.

- Financial systems can be duplicated across all stores.

- Distribution networks can be set up to meet the needs of the business instead of having to rely on other contractors.

- Product development means that a business can stay ahead of the game.

As a result, customers can buy products more cheaply and benefit from up-to-the-minute products in smart new stores on the high street. Competition between large companies may lead to lower prices and a better product range.

Equally, it is also possible that, if there are only a few competitors, they may develop arrangements which mean that they do not have to work so hard to compete.

Any large organisation is likely to have more power than a small one unless the latter has a distinctive way of adding value or a unique product which gives it monopoly power.

The down side

Figure M4.34 shows a continuing downward trend in the number of independent chemists. What is more worrying is that it also shows a similar trend in the total number of chemists.

The increase in large branches of the multiples makes the community chemist less sustainable. Many local chemists have closed because of the pressure of

bigger stores in towns and out-of-town shopping centres. This has led to a reduction in services where people need them.

This pattern is apparent in many spheres, from greengrocers to electrical shops. Often the degree of expertise of the staff is reduced and therefore the level of service does not compare with the standard that was available previously.

As a result, there tends to be a trade-off between the lower prices available in the multiple stores and the quality of service provided by an independent retailer. As multiples move in, the choice between these alternatives disappears because the independents cannot cope with the competition. Once they have gone, there is even less pressure to maintain high standards of service, unless it is the way in which the chains are competing.

Barriers to entry make it difficult for a small shop to set up in competition. The economies of scale gained by the multiple create a level of price competition which an independent shop finds impossible to meet.

Going international

The global box

Washing powders come in a range of large boxes. One of the major manufacturers has many ranges of soap powders which are supplied round the world. The economies of scale are stupendous.

Boxes are made to standard sizes in one factory which serves much of the world. The design can be universal, with appropriate adaptations for language and culture. The flat-packed boxes can then be shipped to wherever they are going to be filled. This may happen in India, Russia or Europe.

Your agenda

1 What economies of scale can be achieved by this approach?

2 How does such scale advantage build barriers to entry for more local suppliers?

3 Why might local suppliers have some advantage?

Multi-nationals can have opportunities for economies of scale of great dimensions. The market for their products can be many multiples of a national business in the same field.

There are many advantages in developing products in such a large market place because costs are spread so widely. From the company's point of view, market research has to be carried out thoroughly because of the importance of adapting to the culture and language of different countries. There are some infamous examples of products being given names which have most unfortunate connotations when used in another language!

As a source of power, a multi-national structure provides business with many opportunities:

- Risks are spread between both countries and products.

- Production in low-cost economies gives an international competitive advantage.

- Economies are often at different points on the business cycle so when demand is low in some areas, it is high in others.

- Legislation varies from country to country so products and production can be managed flexibly.

- Products may have a longer life cycle because of the nature of different markets.

Multi-nationals, however, do not always feel the same degree of commitment to production when it is taking place in another country. A possible scenario is that a global business may cause the demise of a local business because of the degree of competition and then pull out because it becomes cheaper to produce elsewhere.

There are, of course, benefits to the local community in that a multi-national will bring in employment and training which can have a multiplier effect. As always, there are trade-offs in terms of competition when firms go international.

2 Setting the limits

A diamond deal

Diamonds aren't really as scarce as you think. Clever business practice has made them scarce. De Beers, the diamond company, has set up a system which keeps supply short.

At one time, de Beers mined all the diamonds and therefore supply was fixed. It sold them through the Central Selling Organisation. Buyers were sent packages of mixed-quality diamonds which they had to buy if they wanted to stay in the game. This meant that the poorer diamonds were sold as well as the best.

As new diamond mines set up, de Beers bought them to keep control so all diamonds continued to pass through the Central Selling Organisation. More recently, producers have been put under pressure to sell their output to de Beers.

If demand fell, de Beers put fewer diamonds in the packages. To maintain this system, de Beers had to be prepared to hold enormous stocks if price levels were to be maintained.

Buyers couldn't object because there was no one else to buy from. If they are caught buying from other sources,

de Beers will cut off the packages. The rest of the diamond world is too unpredictable to risk being without their little packages.

At the retail end of the business, no one complains. De Beers spends US$200 million a year to keep diamonds precious – to ensure that they really are forever.

Trouble set in when the Russians started cheating on the system. They sold their agreed quantity to de Beers but they sold the rest elsewhere. After protracted discussions, Russia was persuaded to stay on side.

Your agenda

1 Draw a demand and supply diagram to demonstrate the workings of the diamond market.

2 Explain how the demand side and supply sides of the market work.

3 What would happen if the Russians broke away from the system?

4 Why do you think the system has lasted so long?

5 What do you think the market would be like if de Beers did not exist?

6 Who are the winners and losers in this market?

As the interaction of demand and supply creates price, if one of them is fixed, price will behave very differently from the way it would in a market where both are flexible.

Supply can be fixed for all sorts of reasons. Nature plays its part in many markets. The supply of hard wood, for example, cannot be changed quickly once the trees are planted. Trees take a very long time to reach maturity so the supply of teak is strictly limited. Environmental issues reinforce this as timber is only acceptable if it is from sustainable forests.

If everyone suddenly wanted to buy teak garden furniture, the price would rise very rapidly. Inelastic supply will always lead to large price changes if demand changes.

Just as demand has varying elasticities, so does supply. The formula follows the same pattern.

Elasticity of supply = $\dfrac{\text{\% change in quantity supplied}}{\text{\% change in price}}$

So if a 10 per cent increase in price induces firms to increase output by 20 per cent, the elasticity of supply is 2.

If supply can change easily, elasticity will be high or more than 1 in numerical terms. If it is very inflexible, the figure will be below 1. An increase in price will lead to a less than proportional change in quantity supplied. (Figure 4.35.)

Essentials

Elasticity of supply measures the responsiveness of quantity supplied to a change in price.

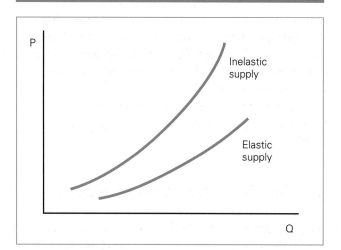

P

Inelastic supply

Elastic supply

Q

Figure M4.35 Elasticity of supply

Elasticity of supply depends very much on the length of time involved. A firm may be considering whether it can expand output this week. It will be able to do so if it has resources available for the purpose. It will need labour, raw material and component inputs, and sufficient spare capacity in the capital equipment. If it is already working flat out, some or all of these things will be unavailable in the quantities required. If the firm is unable to increase output at all, supply is perfectly inelastic. This is quite likely to happen over a short period of time. The time for which supply is perfectly inelastic is the **market period**.

Essentials

The **market period** is the length of time within which supply is absolutely fixed.

In the short run, the firm can get more variable factors of production (labour and raw material and component inputs). In this way it may be able to expand output somewhat. Supply will probably be inelastic. In the long run, all factors of production are variable. The firm can invest in more capital equipment and perhaps build a new factory. Supply will probably be elastic, possibly even perfectly elastic. In other words, by duplicating all the resources needed for production, it may be possible to expand output and still charge the same price.

Supply can be inelastic for a whole range of reasons. The supply of diamonds is very inelastic because De Beers makes it so. Not many businesses can preserve their power so effectively. More often, supply is inelastic because it takes time to organise extra factors of production.

Sometimes supply remains more or less fixed when demand falls. This can be observed in the housing market, where prices may fall quite sharply.

Work in progress

Any Room at the Inn?

Tourists are quite sensitive to price changes. A fall in the exchange rate of a popular destination country can increase the number of potential tourists considerably, and boost export earnings from tourism.

But will there be room for them all? London has at various times had a shortage of hotel beds. What needs to be done to start up a hotel? A suitable building must be bought or built. By next summer? Clearly, this is going to take time.

Q

1 What factors will affect the increase in supply of hotel rooms?

2 What is likely to happen to hotel prices in the short run?

3 If tourists are sensitive to price changes, what is likely to happen to their numbers? What does this tell you about the price elasticity of demand for tourism?

4 What might be the end result of the movements in demand and supply in this very dynamic market? Draw a row of diagrams to show the movements.

5 How long would it take for exporters generally to increase their export sales? How long will it take to increase exports of aero-engines? Explain using elasticity of supply.

What about the producers?

Producers of natural products live in a world of swings and roundabouts. If demand rises, they gain, If demand falls, they lose. This has been seen very clearly whenever a food scare hits the headlines. Such scares are always followed by stories of farmers who have gone bankrupt because the stock that they had invested in was suddenly worth a fraction of their expected value.

When inelastic supply is the result of natural phenomena, it can be a source of power but equally, it can be a threat. An inelastic supply can turn into an excess supply if no one wants it. It must always be remembered that the consumer is a participant in the game and therefore price movements are unpredictable.

When supply is made inelastic by participants in the market, it is because it results in higher profit margins. As shown in the case study on page 331, De Beers has set up a system which fixes the supply in order to control the market.

In any business where this occurs, it is a major source of power because it allows the supplier to adjust the market according to changes in demand. It is, of course, more powerful when related to monopoly power. If all the diamonds are in the hands of one organisation, price is controlled more easily. If they are in many hands, it is probable that someone will take the opportunity of making a fast buck by undercutting a little, and prices will fall.

What about the customer?

When supply is inelastic, the customer can be on the receiving end of price rises if demand increases. Equally, the price will fall if demand falls. The market is clearly working.

When inelastic supply is combined with monopoly power, the situation changes. When demand rises, price rises, but it tends not to fall if demand falls as the business is able to restrict the amount that it offers to the market.

Other elements of the product may change too. The privatised train operators are a case in point. Not only do they have monopoly power on the routes for which they hold the contracts but they can determine how many trains to run, within the limits of government guidelines. As they took over from British Rail, services often improved in the short run. As time has gone on, the quality of services has declined and customers have suffered. Some services have become more erratic and dirty.

Monopoly power plus inelastic supply is a combination that creates power which needs to be scrutinised.

How does it affect competitiveness?

Many countries are affected by natural sources of supply inelasticity. Therefore many problems are common. Foreseeable shortages can benefit from careful planning by both business and government, but the unforeseeable are more difficult to deal with. The weather is often a source of such problems. When banana crops are wiped out by hurricanes, the economies of Caribbean islands can be badly damaged.

Where the combination of inelasticity and monopoly power are united, the issues can be serious. While sales of gem diamonds may not concern many, an inefficient rail network has a more negative effect.

If prices are higher than in a competitive market or the services are poorer, businesses which are seeking to develop will look elsewhere. People will have less disposable income because they have to pay above the market rate for travel. As a result, demand in general will be lower and the criteria for creating competitive advantage will be difficult to achieve. Low-quality, expensive infrastructure is a great deterrent to both existing and potential investors in a country.

What a fix?

Press release: US Department of Justice   **May 20 1999**

A Swiss pharmaceuticals giant, F Hoffman–La Roche Ltd today agreed to plead guilty and pay a record $500 million criminal fine for leading a worldwide conspiracy to raise and fix prices and allocate market share. A German firm, BASF will also plead guilty and pay $225 million fine for its role in the same conspiracy.

The charges are that the conspirators:

- agreed to fix and raise prices on Vitamins A, B2, B5, C, E, Beta Carotene, and vitamin premixes
- agreed to allocate the volume of sales and market share of such vitamins
- agreed to divide contracts to supply vitamin premixes to customers in the US by rigging the bids for those contracts
- participated in meetings and conversations to monitor and enforce adherence to the agreed-upon prices and market shares.

The conspiracy lasted from January 1990 to February 1999 and affected the vitamins most commonly used as nutritional supplements or to enrich human food or animal feed.

'The conspiracy has affected more than five billion dollars' worth of products which are found in every American household,' said Joel I. Klein, Assistant Attorney General.

Source: Adapted from US Department of Justice website, (www.usdoj.gov/atr)

Your agenda

1 Explain exactly what these businesses were doing.
2 What effect has the cartel had on 'the products found in every American household'?
3 Why were Hoffman–La Roche and BASF prepared to take the risk?
4 Why do you think that a record fine was handed down?
5 How does the existence of cartels prevent a country having competitive advantage?

Except in certain circumstances, monopolies are not allowed because of the power that they put into the hands of the business. However, if a business is determined to avoid competing, it may adopt one of a range of **restrictive practices**. These include any method used to reduce competition. They can be encountered in many different sorts of markets. (Later on in this module government actions to prevent this type of activity will be discussed, see page 349.)

Essentials

Restrictive practices include any way in which a business or a group of people interferes with the free working of market forces. This may be done by reducing supply, or by agreeing to share markets out instead of competing.

Competition is an expensive business. All companies know that 50 per cent of their advertising is successful. What they don't know is – which half! If they did not have to compete, they would not have to spend either 50 per cent. The investment that any business makes in matching its products to the market can be avoided if there is only one supplier, or if a group of suppliers acts in unison. There are two well-known ways of doing this:

- tacit agreements
- cartels.

■ Tacit agreements

One solution is for the interested businesses to get together and sort out the market between themselves. There has been a long history of **tacit agreements**. In the eighteenth century the economist Adam Smith said:

'People of the same trade seldom meet together, even for merriment and diversion, but the conversation ends in a conspiracy against the public, or in some contrivance to raise prices.'

Essentials

Tacit agreements are unwritten agreements between firms to fix prices or limit output.

Tacit agreements are hard to prove. The businesses concerned may never have met or discussed their pricing strategies at all. They simply find other ways to compete. The Sunday papers often have stories about products which have identical prices in all the shops. It can be difficult to find the evidence that fixing is going on because it is in the interests of both the producers and the retailers.

■ Cartels

Hoffman–La Roche and BASF went a step further. They set up a **cartel** and made formal agreements about the allocation of the market and the prices that would be charged. Agreeing a price removes all need for speculation about what other firms will do in the future. Deciding the amount that each company will sell in each area gives the group monopoly power. This means that the companies are therefore able to push up prices as well as reducing the costs of trading. This is a very appealing concept for business but, unfortunately for them, it is illegal because it shifts the balance of power between the consumer and producer.

Essentials

Cartels are agreements between companies which fix prices or output and therefore restrict competition. They are illegal.

Price fixing and competitive advantage

A country in which firms fix prices is likely to be paying over the odds for products which people need on a regular basis. This has a general effect on real incomes. It may discourage overseas companies which are planning to set up a branch plant because the cost of inputs will be higher. This, of course, works against the requirement of a competitive home market needed for an economy to have competitive advantage.

If people are paying over the odds for staple parts of their spending, they will have less to spend on other products which will lead to a less vibrant economy. People will have less scope to experiment with their spending patterns. One of the factors which contributes to competitive advantage is an adventurous pattern of home consumption.

3 Is it protection?

Down Tijuana way...

A drive round the industrial areas of this Mexican city flags up the presence of many international names. Companies like Sony and JVC are flooding into Mexico. Why, you may ask? As you have probably guessed, it is not simply the attraction of tequila and sombreros. It is the fact that the USA is just across the border and both countries are members of the North American Free Trade Area (NAFTA).

As NAFTA members, goods can be traded duty free. If it weren't for NAFTA, JVC would be selling televisions from the Far East in the USA. These televisions would attract duty and therefore be less competitive than those from NAFTA members. By assembling them in Mexico, there is no duty and prices can therefore be lower.

Labour is cheaper in Mexico than in the USA but not nearly as cheap as in parts of the Far East.

The one catch is that there are rules of origin about where the component parts come from.

A television made by JVC in Mexico must have some crucial parts that come from within the member countries. So, down Tijuana way, there are factories making tubes standing close to the ones which assemble the tubes.

Your agenda

1 What advantages are there for NAFTA members in trading with each other?

2 What would happen if NAFTA did not exist?

3 Who would gain if trade were free?

Regional trade agreements

Regional trade agreements are being set up rapidly throughout the world. Figure M4.36 shows their proliferation.

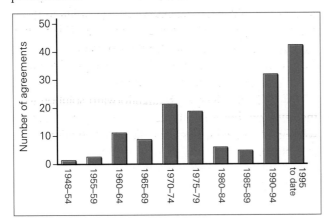

Figure M4.36 The number of regional trade agreements registered with the World Trade Organisation   Source: World Trade Organisation (WTO) *Economist* 3.10.98

What effect do these trading areas have on business and industry?

The North Atlantic Free Trade Area has led to the USA buying televisions, which they once would have made themselves at greater cost, from Mexico. This is 'good' because it is more efficient. People are getting more for their money. It is known as **trade creation**.

Essentials

Trade creation is an increase in trade caused by people buying goods from another country where costs are lower.

If there were no trade agreements, where would the USA go to buy its televisions? Probably, it would buy them from the Far East. Why? Because the price is lower. So what has happened? Although the cost of making televisions is cheaper in Mexico than in the USA, they are cheaper still in the Far East. If Americans' televisions came from the Far East, everyone would have more to spend on other things. It would be more efficient.

NAFTA, on initial investigation, has resulted in trade creation but, in fact, it is only an intermediate step. If the USA were open to free trade with all countries and not restricted by NAFTA, it would buy more from the Far East. This would be real trade creation. In these circumstances, the existence of NAFTA is really **trade diversion**. It stops countries trading with those who could offer them the same products at a lower price.

Essentials

Trade diversion is caused by trade barriers which raise the price of goods from certain countries so people do not buy from the country with the lowest costs.

Building blocks or stumbling blocks?

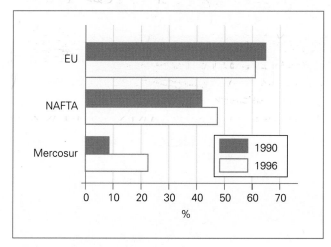

Figure M4.37 Trade within blocks as percentage of total exports
Source: World Trade Organisation (WTO) *Economist 22 Feb 22.8.98*

Figure M4.37 shows the importance of trade within trading blocks. Within the EU, the proportion of trade has fallen slightly but forms a high percentage of internal trade. Trade within NAFTA and Mercosur, the South American group, has grown.

In order to evaluate whether these free trade areas are building blocks or stumbling blocks in the move to free trade, the pattern of trade and the development of the groups must be investigated. Some questions to be answered are as follows:

- What was the pattern of trade before the group was set up? Has it changed?
- Does the external tariff cause trade diversion?
- Are the areas experiencing economic growth?
- Are countries outside the groups lowering tariffs to attract trade?
- Are there pressures from within to maintain high tariffs?
- Do they deal with competition policy?

The answers to these questions combined with the attitudes of governments will determine the path which is being taken.

Some countries are faced with strong internal pressure from business to maintain high tariffs to give protection to industry. Farmers within the EU have led a strong campaign to maintain the Common Agricultural Policy because it has always provided a minimum payment for their products.

There is obviously no straightforward solution to the question, but if free trade areas are open to the world and general tariffs are falling, the situation is improving.

What about the European Union?

Any trade grouping has the same effect. The members of the European Union have formed the European Economic Area with European countries which are not within the Union. It has developed relationships with countries in northern Africa and central Europe. This relationship means that trade still takes place on preferential terms within this grouping.

This leads to issues over particular products which are excluded by one grouping because of being attached to another. Bananas in the US market are cheaper than in the European market. When Europeans pay more for their bananas, trade diversion is taking place. It is, however, based on a sense of responsibility that European countries have towards the Caribbean countries which have built up banana production on the basis of having a safe market. If they lose this market to cheaper producers, there will be considerable hardship in these islands.

The economic answer is that they should produce something that can be done more efficiently, but as these island economies depend on bananas, it is not easy to change direction quickly.

The other countries which produce bananas are seeking access into the European market. Their rejection led to a vitriolic counterattack against European products by the USA.

The EU as a whole has external barriers which discourage primary producers from processing their products. Raw sugar, tea and coffee will be subject to much lower tariffs than if they are ready for the supermarket shelves. This protects the European food-processing industry and prevents developing countries from earning the greater rewards which result from adding value to their raw materials.

It has been estimated that the EU reduces other countries' GNP by 3 per cent or a total of at least US$80 billion. As the EU grows, international trade may become further distorted as the extent of trade diversion grows.

But what about competitiveness?

A country within a regional trade group will have the benefit of free trade with other member countries. The rules and regulations of the EU aim to create a level playing field so that members can compete fairly. This may have two effects:

- If the EU creates standards for products, the group as a whole will have elements of competitive advantage because the rest of the world will know that European goods are of a high standard.

- A protected market can become complacent. If businesses know that the European market is reasonably safe, they may not be pushed into innovation. Innovation may equally be focused on the existing direction with the trading group rather than looking at the needs of potential markets beyond.

Any activity which leads to trade diversion will reduce competitive advantage in areas beyond the protected area. Tariff walls are often reciprocated. NAFTA has tariffs which make European goods more expensive in the USA, Canada and Mexico.

Enquiry 3 Is the market competitive?

1. Who's in the contest?

767 ++++++?

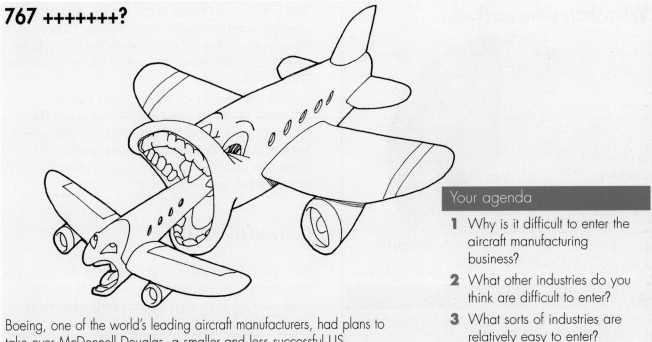

Boeing, one of the world's leading aircraft manufacturers, had plans to take over McDonnell Douglas, a smaller and less successful US competitor. The US competition regulators had no problem. They could see a strong business arising from the project.

The European competition regulator was by no means so happy. If these two firms joined forces, it would create a stronger challenge to Airbus, the European aircraft builder.

Your agenda

1 Why is it difficult to enter the aircraft manufacturing business?

2 What other industries do you think are difficult to enter?

3 What sorts of industries are relatively easy to enter?

4 Why do problems arise if industries are difficult to enter?

5 Is it a national or international problem?

6 What could be done about it?

Contestability measures the ease with which firms can enter and leave an industry. Markets in which new businesses can set up readily are contestable. This can be thwarted in a variety of ways. The barrier of high investment costs is often a significant factor in industries which are non-contestable. Natural monopolies and entrenched oligopolies and monopolies also create high barriers to entry.

Anything that makes it difficult for new businesses to start up in a particular market reduces competitive advantage. It allows firms already in the market to charge higher prices or behave in a way which does not move the market forward as quickly as it might. Lack of competition may therefore leave the customers of one country in a worse position that those in another country.

Many highly capital-intensive industries are multi-nationals or trade internationally. The domination of international markets by a company or companies based in one country is an even greater challenge for other countries. That was why the European regulator was concerned about the reduction in competition in the aircraft industry. However, despite the objection, the take-over went ahead.

Contestability is a useful way of measuring market power but it is complex to measure. It is also somewhat suspect because when the main players in a market are threatened by new entrants, there is a strong tendency to lower prices and therefore repel them. As a result the barrier is maintained and after a while, when the threat has diminished, prices may return to the original level.

Contestability data are of a different order when compared with market share and other ways of measuring power because they are less concrete and more subject to interpretation about the outcome of changes in a dynamic market. Their value as a predictor must therefore be questioned.

2. Shares and concentration?

Who shares the market?

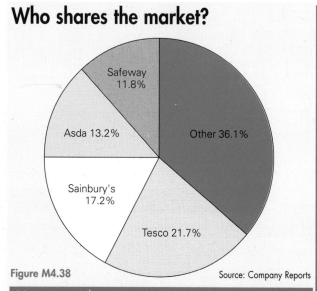

Figure M4.38   Source: Company Reports

Your agenda

1 What do the data in Figure M4.38 tell you about the nature of the market?

2 Why is it difficult for other companies to compete in the retail food business?

3 Are there any limitations to the use of market share to measure the power of companies?

Market share

Market share is a key indicator of market power. A business with a 70 per cent share of the market will probably behave differently from a business with 25 per cent of the market. The number of large competitors will also affect the behaviour of the dominant company. One big company surrounded by many small ones will generally have more influence than any one of a small group vying for market leadership.

Group of firms	Industry A % of total industry sales	Industry B % of total industry sales
Largest 3	45	45
Largest 5	58	80
Largest 10	63	100
Largest 50	65	100

Figure M4.39 A comparison of two different industries

Which industry in Figure M4.39 has the greater concentration of power? Clearly, Industry B, because it has only ten or fewer firms. Both industries could be described as oligopolies, because of the power of the largest firms.

It is not always possible to predict company behaviour simply by looking at market share. There are many other factors that can influence their power. Some of these influences, such as the power of consumers and other interest groups, will be considered in later enquiries.

Concentration ratios

One measure of market power uses concentration. The percentage of the market accounted for by a certain number of firms is called the **concentration ratio**.

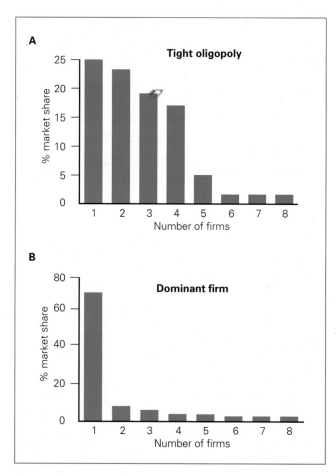

Figure M4.40 Concentration ratios

Figure M4.40 shows two very different pictures:

● Diagram A shows a market with several large competitors who will all be fighting for pole position:
  – The largest has 25 per cent of the market.
  – The top three have 65 per cent.
  – The top five have 88 per cent.

● Diagram B shows a market with one major player and a number of small competitors:
  – The largest has 70 per cent of the market.
  – The top three have 84 per cent.
  – The top five have 92 per cent.

The percentage market share for the top three companies is known as the three-firm concentration ratio. Similarly, the data show a five-firm concentration ratio. These ratios show how valuable the information can be. It is easy to draw conclusions about the nature of competition in markets like these when you have concentration ratios.

This is only one way of measuring the power of individual businesses, but it does give a very quick and easy measure of the structure of an industry.

Essentials

Concentration ratios show the proportion of the market controlled by a particular number of companies in an industry, i.e. a five-firm concentration ratio.

Can they predict?

Market share data and concentration ratios need to be combined with other information if predictions about the future are to be made.

The high cost of shopping in supermarkets in the UK is often related to the market share of the top players. This cannot be the only cause because at the time when Germany's top three supermarket chains had a market share of 43 per cent, in France it was 40 per cent and in Scandinavia it was considerably higher. The UK top three had 42 per cent of the market at that time. High prices seem likely therefore to have other causes. Simply reducing the market share of the major companies may not be enough.

Point of view

There is a range of contradictory data about why prices are higher in the UK:

● Planning laws prevent supermarkets setting up where they want to be so one shop can have control over a large area.
● The restrictions on building new shops puts up the cost of renting shopping space.
● UK supermarkets are half the size of their US equivalents and two-thirds the size of French ones.
● UK supermarkets employ more check-out staff than elsewhere.
● Retailers dwarf their suppliers.
● Europe's top ten have 36 per cent of the market.
● UK's top five have 68 per cent of the market.

Your agenda

Use the above data and any other information available to help decide the cause of the high prices. Are the trends changing?

Hello, dear, I've nearly finished the shopping, but is floor cleaner cheaper in Germany or Italy?

3 But what is the market?

Will it be Alton Towers?

Discussion in the Student Union office

JO   Where shall we go for the end-of-year trip?

SANJAY   How about Alton Towers?

JO   Let's look up the prices. I've got a brochure.

SANJAY   Wow! I think some people might find that a bit expensive don't you? Do you think that they do group discounts?

JO   I wonder what alternatives there are. If we offer a selection, people can vote for the most popular.

SANJAY   So what else can we do?

JO   There are some smaller theme parks, or perhaps some people would like to mark the end of their time here with a touch of culture. What about Stratford? We could go to the theatre.

SANJAY   OK. It could be an alternative. How about a trip to Llandudno? At least it would be cheap. We'd just have to book the coach.

Your agenda

1   If you were working out the market share for Alton Towers, what else would you include?

2   Would you consider a theatre visit or a trip to Llandudno in the same market?

3   Why is Alton Tower's ability to fix a very high price limited?

It can be difficult to gather accurate information about how much power one business has. The first difficulty is how to define the market.

In order to assess the structure of a market and decide whether there is any abuse of power, it is necessary to determine the boundaries of the market. Defining the market means drawing a circle round all the products that belong in the market and excluding all the other products. This is important because determining the size of the market affects the monopoly power that exists within it.

For example, in the market for lending money, the market could be defined as:

1   sources of finance available to a business
2   sources of banking finance available to a business
3   secured sources of banking finance available to a business
4   secured long-term sources of banking finance available to a business.

How would these definitions affect the size of the market?

● The market for sources of finance in general is large. Businesses can borrow from all sorts of organisations so the banks would have relatively little power in the first market.

● These are graded through to the fourth market in which the banks are the most powerful because a business looking for finance of this sort has little alternative but to go to the bank.

In the case of Alton Towers, its market is limited by the fact that there is a wide range of substitutes outside the category – theme parks. For many people a trip to a theme park is a luxury, so they will decide against it if the price seems too high.

Defining a product type can therefore be tricky. If there are significant areas where one overlaps with others, the product may well have substitutes in other 'markets'.

Where's the market?

Markets have changed a lot in size recently. The days when the only option was the high street shop has long since gone. Mail order has always had a significant part to play in increasing the geographical size of the market and e-commerce has taken this much further. It can be quicker to order a book from Amazon on the Internet than placing an order with your local bookshop so book shops have to strive to offer more.

Not everyone has the flexibility to use the larger-scale market place. If you are old and infirm, even the hypermarket may be out of reach. Your market may be restricted to the corner shop.

Can it be substituted?

Market share tells us quite a lot, but the market may have been defined relatively narrowly. Waterstones has a large market share for high street book shops, but the market for books now goes far beyond that.

Substitutability is the key concept in defining the extent of a market. If two products can be substituted, then they are in the same market. They will be competing with each other. The market power of each will be limited by the existence of the other. The closer the substitutes, the higher their elasticity of demand will be.

A product with no good substitutes faces little competition. It will be in a market of its own and will have considerable market power. The demand for it will be very inelastic with respect to price.

4 Who's performing?

What's in a ratio?

	Sainsbury	Asda	Tesco	Safeway
Operating profit margin 1999	4.85	5.32	9.78	4.88
ROCE	16.55	18.13	17.2	11.8

Source: Annual Reports and Accounts

Figure M4.41

Your agenda

1 What does the profit margin tell you about these four companies?
2 What does ROCE tell you?
3 Why are they useful for evaluating the performance of a business?
4 Does each one tell you anything about power or competitiveness?
5 Does the combination of the two ratios help more?

What does ROCE tell us?

Every time a large company reports a profit with many noughts, the media get very excited. What they never tell us is the return on capital employed. A large company with masses of capital would expect to make a substantial profit or it would be failing to use its resources properly.

Return on capital employed (ROCE) shows the relationship between that profit and the capital that the company is using. It is a useful measure of efficiency as comparisons can be made between companies of the same sort and size. It is less useful if very different businesses are being compared.

A small business which needs few resources, such as someone running a wordprocessing agency from home, might have a very high ROCE because they are generating considerable income. A large company, on the other hand, which is investing heavily but has not yet reaped the rewards will have a low ROCE.

In isolation it can tell us little about the power of a company because a small organisation might have the same return on capital as a large one.

Is profit margin useful?

Profit margins are readily available in every annual report and can be used to compare how effectively a business turns sales into profit. Again, it is useful for comparing like with like but in itself, it does not tell us about the size of the organisation.

As a result, we can gain little information about the power of a business from simply looking at the profit margin.

Working together?

Observing the cycle of a company's profit margins and ROCE can be helpful as it paints a picture of changes that are taking place.

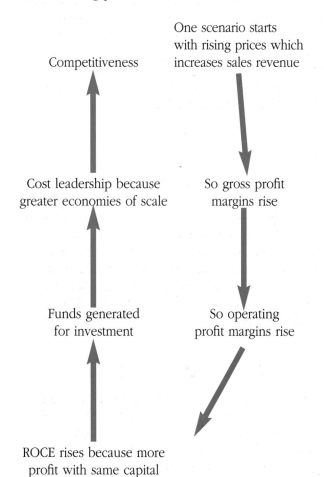

Competitiveness

One scenario starts with rising prices which increases sales revenue

Cost leadership because greater economies of scale

So gross profit margins rise

Funds generated for investment

So operating profit margins rise

ROCE rises because more profit with same capital

It would be possible to track different scenarios in which profit margins and ROCE interacted in this way to tell a story about how the business was functioning. It would also give a clearer picture of where a company was in relation to its competitors.

Work in progress

In Britain supermarket profit margins are double that of their counterparts in Europe. Return on capital is approximately 5 per cent lower.

Q   Can you explain this?

Profitability and power

Businesses which have some power over their prices can generally earn higher profits.
Why?

- The greater the degree of monopoly power, the lower the price elasticity of demand is likely to be.

- A price increase will lead to rising sales revenue and higher super-normal profit.

- Barriers to entry, which are the main source of monopoly power, keep new entrants out of the business so competition does not increase.

- The firms in the industry are likely to continue making super-normal profits.

The existence of powerful businesses can be justified as being in the consumer interest if the profits earned by these organisations are used to develop new products that benefit the consumer.

Another argument put forward is that new products are very expensive to develop and only a large, powerful company could make the necessary investment.

Similar arguments are advanced by the pharmaceuticals industry because of the costs and risks involved in the development and testing of new drugs. Whether such high profits are necessary in order to ensure the development of new products is open to question.

■ So – is it elastic?

Some products are indispensable simply because there are no alternatives. If the price goes up, consumers just have to go on buying them and forego other things.

Businesses are generally seeking to turn their products into ones that consumers regard as indispensable. A swift glance at the advertising budget of many companies tells you just how important this is. By persuading people that they really cannot do without jeans made by a particular company or a certain brand of trainers, the business has succeeded in creating that uniqueness that gives market power.

Such advertising reduces price elasticity of demand and makes other products seem inferior. This reduces the threat of competition and narrows the market by weakening the power of competing products.

If consumers see the substitute products as inferior, it may be possible to raise the price without sales falling much. It all depends on price elasticity of demand:

- When price elasticity is less than 1, a price increase will raise sales revenue because a proportionately smaller number of people will stop buying the product.

- When price elasticity is greater than 1, a price increase will reduce sales revenue because a proportionately larger number of people will stop buying the product.

Figure M4.42 shows the two scenarios. When demand is inelastic, the price increase leads to a gain in revenue which is far larger than the lost revenue from the small fall in quantity demanded. When demand is elastic, the fall in quantity demanded leads to a loss of revenue in excess of that gained from the higher price.

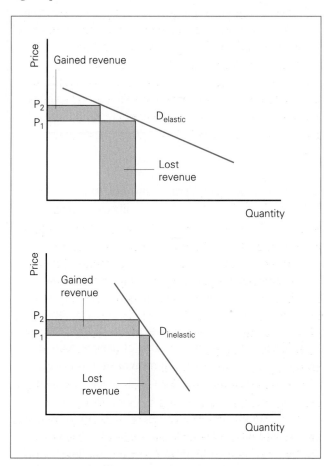

Figure M4.42 Price elasticity and potential sales revenue

This kind of market power can be created in other ways besides advertising. Suchard mini-Easter eggs are made of a higher-quality chocolate than are Cadbury's Cream Eggs with their white and yellow fillings. But both products have a unique appeal. Both enable their makers to charge a relatively high price because customers with a taste for a particular kind of egg will be prepared to pay more for it than they would for other eggs. Effectively, both firms have defined a market niche which allows them to charge a higher price and increase added value.

■ How much revenue?

It is important to remember that decisions about what price to charge depend on potential profit as well as on sales revenue. Profit in turn depends partly on cost structures. If, after a price rise, the quantity bought falls, the new lower quantity will have lower direct costs. In deciding on their pricing strategy, firms need to consider the changes in the relationship between revenue and costs which are likely to result from price and quantity changes.

■ What about competitiveness?

A firm that creates inelastic demand for itself is likely to increase profit margins and ROCE because it can probably charge higher prices for its products, providing it continues to add value in ways which meet customers needs. It will not be able to rest on its laurels as there is always another company which wants to increase its market share.

Provided that the business has to keep working to maintain its position, the customer is not losing out. Once the market becomes more static and competition is reduced, efficiency may be reduced and the consumer starts to pay higher prices.

A company which functions mainly in the domestic market may be safe if imports are not a possibility. The business will have little opportunity to enter international markets and will not survive long if foreign firms start selling in the home market.

The competitive business which has created a brand of international repute will function very effectively in international markets and add to the degree of competitiveness of its home country.

5 Competitiveness: trade-offs

Concentration: ROCE

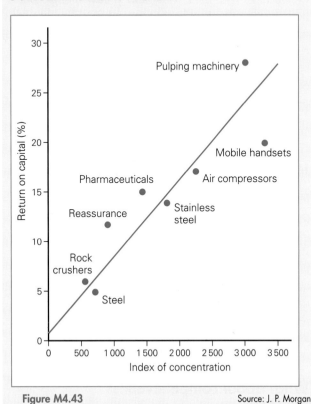

Figure M4.43   Source: J. P. Morgan

Your agenda

1 What relationship between concentration and ROCE does Figure M4.43 show?

2 Why is this relationship likely to occur?

3 Why can an increase in concentration in global industries make the world

  a   more competitive

  b   less competitive?

Mergers and acquisitions have been happening rapidly in Europe. The advent of the euro has simplified many cross-border deals and therefore encouraged this tendency.

There is still a long way to go before Europe matches the degree of concentration that exists in the USA. In the USA there are four firms making tractors compared with 50 in Europe. The USA has five battery makers while Europe has 40.

The pros

These comparisons suggest that European business has a long way to go to achieve the levels of productivity that are to be found in these US companies. Increased size leads to economies of scale which raises the level of returns expected from the business.

Efficiency is expected to increase as the size of a business grows, especially when these mergers demonstrate synergy. Vertical and horizontal integration have recently brought about a greater degree of success on this front than the conglomerate approach. This reinforces the data in Figure M4.43.

The success of such mergers is strongly influenced by the quality of management. Several proposed mergers have fallen apart recently because of the diversity of corporate culture in the two protagonists. A merger requires careful consideration of the structure in order to integrate two groups of people who were recent competitors. As it often involves redundancy, the process needs to be dealt with sensitively or much can be lost because of a dispirited workforce.

If the merger is successful and costs are reduced, ROCE should increase and the business should become a more competitive force in the market place. A larger player in Europe becomes able to compete effectively in world markets with its US counterparts.

The cons

A steady growth in concentration leads to increased competitiveness, but there comes a point at which it becomes a threat. There are many firms producing computer software, but there is only one that has a dominant place in the mainstream market. The dominance of Microsoft is regarded as a threat to competition in the industry.

There are obviously benefits from the majority of people using the same software, but it can lead to a suspicion that the lack of an alternative causes inefficiency. A Microsoft customer has little alternative but to continue buying the company's products and it is therefore possible to reduce quality without fear of losing sales. In a competitive market, a dissatisfied customer would go elsewhere.

Microsoft has therefore created a system in which demand for its products is inelastic. People have little alternative. This creates power which might be regarded as anti-competitive. Greater competition might lead to higher quality.

The trade-off

Concentration is therefore beneficial as long as it does not go too far. Greater economies of scale and increasing efficiency reduce costs and increase competitiveness.

Too much concentration can reduce competition or change its nature so that consumers are not being offered the best products at the lowest prices. If the market is global, there are issues about allocation of resources because everyone is having to pay a high price for lower-quality products. If the market is national, the country concerned will be less competitive than its neighbours because businesses and individuals will be paying higher prices.

1 Putting on the pressure

Who wants to be heard?

Britain's leading environmental pressure group Friends of the Earth today congratulated supermarket chain Iceland on its bold decision to ban genetically modified ingredients from its own-brand food.

Source: Friends of the Earth press release

London, March 10   Reuters
Consumers are frightened about genetics technology because they are being kept in the dark about the developments until they hit the market place.

Source: Gentech web site

For several years now, experiments have been conducted to transfer genes between species. These have included the introduction of:
● fish genes into strawberries
● scorpion genes into maize
● genes from bacteria and viruses into potatoes, apples and nearly all other food crops.

An avalanche of such GM foods is expected to reach our tables over the next five years and it has been estimated that as many as 60 per cent of all food products could already contain derivatives.

Source: *Genetic Engineering – Making Your Views Count*, Genewatch

Your agenda

1 What sort of organisations are Friends of the Earth, Gentech, Genewatch?

2 What is their objective?

3 Who is the material they produce aimed at?

4 Are pressure groups necessary? Why?

Groups have come together to protest since time immemorial. The suffragettes chained themselves to railings, went on hunger strike and one even threw herself under the King's horse in order to win votes for women.

More recently, organisations with a mission to bring about change have taken an increasingly systematic approach to their activities. Many **pressure groups** have national and international networks which spring into action to make the most of opportunities to be in the public eye.

A lot of work goes on behind the scenes and the case study above shows some of the types of coverage. The findings of research are fed into the debate on many sensitive issues. Press releases, web sites and printed material are all available to influence the debate. Pressure groups will take part in conferences, lobby MPs, approach business, appear on the television and radio and use many other strategies to make their voices heard.

There are pressure groups concerned with major international debates and others which are campaigning against the opening of a new supermarket. Some have a long history and others come and go according to need.

Some major organisations like trade unions and employers organisations are pressure groups which have developed a specific role in society. Their objective is always to change things. The result may be on a local, national or international level. It may be new or amended laws or changed business behaviour.

Essentials

Pressure groups are organisations formed by people with a common interest. They have very varied objectives: these might include persuading organisations to change, influencing public opinion, providing services for particular groups of people, or protecting members' interests.

Often the activities of pressure groups seem extreme, but it can take such behaviour to make people take notice. As pressure groups are seeking to hit the headlines, the gentle trickle of information to the public may have little effect. Women might still not have the vote if a small group had not been prepared to take some dramatic action.

2 What does the government do?

> **Competition Commission**   **Press Release**
>
> **THE COMPETITION COMMISSION INVITES EVIDENCE ON THE ACQUISITION OF NEWCASTLE UNITED PLC BY NTL GROUP LIMITED**
>
> **The Secretary of State for Trade and Industry has asked the Competition Commission to inquire into the acquisition by NTL Group Limited of Newcastle United PLC.**
>   **The Commission will be looking at the possible effects of the proposed acquisition on competition in broadcasting and football markets and other public interest matters.**

Your agenda

1 NTL Group Ltd is a communications and media company. In what ways might the take-over affect competition?

2 Who might respond to the request for evidence and why?

3 What is the government's objective in running the Competition Commission?

4 Why does the government publicise its activities relating to competition?

Businesses have always had a desire to reduce the effect of competition one way or another. As the economist Adam Smith had noted in the nineteenth century, it makes profit easier to come by because competition requires strategy and investment.

Restricting competition may be a desired outcome for individual businesses, but it has serious disadvantages for the economy as a whole and for any businesses that are excluded from the conspiracy.

Any business which is thinking of setting up in the UK will look carefully at the structure of competition in its sector. If it finds that a group of businesses seem to be in control or, even worse, just one – it will probably look elsewhere. If the playing field is not level, the game will be unfair. It will prove difficult to compete and profitability will be restricted.

If the UK market is full of businesses which are using anti-competitive practices, the requirement of strong domestic rivals is unlikely to be achieved. Without such rivalry, there is unlikely to be the necessary pressure and challenge to encourage innovation. The UK will not be competitive.

Where such a state of affairs exists, the customers will obviously suffer and potential investors will stay away.

What can be done?

The government has for a long time had structures which aim to control anti-competitive practices. In recent years these have been adapted to fit in with EU legislation. The two organisations which keep control are the Office of Fair Trading (OFT) and the Competition Commission.

■ The Office of Fair Trading

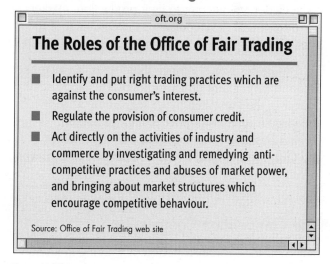

The Roles of the Office of Fair Trading

■ Identify and put right trading practices which are against the consumer's interest.

■ Regulate the provision of consumer credit.

■ Act directly on the activities of industry and commerce by investigating and remedying anti-competitive practices and abuses of market power, and bringing about market structures which encourage competitive behaviour.

Source: Office of Fair Trading web site

Figure M4.44

The activities in Figure M4.44 are taken care of by departments of the OFT and the Competition Commission.

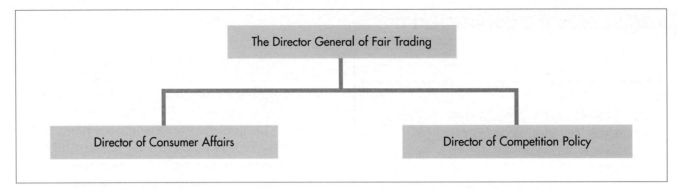

Figure M4.45 The Office of Fair Trading

Within the OFT, the consumer affairs department promotes and protects consumer interests. Its activities range from ensuring that credit is dealt with equitably to maintaining a list of estate agents who have been banned from trading.

The Competition Policy department is the focus for the UK's alignment with EU legislation. The Director General of Fair Trading is now responsible for two 'prohibitions' which are closely based on the European Community Treaty. These are:

● prohibition of anti-competitive agreements – this covers not only explicit agreements but also practices which have been carried out without formal agreement

● prohibition of abuse of a dominant position – this includes any attempt to limit production, markets or technical development to the detriment of the customer.

Businesses which infringe these rules can face fines of up to 10 per cent of UK turnover. This approach is similar to the line taken by US legislation, as shown by the vitamin case about price fixing, (page 334).

If a business does not agree with the findings of the OFT, it can appeal to the Competition Commission which will review the case.

■ The Competition Commission

When businesses are suspected of working in an anti-competitive manner, they are referred to the Competition Commission by the Director General of Fair Trading, the Secretary of State for Trade and Industry or the utility regulators (these are the bodies such as Ofgas which regulate privatised industries).

The type of investigation varies greatly. For example:

● The Commission has looked at the monopoly power exerted by Walls ice-cream through its practice of putting fridges into shops but not allowing other companies' ice cream to be stored in them.

● The take-over of Manchester United by BSkyB was investigated and rejected because it would have put too much power into the hands of one organisation.

In order to investigate the issue, the Commission will gather evidence and invite interested groups to contribute, as the case study at the beginning of this section shows.

Once complete, the report is sent to the Secretary of State for Trade and Industry. The outcome will then depend on whether the protagonists have broken, or plan to break, any laws because the Competition Commission's reports are not legally binding in their own right. Often, however, it is enough for the report to find against a business to persuade it to change its plans.

Some of the cases brought to the Competition Commission are test cases. Once it is clear what the Commission will and will not allow, most businesses will fall into line with its expectations without further action.

Through these mechanisms the UK attempts to create the sort of competitive environment which will attract firms to do business and therefore encourage economic growth.

3 What does Europe do?

VW versus the Competition Commissioner

- Forced to repay an illegal subsidy paid by the state of Lower Saxony, which is a big shareholder in the company.
- Forced to repay a subsidy made by the Spanish government to SEAT, a VW subsidiary.
- Forced to stop preventing cross-border sales from Italy to Austria and Germany.

Your agenda

1 Why might governments want to give subsidies to businesses?

2 Why did the car manufacturer VW want to prevent cross-border sales of its cars?

3 Why did the EU's Competition Commissioner want to prevent these activities?

Three bodies are involved in creating European policy:

- The Council of Ministers is made up of heads of state or their representatives.

- The European Parliament is composed of elected members.

- The Commission is appointed by the governments of the member countries.

The Commissioners propose policy and are responsible for carrying it out once ratified by the Council of Ministers and the Parliament.

The Treaty of Rome, which is the founding agreement of the EU, lays down that a key aim of the organisation is to work against 'the prevention, restriction or distortion of competition'.

The Competition Commissioner is therefore responsible for creating the level playing field on which the efficient working of the single market depends. The objective is to make the business behaviour as close to perfect competition as possible so it can look at a wide range of competitive practices. These generally fall into the following three categories:

- collusive agreements between supposedly independent competing organisations

- power exerted by enterprises with a degree of monopoly

- distortions of the market resulting from government subsidies, legal restrictions or purchasing policies.

How does it do it?

When businesses want to behave badly, they tend to do it in private. The Competition Commissioner therefore needs powers which allow him to find out about what is going on.

How did the EU find out that VW had intimidated at least 50 of its Italian distributors in order to prevent their making cross-border sales? How did it know that contacts had been cancelled with 12 of them because they had sold the cars below the list price?

The Commission has powers to:

- investigate complaints

- initiate complaints

- search and seize documents and records

- produce a reasoned decision on its findings which can be carried out by
  - the national government concerned
  - the Commission itself.

It has the power to impose a fine of up to 10 per cent of the business's annual turnover. Businesses which cannot accept the findings have the right to appeal to the Court of Justice in order to seek to have the decision overturned.

If firms are operating business agreements, which they do not consider to harm the consumer, they can notify the Competition Commission of the agreement's existence. By doing so, they are asking for exemption from the rules. There may be negotiation about the exact nature of the agreement but it avoids trouble which might arise at a later date if the businesses are challenged.

Work in progress

Q The EU has challenged FIFA, the international football organisation, and FIA, the equivalent for motor racing. On what grounds might the activities of these organisations be challenged?

What's the effect?

Is the price of the weekly shopping the same across Europe? Everyone knows that the answer to that question is no. In theory, if the Competition Commission had been really effective, there would be much greater harmony in prices throughout Europe. Taxation is one cause of the differences which exist. As long as different rates of VAT are charged in different countries, prices cannot be expected to be the same.

The Commission itself has been very slow in making its investigations and coming to conclusions. On one occasion, by the time the report was made, the issue was no longer of any significance.

It is also very difficult for the Commission to enforce decisions against national governments. Several European countries have a notorious record for ignoring EU rulings. More recently, however, the speed of activity has increased and the Commissioner has been prepared to take on some of the big names of European industry. For example:

- VW was fined £80 million for its restraint of cross-border activities in Italy.

- Exclusive car dealerships have only been allowed to continue if cross-border purchases are allowed to continue.

- The French government was challenged for subsidising its state-owned bank, Credit Lyonnais.

- Subsidies to Belgian steel-makers have been prevented.

The problem is that the European Commission tries to control restraints on trade by business while many governments want to look after some of their traditional industries. These issues took on a more significant role as the advent of the single currency approached. Price differentials become much more conspicuous when everything is priced in the same currency.

It is difficult to persuade national governments to give up helping businesses, in both the private and public sectors, when jobs and national prestige are at stake. Their own political futures may be at risk when such enterprises have to shut down.

There is inevitably a trade-off for governments between looking after their country's employment situation and fostering efficient competition. The move to efficiency may lead to gains in the long run, but in the short run it can cause regional unemployment and hardship.

The pattern certainly shifted in the last 15 years of the twentieth century. Before that, European industry was to some extent dominated by state-owned firms which lived on a mix of subsidies and protection. In a competitive world, these industries had to learn to live without such support if they were to survive increasingly free trade.

Point of view

- French withdraw a subsidy of £700 to anyone who trades in an old car for a new one.
- French prevented by EU from giving subsidies to Renault.
- Renault closes factory in Brussels with 3000 job losses.
- Renault broke two EU directives by announcing closure before talking to workers' council.
- Renault is determined to become more competitive, provided the politicians will let it.
- Belgium's economy is dependent on the motor industry. It has 34 000 jobs in the industry and output accounts for 15 per cent of exports. All of its five car plants are foreign owned.

Your agenda

1 Write a short paragraph justifying or explaining the significance of each of the statements above.

2 Argue the case.
  a for preventing countries giving subsidies to companies
  b for allowing governments to support industries that are in difficulties.

4 What does the world do?

A success story...

Since 1950 world trade has increased sixteen fold. It has far outstripped growth in GDP.

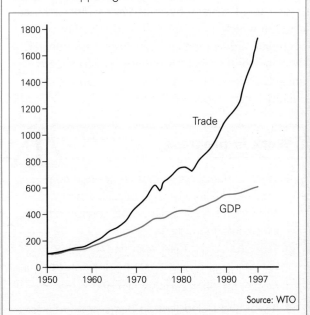

Figure M4.46 Rapid growth (1950 = 100)

Source: WTO

The last round of discussions looked particularly at services and intellectual property which are particularly difficult to control. Since then a telecoms agreement has been reached which prevents national monopolies becoming judge and jury when decisions are made about foreign competition in the domestic market.

The WTO is a club that everyone wants to join.

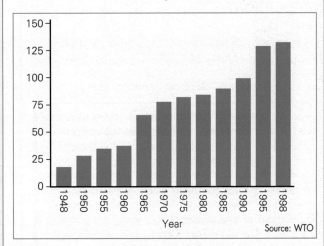

Source: WTO

Figure M4.47 Join the club: members of GATT/WTO

World trade has changed a lot since the GATT was set up. In 1950 no one ever dreamed of the Internet. Even the computer was in its infancy. Today trade takes place in ways that are extremely difficult to regulate – or liberate.

The World Trade Organisation (WTO) and its predecessor, the General Agreement on Tariffs and Trade (GATT), have brought down quotas and tariffs and therefore stimulated trade. (Quotas are physical limits on imports – a maximum level for the product concerned in any one year. Tariffs are taxes on specific imports – sometimes called customs duties. They are dealt with in detail in Option 1, page 407).

Your agenda

1 Why has the reduction in tariffs and quotas led to an increase in trade?

2 What effect does this increase in trade have on national economies?

3 Why does everyone want to join?

4 Why has the information technology revolution changed the way trade takes place?

5 How might these changes affect a country's competition policy?

Freeing up world trade had led to the world becoming a richer place. Everyone gains, in the long run, from the opportunity to sell their products in a freer market. However, the process of reaching the all-round gains can be complex.

The World Trade Organisation is a forum which brings together the majority of the players in world trade. It allows discussion of issues which create friction. In any trade debate there are always two sides because a decision will usually create winners and losers.

The challenge of competition creates a more competitive economy, therefore freer trade will keep business on its toes. It will also lead to companies identifying what it is best to produce in a particular country and concentrating on that field of output.

...but what about the borders of competition?

European and US regulators disagreed about the alliance between American Airlines and British Airways.

The Economist made the following comment:

> A decade ago such clashes were rarities. But as trade and foreign direct investment flourish, national competition policies have taken on global importance. A government's decision to block a merger, tolerate a cartel or prohibit a business practice can have a profound impact on the flow of trade – and can potentially cause economic harm in countries half a world away. This has turned the economic implications of anti-monopoly legislation into a thorny trade issue. The World Trade Organisation, the OECD, the European Union and half a dozen national governments are discussing it intensely. Progress, however, is slow in coming.
>
> *The Economist, 4 July 1998*

Your agenda

1 Why do you think the European and US regulators clashed over the alliance between American Airlines and British Airways?

2 Why is it important for competition policy to be similar in different parts of the world?

3 What effect will a slack competition policy in one country have on the competitive advantage in that country and others?

As the World Trade Organisation has reduced the level of tariffs and quotas, anti-competitive practices have become more obvious. This is an area in which the WTO has no power and yet it can have great influences on trade and competitiveness.

It is also a field in which it can be difficult to reach agreement because national interest can outweigh the greater good. Several bilateral agreements have been made in which countries will work together to overcome anti-competitive practices. Unfortunately, they are not binding. US monopoly busters are unlikely to take the welfare of consumers in other countries very seriously.

Work in progress

● In Japan there are exclusive arrangements between luxury car manufacturers and showrooms so it is difficult for foreign cars to break into the market.

● The USA argued that Kodak was being kept out of Japan by the control that Fuji had on the market for photographic film and paper.

● It was suggested that de Beers and General Electric were fixing diamond prices in the USA and South Africa.

Q 1 Who are the winners and losers in each case?

2 Explain how each of these situations affect competitive advantage.

Where can it go from here?

Although there are strong reasons why competition policy in different countries should be aligned, it is not an easy task.

There are 132 members in the WTO and China and Russia are keen to join. Half of these countries have no competition law and those that do differ greatly in the way they deal with monopoly power.

● Some are concerned with vertical integration – others are not.

● Some accept price fixing – others do not.

● Standards differ on how mergers should be judged.

- Some have laws which are not enforced.

- The process can be very different. It is a legal process in the US but in Europe it is a civil service activity.

If China and Russia are to join the WTO, it is clearly important that their markets are open to foreign trade and therefore they will need competition policy which prevents businesses from behaving in an anti-competitive way.

Other emerging economies need to develop their own systems which fit into the big picture.

Root and branch changes leading to the development of an international competition policy are impossible at the present time. However, there are some simple changes that could be made now. For example:

- The WTO could look at each country's competition policy to identify areas in which its rules are broken.

- Cartels could be banned and disputes settled through the WTO.

- Large mergers could be notified to the WTO and members could express concerns which would have to be considered.

- A list of difficult issues, such as vertical integration, could be drawn up and countries would have to consult when issues relating to them arose.

In the longer run a world system may be possible, but it will take some time to achieve.

Point of view

If resources follow demand, the consumer's wishes are a dominant factor in the allocation of resources. **Consumer sovereignty** is the term used to describe this perspective. It suggests that the consumer is all powerful because without demand, nothing will be produced. This is very true but the idea needs to be considered in the context of activities in the market place.

In the short term, primary products can run out. A ferocious storm might wipe out a region's coffee output for a year. Once a season's coffee has been sold there will be no more until next year. No matter how high demand is, the market cannot respond, except through a price increase.

Consumers are subjected to heavy persuasion by businesses which are very keen to sell their products. The extent to which demand is manipulated through marketing strategies is considerable. Perhaps business persuades us to buy what it wants to sell!

Your agenda

In the light of the above information and international attempts to create a level playing field, evaluate the concept of consumer sovereignty.

Essentials

Consumer sovereignty means the way in which consumers' preferences determine the allocation of resources. Rising consumer demand increases the profitability of the products involved, giving business an incentive to increase production, and vice versa. However, businesses with market power can distort the process.

Enquiry 5   Whose advantage?

1 What's best for business?

Who can cut the cloth?

Going up

Italy's textiles industry is thriving. It supplies its products to countries round the world.

The key is specialization and flexibility. In the many middle-sized family run companies, the managers know about the business from the inside. They have expertise in manufacturing, technical issues and marketing so they look at the market and spot the perfect niche.

Companies study the market place and put the opportunities to work. A new fabric opens up all sorts of possibilities.

Supplier networks are well developed. Benetton is famous for the faithful group of companies that make its products.

Promotion tends to come from within. This way, managers know their stuff.

These Italian businesses are selling their products under their own name. There are many famous Italian names on shops' shelves around the world. However, many also have contracts with big fashion companies like C&A.

Enterprise is, perhaps, just in the blood!

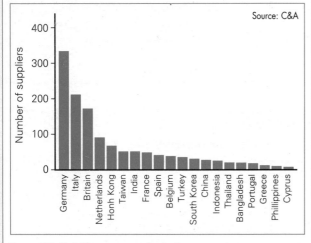

Figure M4.48 C&A international suppliers

Going down

Britain's textiles industry is in trouble. In the last ten years, employment has fallen by a quarter.

Competition from lower-cost economies has won the orders in many cases. UK companies are producing in China and other Far Eastern countries to keep their orders from Marks & Spencer and other high street names.

There are companies which depend on Marks & Spencer for 95 per cent of business. This dependence means that even a small cut in their orders resulted in closed factories and staff reductions.

No one on the high street has ever heard of Gent, Dewhirsts or William Baird. These are the names behind the St Michael brand. They produce in anonymity.

Mergers might have helped to reduce costs but in a troubled industry, there is little spare cash – and no one is very interested in buying into an industry with such a record.

In this fast moving consumer goods industry, in which being up to the moment is crucial, being on the spot should be an advantage but the business is going to have to change to make it work.

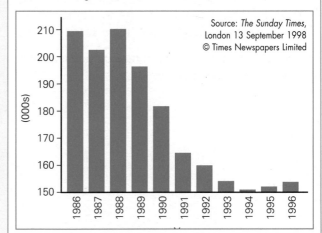

Figure M4.49 Employment in the UK textile industry

Your agenda

1 What is making the Italian clothing industry more successful than the UK equivalent?
2 Are there any economic factors which might contribute to this?
3 How might the UK industry refocus itself in order to achieve competitiveness?

The search for competitiveness can be a threat or an opportunity for business. As everyone searches for lower prices, businesses must search for cost reductions or for new ways of adding value.

In the past, many businesses produced the same range of products for decades. Today, life is very different. The speed of innovation is tremendous and businesses need to be aware of both technical changes and the way the market is moving. As economies become increasingly global, businesses need to look more widely at the competition. They also need to be aware of the changing economic climate round the world. Many businesses have been caught out by economic collapse in far flung parts of the world.

To stay competitive firms must be:

■ Efficient

Any business must look carefully at the relationship between its costs and revenues and its level of output. By monitoring changes, a company can keep control and ensure that projections are being met.

The ability of the firm to maintain profit levels will depend on the nature of the competition that it is facing. In a highly competitive market, profit margins are likely to be lower. However, a competitive industry will probably have a very rivalrous market and therefore businesses will be kept on their toes. This will give long-run benefits because businesses that are in a situation to relax may find that others have quietly usurped their position.

■ Add value

All businesses add value. If they didn't, they would soon go out of business because the costs of the inputs would be greater than the value of output.

The amount of value that is added can be adjusted by organising inputs more efficiently and therefore reducing costs so the gap between the cost of inputs and the value of output changes.

It can also be adjusted by creating products which people value more highly. Business has been very good at this. Who would think that we would pay £2 for a bag of lettuce leaves when you can buy a lettuce for 50p or less? In the greengrocery business little changed

for hundreds of years, apart from a widening range of products. Suddenly, people in the business started looking at lifestyle and decided that there was a market for a product which was more interesting because it contained a mix of leaves and could be tipped out of the bag into the salad bowl or even the bacon sandwich! The extra cost of sorting and packing is very small compared with the £1.50 additional revenue.

Businesses need to be constantly on the look out for ways of adding value if they are to maintain or improve their competitive position.

In some industries that is strongly associated with research and development. New products and modifications of existing products usually come about by research into the product itself, research into the market to see what people want or a combination of the two. Value can only be added if it is what people want. In other words, a company can change the supply conditions but will only be met with success if demand is there. Adding value can only happen if people are prepared to buy the products. If people are prepared to pay an extra £40, £60 or even £100 to have the right label on their jeans, presumably the opportunity cost of wearing other jeans must be high.

> ### Work in progress
>
> Q Look at some of the products that you buy. Explain how value is added. How has the product changed to add more value? How might it, or another product, change to add further value?

■ Flexible

Firms must be flexible, both externally and internally.

Externally, they must look for opportunities and identify ways in which they can meet the market more effectively. The ability to adapt products or develop new ones is an important source of flexibility. A business in a declining sector might be in search of new types of products which have some common elements with its current ranges. This will enable it to build on existing expertise while developing a sounder product portfolio for the future. This takes a creative approach.

The internal flexibility comes from the ability to organise the business to meet the needs of change. This can be either in management or production. As companies de-layer, these two are often combined.

Multi-skilling is therefore an important part of creating a flexible environment. This takes a well-trained workforce which is ready to contribute to rapid change. The culture of the business has a strong influence, of course, on the willingness of people to work in this way.

The advantage that the UK clothing industry has is that it is close to the market. Product ranges change so quickly and no one can be absolutely certain about which lines will really catch on and which will be left for the end-of-season sales. A business which sets itself up with the objective of quick response will make the most of both external and internal flexibility. The business that can move quickly enough to have output of a popular line flowing into the stores within a week will certainly be ahead of the game.

Market aware

Market awareness is more than just knowing about the sector that a business is involved in. This is, of course, very important because, without it, no company would last long.

The bigger picture is also of fundamental importance to any firm when it is making decisions about both current and future strategy. The market is strongly affected by the underlying state of the economy. People have become increasingly sensitive to news of recession, increasing interest rates and other factors which they think might affect their future purchasing power.

Market change can equally happen in one-off circumstances. If, for example, the rules about mortgages are changing to make life harder for people planning to buy a home, suddenly money for clothes is short because many people will speed up their house purchase plans.

As the media are now so full of such news, people respond much more quickly than they used to. Businesses need to be able to identify whether there are any factors on the horizon which will affect demand.

Companies which are involved in trade need to look further afield. Even world leaders like Coca-Cola were caught out by the late 1990s financial crisis in the Far East. Plans had to be changed at short notice because demand was much lower than forecasts had suggested.

Competitive businesses survive or thrive depending on the market conditions and their own effectiveness. The combination of all these attributes will give a greater chance of achieving competitiveness, but much of it comes back to their ability to build on their core competences. Unless a business has identified what it is good at, it will have little chance of success.

etnics → TUS → environer

2 What about the people?

> ### Employment falls by 25% in UK textiles industry.
>
> ### 42 000 shoe workers lose their jobs in Brazil.
>
> ### Demand rises for computer programmers in India.
>
> ### High costs of employing people keep unemployment up in Germany.
>
> ### Minimum wage reduces employment.

Your agenda

1 Explain why these changes might take place.
2 How might life be made better for the first two groups?
3 What effect will the change in demand for computer programmers have on the Indian economy?
4 How can government policy affect competitiveness in the labour market?

A competitive business in a competitive economy is generally good for people. It can mean more jobs and better pay. Growth raises the standard of living for many, but two questions need to be asked:

● Are the benefits equally shared?

● Does growth have other costs?

The search for competitiveness may have led firms to reduce employment because people are the most expensive part of their equation. Both the effects of international trade and the work of governments can have an important impact on people who are caught up in the process.

The effect of trade

We all know that free trade is 'a good thing'. It makes the world a richer place – in the long run. As countries and businesses seek to be competitive, they must move forward by finding the products that they can produce most effectively and processes that keep costs to a minimum.

This will mean that some industries in some countries decline because others can produce the same goods more cheaply. China, for example, has benefited by the growth of its textiles business whereas the UK has lost out. This is 'a good thing' because everyone can now buy clothes more cheaply and have more to spend on other things. The effect on people who were employed in the UK's clothing industry is not so positive. They will be in search of a new job.

It works the other way as well, of course. A thriving new industry in Britain has much greater opportunities because of trade. A company like Vivid Imagination, which always makes the latest range of toys, has export markets across the world.

As economies are always in transition, there will always be some people who are negatively affected by trade and others who are positively affected. Provided that the economy is sufficiently flexible, they should be able to be retrained and reabsorbed into the workforce. This, however, is not always the case. Regions like Liverpool are still suffering, even decades later, from the decline of heavy industry.

The effects of government policy

■ Policies for people

Governments can be very effective in making the transition less painful. The strategies used to help people back into work by retraining assist especially if the training is linked closely to employment opportunities in the region. Enterprise initiatives which give people the skills to run their own businesses are also a positive contribution to the process of regeneration.

There is, however, another side to the story. Some companies view the desire of government to protect the workforce as a hindrance to employment. In Germany the overhead costs of employing someone, mainly social security taxes, are equal to 42 per cent of their total pay. Although such policies are put in place for the welfare of the employee, a government does need to consider whether there is a trade-off between these costs and job creation.

There is therefore not necessarily a positive correlation between competitiveness and an improving situation for people. This is certainly true in the short run because a country may be shaking out the sectors which are not viable while the newer competitive industries, which will replace them, are emerging slowly.

Unless companies and countries do strive to be competitive, the longer-run picture becomes tougher still. Without such endeavour, the country will cease to be an attractive proposition for new businesses which will opt to set up somewhere more vibrant. Existing businesses will find that they are falling behind the competition and will cease to be viable. Government policies need to create opportunities without slowing down positive changes.

■ Environmental policies

As businesses push to be competitive, they may cut corners in order to reduce costs. Environmental damage is one of the external costs which ensues.

It is therefore important that government legislation protects the environment and that there are systems in place to enforce the regulations. Without such programmes, environmental harm will have knock-on effects on the health and well-being of the population.

3 What's best for countries?

What makes winners?

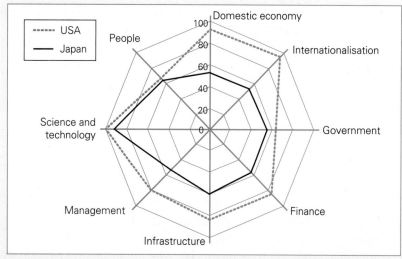

Figure M4.50　Source: The World Competitiveness Yearbook 1999, Published by IMD, International Institute for Management Development, Lausanne, Switzerland, 1999. www.imd.ch/wcy

Your agenda

1 The positions of the USA and Japan in Figure M4.50 have been decided on the basis of the data categories identified. What sort of data would you expect to find in each category on the diagram?

2 How do these two countries compare in the competitiveness stakes? Use Figure M4.51 below for the rank order.

3 Why is the USA more competitive than Japan?

Competitiveness is measured in different ways by different people. One of the most comprehensive measures is carried out by IMD, a business school in Switzerland. Much of the data it uses come from readily available sources which give a picture of the state of economies. However, it combines this with the views of top business people from international companies. They are posed some hard-nosed questions about the nature of the labour force, the climate for doing business, including the nature of corporate culture and the quality of management. Figure M4.51 shows the outcomes for 1999.

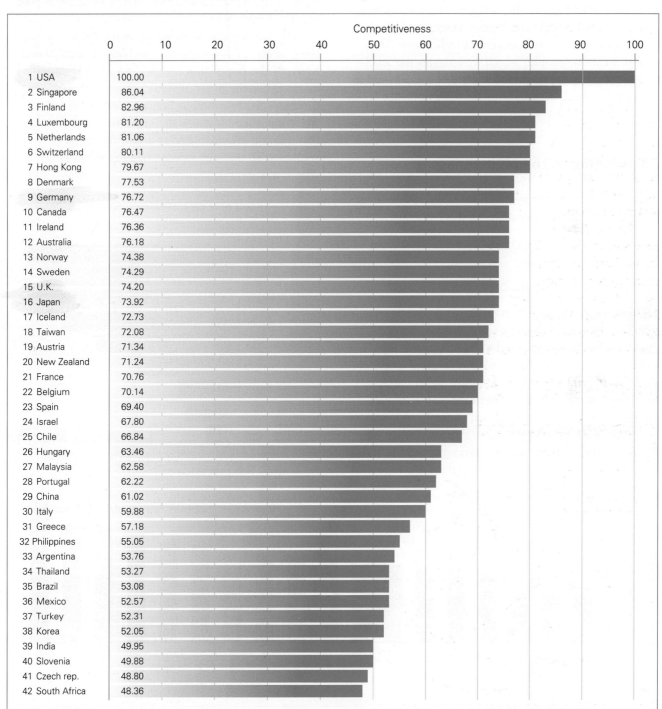

Figure M4.51 The world competitiveness scoreboard (USA = 100)

Source: The World Competitiveness Yearbook 1999, Published by IMD, International Institute for Management Development, Lausanne, Switzerland, 1999. www.imd.ch/wcy

The core competences of any thriving business are a mix of strengths which combine to create a unique environment for success. The same applies to a country. One particular strength is insufficient to become a winner. A combination of different factors has to be involved.

Figure M4.50 shows the strengths and weaknesses of Japan and the USA. The highest point that both economies reach is for science and technology. They almost meet on 'people', which investigates the levels of education, training and flexibility that are reached in the country. In all other sectors the USA outpaces Japan considerably.

Contributing to competitiveness

The mix of factors that lead to a competitive economy are going to change over time but the following provide a sample.

■ Investment in technology

Technological change which facilitates growth is required. The rapid growth experienced by the USA in the 1990s has been attributed to its investment in technology. Figure M4.52 shows the range of levels of investment in information technology. EU countries have been at a disadvantage because both hardware and software have been subjected to tariffs and have therefore been considerably more expensive than in the USA. The tariffs have now been scrapped but they leave all European countries behind the USA.

■ A labour force with appropriate skills

A labour force that meets the needs of business is an essential feature of a competitive economy. When London business people were asked to identify the skills gaps in the labour force, they put information technology, technical and personal skills at the top of the list (Figure M4.53).

The London list is fairly common to most areas of the country. IT is a particular problem in areas where much of the population is office-based. It is important to recognise the areas of weakness and use the mechanisms described in Enquiry 1 (page 314) to overcome them. It is equally important to make sure that training providers are aware of the areas of weakness so that appropriate training is available where it is required.

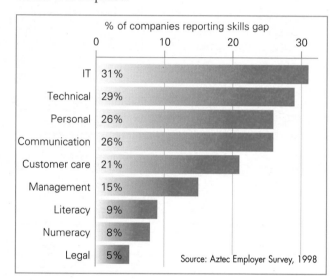

Figure M4.53 Skills gaps in London

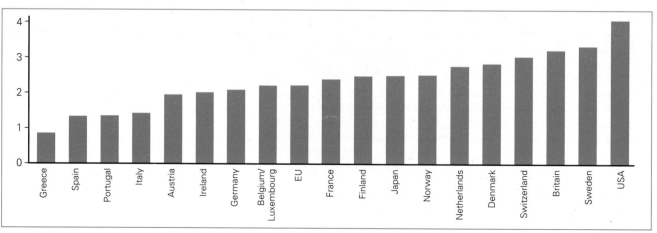

Figure M4.52 Spending on information technology

Source: *International Bank Credit Analyst (Economist page 176 14-11-98)*

■ An enterprise environment

Creating an enterprise environment leads to a culture in which people are prepared to take an idea or use their skills and set up a small business. All businesses were once small. Not all grow into multi-nationals but many develop to provide employment and make a significant contribution to GDP.

There is evidence that there is a relationship between an enterprise culture and growth in GDP. In the USA the level of creation of small businesses is very high compared to Europe. The failure rate is also high but the proportion which survive provides employment and income.

European countries are concerned about the unwillingness of people to take the risk involved in setting up a new business. Americans are apparently less concerned about business failure than Europeans, probably because there is less stigma attached.

The UK government is supporting a campaign to encourage people to become more enterprising. For many years courses have been offered to provide the necessary skills for people who want to set up their own business and there has been a continued rise in the number of start-ups. Efforts are now being made to increase awareness of the opportunities in order to increase the number of successful start-ups.

■ Promotion of industrial growth

Promoting industrial growth by helping companies when they are in difficulties is a delicate matter because it can infringe EU competition law. The deal that was agreed between the UK government and BMW in 1999 to keep the Longbridge plant open was based on growing productivity over a period of years as well as the provision of training by Birmingham City Council and agencies involved in the development of enterprise.

Without such a deal, BMW would have developed a plant in Hungary and a potential half-million jobs might have been lost in the West Midlands. The effect on the area would have been devastating. More than 30 per cent of the region's GDP comes from manufacturing, a figure half as much again as the national average.

The outcome

In a world in which trade becomes increasingly important in every country's agenda, a low competitiveness rating can be a source of great concern. A country which is unable to sell its goods overseas and yet is able to buy imports freely will soon find itself in an unsustainable position.

It is therefore important that both governments and businesses work at maintaining an environment in which business can thrive. The issue of trade-offs arises again because actions that assist businesses to develop and keep costs at a competitive level may reduce support for people.

Lower taxes help keep business competitive but mean that government provision must be reduced. Equally, if business is not competitive, demand will fall, both as a result of falling exports and rising imports so jobs will be lost at home.

The objective must be to achieve an economic climate in which:

- exchange rates are competitive

- interest rates are low

- the workforce is well trained

- businesses are investing

- there is sound infrastructure.

Work in progress

Find data or newspaper stories which give a picture of the level of competitiveness of other countries compared with the UK.

4 Is it right or wrong?

C&A keeps tabs on suppliers

The fashion retailer C&A has suppliers and subcontractors all over the world. It is not easy to keep an eye on them all. The company has set up a monitoring system through an organisation in Belgium that carries out spot-checks and follows up reports of factories which break the Code of Conduct. Suppliers who do not conform will be suspended until changes are made.

The Code of Conduct

The C&A Code of Conduct for the Supply of Merchandise describes the standard of business conduct which we see as fundamental in our dealings with merchandise suppliers. Although our dealings with suppliers often take place in cultures which are different from our own and which have a different set of norms and values, certain standards are universally valid and must apply to all our commercial activities.

Supplier relationships

We seek to develop long-term business relationships with our suppliers who should have a natural respect for our ethical standards in the context of their own particular culture. Our relationships with suppliers are based on the principle of fair and honest dealings at all times and in all ways.

We specifically require our suppliers to extend the same principle of fair and honest dealings to all others with whom they do business including employees, subcontractors and other third parties. For example, this principle means that gifts or favours cannot be offered or accepted at any time.

Legal aspects and intellectual property rights

We will always comply fully with the legal requirements of the countries in which we do business and our suppliers are required to do likewise at all times. The intellectual property rights of third parties will be respected by all concerned.

Employment conditions

In addition to the general requirement that all suppliers will extend the principle of fair and honest dealings to all others with whom they do business, we also have specific requirements relating to employment conditions based on respect for fundamental human rights. These requirements apply not only to production for C&A but also to production for any other third party.

- The use of child labour is absolutely unacceptable. Workers must not be younger than the legal minimum age for working in any specific country and not less than 14 years, whichever is the greater.

- We will not tolerate forced labour or labour which involves physical or mental abuse or any form of corporal punishment.

- Under no circumstances will the exploitation of any vulnerable individual or group be tolerated.

- Wages and benefits must be fully comparable with local norms, must comply with all local laws and must conform with the general principle of fair and honest dealings.

- Suppliers must ensure that all manufacturing processes are carried out under conditions which have proper and adequate regard for health and safety of those involved.

Environmental aspects

The realisation of environmental standards is a complex issue – especially in developing countries. It therefore needs to be continuously reviewed within limits of what is achievable per country. We will work with our suppliers to help them to meet our joint obligations towards the environment.

Freedom of association

We recognise and respect the freedom of all employees to choose whether or not to associate with any group of its own choosing, as long as such groups are legal in their own country. Suppliers must not prevent or obstruct such legitimate activities.

Disclosure and inspection

We require suppliers to make full disclosure to us of all facts and circumstances concerning production and use of subcontractors. All C&A suppliers are obliged to make their subcontractors aware of, and comply with, the C&A Code of Conduct. Additionally, our suppliers are required to authorise SOCAM, the monitoring company appointed by C&A, to make unannounced inspections of any manufacturing facility at any time.

Your agenda

1 What effect does such a Code of Conduct and its implementation have on C&A's production costs?

2 Why is it difficult to implement?

3 Why do you think C&A has such a code and monitoring programme?

4 What effect might it have on C&A's competitiveness?

The search for competitiveness pushes business to seek ever more cost-effective sources for their products. Companies have had to look beyond the UK because of its relatively high costs. It is difficult to monitor the activities of suppliers in far flung corners of the world. C&A has worked hard to set up a system which helps this process. It costs the company more than £3 million a year and inspectors from the monitoring company make over 1000 visits every year to ensure that the code is being kept.

Businesses are often aware of the issues that can arise from a failure to monitor both their own and their suppliers' activities. Many famous names have fallen foul of public opinion when things go wrong.

There has been a growing realisation that building a good reputation with customers and in the communities where production takes place can lead to enhanced shareholder value.

The Prince's Business Forum, which draws together high-level representation from business, has developed a framework for analysing the contribution of business and the way in which adding value to society adds shareholder value. This takes place both through carrying out the business activity as well as broader community activities:

- Business activity injects resources into regions in the form of investment in infrastructure, employment and training.

- Business activity can also disseminate international standards and practices and support the development of legal practices.

- Community activity may take the form of in-kind support as well as financial support to local activities.

This combination of activities can lead to improved results. The business is achieving its targets for output and customers are happy both with the product itself and with the wider factors involved in buying from a company which is perceived to be behaving well towards its stakeholders. Competitiveness, from the individual business's point of view, does not therefore have to be at the expense of others. An ethical perspective can add value in its own right.

Work in progress

Q How do other businesses engage in a social responsibility programme and why do they do it?

---

5 Can governments be ethical as well?

Embargoed!

Myanmar could expect about US$1 billion in aid and a seat at the table for international meetings if it had a democratic government.

Iraq could sell its oil and help its poverty stricken population if it allowed inspection of its military weapons facilities.

USA refuses to deal with Cuba until its Marxist regime moves to democracy

Embargo lifted as Libya hands over bomber

Your agenda

1 What makes a country or group of countries refuse to trade with another?
2 What effects are they seeking?
3 Are there any external effects from such decisions?

Nationally?

A government can participate in creating an ethical environment in a variety of ways. This may be through its own policy, both at home and abroad, and through working with business.

■ Policy at home

A key role of government is to create an environment which enables business to behave in a responsible manner. This may mean regulation in order to create a level playing field. In a highly competitive environment, it will be necessary to lay down minimum requirements in areas such as employment because these are the guides used by companies' codes of conduct.

Despite all the advantage that can be gained by taking an ethical approach to stakeholders, when times get hard, businesses can be tempted to fall below their own expectations. A legal baseline helps to prevent this taking place.

Governments can also use economic instruments to guide the actions of business. The assistance to Liverpool, for example, comes into this category. Taxes, charges, subsidies and grants can all be used to persuade companies to behave in a particular way.

There are, however, trade-offs involved in such policy. Some people argue that regulations can impede a country's competitive advantage because they raise the costs of production compared to its competitors. The Social Chapter of the European Union has been discussed in this light, but its objective is to create the level playing field and protect employees within the EU. The effect would be felt if businesses opted to work outside the area in order to avoid the restrictions it imposes.

The overhead costs of employing people, which include National Insurance and pension contributions, can push up costs: the example of Germany has been given (page 360). While the money taken by the government is used to provide benefits for people, the actual costs will make some businesses think twice before setting up a plant in Germany.

The combined costs of tax and social charges will be a factor which will be taken into consideration when companies are looking for new locations.

Point of view ❝❞

ARTICLE 1

The Community and the Member States shall have as their objectives the promotion of employment, improved living and working conditions, proper social protection, dialogue between management and labour, the development of human resources with a view to lasting high employment and the combating of exclusion. To this end the Community and Member States shall implement measures which take account of the diverse forms of national practices, in particular in the field of contractual relations, and the need to maintain the competitiveness of the Community economy.

Source: EU web site

Figure M4.54 The Social Chapter of the EU Treaty

	% of GDP
France	24.0
Italy	19.5
Finland	19.5
Luxembourg	18.5
Belgium	17.5
Austria	17.5
Spain	16.5
Germany	16.5
Britain	13.0
Ireland	12.5
Netherlands	12.0

Source: Medef

Figure M4.55 Taxes and social charges on business

Your agenda

1 Analyse the positive and negative effects that the above data have on competitiveness.

2 What other information would a business need before deciding where to set up a new plant?

Policy abroad

The political agenda of governments can often have objectives which differ from economic logic. If free trade leads to greater wealth, anything which impedes trade is working against the objectives of competitiveness.

Trade-offs come into play again. In the search for equity and human rights, governments may introduce measures which reduce competitiveness. Economic measures may be more effective or cause less damage than developing a military strategy. Equally, it may take longer to have an effect. The effects may also have impacts on different groups of people. Decisions therefore have to be made about priorities if economic constraints are to be imposed.

Point of view

Select a country which is or has been subject to a trade embargo. Research the effects of the embargo and draw conclusions about its outcomes.

Working with business

Public–private partnerships

'... the overall message is clear: nationally and internationally, the key to growth is with the private sector. The role of government is increasingly shifting to one in which its primary task is creating an enabling agenda for individual energies and initiatives to flourish. This partnership between the public and private sector is now the key to development and prosperity.'
(Kofi Annan, UN Secretary General, India 1997)

Your agenda

1 Why does Kofi Annan believe that the private sector is the key to growth?

2 Why is it difficult to monitor the international activities of business?

3 Why are public/private partnerships likely to be useful vehicles to encourage positive behaviour on the part of business?

Laying down laws about the corporate citizenship role of business is a difficult agenda. It is relatively easy to tell business what it must not do, but it is more difficult to take the proactive approach and say what it should do.

Companies often use their corporate responsibility programmes to create competitive advantage. A business that is seen to be behaving well can attract customers because of its activities. One that is behaving badly can lose customers as in the case of Shell when its behaviour in Nigeria was questioned. Its petrol stations were boycotted and even burnt down.

The difficulty of monitoring these activities has led to the proposal to build a framework for the development of public–private partnerships by the Prince's Business Trust. The framework would contain:

- *command and control mechanisms*, including national legislation and local planning and licensing permits, corporate ownership and governance rules and the legal framework for voluntary associations

- *economic instruments* which use market and financial incentives and disincentives to encourage corporate social responsibilities, including taxes, charges, user fees, subsidies, grants, deposit refund schemes, enterprise zones, eco- and social-labels, public sector procurement policies and environmental trading permits

- *voluntary and self-regulatory standards*, including charter marks, covenants, pledges, guidelines and codes of conduct in areas such as human rights, ethical business practices and environmental management, with parallel systems for measuring, monitoring, and verifying their implementation.

- *public opinion* and the increasing ability of consumer and citizen action to influence the other 'rules of the game'.

The Trust also investigated ways of encouraging such activities. Because of the difficulty of controlling corporate behaviour governments can encourage positive behaviour by supporting award programmes and league tables, for example, which give recognition to businesses that meet the agenda. A strategy for identifying the positive rather than seeking ways of attacking the negative appears to be a useful approach.

The media can also be helpful if they can be

encouraged to give positive coverage to public–private partnerships and other positive behaviour and flag up bad practice.

Internationally?

On the international level, it seems difficult for countries to unite in common purpose. World summits on the environment, for example, produce much rhetoric, but many countries are slow in achieving the targets set.

On issues of competitiveness, countries seem more ready to protect their own agendas than look after the big picture. The USA, for example, threatens trade boycotts of certain European products in retaliation for bans on its products entering the European markets.

The North Atlantic Free Trade Association contains statements on the quality of environmental and employment standards among participating countries, but the objective was to ensure that really low-cost competitors were excluded.

There are, however, some glimmers of light. The desire of members of the World Trade Organisation to come together to discuss ways of achieving an international framework for competition is a start.

What is the global future?

Globalisation is a many-faceted phenomenon. Nations are exchanging more and more of their goods and services with each other. In addition, capital moves freely from one country to another. This makes most nations increasingly dependent on each other. Their economies are becoming steadily more integrated.

1 Who gets to market first?

Tetley in Poland

If you visit Poland and watch television you might well find yourself staring at the cartoon Tetley Tea Folk, their Yorkshire accents dubbed into Polish, telling you that round tea bags are modern but not too flash.

'The Tea Folk in their white coats help us emphasise that Tetley is a quality product,' says Wojciech Pronobis, the marketing manager of Tetley Polska. But marketing needs to adapt fast in countries like Poland because of the speed of development there. 'These are dynamic markets,' he says.

Tetley is not alone there. The Poles are big tea drinkers. Lipton, the Unilever subsidiary and the world's biggest tea bag manufacturer is the market leader. Not long ago, most tea sold in Poland was unbranded and sold loose. Now 34 per cent of it is branded. By value, Tetley and Lipton have 55 per cent of the total market.

To make good in Poland, Tetley has had to work out a distribution strategy that suits the market. Big supermarkets are still few and far between. Poland has 100 000 grocery outlets for its 39 million people. Compare that with the UK which has 37 000 grocery outlets for 59 million people. Tetley has done well in the market by teaming up with a Polish distributor while keeping control of its own brand management.

Tetley is moving on. It is selling tea in India, China and now Russia. The profits are modest as yet. But world tea consumption rose by 8 per cent during the 1990s and is expected to continue rising. That is a lot of tea bags.

Your agenda

1 What were the attractions of the Polish market for the tea bag manufacturers?

2 In what ways did they have to adapt their approach to suit the country?

3 Russia, the Ukraine and the central Asian republics, including Kazakhstan, all have tea-drinking traditions. Would you expect them all to offer enticing markets? Give reasons.

Until 1989 Poland did very little business with western Europe. The tearing down of the Berlin Wall and the shift to market systems in eastern Europe changed all that. Within a very few years many western businesses had spotted opportunities and were well on the way to carving out significant markets.

The **emerging markets**, of which Poland is one, include a wide range of differing countries. There are:

- the former communist countries of eastern Europe, including Poland, the Czech Republic and Hungary

- Russia and the other parts of the former Soviet Union such as Ukraine, Belarus and Kazakhstan

- China, still communist dominated but liberalising its economy to a great extent

- the so-called Asian tigers – Hong Kong, Taiwan, Korea and Singapore – which have been growing strongly for some time (Hong Kong and Korea were badly affected by the Asian financial crisis but seem likely to continue growing over the long run)

- other developing countries which now have substantial manufacturing sectors. The list is long: it includes India, Indonesia, Malaysia, Brazil, Mexico and South Africa.

Essentials

Emerging markets or economies have all adopted policies which encourage market forces and reduce government controls. Many of them have grown fast and thus provide markets for developed countries.

The emerging economies have played an important part in the globalisation process. They have, in many cases, become important as exporters, while opening their economies to imports. Many have adopted new technologies successfully.

There is no definitive list of countries to be included in this category. It applies to economies where a good deal of modernisation is going on and where markets are developing effectively.

Developing markets

Business in China

American Standard produces baths, basins and toilets in seven factories spread across China. Where other manufacturers have encountered problems, its strategy has been a success. Turnover in 1997 was $100 million. The company expected to triple that by 2003. Horace Whittlesay, the general manager in China says, 'Our business grew by 60 per cent last year. Three factories are minting money, three have good earnings performance and one is having a slight struggle. The motto is Never, Never Quit. China can be a frustrating place, so have an enormous store of patience and persevere.'

American Standard started out selling to hotel chains. Gradually, it developed new products specifically to suit the Chinese market. In particular, it changed the design of its toilets so that they could be installed where previously there had been a hole-in-the-floor model. This has been important in its success: the company is market orientated and geared to meeting the real needs of local customers.

Two other elements in the strategy were important. One was the development of a reliable local distribution network. The company set up a network of authorised distributors who had good local knowledge. The second was to put real effort into the organisation and management of people.

Finally, American Standard has had to remember the real nature of the Chinese market. It looks big – all of those 1.2 billion people could do with a nice bathroom. But the 850 million of them who are still living in the countryside have no bathrooms at all. Most of the people in the cities can only afford local-style shower and hole-in-the-floor facilities. The growth potential is there, but it will be a very long time before the market becomes really large.

Your agenda

1 Why does overseas investment in China need to be made with a very long-term view?

2 What are the risks associated with investment in production facilities located in overseas markets?

3 Why have a great many western businesses invested overseas?

Businesses explore potential new markets because they offer chances to expand sales. This is clearly the main motive for American Standard and Tetley. However, new markets can be more problematic than they look. Just because they are new and unknown, the risks are considerable. Many businesses have rushed to get into the emerging markets without realising that the returns were likely to materialise only over a long period of time.

American Standard and Tetley were not simply lucky. Both of them are selling products with a high income elasticity of demand in the relevant markets. Tea bags have a mature market in the UK. Tetley can compete with other producers to get a larger market share, but it probably cannot persuade more people to use tea bags. In contrast, Poland has large numbers of people with growing incomes who are ready to switch from loose tea to the more expensive tea bags.

These experiences highlight the need for market orientation in the development of new markets. Great sensitivity is needed in weighing up customer requirements, as well as in finding appropriate distribution strategies.

Trying to sell luxury goods in countries with relatively low incomes can be difficult. Markets are still small and if all the world's brands are trying for a share, competition can be stiff. Some companies have resigned themselves to investing now against profits in the long run. Others have withdrawn from some markets and cut their losses.

An added difficulty for branded products is the pirate or counterfeit market. American Standard has had to do battle with Chinese producers which put the American Standard name on their own products. To start with, the Chinese legal system had limited power to prevent this kind of abuse. The US government in trade negotiations has put great pressure on China to respect **intellectual property rights** and this situation is now changing.

Essentials

Intellectual property rights refer to the ownership of brand names, patents and copyright items (such as recorded music and books) which cannot legally be used or copied by other businesses.

Where are the markets?

Figure O1.1 shows growth rates in a selection of emerging markets. In some, GDP growth was affected by the Asian financial crisis in 1998–9. They are likely to have resumed their previous pattern of growth after that. Included in the table are some of the large developed markets. In the process of globalisation, the rapid growth of trade between developed countries has been an important part of the picture.

Country	GDP	Exports	Investment
Brazil	3.1	6.0	4.0
China	11.9	15.8	14.1
Germany	1.6	5.6	2.3
India	5.9	13.7	8.9
Indonesia	7.5	9.2	10.0
Japan	1.4	3.9	0.2
Korea	7.2	15.7	6.3
Poland	3.9	11.5	8.7
Russia	−9.0	−13.2	n.a.
South Africa	1.5	5.2	13.0
UK	1.9	5.3	−4.4
USA	2.5	7.0	5.0

Source: World Bank, *World Development Report*, 1998

Figure O1.1 GDP, export and investment growth, average, 1990–97

Here, as elsewhere, data to 1997 has been used because 1998 data was distorted by the Asian financial crisis. This data gives an accurate picture of the trends. As the affected countries recover, they are likely to return to previous trends.

It is easy to see why the rapid growth in the emerging markets has attracted businesses. Standards of living are changing dramatically in some countries. Dynamic companies can make a big difference to their profits if they play the situation skilfully. However, the risks are considerable.

The Asian financial crisis began in 1997 and finally became less of a problem in 1999. The underlying cause was a loss of confidence in certain banks which had overlent to companies which were not profitable enough to repay the money. This precipitated a loss of confidence in some economies generally and rapid selling of the currency. In turn, this completely destabilised the region. The worst hit countries were Korea, Thailand, Indonesia, Japan and Hong Kong, but others felt the side-effects quite badly too. When Russia and Brazil were afflicted similarly in 1998 the crisis began to look less Asian.

For many businesses, the years of crisis were very difficult because spending on some products fell as incomes were affected. The Asian financial crisis will recur throughout Option 1 because it is impossible to analyse the process of globalisation without reference to it. In time its significance will diminish. But this will take several years.

2 What is globalisation?

India and software

India is 3 800 miles away from the European Central Bank. No problem! Indian software companies expected to get US$2 billion-worth of contracts helping banks and companies to adjust their computer systems to the advent of the single currency in 2002. This would be a third of the country's $6-billion software exports.

Tata Consultancy Services, India's biggest software company, won a contract from the Bank of Scotland to makes its systems euro-friendly.

India's 40 000 software engineers sell their services to US and European companies in a big way. They started by flying out to their customers, using their problem-solving skills and devising tailor-made solutions for companies' software needs. That has changed: increasingly, Indian companies offer an 'offshore' service using high-speed data links.

Solving the millennium bug problems associated with computers which were not ready for the change of century was another big money spinner. In the long run, the Indian industry giants expect to be able to sell software packages. Watch out, Microsoft!

Your agenda

1 What reasons can you give for the success of India's software services industry on global markets?

2 Explain the trends which have made the growth of this business possible.

3 Mostly, we think of trade being mainly in goods rather than services. What other services are extensively traded?

Globalisation is an umbrella word which includes a whole range of trends. Part of the process involves greatly increased trade flows. No country would attempt to be self-sufficient now. But globalisation is much more than simply increased trade. Its other strands take in the free movement of capital, funds for investment, and the migration of people.

What has brought these changes about? The Chinese exported silk to the ancient Romans, bringing it across central Asia on a journey that defies imagination, crossing mountains and deserts and braving hostile tribes. Trade is not new, as the flint miners of the New Stone Age would tell you, if they could.

The difference lies first and foremost in the development of new technologies. These have progressively and dramatically increased productivity. They have cut the cost of transport. They have also made communications quick, easy and efficient. These trends have created huge opportunities for dynamic businesses.

Governments have played their part. During the 1930s many politicians realised that trade barriers were destroying rather than creating opportunities. By degrees since the second World War, governments have agreed to cut import duties and other barriers.

While trade has been growing, governments have gradually freed their capital markets. The benefit of this is that it gives businesses access to finance from other countries which they simply could not have if they were restricted to borrowing at home.

The one area where controls are still very significant is in the migration of people. You might think it is difficult to get a work permit for the UK, Canada, the USA and some other countries. You would be wrong. It is almost impossible. You have to have a close relative, very scarce and valuable skills, be a refugee, have money (lots)...

Trade barriers and foreign exchange controls still exist, but they are very much less significant than they used to be. This has had a dramatic effect in increasing the interdependence of the world's nations

Work in progress

Q 1 Why is access to finance for capital investment crucial to growth?

2 Why has changing technology been important in the growth of trade?

3 How have lower import duties contributed?

3 Where are the cheapest inputs?

Who has the lowest costs?

● VW buys its gear-shift components in Shenyang. Some car components consist of masses of small pieces carefully assembled into one larger item. VW's gear-shift mechanisms are like this. The assembly stage is fiddly and labour intensive. Nimble fingers on low wages in north-east China can save VW a lot. The bits are shipped out to the factory, assembled there and shipped on to VW's main assembly plants.

● Mr Li fixes everything for this year's dresses. Li and Fung are based in Hong Kong. The company can help western companies looking for low cost garment manufacturers. It will order undyed yarn, book the capacity in the dying and weaving mills, warn the factories that a big order is on its way, line up supplies of buttons and trim and think of everything in advance. Five weeks before delivery, the buyer company decides the colours and styles. Mr Li has everything ready, suppliers lined up all over south-east Asia. As soon as the final decisions are made, a complete coordinated plan swings into action. The clothes reach the shops only weeks later, and still they are just what people are wanting this year.

● Nike contracts out all its production. Nike doesn't own factories. The company consists entirely of the design and marketing team in California. All the trainers are made in the Far East. Supplier companies make them to Nike's specifications with strict quality control.

● Everyone gets their phones in China. Just take a look underneath the nearest phone. It may have been made somewhere else, but it's not likely.

Your agenda

1 What trends have made the above developments possible?

2 What are the pressures which make western businesses source parts or all of their products overseas?

3 What are the benefits of these developments for consumers?

Outsourcing has become an important way for many manufacturers to cut costs. Some shift the whole of their production to locations where wage costs are lower. Others outsource components. Yet others locate just one stage in the production process elsewhere.

Essentials

Outsourcing means buying in from another business inputs which were previously created within the organisation.

Many businesses have found that they can manufacture abroad with great advantage. They may set up their own factories in countries with low wage costs. Or they may outsource, purchasing what they need from independent, often local, businesses.

Of course, sometimes costs are low because working conditions are not good. Most businesses which work in this way will assure shareholders that their suppliers obey the laws of the country in which they are located. The trouble is that some countries' laws are designed to encourage businesses rather than to protect their employees. Wages can be very low indeed and health and safety regulations more or less non-existent. It has to be remembered, of course, that the alternative of no work at all is not attractive either.

These trends are another important element in the process of globalisation. Many manufactured goods which are officially made in developed countries are actually stuffed with bits from various low-wage economies.

Is it simply a matter of low wages?

Many emerging economies have more on offer than just low wages. China and India, for example, both have education systems which compare well with other countries with similar per capita GDP. The same is true for eastern Europe. The combination of an educated population with low wages can be very potent.

We should not underestimate the impact that globalisation has had on people's welfare. It is very likely that the incomes of most people in emerging economies have not gone up by as much as GDP in Figure O1.1. However, even if they went up by half that, a lot of rather poor people would notice the difference. There is no question that standards of living have improved in the past decade.

Some economies which have been developing well for some time now have substantially higher wage rates. Korea is a case in point. Nike used to manufacture there, but not any more. Wage rates are far too high. It does not matter: Korea can make money from car manufacturing and shipbuilding.

4 How is technology helping the world?

Tractors in India

Graham Edwards is managing director and owner of HST Developments. He had been developing his new tractor for 26 years. He now employs 12 people in Birkenhead on Merseyside, working as consultants on farm machinery. His product, the Trantor, has a special suspension and drive system that enables it to travel at up to 40 mph. It also has three seats, so friends and family can come along for the ride.

The Trantor never really took off in the UK. After all, most farmers have a tractor for the fields and a car for the roads. They don't need a Trantor. In India things are different. Many farmers who are prospering are able to buy a tractor, but they won't then be able to afford a car. A tractor that can take produce to market and accommodate the family as well could be a real asset there.

Now HST is building the model in Madhya Pradesh in central India. The company is in partnership with Gajra Gears and they are sharing the cost. They are starting with an output of 500, which could rise to 6 000 in a few years. They will sell for £5 500, about 10–15 per cent more than an ordinary tractor in India. For that, customers will get the added flexibility.

Your agenda

1 Developing countries often need different products from those of developed countries. Explain why.

2 How does technological change contribute to rising standards of living?

3 How has globalisation hastened the pace of technological change?

Technologies are changing very quickly and most people expect them to change even faster in the years to come. The technologies can actually themselves speed up changes because of the role of computers in design. Computer-aided design (CAD) and computer-assisted manufacture (CAM) have made it possible to vary designs and quantities produced so that manufacturing is much more flexible.

In module 3.2, enquiry 3, 'What makes an economy grow?', we looked at product and process innovation. CADCAM is all about process innovation. It cuts costs and, very importantly, provides ways of improving quality. The Trantor is a product innovation. Sometimes the two go hand in hand – think of e-mail. Adopting new technologies has a big role in the achievement of competitive advantage for the individual business. Businesses which are successful with new product development often have opportunities to charge high prices – skimming the market.

New process technologies increase productivity. They help us to get more of the finished product from a given quantity of resources. They are one of the fundamental ways in which standards of living can be improved for the long term. They do, of course, involve adjustment, which can be painful. They also require care and attention to environmental effects, to ensure that external costs do not outweigh the benefits.

Work in progress

Q 1 You are an Indian farmer. Would a Trantor be product or process innovation? Why?

2 Think of three new products which have made a real difference to standards of living.

3 How does process innovation benefit consumers?

The decision as to what technology should be used is often a difficult one, particularly in developing countries. It involves careful preparation of cost estimates for all the inputs for each possible technology. Sometimes the newest technology is not the cheapest. State of the art machinery only makes

sense if it is either saving labour costs or giving a quality advantage that adds value. If the latter is the benefit, marketing departments have to be involved in the decision-taking process as well as production departments.

New technologies usually involve attention to human capital as well. People may need retraining. People with new skills may have to be recruited. However, this may have useful side-effects as employees become used to doing different kinds of work. It is not so helpful if employees develop **resistance to change**. Usually, this is based on fear, and careful training can reduce it. A corporate culture which is explicit about welcoming constant change can be a prerequisite for successful adoption of new technologies.

Essentials

Resistance to change occurs when employees fear change because they do not like the new ways of doing things, or because their jobs may be threatened.

New technologies can and do result in loss of jobs. Often employers manage this without redundancies but not always. Natural wastage may be enough to reduce the workforce. Sometimes people can be redeployed elsewhere in the production process, though they may resist this because it brings other changes.

The benefits of fast communication

Two views

‘ Because we can communicate instantly with our suppliers in the Far East we can have flexible production arrangements and low costs as well. Of course, we do meet from time to time. Personal contacts are important at the beginning of the supplier relationship because we need to establish quality objectives. But once we have good personal relationships with the managers of our supplier companies and trust has been established, we can communicate from day to day by e-mail and fax with occasional phone calls. Our suppliers' lead times are only a little longer than those we had when we produced here in the UK. ’

‘ In the days when international telephone calls were expensive and took time to organise through an operator, you made a lot fewer of them. Letters gave you time to think. Even faxes provide a short breathing space. With e-mail, I have to do all my normal office work as well as the meetings and tours arranged for me when I'm working abroad. Decisions all have to be made immediately. The pressures are enormous. Responses have to be instant. But there can be no going back. The work we do now would be impossible without today's communications technologies. ’

Your agenda

1   What difference have faster communications made to the location of production activities?

2   What role have improved communications played in the globalisation process?

3   What are the implications of the communications revolution for corporate cultures?

Improved communications increase productivity very considerably. They reduce lead times and so cut costs. Lead time refers to the gap between taking a decision, for example to produce a particular model in greater quantities, and the increased supplies arriving in the market place. This makes it easier for businesses to respond quickly to market trends. It has been particularly important in clothing, where responsiveness to changes in fashion is an important element in competitive advantage.

This is not simply about cheaper phone calls, fax and e-mail. Lower air fares have helped along the globalisation process because people can meet without incurring massive costs. Communications of all kinds grease the wheels of business because they make it possible for very different people to work together towards common objectives.

The benefits of use of English as a common language for business have also helped to speed up communications. It remains the case that those who speak only English may miss out in important markets because they cannot appreciate the finer detail of the local ways of doing things.

Technology in developing countries

Time's up for the mozzy

Pesticides successfully eradicated mosquitos from the USA and Europe in the 1950s and 1960s. In Africa though, the treatment was intermittent and coverage was incomplete. The malaria parasite survived and even developed resistance. The result was continued suffering from disease. Now the World Health Organisation (WHO) has the Roll Back Malaria campaign in place. The objective is to reduce deaths from malaria by 50 per cent within ten years from the start in 1999.

Malaria kills between 1.5 million and 2.7 million people every year: 95 per cent of the deaths occur in Africa, often taking young and active people with the capacity to help others. Yet funding for malaria research amounts to just 1 per cent of the sum spent on Aids research. The WHO is campaigning to increase funding. It is focusing attention on the life cycle of the mosquito, aiming to cut the infection down at its source by preventing the insect from reproducing.

Why is WHO optimistic after years of failure? A few years ago, Glynn Vale, a researcher studying the tse-tse fly, which carried sleeping sickness, discovered that it could be eliminated by the use of a trap baited with cow's urine. He worked on a small island on Lake Kariba in Zimbabwe. His methods – cheap and accessible – have spread right across Africa with excellent results. The new mosquito programme is about to start work on an island just off the coast of Tanzania.

These kinds of strategies get little help from the big drug companies which are much more interested in vaccines.

Your agenda

1 Explain how eliminating mosquitos could raise standards of living.

2 Why do you think malaria research is underfunded?

3 Is the solution to this problem a public good? Explain the implications of your answer.

The scope for technology to improve lives in some of the world's poorest countries is very considerable. Access to some expensive technologies may be out of reach. Labour-saving production techniques are inappropriate if they throw people out of work. However, huge improvements are still possible for ordinary people.

A major advance in the techniques of dry land agriculture could have enormous impact. It is quite likely that this will come from genetically modified seeds. The possibilities of this are explored in enquiry 4 of this option. There are other technological developments in the health field which could bring high returns.

Sometimes **intermediate technology** provides answers. The principle behind this is that low-cost new ways of doing things can be devised which will increase productivity. Innovations like this are intermediate between traditional methods and high technology. The important feature of intermediate technologies is that they are appropriate to the conditions in which they are used. A wheelbarrow is intermediate technology. It increases productivity greatly.

This shrimping raft uses polystyrene in place of wood, gaining in lightness and buoyancy as well as cost.

Essentials

Intermediate technology uses relatively simple and inexpensive ways to make better use of available resources.

Intermediate technology often improves on existing techniques but does not use the highly sophisticated, capital intensive methods found in the developed world. The stress is on use of existing skills and resources so that people do not become overdependent on others.

The Jiko: an energy efficient stove

The traditional Kenyan cooking stove, a jiko, had an energy efficiency of about 20 per cent. As it ran on firewood, which was in increasingly short supply, a programme was set up to develop a more efficient model. A strategy was devised which looked first at the requirements of the stove and its role in the life of users, in order to develop a product which was acceptable and effective.

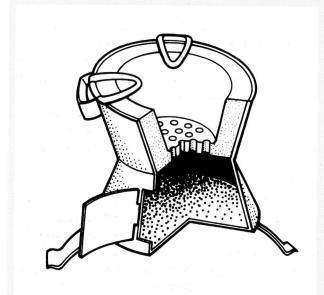

It was essential that the artisans who had made the traditional stove could continue the production process so the second phase was a training programme for them and for people who demonstrate the new product in the community. The artisans were also provided with practical assistance to aid production. The final stage was monitoring and evaluation so that constraints could be identified and impact assessed.

The total cost of the programme was about US$500000. Almost a hundred new jobs were generated by the new processes and households were estimated to be saving approximately $2 million. The demand for charcoal fell by 1.5 million tonnes per year and the toxic output was also reduced. This suggests that the stove provided a very high rate of return on the funds employed. The programme has been successful because of the involvement of local people in all stages of the process. It enabled traditional cooking methods to continue while using resources more effectively.

Your agenda

1 Think of three more examples of intermediate technology.

2 Why are new technologies often not the cheapest solution in developing countries?

5 Where is the best place to invest?

Caterpillar in the UK

In 1996 Caterpillar was trying to decide between four rival sites for its new European plant. The company is the world's biggest maker of construction equipment and its best-known products are earth movers. In the end, it settled on Desford in the Midlands. The Caterpillar factory was started there on a disused airfield in the 1950s. It was to be expanded to produce a new range of machines designed for smaller building projects.

The losers in this contest were the three possible sites in Italy, the Czech Republic and the Netherlands. Jim Waters, Caterpillar's UK managing director, said, 'We are here for the long term. There is a good climate for

business and an existing network of reliable suppliers. We are having some problems with the strong pound, but the damage is partly offset by the lower price of imported components.'

Your agenda

1 Many multi-nationals invest in production capacity close to their major markets. Explain why this is.

2 What are the main likely factors in a decision about location with four possible sites in Europe?

3 The UK welcomes foreign investment. Why?

Foreign direct investment (FDI) is an important element in the globalisation process. Direct investment is spending on plant and machinery for production. This is in contrast to portfolio investment, which refers to capital movements in the form of bank balances. These can be moved from one place to another to get the best rate of interest available.

FDI has increased dramatically over the past few decades. Most countries welcome investment because it brings with it jobs and the potential for increased prosperity. The Welsh Development Agency has been highly successful in attracting FDI in the past. It was saddled with a large legacy of declining heavy industry in the coal-mining and iron and steel areas along the south coast. FDI brought a much larger range of activities to replace these. During the late 1990s Ireland experienced a big inflow of capital as companies sought a location inside the euro zone and also English speaking.

We have already seen that FDI is important in the emerging markets. So where is it not important? Sadly, the least developed countries, the ones which could most do with an injection of prosperity, have had the most difficulty in attracting investment. There has been some, but the amounts are relatively small. Figure O1.2 shows amounts for selected countries. Bear in mind that the UK and the USA have large outflows of capital as well as large inflows. One thing is clear: the least developed countries' share of FDI has remained small.

Country	Total flow (US$ million)
Brazil	19652
China	44236
Cote d'Ivoire	327
Ghana	130
India	3351
Indonesia	4677
Japan	3200
Korea	2844
Poland	4908
Russia	6241
South Africa	1725
UK	32518
USA	47918

Source: World Bank, *World Development Report*, 1998

Figure O1.2 Foreign direct investment inflows, 1997

Investment in the least developed countries

You might think that countries which had very low costs, such as those of sub-Saharan Africa, would be attractive to industry, but it is clear that cheap factors of production do not always lead to a high rate of return on investment. In developed countries the rate of return on foreign direct investment averaged 16.5 per cent between 1987 and 1990, whereas in sub-Saharan Africa it was 6.6 per cent. This can be attributed to a variety of causes.

The least developed countries tend to have a poorer level of infrastructure which slows down the process of producing goods and services and therefore generates additional cost. The labour force tends to be less productive because of lower levels of education and training. The lack of political stability creates uncertainty and often leads to higher borrowing charges and foreign exchange controls, which again raise costs.

Interest rates in developing countries are often much higher than those of developed countries. This may not deter foreign direct investment as multinationals can usually borrow on world capital markets, but it will have a negative effect on local companies which develop to provide goods and services to them. In many cases, these factors outweigh the benefits which are gained by establishing factories in what are thought of as low-cost locations.

Investment in developed countries

Figure O1.3 shows both inflows and outflows for the developed countries. They are the providers of FDI. A good deal of capital is swapped between them. The rest goes mainly to the emerging economies. The inflows and outflows are measured as a percentage of GDP. The US percentage looks low, but the data for the USA in Figure O1.3 show a very high figure. This reflects the fact that the USA has a very large GDP, being both populous and rich. The figures on the right in Figure O1.3 show the net outflow. Many developed countries are net providers of capital to the rest of the world. This is as would be expected since they are all relatively prosperous.

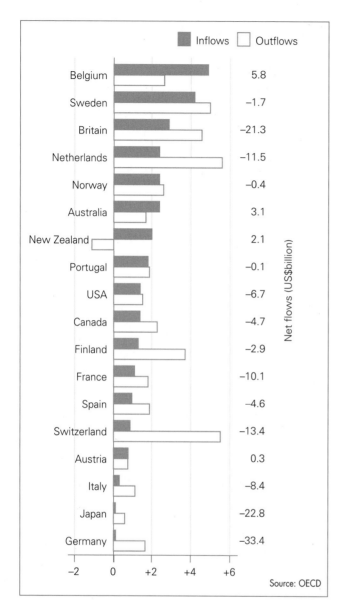

Figure O1.3 FDI as percentage of GDP, 1997

The chart shows Inflows and Outflows with the following Net flows (US$billion):

Country	Net flows (US$billion)
Belgium	5.8
Sweden	−1.7
Britain	−21.3
Netherlands	−11.5
Norway	−0.4
Australia	3.1
New Zealand	2.1
Portugal	−0.1
USA	−6.7
Canada	−4.7
Finland	−2.9
France	−10.1
Spain	−4.6
Switzerland	−13.4
Austria	0.3
Italy	−8.4
Japan	−22.8
Germany	−33.4

Source: OECD

Investment in emerging markets

Some emerging markets have been very successful in attracting investment because their recently liberalised economies have been growing very fast. The experiences of the businesses concerned have varied. For example:

● Some companies have been very successful. American Standard was one (see case study on page 370).

● Other companies are covering their costs and are happy because they now have a share in a market which is expected to grow. Tetley comes into that category (see case study on page 369).

● Another group has made steady losses, but they will stay, because they regard their investment as very long term in nature. Some businesses in China are adopting this strategy.

● A fourth group of businesses decides that enough is enough.

Peugeot in India

Not everyone thinks that expansion overseas is always wonderful. The car manufacturer Peugeot decided to cut its losses in India. In 1994 it had set up a joint venture with an Indian company which provided a factory near Bombay. There Peugeot's 309 model would be assembled, with a view to taking an eventual 10 per cent of India's car market.

It never got anywhere near its expected sales. The 309 is a mid-range car in Europe, but it turned out to be too expensive for most of India's car buyers. Sales were very disappointing. Furthermore, despite careful negotiations beforehand, the Indian government insisted on taxing the imported components separately. With just 23 per cent of the components produced locally, this brought a big cut in profits. Peugeot blamed everyone in sight: the Indians; Fiat, with whom its partners were negotiating other deals; and its own management at the time the decisions were made. Some people blamed Peugeot: it was the wrong car, for a start. Something smaller might have sold. By the end of 1997 it was all over.

Your agenda

1   What particularly important requirements are there for businesses thinking of investing in emerging markets?

2   How might the mistake have been avoided?

6 Where is the finance for development?

Ending river blindness

River blindness is caused by a parasite that is carried from person to person by the blackfly. This concentrates along river beds, so over the years the disease has caused large areas of fertile land in west Africa to be abandoned. Ghana, Cote d'Ivoire and a number of other countries have collaborated with the World Health Organisation, an agency of the UN, to tackle the problem.

The blackfly had become resistant to insecticides, so the programme applied several different insecticides in rotation: 35 million people are now protected from infection. Vacant lands are being resettled. This land can feed 17 million people.

The programme worked because it collected information on the best time to spray. Local people entered the data from sensors on the river bottom into computers. Information was transmitted by satellite to laboratories which, in turn, transmitted schedules to the airline pilots who did the spraying.

An added bonus was that a drug was discovered during the later years of the programme. Only one dose per year is required. The drug company Merck supplied it free. National teams distribute it. This combination of information technology, medical knowledge, community participation and international support has proved very successful.

Source: World Bank, World Development Report, 1998 page 60

Your agenda

1 How does this type of project improve standards of living?

2 What crucial elements brought success?

3 Some aid projects are less successful. What sorts of things go wrong?

While foreign direct investment is of great value for some emerging economies, it clearly will not help the poorer countries to develop. Some still rely heavily on aid. Others do not receive enough of it to rely on.

Some aid is needed for disasters, both human-made and natural. This is humanitarian rather than development aid. The poorest countries, of course, have the greatest difficulties in repairing the damage caused by disasters because their resources are very limited. This aid is for consumption – short-term help to overcome immediate problems of shortages of food and shelter.

Aid for the longer term problems generally falls into one of two categories. Bilateral aid is given directly by one government to another. Multilateral aid comes from several or many governments and is often fed through a donor agency such as UNICEF (United Nations Children's Fund) or the World Bank Group. Aid may be given in the form of either grants or loans. The latter, of course, has implications for future demands on the recipient because repayments must be made.

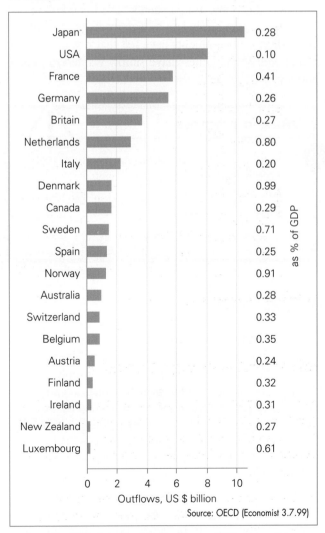

Country	as % of GDP
Japan	0.28
USA	0.10
France	0.41
Germany	0.26
Britain	0.27
Netherlands	0.80
Italy	0.20
Denmark	0.99
Canada	0.29
Sweden	0.71
Spain	0.25
Norway	0.91
Australia	0.28
Switzerland	0.33
Belgium	0.35
Austria	0.24
Finland	0.32
Ireland	0.31
New Zealand	0.27
Luxembourg	0.61

Outflows, US $ billion

Source: OECD (Economist 3.7.99)

Figure O1.4 Official development assistance, 1998

Some aid is for specific purposes and is known as project aid. Alternatively, it may be programme aid, given as general support for the full range of the government's activities. Loans may be concessional, which means that the rates of interest will be below those charged in the financial markets. Non-concessional loans are charged at the market rate.

Technical assistance is an alternative method of giving help to other countries. This involves sending people with specialist skills to assist with a particular development or to train the indigenous population.

The United Nations sets a target of 0.7 per cent of GNP for developing countries to give as aid. Figure O1.4 shows that few achieve the UN's objective. Although the US is the second largest donor in terms of dollars, it comes low down the list when this figure is converted into a percentage of GNP.

Over the years, aid payments have been falling, both in absolute terms and as a percentage of GNP. Some donor governments have felt that it was not being well spent. Others have simply wanted to save money.

Work in progress

Q **1** To what extent have donor governments met the official target for aid payments?

2 What type of aid was involved in the river blindness project?

3 Is aid still needed? Why?

Why give aid?

There are strong economic reasons for aid donations. Many of the recipient countries have a wealth of productive resources but an inadequate supply of finance and foreign exchange with which to carry out investment projects. As a result, the resources are unproductive when they could be helping to increase the growth rate for the country as a whole. This represents an imperfection in the capital market because the supply of funds for investment does not reach those who can put it to use. There is a vicious circle: low investment leads to low incomes, from which little saving can be generated, so that there are few resources for investment. Aid can bridge the gap with the provision of both finance for capital expenditure and technical expertise.

Once the process is set in motion, incomes will increase and therefore gradually permit the population to increase saving. By doing this, the country slowly becomes able to fund further investment projects internally, instead of having to be supported by others. This is inevitably a long-term process, but the multiplier effect on the initial injection of assistance will generate further growth. Investment projects must be carefully chosen so that those with the greatest potential returns are selected.

Technical expertise is often needed if new investment projects are to be carried out successfully. Many developing countries have a 'manpower gap' because education and training are not sufficiently sophisticated to enable people to cope with the technology employed. For aid to be effective, expertise must be passed to the local population so that the development becomes self-sustaining.

Giving aid is not always an altruistic process. Donors often expect something in return. Both economic and political motives play a large part in the structure of international aid transfers. Assistance has been given to 'friendly' countries and those of strategic importance.

Aid which is provided by governments is termed official development assistance, or ODA. Bilateral aid, which forms about 70 per cent of all ODA, often has strings attached and is known as tied aid. This may be a formal part of the agreement or an implication of a particular type of support. A donor country may supply a developing country with funds or resources, but there may be a reciprocal agreement for the purchase of certain goods. The installation of a new factory will certainly help a developing economy, but spare parts and updating will then have to be bought from the donor.

The recipients

Each year approximately US$54 billion is given in aid. Figure O1.5 shows how significant aid is in selected economies. Aid does not necessarily go to those that need it most. Some aid has been given for military reasons. Nevertheless, it can be a crucial element in the development process.

	Real GDP per capita (PPP$)*	Aid as % of GNP	Aid per capita (US$)
Bolivia	2880	9.2	106
Congo	1620	14.7	117
Cote d'Ivoire	1840	4.7	37
Gabon	7550	0.9	40
Honduras	2220	6.7	61
Jordan	3450	6.8	130
Lao Republic	1300	19.5	82
Mauritania	1730	23.9	120
Namibia	5010	5.0	119
Papua New-Guinea	2654	8.6	88
Senegal	1730	9.6	56
Zambia	960	16.9	77

*PPP$: Purchasing power parity, i.e. an amount representing equal purchasing power in each county.

Source: UN, *Human Development Reports*, 1998 Oxford University Press

Figure O1.5 Selected aid recipients, 1997

Some very poor countries receive relatively little aid. Bangladesh, for example, with per capita income of US$1050 recieves US$9 per capita.

The motives of recipients

Developing countries generally accept the view that aid is necessary to achieve a higher level of economic growth. Many need better infrastructure and are therefore willing to accept assistance despite the fact that it may have considerable strings attached to it. There are many cases where economies have taken off as a result of sustained injections combined with appropriate government policies.

Evaluating the effect of aid is not easy. The question which always crops up is 'What would have happened without it?'. The answer is not straightforward for a variety of reasons. First of all, the type of aid which has been provided will affect the expected outcomes. Emergency aid is intended to provide short-term relief in crisis situations and although it may contribute to re-establishing the economy, it is not a direct contributor to long-term growth. Figure O1.5 suggests that there is little relationship between the amount of aid as a proportion of GNP and the level of per capita GDP.

In countries where aid has generated growth, the distribution of benefits is unlikely to be equitable. People who are working in the new industries may find themselves in a very different world compared to the rest of the population which is still employed in agriculture or indigenous industries. A dual economy may be the result; in any process of development it is a possible outcome. The shift from being a rural, low-income economy to an industrialised country is inevitably gradual.

Debt: the outcome of aid?

Aid can be granted in the form of loans as well as grants. Borrowing necessitates repayments as well as incurring interest charges. Lending to developing countries by aid-giving organisations is generally on a concessional basis. In other words, the interest to be paid is lower than would be paid in the money markets.

Tied aid, even as a gift, may cause difficulties because the recipient is committed to purchase machinery, for example, from the donor country. The training of staff and maintenance will lead to further expense which may have to be funded by borrowing. However, much of the debt which has exacerbated the problems of the developing world has been the outcome of commercial borrowing rather than being aid associated. The debt problem is explored in more detail later (see page 414).

The role of non-governmental organisations

Lifelines

Credit in rural China

The Development Organisation of Rural Sichuan runs the Women's Rural Credit Scheme in a poor minority area. Fifty-nine women received loans and made repayments on a monthly basis. The scheme is flexible. One woman was unable to make her full monthly repayments because her husband fell sick. The women in her group met to decide what to do. They said she could make smaller repayments until one of the three piglets which she had purchased with her loan was ready for market. Overall, loan repayments were made ahead of schedule.

Source: *DORS Newsletter*, 1998

...and in Haiti

⁶ Without the Methodist Church's Rural Development Programme it would be different. I used to borrow from loan sharks, paying back much more than I borrowed. Then the church set up a community bank for women like me. It has taught us how to plan financially, how to calculate profits and costs. It gave us loans at low interest rates. I can take ingredients to the bakery and arrange for the bread to be made. I sell the loaves and I make peanut butter to sell with them. In time I hope to save enough to build my own large oven. That's my ambition. ⁹

Source: *Christian Aid News*, Spring 1999

Your agenda

1 What advantages do rural credit schemes have from both the donor's and the recipient's points of view?

2 Can charitable flows replace ODA?

Non-governmental organisations (NGOs) have an important role in the development process. Typically, their efforts are based on genuine donor concern and not on political considerations. (Some NGOs have a religious affiliation, of course.) The charitable money which they bring is of some value. Some NGOs such as Oxfam are very experienced in monitoring the success of their aid donations. Some bring very dedicated people into the development effort and they can help with technical assistance.

Many small local NGOs have sprung up too. These vary in origin, but many have emerged from trade unions, self-help groups, church organisations, the cooperative movement or lobbying groups. Although this process has drawbacks because it may lead to fragmentation of provision, it gives opportunities for local people to develop and control their own existence.

Where credit and marketing schemes have been set up, success seems to come to the ones which promote labour-intensive trades and therefore open opportunities for small-scale industry to be established on a local basis. Such NGOs will also act as intermediaries and negotiators with the government, providers of aid and the area's elite.

Need or efficiency?

As the total amount of aid declines, the debate about its use becomes more pertinent. Should aid be given because there is a need for it or should donations be evaluated on the basis of their effectiveness? Emergency aid is not generally questioned in this way because people need short-term relief in disaster situations.

Most projects have a considerable period devoted to planning and projection of outcomes and all donors insist that progress is monitored, but this is carried out within the remit of the donor organisation. Need and efficiency will be interpreted differently by different people and organisations. Countries with high levels of military expenditure receive about twice as much aid per capita as those with lower levels. The data have already shown that much aid goes to countries that are not exceptionally poor. The availability of assistance is unpredictable and is not necessarily related to human priorities.

Enquiry 2   What is the role of business?

This enquiry addresses the ways in which businesses expand their markets and develop global products and markets. It traces the development of multi-nationals and the impact of globalisation on business. Lastly, it examines the sources of competitive advantage.

1 Global brands

Coca-Cola

- In 1996 Coca-Cola sold 329 billion bottles, 8 per cent up on 1995, double the growth rate for the industry as a whole.

- Coca-Cola had 48 per cent of the world market for soft drinks.

- Coca-Cola outsells the leading tea in Britain, the leading bottled water in France and the leading coffee in Brazil.

- The chief executive of Coca-Cola once said that he would never rest until the C on the kitchen tap stood for Coke.

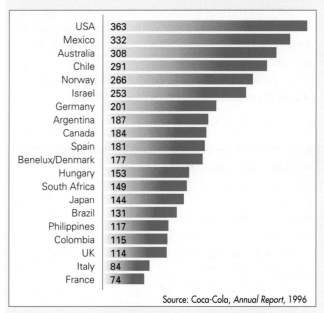

USA	363
Mexico	332
Australia	308
Chile	291
Norway	266
Israel	253
Germany	201
Argentina	187
Canada	184
Spain	181
Benelux/Denmark	177
Hungary	153
South Africa	149
Japan	144
Brazil	131
Philippines	117
Colombia	115
UK	114
Italy	84
France	74

Source: Coca-Cola, *Annual Report*, 1996

Figure O1.6 Coca-Cola product consumption, servings per person, per year

- The average person requires 64 ounces (1.8 litres) of liquid per day. Coca-Cola supplies 2 of those ounces (0.057 litres). The chief executive said, 'We remain resolutely focused on getting after the other 62.'

Coca-Cola is the world's best-known brand name. Name recognition levels are a major asset for the company. It also has an incredibly powerful distribution system. Its bottling partners buy the soft-drink concentrate, mix it with water and bottle or can it for local markets. Distribution has been strengthened recently as the company bought many of its smaller bottlers, invested in them and then sold them to more powerful regional bottlers.

The company has a portfolio of different adverts aimed at a whole range of audiences. It markets aggressively. In 1997 it tried to elbow Cadbury Schweppes out of its way by offering McDonald's franchises huge free gifts of soft-drink syrup, on condition they served only Coca-Cola products.

Your agenda

1 Is Coca-Cola operating in a competitive market? Explain the nature of the competition the company faces.

2 To what extent can a single brand suit all markets?

3 Is Coca-Cola selling a product or an image? Explain your view.

4 How much further do you think Coca-Cola can expand?

5 To what extent do you think that Coca-Cola is market orientated?

An important part of the impetus for globalisation has come from companies which want to expand their markets. A successful product can approach **market saturation** in its home market. One obvious way to expand sales is to sell abroad.

Some companies such as Coca-Cola have been able to create **global brands**, which sell worldwide. Their strategy is to develop an image which will appeal to people everywhere. Coke is perhaps an unusual product in that it can sell in large quantities even in countries with low incomes. Many global brands are prestige products which sell mainly to people with well above average incomes. Global brands are by their nature fully **standardised**. The Coke selling in Thailand is the same as the Coke selling in the USA.

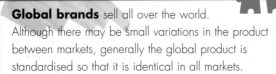

> ### Essentials
>
> **Market saturation** occurs when it becomes impossible to expand sales further in that particular market. If the product is a durable good, for example a washing-machine, market saturation means that it will only be possible to sell replacement machines.

> ### Essentials
>
> **Global brands** sell all over the world. Although there may be small variations in the product between markets, generally the global product is standardised so that it is identical in all markets.

> ### Essentials
>
> A **standardised** product is one that is identical wherever it is sold, regardless of variations in the nature of the market.

Regardless of whether the business sells a standardised product or one which meets local needs, choices must be made as to where it will be produced. Coke is bottled close to its market because the process of adding water to the syrup increases bulk and weight and therefore also transport costs. However, products with a relatively low bulk to value ratio, such as trainers, do not need to be produced close to the market. Nike locates production where wages are low, in Indonesia and the Philippines for example, then sells the product all over the world.

> ### Work in progress
>
> **Q 1** How can Coca-Cola sell at prices low enough to attract relatively poor customers?
>
> **2** Explain the component parts of Coke's marketing mix.
>
> **3** How does Coke's marketing mix differ from that of Nike?
>
> **4** Could Dandelion and Burdock have become a global product with a little more effort? What about Irn Bru? Think through the reasons.

Global markets

The business which has a well-known brand in its domestic market can always consider turning it into a global brand. An alternative strategy for the company which wants to expand into global markets is to tailor the product to the market. This means doing extensive market research in each individual market in order to determine how the product may best be adapted to suit local customers.

In either case, the company could have a number of objectives driving its expansion, including:

- increased sales and revenue
- a chance to sell in markets where incomes are growing most strongly
- shareholder pressure to maintain profit growth
- an opportunity to diversify into a range of markets so that heavy dependence on one or a few markets, which could decline, can be avoided. This reduces risk.

A different story

McDonald's is a global brand too. For many years, it really didn't need new products. Its profits grew as it opened ever more outlets. Then in the mid-1990s things began to change. Sales growth in the USA slowed down; it couldn't keep pace with the growing number of outlets. Sales per outlet actually fell. The company lost market share to Burger King and Wendy's.

Something had to change. Under the new chief executive, Jack Greenberg, new computerised kitchen equipment was installed so food could be cooked to order. This meant that the menu could be more varied – it wouldn't matter if some items sold less well than others. Then McDonald's bought Chipotle, a Mexican food chain. These were revolutionary departures from the company's previous policies. As Mr Greenberg said, 'Given our competences and our resources, I think we owe it to our shareholders to experiment with other concepts, maybe at different price points, and see if we can find another global brand.'

Your agenda

1 What does this case study tell you about the need for brand management?

2 Why is McDonald's position perhaps quite vulnerable, in your view?

3 McDonald's now varies its product mix depending on the location. How might this benefit the company?

Coke and McDonald's are emerging as two rather different global brands. Coke has a one-size-fits-all approach. Gillette works that way too, and it has 70 per cent of the world market in shaving products. It looks as though McDonald's best strategy might be quite different. All three companies produce and market all over the world and are impressively experienced in making profits.

These companies are actually using branding in different ways. Gillette and McDonald's are using their brands to cover their whole product range. Gillette wants its name associated with a high-technology approach to shaving, one which will provide speed and comfort. McDonald's branding covers the Big Mac, the fries and all the other menu items. In effect, the brand is intended to define a particular eating experience rather than a single menu item.

Coke is Coke. It might come in a can or a bottle, but the flavour will be the same. Coca-Cola sells other products – such as Fanta and Sprite. Each product has its own brand image. Coca-Cola's objective is to corner the world market in soft drinks. Sales of any of the products in its range will contribute.

Work in progress

Q Come up with three other examples of global brands. Explain the appeal of each, and why they have been highly successful. Compare them with the three examples just described.

2 Getting into the global market place

A joint venture in China

Fedders produces room air-conditioners for the US market. Unlike many companies, this is its only product. The air-conditioner fits into a window and runs off the household electricity supply.

By 1995, Fedders felt it was facing problems. Although it was the biggest producer of room air-conditioners in the USA, it faced a mature market. Only replacement sales could be expected, and sales are highly seasonal. In winter sales revenue will not even cover fixed costs. Furthermore, the company was in competition with central air-conditioning systems which are installed in most new buildings. Fedders decided that it should try to branch out. Asian summer weather and rapid growth in incomes provided strong prospects. It settled on China as the place to look. In 1991 annual sales of air-conditioners in China were 500 000. By 1995, they had risen to 4 million. That made the Chinese market as big as the US one, but still with vast growth potential because of China's 1.2 billion population.

Entering a foreign market is never easy. First, Fedders hired 20 Chinese-speaking US citizens. With their help the company found a potential Chinese partner, the Ningbo General Air Conditioner Factory. It was looking for a joint venture partner because it faced mounting competition in the Chinese market.

The two partners spent some time establishing personal relationships so that a sense of trust could develop. This is an essential part of Asian business deals, often neglected by western businesses. The standard way to solve problems is over a good dinner. Fedders needed the support of the regional government, and promised to provide housing for all employees if needed.

Then Fedders turned its attention to quality issues. It had to develop a new model to suit the Chinese market, where an air-conditioner is a major consumer purchase and often a status symbol too. This meant that a more sophisticated design was needed, in contrast to the utilitarian US product.

What's in it for the two partners? The Chinese company gets an injection of funds for investment and access to new technologies which should cut costs and make it very much more competitive. Fedders gets a chance to sell in the vast Chinese market and to export to other Asian countries. It gets local expertise for its operations in China and new relationships with Chinese component suppliers which may be able to meet demand for lower-cost components in the US factories. Both partners are likely to find that they can expand together much more than they could separately.

Your agenda

1 What do you think would be the main hazards in attempting to set up production facilities overseas?

2 What are likely to be the main advantages of producing in a country such as China?

Joint ventures have become a well-established way for businesses to expand their activities in countries where they have not previously been active. They are particularly useful where language and political barriers exist. They allow owners of capital to invest it in places where the return on capital is high, typically because wage costs are relatively low. Equally, they create possibilities of increased incomes for employees in the host country. This can do wonders for the profitability of companies based in developed countries where wage costs are usually high. Equally, it can bring big improvements in the standards of living of developing countries too.

China has favoured the joint venture as a way of encouraging **technology transfer**, enabling its factories to exploit new technologies. This is very important to developing countries which do not have easy access to new ideas.

Essentials

Joint ventures involve businesses in a collaborative relationship with a local producer. They are of particular value where the business wants to produce and sell in an unfamiliar market. They can be used as a way to spread risks.

Technology transfer refers to the way in which countries which do not have access to modern technologies may acquire expertise when multi-national companies locate there. The company then trains local people in the new methods of production, gradually creating a group of people with the skills needed to make use of the new technology.

The joint venture is one form of alliance which companies can create in order to meet their objectives. One major advantage is that a joint venture enables businesses to share the risks of a new development. Coca-Cola has entered into a large number of joint ventures through its alliances with local bottling companies. It trades brand power for local knowledge of the distribution system.

One particularly successful partnership has been the alliance between Samsung, the Korean electronics company, and Corning, the US glassmaker. This started in 1973 with one plant making television tubes in Korea. It has grown into an agreement covering much of east Asia.

Joint ventures are not simply for multi-nationals seeking entry to an unfamiliar market. Siemens of Germany has a joint venture with Corning in the fibre optics field. This was a new and risky product when they first started in 1980. Collaboration reduced the risks. All these alliances provide examples of the way globalisation has actually occurred.

Franchises

For many businesses, the best way into international markets has been through **franchises**. This enables a local business (the franchisee) to start up under the name of a major organisation (the franchisor) which has been successful elsewhere. Fast-food chains McDonald's and KFC and the fashion retailer Tie Rack all make extensive use of franchises. It is a form of organisation which is particularly appropriate in the service sector, especially retailing.

The franchising company makes a legal contract with the local business. This contract establishes very strict rules for the operation of the business. The franchisee has to pay an initial lump sum fee and then an annual payment based on a percentage of the turnover. Typically, the premises will be given the characteristic appearance dictated by the franchisor.

The local business benefits from this arrangement because it gets the local rights to a recognised trade name and reputation. Unique selling points are tried and tested. Furthermore, the franchising company uses part of its income to run an advertising campaign. This benefits all the franchisees because they gain from the marketing economies of scale which can be secured by the franchisor. The franchisor benefits because it operates in widely diversified markets without having to have business expertise in individual local economies.

The franchisor in this way can expand its operations without having to find large amounts of capital for investment. Communications with individual franchisees are easy and the local managers are likely to be strongly motivated. They know their local market well. Some franchisees may lack the necessary business experience, but this can be guarded against by the franchisor at the selection stage.

Franchises are legal agreements by which local businesses are allowed to set up using the name, logo and trading method of a well-known company. They are usually restricted to a well-defined area. They gain all the benefits of a strongly branded product. In return they pay a lump sum and an annual percentage of turnover.

Work in progress

Q 1 Take the three examples given (McDonald's, KFC and Tie Rack) and any others you know about, and consider the sources of competitive advantage for each one.

2 What do these companies have in common?

3 Does The Body Shop use franchising for the same reasons?

Licences

A looser link with businesses worldwide can be created by selling the right to produce under **licence**. The owner of a patent or a copyright can license other businesses to create and sell its product, or to use its technology. This means that an innovative company can expand into international markets without actually having to invest in locally based production facilities. For example, Heineken lager is brewed under licence by Whitbreads in the UK.

This is one way to preserve intellectual property rights. This is the name given to the ownership of an innovative product or process which can be protected. Books and other publications are protected from copying by copyright laws. Recordings similarly belong to the company that made them. (This is explored in more detail in Option 3, page 540).

New inventions can be protected by patents, which guarantee exclusive rights to the design for a period of years. These allow the company to recoup the development costs by giving them a temporary monopoly.

Equally, the business which is licensed to use a new technology gets the benefit of it. It pays for it in licensing fees, but it does not have to invest in a risky development process.

> **Essentials**
>
> A **licence** allows a business to make and market a product, or use a production method, which is protected by copyright or patent.

A global company

Ford

The 'Ford 2000' plan combines in a single organisation Ford's European and its North American businesses. Hitherto, the two have had their own management structures, products, factories and cultures. It will be organised on the basis of products rather than geographical regions. This should enable it to dispense with duplicated management functions and to reap massive economies of scale.

New technologies have made it possible for the company to introduce a new kind of globalisation. Computer networks and video links will allow people who are widely separated by distance to work together on the same car.

Ford was in a highly successful position when this strategy was first planned. But the market for cars in Europe and North America is a mature one, whereas in Asia it will expand faster as incomes rise. Furthermore, even after all car manufacturers had embraced lean production, Toyota still produced 37 cars per year per worker, as against Ford's 20. So there was no room for complacency. In order to ensure that it did not lose market share, Ford needed to take action.

Having different models for Europe and North America meant that Ford's engineering costs were three times as high as they could be with a unified range. All the evidence pointed towards the need to become a fully global company.

The hope was that there would be savings of $3 billion a year on costs, shortened product development times and new creative approaches to design through teamwork. To date, the benefits in terms of profitability look unimpressive. However, it may be that Ford had no choice but to change, and the benefits will show in the long run.

> ### Your agenda
>
> **1** Are cars different from other consumer goods? Are there good reasons why it is not necessary to produce for particular national markets?
>
> **2** What drawbacks would a global structure have for a car company?
>
> **3** What other products might lend themselves to the Ford approach?

The conventional wisdom is that multi-national corporations should be highly sensitive to local variations in their market. For many businesses, this is clearly true. As we saw, even McDonald's is considering local product changes. At the other extreme, UK breweries produce their ales to quite different recipes for different regions. Yet other brewers run successfully with a truly global approach.

It seems likely that integrating the US and European operations of Ford could work. The US liking for large cars has become less and less marked. The cost advantages of integration look solid. However, Ford could anyway be vulnerable in an increasingly competitive industry.

Reorganising a company requires great attention to the detailed aspects of communications with employees, otherwise the necessarily difficult aspects of the reorganisation can alienate many of the people involved. The management at Ford went out of its way to involve employees in the changes so that they would understand the underlying objectives. Without this kind of effort, employees may resent the impersonal nature of a global organisation.

In general, global products may turn out to be unattractive because they do not reflect the real needs of any particular market. So the right strategy for a multi-national needs to be determined in the light of its product, its cost structures, its market and its competitive position. Ford's experience will be worth watching.

3 How did multi-nationals develop?

Caterpillar, Coca-Cola and others

During the Second World War, General Eisenhower asked Coca-Cola to supply the US troops. The idea was to improve morale. By the end of the war, Coca-Cola had bottling plants everywhere the US army had been, i.e. just about all over the world.

Meantime, the US army was using Caterpillar machines in the course of the fighting. After the war was over, they were put to use rebuilding the shattered infrastructure. They needed spares, though, so Caterpillar got established supplying them.

US engineering and construction companies were heavily involved in the rebuilding process. Some of the projects were financed by US aid, the terms of which required the participation of US companies.

This process undoubtedly gave encouragement to the development of a number of multi-national corporations (MNCs). For example, US construction, mining and forestry businesses wanted Caterpillar's earth movers – the ones they were familiar with. In due course, Caterpillar identified markets in Europe and elsewhere which were potentially profitable. To start with they built factories in countries which had high tariff walls which made imports expensive and uncompetitive. Much foreign direct investment reflected this up to the 1970s.

Later, it became clear that multi-nationals could benefit from lower wage costs if they chose their locations carefully. As tariffs became less problematic, the search for low-cost locations became more important. It remains the case that US and Japanese companies locate in Europe, often in the UK, to avoid the Common External Tariff of the EU.

Your agenda

1 What benefits do multi-nationals bring to the host country?

2 Many multi-nationals are very large producers. What advantages does this have for their customers?

3 What are the main motivating factors for businesses which extend their operations to new countries?

What is a **multi-national enterprise**? When companies invest abroad, there is direct foreign investment. The company sets up factories or sales outlets, or acquires other revenue-generating assets, in more than one country. So what is the objective?

Essentials

A **multi-national** enterprise has business interests located in several countries.

There can be many reasons for direct investment:

- Some multi-nationals are locating in a particular target market. There may be advantages in being close to the market, or they may want to escape import duties.

- Others may be seeking the lowest cost location for their production facilities, and may be attracted by the availability of skilled labour or large areas of cheap flat land. Low wages are often the draw.

- Other businesses may want to invest in their own sales outlets so as to reach their foreign markets more effectively. The Body Shop, Marks & Spencer, Laura Ashley and Church's Shoes all do this.

- Some large firms, such as ICI, Siemens, Ford, Hitachi and Phillips, produce goods with a worldwide market and are large enough to exploit its potential. They are also able to achieve significant economies of scale. They look for production possibilities, as well as marketing possibilities, virtually everywhere.

Looking closely at multi-national enterprises, one thing is clear. Transport costs are usually not very important in the modern world. Only very heavy or bulky items, such as bricks, must be produced close to their market. Avoiding transport costs is not usually a major motive for foreign direct investment, although it can be one of a number of considerations.

How do multi-nationals operate?

A multi-national may acquire a green-field site and build its factory from scratch. This is what happened when Henry Ford built the Dagenham car plant in the 1930s. It is organic growth.

Alternatively, firms may invest abroad by buying foreign companies: they acquire control by buying the shares. For example, in 1988 the Swiss company Nestlé acquired the UK confectionery manufacturer Rowntree. Acquisitions of this sort can lead to restructuring on a worldwide basis, which can cause people to feel that the activities of multi-nationals are both unpredictable and destabilising for their employees. In fact, in the UK, it has been found that job losses are as likely to come from UK-owned as from foreign-owned employers.

Multi-national hotels

Accor is a French hotel and travel company. It pioneered budget hotels: Formule 1 is now a world leader in its field. Jean-Marc Espalioux, chief executive, explains the company's development:

'Accor has to be a global company, in view of the revolution in the service sector which is taking place. I do not see any future for purely national hotel chains, except in niche markets. They cannot invest enough money.

Having globalisation as an objective has the advantage of spreading our risks and compensating for any short-term problems we may encounter. We are expanding in countries such as Poland, Brazil, Argentina and Indonesia.

We cannot exclude the possibility that there is a devaluation crisis or other problems in one of these countries, but with a good geographical spread we can avoid worrying about the next two years and concentrate on the longer view.

Globalisation brings considerable challenges which are often underestimated. The principal difficulty is getting our local management to adhere to the values of the group. Our Indonesian managers must understand our market and culture and we have to learn about theirs.

Our executives use video-conferencing and travel non-stop to keep in touch.'

Your agenda

1 What are Accor's main objectives as a global business?

2 What advantages can it offer its customers?

3 Some hotel chains use franchising as their way of working. What advantages would this have?

4 Multi-nationals in developing countries: a cause for concern?

Singapore

With just one small island for its 3 million people, Singapore had to work out a strategy for development. It was clear that land would be in very short supply. The newly independent government saw an immediate solution in foreign direct investment. It decided on a range of tax incentives. These included tax exemption on profits for five to ten years and extra tax incentives for exports. The results were impressive:

- By 1979, incomes were growing at around 7 per cent a year in real terms and standards of living were similar to Spain and Greece at the time.

- By the mid-1980s, foreign firms were responsible for 70 per cent of gross output in the manufacturing sector, employed more than 50 per cent of the workforce and generated 80 per cent of direct exports. In fact, more than 25 per cent of Singapore's GDP was produced by foreign-owned companies.

Wage rates were rising. The original motive for locating in Singapore was no longer operational. Some companies left, locating their production in lower-wage economies such as Thailand and Mexico. Many people felt this was evidence of the fickle behaviour of multi-nationals.

In spite of many changes, Singapore has never really stopped growing. It left the ranks of the developing world long ago. The World Bank data for 1998 per capita GNP shows Singapore ranked slightly higher than the USA.

Your agenda

1 What possible reasons can you think of for Singapore's success, other than high levels of foreign direct investment (FDI)?

2 Which other countries have had very high growth rates?

3 To what extent was FDI important for those countries too?

Many multi-nationals are large in relation to the national income of some of the countries in which they operate. This means that it is not always as easy for governments to control their activities as they would wish. It raises awkward ethical issues about power in the market place. On the other hand, governments may want foreign investment, because it generates jobs and income, and because it can lead to local people being trained in new skills – technology transfer.

In a highly competitive world market, companies seek locations where they can establish plants which will give them a cutting edge in pricing their products. Many governments found the prospects of factories being set up by large overseas companies appealing. They would move the economy higher in the growth league tables.

Larger developing countries, such as Brazil, have felt able to negotiate with foreign investors, so regulating their activity. Smaller, weaker countries such as some southern African nations cannot do this.

These questions become highly political and very hard to resolve. Evidence is often conflicting. Weighing up the balance of the pros and cons can be almost impossible.

The case for encouraging multi-nationals to invest

- Foreign investment provides funds which businesses in developing countries cannot access. Where incomes are low, savings are often low too. Local banks cannot provide loans to very many businesses and when they do, they avoid taking risks.

- The generation of saving is generally inadequate to permit large-scale industrial investment so the introduction of finance from elsewhere allows it to go ahead. By doing so, the economy will grow and generate further income, so the multiplier effect of such an injection is to be welcomed.

- FDI brings in firms which want to produce for export. Even if they import capital goods and other inputs, there should be a net gain on the foreign exchange available for imports.

- Technology transfer opens up additional opportunities.

- Developing countries often have an inadequate supply of appropriate skilled personnel to staff a modern plant so the introduction of overseas staff will provide the basis for training a future workforce. Not only will technical experts be installed but managerial staff will be brought in as well. Their duty will be to train the local employees in coping with the complexities of decision-making and dealing with international markets.

- Foreign companies add to the country's tax revenue and therefore assist in the provision of funds for developing new infrastructure and the provision of other facilities which will help in improving the quality of life for the resident population.

The case against

- Multi-nationals may take the profits they make from the country where they were made, and distribute them to shareholders, or re-invest them in other countries.

- They may transfer their products to other countries at artificially low prices, so avoiding some local taxes. If they have received substantial tax breaks, their contribution to the country's revenue may anyway be less than expected. Long-established companies often continue to negotiate special terms in order to maintain their position.

- Semi-finished goods are often imported to be assembled and exported again. However, if the profits are remitted to the country of origin, the local gains may be very limited, consisting of the creation of some very poorly paid jobs.

- There may be little need to train the local workforce if the company brings in the experts that are required. The jobs which are carried out by the country's nationals tend to be low skilled. This reduces the impact of technology transfer.

- Importing the latest technology may have little effect on the local population. In fact, it may undermine existing companies which are trying to compete using less sophisticated equipment.

- Some companies use their economic power to influence decisions that are taken by the government. They can play one country off against another to gain the best package of concessions and incentives.

- Multi-nationals can increase income inequalities by creating a prosperous managerial class while paying very low wages to the majority of employees.

- Local businesses may feel that they have suffered because the multi-nationals can bring in products with famous brand names and sell them as loss leaders in order to capture the market. This can discourage local investment.

- Some multi-nationals may be taking environmental risks in developing countries which would not be allowed in developed countries.

There are many difficult ethical issues. Nestlé continues to advertise its baby milk in developing countries. Bottle-feeding is not very desirable in developing countries because there are hygiene risks, and a danger of babies being undernourished, both of which are reduced by breast-feeding. The tobacco companies are targeting poor countries where smoking is still on the increase, now that life in the developed world is getting more difficult for them. These are not the only problems.

Work in progress

Q 1 What benefits do multi-nationals bring to the host country?

2 Sometimes multi-nationals are allowed to do things in their host country which would be illegal in their country of origin. What are the arguments for and against this?

3 Do multi-nationals help or hinder the economic growth of a country? Explain.

5 How has globalisation affected business?

An improbable story?

We used to assume that cement was so heavy that it would not be economical to trade it internationally, and it would always be dominated by national or local interests. Quite wrong. During the 1990s, there was a phenomenal burst of acquisitions. The big players got bigger and most of the small players went. The world market has been divided up between the UK's Blue Circle, Cemex from Mexico and four others based in Switzerland, Germany, France and Italy.

Cemex went on a buying spree all over Latin America during the 1980s. Then it rationalised production and really improved efficiency. When the Mexican peso crashed in 1995, Cemex reckoned it was saved by its subsidiaries. The Mexican side of its business could not have survived the resulting slump.

The European cement makers bought up most of the capacity in North America during the 1990s. Then the Asian financial crisis put a stop to much construction work there. The bottom dropped out of the local cement business. The Europeans bought countless cement works at bargain basement prices. Then when the USA ran short of cement for its building boom, they could ship it from Thailand across the Pacific. (Cement is too heavy to transport far by land but can be transported easily in container ships. With Thailand's low labour costs, it made economic sense).

If there is another Far East building boom, the big players will make a killing. Cemex is moving into Asia too.

Your agenda

1 What kind of growth is being described here?

2 Can these mergers and acquisitions have any benefits for customers?

3 What advantage does this approach have for the companies?

4 What is the scope for technology transfer in this situation?

The process of globalisation has three distinguishable phases for the individual business:

- Companies with a national focus look to expand their markets by selling abroad.

- They develop bases in overseas markets from which they can service their sales activities.

- They go on to develop sources of inputs based on the cost advantages of a wide variety of locations.

Global companies have passed through each of these phases and have fully integrated operations. They may then go on to expand through inorganic growth as Cemex did.

Inorganic growth

Globalisation presents fantastic opportunities for some businesses. If they have a real competitive advantage in their core business, they will be able to acquire capacity in places where demand is growing fast. They can use their expertise to increase productivity and cut costs. In any business where economies of scale are significant, there can be real scope for improvements.

Cement provides an interesting example because it is of particular importance in the emerging economies. It is they that provide the biggest markets as they invest in infrastructure. If incomes are rising quickly, they can also make big improvements in housing.

Inorganic growth is sometimes seen as being an easy way to develop globally. The businesses which are bought outright are already operational; no start-up is needed. However, the parent company has got to know enough about local production and marketing to make a success of the business. This is not a foregone conclusion, even if good local people are recruited.

Buying outright – acquisitions – gives the parent company full control. Mergers, by contrast, require collaboration. They may take some time to get right, as the organisation of the two businesses has to become integrated. This is one reason why alliances such as joint ventures have become more important in recent years.

The forces of globalisation

There is no doubt that globalisation has increased competitive pressures. Many businesses get involved in overseas markets because they are finding it hard to expand against the competition at home. The end result is that for many products there are simply many more competitors in any one market. This can mean that quality improves and price goes down. Washing-machines, televisions and so on are definitely cheaper and better because of international competition.

Some businesses look for new markets to help them cope with the competition. Others are simply looking for expansion. The success of the emerging economies has created opportunities. It is a two-way process because the foreign direct investment helps the emerging economies to grow.

Selling into unknown markets is difficult and the case studies so far have shown some possible strategies. Very importantly, companies need to forge appropriate alliances. Joint ventures, franchises, licensing agreements, mergers: partnerships of all kinds become very important.

Increasing transparency

Multi-nationals now operate in a much more visible way. News media can report events all over the world. People take notice. Many people are not sure about whether multi-nationals always act in ethical ways. Many others are quite sure: they reckon they don't, and many of these people belong to pressure groups which can protest.

This has had a good effect on the multi-nationals. It has made it harder for them to get away with unethical practices. These issues are explored elsewhere in more detail (see page 420 and Option 3, Enquiry 4).

6 How do companies get competitive?

Communication

A US family invites a Japanese man to dinner, 7.30 for 8pm. Knowing it would be rude to arrive on time (his hosts might not be ready), he rings the doorbell at 8.45pm. Concealing their irritation – and their worries about the dinner – the Americans invite him in, take his coat and enquire if he would like to 'use the bathroom' (a US term for the 'toilet') before the meal. Their Japanese visitor beams and accepts. This is exactly what would happen if he were invited to an unusually courteous Japanese family. Imagine his hosts' consternation when, a few minutes later, they hear the bath taps running! Refreshed and relaxed, he emerges at 9.30pm. to face his glowering hosts and a ruined meal.

Your agenda

Can you recall situations in which there has been a total failure of communication? What was the cause of it all?

Who are your five best friends, the people whom you find easiest to talk to? Chances are, they are roughly the same age as you, of approximately the same income level – and grew up in the same country as yourself. 'Like-minded' people are easy to talk to: we share their attitudes, their unspoken assumptions about the way things ought to be, their interests, their hopes and fears.

This simple observation creates a significant problem for multi-nationals. They are, by their very nature, trying to communicate *across* cultures, to sell their products to people with whom they often have little in common in terms of language, religion, ethnic origin and history: the factors that make up what we loosely refer to as 'culture'.

So what exactly is 'culture'? Geert Hofstede, a Dutch business theorist, has identified four key elements that the multi-national sales force can use as a guide to work out how best to approach their counterparts in other countries:

● *Attitude to relationships.* Generally, Asian cultures value the buyer/seller relationship as much as the immediate deal in prospect. Time spent socialising is expected before any business is discussed. By contrast, westerners will commonly move to discussing terms after the briefest of introductions.

When GEC-Alsthom sales executives went to North Korea to negotiate a contract for a high-speed train link from Seoul to Pusan, they included karaoke sessions in the salesperson activities. This proved very helpful in establishing trusting relationships, even though the sales executives found it quite difficult.

● *Attitude to risk*. The French spend a great deal of time establishing precise customer requirements before closing the deal. Why? The possibility of selling the product with unsuitable specifications is a risk they are not prepared to accept. By contrast, the typical Anglo-Saxon salesperson will be less concerned. Some customers may end up unhappy, but most not. Win some, lose some.

● *Attitude to authority*. The US seller will try to contact the decision-maker, the person with authority to place an order. People lower down are, frankly, a waste of time. But the French adopt the opposite approach. Why disturb a figure of great importance? Better to find a contact lower down with whom friendly relationships can be established. Time enough to approach the boss when details have been thrashed out and a signature is required.

● *Attitude to the individual*. Japanese society is essentially collective: the individual's self-worth derives from membership of groups – and particularly the company. Its rival across the Pacific, the USA, adopts a much more individualist approach. In broad terms, the USA has famous entrepreneurs. Japan has famous companies. It follows that the US business community has a natural sympathy for the one-to-one approach, whereas the Japanese are more interested in a relationship between teams.

Work in progress

Q 1 Using the above analysis, advise James Dyson, inventor of a novel design of vacuum cleaner, how he should go about selling his product:
   a in Japan
   b in the USA.

2 What issues might Ford consider when deciding whether its German sales operation should be run by a German, or by an American from its Detroit Head Office?

3 On the basis of the above analysis, why do you think just-in-time stock control (see page OO) originated in Japan? Can you envisage any problems transplanting the idea to a British setting?

4 Hofstede's analysis is based on national stereotypes, i.e. statements about the *average* American or Japanese. Are such stereotypes likely to be a help or a hindrance to our understanding of cross-cultured communication?

■ Selling effectively

Sensitive communications are absolutely vital to successful marketing. Multi-nationals which have overcome problems have much going for them. The basic choice, between adapting for different markets and going with a global product, has already been explored. Studying the need for effective communication can help to inform the decision-taking process.

The food manufacturer Nestlé says: 'Marketing cannot be a head office activity. Giving life to our brands, making them relevant to our consumers, is the responsibility of local managers.' That means local managers and head office need to understand each other.

■ Recruiting the right people

Creating a global company takes a long time – maybe ten years. It means having good employees in all the areas of interest.

ABB, a Swiss-Swedish engineering company, says: 'Globalisation is a long-lasting competitive advantage. If we build a new gas turbine, in 18 months our competitors also have one. But a global company is not so easy to copy. Our main task now is to bring more executives from emerging economies in eastern Europe and Asia into the higher levels of the company. We have 82 000 employees in emerging economies. We have to bring the best of these to the top.'

Being flexible

Global companies have to be just as flexible as their local competitors. Their sensitivity to changing customer requirements and their speed of response have to match up. Product life cycles are getting shorter. New technologies are coming along faster.

Giant is a Taiwan bicycle manufacturer which has made good use of low Asian wages. Now it is investing in sites closer to European markets. It says:

'Fashions are changing quickly and market trends must be followed closely. Having a production base next to the market means we should be able to satisfy our customers better.'

Knowledge and information: a big priority

Michael Porter, in his book *The Competitive Advantage of Nations*, emphasises the importance of acquiring and using knowledge:

- Watching for trends in the market place is one priority. By examining the varying regional trends in all its markets the company may become aware of change before its competitors do.

- The business with highly dispersed production, i.e. factories in many countries, needs to gather the information needed to coordinate those activities. Where economies of scale are possible, specialisation can take place. Ford is doing this: its factories in Europe are specialising in particular models and then swapping them so that each country has the full range to choose from.

- Some multi-nationals shift production to the countries with the lowest exchange rates.

- On a very simple level, lessons learnt in one country can often be used to advantage in other countries.

Making knowledge and its analysis a high priority can become part of the culture of the business. Information is expensive to collect, but better software is reducing that problem. Many businesses could now build their competitive advantage on the quality of the information they have at their fingertips.

Knowing your limitations

The thread that runs through all these important aspects of global competitiveness is communication. The really difficult thing about communications is the time it takes to set up structures which improve them. For some companies, the best strategy is not to be multi-national. It is to concentrate on defending the home market. However, this too requires a thorough awareness of market trends, a willingness to find the cheapest components and openness to new technologies. Competing locally requires global knowledge.

7 How do countries stay competitive?

Motor components hit by strong pound

Early in 1998 the pound was rising. Over the previous year the sterling index had appreciated by 9 per cent. But that was not all. Some other currencies, including the deutschemark, had been falling, so UK companies had lost competitiveness in a serious way. Car maker VW's purchases in the UK dropped sharply.

The car components manufacturers were particularly badly hit. Some of them were having difficulty in meeting quality standards anyway. Sales of engineered components designed for particular models were not too badly affected, but batteries, lighting equipment and other standard parts were being re-sourced by the car companies.

The worst effects were felt in the new model production programmes, where a decision to buy elsewhere would mean years of lost sales.

Your agenda

1   Explain why appreciation has an adverse effect on competitiveness.

2   What options are available to the business which is faced with an unfavourable exchange rate?

3   How can businesses protect themselves from the adverse effects of exchange rate changes?

Having a low exchange rate is a great advantage, especially to manufacturers. They will find it easy to export. Similarly, it helps businesses which are in competition with imports. For a while, the UK belonged to the European Exchange Rate Mechanism (ERM), as part of its overall macro-economic policy. In 1992 it had to leave the ERM because it could no longer resist market pressures on the exchange rate. Too many people were selling their sterling bank balances. Immediately after the pound dropped out of the ERM, it depreciated by about 9 per cent. The beneficial effect on demand for UK products can be seen in the strong growth rates in the period 1993–7. (See page 198).

By 1998 the beneficial effect had all gone. The pound had risen well above its previous level. UK manufacturing had to endure two very difficult years.

Sometimes governments can decide upon an exchange rate policy and help to bring about change. The trouble is that not everyone can have a favourable exchange rate. When the Asian financial crisis started, and many people and businesses were selling Asian currencies, one of the currencies they bought was the pound. The dollar went up too.

Exchange rate stability does at least make the situation predictable for businesses, but that is elusive too. The UK may or may not join the Economic and Monetary Union (EMU). Not joining will mean less exchange rate stability for the UK, at least in relation to the euro.

Keeping a competitive economy

Michael Porter says that the biggest spur to competitiveness is domestic competition. Rivalry between businesses does wonders for keeping them on their toes. They watch each other, copy each other and poach each other's employees. They toughen each other up. In this way, expertise in the management of the business is transmitted throughout the industry. If the rivals are forcing each other to compete effectively, then they will be able to compete internationally.

It follows that countries which have tough competition legislation are actually more likely to be competitive internationally. Letting big businesses enjoy an element of monopoly power may make their profits look good, but quite soon they become flabby and complacent. The chances of their exports competing well are poor.

Developing countries which have reduced import controls and gone for export-led growth have generally done well. Hong Kong, Taiwan and Singapore, three of the Asian tigers, went along this route with results which promise well for the other countries now trying to do the same. Letting in imports forces domestic businesses to become lean and fit in the same way that Porter describes. For a long time, India protected its domestic industries, and grew rather slowly. Since liberalising its trade regime, its growth rates have risen despite the problems in Asia.

Supposing it doesn't work?

Some countries stand little chance of exporting manufactures at the present time. The least developed economies, including many in sub-Saharan Africa and some Asian economies, are dependent on exports of primary products. World commodity prices are notoriously variable, depending on levels of demand and production in competing countries.

Discussing the need for competitiveness with a government official in a country dependent on primary export earnings is irrelevant. Of course, it is important to try to ensure that the exchange rate is not overvalued. This is no laughing matter in some African countries where exchange rates have been kept high to make imports cheaper. This is not a good idea even if the cheap imports make local people living in the towns happier and prevent riots.

In such situations aid has a part to play. These issues are taken up in later enquiries.

In order to look at how people are affected, this enquiry starts with an analysis of how trade affects the way resources are allocated. It weighs up the benefits of more and less trade and how incomes are affected. The prices at which products sell and the way trade is financed are both important, especially to poorer countries. Lastly, the impact of trade on employment is explored.

1 Can trade bring growth?

Export expertise

What can the UK sell?

Traditionally, the UK exchanged manufactures of all kinds for a range of imported primary products. It isn't so simple any more.

- Many other countries export manufactures.

- In the meantime, the UK got its own oil from the North Sea. That reduced imports and increased exports of a major primary product.

- Then UK farmers started to produce much more food: fewer primary imports again.

- Services, especially the financial kind, had always been important for the UK. They became more so.

UK manufactures which sell well overseas include items such as scotch whisky and high-quality wool cardigans. They also include aircraft and aircraft parts. British Aerospace and Airbus Industrie have proved their success as exporters, so have a lot of specialist chemical companies. In fact, many successful exporters are very specialised indeed.

The advantages which give the UK its chances in export markets are so many and various it is hard to define them, but it is clear that the UK does have some advantages in knowledge-based industries. Media, financial services, pharmaceuticals, education services and many others rely on knowledge as their stock in trade.

What can Australia sell?

Have you bought any Australian products lately? You probably didn't even notice. Australia has specialised in agricultural exports. No question, it can sell wheat and wool. Australia is still sparsely populated. Its land produces farm products of all kinds and exports them all over the world. In 1999 production of wheat was 23 million tonnes, of which only 5 million were consumed within Australia.

Your agenda

1 Identify three successful UK exporters and think about the reasons for their success.

2 What are the advantages of exporting?

3 How do you benefit from international trade, personally?

4 Do you think trade should be encouraged?

It is easy to see that both importers and exporters gain from their activities. There is also a more formal way of looking at the gains from trade. First, it is obvious that some countries are better at producing particular products than others. The USA clearly has an advantage in the production of computers, compared to a country like Nigeria. This advantage is defined in terms of resources: one country has an **absolute advantage** over another if it can produce the product using fewer resources. When this is the case it pays countries to specialise, producing more of the products in which they have an advantage, and trade.

Essentials

An **absolute advantage** exists if the real resource cost of a product is lower in one country than in another.

How much land, labour and capital does it take to produce bananas in the UK? Rather a lot, because we would be very inefficient producers of tropical fruit. These resources could be much better used producing aircraft or insurance. The cost of producing bananas in the UK is extremely high, because it would be necessary to build and heat glasshouses. Large quantities of resources would be tied up in inefficient production. This is an example of an absolute disadvantage. However, even if they do not have an absolute advantage, countries can still gain from trade.

Comparative advantage

It is possible to show that trade can almost always increase real incomes using the theory of **comparative advantage**. This is so even if one country has an absolute advantage in both, or all, products.

Essentials

The theory of **comparative advantage** states that if two countries each specialise in the product with the lowest opportunity cost, and trade, then real incomes will increase.

Comparative advantage relates to the opportunity cost of production. Provided opportunity cost

structures differ between countries, every country will have a product for which its opportunity cost is lower than that of other countries. This is the product it can produce relatively most efficiently, in which it should specialise.

Figure O1.7 Comparative advantage

The theory of comparative advantage is one of the oldest economic ideas around. It was developed by David Ricardo (1772–1823). He was working on the Stock Exchange by the age of 14 and had little formal education. He was extremely successful on the money markets, and made a sufficient fortune to retire at 42. He was an MP and active in debates on the economy. Once retired, he began to write about his ideas on economics. Comparative advantage was his most far-reaching idea. He used the example of Britain and Portugal, producing cloth and wine. Figure O1.8 shows how the theory works.

Country	Output of good		Opportunity cost ratio	
	Wine	**Cloth**	**Wine**	**Cloth**
Britain	60	40	$\frac{2}{3}$	$1\frac{1}{2}$
Portugal	90	45	$\frac{1}{2}$	2

Figure O1.8 The theory of comparative advantage

The output shown refers to the amount obtainable from one unit of resources in each country. It is clear that Portugal is better at producing both wine and cloth. Nevertheless, Britain has a comparative advantage in the production of cloth, because there the opportunity cost of cloth is one and a half units of wine, as against Portugal's opportunity cost of two units of wine. Portugal has a comparative disadvantage in cloth. If Portugal specialises in wine and Britain in cloth, it will be possible for both countries to be better off.

How much better off?

In Figure O1.9 it is assumed that before trade, both countries split their resources evenly between production of the two products, and that after trade both countries use all their resources (ten units for Britain and eight units for Portugal) for the product with the lower opportunity cost. So long as the two countries have different opportunity cost structures, they will produce more if they specialise and trade.

Country	Output of good			
	Before specialisation		After specialisation	
	Wine	Cloth	Wine	Cloth
Britain (10 units)	300	200	0	400
Portugal (8 units)	360	180	720	0
Total output	660	380	720	400

Figure O1.9 The outcome of specialisation

Ricardo's model is very simple. It assumes that transport costs are not significant and that resources are mobile and can be reallocated. Nevertheless, its prediction of an increase in output resulting from specialisation has been born out by experience. Ricardo's thinking has had a profound influence.

Work in progress

Q 1 What are the implications of the theory of comparative advantage?

2 Does France still enjoy a comparative advantage in fine wines?

Resources

Countries have different resource endowments. Some are rich in natural resources, as is the USA. Others have very few natural resources, but a well-educated, skilful labour force, for example Japan. Some have accumulated large stocks of highly productive capital. This applies to some degree to all the developed countries. Some countries have an advantage because they have knowledge of technologies which other countries do not have. The UK falls into this category, although it has not always developed its know-how into manufacturing capacity.

Different products require different kinds of resources in different proportions. Which resources are most crucial to efficient aircraft production? The most important items are design skills, engineering skills, management skills and capital. The countries with the lowest opportunity costs in aircraft production will be those which possess these resources in abundance. Similarly, countries with a concentration of skilled computer programmers will produce software most efficiently.

Often a crucial factor is cheap labour: this is true for all kinds of clothing. Countries with low labour costs can produce many manufactured goods with a low opportunity cost. However, cheap labour is not the only factor. Other inputs may have a very high opportunity cost. It pays countries to export those products which they can produce with the lowest opportunity cost overall. This makes it possible for the UK to continue having an advantage in high-quality knitwear.

When countries specialise, using their resources in their lowest cost uses, they maximise their overall output. Because all resources are used in specialised ways, they are able to produce more goods and services than they can if there is no trade. This overall increase in the quantity of goods and services produced helps the economy to grow. Both importers and exporters gain.

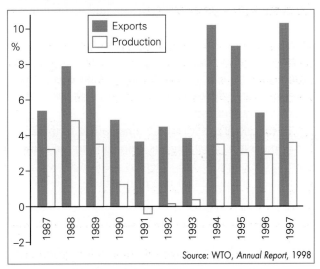

Figure O1.10 Trade and growth, worldwide, 1987–97

Figure O1.10 shows how trade and growth have moved together. Growth implies more trade: people have more money to spend on imports, everywhere. Trade brings growth: the increase in specialisation allows a country to get more output from the same resources, because it is producing more efficiently. The link between trade and growth is well established overall, although it is always possible to show that there are individual instances in which trade has created problems.

Work in progress

Q 1 Which countries have a comparative advantage in tourism? Why?

2 How does trade benefit consumers?

Competitive advantage

The theory of comparative advantage is very good at explaining why countries trade in order to obtain goods which they cannot produce efficiently themselves. It shows clearly why some countries specialise in producing bananas and some in scientific instruments. But can it explain the way countries trade office equipment with each other? A large part of the growth of trade which has taken place over the past 40 years has come from developed countries swapping manufactured goods with each other.

For manufactured goods, design and technology have become more and more important factors in competitiveness. Often we find that it is not a particular nation which has an advantage, but a particular firm. It is the firm which develops effective management techniques, not the nation, although the education system can help.

In this situation, it is more appropriate to think of the comparative advantage as belonging to the firm than to the country. Then there is a competitive advantage, meaning that one firm is better able to compete than another.

Exploiting a competitive advantage: the EU

The idea behind the EU is to promote free trade within the Community. That way, member countries can buy from the most efficient supplier within the area. Consumers have access to the goods which are produced most cheaply, and their real incomes can increase more.

Since the UK joined the EU, trade with member countries has grown enormously:

- Before membership in 1973, about 30 per cent of UK trade was with EU countries.

- By 1990 this had grown to 53 per cent of trade.

Many more UK businesses have got involved in both importing and exporting. This change represents a real shift in the UK trade pattern. Traditionally, the USA was the UK's most important trade partner, and trade generally was biased towards the former colonies. This is no longer the case.

On a very simple level this has increased consumer choice. It has intensified competition and brought some prices down, relatively, thus raising real incomes. It has also enabled some firms to exploit greater potential economies of scale because they have a larger market.

Work in progress

Q 1 How can the EU help member countries to exploit their own comparative advantages?

2 Why might exploiting a comparative advantage raise real incomes?

3 How is comparative advantage shifting in tourism? Why?

4 Give examples of other shifts in comparative advantage.

2 Shifts in comparative advantage

San Miguel Glassworks

San Miguel is a traditional glassworks situated in the heart of Barcelona in Spain. The company hand-produces high-quality lead-crystal glasses, ornaments, carafes and trinkets. In the early 1970s a fierce recession hit Spain and the glassworks faced closure due to depressed demand for its luxury items. The workforce responded by joining together to buy out the existing owners. In the short run profits were low and so were wages, but the employees were guaranteed a job in the long run.

During the 1970s and 1980s the workers employed a succession of managing directors to run the company, but there were many structural problems that could not be overcome. The workers, while motivated to work in the best interest of the company, were no longer able to compete. New technology had swept the industry. San Miguel's competitors were using machines that could mass-produce glass at high speed and low cost with a reduced demand for labour. A possible strategy could have been to focus and re-target their market to a more exclusive audience.

Meantime, the San Miguel Company faced lower profits, for the following reasons:

- It was using specialised batch production techniques. These were efficient in terms of productivity, but once the mould was installed it was too expensive to change it again that day. It took over 20 hours for the glass to cool in one of two coolers.

- The skilled workforce used very little machinery: batches were produced by labour-intensive methods and to order. In spite of this the brand was not perceived as high quality in comparison to Wedgwood or Waterford.

- Although San Miguel operated on low margins, competitors in Czechoslovakia, Poland and Russia seemed to be capturing the market.

- San Miguel was a price-taker with no obvious way to increase value added.

- Costs had already been pared away: all waste glass was recycled.

The company retained a well known Argentine sculptor to design its top of the range sculptures. It realised that it could cut costs by 50 per cent if it installed machines and mass-produced.

Your agenda

1 What had happened to San Miguel's advantage in the market place? Why?

2 Think of three possible strategies with which the company might respond. Which is likely to be the most promising? Why?

Sometimes, a comparative advantage can last a long time. Take France, with its advantage in wine production, well established in Roman times. In other cases, the comparative advantage moves on, to another country, when circumstances have changed. During the 1890s the great majority of the world's ocean-going merchant ships were built in the UK. Over the years that comparative advantage was gradually lost, recently to countries such as Poland and Korea.

When comparative advantage shifts, for whatever reason, the pattern of trade alters, and structural change follows.

- When trade increases, people feel the benefit as consumers. There is an increase in the availability of relatively cheap imports and in the choice available. Also, for some, the increase in demand and in productivity may make higher wages possible. If demand for exports is growing, jobs will be created in exporting industries.

- Some people will feel only the costs of the structural changes. First and foremost are the people who lose their jobs. Shareholders in adversely affected firms will also feel the draught as profits fall. (These problems are looked at in more detail later in this enquiry.)

The workforce at the glassworks in the case study might or might not survive the intensified competition. What is certain is that change is essential. This could mean closing down, but it could also mean rethinking the strategy so that an advantage can be regained in a new way.

Some problems with comparative advantage

The theory of comparative advantage rests on a number of assumptions. One is that there are two countries and two commodities traded. This is, of course, an oversimplification. Nevertheless, the theory helps us to see why trade can improve standards of living.

There are other problems with comparative advantage as an idea. In analysing real world events we need to keep these problems in mind as they apply to specific markets:

■   The theory assumes that resources are mobile. Specialising means that some industries decline while others grow. In practice, people are often not very mobile.

■   The theory tells us nothing at all about who will actually receive the gains from trade. They could all go to the people who make profits. This is unlikely because the increase in competition should mean lower prices and consumers should get some benefit. However, it must be remembered that some groups of people gain much more than others.

■   The theory of comparative advantage assumes that the prices at which things are sold reflect their true costs of production. This is not always true. The full social cost of an export will be higher if there are negative externalities involved. For example, there is a good deal of international trade in tropical hardwoods. Deforestation has a number of environmental costs which cannot at the present time be calculated in money terms. These are not included in the price: they are negative externalities. The trade in timber would not be nearly so profitable if these costs were included.

Work in progress

Q 1 What other examples are there of trade which involves negative externalities?

2 What are the implications of increasing trade when resources are not very mobile?

Adjusting to change

In module 3.1 we considered how resources are reallocated away from the production of things people don't want, and towards things that they do want. When demand for a product falls, its producers become part of a declining industry. Equally, growing demand leads to growing industries. This is structural change.

Much of the time, the job losses in declining industries are balanced by job gains in growing industries. But economies often take time to adjust, and when they do there is structural unemployment. This can be made very much worse by immobilities of labour, be they geographical or occupational, and by inadequate arrangements for retraining.

Trade benefits consumers, who get more choice, cheaper products and higher real incomes. It may benefit producers: if they are able to make use of profitable opportunities to import or export, or if they can go to work for someone else who exploits these opportunities, they will gain, but if they are made redundant through competition from abroad, they may become losers. People who are unable to find another job may lose substantial amounts of real income.

It is impossible to say how many of the unemployed are made so by international trade, because there are so many other reasons for unemployment. The biggest single cause is probably technical change.

Work in progress

Q 1 What types of employment are likely to have been affected by competition from imports?

2 What other important influences on employment in different industries have there been?

Trade and structural change are closely connected. Changing trade patterns cause structural change as demand shifts. But structural change, the growth of some industries and the decline of others, enables competitive industries, producing things which are in strong demand, to expand. Areas which lose comparative advantage decline. Resources then gradually shift into the areas of the economy where competitiveness is growing. However, this can be a rather slow process.

3 Why restrict trade?

Spreadable butter

New Zealand has a comparative advantage in dairy products. Traditionally, its main market was the UK, partly because of its close relationship with the old colonial power, not to mention a lot of kith and kinfolk.

When the UK joined the EU, it also joined the Common Agricultural Policy (CAP). The CAP guarantees prices to farmers inside the EU. Imports are taxed via the Common External Tariff (CET). This means that imports of New Zealand butter pay a hefty import duty.

Then the New Zealanders invented spreadable butter. It was a real breakthrough – butter you could spread straight from the fridge. For a little while they had good sales because no one else in the EU was marketing a comparable product. Then the Danes produced their version. The EU responded by raising the duty on spreadable butter.

The New Zealanders felt they had been discriminated against. They had used their brains to make a really useful product and what happened?

Your agenda

1 What was the impact on the consumer of the invention of spreadable butter?

2 Why would the EU increase the duty on spreadable butter?

3 What effect would this have on the price to the consumer?

4 How would the whole episode have affected farmers in:
  a New Zealand
  b Denmark?

When jobs and incomes are threatened it is very tempting for governments to try to protect them. The obvious way to do this is to control imports. This can be done using **tariffs** or **quotas**. The snag with import controls is that although they do reduce imports, they also annoy the exporter. If that leads to your own exports being controlled, then sales are lost. Many governments and the World Trade Organisation (WTO) have put a lot of effort into encouraging trade, so discouraging it needs a strong argument.

Essentials

Tariffs are taxes placed on specific imported goods. They are also called import duties.

Essentials

Quotas are physical limits on the level of imports in any one year for specific imported goods

Agricultural trade is one area where trade restrictions are common. The CAP is for some products very restrictive indeed. As a consequence, some food prices within the EU are well above world prices. This means that real incomes are reduced by the trade restrictions. The EU is not the only developed area to protect agriculture.

Although the EU has cut its subsidies to agriculture in recent years, countries such as the USA and Australia find EU protection hard to take. They feel they could export a lot more to Europe if restrictions were lifted.

There are alternatives to restricting trade.

■ Farmers can be paid to undertake environmental work on their farms. This raises their incomes without affecting food prices.

■ With forest products it may be possible to provide incentives to countries which manage their forests sustainably. Their timber products could command higher prices or arrangements could be made for them to receive extra foreign aid money, if an international organisation certified those forests which were well run. But this will take time to organise. Meantime, deforestation is increasing.

How tariffs work

When tariffs are levied in order to curb imports, the intention will be to protect a domestic producer of a substitute. The substitute may or may not be a good one. But if it is, as with Danish spreadable butter, then demand will be elastic, prices will rise, imports will fall substantially and the domestic producer will sell more at a slightly higher price. Figure O1.11 shows what happens.

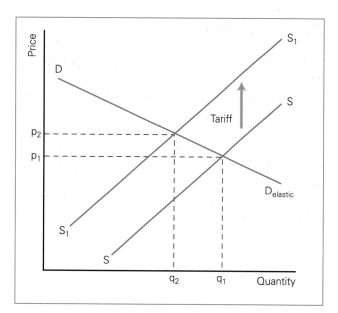

Figure O1.11 Tariffs with elastic demand

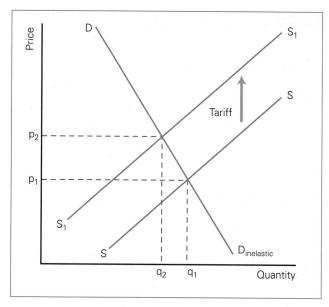

Figure O1.12 Tariffs with inelastic demand

Arguments in favour of tariffs include the protection of domestic producers, of jobs, and sometimes of **infant industries**. These occur when production is just getting started, and as yet, firms have not had time to develop economies of scale or to become expert in what they are doing.

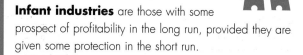

Essentials

Infant industries are those with some prospect of profitability in the long run, provided they are given some protection in the short run.

But supposing the domestic product is not a very good substitute. It may be unreliable, poorly designed and much dearer than the import. Then what does the tariff do? The demand for the import is inelastic, and people continue to buy it anyway, because it is so much better. Only now they have to pay a higher price than they did before the tariff. This is all right for the government. The more inelastic the demand for the imported product, the higher the government revenue from the tax. Figure O1.12 shows what happens.

Tariffs can reduce real incomes by making people pay more for the items they want. This means that their spending on other things will be reduced.

So tariffs on cars or video recorders may make domestic manufacturers happy, but if people then have less money to spend on restaurant meals, restaurant owners and employees will be unhappy.

This is the snag with tariffs, generally. They cause a welfare loss (i.e. a loss of real income) to the consumer. People lose real income because the higher prices lead to their losing purchasing power.

Work in progress

Q 1 Think about Nike trainers. How elastic is the demand for these? Would you be able to find a suitable UK-produced substitute for the Nike version? If not, what implications does this have for your elasticity estimate? Draw a diagram, making sure your demand curve reflects your elasticity estimate. What happens to the equilibrium price if a tariff is imposed?

2 Under what circumstances will a tariff be successful in curbing imports?

3 Identify two imported products with elastic demand, and two with inelastic demand. Show what the effect of a tariff would be on each. Draw a diagram and explain your conclusions.

Dumping: is it unfair competition?

Dumped grey cotton

Grey cotton is the basic textile material from which clothes and other textiles products are made. For some time, some EU countries including France wanted to block imports of cloth from the Far East on the grounds that they were being sold at less than cost price.

In the past, EU anti-dumping measures have been used to block imports of microchips, office equipment, televisions, footwear and minerals. Now, however, most of the northern EU members feel that this excuse has been used for long enough. Some governments have been lobbied by big retailers such as Carrefour in France and Marks & Spencer in the UK. These companies see anti-dumping rules as the cause of high costs for the EU clothing manufacturers and retailers.

Your agenda

1 Why would Marks & Spencer be against import controls on fabrics and clothing?

2 What happens to real incomes when clothing prices rise?

If producers sell their exports at a price lower than that at which they sell in their home markets, then we say that they are **dumping**. A firm which is competing with a foreign supplier who dumps will probably feel very aggrieved about it. On the other hand, consumers of dumped products will probably be very pleased with the prices they are paying.

Essentials

Dumping means exporting at a price which is less than the cost of production.

The problem with dumping is that it may be quite difficult to prove that it has happened. Information about producers' costs is not usually available. Sometimes the Japanese are accused of dumping, when they sell some manufactured items at lower prices in Europe than in Japan. The EU levies anti-dumping duties on Japanese and Korean video recorders and on Japanese photocopiers and printers, but many people think that these imports are a good way to keep prices down and that the EU exaggerates in its dumping accusations.

How quotas work

Because quotas set a physical limit beyond which supply can expand no further, above the level of the quota, the supply of imports will be perfectly inelastic: they cannot expand at all.

If demand is at a low level, less than that of the quota at the prevailing price, then obviously the quota has no effect, but if demand is high, as in Figure O1.13, the price will be pushed above its free-market equilibrium. Here again there will be a welfare loss, with consumers paying a higher price for a smaller quantity than they would ideally choose to buy. Figure O1.13 shows the outcome.

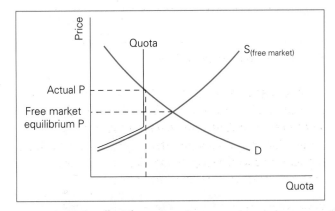

Figure O1.13 The effect of quotas

Work in progress

Q 1 If a quota on imported video recorders limits imports, what will happen to the price ?

2 Who will benefit from the quota?

Quotas are just one type of non-tariff barrier (NTB). There are other possibilities for countries looking to make exporting more difficult for their competitors. An important one is the qualitative control. Some of these are genuine: no one wants unsafe toys or electrical appliances to be imported. Others are more questionable.

Some countries create a lot of red tape around any importing, simply to make delays more likely. Some governments award contracts for the provision of goods or services only to firms in their own country. Sometimes trade is restricted by the use of subsidies on exports. (This may result in dumping.) All of these measures can become the subject of a complaint to the WTO.

Surviving the competition

Given time, many industries have shown that they can adjust to competition from abroad. New management strategies, more efficient production and attention to quality and the product portfolio can all keep them going. In other cases, large numbers of businesses shut down.

Protecting domestic industries usually makes them less efficient in the long run. The countries with a competitive advantage in particular products often have it because those industries were highly competitive. (remember Porter's view, page 398?) This is why, on the whole, most governments have tried to negotiate the reduction of trade restrictions. It also explains why countries want to join the WTO. Still, businesses often try to pressure their governments into giving them special treatment.

4 Must inequality increase?

Who gets what?

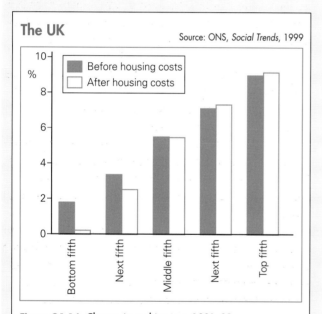

The UK

Source: ONS, *Social Trends*, 1999

Figure O1.14 Change in real income, 1981–93

Between 1971 and 1996, average incomes rose by 55 per cent in real terms. Focusing on the 1980s, the top 10 per cent of incomes improved by 47 per cent. The bottom 10 per cent grew by 6 per cent. Some of this disparity reflected the serious loss of income occurring when people were made redundant. There has been some improvement during the 1990s. This probably owes something to the generally lower level of unemployment.

Figure O1.14 charts a part of the increase in inequality.

China

	1988	**1995**
Top 3%	5567	8533
Bottom 20%	724	721

Source: *Increasing Income Equality and its Causes in China*, Zhao Renwei, Chinese Academy of Social Sciences, 1998

Figure O1.15 Mean wages, yuan (1988 prices)

China had a lot of inflation and the data in Figure O1.15 do not mean much in terms of today's exchange rates. They do show which people benefited most from China's growth.

Your agenda

What conclusions can you draw from the above data concerning:
a income growth
b inequality?

Whichever data one looks at, it is clear that in most countries, there has been an increase in inequality. While on average incomes rose quite substantially, the bulk of the increase went to those on average incomes and above. In particular, there was a big increase in the incomes of the very rich.

This trend reflected the opportunities created by **market liberalisation**. Removing government controls gave opportunities to people who were prepared to take risks. If they used their chances skilfully, they made a great deal of money. Some of the people who made a lot of money also created a lot of jobs.

> ### Essentials
>
> **Market liberalisation** means the progressive freeing of markets from government regulation.

When markets give people an incentive to invest and make money there is often a trade-off between efficiency and equity. If those markets are competitive, the chances are that businesses will have to be efficient to survive. If they are not competitive, then they may make money even though they are not efficient.

In the developed countries, most people have benefited from the growth in incomes. However, there are groups of people everywhere who have been left on the margins of society, excluded from the benefits. Perhaps about 10 per cent of the population of the developed world has experienced this. They rarely or never have steady jobs, their housing may be poor, they may not speak the language of their country of residence well or at all. They are the people who have borne the brunt of the structural change because they lack the skills and life chances which would make them occupationally mobile. They cannot adjust therefore to the new pattern of economic development.

In developing countries, the majority of people on low incomes have become better off. There is really no question that trade and development have brought benefits to most. It is just that some have benefited more than others.

While economies have been adjusting to the impact of increasing trade and specialisation, they have also been adapting to new technologies. So it is impossible to say that increasing inequality is a direct consequence of trade. Increasing productivity has been accompanied by a fall in demand for unskilled labour. We have to look at the big picture, the whole story of structural change. The fact remains that not everyone has done well in the growth process.

Income distribution between countries

As countries move along the continuum of growth, they progress through various stages of development. The largely agricultural society where the majority of the population lives in rural communities gives way to an increasingly urban structure in which manufacturing industry grows to be dominant. The stage beyond this is identified by an increasing number of people working in service industries, while the manufacturing sector shrinks relatively. Throughout the process, there is generally a steady decline in the number of people involved in agriculture although output and productivity continue to increase.

In all developing countries, except those which are struggling with a serious Aids problem, life expectancy has increased. In the countries which are growing well, life expectancy is approaching developed country levels.

Overall though, the developing world has split into two groups. There are a number of countries with high growth rates which seem likely to be able to catch up with the developed countries eventually. Singapore provides the strongest example. Many others are following. Some, like China, started from a low base and are growing well but will take a long time to achieve acceptable standards for all their people. Something may yet go wrong, too.

The other group is not in such good shape. Most of Africa, Pakistan, Bangladesh and Cambodia are all still very much in the grip of serious poverty. To a large extent, they have been left out of the development process. High birth rates are keeping per capita incomes low in many countries. The birth rate will not fall until incomes start to rise. There is a vicious circle which is not yet broken. It is often made worse by wars and natural catastrophes. Birth rates are subject to many influences, but in general, they have fallen in the countries which are developing well.

Food insecurity

During the 1970s and 1980s many people thought that food was becoming less of a problem. It is true that in some countries, it is. In others, degradation of the land, population growth and climate change between them have reduced hopes of food security. Figure O1.16 shows both progress and expectations.

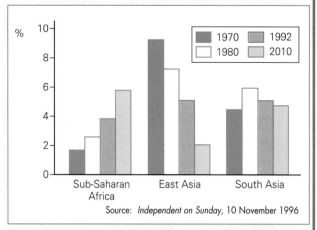

Source: *Independent on Sunday*, 10 November 1996

Figure O1.16 Number of chronically undernourished people

Your agenda

1 Why is there a marked disparity between the food security situations in sub-Saharan Africa and east Asia?

2 What measures might help to reduce the problem in Africa?

The low level of education and health in the least developed countries makes rapid development an unlikely prospect. Low levels of investment in human capital result in low levels of labour productivity. Employees may be cheap but if they do not have the necessary level of education or physical health to cope with the work or training, there is little incentive to induce a company to move in. The provision of roads, railways and other forms of infrastructure are equally undeveloped and therefore it would be difficult to attract industry. The political instability of some of these countries has also contributed to their lack of appeal.

All these factors would, of course, add to costs for any firm which considers investment in these extremely poor countries. Equally, local entrepreneurs are hardly in a position to take risks. The end result of these trends is a situation of very real inequality between nations.

Inequality within developing countries

Job losses in Chengdu

During the late 1990s, many Chinese lost their jobs. The problem was that the old state-owned enterprises (SOEs) were clearly not able to compete with the newer, market-driven sector. The Chinese government wanted to reform the loss-making SOEs because of the cost to the public purse of keeping them going.

During the first eight months of 1997 a total of 16 state companies went bankrupt, declaring 16 000 redundancies. A New York-based human rights group reported that 300 workers from the Number Two Radio Factory in Zigong gathered to demand payment of wages for the past year and health expenses for two years. Local government officials denied all knowledge of the incident. The Chinese government has been concerned to keep unemployment below 4 per cent. The Labour minister said, 'Although deepening economic reform will cause certain pressure on employment, it will by no means touch off social unrest.'

Your agenda

1 Developing countries have little provision for unemployment benefit. What effect would these trends have on income distribution?

2 How will market forces affect Chinese consumers?

3 What long-run solutions can you see in this situation?

In many developing countries, some people have left the land in search of work in the cities. Initially, they may appear to be better off because they have higher money incomes. However, their living costs are higher too and the benefits may be quite limited. They do have more choice and may be able to get a better education. If they lose their jobs though, they will face big difficulties.

Figure O1.17 shows how income distribution varies within selected countries. The figures for the industrial countries together give a basis for comparison. Many developing countries are not able to redistribute income effectively through taxation. However, industrial countries can easily do this if they have the political will.

	Poorest 20% 1980–94	Richest 20% 1980–94
China	722	5114
Colombia	1042	16 154
India	527	2641
Indonesia	1422	6654
Kenya	238	4347
Mexico	1437	19 383
Senegal	299	5010
Sri Lanka	1348	5954
Singapore	4934	47 311
South Africa	516	9897
Industrial countries	4811	32273

Source: UN, *Human Development Report*, 1998 Oxford University Press

Figure O1.17 Income distribution (US$)

It seems clear that countries are unlikely to follow a well-defined pattern as to the way in which income distribution changes during the course of their development. Much depends on the political situation, but even then the situation is not clear. You might expect China to have a reasonable degree of equality.

Within developing countries big differences have developed between rural and urban populations. Figure O1.18 shows how rural areas in a range of developing countries compare with urban areas in the same country. Clearly basic needs are not well catered for in the countryside.

The poverty of many of the least developed countries has not stopped some of their residents from becoming extremely wealthy. Sadly, some of these have chosen to invest their wealth in developed countries. In some countries, corruption makes inequalities worse and hinders the implementation of development policies.

Many countries are not really addressing the possibilities of income redistribution. There are some interesting projects. In Brazil banks supported by the World Bank are lending to landless labourers so that they can buy land and farm. The policy has so far been highly successful. But such developments are still rather rare.

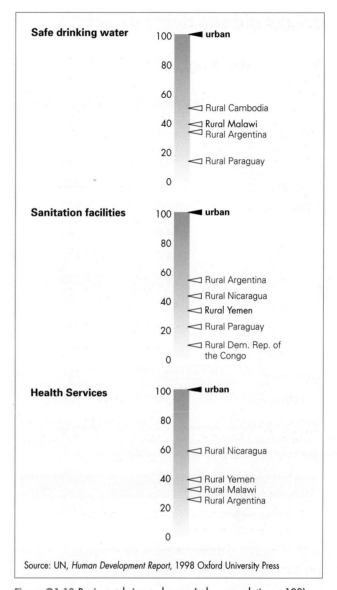

Source: UN, *Human Development Report*, 1998 Oxford University Press

Figure O1.18 Basic needs in rural areas (urban population = 100)

Sometimes poverty is a reflection of the quality of life rather than simply a matter of low income. The Human Development Index (HDI) is a U.N. measure of development which takes into account many factors besides per capita income, such as education, literacy and life expectancy. (The HDI is on the Nuffield database.) Inequality within developing countries can mean lower standards of living for the less fortunate.

5 How did the debts grow?

Where's the trouble?

	US$ (billion)	As % of GDP
Angola	11.5	275
Bangladesh	16.4	56
Congo	6.0	366
Cote d'Ivoire	19.0	252
Ecuador	14.0	84
Jamaica	4.3	135
Mauritania	2.5	243
Mexico	165.7	70
Mozambique	5.8	444
Nicaragua	9.3	590
Nigeria	35.0	141
Zambia	6.9	191

Source: UN, *Human Development Report*, 1998 Oxford University Press

Figure O1.19 Total external debt, selected countries, 1995

Your agenda

1 What do the countries in Figure O1.19 have in common?

2 Why is it difficult for seriously indebted countries to repay their debts?

In order to develop, many countries borrowed from overseas sources. The level of savings within the country was inadequate to supply the funds needed to allow industrialisation to take place. In low-income economies, consumers spend a high proportion, if not all, of their earnings to maintain a moderate standard of living. Only a small sector of the population receives an income which is large enough to allow them to save.

In a developed economy, savings would be transmitted, via the banking system to individuals who sought to invest. Developing countries with low savings therefore found the generation of sufficient funds for investment impossible. There were other problems:

- In areas where money was available, the embryonic banking system was not adequate to channel the surplus to those who could use it for development. This is a common problem as countries industrialise. In the UK, the emergence of the banking system had allowed agricultural surpluses to be used to fund the industrial revolution of the late 18th century.

- Development required the purchase of capital goods and expertise from overseas. Foreign exchange was needed to pay for these imports, but most countries found their supplies inadequate. Many primary producers experienced a fall in the value of their exports which compounded the problem. Borrowing became the only solution.

- Borrowing was initially in the form of aid, with concessional rates of interest, for imports of capital goods and development projects. This was beneficial and repayments were under control. Then in the mid- to late-1970s and into the 1980s many governments borrowed at commercial rates from banks in the developed world. Initially, interest rates were low. But when the developed country governments raised interest rates as part of their counter-inflation policy, the interest payments and repayments together created a burden which many borrowers proved unable to meet.

- To repay such debts, a country needs a strong currency, low interest rates and a good price for its exports. Commodity prices have been low at times and always fluctuate. Many loans have been made at commercial rather than concessional interest rates. The major debtors had little chance of even paying the interest on their debts.

- The nature of the investment which developing countries carried out on the strength of their borrowing did not help the situation. A commercial organisation which borrows money always ensures that the return on the investment will cover the interest that has to be paid and provide some profit. The debtor countries were generally using the funds to invest in projects to improve the infrastructure. Building a dam will provide water and electricity for the population and industry but may not provide the return that is needed to pay off the debt. In the longer term, the improved facilities may encourage new industry to set up, but this time scale was too long for the lenders.

On the whole, the emerging economies were exporting successfully and could pay their debts. Mexico is a case in point. There were some crises during the 1980s and 1990s but the problems eventually subsided.

The debt problem

In Africa and some of the least developed countries elsewhere, it was different. The annual flow of interest and repayments began to outweigh the annual inflow of aid. Exports grew slowly or declined. This situation was partly responsible for the negative growth rates suffered in some African countries during the 1990s.

The traditional way of coping with this problem is to reschedule the debt. This is done by delaying repayments or adding the unpaid interest to the capital sum. Both strategies make the problem worse in the long run as the debt grows and increases the proportion of future GDP which has to be spent on meeting the repayments.

A fresh solution

At the time of writing serious efforts are being made to end this situation. The 1999 UN *Human Development Report* pointed up the facts very starkly. Figure O1.20 makes it clear.

- In 1997 the richest fifth of the world's population, those living in developed countries, produced 86 per cent of the world's income. The bottom fifth produced 1 per cent.

- In 1820 the ratio in living standards between the richest and the poorest countries was 3:1. By 1913 it was 11:1, by 1950 it was 35:1. It is now 72:1.

- Meantime, many countries have begun to grow faster than the developed world. China and India, with two-fifths of the world's population between them, are in this category. There is hope.

In more than 80 countries income per head was lower at the end of the 1990s than it was at the beginning. Aids and malaria reduce their capacity to find solutions. Approximately 1.3 billion people have less than a dollar a day to live on. Yet a solution is within reach, if we have the political will. The amounts needed to cancel the debt for the poorest countries are not huge.

In 1999 the donor countries agreed that the International Monetary Fund (IMF) should sell 10 million ounces of gold to fund a programme through which the poorest countries can apply for debt relief. The funds so raised will be about US$2 billion. The countries will have to meet IMF conditions. This may not be easy, or even in their best interests.

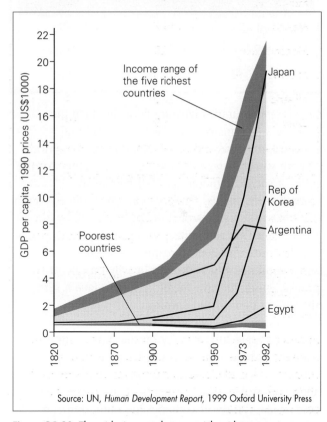

Source: UN, *Human Development Report*, 1999 Oxford University Press

Figure O1.20 The widening gap between rich and poor

Work in progress

Q1 This story is not over. Has debt ceased to be a problem since 2000?

2 Why was it important to find a solution?

6 The commodity rollercoaster

Selling cocoa

Sacks of cocoa are sitting in the warehouse in the Cote d'Ivoire, but no one wants to buy them. The next crop of beans is nearly ready for picking, but no one knows whether it is worth bothering. The buyers received so little money for last year's crop that they have insufficient cash to pay for this year's. The farmers cannot afford to buy meat or new tools. The children are without school books. If things do not improve, the villagers will have no choice but to head for the towns.

Your agenda

1 What effect will the fall in cocoa prices have on the local economy?

2 How will the national economy be affected?

Developing countries have traditionally been the producers of primary products (i.e. agricultural products, minerals and fuels). Apart from the periods of both world wars, there has been a tendency for the price of such commodities to fall relative to manufactured goods. This took on a new dimension in the 1980s when prices of some products fell by almost 50 per cent. Tea and coffee, for example, fell to prices which were equivalent in real terms to pre-war levels. Some countries which depend heavily on one or two primary products have therefore had to face a serious shortfall in their export earnings.

All through the twentieth century, commodity prices fluctuated erratically. Primary products have always tended to suffer price variations because they are so subject to changes in supply caused by the weather and other factors which are difficult to control. In the case of glut, producer countries are often desperate to sell their output as they need foreign currency: they cannot wait until a better price can be obtained.

Economic and political factors can also affect prices. Recessions in the industrialised world have led to falls in demand for raw materials. The changes in eastern Europe and Russia during the early 1990s caused increased demand for some commodities while increasing the supply of others. The prices of grain and meat, for example, were kept high because of the former Soviet

Union's inability to maintain food supplies, but in order to earn foreign currency it sold more bauxite and copper. This had an adverse effect on the prices which Ghana and Zambia could obtain for their exports.

Over the years there has also been a worldwide tendency for supply to increase in general because production has become more efficient and new countries have entered the market despite the trend of falling prices. Figure O1.21 shows how this affects the markets.

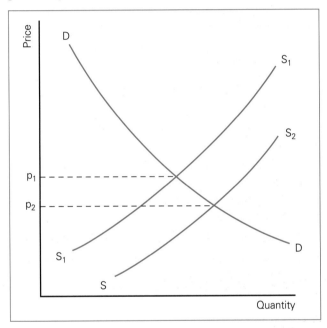

Figure O1.21 The effect of increasing supply

The second unfortunate trend for primary producers has been the fall in demand. This has been caused by the development of substitutes such as glass fibre which replaces copper wire in the telecommunications industry. Manufactured fibres have replaced cotton and linen and plastics have been substituted for rubber and some metals.

As exporters of primary products and importers of manufactured goods, such countries will suffer when the price of primary products falls in relation to the price of manufactures. The relationship between the price of imports and exports is known as the **terms of trade**. The following formula shows how the index of the terms of trade can be calculated. The indices are calculated using weighted averages of a wide range of imports and exports.

$$\text{Index of terms of trade} = \frac{\text{Index of export prices}}{\text{Index of import prices}}$$

The trends described above have badly affected the terms of trade of many developing countries. In Figure O1.22 both the trend and fluctuations can be seen. The Second World War boosted their relative value, but by the late 1980s they had fallen back to pre-war levels. The evidence suggests some decline even when allowance is made for the improvement in quality of manufactured imports.

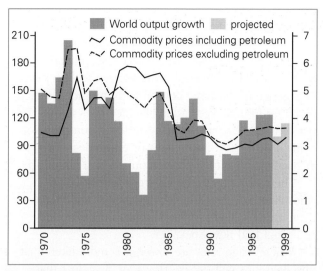

Figure O1.22 World commodity prices (1990 = 100)   Source: IMF

Work in progress

Q 1 What has been the overall trend in commodity prices?

2 What happens to commodity prices during recessions?

3 How are commodity producers affected by price changes?

4 What can you say about the elasticity of supply of:
  a agricultural commodities
  b minerals?

5 What implications does this have for prices?

Essentials

The **terms of trade** express the relationship between export prices and import prices. When export prices fall, terms of trade are deteriorating.

7 Are there solutions?

Ghana

A recent study of the returns to education in Ghana yielded interesting results. It found strong evidence that in the Ghanaian manufacturing sector, the more educated the worker, the more productive he or she is. Workers with secondary education are 46 per cent more productive than workers with no formal schooling. Other findings were as follows:

● A one-year increase in the average level of education within a firm is associated with a 7 per cent rise in worker productivity. This, in turn, means an increase of the same amount in pay.

● Workers who completed higher education were roughly 25 per cent more productive than those who only went as far as secondary school.

● Similar results were obtained when investigating the value of vocational training. On average, workers with vocational training were 72–78 per cent more productive than those with no formal schooling.

● Ghanaian employers paid wages which reflected the effects of education and training on productivity.

● On average, workers in OECD countries gain 7 per cent in earnings for every extra year of schooling.

Source: *Centre Piece*, Volume 4, Issue 2, published by the Centre for Economic Performance (Tel: 0171 955 7673)

Your agenda

1 How are educated workers affected if their employer makes them redundant?

2 How does education affect development opportunities?

3 Evaluate the role of education in the development process.

We have already seen that education and training make people both more flexible and more productive. In developing countries where access to primary education is not universal, adult literacy will be low. This is one of the basic development problems which is still far from solved. Adult illiteracy rates above 50 per cent are common in many African countries. Not being able to read instructions or good ideas for increasing agricultural production is a real handicap.

The real losers in the UK from the structural adjustment which follows the growth of trade have been the unskilled people who lost their jobs and could not find new ones.

Where wage rates are lower, it is more likely that unskilled jobs will persist. However, it is clear that many developing countries do have problems with unemployment and also with underemployment. This last is what happens when people cannot find work enough of the time to give them a decent wage.

Availability of unskilled jobs is not, anyway, such a good thing. As earlier case studies have shown, unskilled work is usually poorly paid wherever it is. All over the world, people need jobs which will help them to avoid poverty. That means acquiring skills, increasing productivity and earning more.

Although there have been aid projects directed at improving access to education, progress is very patchy, especially for women. Improving education is a very long-term project.

Some commentators are beginning to suggest that what many of the least developed countries really need is a more efficient apparatus of government. Poverty on its own does not have to imply that many people get no schooling. India has always managed to score relatively well in this area. It has 100 per cent primary enrolment, despite rather low incomes. This is one reason why it is succeeding in a knowledge-based industry – software. It is possible that measures to foster improved government may have an effect.

Compared to the developing countries, most developed economies have high levels of access to education and training. Nevertheless, further enhancement of skills is vitally important there too. Education and training is the way for developed countries to accommodate increased competition from low-wage economies.

Addressing the long-run problems in developed countries

Getting education and skills

	Secondary enrolment (%)*	Full-time students per 100 people, age 5–29*	Education spending as % of GNP
China	67		2.3
India	49		3.5
Mexico	58		5.3
Nigeria	36		n.a.
Singapore	n.a.		3.0
Zambia	28		1.8
UK		53	5.5
USA		59	5.3
Japan		56	3.8

* Measuring access to education in both developed and developing countries needs different figures. Secondary enrolment in developed countries is usually close to 100 per cent, so we need to use a measure which takes in the wider age group.

Source: UN, *Human Development Report*, 1998

Figure O1.23 Education provision, selected countries, 1995

The New Deal

Anne Mason, a 33-year-old single mother, has for the first time got hope of permanent employment. Under the New Deal, she is working at jewellers H. Samuel. 'Meeting people has meant my self-confidence and self-esteem have built up again. It really diminishes if you're stuck at home and not in contact with people. Now I am enjoying myself and no longer feel alone,' she said.

The greatest practical help she received from her lone-parent adviser was how to balance her books. 'He showed me my outgoings so I could work out how much I had to earn to survive,' said Ms Mason.

Your agenda

1 Employers are often unwilling to take on people who have been unemployed for a long time. Why is this?

2 What are the consequences of this for the economy?

3 What kinds of help do people who have been out of work for a long time need?

When structural change began to create large numbers of redundancies, unemployment was for a time very high indeed in the UK. The result was that many people joined the ranks of the long-term unemployed. They eventually became discouraged workers – people whose work expectations had been so diminished that they had lost their skills and their commitment.

The New Deal is a way of breaking a cycle of long-term unemployment. It addresses the need for improving skills before work can be found. It offers opportunities to go back to education. It is too soon to say whether it will succeed where other schemes have failed. It does look quite promising, however.

Flexibility

Businesses which have deliberately organised themselves in ways which foster adaptation to change do have a competitive advantage. Flexibility of this kind comes in a number of forms:

- *Functional flexibility* allows employers to transfer employees from one task to another within the production process. Multi-skilling makes it possible for each employee to do a range of different things according to need. (It also reduces the boredom associated with constant repetition, but that is not our concern here.) This kind of flexibility is particularly useful when it comes to problem-solving and teamwork. Quality control can improve when teams are made responsible for it and for solving related problems. Herein lie many possibilities for reducing costs by increasing productivity.

- *Numerical flexibility* allows businesses to adjust the size and the composition of the workforces according to the level of demand for the product. This means that large numbers of employees will be part-time or on short-term contracts.

- *Financial flexibility* means being able to vary wage costs. When extra effort is required, employees can be motivated by bonuses and productivity payments. This means that pay is more often locally negotiated than nationally. It involves widening differentials between skilled and unskilled employees and between similar occupations in different regions.

Flexible labour forces are not always the very best thing for employees. They may lose some of the benefits of protection under the law and they may have poorer working conditions. However, the EU countries which have more flexible labour markets, the UK and the Netherlands, also have somewhat lower unemployment rates than neighbouring member countries.

Flexibility is partly a matter of culture. Some businesses have a corporate culture which assumes openness to change. This can be invigorating to the workforce if it is combined with a commitment to develop employee capabilities. If staff are valued and motivated, it may be possible to pay them well rather than cut wage rates. Much depends on the type of production involved.

Conclusions

Globalisation has brought many helpful trends and also much unwelcome change. The impact on standards of living is not really in question but the extent of the changes means that there is much to be done to alleviate the more harmful effects. Awareness is important.

The World Bank, in one of its *World Development Reports*, gave general policy advice that if markets are working smoothly, they should be allowed to continue, but if imperfections appear, corrective action should be taken:

- Competition should be protected through anti-monopoly legislation which should be policed efficiently because it is never villain-proof.

- Consumers should be protected by legislation to control product safety for the pharmaceuticals, food and motor industries, for example.

- Workers should be protected by trade unions and government legislation.

- Specific groups, such as women and ethnic minorities, should be protected and enabled to take their rightful role in the market.

- The environment should be protected to prevent its degradation at the expense of industrial production.

As more and more people are drawn into the global economy, their need for some protection is clear. Some would say that the forces of globalisation are largely evil, but without them, many promising developments would be lost.

This enquiry focuses on the effects of trade and growth on the environment. It discusses the meaning of sustainable development and what can be considered desirable and necessary for future generations to survive and prosper. Progress towards sustainability is discussed both in the developed and less-developed world. Alternative methods of providing energy and transport are examined and the role of technology in putting things right is explored. The trade-off between environment and economics is addressed at the end of the enquiry.

1 Trade and growth equals degradation?

Taiwan is paying for growth

Taiwan is approximately twice the size of Wales, but accommodates 20 million people, mostly squeezed into a fairly small lowland area. The capital city of Taipei has been described as unfit for human habitation because blocks of flats are only feet apart and there are no green areas for children to play or adults to relax. The streets are constantly gridlocked and whole family groups balance on one moped to avoid the jams.

The economic growth rate of Taiwan was in double figures for about 20 years and in 1995 was still at 6 per cent, making it the fourteenth largest trading nation in the world. This relatively small island has become the victim of its own success.

Taipei, the capital, has a major transport problem because the only public transport alternative to the car in 1995 was the bus, which got stuck in the jams with the cars and was not therefore a serious contender for the commuters' custom. Mountains surround the city and it is not unusual to see children wearing masks to protect them from the pollution caused by the constant traffic. Dr Y. F. Liang of the government's Environmental Protection Administration stated that 'Taipei's air quality is perhaps the worst in the world'. There were 5 million cars on the island in 1995 and this number was increasing at a rate of 10 per cent per year.

The Taiwanese are well aware that their wealth and success is actually literally choking them. They see the problems stemming from lack of long-term planning. Taipei was designed for 300 000 people and accommodates in excess of 3 million. Paddy fields and coastline have been spoiled by development in the north of the island to provide shops, factories and flats. The mountainous interior of the island is also suffering from Taiwan's success. The area is used for cement-making, quarrying, house-building and golf courses, and the forest areas are being destroyed in the process. The rains trigger landslides, soil erosion and floods.

Industries in Taiwan do not always abide by environmental regulations and threaten to relocate to China if officials try to force them. Land-use regulations are also changed regularly so that industry can encroach on to the National Parks. Of the 100 golf courses around the island, 48 of them illegally use land belonging to the National Park. Most of these courses are far too expensive for local people to join and were built at great expense to the environment as they require land to be levelled, forests to be felled and a cocktail of chemicals to be put in the soil. According to the 'Homemaker's Union and Foundation', a fledgling environmental group, the golf courses were built by developers in return for favours from politicians and government officials when they applied for land-use changes.

The people of Taiwan are now realising that environmental education and awareness are vital to halt the growth of pollution. The idea of a pressure group to fight for the environment is relatively new to Taiwan: 1987 saw the first group start, but people are still wary of joining in any action.

Source: *The Guardian – Society Supplement* 11.1.95

Your agenda

1 What are the main environmental concerns highlighted in the case study?

2 What measures could be used to sort out the pollution of the city of Taipei?

3 Environment versus economy: has Taiwan got its priorities right?

4 How can the Environmental Protection Administration convince the people of Taiwan that they have a problem that must be addressed?

Taiwan has been described as one of the 'Asian Tigers' because of its rapid growth, fuelled by increased trade with other countries. However, the economic growth has led to environmental problems that actually threaten to asphyxiate the population. It can take up to 12 hours to travel by car from the capital to the north of the island, a distance of about 200 miles. Congestion increases emissions from vehicles, but more roads would further damage the environment of this island.

Is environmental degradation quantifiable?

The reduction of emissions into the atmosphere is an important part of any plan for sustainable development because of the threat of global warming and the problems, which will come with it. Damage to our environment is not easy to measure because it cannot always be valued in money terms. Global warming and the depletion of the ozone layer will cause quantifiable physical effects on our way of life, for example the failure of a particular crop can be given a monetary value because there is a market for that crop. When losses can be quantified, producers can in theory be compensated for their losses.

The destruction of a forest to build a road to ease congestion raises a different question. The benefits to business can be measured because goods will arrive at their destination more quickly, and so reduce a firm's private costs, but how do we put a value on the natural habitats lost when the bulldozer cuts through the forest? There is no real measure of value for the loss of nice scenery, an animal's habitat or a country walk! There is no way that we can translate these things into 'costs' using market prices. These are external costs which society, as a whole, will pay for.

In order for the firm to realise the total cost of the product it must add the social costs of production to the private costs. This will give the true cost of the product to everyone involved. A clearer notion of the product's worth can then be seen. If social costs exist, and a value can be attributed to them, should the firm be made to pay?

Pollution reduces productivity

Health is an issue to be included on the agendas of environmental and economic meetings of the future. The World Health Organisation, headed by environmentalist and Norwegian Prime Minister Gro Harlem Bruntland, is set to ensure that health issues receive high priority in the future.

She argues that sick people are unproductive people and, consequently, pollution does not make economic sense. In 1999 in London, the largest-ever gathering of health, environment and transport ministers attended a conference to negotiate, set targets and sign agreements concerning health issues across Europe. Bruntland aimed to highlight the plight of people in eastern Europe facing unsafe water, damaging air pollution and the recurrence of diseases like cholera. Holiday travel has broadened peoples' horizons and exposed them to new dangers, making issues concerning just one country an outdated notion.

Children's health was on the agenda and pressure to recognise their vulnerability was strong. Young people receive greater exposure per unit of body weight than adults do and it has been argued that their future fertility and growth are at risk from hormones present in our polluted environment.

The conference also debated the issue of paying for pollution with our health whether we are driving or walking. Children living beside busy main roads have a 50 per cent greater chance of suffering chest problems.

The external costs of traffic pollution have been estimated as 4.1 per cent of the GDP of the European Union, and the potential savings from cutting back road use would be increased further by the lowered medical costs when people become healthier by walking and cycling to work, rather than driving.

Other issues on the conference agenda included climate change caused by global warming, the damage to health of heatwaves, floods and skin cancers. The delegates were expected to sign a legally binding agreement to secure safe water for all and reduce the spread of diseases like cholera and typhoid.

Your agenda

1 Why have 'medieval' diseases like cholera and typhoid started to affect us again today?

2 How does increasing pollution affect standards of living?

3 Should we forego some trade in order to reduce pollution?

If the standard of living of future generations is to improve, then health issues, such as those mentioned above, need to be part of the agenda of governments. There are also issues concerning human rights, poverty, inequality, unemployment, crime levels and mental health which, it could be argued, need to be included in plans for the future expansion of trade between nations. Closing down a factory that pollutes our atmosphere will reduce pollution, but at what cost? The improvement to our environment may be far outweighed by the social problems the shut-down will cause.

The previous case study mentions an agreement about water safety across Europe and diseases that have shown themselves after a long period of absence. Business management writer Tom Peters refers to the 'nanosecond nineties' to emphasise the speed at which business managers now have to make decisions, but the consequences of these decisions are far reaching in their impact upon the environment and our future. If companies are made accountable for their external costs, then the clean-up operation will be charged to those causing the pollution. The resulting increases in costs will cause a reduction in profits or an increase in selling price which will be borne by the consumer.

No more food from the sea

The oceans of the world are being overfished to such an extent that certain species may disappear altogether. Many of the traditional fish are not being allowed to recover their numbers sufficiently to assure future catches.

A US study in 1995 suggested that fishermen actually catch and discard approximately 27 million tons of fish per year. The fish are discarded because they are not the valuable varieties that the boats go out to catch and because they take up ice and space that could be used by more lucrative hauls. This means that these fish are lost both as food and income for other boats. The UN Chief of the Food and Agriculture Organisation (FAO) believes that this practice should be outlawed by making a rule that boats would be obliged to bring in their entire catch.

The major fishing territories throughout the world all tell the same story

- The Northern Pacific shows total landings to be the highest in the world with the decline of salmon being a major concern. There is also a more gradual decline in other varieties of fish such as cod, pollock and hake.
- The North Atlantic is generally overfished, with most pressure on high-value fish such as cod, but it also shows a decline in other species of lesser value.
- The Mediterranean and the Black Seas show stocks fully exploited and a collapse of the fish catches in the Black Sea.
- The Indian Ocean shows that the most important species are over-exploited.
- The Central and Southern Pacific tell a similar story.
- The Southern Atlantic is only moderately exploited, but this is rapidly changing due to the increase of visits by international fleets.
- The Central Atlantic is generally fully exploited.
- The Southern Ocean, used mainly by the former Soviet Union and Japan taking mostly krill. This area is very vulnerable to over-fishing.

Your agenda

1 Why are governments unwilling to cut back their fleet sizes?

2 Throwing back low-value fish catches benefits the fishermen because they have room and ice supplies for more high-value fish. How could making this illegal affect a small business?

3 Allowing the stocks of a high-value fish like cod to be depleted will attract a high reward for the successful fishermen. Explain this using your knowledge of supply and demand.

The general economic consequences of reducing fleet sizes and limiting catches make governments very reluctant to act upon environmental advice or concerns. The loss of jobs and income would be very unpopular with the voters. Pressure from environmental activists is always very high profile news, but is this less damaging to the political process than a high unemployment rate?

Production can cause a wide range of problems for future generations to have to try to deal with and these problems are not going to disappear without action. Unregulated markets work well in the short run because competition reduces prices and increases quality. In the long run markets can cause a shortage of resources, as shown in the case study, because there are no limits imposed upon the competitors.

Tradeable permits can provide a possible way forward and have been used successfully in New Zealand (see Module 2.2 page 146).

Point of View ❝❞

'Defend the Wee Bankie'

In 1980 there were 55 boats fishing from Pittenweem, on Scotland's Fife coast, and in 1996 there were 17 remaining. The protest banners were flying and the battle lines drawn to stop the Danish fishermen taking the remaining fish.

Danish fishing boats have over-fished the estuary and removed most of the sand eels, which feed the cod, haddock and other fish that used to inhabit the area. The sand eels are a vital base for the food chain and without them, the fish stocks have become depleted. The local fishermen are losing their livelihood and the fleet of small boats is fast being sold off. These people have a history of fishing the Fife coastline but cannot compete against the Danish commercial boats.

Various groups have campaigned to rid the Firth of Forth of the Danish boats in order to protect the food they take. Many species of birds used to breed in the Firth but they are disappearing nearly as fast as the sand eels. The Royal Society for Protection of Birds (RSPB), the World Wide Fund for Nature (WWF) and the Royal Society for Nature Conservation have all warned of the dangers to the other life forms that inhabit the estuary. The local fishing communities face huge losses to their income and heritage, but nothing has been done to change the laws that allow the Danish to commercially fish the area. The main sand eel fishery is the Wee Bankie, followed by the Marr Bank, off the south-east coast of Scotland. There is another small fishery off the Shetland coast, but this is restricted to British registered boats only. The locals from Pittwenweem want the same restrictions to apply to the Wee Bankie, before it is too late.

The Scottish Office denies that the loss of the sand eels is a real problem, but local fishermen will verify that when they began fishing in their youth, cod were often seen with sand eels hanging out of their mouths. The locals argue that the sand eels must be a necessary part of the environment that attracted so many fish, and without them the fish will not return.

Source: *The Guardian – Society Supplement* 1996 10.7.96 page 4

Your agenda

1 What do the various groups stand to lose because of the Danish boats?

2 The local fishermen want the sand eels protected for a different reason to the RSPB. Explain how the two groups can help each other in this fight.

3 How would the effects of the lost fishing fleet be noticed in the local community? Explain using the downward multiplier.

4 The UN has helped Asian communities to preserve fish stocks by imposing limits on commercial fishing and introducing patrols to make sure of compliance. Have the Scottish fishermen as strong a case for such measures? Find out how the EU rules affect small fishermen in Scotland and elsewhere.

5 As a group, debate the issues highlighted by the case study and suggest a way forward for these communities.

The various groups involved in the Wee Bankie protest were taking action to try to change the rules by means of demonstrations and stimulating media interest to gain support for the cause. Are pressure groups alone likely to make a difference?

- The fishermen are losing their income and traditional occupation and are therefore against the freedom to fish the estuary without any controls.

- The RSPB, WWF and the Royal Society for Nature Conservation are concerned about the loss of the sand eels to the eco-system and the consequential loss of other species to the area.

- The Danish fishing fleets make profits from their fishing and do not pay the external costs, so they want things to remain the same.

The free market could result in the end of the fishing industry in the area and everyone would lose in the long run. One solution would be to impose quotas on the Danish boats, but this would produce its own social costs. The job losses would be in Denmark rather than Scotland, the price of fish would increase because the small boats will not bring in enough for mass markets and the long-term future of the fishing villages in the area is therefore still not guaranteed.

2 Do people respond?

Progress?

What happens when people get trucks...

In many parts of the world people are short of firewood for cooking and heating. With growing prosperity, people are able to buy trucks. Instead of collecting firewood on foot, they can drive to places where it is easy to get a truckload. They will have plenty for their own use and more to sell when they get back to their towns and villages.

Unfortunately, large areas in the foothills of the Himalayas in Nepal are being denuded of their forest cover. Where tree roots once held the soil together on the mountainside, there is now bare soil. When it rains the topsoil is washed away. The ground becomes arid and eroded and trees no longer regenerate themselves. Rain which no longer soaks into the mountainside creates floods lower down the valley. Firewood becomes scarcer and so does grazing land. But the people of Nepal are generally very poor and have few opportunities. What are they supposed to do?

... and an overview...

Peter McCawley was the Australian representative at the Asian Development Bank. This is an international organisation similar to the World Bank, which specialises in finance for development in Asia. He said:

'I try to encourage the representatives of Asian governments to consider the likely environmental problems which arise when natural resources are exploited in an unconstrained way. But they find the problems hard to understand. Most of the populations in developing countries are poor. They consume relatively few resources. If they are told that they should be consuming even less, they find it hard to believe. They look at the resources consumed in the US compared to the resources they consume, and they simply don't believe that it is their problem. I have to be very cautious in mentioning the subject.'

On GM foods...

Many farmers have enjoyed an improvement in their standards of living over the past 20 years. The Green Revolution brought about big increases in yields from the use of improved seed in areas with adequate rainfall or irrigation. Unfortunately, the people farming on drier land had to wait longer for improvements.

When incomes rise, birth rates generally fall. But in the many areas where incomes are still growing very slowly if at all, birth rates remain high and the population increase is in the range 2–3 per cent per year. (Contrast this with 0.7 per cent growth in high-income developed countries.) These people need more food.

Genetically modified (GM) food could improve yields dramatically for many of the world's poorest farmers. This is what the Nuffield Council on Bioethics had to say in its 1999 report, *Genetically Modified Crops: the Ethical and Social Issues*:

'Just as the world could not feed itself today with the farming methods of the 1940s, so farmers can hardly expect to meet the increased global demand for food in 20 years time using today's crop varieties and agricultural technologies. In 1961 the amount of cultivated land supporting food production was 0.44 hectares per person; today it is about 0.26 hectares. Based on population projections, by 2050 it will be approximately 0.15 hectares per person. The rate of expansion of arable land is now below 0.2 per cent per year and it continues to fall.

The UN's Food and Agriculture Organisation expects 680 million people, 12 per cent of the developing world's population, may still be 'food insecure' in 2010, down from 840 million in 1990–92.

GM crops may help alleviate world hunger. Some progress has been made, but significant inroads require radical changes in the current focus on research. At present, most research is done by a small number of large companies which are working on consumer quality, herbicide tolerance and the other requirements of labour-saving farms in developed countries. What is required is a major increase in support for GM crop research directed at employment-intensive production of food staples within developing countries. This should involve public sector research in developing countries and international institutions. The resulting spread of GM food staples would be highly beneficial to consumers' health and the environment in developing countries. However, safety concerns require improved regulation, both of field trials and of the use of GM crops in the food chain.

The UK is ideally placed to take a lead in addressing this situation. If it is not tackled, the world will be hungrier and more disease prone. It will also be more unstable, ecologically threatened and politically dangerous, for rich and poor alike.'

Your agenda

1 The people of Nepal are making progress if they get trucks, but they are also causing problems. What do *you* think they should do?

2 Are people from the less developed countries paying a higher price to protect the environment than the rest of the world?

3 What can be done to aid the development of GM foods so that the outcome benefits third world farmers?

The people of Taiwan are grateful for the economic benefits growth has brought them and relatively ignorant of the problems. It is often difficult to convince people that something has to be done to stop environmental degradation. There have been attempts by international organisations to start to put things right, but have we moved fast enough to make a difference? Are people from places like Nepal paying a higher price than countries of the developed world?

The term **sustainable development** is not simple to define but is not a new concept. The Bruntland Report, 1987 *Our Common Future*, defines it as '...development that meets the needs of the present without compromising the ability of future generations to meet their own needs'. Translated into everyday terms it means that we must not further our own economic growth at the expense of future occupants of the planet. If we use up scarce resources, then we need to replace them or find an alternative to leave for the people who come after us. Sustainable development requires us to think about the future and to plan with the environment at the forefront of our minds.

Essentials

Sustainable development involves economic growth which does not degrade the environment in such a way that the costs of that growth have to be paid in the future.

	Thousand metric tons of oil equivalent		Carbon-dioxide emissions per capita (metric tons)	
	1980	1995	1980	1995
Indonesia	25 904	85 785	0.6	1.5
USA	1 801 406	2 078 265	19.9	20.8

Source: World Bank, *World Development Report, 1998–99*

Figure O1.24 Commercial energy use

Indonesia and the USA have a comparable population size, but Figure O1.24 shows that there is a disparity between them regarding energy usage.

Work in progress

Q 1 Work out the percentage increase in energy use and emissions for the two countries.

2 What do the results tell us?

Environmental degradation does not take long to affect local people in some way, but Figure O1.24 shows that double standards seem to apply. The energy use figures for the USA far outweigh those for Indonesia, but both countries will need to take steps to reduce the harm done to the environment by the processes involved in everyday production of goods. Both countries are making a contribution to global warming.

Developing countries do degrade their own environments by deforestation, over-fishing, over-grazing and so on; they are not naturally geared towards sustainability. But in terms of relative contributions to global warming, it is easy to see why many poorer countries disclaim responsibility. However, the figures do show that emissions are actually increasing as Indonesia develops, rather than decreasing.

- Intergenerational sustainability requires us to look after the environment for our children and grandchildren and one suggestion put forward has been to create traffic-free and therefore pollution-free zones around schools.

- Children are our future human capital and we must look after their well-being so that their value does not depreciate.

The notion that education and training increase the value of human capital can be extended to include degradation caused by pollution and illness. If a business invests in a piece of machinery to increase productivity, it must save to replace it when depreciation makes it no longer usable, otherwise production will cease and the business close down. Polluting the environment, and damaging peoples' health works on the same principle. Sustainable development requires that we 'save' for the future of the planet by protecting our children, and theirs, from health problems brought about by environmental hazards.

Recycling our waste

We cannot escape the fact that we pollute the environment even by breathing because we produce waste products. The key to sustainable development is to reduce the impact of the waste products produced by industry and households. In the carpark of most supermarkets there are waste recycling collection points for bottles, aluminium cans and paper, but do we all take the trouble to use them? Charities have used waste-paper collection as a lucrative means of raising money, but this has declined in recent years because they cannot get as much money for their efforts.

We are all willing to collect waste for recycling if someone makes it worthwhile in money terms, but not so ready to cooperate to save the environment if there is no immediate reward. The problem with recycling schemes began when the rewards started to decline because the supply grew too big. Firms using waste paper would pay high prices when the supply was small, but once they could get enough easily they dropped the price.

Work in progress

Q 1 A local Scout group raises money for charity on a regular basis. In 1995 it could get £50 per ton of newspaper collected, and a jumble sale would raise approximately the same amount. Why would the scouts choose to collect the newspapers?

2 The 1999 reward for collecting newspaper would be more like £20 per ton, and the jumble sale might raise about £100. What effect has this had and why?

3 A great many organisations started to collect newspapers for recycling, but the rewards fell dramatically. Why do you think this occurred?

Illustrate your answers using supply and demand diagrams.

3 What is not sustainable?

Getting there faster

Europe has a major transport problem and, as a solution to this, the European Parliament and the Council of the EU adopted a proposal to develop TENs (Trans European Networks). This is an ambitious plan to develop all the transport systems across Europe to:

- contribute to the development of the EU internal market and strengthen social ties

- ensure the mobility of persons and goods under the best possible social, safety and environmental conditions

- interlink different modes of transport in an attempt to make best use of the advantages of each.

So, what does this mean? One of the consequences will be that new major roads, such as the Birmingham Northern Relief Road, will have to be built and large sections of our motorways will have to be widened to take account of the predicted increase in traffic.

Advantages of the TENs

- Goods will be delivered on time.

- Manufacturers will be able to transport more goods, more often.

- Workers will be able to get to work on time – increasing their productivity.

- Firms' costs will fall.

Your agenda

What are the implications of the plans to build more roads across Europe:

a to companies

b to local residents

c to the environment?

The benefits to industry of efficient road transport networks are numerous, not least the reduction in wasted man-hours due to congestion. The profit-maximising organisation will gain the confidence of consumers and reduce costs of transportation if it can guarantee delivery on time. The fact is that road transportation of goods is the most flexible and trouble-free method. The delivery vehicle can deliver 'door to door' making multiple drops possible and therefore saving money for the firm, but only if the roads are free from congestion. Improving infrastructure increases competitiveness.

Carbon-dioxide emissions from vehicles are a problem for the world, but job losses are a problem for governments and the unemployed. The Budget in 1999 saw the Chancellor putting some environmental promises into action.

Tax increases drive hauliers to Europe

Following the 1999 Budget British hauliers threatened to move their operations to mainland Europe to take advantage of lower fuel and excise duties. The cost of refuelling in the UK in 1999 was nearly double that of France or Belgium and, as an average lorry can travel about 1200 miles on a full tank of diesel, many hauliers have been organising their business to avoid paying UK prices. The Treasury is losing revenue, but the roads are still congested.

The Road Haulage Association stated that the cost of registering a truck in the UK was ten times that of registering in France. The Association warned that many hauliers would move their operations to Europe and predicted 53 000 job losses by 2002.

Carlisle-based haulier Eddie Stobart estimated that a rise of 6p per litre would cost his firm about £2 million per year. He then compared the £500 cost of registering a truck in France to the UK charge of £5750 and stated that he was considering registering half of his fleet in either Belgium or Luxembourg in order to save costs and stay competitive. (Legislation states that a vehicle only has to return to its registered base six times per year, so the option is easily available to companies who wish to operate in the UK.)

Your agenda

1 What are the trade-offs involved in increasing the tax on diesel?

2 Congestion and pollution would be reduced if more goods were transported by rail. What problems can you identify with this idea?

3 What are the costs and benefits involved for Eddie Stobart if he moves his base?

4 Are the tax changes achieving the desired effect? Debate the issues in a group.

The government has tried to use incentives in the pricing structure to persuade companies to economise on their fuel use. The response shows that the profit and competition motives took precedence over environmental considerations due to inequalities between the policies of the various governments throughout Europe.

Phasing out leaded petrol caused some problems for the government. The component manufacturers advertised products to convert leaded-petrol vehicles so that they could use unleaded fuel. These businesses obviously gained from the initiative, but many others lost when they had to pay to convert their older cars and vans. Changing to unleaded fuel will reduce environmental damage considerably. Ethical growth is possible, but is it popular?

Work in progress

Find out what a local business is having to do to meet environmental regulations. What do they think about it? What will the benefits be? How will the changes be paid for?

Ultimately, the cost of environmental sustainability has to be passed on to consumers. The question is, will they pay? Society, as a whole, suffers the negative externalities produced by firms but would also have to suffer the price increases caused by making business accountable.

Ethical multi-nationals?

The Chiquitano forest in Bolivia lies in the path of a gas pipeline planned to transfer natural gas from Rio San Miguel in Bolivia to Cuiaba in Brazil. The forest is home to many endangered species including the ocelot, the jaguar and the extremely rare hyacinth macaw. The World Wide Fund for Nature (WWF) warned the consortium (which included Shell) planning to build the pipeline that it was acting irresponsibly and totally against its promises to conserve the environment.

'This area has been identified as one of the richest, rarest and most biologically outstanding examples of the Earth's diverse habitats and a priority region for conservation efforts.' (Clive Wicks, head of international programmes for WWF-UK).

In Peru natural gas has meant problems for local villagers hunting and fishing. They have complained that the normally chocolate-coloured river sometimes becomes black. Activists have complained that they were not given complete information about the extent of the mining and their representative argued that the agreement was signed in a hurry and there was no time to consult a lawyer. The reply from the company:

'The communities keep their hunting grounds secret from other communities in order to protect scarce resources. How are we to decide what just compensation to give them when we cannot determine the *exact* impact on their life?'

Source: *The Independent* 12.6.99 NOT Independent ©

Your agenda

1 "Many large businesses have ethical policies but will be guided by other motives." How true do you think this is?

2 Examine the annual report of a multi-national company and find out how many promises it is making about the environment.

How committed are the multi-nationals to following ethical, environmentally friendly policies? There is a conflict of interest between profit and ethics. Being ethical can bring extra costs to bear on the company, which could make it less competitive. Promoting ethical principles involves abiding by certain standards, which are seen to be morally right for an industry. Many companies now have an ethical code of practice which employees are expected to adhere to. These codes usually include four main areas:

- Corporate integrity – the company will not attempt to use unfair tactics in the name of competition. Collusion between two large firms could drive a competitor out of the market.

- Social responsibility – this means that prices will be fair and advertising honest. The firm will not try to sell goods which do not perform as they should.

- Personal integrity – this includes relationships with suppliers, who must be afforded fair treatment.

- Environmental responsibility – the firm's relationship with the environment must be a fair one. Emission levels, pollution and recycling come under this heading.

Ethical actions include protecting the environment from pollution and decay because these harm society. The modern consumer is well informed and companies can gain good publicity by being seen to be advertising an ethical product. It is good for public relations to be ethical, but the temptation to cut corners, and so reduce costs and keep shareholders happy, can be too great to ignore. The opportunity cost of caring for the environment can be too high to consider!

Some companies have used ethical policies to promote their business successfully. The Body Shop, for example, has a reputation based on environmentally sound policy. The employees of ethical firms are usually proud to be associated with their employer because society is more aware of the problems of degradation and pollution. There are gains as well as losses to be made by carefully planning and advertising an ethical policy.

Weak sustainability

This is often the path chosen by the multi-national. The theory is that we should leave behind us the same stock of resources, but the make-up of those resources does not have to be the one we inherited. If we look at this from the company's point of view, then we can use up resources like coal and oil but we must replace them with alternative sources of energy.

The multi-national can invest in research and development of substitute fuels while at the same time profiting from the non-renewable resources.

Strong sustainability

Ecologists argue that we must pass on an unadulterated set of resources to the next generation because the substitutes may be adequate alternatives for energy purposes but not for the continuation of eco-systems.

This makes life much harder for the companies that use depletable resources to justify their position. If we want strong sustainability, then the limits on the use of scarce resources are very close, or even at the point of no return. Using non-renewable energy sources has been connected to global warming and climate change and we do not really know if the adverse effects are reversible. The fact is that scientists do not really know for sure how much damage has already been caused.

Global warming – the consequences?

- The Scottish and Australian ski industries will disappear through lack of snow! The lower slopes of the Alps will not see any snow for most of the winter.

- The land at sea level will disappear – much of the Netherlands and East Anglia will be lost.

- Maize, the staple food for 100 million people in southern Africa, will not be available to them due to a shortened growing season caused by longer, drier summers.

- The Sahara Desert is expected to cross the Mediterranean into southern Spain and Italy.

- The climate will be more erratic and 'severe weather events' more numerous.

- Other types of plants and trees will drive out many mountain-top species of plant.

- Two thousand miles of railway are held together in China by permafrost but this is melting and will eventually cause rockfalls.

- Some European rivers are ice free for longer than they were 50 years ago.

In Geneva, in June 1996, at the Climate Change Convention, a cutting from a newspaper in the Solomon Islands (north-east Australia) was passed around the representatives present. It reported that the Carteret Islands, home for 1700 people, had been washed over by a freak tidal wave that had ruined the whole vegetable crop by washing away all the soil from gardens. Emergency supplies of rice had been sent, but the article added that the sea level had risen 30 cm per year since 1991 and there was a real danger that the islands could soon be submerged. The Australian government is faced with the task of relocating these people on other, higher, islands as soon as possible.

Your agenda

1 Over-populated nations will soon be faced with the problems of global warming. How can they cope with extra people to locate when they have no room for the present population?

2 China could lose 2000 miles of railway track. What sort of problems would this present to:
   a the government
   b the people of China?

4 What *is* sustainable?

Community-based fisheries management

Phang Nga Bay on the sea coast of Thailand produces the livelihood for many fisherfolk from the villages along the coast. Overexploitation of the available stocks and pollution of the water by local industry and tourism were depleting the fish stocks. They needed a better management regime to ensure continuation of the species found in the area so that the fisherfolk could maintain their incomes.

The community was encouraged to work together to maintain, monitor and improve the situation for the benefit of all concerned. The Andaman Sea Fisheries Development Centre, working with the locals, banned the use of trawls and motorised push-nets within 3 km of the shoreline, introduced new cultures of fish and shellfish and patrol boats to police the shore. The locals gave up their resource-destructive fishing gear in return for the more environmentally sound gillnets donated by the government and are encouraged to take part in the policing of the Bay. The villagers have a sense of ownership and pride in the scheme and have agreed to return rare species back to the sea if they are accidentally caught. Waste disposal schemes have been set up to stop industry and tourism using the sea.

There have also been 40 artificial reefs installed at the entrance to the Bay to keep trawlers and push-netters out of the inshore zone. The local fisherfolk can now fish in peace and live in harmony with the commercial fishermen because they are no longer a threat.

Your agenda

1 How does this scheme improve human and social capital and 'save' for future depreciation?

2 How does this scheme demonstrate the requirements of sustainability?

The above case study demonstrates how a developing country is making the effort to develop sustainable fishing communities. These developments have been initiated through organisations committed to the environment and protecting it for future generations. Education has played a major role in these countries and is a requirement for further advances.

Consumers in the UK are becoming more aware of the value of ethical business management, and adverse publicity will continue to play a vital role in the education of consumers. More and more companies are undertaking environmental audits and producing policy statements in response to consumer pressure. The question is: do they really intend to implement them regardless of reduced profits?

Natural Step

Sweden's Dr Karl-Henrik Ròbert would like all companies to follow his 'Natural Step' programme. He is a cancer specialist who became frustrated about arguments over precise effects of environmental damage and wanted a straightforward approach companies could follow. He went back to basics and came up with four 'rules' an environmentally friendly firm should follow:

● Fossil fuels, metals and other materials should not be extracted faster than they can be redeposited.

● Substances should not be produced faster than they can be broken down by nature.

● We must not take from nature more than we can replace.

● We must be fair and efficient in meeting basic human needs.

His ideas are not new, and companies such as the furniture chain Ikea and domestic appliances manufacturer Electrolux, who joined early in the scheme, are still struggling to meet the criteria. McDonald's in Sweden has changed to paper packaging, rather than polystyrene and plastic, and many of its outlets have a windmill on the roof to generate power.

Yorkshire Water, one of the UK companies signed up to the scheme, already uses wind energy and generates power by burning sewage sludge. Other UK organisations who have signed up for Natural Step include Tarmac, the Environment Agency, Sainsbury's and The Body Shop.

Source: *The Observer* 23.3.98

Your agenda

1 The Natural Step scheme has been criticised because the benefits of following the 'rules' have not been scientifically proven. What are the likely benefits and costs?

2 Fast-food outlets produce huge amounts of waste packaging but have to meet hygiene requirements. Is there a solution?

Companies have been accused of exploiting workers and ignoring environmental damage in the pursuit of bigger profits. The fact is that they could not do this without the agreement of the consumer. When we buy a pair of trainers stitched together by a child earning no more than a few pence per hour, we are actually encouraging the exploitation. Who is wrong here, the consumer or the company? The fact that companies are joining 'Natural Step' shows a commitment by these firms to act in a socially responsible and ethical manner, but will consumers pay the possible increase in price?

Ethical trading is becoming a selling point because people are being made more aware of the issues, through education and the media. Modern firms need to be aware of public opinion and react quickly to new, environmentally friendly developments. The companies registered with the Natural Step scheme are showing a caring image to the consumer – the fact that they may not be meeting the requirements will not be publicised as much as the fact that they are willing to try.

5 Does technology help?

Tyres to electricity!

Near Wolverhampton, in the West Midlands, there is a very strange-looking power station which burns scrap tyres – something we have a problem disposing of – and produces electricity. Wolverhampton was chosen as the site for this facility because it is in an area which produces 90 per cent of the nation's tyres.

The power station was designed to burn approximately 94 000 tons of scrap tyres per year to produce approximately 175 000-megawatt hours of electricity. It also produces about 15 000 tons of steel wire and 2 000 tons of zinc oxide, and all without going above the allowed environmental guidelines for emissions.

The plant is constantly monitored for emissions and there are agreements with the local community about the timing of deliveries and the allowed noise levels. The facility also created in excess of 300 jobs for local people during construction and employs 90 workers now that it is operational.

Your agenda

1 Technology can help us to solve some of our environmental problems, such as waste tyres. Make a list of any other innovations that have made it easier to protect the planet from harmful pollution.

2 'Research and development into alternative technology should be funded by governments.' Is this fair comment?

If we are to make progress towards sustainable development, then technological advances must take into account the current problems of a particular area or country. The case study states that Wolverhampton was chosen because of its relationship with the tyre manufacturing industry. Technology must fit into the overall scheme of things. Existing producers in less developed countries would not be happy to be told that their methods were substandard. They need to be able to see how technological progress can be used by them to improve their products.

Transport is vital to everyone wherever they live. It gives us access to the goods and services we need and want. Many rural communities in the less developed areas of the world are cut off from the markets where they could sell their produce and raise their living standards. In Sri Lanka approximately 70 per cent of the population live in the countryside and were cut off from the markets of the towns. The Intermediate Technology Development Group (ITDG) has been helping them to build cycle trailers and, as a result, many villagers have set up small businesses such as passenger transport or mobile shops. There has been no harm done to the environment by the use of fuel and the trailers have been made in local workshops, following the training they received from ITDG.

Intermediate technology in Zimbabwe

ITZ (Intermediate Technology Zimbabwe) began in 1989 and aims to help the country develop through education in the use of different technology. It has experts in various fields working to assist the country to grow economically but in an environmentally secure way:

- The building materials team is helping to develop alternative building materials such as stabilised soil blocks.
- The mining programme is helping small firms to ensure a sustainable industry.
- The agriculture scheme puts emphasis on community ownership and encourages links between farmers and the government so that research is carried out to help feed the most needy.

- The light-engineering project seeks to upgrade skills and increase the quantity and quality of goods produced.

All of these projects are moving towards the same goal – a sustainable development programme for the nation as a whole.

Source: ITZ Website (Intermediate Technology Zimbabwe)

Your agenda

1 If we have the technology in the developed world, then why not simply give it to poorer nations?

2 Which is more beneficial in the long run, training and education or foreign aid?

Intermediate technology is so called because it is the middle ground between traditional methods used in many developing countries and the high technology used in the west. Advanced technology is usually capital intensive and would not be an option for poorer countries. The idea behind this type of development process is that the current workforce can use its existing skills and resources but in a much more efficient way. This means that the projects succeed in achieving sustainable growth.

6 Can prices be ethical?

Switch to Fairtrade

‘Quality of taste should always go with quality of life.’ (Gary Rhodes)

This is the endorsement found in a leaflet published by the Fairtrade Foundation and found by the coffee in a Sainsbury's store in the Midlands. The Fairtrade Mark is put on to the labels of coffee, tea, chocolate, cocoa and honey produced by third world farmers who have been given a fair price for their produce.

‘From the money we got from cocoa we have made a concrete floor in our house, instead of the dirt floor, and our children are now able to go to secondary school in Punta Gorda. Because Fairtrade guarantees a fair price we have planted more cocoa.’ (Christina Peck, a Maya farmer, speaking after Maya Gold chocolate was awarded the first Fairtrade Mark in 1994)

Source: Fairtrade Foundation leaflet

Your agenda

1 The quality of life for the Maya farmers has improved vastly due to a British initiative, but this will only continue if we look for the Fairtrade Mark. What are the benefits to the consumer?

2 Would you pay more for an ethically produced product? How much more?

The campaign run by the Fairtrade Foundation is aiming to make sure that a fair price is paid for goods produced by people without the bargaining power to refuse low prices. The idea is to give these people their independence and make them self-sufficient. It allows third world farmers to continue their traditional, sustainable lifestyles and allows them to look after their families without outside help. Encouraging British people to buy their goods, and pay fair prices for them, is the alternative to asking for aid to help them to survive without an income.

The fashion industry...

Many of the fashion items we buy have been produced in sweatshops by women and young children earning an extremely low wage. It is only when we are informed by the media or through education that we think about the consequences of our purchases. People are prepared to pay far more for a well-known branded label, but is the extra money for the extra costs involved?

Highly competitive markets will lead to lower prices for the consumer, but at what cost? The most obvious cost for a business to cut is the largest one, which is usually labour. Competitive markets will lead to low wages if firms can get away with it. The introduction of the minimum wage in the UK may have led to job losses because of the escalating costs to the firms. We, at least, have some regulation as to the setting of wage rates but the less developed countries do not. Many of the workers in the sweatshops have no choice but put up with the low wages and poor conditions because the alternative is starvation.

Work in progress

Complete a survey to find out how much more people would be prepared to pay to wear a fashion sports item produced for a fair wage.

Q Discuss your results with the group. Are they as you expected?

Unregulated markets will allow exploitation of the workforce and of the other resources used in production. If there are no controls on the use of

chemicals or the destruction of forests, then the planet will suffer along with the people.

In the UK and other developed countries we are told that competition is healthy because it benefits the consumer by forcing prices down and quality up. Price wars between supermarkets mean that we shop around for bargains and our wages buy more products. It also means that in order to reduce costs enough to gain a healthy profit the supermarkets will need to find a way to reduce their costs. The question is: does competition always provide the best for the consumer?

The 'Labour Behind the Label Campaign'

This is the title of a campaign being run by a network of organisations from around the world that are interested in stopping the exploitation of garment workers. Many of them work in appalling conditions and risk poor eyesight and chest problems, as well as putting up with low wages.

Here in the UK a homeworker may only earn about £1.50 per hour and be expected to work in excess of 50 hours per week. Dust from the materials used is causing their children, as well as themselves, to suffer from respiratory problems but they carry on because they need the money.

Retailers are being asked by the campaign organisers to acknowledge the need for the consumer to know how their garments were made and to improve pay and conditions to an acceptable standard.

❛ I sewed on collars. I was paid £4.64 a month. I often worked overtime. I worked from 7am to 10 pm or sometimes all night, for seven days a week. I had 30 minutes for lunch and we had to eat at our machines – we were not allowed out of the factory.❜

(Bokul, factory worker in Bangladesh)

Your agenda

1 How are the consumers expected to change the way workers are treated?

2 What will happen to prices if the campaign is successful?

If we want firms to conduct their business in an ethical way, then we must exert pressure on them to be fair to their workers. The consumer will be expected to pay higher prices for goods so that companies can continue to make profits. The question is how big a profit are we going to allow them to make at the expense of the worker or the planet.

Not only do we have to consider pollution and extinction but we have also to consider the human element.

Work in progress

Q 1 Find out what other initiatives have been taken by groups such as Traidcraft to ensure that business becomes more ethical.

2 Research a large company and find out what its policies are concerning ethical trading and environmental issues. Evaluate its claims.

The problems highlighted in the case studies in this enquiry show how complex the issues concerning sustainability are. They also show that pressure groups and individuals need help to make changes. The way forward for the world to move towards sustainable lifestyles can only be through international cooperation. Without this, the difficulties in enforcing new regimes will not be resolved. Countries need to agree on the targets and put together a plan for the future. The progress towards international agreement is examined in the next enquiry.

Many developing country governments are concerned that if developed countries insist on higher wages being paid, job opportunities will be reduced. They see poorly paid jobs as better than no jobs at all. This is likely to be a continuing issue in trade negotiations in the future.

In studying this option, it becomes clear that global prosperity and stability are two very major goals requiring international cooperation. This enquiry examines a whole range of negotiations and agreements. It outlines areas of progress and areas of controversy.

1 How has trade changed?

WTO versus NGOs

A number of non-governmental organisations (NGOs) are hoping to stop the World Trade Organisation (WTO) from extending its powers. They include Oxfam, Friends of the Earth and the Japanese Consumers' Union. They have many anxieties. They say, 'The WTO has prised open markets for the benefit of multi-national corporations at the expense of national economies, workers, farmers and other people.' They cite a selection of the problem areas:

- The WTO ruling in favour of the USA in the dispute with the EU over hormone-fed meat. The USA was authorised to impose trade sanctions on EU products such as Roquefort cheese, raspberry jam and motor cycles.

- The WTO stopped the USA from requiring imports of shrimps to come from nations which would regulate their fishing industries to ensure that their boats did not catch endangered sea turtles.

- Major disputes are expected over genetically modified foods.

Your agenda

1 What are the WTO's primary objectives?

2 What benefits has the WTO brought to ordinary people?

3 In what sorts of situations can these objectives run counter to the interests of human beings?

4 What is the best way to reconcile differences of opinion in trade matters?

The World Trade Organisation started life as the GATT, General Agreement on Tariffs and Trade. During the 1930s, many governments tried to cope with the slump by bringing in tariffs and quotas on imports. Because so many of them were doing the same thing, trade was greatly discouraged, and worldwide the amount of goods traded fell sharply. Imports fell as intended by the policy-makers, but of course exports fell too. The loss of income from exporting meant that demand for imports fell. A vicious circle was created.

Towards the end of the Second World War, policy-makers realised that it would be important to try to avoid a repeat of the 1930s problems. They set up the GATT in order to reduce barriers to trade, and encourage a stable and predictable trading environment. The idea was to create a level playing field for trade.

In 1995 GATT became the WTO. It was strengthened and enlarged to accommodate a much more comprehensive system for settling trade disputes.

The WTO has encouraged its signatories to:

- reduce international trade restrictions in general

- not grant trade advantages to some of their trading partners while restricting trade with others

- settle disputes with other signatories by negotiation.

Using negotiation to decide trading arrangements has proved to be a powerful principle. Simple retaliation escalating into full-scale trade war has become less of a problem since 1945 than it was before.

Pressure to bring in more import controls is called protectionism. It is often a controversial issue. Many people think that competition from cheap imports is a bad thing. They may not realise how much they have gained from them.

Work in progress

Q 1 Describe in your own words how a cut in tariffs on sugar might lead to higher real incomes. Do the same with cars. Do you have to consume these products yourself in order to benefit from the change in tariffs?

2 If you benefit, what will you do with the extra real income?

3 What trade disputes are you currently aware of? What issues are currently being negotiated?

What has trade liberalisation achieved?

There have been three important rounds of international trade negotiations. In the 1960s, the Kennedy Round led to a considerable cut in tariffs worldwide. In the 1970s the Tokyo Round achieved further reductions. It brought the average tariff on manufactured imports into developed countries down from 7 per cent to 4.7 per cent. In 1986 a further round of negotiations opened in Uruguay, aiming to open up trade much further. The Uruguay Round was very long and drawn out, finally finishing in 1994. The talks were acrimonious, with particular areas of dispute involving EU restrictions on trade in agriculture.

The growth of trade is a major factor in globalisation. A large part of this growth consists of increasing trade in manufactures between developed countries. Often large businesses have acquired a comparative advantage by developing expertise in design and production. They use a global market to allow them to expand production and to reap very large economies of scale. This makes them very competitive. Low prices can improve consumers' real incomes and generate substantial growth.

The Kennedy and Tokyo Rounds were most successful in reducing tariffs on manufactures. The Uruguay Round extended this liberalisation to services, and to some extent, to agriculture.

What the Uruguay Round did

The Uruguay Round, with 117 participants and an agreement which stretched to 500 pages, has contributed to freedom of trade in the following ways:

- It succeeded in cutting tariffs by around 40 per cent, significantly better than the one-third reduction that was originally sought.

- It made agricultural tariffs more explicit. (The EU's Common Agricultural Policy has always been a bone of contention because it gives European farmers high levels of subsidy and protection.)

- It brought intellectual property rights within the system.

- It opened up some government purchases to international competition.

- It relaxed the rules on cross-border investment.

- It streamlined the world's trading system.

It was estimated at the time that all these movements towards trade liberalisation should add US$220 billion (at 1994 prices) to world income in the year 2002 and each year after that date. These benefits would, however, be unequally distributed. Developed countries, for example, were expected to gain almost two-thirds of the total. Although the agreement was expected to benefit many poor countries, the benefits were rather small in comparison.

Extending WTO membership

The benefits of WTO membership are not lost on most countries. Developing countries which were not WTO members often found that their trading arrangements were dominated by bilateral agreements which were much less favourable than WTO agreements. So they flocked to join. At the time of writing China is engaged in protracted entry negotiations. These have been difficult because WTO does not easily accommodate economies which have large non-competitive sectors (see Module 4.2, page 353).

WTO could give China improved access to developed country markets, and a multilateral disputes settlement procedure. Both can help to make trade easier.

WTO's work is exceedingly complex and many-faceted. Small, poor countries have difficulty in keeping up with the discussions and the changes because they cannot afford to keep large delegations in Geneva, or to send their own experts. Geneva is a very expensive location. The WTO is aware of this and is setting up Internet connections which will keep small member countries informed. There is much to be done in this area, because knowledge gives power and lack of knowledge can disadvantage countries with very poor prospects to start with.

Settling disputes

The WTO has become increasingly important as a forum for settling disputes. As trade has increased, so has the number of disputes. Sometimes these disputes seem unbelievably vicious. It is worth remembering one of the most acrimonious disputes was that between Canada and the USA over fishing along the Pacific coast. Now, these countries are older friends than almost any other pair of neighbour countries in the world. They settle their disputes by having a fierce argument. It's a good precedent.

Where next?

The Millennium Round might have a life about as long as that of this book. It was first suggested by US President Clinton in his State of the Union address in January 1999. The world was already committed to further negotiations on agriculture and services. Other areas for deliberation include:

- elimination of tariffs
- further opening of markets for government procurement
- promotion of competition
- curbs on anti-dumping measures
- improved conditions for foreign direct investment.

The opening meeting of this new round of negotiations in Seattle in November 1999 collapsed in argumentative chaos. The WTO still thinks progress is possible. Watch this space.

Point of view

Some problems with WTO approaches

The environment: not all governments care deeply about the environment. By encouraging trade and growth, the WTO is sometimes encouraging developments which are actively harmful to the environment. Furthermore, it tends to be against the sort of trade restrictions (such as prohibiting imports of tuna which have been fished in dolphin-unfriendly ways) which might be considered more in the coming years.

The WTO view:

❛ Some practices may simply be unacceptable to certain people or societies, so they oppose trade which encourages such practices. These can include killing dolphins in the process of catching tuna, using leg-hold traps for catching animals for their furs, or the use of polluting production methods which have only local effects.

On the other hand trade liberalisation may improve the quality of the environment. Trade stimulates growth and growing prosperity is one of the key factors in societies' demand for a cleaner environment. Growth also provides the resources to deal with the problems – resources which poor countries often do not have. Trade and growth can also encourage the dissemination of environment-friendly production techniques. ❜

Labour standards: trade can encourage multi-nationals to locate in low-wage economies where they can employ people in very poor working conditions. This can, in turn, put pressure on employers in higher-wage economies to downgrade their own standards in order to cut costs.

The WTO view:

Developing countries fear this argument as a possible way to exclude their products from developed country markets. The WTO was not designed to set labour standards: that is the job of the UN's International Labour Organisation. The ILO has agreed a Declaration of Fundamental Principles and Rights at Work.

Trade can actually contribute to improving labour standards and their enforcement. Trade promotes growth, which in turns increases people's demand for better working conditions. Growth and prosperity also provide the means to finance improvements in labour standards and to send children to school instead of factories.

Your agenda

1 Have other controversies developed, similar to those outlined above?
2 What would be the implications of creating trade restrictions which address these anxieties?

The facts and the controversy

Few people doubt that trade increases standards of living. People do however worry about quality of life. The great difficulty lies in working out which points of view relate to vested interest, which to personal preference and which to genuine concern for others.

Unfortunately, many of the issues reflect fundamental cultural differences. When we oppose an established point of view we may be being totally objective, or we may be trying to impose our personal views on others. Two approaches can help us. (1) We should not discount the data even if they have to be qualified. (2) Before deciding what is best, it is important to try to imagine what the other person's point of view will be.

2 How has Europe changed?

Exports and the single market

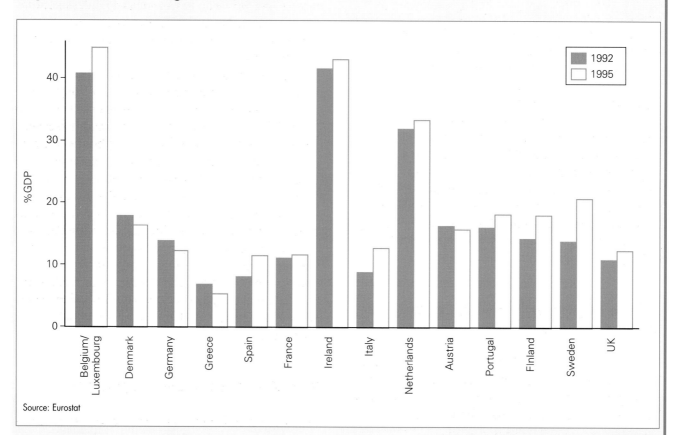

Figure O1.25 Intra-EU exports as percentage of GDP

The European Union economy is becoming more integrated. The introduction of the single market in 1992 was, to some extent, psychological in its impact. Effectively, it was a relaunch of the EU. It played a part in educating EU exporters to the possibilities. But some of the cost and price cuts which resulted were real. Reduced bureaucracy at border crossings, harmonised safety standards and reduced non-tariff barriers really did make trade easier. Figure O1.25 shows how much EU member exports to each other increased in the first three years of the single market.

Your agenda

1 What impact would you expect the single market to have on growth in the EU?

2 How would businesses react to the regulatory changes which the single market entailed?

The European Union is a customs union which has steadily removed trade barriers between the member countries, while maintaining an external tariff against imports from the rest of the world.

The EU is at once a recognition of existing interdependence and a move to strengthen that interdependence further. It goes beyond policy coordination to achieve unified policies in a number of areas. The most important are monopoly policy, the environment, employment protection, product regulation and agriculture. Most of these are dealt with specifically elsewhere in this book.

The single market can reasonably be expected to further the international division of labour, encouraging the development of more intense specialisation. It should also increase competition in many markets and reduce market imperfections. Some businesses should reap further economies of scale.

Customs unions lead to both trade creation and trade diversion. Trade creation occurs because new opportunities to specialise become apparent. Businesses with a competitive advantage get more chances to expand. Trade diversion occurs because some trade becomes relatively more profitable within the customs union, resulting in EU buyers switching to EU suppliers instead of non-EU suppliers. This reduces trade with the rest of the world. (See Module 4.2 page 336.)

Did the single market live up to its promise?

Reduced trade barriers did have an impact in the EU. This is clear from the data in Figure O1.25. However, the single market is not quite what it was supposed to be. Common technical standards have been implemented in some industries but not in others. Despite the Social Chapter (see Option 3, page 564), there are still differences in some aspects of labour law. VAT rates vary, as do environmental regulations. Most government contracts still go to domestic businesses. These are all areas which the European Commission will continue to work on.

The EU and developing countries

With world trade growing so fast, it is hard to find evidence of trade diversion. However, it is probably taking place. Intra-EU trade is likely to reduce some member countries' trade with the rest of the world. It may have had a negative effect on trade with the developing world.

The structure of the EU's external tariffs is designed to discourage primary producers from processing their products. Raw coffee, tea or sugar, for example, will be subject to a much lower tariff than if it is ready for the shelves of the supermarket. This protects the European food-processing industry and prevents the producing countries from earning the greater rewards which result from adding value to the raw materials.

Members of the EU had strong trade links with their colonies, often to the extent that the latter had become dependent. In theory, these should have been severed when the Treaty of Rome, which established the European Community, was signed by the original six members. In order to overcome the political problems which would result, the Treaty gave these colonies continued rights to trade and aid. As the countries became independent a series of Conventions, concluding with the Lomé Convention, continued this special relationship. The 69 members are from Africa, the Caribbean and the Pacific (ACP). Many of them have continued to be highly dependent on trade with the EU and any suggestion that the relationship should end causes uncertainty about the future of their economies.

Will EMU mean closer integration?

Monetary union implies that member countries' macro-economic policies must be closely coordinated. Any country which falls out of line with the majority will experience difficulties. For example, if one country faces weak demand compared to the rest, it will want lower interest rates. But the euro rate will not be reduced unless such a change also suits the other member countries. The country in difficulty will have to find other ways of increasing demand by becoming more competitive. Inevitably, therefore, EMU creates a greater degree of interdependence.

Point of view

A letter to the *Financial Times*, 17 June 1999

Sir, I was disappointed that your leader has a flawed piece of analysis in it. You say 'had Britain joined the euro-zone in January 1999, the weakness of the euro would, on balance, have helped the economy'. This is based on the proposition that an over-valued pound is not good for Britain, since it squeezes exports and damages manufacturing industry.

It is worth pointing out that if Britain had joined the euro-zone in January, short term interest rates would immediately have been reduced to 3% and probably later on to 2.5%... I would submit that the inflationary damage caused to the British economy by interest rates at such a low level would have far outweighed any benefit to the exchange rate.

Tim Melville-Ross, Institute of Directors

A personal view

❝ The Bank of England's Monetary Policy Committee is very well designed and it is conducting UK monetary policy in a competent way. Nevertheless, for a small economy like Britain, which is quite open to international trade in goods and services, and very open to international capital flows, the cost-benefit analysis of monetary union is simple. A national currency and an independent monetary policy are a costly way of expressing a preference for national sovereignty.

Opponents of monetary union point to the usefulness of exchange rate flexibility as a mechanism for adjusting to fundamental economic shocks. But even when foreign exchange markets have been working really efficiently, independent national monetary policies have been a source of divergence.

A floating exchange rate can create shocks and instability. When the pound rose in 1996 and 1997, it created an imbalance between manufacturing and those services which were internationally exposed, and the rest of the economy. An independent monetary policy could not help with this. Within EMU, monetary policy will maintain price stability and prevent crises; it will not make the business cycle worse.❞ (Willem Buiter, Monetary Policy Committee member)

Your agenda

1 The euro was worth 65p on the day the above views were published. What is it worth now (if the UK is still outside EMU when you read this)?

2 How has the EMU affected
   a the UK
   b the eurozone?

3 Some companies, for example Unilever, were unhappy that the UK did not join EMU from the start. They considered gradually relocating more of their activities in the eurozone. What impact has this view had?

4 When you read this the UK will be either inside or outside EMU. Whatever the decision to date, what do you think have been the costs and benefits?

5 Do these questions look silly? Explain your reasoning.

Making EMU work will not be easy. If it does work well, it will certainly make its members very much more interdependent. In time, the euro-zone will resemble a single economy.

In an integrated European economy it will be more important to ensure that the European Parliament works well. The 1999 election, though not well supported by the voters, did return to the Parliament many members who wanted to see its power enhanced. UK voters may be mistaken in thinking it is not relevant to them.

3 What does interdependence mean for the world?

Manchester United in China

The world's richest football club was on the move again. The club wants to build a global image. With fans all over the world, the commercial possibilities are enormous. In the past, people supported their local team. That is no longer true. Fans may come from anywhere in the world.

Satellite television has brought football to a much larger market. Old Trafford megastores will attract new members, operate football schools and provide 'Red Cafés' so people can watch games live all across Asia. The team will tour China every two years. Their only problem is counterfeit goods. Chinese producers have been selling replica versions for a while.

Your agenda

1 In what way is football part of the globalisation process?

2 Globalisation involves increased trade in goods and services. What are the other important elements in the process?

3 What are the benefits for Manchester United?

Growing interdependence is about trade, the activities of multi-national corporations and capital movements. It means that most countries are increasingly dependent on imports. Another way of saying this is that they become more open. The Manchester United case study simply illustrates how far the process has gone.

Multi-nationals have expanded their activities enormously in recent years. They contribute to the major shifts in the international division of labour which result from the growth of trade. These shifts create a need for major adjustments and these are easier for some countries to accommodate than for others.

Financial capital can move from one country to another very quickly: it is very mobile. There is much potential in this for destabilising both exchange rates and national economies. The reality of this became apparent during the Asian financial crisis, 1997–9. An important implication of these trends is that each country becomes vulnerable to changes in the economies of its trading partners. If China's economic growth had been stopped by the crisis, could the fans have afforded the tickets?

Growing interdependence creates a need for mechanisms for collaboration. So far, most of these are embodied in the international institutions.

International institutions

Ever since the Second World War, many governments have wanted to maintain international institutions which allow countries to collaborate in finding solutions to problems. Initially, the objective was to avoid anything like the worldwide slump of the 1930s.

By 1944 the Allied governments wanted to design a new international monetary system which would provide a stable framework for the future growth of prosperity. The interdependence of trading nations was recognised. It was clear that policies carried out in one country would have crucial effects on prices, and therefore on the allocation of resources, in other countries with open economies. So an institutional framework was needed that would deal with problems of adjustment both to trade surpluses and deficits and to capital movements. Interdependence meant that policies would have to be coordinated: governments could not function completely independently.

The eminent economist J. M. Keynes played a substantial part in designing the system. The objective was to establish rules to govern the movement of goods and services. The system was to have three vital components: the International Monetary Fund (IMF) would create an international payments mechanism; the International Bank for Reconstruction and Development (the World Bank) would provide funds for investment in countries needing finance for development; the World Trade Organisation would create rules governing trade. The last did not happen at first, but GATT performed some of the functions intended for it.

The international monetary system

The need for cooperation has never grown any less. Changing inflation rates, shifting trade patterns, and changes in oil prices and interest rates have combined to force numerous changes in the ways in which international trade and payments are organised.

Keynes once suggested that economists are at their most useful when producing humble technical services, rather than when they pontificate about policy. He said they should be the plumbers and maintenance staff of the world economy. It was the role he had in mind for the IMF.

The main concern of the IMF is to help maintain stability by lending to countries in crisis. Each member country contributes an amount to the Fund, set in proportion roughly to the value of its trade. This gives the IMF resources with which to help finance deficits. A loan from the IMF often restores confidence during a currency crisis, when holders of the currency are selling it fast, believing that its value is about to fall. Such loans therefore have a stabilising influence. Note the present tense: this aspect of the IMF's work has continued throughout its life.

The other important aspect of the IMF's work is surveillance. It continuously observes members' policies (both internal and external). It reports on events and comments on members' policies. This can affect governments' freedom of action and does not always make the IMF popular. But it has helped to make clear the need for collaboration in national policy-making.

Early on in its life, the IMF supervised a system of fixed exchange rates. This broke down in the early 1970s as the world shifted to a system of floating rates. At this point, it seemed that the IMF might be partially redundant. Indeed, its influence and centrality to the system have been reduced for developed countries. The Group of Seven (see below) and European Monetary Union both became important to the process of policy coordination. The IMF remains important for developing countries, as a source of funds and advice.

The foreign exchange markets do not always produce an exchange rate appropriate to long-run trade prospects, for at least three reasons: capital movements affect floating rates substantially; central banks manage them; and developing countries have in many cases retained fixed rates. As a result, many balance of payments deficits have developed and IMF loans have been made to tide countries over, and to restore confidence in their currencies. These help to prevent destabilising short-run lurches in currency values.

Conditionality has always been an established principle of IMF lending. The larger the loan, the tighter the conditions. The negotiation of conditions is an essentially political process and there is room for much variation of opinion about the outcome. Typically, IMF conditions will include restriction of public spending or borrowing, and of the growth of bank lending. It may also insist upon exchange rate devaluation. These kinds of conditions are unlikely to be popular with the electorate.

Essentials

Conditionality refers to the way in which the IMF requires countries to conform to its required policies before financial help is given during a crisis. It often requires cuts in interest rates and government spending which can be very damaging for developing countries.

Some governments have been glad of the IMF, because they can blame it for forcing them to adopt necessary but unpalatable policies. But many developing countries have argued that the conditions applied to them when they borrow are much more stringent than those applied to the developed countries. They point out that the policies are inappropriate to the special needs of developing countries. Many experts in the field support this view in whole or in part.

Other groupings

■ *The Group of Seven* (G7). Its members are Canada, France, Germany, Japan, Italy, the UK and the USA. Generally, Russia now joins in and it may be more commonly referred to as G8. Every six months, the Group of Seven meets to discuss matters of global importance. Sometimes the focus of discussion has been on economic matters, such as unemployment. Sometimes it is on security matters of a pressing nature. It is mentioned here because it can be used as a forum for the discussion of difficult economic issues. It draws together the most powerful economies. It may have a limited lifespan in its present form if fast-growing developing countries think they ought to be included.

■ **The OECD**. The Organisation for Economic Development and Cooperation is a group of developed countries, primarily concerned with economic research, but sometimes acting as a forum for discussion. It is sometimes used to coordinate aid payments or to give special help to developing countries in crisis.

■ **The United Nations**. The UN is an umbrella organisation with coordination responsibilities in many fields, including peace-keeping, health, education, telecommunications, weather forecasting and so on. The UN Development Programme (UNDP) has a particular economic function as it provides technical assistance to developing countries.

■ **The World Bank**. The International Bank for Reconstruction and Development. It isn't really a bank at all. It can raise money cheaply on western capital markets and lends it to developing countries which find access to capital difficult for some of the investment projects they want to undertake. Through the International Development Association (IDA), the World Bank gives aid (grants, not loans) to the poorest countries. It does much economic research and gives advice to developing country governments. The advice is not always popular.

■ **The Asian Development Bank**. The ADB and other regional development banks have similar objectives to those of the World Bank but operate on a smaller scale.

■ **NAFTA**. The North American Free Trade Area is a much looser grouping than the EU. However, it is emerging as a significant influence on the way businesses locate production within Canada, the USA and Mexico.

4 Can we collaborate on the environment?

Earth Summit, 1992, Rio de Janeiro

The United Nations Conference on Environment and Development (UNCAD) took place in Rio de Janeiro in 1992. It was planned to assess the state of the environment and to look at ways to conserve it for future generations. The main aim of the conference was to come to an agreement over the measures needed to ensure equitable, secure and sustainable development.

These were its five outcomes:

1 *The Climate Change Agreement* – this set voluntary targets for freezing carbon dioxide emissions at 1990 levels by 2000.

2 *The Bio-diversity Agreement* – this aimed to protect endangered species and to share the profits from global genetic resources more fairly.

3 *The Statement of Forest Principles* – this aimed to save the world's forests.

4 *The Rio Declaration* – this covered sustainable development and examined the principles which link economic growth to environmental issues.

5 *Agenda 21* – this was the blueprint for carrying out the Rio Declaration. It was aimed at achieving economic growth without destroying the environment for future generations.

Agenda 21 was an action plan for the environment and a major step forward for future discussion. The treaties on climate change and bio-diversity were signed by all the countries present and are legally binding agreements to implement changes to the way we treat our environment.

The object is to look after the world so that it can be passed on, intact, to the next generation. The Rio Declaration was a major step towards sustainable development. The countries present at the conference had pledged their support for the five initiatives and went away to try to convince the populations of their respective countries that they must also make a commitment.

Your agenda

1 Why is it important for the leaders of the various nations present at the summit to convince their populations that we need to act upon the agreements made?

2 What problems are there in convincing people?

The UK Budget, which followed the second Earth Summit in New York in 1997, was expected to be hard on the motorist. The government wanted to put environmental issues at the top of the agenda. Radical measures to reduce the level of carbon-dioxide emissions were discussed. The motoring organisations predicted a large increase in vehicle excise duty coupled with higher fuel duty.

These forecasts were welcomed by environmental groups who actually wanted to see excise duty linked to engine size so that the 'gas guzzling' cars would be punished more than the smaller, less damaging ones.

Company cars account for 10% of the UK car population but 20% of the total mileage covered. There were calls for the 18,000 miles a year threshold, which reduces the tax charged, to be abolished or lowered.

Environmentalists argued that many company car drivers undertake unnecessary journeys in order to qualify for the reduction in their tax bill.

The Transport Minister began the process of introducing urban congestion charges and taxes on parking in city centres in an effort to gain revenue to improve the public transport network.

Meantime, trouble developed. The UK government was afraid of being seen as 'anti-car'. Petrol taxes were already above levels prevailing in the rest of the EU, and well above those in the rest of the world. Petrol taxes hit consumers' pockets directly. Democratic governments were being very slow to discourage car use in any very serious way. The only country which tried hard was Singapore, which had an added incentive because it has not got room for all its cars anyway.

The failures of the Rio Earth Summit

'Environmentalist groups say that none of the five main agreements made in Rio have been fulfilled.

The Climate Change Agreement called for emissions from vehicle exhausts and industry to be frozen at 1990 levels by the year 2000. Britain and Germany appear to be set to achieve this target but most other G7 countries are likely to miss it. They argue that American emissions have actually increased by more than 13 per cent since 1995.

The Bio-diversity Agreement was introduced to protect endangered species but deforestation still wipes out three species every hour.

Since the agreement was made to save the world's forests an area equal to twice the size of Belgium has been deforested in the Amazon.

Agenda 21 set a target for overseas aid for sustainable

development of 0.7 per cent of GDP, equal to approximately £78 billion, the actual figure has fallen to 0.27 per cent, a massive reduction on the promised amount.'

Source: *The Electronic Telegraph*, June 1997

Your agenda

1 Why is it important that *all* the participants work together to achieve sustainable development?

2 The article above was written five years after the summit took place and it emphasises the failure of nations to keep to their agreements. Why would pressure groups concentrate on the negative aspects?

3 Contact an environmental pressure group and obtain its views on the progress since 1997. Present your findings to your group.

In June 1997 the second Earth Summit, held in New York, was convened to enable delegates to talk about the progress made since Rio. At this conference, officially known as the United Nations General Assembly Special Session (UNGASS), each of the 166 delegates gave a short speech about the initiatives already in place and the plans for the future. The speeches showed that nations were working in a variety of ways towards the achievement of sustainable development.

Governments were shown to have made improvements. They have set up councils for sustainable development, establishing protected areas, included environmental education in their school curricula and introduced legislation to protect endangered species.

Work in progress

Q 1 Why do environmentalists want excise duty linked to engine size?

2 Company car drivers would not be the only 'losers' if they were forced to pay more tax. Who else would be worse off following the predictions made in the article in the case study above?

3 What alternatives are available for the transport of goods around the UK? Explain why road haulage is the preferred option.

4 Why is progress so slow?

A global approach to the environment

It often happens that environmental problems cross national boundaries. Acid rain created in the UK falls on the Scandinavian forests. The hole in the ozone layer which has probably been created by developed countries generally is expected to cause increased incidence of cancer in Chile. This means that international collaboration on the environment is absolutely essential.

It would be pleasant to be able to report that negotiations are leading to swift action in a number of fields. Unfortunately, the process is slow and although it has at least been under way since the Rio Earth Summit, it would appear that many governments are not actually taking action in the way intended. There is progress, but it is certainly not fast enough to satisfy environmental pressure groups. It may not be fast enough to prevent some serious losses.

When the reality of environmental policies is confronted, vested interests object to the costs. This makes the necessary political agreement very hard to achieve. If all nations do not implement their policies together, then those that do face the possibility of losing competitiveness relative to those that do not.

There is some further discussion of environmental issues in Option 3, page 589.

Moving and stalling in the EU

About nine million cars reach the end of their lives in the EU each year and a quarter of them finish up in landfill sites. The result is contamination of the ground with hazardous substances. Recycling cars has become less profitable in recent years as more use is made of plastic and other non-recyclable materials and scrap steel prices remain low.

Just as the EU was about to implement an agreement on vehicle recycling, VW contacted German Chancellor Schroder and asked for a delay. It will now be 2003 before manufacturers can be required to take cars back at the end of their lives. The requirement to recycle or reuse 80 per cent of car weight starts in 2005. That proportion rises to 85 per cent in 2015. Car makers feel they are being punished. A EU official said, 'we are not trying to punish the manufacturers. In the long run we want all cars to have a positive value. If car makers know they will have to meet end-of-life costs they are more likely to change the design.'

International agreements are not easy to achieve. Pressure from businesses can make it even harder.

Your agenda

1 Enterprising businesses naturally oppose measures which threaten profits. What is the solution?

2 Should consumers be made to pay the costs of the pollution they create? How?

5 Is stability possible?

Learning from a crisis

The crisis began in Thailand in July 1997. It spread through east Asia, infecting Russia and then Brazil. It took just a few months for badly affected economies to go from strong growth to deep recession. Children dropped out of school, millions of people returned to a level of poverty they had only recently left. In Thailand and Indonesia alone the crisis may have pushed 25 million people back into poverty.

There was no easily identified single cause. What happened was that the affected countries were caught between difficulties with their liberalisation programmes and the ease with which international capital can move from one currency to another. When they discovered that many Asian banks had a backlog of bad loans, the international financiers pulled out. Figure O1.26 shows the impact.

The rich world slows...

G7 GDP growth forecasts

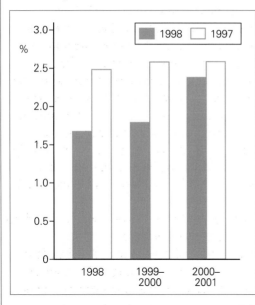

the poor fall back

World output growth (annual % change)

	1997	Forecast average 1998	1999	2000	2001–7
All developing countries	4.8	2.0	2.7	4.3	5.2
East Asia crisis countries*	4.5	–8.0	0.1	3.2	5.2
Transition countries of Europe and central Asia	1.7	0.4	–0.6	3.0	4.8
Developing countries (excluding transition countries)	5.3	2.5	3.2	4.5	5.2
Developing countries (excluding transition and east Asia**)	5.5	3.9	3.6	4.7	5.2

*Indonesia, South Korea, Malaysia, Philippines and Thailand
** East Asia crisis countries (excluding South Korea)

Source: World Bank

Figure O1.26 Expectations dashed

The then vice-president of the World Bank, Joe Stiglitz, suggested that many lessons had been learned. When it became clear that the rescue measures used by the World Bank and the IMF had not been entirely successful, he said that in future international institutions must be flexible and open-minded, tailoring the policies to suit individual country needs.

Your agenda

1 Some countries were very badly affected by the crisis. What were the indirect effects on the rest of the world?

2 During the crisis, in order to restore confidence, the IMF required afflicted countries to raise interest rates. What was the purpose of this? What effects would it have?

The Asian financial crisis was followed by a great burst of suggested measures to ensure that, in future, the international community handles problems in ways that keep them small. It may be possible to create greater stability in the future but doing so will require action on many fronts.

The banks

One very important area for development concerns banking regulations. All banks are supposedly supervised by their central banks, which impose regulations designed to ensure that they do not make too many loans, especially to dodgy borrowers. In practice, even the most experienced central banks have been known to make bad mistakes. The Bank of England made mistakes in its handling of the Barings merchant bank crisis, but it did not try to rescue the bank!

Many central banks have at times rescued banks which have a lot of loans to companies which cannot repay. They do this by lending banks money to tide them over the worst. Unfortunately, the effect of this is to make the banks more casual about the dodgy borrowers. If they get too casual, they will be threatened with collapse, confidence evaporates, people withdraw deposits, panic sets in and people sell the currency. The technical term for this is moral hazard.

The Bank for International Settlements (BIS) – the international bank which coordinates the activities of the central banks of the G7 countries and acts as a forum for discussion of banking issues – suggests a remedy. Closer supervision by central banks and a requirement for banks to have more liquid assets to balance very risky loans would together reduce the likelihood of banking problems.

The World Bank

As a major source of development finance, the World Bank is involved in rethinking approaches. Ideas which have been circulating include:

- better bankruptcy laws, which would provide ways for winding up failed businesses so that as much money as possible goes back to the creditors

- more willingness to help countries with excessive debt by arranging repayment standstills and equitable ways of sharing burdens

- better regulation of financial systems (much as suggested by BIS)

- particular attention to social protection, providing

benefits or insurance against unemployment and extreme poverty. Asian developing countries are beginning to put safety nets in place, but as yet they have not nearly solved the problem.

Work in progress

Q Difficult one, get your teacher to help. To what extent have the ideas mentioned so far been put into effect?

The UN Development Programme

The UN Development Programme (UNDP) is particularly concerned with the welfare of the least developed countries. Its 1999 *Human Development Report* advocated performance standards for multi-nationals, fair trade and environmental protection and ways of reducing the negative effects of globalisation for poorer countries. It called for a 'global forum' to bring together multi-nationals, trade unions, non-governmental organisations and governments to help create ethical codes of conduct. It sees the multi-national as too powerful and deplores the increase in inequality.

The outcome should be a system with rules which protect the poor. The Report says:

'The new rules of globalisation – and the players writing them – focus on integrating global markets, neglecting the needs of people that markets cannot reach. The process is concentrating power and marginalising the poor, both countries and people.'

The UNDP has an additional worry: it is that the information revolution is acting to create an information system which only the well-off and educated can access. Poor people will be left with only the more expensive means of communicating. This will create further disadvantages.

The IMF

The Fund defended its high interest rate policies, saying that they were necessary because the first priority was to restore confidence in the affected currencies. Like everyone else, though, it saw some lessons for the future. It suggested:

- more surveillance of government policies in good times as well as bad

- regional collaboration between neighbouring governments

- better banking supervision

- easier access to international capital markets

- strengthened international institutions.

Conclusions

Not everyone would agree with the IMF. Some people suggest abolishing it and the World Bank too. Some say that the private sector could do a better job at less cost. No one is suggesting abolishing the BIS, yet, and there is widespread agreement on the need for better banking supervision. Improved regulation would make confidence less fragile.

Unfortunately, policing the global economy is probably not enough to ensure stability even if well done.

A much greater effort to mobilise international help for those affected would be a step forward. Unfortunately, the miserable amounts of aid on offer (enquiry 1, page 381) do not promise much. Even the efforts to solve the debt problem look inadequate.

Some of the poorest countries get enmeshed in vicious wars which make matters much worse. It seems improbable that we shall be able to persuade those who go to war of the need to abandon nationalism. There are proposals to take a stronger line with corrupt governments. These may run into popularity problems.

Work in progress

Q Apathy is the worst outcome of all. Make two lists of changes since the above was written. Think of four things which have got better and four things which have got worse. Identify possible solutions and assess their realism. Ask yourself whether you can do anything about the problems; if so, which, and how? Take the long view.

Can there be certainty?

Opportunities or constraints?

Option 2 opens with an exploration of the way the business environment changes over time. Decision-takers need to be aware of current events and the way they may develop in the future. There are various strategies for ensuring that decisions are realistically based on trends and expectations. These trends themselves need careful consideration. The enquiry examines the uses of business, national and international data as well as the reactions of individuals and businesses.

1 What will the future bring?

Barbour and a chill wind

The Barbour jacket has had a long life. This heavy waterproof waxed garment had a timeless reputation as a practical and very durable jacket for countryside pursuits of many kinds. Then it became a fashion item. People who never left the city were just as likely to buy one. The company increased its range so that enthusiasts could have complete Barbour outfits.

Originally founded in 1894 to make oil skins, the company took off in 1974 when it obtained a royal warrant. Its heyday came in the 1980s. The real trouble started in 1996. Sales fell from £60.7 million in 1996 to £43.8 million in 1997. Exports fell by £12 million to £26 million. Profits were seriously reduced, from £11.6 million to £2.6 million in the year to August 1997. Two plants, in Newcastleton on the Scottish border and at Hebburn, South Tyneside, had to close with the loss of 83 jobs. Some workers were moved to another factory.

The managing director, Margaret Barbour, said in the Annual Report and Accounts that the cause of the problem was the strong pound. The company relies on exports and also sells to tourists visiting the UK. Other possible causes identified by the company included dry weather, early high street sales and the Asian financial crisis. 'At the end of the day, if it isn't raining, people might not buy raincoats,' said one of the directors.

It is hard to avoid drawing the conclusion that fashions changed too. The company expanded its range in 1998, saying 'it's not all doom and gloom. We have been developing our overseas markets, diversifying the brand and consolidating our workforce. Our commitment to manufacturing in Britain, while competitors make savings abroad, has had an effect'.

Your agenda

1 To what extent was Barbour dependent on overseas sales?

2 Explain how the high pound would have affected sales. Use a supply and demand diagram as part of your explanation.

3 How could Barbour protect itself from the problems associated with dry weather?

4 Were the problems predictable?

5 What information might have helped Barbour to avoid falling sales?

Businesses can experience serious changes in their sales and profits. What went wrong for Barbour? What information might have been helpful if the company had had access to it? The company was very clear about the causes of its problems, citing the exchange rate as the major factor. Figure O2.1 shows the changes in the sterling index from 1988 onwards.

Year	Index
1988	118.1
1989	114.7
1990	112.0
1991	113.0
1992	108.7
1993	99.7
1994	100.0
1995	95.1
1996	96.7
1997	112.7
1998	116.5

Source: *National Institute Economic Review*, May 1999

Figure O2.1 The exchange rate index (1994 = 100)

Market-orientated businesses keep in touch with their customers. They use focus groups and other ways of finding out what people actually want. Did Barbour do this? We cannot know, because the company's public statements did not recognise the possibility of its products having gone out of fashion.

Could the Asian financial crisis have been foreseen? It is likely that the main market in the Far East is Japan. Barbour jackets would feel a bit hot in Hong Kong, even in the winter. They certainly would not sell much in the Asian developing countries, where incomes tend to be low and temperatures high. Figure O2.2 shows how GDP changed in Japan. The financial crisis began in 1997. 1998 was a very difficult year. Quite a number of UK exporters faced a big drop in sales to Asian customers. Tentative assessments in mid-1999 suggested that by then the worst was over.

Year	GDP
1995	101.4
1996	106.6
1997	108.1
1998	105.0

Source: *National Institute Economic Review*, May 1999

Figure O2.2 GDP, Japan (1994 = 100)

Work in progress

Q 1 What conclusions can you draw as to the likely effect of the exchange rate changes on Barbour's profits in the year to August 1997? Keep in mind that the customer response to exchange rate changes can be lagged if overseas suppliers still have stocks which can be sold at the old price.

2 What effects might the Asian financial crisis have had on Barbour?

3 What is your overall conclusion as to the likely causes of Barbour's problems?

4 What kinds of remedial action might Barbour have taken?

Dealing with uncertainty

Some events are very difficult to predict. The Asian financial crisis would have been impossible for most businesses to predict. The sequence of events went like this:

● A number of banks got into difficulties because they had too many bad loans.

● People lost confidence and tried to withdraw their money. When the banks concerned found themselves with too few liquid reserves to meet all possible demands for withdrawals, the loss of confidence spread to the entire financial sectors of the countries concerned.

● Holders of currency started to sell, as they too lost confidence. The result was a sudden fall in several countries' exchange rates.

- As people became more nervous, there was a serious decrease in consumer spending.
- Trading conditions became very depressed for both local businesses and exporters elsewhere.

The business cycle is somewhat more predictable in most developed countries. Big businesses have forecasting departments which keep an eye on the trends and aim to predict changes in spending. Forecasting is difficult, but not impossible. Most businesses can hope to avoid expanding just when the economy is going into recession. This is particularly important for those products with a high income elasticity of demand.

Serious exporters concern themselves not only with the UK business cycle but also with trends in all their other markets. Exchange rate changes are very hard to foresee, but businesses can have contingency plans which help if change comes. For example, they do not have to raise prices in overseas markets when their own exchange rate rises. They have the option of keeping the foreign currency price the same and accepting a cut in profit margins. This may turn out to be less harmful than the fall in sales which results from a price increase.

Planning for the future

Planning involves more than simply being well informed about current trends in the economy. Businesses have to know and understand their markets. This is particularly true if their markets are subject to changes in fashion.

Much depends on the quality of forecasting. Analysis of current trends and their accurate projection into the future:

- reduces uncertainty
- increases confidence in decision-making.
- cuts the value of 'insurance premiums' necessary for reasonable security.

However, economic and business forecasting is generally difficult. The future frequently does not resemble the past; trends can shift their pathways unexpectedly; shocks of all sizes abound. This is a problem that affects small and large firms alike, albeit on a different scale. For the small firm the question may be: what are likely takings over the coming year? The large firm might ask: when will continental export markets recover from recession?

2 Which way forward?

Asian flu

Lanemark International makes gas burners. They are sold to a wide range of businesses in such diverse areas as food processing, petrochemicals and metal treatment. The company has thirty employees and an annual turnover of £2 million. Lanemark had always seen its Asian markets as being very important to the business. Its agents in Singapore, Malaysia, Thailand and South Korea accounted for 10 per cent of sales.

By summer 1998, John Spencer, the managing director, summed up the situation thus:
'There is clearly a slowing of demand. We are a capital equipment supplier and if that equipment does not have to be replaced, in the current situation, it won't be. Our Asian sales are down by a quarter, and those orders taken are at gross margins also about 25 per cent lower. Profitability on these sales is borderline. We are switching our efforts elsewhere – for example to mainland Europe, where prospects are good.'

The Harris Tweed industry gave similar reports. Ian Mackenzie, chairman of the Harris Tweed Authority, said: 'It's a bad situation. Japan in particular was important because, there, Harris Tweed was a high value garment. Our aim must be still to be there when this is over – I think we will.'

Your agenda

1 How would you expect falling demand in Asia in the period 1997–9 to affect UK companies?

2 How can businesses protect themselves from falling demand?

3 In general, why would the Asian market be important to some businesses?

Economies, and business prospects within them, are always subject to considerable uncertainties. In many ways these have become greater as time has gone by, because of the increasing importance of international trade. National economies have become steadily more interdependent as businesses have come to rely more and more on foreign markets.

Of course, businesses need to understand their markets. This does not only mean being market orientated – knowing the real needs and requirements of potential customers and responding to that knowledge. It also means understanding the economies in which they are operating. It means being able to foresee problems and plan for them, as much as possible. All this points to the importance of understanding the data which are available and knowing how to interpret them.

What happened in Asia?

Figure O2.3 shows how GDP in the selected countries was affected by the Asian financial crisis. (US and UK figures are shown for comparison.) Some countries managed to stay free of the contagion, but many experienced the sequence of loss of confidence, falling stock exchanges, flight of foreign investment, falling currency, bankruptcies, reduced expenditure, reduced incomes and falling industrial output.

Percentage GDP growth, Average		
	1990–97	1997	1998
China	11.9	7.2	8.3
Hong Kong	5.3	−2.0	−3.4
India	5.9	4.3	5.0
Indonesia	7.5	−6.2	−10.3
Malaysia	8.7	−1.8	−1.3
Philippines	3.3	1.7	1.2
Singapore	8.5	5.6	1.2
South Korea	7.2	−3.8	4.6
Thailand	7.5	−0.4	−8.0
Japan	1.4	−3.7	0.1
UK	1.9	3.0	0.6
US	2.5	3.9	4.0

Source: World Bank, *World Development Report*; *The Economist*, 18 July 1998 and 3 July 1999.

Figure O2.3 Percentage GDP growth, Asian countries

When it comes to trying to unravel the causes of the crisis, there are varying reasons in each country concerned. Very roughly, it is possible to discern common threads in the sequence of events. But a summary such as the following is a very great simplification and should be read as such. What is clear is that information, or lack of it, was at the heart of the problems. Here are some of the contributing factors:

● Spectacular growth rates in many Asian countries had given many governments a sense that the Asian approach to business was working well. The Asian approach places great faith in personal relationships and the establishment of trust between business partners. Unfortunately, this had not stopped many Asian banks from making large loans to companies which did not have good long-term prospects of profitability. Eventually, these loans became bad debts. The bad debts mounted up, and began to threaten some of the banks with insolvency crises, i.e. not enough liquid assets to meet their own liabilities.

● Once this became apparent, some people in Asian countries grew nervous and tried to withdraw their bank deposits. Businesses all over the world which had invested in Asian countries became nervous too. A crisis of confidence developed. The flow of capital from western countries into Asian countries began to dry up. Many holders of Asian currencies sold, as did shareholders in Asian businesses. The loss of confidence spread all over the world.

● With a wave of selling on the stock exchanges and the foreign currency exchanges, share prices and exchange rates dropped very sharply indeed. The losses forced some businesses in the financial markets to close immediately. The loss of finance for business caused bankruptcies of all kinds and the resulting cuts in spending reduced demand for all sorts of goods and services. Businesses generally were faced with falling demand and profits. In some countries, especially Indonesia and Thailand, ordinary people were badly affected. Political problems developed in Indonesia.

Work in progress

Q 1 Which countries were badly hit by the Asian financial crisis?

2 How does falling demand affect businesses?

3 Why is confidence in the financial system so important?

4 What effect did the crisis have on countries outside Asia?

What are the lessons?

Businesses everywhere need to be prepared to face change. The world is unpredictable and a certain amount of caution is required. From the point of view of western businesses with export markets in Asia, it may be appropriate to aim for a diversified market. Lanemark International turned to Europe. The Harris Tweed Association looked for ways of weathering the storm so as to be ready when improvement came. In general, the crisis underlines the need to have the best understanding possible of world events so that decision-taking can be informed and sensitive to reality.

Many UK exporters experienced sharp falls in their export sales to the affected Asian economies. This was just the beginning, a result of falling spending at the time. But because so many Asian countries experienced falling exchange rates, they became significantly more competitive. At the time of writing, the impact of this is still largely to come.

Could the Asian crisis have been foreseen? Some people knew that the banks were overlending. Michel Camdessus, managing director of the International Monetary Fund (IMF), visited Thailand four times before the crisis broke, but the Thai government had political problems and ignored his advice. When it came to South Korea, the IMF knew that the banks there had concealed their rather low levels of liquidity. The IMF has tried to get Asian governments to impose tighter controls on their banking systems, and to require the disclosure of more accurate information.

Underlying the stories of individual businesses and countries lie two important factors. Governments need to be careful to control the growth of their banking systems and ensure that banks abide by rules to ensure prudent lending. International capital markets are very volatile: loss of confidence can lead to large-scale capital movements which are very destabilising. The way international organisations are working to promote stability is examined in more detail at the end of Option 1.

Although some people knew that there were problems in Asia, they could not know in advance if or when a crisis might develop. Many economic problems are solved before they acquire critical dimensions. For both businesses and governments, the trick is to know what the problems might be and devise strategies which accommodate a range of possibilities.

Work in progress

Q Find data on growth rates in Asia since 1998. To what extent have the affected economies recovered? Has the situation been further destabilised by unforeseen events? How have UK exporters responded to recent developments?

Forecasting the future

The Asian financial crisis could not have been predicted by businesses generally. The ups and downs of the business cycle are a different matter. Usually, there are signs that change is coming. A careful reading of the available data may allow managers to plan for the future.

Accurate forecasts are very valuable. Organisations forecast such variables as sales, expenses and cash flow. Governments forecast changes in the economic variables that shape its taxation and spending decisions. Forecasting the behaviour of a system as large and interactive as the UK economy is extremely complex.

First, a model must be constructed to represent the system and its behaviour. Countless millions of decisions by organisations and individuals have to be condensed into key generalisations and take the form of mathematical equations. For example, suppose that evidence shows that an x per cent change in the rate of interest leads to a corresponding $0.25\,x$ per cent change in the level of consumer spending in the first month and an $0.5\,x$ per cent change after one year, *other things being equal*. But does the relationship vary with the original rate of interest? Is the outcome affected by the rate of inflation? How is the link affected by the climate of economic expectations?

Having designed a model of best fit, the most accurate and up-to-date data can be entered. Government data come mainly from the Office for National Statistics (ONS). Although carefully collected and analysed, it is subject to significant error, especially for the most recent time periods. Next, a whole range of assumptions must be made and entered into the model. This involves political as well as economic forecasting and is subject not only to margins of error but to the impact of shocks. No model will predict the impact of wars or financial crises. Finally, the raw predictive data produced by a model may be adjusted for the forecaster's own judgement of novel or one-off factors.

Economic forecasts have grown quickly in sophistication and number since the 1960s. Today they are produced by government, research institutions, universities and business schools using increasingly refined computer programs. The best known is the Treasury model which is the government's own source of forecasts.

Which indicators help?

Information needs to be appropriate to the use for which it is required. Businesses need a variety of **time series**. They require economic growth data for the countries in which they sell. They also need their own sales data. The link between the two will be much closer if the product has a high income elasticity of demand.

Essentials

Time series provide short- and long-term data which allow us to analyse trends over a period.

Many businesses want to know where they are in relation to the business cycle. This can help them to avoid making mistakes in the timing of their expansion plans. They will not want to invest at a time when accelerating inflation makes it likely that interest rates will be raised as a matter of policy. Figure M3.48 on page 233 shows economic growth rates in the UK. Using this information, managers can work out which

phase of the business cycle they are in. If they have experience of past phases of the cycle they will know how to interpret current figures.

With some understanding of the phases of the cycle, managers may be able to make good use of **leading indicators**. Some of these are shown in Figure O2.4. Leading indicators are selected because they provide advance warning of possible changes.

Essentials

Leading indicators are variables which are known to give good indications of later changes. They are known to precede future events by a predictable time period.

Year	Investment in plant and machinery	Export optimism	Skilled labour
1995	+17	+21	10
1996	+12	+11	11
1997	+2	−28	13
1998	−21	−50	8

Source: *National Institute Economic Review*, May 1999

Figure O2.4 CBI Industrial Trends survey

The figures for plant and machinery in Figure O2.4 show the difference between the percentage of respondents expecting to increase investment over the next year and those expecting to decrease investment. Similarly, the export figures give the difference between those expecting to export more and those less. For skilled labour, the figures give the percentage of respondents expecting shortages of skilled labour to be a problem.

Work in progress

Q 1 What signs can be detected in Figure O2.4 of the impact of the Asian financial crisis on UK business?

2 What changes in UK GDP would you expect to find accompanying the data?

3 Would there be time lags in the response to changes? How long might they be?

Trend analysis

Sometimes what businesses really need to know is not how much fluctuation there has been, but what the long-term trend is. Figure M3.48 on page 233 showed both the annual growth rate for UK GDP and the long-term trend rate of growth. This tells us that the economy can reasonably be expected on average to grow at a little more than 2 per cent per year. This growth reflects the long run growth of productivity as investment in capital increases productive capacity, and the benefits of improved technologies and business organisation.

In business, the long-term trend in sales turnover can help to show what can be expected. However, it is frequently difficult to decide which changes are temporary and which are part of the long-run trend. One way to get around this is to use **moving averages**. This technique 'smooths out' the peaks and troughs in the data and enables us to see the underlying trend. It takes the data from a number of consecutive time periods and plots the average. For example, the average from time periods 1, 2 and 3 is plotted, then the next number that is plotted is the average from time periods 2, 3 and 4. This would give a three-year moving average. By continually adding the newest piece of data and removing the oldest piece of data, a new line develops showing the trend.

Five-year moving averages can also be useful if we want to smooth out the fluctuations further. The same method can be used to smooth out seasonal fluctuations if needed.

Essentials

A **moving average** removes the sharp fluctuations from the data, giving a picture of the underlying trend.

Work in progress

Bookings at Picton's Country House Hotel varied strongly over the course of the business cycle because it is one thing which people can cut back on if incomes are falling. On the other hand, better-off customers have mostly been doing well for the past decade or so, and the hotel could expand if the growth of bookings could be relied upon.

Q 1 Use the data to construct a three-year moving average for the years 1988–98.

1988	**1989**	**1990**	**1991**	**1992**	**1993**
18 250	17 600	15 300	15 200	16 100	17 600

1994	**1995**	**1996**	**1997**	**1998**
18 900	20 400	21 600	21 100	21 200

2 Would a five-year moving average be more appropriate?

3 On what rate of growth can the hotel rely in the long run?

What the data will not tell us

Making sense of the data means bringing an informed mind to bear on it. Without an understanding of the way businesses and economies work, the data will be meaningless. In particular, misinterpretation is likely unless the time lags are understood. Chancellors of the Exchequer have always complained that economic policy for the future had to be based on information about the past. In between the past and the future everything can change as unforeseen events occur.

Shocks of one sort and another do create difficulties. Political changes can be very important. The reunification of Germany in 1989 affected the whole EU for years afterwards, in ways which were not at first well understood. More subtle changes are not at first recognised as such but can have a major long-term impact. Changes in demand affect individual businesses dramatically and often have knock-on effects elsewhere. Data must be interpreted carefully in the light of events and with a full understanding of the relationships involved.

3 The bigger picture

Predicting the impact

For many years, up to 1999, travellers were able to buy duty-free alcohol, tobacco, perfumes and luxury goods when travelling from one EU country to another. They still can get them if they travel outside the EU. In 1991 the European Commission decided that duty-free sales were contrary to the spirit of the Single Market. They gave an unfair competitive advantage to organisations which could provide duty-free goods. They increased the cost of goods to people who did not travel. All member countries agreed that duty-free in the EU must go.

The ferries, airlines and airports were dismayed, not to mention the transport trade unions. All they could see was lost jobs. A whole industry had grown up on the back of the concession. Between 1991 and 1998 European duty-free sales grew from £2.4 billion to nearly £4 billion. In Britain it was said that 30 000 jobs were at risk. The tobacco companies and retailers joined forces with the transport industry to fight the decision by setting up the European Travel Research Foundation. This was to provide figures to back up the campaign against the change. It argued that ferry companies and ports would have to shed 10 800 jobs. Knock-on effects in other parts of the tourist industry were expected to take a further 20 000 jobs; 700 of these job losses were expected in Scotland as the effects took their toll on the Scotch whisky industry.

In contrast, the European Commission estimated that 50 000 jobs would be lost across the whole of Europe. It argued that duty-free sales amounted to a £1.4 billion annual subsidy to parts of the transport industry. In 1999 duty-free within the EU was duly abolished.

Your agenda

1 If you smoked but could not get your cigarettes at duty-free prices any more how do you think you would react? Would you give up smoking? If so what would you spend the money on instead?

2 How did duty-free sales affect tax revenues?

3 Explain who were the gainers and who were the losers in the abolition of duty free in Europe.

Change means trouble for someone, but exactly how much trouble? Data are always needed to build understanding and arguments, but some data present problems:

● Data may be uncontroversial and cause no problems.

● Data may not be very accurate or helpful.

● Some data have actually been manipulated to suit the user's objectives.

● Some data series are much better than others at giving a clear picture of what is going on.

In this section we look at a selection of data series and comment on the background. The real lesson to be learnt is that all data need informed judgement and great care in the interpretation.

An important factor in evaluating data is the reliability of the source. It is easy to see why the data relating to duty-free sales differed between sources. Vested interests were involved. The data suggesting large-scale job losses is probably fairly accurate regarding the job losses in the transport sector: after all, those duty-free sales really did stop and the sales assistants were no longer needed. But the data probably overlooked the fact that people who had been spending in duty-free outlets would take their money and spend it elsewhere. Depending on how they spent it, it would create other jobs. Of course, the new jobs might not be suitable for the people who had lost their old jobs.

There are a number of objective reasons why data can be misleading. However, it is important not to reject the evidence of the data simply because it needs careful interpretation. Most data are better than nothing and when more than one source is available, an accurate picture is likely to emerge from a comparison.

What data are available?

The collection of data has become increasingly important to many kinds of organisation. Information is often available from more than one source. Data from international sources have been based on national data which are adjusted so that the figures are broadly comparable across the range of economies. This is particularly important for unemployment data, because different governments use different definitions of unemployment.

Even in developed countries with very good data collection services, data can be unreliable at times. The UK statistical service, the ONS, had to admit in 1998 that its average earnings data were out of line with reality. The reasons were complex and technical – there was no intention deliberately to mislead. However, monetary policy had been based for some months on the faulty figures and it was clear that improvements in data collection were needed urgently.

Data from developing countries

In developing countries it is much harder to collect good data because accounting systems are less well organised. In studying development issues the data are often a guide, which should be considered alongside qualitative information in order to build a clearer picture.

Did you notice that in Figure O2.3 (page 452) the Chinese economy had grown spectacularly and was virtually unaffected by the Asian financial crisis? Everyone agrees that China has grown fast, but some specialists think the economy may not have grown quite so much as the figures suggest. The communist government is still able to control flows of information to some extent and it is quite likely that growth rates have actually been rather lower than the official figures suggest.

OECD data

The Organisation for Economic Cooperation and Development (OECD) is the international organisation which includes most developed countries. It undertakes detailed adjustments to unemployment data because many governments, including the UK, particularly in the 1980s, have at times 'massaged' their unemployment data to make them look better than they really are. One of the best places to look for accurate trends in unemployment is the OECD web site. Figure O2.5 shows how the USA and Japan compare with Europe for both unemployment and job creation.

	1996	1997	1998
USA	5.4	4.9	4.5
Japan	3.4	3.4	4.1
EU15	10.8	10.7	10.0
France	12.4	12.3	11.7
Germany	8.9	9.9	9.4
Italy	12.0	12.1	12.3
UK	8.2	7.0	6.3

Source: OECD, http://www.oecds.org/news_and_events

Figure O2.5 Standardised unemployment rates

EU data

You can see at once that country comparisons within the EU will be vital in the making of EU policies. The member countries actually have widely differing economies and needs and the impact of policy is correspondingly varied. Businesses use EU data to inform their strategic planning. Much EU data comes from Eurostat, which offers a good web site, and Eurostat data are available in public libraries.

Figure O2.6 shows the relative importance of employment in the primary, secondary and tertiary sectors for all EU member countries. Comparison with data for the most recent year you can find will show how change continues.

	Agriculture % of employment	Industry % of employment	Services % of employment	GDP % of EU
Austria	6.9	35.4	57.7	112
Belgium	2.9	28.9	68.2	113
Denmark	5.0	26.4	68.1	112
Finland	8.6	26.3	65.1	91
France	5.2	26.8	67.9	110
Germany	3.3	37.0	59.7	108
Greece	20.8	23.6	55.6	63
Ireland	13.1	27.1	59.7	81
Italy	7.7	32.1	30.2	102
Luxembourg	3.1	26.8	69.5	160
Netherlands	3.9	22.8	71.1	103
Portugal	11.8	32.5	55.8	69
Spain	9.9	20.1	60.0	78
Sweden	3.4	25.0	71.6	98
UK	2.1	27.6	69.7	99

Source: ONS, Regional Trends, 1996

Figure O2.6 EU employment by sector

Work in progress

Q 1 Using Figure O2.6, which countries have the largest service sectors? What does this tell you about them?

2 In which countries might a seller of luxury items be most likely to locate a sales outlet? What other information would you need to help with this decision?

3 Which countries are likely to benefit most from the Common Agricultural Policy?

4 What would you expect to happen to the GDP figures once the single market has been in operation for some time?

Work in progress

Q 1 Give as many reasons as you can for the ranking of trading nations in Figure O2.7.

2 Which are the countries where trade has increased the fastest?

3 In 1997 the above nations together accounted for 77 per cent of all world trade. How has trade affected standards of living for these countries?

4 The US share of world imports in 1997 was 17.2 per cent. How could this be? What implications does this have for exporters in other countries?

World Trade Organisation data

The WTO publishes details of imports and exports for all member countries. Figure O2.7 shows the figures for the world's leading 15 exporters/importers. Exports generate foreign exchange which is used to pay for imports. Although exports and imports do not usually balance in any one year for any one country, overall, the big exporters are also the big importers.

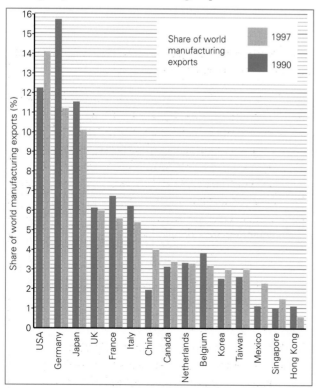

Figure O2.7 Leading exporters of manufactures

Source: World Trade Organisation, *Annual Report*, 1998

Demographic data

Demographic data are currently being used to predict a major need for additional homes in the UK. It isn't just population growth although there is still some of that especially in south-eastern England. It is the fact that people are living for longer on their own, rather than going into rest homes or living with sons and daughters as they grow older. Then, there are more divorced and single people generally living in one-person households. Fewer young people stay in their parents' homes. All of these factors lead to increased demands for small housing units in particular areas.

Figures O2.8 and O2.9 give the flavour of some of the trends which contribute. For some businesses, demographic trends can be an important indicator of potential markets. In particular, the age structure of the population may affect different segments of the market.

Year	% Under 16	16–24	25–34	35–44	45–54	55–64	65–74	75/over	All ages (millions)
1991	20	13	16	14	11	10	9	7	57.8
2001	20	11	14	15	13	10	8	7	59.6
2011	18	12	12	14	15	12	9	8	60.9
2021	18	11	13	12	13	14	11	9	62.2

Source: ONS, *Social Trends*, 1999

Figure O2.8 Percentage of Population by age, UK

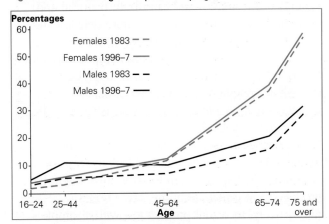

Figure O2.9 Percentage of people living alone 1983 and 1996–7, UK

Source: ONS, *Social Trends*, 1999

Work in progress

Q 1 What types of businesses are likely to be interested in demographic data? Evaluate their likely importance to them.

2 What planning issues arise from projections into the future?

3 What sorts of changes might make the projections invalid?

4 What will people buy?

Finding a product to fit the future

People at Kellogg's, the breakfast cereal manufacturer, are very proud of the fact that they do not make any products which are not sold under the firm's own brand name. They have consistently resisted the temptation to make cereals for supermarkets to sell as 'own-label' products. Because they have chosen this approach, the firm is constantly seeking ways of protecting its substantial market share against the threat posed by supermarket own brands. One problem Kellogg's faces is how easily cornflakes can be copied by other manufacturers.

In an attempt to strengthen its position relative to competitors Kellogg's developed a new marketing initiative. The 'big box' promotion simply meant making packages much larger than the usual size offered to customers. The bargain value was intended to tempt customers into purchasing more cereal than was usually their habit. This would allow Kellogg's to maintain production and utilise its machinery fully, maximising productive efficiency. In turn, the result would be low costs of production, allowing the firm to keep its prices competitive in comparison to those of supermarket 'own-brand' products.

Did the 'big box' promotion work? Surely, no one could lose out? The customer got improved value for money, while Kellogg's maintained its competitive position. Sadly, it wasn't that simple. Customers didn't like the larger packaging because they could not fit it between the shelves in their kitchen cupboards. It was an inconvenience to them because they had to change their normal habits. Soon it became clear that sales targets would not be met and the campaign was doomed to failure.

Your agenda

1 Could Kellogg's have anticipated the failure of the 'big box' campaign?

2 Why did it happen?

3 What information would have helped the firm to avoid the disappointment of devising a promotional campaign that failed to meet its targets?

Market-orientated businesses need detailed knowledge of their potential customers and the nature of their wants. The gathering, processing and interpretation of this information – market research – has become a major industry as specialist firms exploit the growing power of information technology.

To be effective, the collection of data needs a systematic and scientific approach. The first need is to clarify and define the goal of research. There is a real danger that managers will misinterpret a problem and then pursue irrelevant lines of research. For example, disappointing sales of a powdered hot drink might prompt research into the recipe and taste when the real problem is the packaging and the unfortunate psychological impact of its colour.

Research itself can be of several types:

- *Exploratory* research is open-ended, aiming to improve understanding of the market. It may clarify future research needs and generate hypotheses for testing. For example, a greetings card manufacturer might be considering the possibility of new designs suitable to be received by boys and men.

- More common is *descriptive* research that collects information to assist in decision-making. The card manufacturer may wish to know more about the age, sex and educational background of customers purchasing at newsagents.

- By contrast, *causal* research actually tests hypotheses and aims to identify specific relationships. Perhaps the need is not for cards that appeal directly to men but for those that appeal to the women who buy cards *for* men?

All market research and internal information systems use resources and carry both financial and opportunity costs. Generally, the more detailed and accurate the data required, the higher the costs. For each research need the firm must attempt to optimise the trade-off between accuracy and cost. There is also the risk of generating an overload of data such that managers feel unable to extract what is valuable from the material collected.

In Kellogg's case, it would seem that market research surveys which targeted loyal and regular customers, perhaps through focus groups, might have produced a warning about the larger boxes. Alternatively, an actual product test with a sample group might have revealed consumer resistance.

Sometimes a marketing problem is linked to much wider problems involving every aspect of the activities of the business.

Marketing or strategic planning

The future is all in the name

Marks & Spencer is a household name. The profits the business could command by selling its wide range of quality products such as clothing and food stuffs were the envy of other major high street retailers. The business seemed to be able to differentiate its products in the eyes of customers, while at the same time producing sufficient volume to drive costs of production down. Premium prices and low costs are a sure way of achieving long-term financial success.

Then, in early 1999, disaster struck. The business faced a 50 per cent slump in profits. What was going wrong? It seems that Marks & Spencer may have grown a little complacent about the strength of the firm's own-brand St Michael. It had long been the strategy of the business to employ top designers such as the knitwear specialist Julian McDonald, but in contrast to its competitors the business preferred to maintain the St Michael name rather than developing designer labels.

Slowly, the market place for mass-produced fashions was evolving in a different direction than the one mapped out in the minds of Marks & Spencer's managers. Debenhams introduced a designer range by Jasper Conran, while Top Shop launched styles developed by Hussein Chalayn. Dorothy Perkins responded by signing up Clements Ribeiro, and Principles fought back with Amanda Wakeley. The high street fashion war was hotting up as the battle to capture the big name designers became increasingly fierce, but Marks & Spencer was nowhere to be seen.

Increasingly the St Michael brand name seemed rather traditional and unimaginative to the shop's usual customers.

Reluctantly, in March 1999 the newly appointed chief executive Peter Salsbury was forced to make 31 of the senior managers at Marks & Spencer redundant. At the same time he launched a formal strategic review of the decision to stick with the St Michael brand. It was clearly time for a major shake-up in the firm's thinking if it was to continue to be the dominant force in high street retailing that it had been in the past.

Your agenda

1 Could the senior managers of Marks & Spencer have anticipated the changes in the high street fashion market?

2 Why did they maintain such a strong belief in the St Michael brand despite the growing evidence that it was no longer the asset it had once been?

3 What should Peter Salsbury encourage his managers to do at this point? Would it be a good idea to launch designer labels or is it too late?

4 What kind of information would help Marks & Spencer to make this decision?

5 What has happened to Marks & Spencer since 1999?

Marks & Spencer's strategy following this disaster involved much more than just marketing. The company developed a sense that the outgoing chairman, Sir Richard Greenbury, had been autocratic in his management style. This discouraged local managers from being fully responsible for their own stores. However, the early warnings which might have prevented the slump in profits could have come from accurate and penetrating assessments of customers' current preferences.

The point is that a tried and tested formula can suddenly look tired and unimaginative. This can be of particular importance in the fashion business. We have already seen that businesses can use either cost leadership or differentiation as a winning strategy to give competitive advantage. Marks & Spencer eventually drifted into a position where it was not the cheapest, neither was it clearly differentiated. The outcome could be a classic story of how a new strategy is implemented.

A different problem

A product under fire

British American Tobacco (BAT) has been making and selling cigarettes for a long time. When the health risks of smoking began to become really clear, the tobacco industry's first response was to deny the problem. Eventually, that became more difficult. Governments began to tax tobacco more heavily and to ban advertising in some media. The companies were made to put health warnings on both packs and adverts. BAT, like many other tobacco companies, at first responded by diversifying into other markets. Then it changed tack. Perhaps searching for focus, it divested itself of all its non-tobacco activities and concentrated on expanding markets overseas.

Many developing countries are still increasing their tobacco consumption. Their markets are attractive to the western tobacco companies which can take market share from local businesses producing rougher brands. BAT can increase sales because its products have a distinct and attractive image supported by extensive worldwide advertising.

Your agenda

1 In what ways do the tobacco companies differentiate their products?

2 Why would the developing countries of the Far East provide lucrative markets for BAT?

3 What kinds of strategies might be needed for exploiting these markets?

One of the most famous writers on business strategies was Igor Ansoff. His path-breaking book, *Corporate Strategy*, was published in 1965. He argues that a firm must clearly identify the direction of its strategic development. This is shown simply in Figure O2.10.

● *'Market penetration'* relates to the firm's intended market share: this is often intended for expansion but it may also be appropriate to consolidate or even to withdraw from a market. Sometimes the firm recognises a disproportionate cost in increasing market share or realises that its competitive advantage is exhausted. The basic strategy is to continue selling existing products in existing markets, but to do it more effectively.

● *'Market development'* means that the firm retains its current products but attempts to find new uses and customers for them. This might imply entering a neighbouring market segment or a new geographical territory, say through exports.

● *'Product development'* involves remaining within existing markets and achieving growth through a steady stream of modified or new products.

● *'Diversification'* means that the firm is developing through both new markets and new products. This may be *related* diversification, where the firm moves into markets and products that are in some sense an extension of its existing activities. Alternatively, it may be *unrelated* where the markets and products are entirely new and the only link is the managerial skills or the potential for financial synergy.

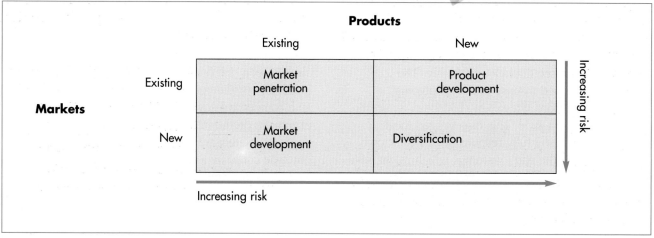

Figure O2.10 Ansoff's matrix

The whole point of this approach is to match the strengths of the business to the nature of the competition which it faces. The key features of its competitive advantage are identified, and then developed in the most effective way possible. The low-risk strategy is to stay with the existing product in the existing market. However, this may also be a strategy for low returns – it certainly seems to have been for Marks & Spencer in the late 1990s. The high-risk strategy is to diversify in both products and markets. One way to limit the risk is to test market a new product in one region before launching it nationally or internationally. Chocolate companies do this, among others: Yorkie was a classic case.

Of course, some companies can and do stay in the low-risk area, aiming for market penetration with an existing product in an existing market. Obviously, attention has to be given to cost and price with this strategy, as well as to the overall marketing plan.

Work in progress

Q1 Show how the strategy employed by BAT relates to the options identified by Ansoff.

2 Go back to the Barbour case study at the beginning of the enquiry. Use Ansoff's approach to identify a possible strategy for the company, explaining why it will work.

Just doing things better, maybe

Marketing the future

In 1995 Heinz made a key decision. The famous manufacturer of food products such as baked beans and ketchup was finding the £15 million cost of financing the TV advertising for its growing product range increasingly difficult. It decided to depart from the existing marketing strategy and abandon both corporate and product advertising.

'Heinz at Home' was conceived as the answer to the problem. A magazine would be delivered free to the four million homes of families identified as loyal Heinz customers. Each feature in the magazine was to be targeted specifically at encouraging the purchase of a particular Heinz product. This included special-offer gifts and money-off coupons with a unique bar code so that if the customer used it Heinz would know exactly what products that customer was interested in.

Heinz believed it could establish two-way communication with its loyal customers. It would no longer need to spend large sums on developing TV advertising without a clear understanding of its impact on the customer base. Instead it would be able to speak directly to individual families about the products it knew interested them, while at the same time receiving vital feedback about the way people felt about the goods they had bought.

The new marketing strategy was a big risk. Did it work? Heinz said nothing but by 1998 it was again investing heavily in TV promotion. A large-scale series of advertisements was launched, based around the theme of returning home to enjoy the benefits of a supportive, friendly, home atmosphere in which Heinz's familiar products played the key role.

Could Heinz have anticipated the impact of its direct marketing campaign? Some critics suggested that in a mass consumption good market like baked beans, direct customer contacts could never be cost effective. Others suggested that the reduction of TV advertising could have led to the Heinz brand name losing its prominent position in the minds of consumers.

Your agenda

1 Explain the logic underlying Heinz's strategy.

2 Why was the strategy a big risk?

3 Why did the company return to advertising?

4 Suggest an alternative strategy which might help the company to compete at lower cost.

5 Are expectations changing?

What happens next?

Think about it. If you expect share prices to rise on the Stock Exchange, what do you do? You buy, of course, and the increase in demand for shares from all the people who are thinking like you do makes the price rise. A self-fulfilling prophecy, this is called. That's in a bull market. Supposing confidence is tumbling, the way it did in the Asian financial crisis, and people are starting to sell. Prices are falling. What do you do? Sell, of course. Prices fall further. This is a bear market and it can happen any time if share prices get out of line with the fundamental profitability of the companies concerned.

Now, if you expect the prices of the goods and services you buy as a consumer to go up, what do you do? You might rush out and buy now before it happens, but this is awkward if it applies to everything. It might be better to try to get a pay rise which will cover the cost of whatever you expect the inflation rate to be. But what will you do if your employer says there is no money in the kitty?

Your agenda

1 What expectations do you have about your own future? What assumptions are you making about the way things will be?

2 Are there any possible changes which might cause your expectations to have to be adjusted?

3 Are you prepared for possible changes? How would your decisions change if the underlying expectations were disturbed in some way?

Expectations play an important role in many aspects of economic and business life. Our expectations influence the way we behave. Theories about expectations influence policy-makers and decision-takers in business. It is important to understand the different ways in which expectations may influence people's behaviour. Unexpected changes create unpredictable situations, but normally most people's expectations are formed in a predictable way. Decision-takers rely on the predictability of expectations to give them a reliable basis for future action.

First, we look at the way expectations of likely future profit affect business decisions to expand. Then we turn to the way expectations can affect the process by which inflation is controlled. Lastly, we consider how consumers' expectations can change in ways which make marketing decisions rather difficult.

Time to invest?

Businesses invest when they have reliable expectations of making a profit. A fall in demand for the product can make them backtrack. So can a rise in interest rates. Unfortunately, these sorts of events generally hit quite a wide range of businesses at the same time. Once a few companies have cut back their investments, prospects for other companies look less good. First their supplier companies have to follow suit. Then some employees will probably be made redundant and they will experience falling incomes. This will lead into falling demand for consumer goods generally – or with luck, maybe just demand growing more slowly.

This sort of malaise is catching. Gloomy expectations can spread fast. The point of contact with reality is often seen early on in share prices. Expectations of falling profits make some people sell shares, share prices then fall, and that enhances the gloomy expectations.

There are various measures of business confidence. The Confederation of British Industry (CBI) in its Industrial Trends Survey collects data on the number of businesses which have become more optimistic over the past four months, and the number of those which have become less optimistic. The difference between the two is shown in Figure O2.11. It is clear that the threat of recession was building fast in 1998. Although growth slowed that year, by mid-1999 optimism was returning, so it was a short-lived recession. Still, it generated a lot of gloom.

October 1995	−11
April 1996	−3
October 1996	+8
April 1997	+4
October 1997	+2
April 1998	−22
October 1998	−58
April 1999	−6
October 1999	+13

Figure O2.11 Business optimism?

Source: *National Institute Economic Review*, May 1999

It is hard not to conclude that gloomy expectations on their own can depress a whole economy. If those expectations are based on a realistic assessment, they may be healthy in that they prevent businesses from taking decisions they may later regret. If they become exaggerated, they may do real damage.

Expectations and monetary policy

What does the Bank of England think?

The Bank of England tries to make the way the Monetary Policy Committee thinks as open as possible. It publishes the minutes of its meetings. It has also published details of the models which are used to predict likely outcomes. It sees the analysis of labour market changes as a crucial input to the decision-making process. Another major factor in its thinking is the role played by market expectations about the likely effects of changes in interest rates, exchange rates and inflation.

The size of any necessary change in interest rates is determined by the impact the committee thinks it will have on businesses and markets. Higher interest rates make borrowing for both consumption and investment more expensive. But how quickly will these be affected? And how much? Some kinds of investment are very interest sensitive indeed, some less so. It depends partly on the extent to which the finance for investment would

have been borrowed, and partly on how sales might be affected by the change. Importantly, though, business expectations create feedback effects. If businesses think that rising interest rates herald a downturn in the economy, they may make cutbacks even before the full effects of the change become clear.

The Bank of England is very much aware of the influence of expectations on decisions. In fact, it thinks expectations are becoming steadily more important as information becomes more easily available.

Your agenda

1 What are business expectations like right now?

2 Are interest rates likely to rise, fall or stay the same, next time they are reviewed?

3 Would the situation you are describing be affected if the UK joined the Economic and Monetary Union (EMU)?

It is sometimes said that the only way to control inflation is to reduce expectations of inflation. If inflation has already started to accelerate, that can be quite difficult. People will expect pay rises which at least preserve their real incomes. So inflation becomes built in to the pay bargaining system. The way round this is to reduce demand in the economy by raising interest rates and reducing pressure in the labour market. Then people become fearful about their jobs, so they settle for smaller pay rises and the rate at which costs are rising will fall. Prices then follow suit. This process is covered in more detail in enquiry 3.

Clearly, the way expectations of inflation are formed in people's minds is very important in determining the impact which monetary policy will have. Similarly, the way businesses respond to changing expectations is also vitally important. More

information is becoming available but also, the media analysis of financial information has become more detailed. Many more people are now in a position to base their decisions on their own assessments of future prospects. Sometimes expectations change gradually. People adjust by degrees to new information. This is a major reason why there are time lags in the macro-economic system. People who have got used to expected inflation take time to reduce their expectations of a pay rise.

The MPC now tries to adjust interest rates *ahead* of the time inflation is likely to accelerate, so allowing for the time lags. This way, the inflationary pressures could be reduced before people develop serious expectations of inflation.

Point of view

Mutant spenders

Marketing specialists have long relied on the predictable ways in which people behave as being a source of useful evidence for marketing trends. This may be changing. Martin Hayward, director of consumer consultancy at the Henley Business Centre says:

'The scope of change is accelerating on a daily basis. We try to help clients to make sense of what is happening, but we are running to stand still at the moment. Life used to be very ordered. You got married in your late teens and had a family, which kept you fairly busy until you were about 60. You had ten years left and that was it. We have now reached the position where it is perfectly ordinary to be in your mid-30s leading the life-style of a 19-year-old. You have got nobody to go home to and no reason to go home. Marketers will have to tear up their rule books. People are in and out of their pigeon holes all day long. They step into different roles because they are allowed to. For every trend there is a counter-trend. Society is now incredibly fluid, and determining who somebody is will depend on the time you talk to them.'

Your agenda

1 Why have marketing specialists generally expected different types of people to have predictable consumer preferences?

2 How will they react to people being rather less predictable than before?

Marketing specialists work to reduce the risks involved in selling the product. They are trying to ensure that what is produced actually does sell. It follows that unpredictable people will destroy the stable expectations of marketing people and make business more risky! While many of us might feel secretly pleased that marketing specialists can no longer put us into neatly labelled boxes, it is easy to see that the trend towards a more diverse society could make business decision-taking more difficult.

Work in progress

Q Go back to the Barbour case study at the beginning of this enquiry. Which of the company's problems were predictable? What could have been done to plan strategies to deal with them in advance?

The focus of this enquiry is upon the ways in which businesses expand when circumstances are favourable. Managers must be aware of the need for caution in the face of economic uncertainty but their plans can be made with reasonable optimism. These plans must cover finance and investment, production, the sourcing of inputs and the training of the workforce. Quality issues must also be addressed.

1 How do businesses expand?

Going for growth in 1998

EasyJet, the low-cost airline, yesterday announced pre-tax profits of £2.3 million. This compares with a loss of £3.3 million last year! The number of passengers flown has increased by 65 per cent relative to the previous year and by 309 per cent relative to the first year of operation, signifying considerable acceptance of the 'easyJet product'. Mr Stelios Haji Ioannou, the chairman has attributed the success of the firm, in part at least, to the fact that the company is a private one. This allows him to take long-term decisions without worrying about 'City reaction'.

He operates a fleet of eighteen Boeing 737-300 aircraft. The growth plan for the company commits the firm to using only brand-new aircraft purchased from Boeing. A further 15 next generation Boeing 737-700s with an option to take 15 more is already in the pipeline. EasyJet is increasingly capturing the business traveller market. Mr. Ioannou launched the firm to take advantage of the liberalisation of the EU aviation market. It is expanding rapidly. The chairman has not ruled out a flotation to raise finance but has no immediate plans to do so.

The company is constantly striving to create value for the consumer. This year alone 10 per cent of all sales were sold using the Internet. On particular days 'on line' sales have accounted for 40 per cent of the day's total. Management initially invested heavily in marketing to establish strong brand recognition. Recent surveys suggest that this has been successful.

Figure O2.12 shows how easyJet has grown.

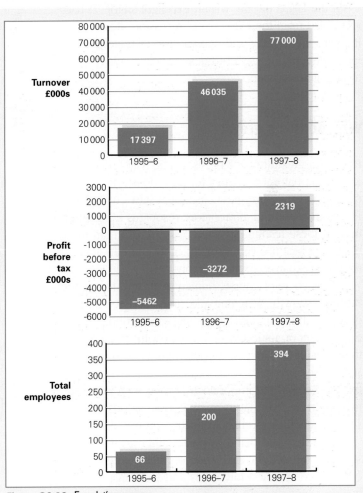

Figure O2.12 EasyJet's progress

Source: Adapted from the EasyJet Airline Company Limited Directors' report and financial statements, 1998

Your agenda

1 What are the advantages and disadvantages for a business like easyJet of staying as a private company?

2 How has easyJet created a competitive advantage?

3 Under what circumstances might easyJet be able to expand further? What economic conditions would be most favourable for the company?

The story of easyJet's expansion is very impressive. Within a few years of its start-up, the company had established a recognised brand image and made significant progress in gaining market share. This organic growth, based on growth in sales rather then on mergers within the industry, has, so far, been supported by private equity rather than a public share issue. Of course, when easyJet began operations in 1995, the UK economy was in excellent shape. It had recovered from the early 1990s' recession. Real incomes were rising and demand for air travel was increasing among both business travellers and individual customers.

Why do firms grow?

Profit is a great attractor of resources. A good business idea has a natural tendency to grow. Existing customers buy more, new customers start buying. Profits increase and attract more resources from other uses. If these resources earn a better return than in their next-best-use (opportunity cost), then another round of expansion will probably occur.

In practice, of course, human goals and hopes fuel business growth. Watching a business succeed and grow can bring immense personal satisfaction. Usually, the owners of a successful firm will want to increase their wealth and income through the expansion of total sales. They may also want to increase their power in the market and the importance of their own job. They may even believe that as many people as possible should benefit from their distinctive product.

It is often said that a business either grows or dies: standing still is difficult. Market segments shrink and expand; competition intensifies and weakens; the business environment becomes more or less favourable. Even if the firm intends no change in its size, it is unlikely that its sales will remain constant for long. Almost inevitably, increasing sales pull resources into the business while falling sales release them. The opening of an additional shop, branch office or factory has almost always been preceded by rising or record sales. Equally, most people have seen the words 'Closing down sale' across the window of a small business. Often this is the last act in a long drama of falling sales.

There are certain underlying trends or principles that give firms their tendency to grow:

- *Competitive advantage*. Once a competitive advantage has been built, a business will normally try to extend its application. The extent to which this is possible varies widely. For successful extension, the potential market size must be large enough while the competitive advantage itself must be strong and hard to copy.
- *Economies of scale*. In general, the average cost of any product falls as output increases (see Module 2.1, page 103). A business therefore has an incentive to increase output and sales in order to gain a cost advantage. This is most likely to be valuable if only achieved by the one firm.
- *Economic growth*. Economic activity tends to move in a continuous cycle of upswings and downswings, booms and slumps. Over the longer term, the economy grows. In Britain, this economic growth trend means – very roughly – that real incomes rise by just over 2 per cent per year. The result is a steady underlying rise in demand for the products of many firms. Obviously, the impact of this growth is greatest during the upswing of the business cycle.

There are many other possible drivers of growth. We saw in Module 3.1, page 162 how demographic and cultural forces bring change to national, regional and local markets. While the long term growth process raises incomes over time, there are always short run changes in the pattern of demand. These bring growing or declining sales for individual businesses and contribute to the process of structural change. Some businesses benefit particularly from having a product which gains in popularity as incomes rise. Others can plan expansion on the basis of improved technology leading to enhanced competitive advantage.

2 How can growth be financed?

EasyJet's finance

As a private company, easyJet avoided raising capital from the public through equity finance. At the end of 1997 it had just under £5 million in shareholders' funds, and to this was added a further £2.3 million during 1998. To start with, the company took out short-term loans. This enabled it to finance a major marketing effort with extensive advertising. The objective was to establish a high degree of brand recognition and then sell through the Internet.

The directors' report says:

'Due to this innovative marketing approach, adopted since easyJet's inception, the airline has been able to differentiate itself from its competitors and this approach has been rewarded both through the significant growth in sales and through the high level of brand awareness. A recent NOP poll indicates a recognition rate of 72 per cent.'

The brand-new aircraft of which easyJet was so proud were financed through leasing. That means that they had a long-term rental agreement with the company which owned the aircraft. The advantage of this is that it greatly reduces easyJet's need for finance.

Once the company was making profits it was able to pay off its start-up loans. The figures for operating profit in 1997–8 shown in Figure O2.12 on page 467 were calculated after £7 million's worth of payments to creditors had been made. These figures were all available on the company web site, which has detailed cash flow information.

For 1997–8 the company paid no dividends. Being a private company, easyJet did not have to worry about shareholders' short-term objectives. The shareholders would all be known to the directors and no doubt the prospects of long-term growth would keep them very happy.

Your agenda

1 How has easyJet's expansion been financed so far?

2 What important sources of finance would be available to the company after the period described?

3 What would be the main advantages of a share issue as a way of financing expansion?

Every day hundreds of intending entrepreneurs launch business enterprises with their own funds or make requests to the banks for advice and support. A key role of the banks is to recycle as loans the money that other people and firms have deposited with them as savings. An important part of this lending is to small businesses, and in making decisions about requests for loans, the bank must – as always – balance risks against return.

A business plan is an important factor in persuading a bank to lend. The more detailed the projections and the more specific the evidence on which they are based, the better. In practice, the great majority of firms, not just business start-ups, make use of external sources of finance such as bank loans. The terms, conditions and rates of interest attached to loan finance vary widely.

Sources of external finance

Loan capital

For most firms, loans are obtained from the banks. They are especially interested in lending when the economy is growing healthily. Interest rates can be fixed, variable or renegotiable at agreed dates. The scheduling of repayments may also be flexible and related to the expected stream of additional income to be generated by the business. In general, a longer term and a higher element of risk will carry a higher rate of interest and a greater demand for security by the bank.

The need to provide a bank with adequate security is a major issue for many small firms. There can be a lack of readily marketable assets within the firm and the owners may need to use their homes as security. Mortgage loans are usually very long term and used for purchasing land or buildings which then represent specific security for the lender. By contrast short-term loans are often related to items of equipment with a short life. An overdraft may provide a source of extra working capital.

Venture capital

Venture capital provides another source of start-up capital for smaller firms – often those involved in technological innovation. This is provided by specialist institutions including subsidiaries of merchant and commercial banks. Both share and loan capital may be supplied, but the venture capitalist often expects to be closely involved in the management of the growing enterprise. Venture capital has been increasingly used to finance management buy-outs. These occur where one firm is wholly, or partly, owned by another and its managers wish to buy their independence.

Leasing

In some cases **leasing** or hire purchase can provide a potential source of finance. Leasing involves another company (the lessor) buying an item of plant or equipment and allowing its use by the lessee in return for a rental charge.

A hire purchase agreement

A firm purchasing a particular asset pays a deposit to a finance house which then settles the amount outstanding in return for a stream of repayments by instalment, typically over the three to five years ahead. After all the repayments are made, the machinery becomes the property of the business.

Essentials

Venture capital is risk capital, usually a combination of loans and equity funds, for small and medium-sized companies involved with innovative products.

Essentials

Leasing enables the company to rent its equipment from another company which owns it. This avoids the cash outlay required to buy the equipment outright.

Work in progress

Q 1 Virgin Atlantic leases all of its planes. What advantages does this have for the company?

2 What other types of business might find leasing appropriate? Why?

3 What are the disadvantages of leasing?

A share issue

Once a business is established, the directors can raise additional finance to fund a planned expansion by selling additional shares to existing or new shareholders. In a private company the shareholders are usually members of the family or close business associates. Some of them may well be willing to increase their stake, especially if the company's prospects appear favourable.

When the scale of proposed investment exceeds the funds available from this source, the company may decide to 'go public'. This means taking on the legal status of a public limited company (plc) with an issue of shares to investors and the general public who can then buy and sell them on the London Stock Exchange. An issuing house (usually a merchant bank) is appointed which will publish a detailed prospectus explaining the nature of the firm's business with a record of its financial performance.

Although a public company has easier access to sources of new finance, there are pressures and responsibilities. Shareholders and 'City opinion' (the views of investors, brokers and commentators in the City of London) must be satisfied with the firm's performance in terms of profitability, dividends and share price. This can drive management to seek short-term results rather than strategies for long-term investment. Indeed, the City has often been accused of causing 'short termism' in British business management. Yet investors must have confidence in the company if future share issues are to succeed. Institutions such as insurance companies and pension funds may take major stakes in the firm, making their investment managers significant players in the delicate calculations of decision-making.

Existing public companies normally sell new shares through a rights issue. This means that all shareholders are given the opportunity to buy new shares in proportion to the size of their current holding.

Internal finance

For nearly all established businesses easily the most important source of new finance comes from within the firm. The main internal source of finance is retained profit. It appears in the balance sheet as 'Profit and loss account', in the reserves section. It has the great advantage of being unconditional, with no external parties to satisfy and no interest to pay. However, it is not 'free' of any cost.

As a use of scarce resources, retained profit carries an opportunity cost, which, at the barest minimum, is the current rate of interest available. Any addition to the net resources controlled by a firm places an obligation on the management to use it in a way that generates an adequate minimum return. Retained profit accumulates within a successful firm relatively quickly. Say a business achieves an average 20 per cent return on capital employed; if 7.5 per cent is distributed in dividends, then a 12.5 per cent retention rate will double the firm's capital in six years without any borrowing.

The business which finds itself short of working capital should examine carefully the possibilities for collecting its debts more quickly. It may be able to reduce the finance needed for stocks of both inputs and output – just-in-time strategies may be appropriate. Perhaps it can give credit more sparingly. Such measures will reduce the need for finance for working capital. Performance on all three fronts can be evaluated by comparing aspects of the balance sheet with that of the previous year.

Gearing

The Arriva Bus Company plc

Arriva plc is a total transport solutions supplier embracing bus operations and distribution, urban transit systems, motor retailing and vehicle management. One of Britain's top 200 companies, Arriva changed its name from Cowie Group in 1997.

Arriva spent £74 million on acquisitions in the first half of 1998. The principal aim of this was to further the growth of its international bus operations. Strong cash inflow from its operations and the strength of its balance sheet allowed this expansion. This strength came from the Group's operating activities which brought in a net cash inflow of £354 million in the first half of 1998, compared to £320 million in the same period in 1997. A further £128 million was received from the sale of ex-contract hire and daily rental vehicles.

The firm has a £400 million loan facility and shareholders' funds of £333 million. In addition, it has borrowed £104 million on the US capital market. Given this, Arriva feels well placed financially for further growth, both organically and through acquisition.

Your agenda

1 What is organic growth?

2 Why might shareholders have reservations about the amount of borrowed funds which Arriva is using?

3 What are the risks associated with the kind of capital structure created by Arriva?

Loan finance as a proportion of a firm's capital employed is called the **gearing ratio**. A firm is said to be highly geared when a large part of its capital employed is provided by loans. Capital employed consists of long-term loans and shareholders funds. The formula for calculating the gearing ratio is:

$$\frac{\text{Long-term liabilities (loans)}}{\text{Capital employed}} \times 100.$$

The gearing ratio is important because the interest payments needed to service loans will impact upon the level of profits within the firm. This will show up in the accounts as the difference between operating profit and profit before tax. The ratio of bank lending to equity finance tends to rise sharply during a boom as firms find banks keen to lend to them.

Essentials

The **gearing ratio** measures the proportion of capital employed which is covered by long term loans. Excessive reliance on loan rather than share capital is risky because interest must always be paid.

Work in progress

Q Calculate Arriva's gearing ratio for 1998. Comment on the figures. Compare Arriva's gearing ratio with those two other companies for which you have balance sheet figures.

K employed → covered by long term loans

Problems arise if the rate of interest on the loan rises, increasing cash outflows. This can happen if the economy is overheating and monetary policy calls for all interest rates to go up. Then the impact may be exacerbated by the way consumer spending falls when people are having to pay higher interest rates. Obviously, profits will be badly affected if gearing is high. (Gearing over 50 per cent is generally regarded as high.) Firms which had their fingers burnt in the late 1980s will have learnt to factor into their cash flows a number of different interest rates and to have contingency plans in case of a change in expectations. High gearing increases risks.

Booms in the last two decades have been characterised by intense merger activity or inorganic growth, as firms have sought to expand through acquisitions. Much of this activity has been financed by the banks. If interest rates are stable there may be no problem, but a monetary squeeze will produce bad results.

3 How can the business meet its need for cash?

A watchful eye

Remember Manicmixers? We left it in Module 3 at the point where Steve and Gina had taken their business plan to the bank. In fact, things had not gone according to plan right from the first day that Steve and Gina began running Manicmixers as a full-time business. Chris Dixon was not as prompt in paying for their work at his nightclub as they had expected. It soon became clear they would not see any cash from this part of their business until October, and even then it seemed inevitable that payments would always be one month behind. This was not their only worry: two of the private party bookings that they had taken in September showed no sign of paying at all!

Gina was annoyed because she had said all along that this kind of problem would arise as soon as they started doing work for people they did not know. Despite this, Steve insisted they would have to get used to a few customers not paying promptly now that they were operating full time.

In the last week of September they received a letter from Graham Wharton, the small enterprise adviser at their bank. The firm's account was overdrawn and the cheque for the new effects unit had 'bounced'. A quick glance at the actual cash flow for the business was enough to show why.

Gina and Steve knew their business was still making a profit and found it difficult to accept that despite this they could not pay the outstanding bills. It was only after an interview at the bank that an overdraft facility was arranged so that the business could continue to operate.

	September (£)	October (£)
Opening balance	8000	(180)
Money in		
Night club bookings	0	1600
Private bookings	1000	1200
Total in	1000	2800
Money out		
Night club bookings:		
Variable cost	40	40
Private bookings:		
Variable Cost	240	240
Wages	1600	1600
Advertising	200	200
Equipment	2000	0
Van	5000	0
Interest	100	100
Total out	9180	2180
Difference	(8180)	620
Closing Balance	(180)	440

Figure O2.13 Manic mixers

Your agenda

1 To what extent could Gina and Steve have anticipated the working capital problem they faced at the end of September?

2 What actions other than securing an overdraft might Manicmixers have taken to deal with the cash flow difficulty it faced? How would these impact upon the cash flow forecast in the business plan?

3 Why is it possible for a business to face a shortage of cash at the same time as generating a profit, in the way that is illustrated by the experience of Manicmixers?

4 Why is it that expanding too quickly can lead to cash flow problems?

Businesses can easily find themselves with insufficient cash flow. They may have excellent prospects of achieving profitability in the long run, but if they do not have enough cash to pay the bills in the short run, they may still fail. The basic problem is insufficient working capital. In fact, Manicmixers should have been able to see that with so many large items to be paid for, it was very vulnerable to unforeseen delays. Business managers have to learn from experience what sorts of time lags they must expect.

Overtrading by businesses during times of rapid economic growth has been the undoing of many otherwise successful firms. Ironically, it is a problem caused by success, or rather the inability to manage success. Put simply, it occurs when a firm spends sales revenues immediately on capital items such as equipment or premises, perhaps in a desperate attempt to keep up with demand. As happened to Gina and Steve, working capital soon reaches a dangerously low level and there is not enough in the bank to pay suppliers, staff or overheads.

The result is that eventually creditors are left with no choice but to have the firm wound up, in order to get what they are owed. If the business builds its working capital needs into its plans from the start, there is less risk of this happening.

Essentials

Overtrading occurs when the business expands without sufficient finance. If it does not have enough working capital to cover its bills, it will face a liquidity crisis and may become insolvent.

4 Investment... can it earn its keep?

Lets mix it again...

Ten months after going into business on a full-time basis, it became clear that Manicmixers would have to have a completely new sound system. Steve and Gina explored the products available. The state of the art, Rolls Royce product could be had for £4000. A less sophisticated version, very much better than their existing system, would cost £2500. The cheaper version would enable them to carry on what they were doing with obvious improvements in sound quality. The pricier equipment would probably permit them to expand their activities further.

Once again, they had to start estimating future cash flow for these two scenarios. This time they were aware that there were a lot of uncertainties. How could they be sure that their estimates of likely ticket sales were realistic? And what would be the best way to compare the projected returns with the cost of the investment? To what extent would they need to rely on bank finance? They knew it was important for them to keep up to date with new kit, but there were difficult issues to consider.

Your agenda

1 What uncertainties would Manicmixers face in making its estimates?

2 Is it sufficient for the business to get back the cost of its investment over a period of, say, four years?

3 How can the business make allowance for risk in its calculations?

Companies buy machinery, premises, tools and equipment. These are the assets of the business, which are used to make a profit. The most successful and profitable companies make the most efficient use of their assets, so decisions about which assets should be acquired and how much money should be invested are vitally important.

A business will have only a limited amount of capital available at any one time and there will be a range of possible alternatives on which to spend it.

The business has to make a decision about which project to undertake and the managers will need to look at the costs of each alternative and the possible revenues.

Decisions about an investment are based on predictions concerning the future. These are both quantitative – about such things as interest rates and costs – and qualitative – about how well a product will perform against its competitors and about how consumer tastes will change. Several techniques have been developed to help businesses to make investment decisions.

Initially, accountants will be asked for a view on the likely financial returns from the outlay. The results of this investigation can take a number of forms. Most investments are intended to generate money over a period of several years, so the first step is to predict the amount of money which the investment should generate each year. This is known as the net cash inflow, i.e. cash inflows net of outflows.

Payback period

Calculations may simply focus on how long it will take for the firm to recover its initial investment. This **payback period** may be used as an initial test of whether the investment has a chance of justifying its cost. It can also be used as a way of deciding between two alternatives.

Essentials

The **payback period** is the length of time needed for the cost of an investment to be recovered by the net cash flow that it generates.

For example, Malvern Mats Ltd is trying to decide which of two possible cutting machines it should purchase. Both machines cost £45 000. Figure O2.14 shows the likely savings (i.e. net cash inflow) expected to result from the investment. The outcome on this test is clear: the shorter payback period will mean reduced risk for the business.

	Year 1	Year 2	Year 3	Payback period
Machine A	£10 000	£20 000	£30 000	2.5 years
Machine B	£30 000	£20 000	£10 000	1.75 years

Figure O2.14 Malvern Mats' payback period

Work in progress

Steve and Gina estimate that if they invest in the more expensive £4 000 sound system they will be able to add £1 500 to their annual sales revenue. If they buy the cheaper £2 500 system, they will gain just £750 per year. All other costs will stay the same, so these amounts will be the expected net cash inflow resulting from the investment.

Q 1 What are the payback periods for the two outcomes?

2 Which purchase is preferable?

Average rate of return

A second possible way of evaluating the likely outcome of an investment is to use the **average rate of return** (ARR). This is found by taking the average net cash flow (i.e. additional profit) earned by the investment over the years of its life, dividing by the original cost of the investment, and expressing this as a percentage.

Essentials

The **average rate of return** is a measure of the annual profit generated by an investment as a percentage of its initial cost.

Example 1

A firm has a choice between two projects, A and B. Project A needs £3 000 investment while Project B needs £6 000 investment. The resulting net cash inflows are set out in Figure O2.15.

		Project A (£)	Project B (£)
Investment (now)	Year 0	−3000	−6000
Net cash inflows	Year 1	+2500	+3500
(End of year)	Year 2	+4000	+4000
	Year 3	+4000	+4500
Total net cash inflows		+10 500	+12 000
Net cash inflows less initial investment		+7500	+6000
Average annual return` (Net cash inflow/no. of years)		+2500	+2000
Average annual rate of return		$\dfrac{2500}{3000}$	$\dfrac{2000}{6000}$
		= 83%	= 33%

Figure O2.15 Average rate of return on two projects

The percentage figures in Figure O2.15 represent the percentage of the initial investment which is returned *on average* each year of the project. If you were choosing between Project A and Project B on financial grounds alone, you would choose Project A because, on average, you get a higher return on your investment in each year of the project.

Example 2

There is a problem with average rate of return as a method of investment appraisal. Suppose you had to choose between Projects C and D using ARR in Figure O2.16.

		Project C (£)	Project D (£)
Investment	Year 0	10 000	10 000
Cash inflows	Year 1	6000	2000
	Year 2	5000	5000
	Year 3	2000	6000
Total net cash inflows		13 000	13 000
Net cash inflow less initial investment		3000	3000
Average annual return		1000	1000
Average rate of return		$\dfrac{1000}{10000}$	$\dfrac{1000}{10000}$
		= 10%	= 10%

Figure O2.16 ARR and cash flow over time

The ARR of each project is the same, but there is a very good reason for preferring Project C.

If you chose Project C, you would get your money back much more quickly than if you chose Project D. The high cash inflows for Project C are in Years 1 and 2; the high cash inflows for Project D are in years 2 and 3. The more quickly you get your money back, the sooner you can reinvest it in new projects and make even more money. The ARR hides the timing of the cash flows. As far as ARR is concerned, £6000 in three years' time is as good as £6000 now.

Having to wait longer for the returns to an investment does matter. The longer the wait, the greater the risk. This means that businesses will use the payback period to help size up the risks involved in the project. They find ARR useful because it is easy to understand. But the payback period gives added information. The sooner the returns come in, the less risk there is of something going wrong and interrupting the flow of cash.

Work in progress

A business has two possible investment projects – Project A and Project B – and is going to make its decision by comparing the average rate of return of each project. Project A involves investment in new machinery. Project B is a new product development.

The capital outlays and net returns for each project are:

		Project A	Project B
Capital outlay		£50 000	£180 000
Return	Year 1	£12 000	£75 000
	Year 2	£12 000	£30 000
	Year 3	£12 000	£30 000
	Year 4	£12 000	£30 000
	Year 5	£12 000	£30 000

Q 1 On the basis of ARR only, make a recommendation about which project the business should select.

2 What criteria, other than ARR, might you take into consideration when making your decision?

Money now or money later

An investment decision today will be made on the basis of the amount of money invested and the amount the firm expects to make from it. But this is not comparing like with like, because the initial outlay must be made in the present, while the returns are all in the future. Having to wait for a sum of money reduces its value, for three reasons:

■ the risk that circumstances prevent your receiving it

■ the effect of inflation on its value

■ the opportunity cost, i.e. the value of the profits you could have made if you had been in possession of the money.

One way to decide how much forecast cash flows are worth is to use a discount rate. This involves reducing future income by an amount which reflects the cost of waiting for it. Then the present value of the future income can be compared with the capital outlay needed before production can begin.

5 Can the business stay efficient?

Flagging up the future

AA Flags is a small company based at Consett in the north east of England. Mandy set up the business in 1990 and is confident that she has her 13 employees so efficiently organised that she can produce a batch of flags within 24 hours of receiving an order. Despite this, even she was astonished by the events of April and May 1999.

In just a few weeks the turnover of her business increased by 200 per cent and the order book was bulging. What caused this sudden explosion in demand for flags in the north east of England? In the space of a month, Sunderland Football Club won the first division championship and Newcastle United appeared in the FA Cup final. Every self-respecting north-east soccer fan wanted to celebrate the club's big day.

Could Mandy have anticipated this massive surge in demand for her product? What should she do now? Her main business is making corporate flags and bunting for organisations like golf clubs and hotels. If she bought extra machinery to meet the new demand created by the success of local football teams, would she be able to utilise it fully in the future? On the other hand, could she afford to miss out on the demand while it was there?

Mandy actually coped with the orders by getting her staff to work night-shifts. Her strategy of turning orders around within 24 hours, normally, where other flag-makers take up to eight weeks, worked. 'The staff are very good and will always work night-shifts if they have to complete an order,' she said. 'They have worked flat out.'

Mandy is now getting orders from Japan. 'I don't know what it says, the writing is all in Japanese,' she remarks.

Your agenda

1 How could Mandy have achieved this level of flexibility?

2 How has the business achieved its competitive advantage?

3 What important features will efficient organisations have in common?

4 What are the main ways of increasing efficiency?

5 How would Mandy decide between getting the staff to work overtime and buying more machines?

When the subject was increasing productivity, you learnt about business organisation, motivation, lean production, quality, investment: all the important elements in the organisation of production. The key message here is that there is a range of strategies which are closely related, all of which need to be considered by the well organised company. For efficient production depends not only on having all the technical inputs organised appropriately, but on having good human resource management and supplier relationships as well.

AA Flags had to have a flexible labour force. If Mandy had been unable to find enough people to work overtime, she could not have coped with the orders. Yet clearly her organisation had to be technically competent, in order to meet orders quickly.

Lean production

In larger businesses, efficient production may imply giving attention to the techniques involved in lean production. This encompasses cell production, just-in-time supply systems and Kanban. Cell production in manufacturing involves firms in creating clusters of different kinds of equipment. Each cluster or cell is responsible for creating a finished product. These ideas were dealt with in detail in Module 2.1, pages 95–99.

Cell production has many advantages, including:

- shortened lead times – the business can respond faster to changes in the market
- reduced inventories and work in progress
- lower costs, improved quality and increased job satisfaction
- better teamwork.

Evidence of benefits

Performance measure	Total no. of responses	Indicated performance improvement	Claimed no improvement	Improvement unknown or not measured	Provided numerical estimate	Average % improvement	Minimum % improvement	Maximum % improvement
Reduction of move distances / move times*	37	35	0	2	24	61.3	15.0	99.0
Reduction in throughput time	40	34	0	6	27	61.2	12.5	99.5
Reduction of response time to customer orders	37	31	1	5	17	50.1	0.0	93.2
Reduction in work in progress inventory	40	37	0	3	29	48.2	10.0	99.7
Reduction in setup times	33	24	2	7	22	44.2	0.0	96.6
Reduction in finished goods inventory	38	24	6	8	21	39.3	0.0	100.0
Improvement in part/product quality	39	33	1	5	22	28.4	0.0	62.5
Reduction in unit costs	38	28	1	9	20	16.0	0.0	60.0

*Of the 37 firms that responded to this question, 35 indicated that improvement had taken place and two indicated that improvement was either unknown or not assessed (none of the 37 firms expressly claimed that improvement had not taken place). Further, 24 firms provided quantitative estimates, with an average improvement of 61.3%.

Source: U. Wemmerlov and D. J. Johnson, 'Cellular manufacturing, a survey', in International Journal of Production Research 35 (1), 1997; Taylor and Francis Ltd, http://www.tandf.co.uk/journals/prs.htm

Figure O2.17   Reported performance improvements

In a survey published by U. Wemmerlov and D. J. Johnson in 1997, 94 per cent of businesses responding to their questionnaire stated that improvements had occurred after reorganisation into cells in the production process. Figure O2.17 shows the responses of reported performance improvements.

It is worth noting that only 29 per cent of the firms questioned had achieved anything without also investing in new plant and machinery.

Your agenda

1 What conclusions can you draw from the evidence provided in Figure O2.17?

2 How might businesses moving to cell production overcome resistance to change?

3 Give one example of a company you know about which has adopted cell production.

There is a human issue to address when considering the move to cell production. Will employees feel more involved? Will satisfaction increase? There may be implications for labour management relations and there may be resistance to change. Some of these were considered in Module 4.1, page 277. All the ideas about how people can react positively to change apply here.

There is a need for thorough planning before implementing cell production. The selection and physical placement of cell equipment in itself is a major planning issue. It is also important to plan the role of humans in cell design and operations. Most of the problems faced by firms which reorganise production relate to people rather than to technical issues.

The introduction of cell production and just-in-time can involve quite dramatic changes in the management structure of a company. There may be de-layering, increased spans of control and a general flattening of the hierarchy of a company.

Time-based management

Some manufacturing businesses have in recent years tried to shorten their production runs with a view to increasing customer satisfaction. Goods are produced as they are required in response to known levels of consumer demand.

To do this, the business needs equipment which is flexible enough to switch from one model to another at short notice. Staff have to be multi-skilled, so that they can adjust as necessary to changes in production. The advantage lies in being able to offer a varied product range without losing economies of scale.

Some car manufacturers are able to make good use of time-based management. They can produce each car with the precise combination of accessories desired by the customer yet with a short waiting time for the order to arrive. Few cars have to be stored and this cuts costs.

A well-trained workforce is essential to the successful operation of this approach. Suppliers have to be flexible too. The level of orders for specific inputs can change at any time.

Point of view

It looks as though a key factor in staying efficient will be in the management of information. Bill Gates, in his book *Business @ the Speed of Thought: Using a Digital Nervous System*, says this:

❛ I have a simple but strong belief. The most meaningful way to differentiate your company from your competition, the best way to put distance between you and the crowd, is to do an outstanding job with information. How you gather, manage and use information will determine whether you win or lose.

I can anticipate your reaction. No, it's efficient processes! It's quality! It's creating brand recognition and going after market share! It's getting close to customers!

Success of course depends on all these things. Nobody can help you if your processes limp along or… your customer service is poor. But no matter what else you have going for you today – smart employees, excellent products, customer goodwill, cash in the bank – you need a fast flow of good information to streamline processes, raise quality, and improve business execution. ❜

Of course, Bill Gates hopes we shall all buy our information software from Microsoft. But he goes on to say:

❛ McDonald's is well on the way to installing a new information system that uses PCs and web technologies to tally sales at all its restaurants in real time. As soon as you order two Happy Meals, a McDonald's marketing manager will know. Rather than superficial or anecdotal data, the marketer will have hard, factual data for tracking trends. ❜

Your agenda

1 What suggestions is Bill Gates making about the best way of improving efficiency?

2 How might a car manufacturer be helped by improved information flows?

3 Evaluate the likely impact of improved information flows on the marketing effort of a producer of greetings cards.

It is likely that many large organisations will reinvent their production processes around new digital developments. However, to do this they will have to have an appropriate corporate culture in place. Employees will need a common ethos and a sense that they are all headed in the same direction. This will make it possible for an atmosphere of trust to flourish.

Keeping in mind that having the right capital equipment, good stock control, a well-motivated workforce and good communications are all essential to business success, the rest of this enquiry focuses on the need for quality and for a flexible and skilled workforce. The role of **supply chains** in contributing to quality enhancement is also explored.

6 Supply chains and core activities

Businesses have always needed to buy inputs from other businesses. But in recent years there has been a trend away from producing both components and finished products under one roof, or even within the same company. Increasingly, businesses will focus upon their core capabilities and will **outsource** many of their requirements from other companies.

A supply chain may have few or many contributing businesses. Charles Handy, in his book *The Age of Unreason*, suggests a shamrock structure as a way of looking at how businesses organise their inputs.

Figure O2.18 shows how the business consists of three groups. There are the core workers, the people who contribute to the main activity of the company, reflecting its chief sources of competitive advantage. There is the contractual fringe, all those activities which can be outsourced and bought from other businesses. Then there is the flexible workforce, the part-time and temporary employees who can assemble products according to the level of demand.

Essentials

Outsourcing means buying necessary inputs from independent suppliers. It can apply to components or to business services, indeed to anything which was previously produced within the business.

Essentials

Supply chains consist of the businesses which work together to contribute each element in the production process.

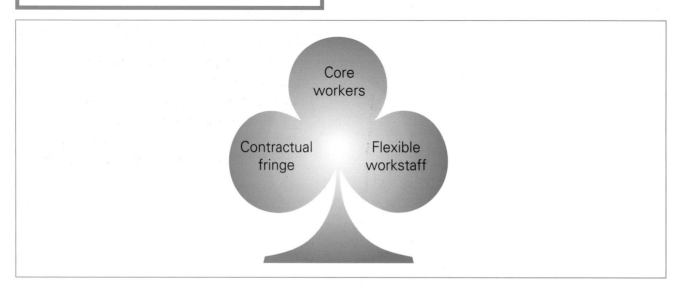

Figure O2.18 Charles Handy's shamrock

Source: Charles Handy, *The Age of Unreason*, Vintage, 1980

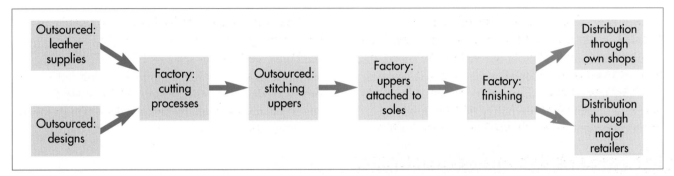

Figure O2.19 Shoes in a supply chain

Figure O2.19 shows how a supply chain might look for a high-quality shoe manufacturer such as Church's. The company makes traditional brogues and other men's shoes of a very high quality. For some shoes, the uppers are sent to be stitched in Thailand, because of the comparatively low labour costs there.

JIT and supplier relationships

For many rapidly expanding firms in growing markets just-in-time (JIT) and Kanban are an excellent way of transferring the burden of input supply management to the suppliers. Suppliers guarantee a JIT delivery system. They store the materials and have a vested financial interest in ensuring that their customers are happy. This may mean that their costs rise. The customer firm which benefits from the reduced costs associated with JIT may well be larger and have more market muscle than the supplier firm. Its profits will rise but at the expense of the suppliers' profits.

Staying on track...

AT & T may shift to multiple suppliers

AT & T is a large US telecommunications company operating in a rapidly expanding industry. It announced that it was looking for alternative equipment suppliers. AT & T had long depended on Lucent, the company it spun off in 1996, to meet its core equipment requirements. This latest move would enable it to purchase equipment from any number of suppliers and would reshape its supplier relations.

The company realises that managing a multiple supplier network is more difficult. However, it believes that the change will help it to buy the most appropriate technologies at the best price. It is likely that the trend to multiple supplier relationships will gather pace as the industry adopts new technology. It needs to do this in order to respond to the big increase in data traffic. The move has given suppliers in this market an opportunity to establish relationships with AT & T that have not been possible in the past.

Your agenda

1 What are the likely advantages of a single supplier system?

2 What difficulties may arise when trying to manage a multiple supplier chain?

3 Is the adoption of such a policy something that all firms in rapidly expanding industries could try out?

Growth of a firm at a time when the economy is growing would seem to be something easily achieved. Consumers, confident about the future, will spend, and firms, with some confidence in the expected payback from any investment, will create new capital by investing in plant and machinery. However, getting production right in these conditions is not always as easy as one would think. Increased orders from its buyers will put pressure on the business's ability to meet the order and to maintain the quality that its customers have become used to.

In a boom, suppliers of materials will find themselves under pressure to meet their increased orders. How can a business avoid the situation where its production targets are not reached because its supplier could not get sufficient quantities and qualities of raw material to the business in time ? How does a business ensure that the quality standards its customers have come to expect are maintained, as ever more ambitious production targets are set?

Maintaining good relationships with suppliers may help particularly if companies are interdependent. However, in a rapidly growing economy which provides a small firm with the opportunity to expand, the current supplier may not be big enough. In the USA it is now more common to have multiple suppliers. This enables firms to purchase equipment and materials from any number of businesses and increases flexibility. It does mean that if quality is to be maintained, supplier relationships become more complicated and perhaps a higher priority for the business.

Supplier relationships can be supportive and collaborative, or they can be adversarial. To some extent, this depends on trading conditions. When demand is growing it is easy for everyone to be pleased with the progress. If times become more difficult, some businesses may find that their margins are being squeezed.

Some supplier companies find that large customer companies are slow to pay them, but because they depend on the customer company, there may be little they can do about it, even though the lost liquidity can be fatal. In a recession, large customer companies may delay payments to strengthen their own position while supplier companies are becoming insolvent and in some cases closing down.

There is no doubt that customer companies such as Marks & Spencer have been able to improve quality by insisting on their suppliers adopting their own high standards. Many other retailers have done the same. In a well-managed supply chain, businesses match processes directly to the product qualities which customers are seeking. There are excellent opportunities for market orientation to be transmitted back down the supply chain to the individual suppliers.

Work in progress

Developing good relationships with suppliers can be beneficial to both businesses. Boots the Chemists has worked closely with Jackel Ltd to develop a range of baby products which exceed minimum safety standards. Product quality is central to the company's strategy of gaining consumer confidence in the product's quality and in giving Boots a competitive advantage. Jackel has benefited because it has benchmarked its own products against the products it has made for Boots own label brands. This has given its Tommy Tippee brand a competitive edge over rival brands.

Q 1 Benchmarking means setting a competitive performance standard based on other companies' products or processes. How did benchmarking help Jackel?

2 What advantages did the relationship have for Boots?

3 Could Boots have achieved its objectives without a collaborative supplier relationship?

7   How do people contribute to growth?

Our business is people

When Keith Greenough was appointed chief executive officer of Mortgage Express he faced a tricky problem – how do you manage and motivate a company which is faced with closure, whose staff are facing redundancy and which has losses of £66 million?

Mortgage Express was part of the TSB group. The parent company in a shift in corporate strategy had decided to concentrate its mortgage lending through its branches. Mortgage Express had no distribution network, so it was no longer a part of the company's long-term strategy. The decision was taken to cease operations within two years.

When Kevin Greenough took charge at Mortgage Express he found that problems were worse than he had anticipated. The firm was losing £1 million per week. Management of payment arrears became an immediate focus for the new chief executive. He also recognised that if he was to turn the company around, then he must improve morale. Like many chief executives before him, Greenough announced that, 'Our people are our biggest resource'. The difference was that Greenough actually believed it. He organised opinion research and sought to improve morale by creating a culture which was based on trust, openness and good communications. Then he responded to the survey results. A 'strong people management structure' was introduced. This was the antithesis of the 'mushroom management,' employed by some UK firms, which seeks to keep employees in the dark.

Employees of the company have been complimentary of the changes in management style. They are convinced that the changes in the style and quality of communication have been the most important factor in the company's turnaround. A structured communication process was introduced, providing the opportunity for face-to-face contact between management and staff. Monthly formal briefings were arranged in order to keep staff informed and to enable them to ask questions. Greenough also arranged formal staff presentations every quarter.

One employee said, 'Things are a lot more professional, there's lots of training. We also feel that we're working in a better environment and we know what we're doing... motivation has increased as a result.'

Staff annual conferences and black-tie dinners became an opportunity to have a good time and to recognise the work of staff with the award of performance prizes.

The success of management by motivation can be clearly seen. When Greenough took over the company had announced a loss of £66 million. Three years later the company was able to announce a profit of £38 million. Improvements in the economic climate and reductions in interest rates have contributed to the company's reversal of fortunes, but the situation has been enhanced by improvements in staff morale.

Mortgage Express actively encouraged staff through a sponsorship initiative to develop through formal training. Susie Every started work with Mortgage Express as a temporary worker in the Collections Department. She subsequently completed an MA in Human Resource Management focusing on the problems of downsizing at Mortgage Express. Training and professional development brings its rewards – Susie Every gained promotion to become a litigation supervisor.

Keith Greenough summarised the company philosophy, 'Of course the more training they do and the more they are encouraged to participate and become involved at all levels, the more they are enhancing their own future prospects of employability.'

Mortgage Express became a success despite uncertainty over its future. Greenough is convinced that success has been achieved through openness. He thinks that staff at Mortgage Express are performing better than their counterparts working for other firms. He is proud of the progress made by his company, but he remains adamant that all credit for the firm's success goes to his staff.

Your agenda

1   How could the management techniques used at Mortgage Express have a positive impact on the quality of the service on offer? Explain the reasons for their success.

2   Do these measures increase productivity? How?

3   How do such activities help a business to deal with demand in a growing market?

4   What other kinds of business might benefit from the same approach?

Nimble businesses know that performance depends on good decisions not just in certain areas of management but in the whole range of management functions. At Mortgage Express the key developments were in communications. In general, many businesses find that the most sustainable forms of competitive advantage come from their approach to human resource management.

People develop a knowledge of the job through taking continuous decisions. They learn what works and what does not. It is difficult for competing companies to replicate a successful human resources strategy because they cannot give their employees exactly the same experience. Each business has to create a training experience of its own. Then it has to recognise its employees' firm-specific skills and reward them in ways which are genuinely motivating. This may imply paying them more or it may involve other strategies.

The need for training

Some UK companies now devote a great deal of effort to training their employees. Others still neglect this area of management. A recent study by the Food and Drink Federation, an employers' organisation, found that UK food and drink companies are 10 per cent less efficient than their overseas competitors because their employees are less well trained. The report was based on a benchmarking exercise involving comparisons between UK businesses and others in Japan, the USA and the rest of the EU.

Lack of skills means that employees have difficulties with up-to-date production equipment, and few are multi-skilled. They may not be able to cope when things go wrong. There is often a shortage of skilled engineers to install and maintain equipment, so investment in new equipment often yields disappointing returns.

Comparisons between employees' education levels in the countries concerned revealed that at every level, UK food and drink businesses had fewer people with formal qualifications than those in other countries.

Skill shortages mean that workforces are less flexible than they could be. Multi-skilling enables machine operators to fix minor malfunctions when they occur, instead of waiting for help to arrive. The value of skills and training will appear again and again throughout this option.

In some occupational areas there is a constant need for more skilled people. Some computer and other high technology skills remain scarce wherever the economy is in the business cycle. Other skill shortages become apparent when the economy is in the recovery phase and acute if there is a boom. The idea of lifetime learning is encouraging both people and businesses to undertake training at various times during their working lives. Still, there is a real need for further development of training programmes.

Teleworking

BT

One in ten of British Telecommunications' 100 000 strong workforce could find their homes transformed into their office in Britain's most ambitious experiment to date in 'teleworking'.

It is hoped that 10 000 office workers can be persuaded to work from home, communicating with customers and managers by fax machines, telephone and the Internet. The savings are estimated at a possible £134 million a year, excluding the unquantifiable effects of reduced stress and reduced commuting and fuel costs.

Line managers have been trained to counsel potential home workers on the likely problems including lack of space for equipment, the demands of the family and the difficulty of working while divorced from the office culture.

A principal reason behind the initiative is BT's need to dispose of hundreds of surplus properties across the country. Telecoms equipment now takes up very little space and requires far fewer support staff.

Source: Adapted from the *Financial Times*, 12 May 1999

The solicitor

Christopher Davis runs a 'virtual' law firm from his home in Hampstead in London. The 40 lawyers and six support staff who work for him are all based in their own homes. This cuts overheads and allows the firm to reduce its fees by a third compared with city firms.

British Gas

British Gas moved 5000 of its service engineers to teleworking four years ago, enabling it to close 440 depots and reporting stations. The firm invested £20 million in the hardware and the back-up for the changeover, but says that it has recouped that many times over. In the words of Chris Wright at British Gas services, 'The increase in efficiency is staggering. It has made a significant and material difference to our return to profitability.'

Teleworking managers admit, '... it is harder to monitor the time that people spend on things and whether you're getting value for money, but you save so much money, you have built in a margin for that.'

Your agenda

1 How can teleworking enable a firm to expand more easily?
2 Are there any drawbacks to the practice which may hinder the future expansion of the firm or curtail its growth forecasts?
3 What kind of corporate culture is most suited to a teleworking business?

There are obvious cash savings to be made from encouraging individuals to work from home. The added bonus of staff who are less stressed by journeys to and from the office and by the 'office environment' is less measurable and may in fact prove to be less of a bonus than companies first envisaged. Nevertheless, teleworking is becoming more and more popular.

It is obvious that teleworking will be most effective where there is an atmosphere of trust in the business. People need to be empowered to take their own decisions and a democratic leadership structure will help to ensure that communications work well in both directions. Operating at its best, teleworking can give the business a degree of cost leadership.

Labour market flexibility and aggregate supply

Flexible labour markets help employers to make efficient use of their employees. People can be deployed to do the tasks which need doing. They can move from one type of task to another without delays. Extra people can be taken on on a temporary or part-time basis at times of peak demand. These kinds of flexibility can increase productivity and contribute to cost leadership.

Whenever it is possible to increase productivity, the capacity of the economy to supply goods and services is increased. The people and the capital equipment available at the time can be made to produce more. Aggregate supply increases. If many businesses are exploiting these possibilities, the effect on the economy as a whole will be significant and real incomes will rise.

Labour market flexibility can be a response to poor trading conditions and the need to cut costs to stay competitive. Economic recovery, equally, provides incentives to organise the workforce effectively. The need to meet delivery schedules when demand is expanding encourages businesses to implement changes, looking for good ways both to motivate and to organise the workforce. Expanding production while simultaneously retaining competitive advantage opens up many possibilities.

This option began by looking at how businesses plan for the future in normal circumstances. Now it is time to examine what happens when short-term changes in the business environment begin to affect decisions. As the economy grows, supply constraints become a problem and prices may rise more quickly. Businesses and individuals will be affected and the government will use macro-economic policy.

1 Running into the buffers

Pfizer's growth plan

Pfizer, the US healthcare company, has been located at Sandwich in Kent since 1954. It has brought steady inward investment and created 4500 jobs. Between 1996 and 1999 it hired nearly 2000 staff, and it followed that up with a new research facility which could employ a further 1000. Viagra was discovered on this site, and capacity was set to double by late 2000. The company says every job there supports another five in the surrounding area. There is generally high unemployment there and the jobs are welcome.

Meantime, the company was conscious of problems developing. Ken Moran, Pfizer's UK chairman, said, 'We are outstripping the ability of infrastructure to meet our day-to-day needs. This is not just about roads, it is about train services, hotels, cultural things. It's about housing and schools. If we were to double in size, the infrastructure would crumble.'

The company discussed the issues with Kent County Council, the train and bus operators and the South East Development Agency. It gave employees incentives not to drive to work in a single occupant car. The company expected increasing sales of its newer drugs. However, constraints could limit its growth in the Sandwich area.

Your agenda

1 If many businesses are growing and successful, what local problems may be created?

2 Pfizer decided to recruit some of its employees from other parts of Europe. How would this affect the local area?

3 There are solutions for the problems identified. What are they? What are their implications for the company and the community?

During a recession, trading conditions are difficult. But once demand starts to grow, optimism returns and many businesses try to expand to meet the demand. If they have investment plans, they will activate them as quickly as they can, once they are confident that the increases in demand are likely to continue.

At any one time, there is a finite limit to what can be produced in an economy. The resources of labour and capital are there. They can be increased in quantity by means of investment and training, but both these take time. The maximum output that can be produced now is termed full capacity output.

As aggregate demand increases, businesses respond by expanding production. The economy moves closer to its full capacity output and as it does so, various kinds of supply constraints start to become a problem. The Pfizer case study highlights some likely problems for an area where facilities are not really sufficient. But it is not alone: Cambridge has become the European answer to California's silicon valley and the choices there are difficult.

A new town?

Cambridge Futures, a joint venture between local businesses, Cambridge University and the local government, is analysing ways to cope with local population growth using computer simulations. It has a number of proposals. A new town would help to curb car use in Cambridge, which is very congested already. The alternatives could be to restrict growth, or allow surrounding towns and villages to expand, or build more densely in the city. None of these options is entirely satisfactory. The plain fact is that further growth raises costs. John Prescott, the Minister for Transport and the Environment, favours building along public transport routes. But this means investing in railways and hoping that people will use them rather than their cars.

Your agenda

1 What are the constraints that the area is up against?

2 Local businesses could be persuaded to relocate to areas of declining employment. Why is it unlikely that this strategy would be successful?

3 What might finally push businesses to seek other locations?

4 It seems odd to be talking about restricting growth, when growth brings jobs and prosperity. Is it a serious option? Why?

Supply constraints

The two case studies here are stories of supply constraints which affect particular areas. There are many parts of the UK which are not afflicted in this way. Yet the companies which locate in them have done so for very good reasons. When the economy picks up, supply constraints appear at first in small areas, then in particular sectors. Eventually, most of the economy begins to overheat.

Figure O2.20 shows the overall picture. Aggregate demand shifts to the right. As it does, the quantity of unemployed resources – unemployed labour and underutilised capital – shrinks. To start with, there were enough resources lying idle in the economy to produce an extra quantity of output, XZ. As demand

increases these unemployed resources are put to work. With aggregate demand at its higher level, only enough unemployed resources remain to produce an extra YZ of output. By this time, some particular types of resources will be getting scarce. If demand goes on rising fast, all sorts of supply constraints will develop.

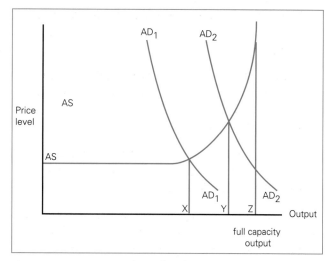

Figure O2.20 Aggregate demand and supply constraints

The closer output gets to the full capacity level, the larger the number of businesses which will have difficulty expanding. It is easy to see that this kind of pressure on resources will tend to push up prices. Often, you can see it coming as house and commercial property prices start to rise faster.

The last big boom

If you refer back to Module 3.1, page 187, you can review the main events of the business cycle for the past 20 years. You will notice that the cycle of boom and bust does not proceed with regularity. Events intervene. Sometimes the boom and the bust are acute in quality. Recently, they have been rather more muted.

The big overheating story of 1988 tells us what happened when the economy was allowed to grow unsustainably fast. You can see exactly what happened in Figure O2.21.

● The economy was warming up anyway, proceeding through the recovery phases of the cycle.

- In 1987 a substantial tax cut and a year of relatively low interest rates gave demand a real boost. For some reason, the government ignored the evidence of mounting supply constraints.

- Growth in 1988 was nearly 5 per cent – quite unsustainable in a developed economy at any time. (Remember the 2 per cent long-run trend rate of growth, based on real increases in productive capacity?)

- The supply constraints got worse and inflation got going with vigour. The government saw that its flagship policy, stable prices, was about to be blown out of the air.

- Interest rates were raised sharply and, quite suddenly, the boom was at an end. The economy went down and down…

This is a long time ago now, but unless something similar happens in the next few years, it is still the best example of unsustainably fast growth in the UK.

Work in progress

Q1 With an economy growing well, why might the government not try to slow it down?

2 What happens to imports and investment during a boom? Why?

3 How was 1988 different from 1997?

4 What has happened since this was written?

1993–9

The recession which followed the late 1980s boom was a long and deep one. Business confidence took a real beating and was a long time recovering. You can see though that the years 1993–7 were good ones for growth. There were plenty of unemployed resources. Businesses had overdone the investment in the late 1980s and they had spare capacity. Unemployment was relatively high. The private sector set about putting people back to work. Inflation was comfortably

	GDP* growth (%)	Investment growth (%)	Inflation (%)	Unemployment (%)**	Import growth (%)
1985	4.0	4.2	6.0	11.8	2.6
1986	4.0	2.6	3.4	11.8	6.9
1987	4.6	10.3	4.2	10.5	7.8
1988	4.9	13.9	4.9	8.4	12.6
1989	2.3	6.0	7.8	6.3	7.4
1990	0.6	−3.5	9.4	5.7	0.5
1991	−2.1	−9.5	5.9	8.0	−5.2
1992	−0.5	−1.5	3.8	9.7	6.9
1993	2.2	0.6	1.6	10.3	3.0
1994	4.5	4.3	2.5	9.4	5.5
1995	2.8	1.5	3.5	8.3	4.2
1996	2.5	1.5	2.4	7.5	8.4
1997	3.1	4.8	3.2	5.5	9.2
1998	2.4	0.1	3.5	4.7	1.9
1999 estimate	1.3	0	1.3	4.6	n.a.

* Gross domestic product at constant factor cost ** Claimant count

Source: ONS, *Monthly Digest Statistics*

Figure O2.21 Main economic indicators, 1985–98

inside the government's target range…

… until 1997. Signs of overheating reappeared. Monetary policy damped things down a bit and the Asian financial crisis blew up too. The UK economy entered a period of complex and conflicting indicators which will be explored in more detail through the rest of this enquiry. First, though, there is more evidence to consider.

2 Where are the skills?

Very special people

There is an acute shortage of sheet-metal workers. They are a crucial input for aircraft manufacturers. For some reason they are not being trained. Recruiting teams from Canada and the USA have been attracting them to work at Boeing, among others.

Construction workers are always in short supply during a boom. Take bricklayers, and many other construction skills. Building work suffers greatly during recessions but recovers as prospects improve. During the recovery many building projects are started. After a while, shortages of skilled construction people become a major constraint. The Construction Federation, an employers organisation, says that with more young people going to university it is sometimes hard to find suitable apprentices.

There is a permanent shortage of civil engineers in the UK. Entry to the training is relatively easy, provided you have mathematical ability. Starting pay is £24 000. Sometimes French engineers have been brought in to fill the gap. Maybe all the numerate types are going into the financial sector. That's what the Engineering Employers' Federation says, anyway.

Teachers are being recruited from Australia and Holland, among other places. When job opportunities are numerous, teachers leave to do other things. In London particularly, the shortfall is to some extent made up from overseas.

Your agenda

1 What would you expect to happen when employers find it hard to recruit the people they need?

2 What other skill shortages do you know of? Why do they exist?

3 What is the long-term impact of skill shortages?

4 Is there a solution to the problem?

5 Go back to Figure O2.21. In which year of the recovery do you think skill shortages might have begun to become a problem?

Just as some areas experience local physical constraints on growth, some companies have difficulty recruiting the people they need. If they are trying to attract people with very scarce skills, they may have a problem even during recessions. The difficulties can be seen in the data from the CBI Industrial Trends Survey in Figure O2.22. The number of businesses which expect skill shortages to limit growth gives an indication of the seriousness of recruiting difficulties over time.

Year	% of respondents expecting skilled labour to be a limiting factor within the next four months
1987	18
1988	24
1989	24
1990	15
1991	4
1992	4
1993	5
1994	8
1995	10
1996	10
1997	13
1998	12
1999	10*

Source: *National Institute Economic Review*, May 1999
* By the end of 1999 the figure was 11 and rising

Figure O2.22 Expected skill shortages

To some extent, the problem of scarce skills reflects a mismatch between the skills people actually have and the skills employers want. There have been times when skill shortages were clearly a problem, yet large numbers of people remained unemployed. The process of structural change has led to some industries declining. Skilled people, like welders working in the Clyde shipyards, have been unable to find work. The growing industries were looking for people such as computer systems engineers in London and the Thames valley.

When this happens, it is clear that much of the unemployment is structural rather than cyclical in nature. The unemployed people are affected by occupational and geographical immobilities which make it impossible for them to find work. Relatively few employers are looking for unskilled people and those that are tend to be looking elsewhere than in the areas where unemployment is high.

Work in progress

Q 1 Using Figure O2.22, why did few employers expect skill shortages in 1991–2?
2 What was the problem in 1988?
3 Are skill shortages a problem at the present time?
4 In which years were skill shortages and unemployment both problematic?
5 What is the solution to this problem? Why, in your view, has it not been implemented?

Why not train people in scarce skills?

Skill shortages have been around for quite a while, so you would think that training programmes would have sprung up to meet the need. Up to a point, they have. The government has set up new vocational training systems, which have brought a wide range of qualifications into the unified system of National Vocational Qualifications (NVQs). Many businesses do have good training programmes.

There are several aspects to training:

- General skills and knowledge are mainly acquired off the job, sometimes within a business, often at a local college or university.

- Firm-specific skills are acquired during on-the-job training.

- Staff development occurs when various means are used to help employees to reach their full potential.

Unfortunately, repeated research programmes have shown that training in the UK does not receive enough attention. The government tried to address this with its Investors in People scheme, which encourages businesses to involve all their employees in training and development. This was a step in the right direction and many businesses have responded. The Internet is providing new, time-saving ways of approaching training. The fact remains that skill shortages are still a serious problem in some occupations.

The costs of not training adequately are well

known. For individual businesses, recruitment costs are higher, employees are less productive than they might be, they are also less flexible as to the tasks they can do and accident rates may be higher than they should be. Nationally, productivity grows more slowly than it does in some competitor countries.

So why is training neglected?

There is an obvious solution to the problem of skill shortages. It is to train people. However, it is always expensive to do this. Some employers argue that if they train people they will simply lose them to other employers just when they are becoming most productive. Small businesses feel they do not have the facilities for extensive training. Many employers argue that the government should do more.

Some people argue that the government has put all its efforts into improving access to academic education and neglected vocational education. It is difficult to tell whether this is true. Research has shown though that vocational training is not as effective in the UK as it is in Germany.

Work in progress

Q 1 We know what happens when demand rises for something which is in fixed supply in the short run. Draw a diagram which gives a prediction.

2 Go back to the opening case study on page 487. Pfizer was expanding in an area of high unemployment, yet for some reason it was recruiting in continental Europe. Why could this be?

Is it just training that is at fault?

Sometimes, particular kinds of people are scarce. Take biotechnology. European companies are all having difficulty finding suitable managers for this. The problem is that they need people who are good at science but who also understand the world of business.

As the scientific discoveries created opportunities, venture capitalists collaborated to get new companies up and running. The problem was that the products tended to be very risky. Their likely commercial success was very hard to predict. Where new drugs are involved, clinical trials, which may or may not work out well, add additional uncertainty. Managers who are able to assess the risks reasonably accurately are hard to find.

A number of managers from the big pharmaceuticals companies such as Glaxo SmithKline have gone on to head smaller businesses. Meantime, if weak management leads to poor results, European venture capitalists may take their funds elsewhere, leaving the biotechnology field wide open for US companies.

Your agenda

1 Why are people unwilling to get involved in risky businesses?

2 What skills are needed to make sound judgements?

3 How might these problems be overcome?

What happens next?

The business which does not attempt to train its own employees must recruit people when it needs additional skills. If lots of other employers are looking for the same skills, it is clear that wages will be bid up as they try to poach key workers from each other. This is easily observed among construction workers during a boom. Many Irish construction workers went back to Dublin in 1998 as there was so much building work to be had there. (Businesses that wanted to be in the euro zone and in an English speaking country were moving to Dublin in a big way.) That must have meant that wages had risen in Dublin to the point where employers could compete with London construction companies for the scarce skills.

There is an element of short-termism in business attitudes to training. Ideally, employers should be able to predict their need for skilled people, promote people with potential in scarce skills and anticipate their training needs. Unfortunately, more often, they see poaching as cheaper and try to recruit instead.

The supply of skilled workers is perfectly inelastic, i.e. fixed, for the length of time it takes to train more. This means that wages in the short run are demand-determined. They can rise sharply when the economy is in its recovery phase and employers are actively recruiting. The business which has not predicted its training needs and taken steps to meet them internally will be competing with other employers for a fixed pool of skills. People who have the scarce skills can negotiate pay increases very easily.

As pay rises in some sectors where skill shortages are a problem, it may also rise elsewhere. If pay has traditionally been determined by reference to what other types of workers are getting, the general tendency for pay to rise may spread across the economy.

3 Will prices rise?

Skills shortages: a crucial issue

Spring 1997

The *Financial Times* reported that the UK's skilled labour shortage was worsening. It warned that this might lead to higher inflation: employers would be likely to raise wages in order to retain key staff. Reed Personnel Services, the recruitment company, was reporting a lack of skilled job applicants. The biggest problems were in East Anglia, the Midlands, Wales, the south and the London area. Alec Reed, the organisation's chairman, said, 'Skill shortages have clearly emerged as one of the most crucial issues facing UK business today. Rising requirements for multi-skilling across the board and increasing demand for new staff as the economy continues to recover from recession have all combined to create a major problem.'

January 1998

A survey carried out by the British Chambers of Commerce reported widespread skills shortages. Sales and management staff, clerical and office workers are all hard to find. The report said that wage inflation might rise as companies fought to find recruits from a diminishing pool of qualified people. The government had failed to hit its 2.5 per cent target for inflation in December. Ian Peters, deputy director of the British Chambers of Commerce, said, 'Skills shortages create major capacity constraints in the economy, giving rise to inflationary pressures, just what the UK does not need at the present time. Meantime the education system appears to be failing to meet the needs of the small business which tends to be hardest hit by skills shortages.'

Your agenda

1 Go back to the case study 'Very special people' on page 490. What was your answer to question 5? Did you predict the timing correctly from the data?

2 Why did the UK economy develop skill shortages this time?

3 Why were skill shortages 'just what the UK doesn't need at the present time'?

4 Why did these skill shortages become less of a problem in 1998? (Go back to Figure O2.22 for the data.)

A pay increase for the employee is a cost increase for the employer. During the recovery phase of the business cycle, many businesses find it easy to pass increased costs on to the consumer in the form of higher prices, so they may not be unduly disturbed at having to put prices up.

Figure O2.20 (page 488) showed that prices would rise as the economy approaches full capacity output. It certainly looked as though this was going to happen at the time of the two reports above. Thinking again about what happened in the period 1988–90, the prediction definitely fits. Figure O2.21 (page 489) shows that after the boom year, inflation accelerated for two more years. By the time it reached its peak of 9.4 per cent in 1990, businesses were certainly not happy.

The impact of inflation on businesses

The trouble with inflation is that once it accelerates, it is very hard to stop. Expectations of inflation cause people to seek wage bargains which will preserve their real incomes. These wage bargains involve increased business costs and further increases in prices. So inflation gets built into the system.

For businesses, there are a number of implications:

● High inflation tends to be variable and to accelerate further. It becomes unpredictable.
● The higher the rate of inflation, the harder it is to make plans for the future. Uncertainty creates problems for businesses. Expansion plans have to promise higher profits in the future before they can be implemented.
● There are gainers and losers: businesses which depend on borrowed funds may find the interest rates needed to compensate lenders for the loss of value of their money create cash flow problems.
● Inflation brings a variety of economic, business and social problems in its wake and governments may raise interest rates to combat it. This 'in turn' will cause the economy to slow down.

Most people in business would regard 9.4 per cent inflation as much too high for comfort.

For the Conservative governments of the 1980s, controlling inflation had always been the highest priority, so the Cabinet was deeply dismayed when it realised that the boom had turned nasty in 1988. Interest rates were raised and kept high while the economy cooled down. That meant aggregate demand fell sharply and businesses were, in many cases, thrown into deep distress. The rate at which they went bankrupt rose and so did unemployment. The resulting reductions in many people's incomes caused a good deal of suffering. They also created downward multiplier effects, further reducing demand for goods and services.

The instability of the late 1980s and early 1990s did not at all suit the business world in general. Businesses want a predictable and stable business environment. They want to concentrate on expanding their markets without the disruptions caused by recession, which at best has a very detrimental effect on profits.

The impact of inflation on people

The real costs of inflation to people are a matter for debate. There is no doubt that, in general, people do not like inflation, especially if they are older. It becomes a nuisance to try to keep track of price changes and consumers become confused. On the other hand, if their pay is keeping up with prices and their real incomes are not affected, what is the problem? The fact is that there are gainers and losers, but it is not always quite clear what the overall effect is for each individual:

■ Borrowers find the real value of their loans falling. They have less to pay back in real terms. People with mortgages benefit, unless interest rates are high.
■ Savers' bank balances lose their real value. Unless interest rates are comfortably above the rate of inflation, they lose.
■ Older people with incomes which are fixed in money terms lose. This may happen if they have pensions which are not indexed.
■ Money does not work well if its value is unstable. People try to find other ways of holding their savings and paying for the things they want. Decisions become more problematic and many tasks which are normally straightforward become more complicated.

Low rates of inflation do not seem to have serious effects on individuals, for the most part. However, the higher the rate of inflation, the more likely it is to become part of people's expectations and therefore to rise some more. The consequences of hyperinflation are very serious indeed for the economy as a whole. Hyperinflation occurs when prices are rising daily. For example, in Israel during the 1980s inflation rose to 1000 per cent. At that point, people began to use US dollars instead of their worthless shekels. Germany has retained a lasting abhorrence of hyperinflation since its experience of 1923: middle-class Germans lost most of their savings, which simply became worthless. The conclusion must be that controlling inflation is essential to maintaining a stable economic and business environment.

What actually happened in 1998?

By now you have probably realised that 1997–8 was not at all like 1988–9. Figure O2.23 shows what actually happened in 1997 and 1998, but keep in mind the Asian financial crisis as well. Asian markets are large and very important to UK exporters. As one country after another developed problems, starting in mid-1997, investment was cut back and demand for imports plummeted. That meant that just as the UK economy was coming up to the boil, it cooled off again.

- *Average earnings* is a useful measure of wage inflation. (It had some problems in 1988 due to technical difficulties affecting data collection – it seems to have overstated the wage increase. However, it is better than nothing.)
- *Vacancies* are a measure of labour market tightness.
- *Unemployment* shows the extent to which changing output is affecting employees.
- *Inflation* shows how the upward pressure was developing.
- *Base rate* tells us what the Bank of England was up to.
- *Quarterly data* help to show the changes in detail.

In mid-1997 the rise in inflation produced a very swift response from the Bank of England. Base rates were raised. Even with a time lag, we would expect unemployment to be affected by late 1998. Yet it wasn't – it was still on its way down. Perhaps even more surprising, vacancies were still on their way up. The labour market data suggest continued overheating, but then we would expect to see average earnings and inflation reflecting the strong demand for labour and more bidding up of wages. Do we see this?

	Average earnings (% growth)	Vacancies (000s)	Unemployment (%)	Inflation (%)	Base rate (%)
1997					
Q1	3.8	278	6.2	2.7	6.0
Q2	4.1	284	5.7	2.7	6.0
Q3	5.1	296	5.3	3.5	6.9
Q4	4.7	282	5.0	3.7	7.2
1998					
Q1	4.9	284	4.8	3.4	7.3
Q2	4.9	298	4.8	4.0	7.3
Q3	4.4	302	4.6	3.4	7.5
Q4	4.9	309	4.6	3.0	6.8

Source: *National Institute Economic Review*, May 1999

Figure O2.23 Was the economy overheating or cooling off?

We see inflationary pressures only to a limited extent. Inflation did rise, but then fell back again. Before we can really make sense of this, we need to look again at the international dimension.

Work in progress

Q Summarising the work of this section, the 1988 boom offers a textbook case of an economy generating rapid growth, accelerating inflation and serious skill shortages. In the 1990s, we have a challenge. There is a complex unfolding story. The textbook can only take you so far. To understand what happened you need to study the data for the gap between when this book was written and when you read it. Very recent data is published in many Sunday broadsheets, as well as in the *Financial Times* and *The Economist*.

4 Expand or import?

Where to get the goods?

'I'm sorry Mr White, I understand that you need regular supplies of meters if you are to complete your orders. But we cannot possibly supply them in less than ten weeks. We have a long order book and we are already working flat out.'

This sort of conversation can be heard when the economy is getting close to full capacity. The solution for many businesses is to find an overseas supplier. Bottlenecks of this sort do not only encourage rising prices. They lead to a rapid surge in imports as businesses try to obtain the supplies they need.

Your agenda

1 Look at Figure O2.21 (page 489). What do the data tell us about the likelihood of imports rising during a boom?

2 What would you expect to happen to exports at such a time?

3 What impact would these changes have on the exchange rate?

4 What is the likely future impact on UK business?

Imports rise as the economy grows for a number of different reasons:

- If incomes are rising, many consumers will buy imports. Foreign holidays and luxury imports become more affordable. Many such products have a high income elasticity of demand, so if consumption is rising, imports rise.

- If **bottlenecks** are developing in the economy, it makes sense to try to remedy the situation by importing. This means that any business which has been buying inputs on the domestic market will consider importing if shortages develop.

- If prices are rising, competitiveness may be affected. Accelerating inflation can make imports look like a much better buy. If the inflation rate is on the way up while competing countries have relatively stable prices, then competitiveness will be lost quite quickly. Within a few months imports will rise, unless the exchange rate is falling to compensate.

Typically, the income elasticity of demand for imports in the UK is quite high. So we would expect the level of imports to move with GDP growth.

Meantime, what can be expected of exports? Exports are greatly affected by exchange rates. A fall in the exchange rate increases competitiveness. For most manufactured products world markets are very competitive indeed, so export levels depend very much on whether sterling is high or low relative to the currencies of the UK's trading partners.

The other important influence on exports generally is how easy it is to sell on the domestic market. Selling in your own market is relatively easy. Communications are close, the market is well known, there are no language problems. Sometimes, the home market is more profitable. Many businesses make less effort to export when domestic demand is buoyant. They redouble their export effort when home sales are falling.

Other things being equal, we can predict what will happen to the current account of the balance of payments over the course of the business cycle. It is much more likely to be in deficit during a boom than during recession. Figure O2.24 shows the current balance, which includes all trade in goods (visible trade) and in services (invisible trade). Services are important to the UK because they help to reduce the permanent deficit on visible trade.

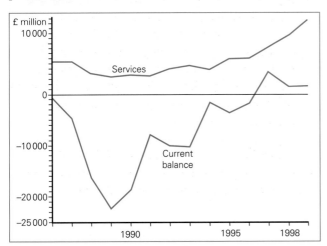

Figure O2.24 Balance of payments on current account

Source: ONS, *Monthly Digest Statistics*

Does the current account deficit become a problem? On the whole, not often, is the answer. Over the years it has usually been balanced by an inflow of capital. This is partly composed of funds invested on the London money market and partly of direct investment by multi-nationals.

Work in progress

Q 1 What happened to the current account of the balance of payments during the 1988 boom? Why?

2 In 1992 the pound was taken out of the European Exchange Rate Mechanism (ERM), after two years of being fixed against the deutschemark and other currencies. Immediately, it fell sharply (see Figure O2.25). How did this affect importers and exporters?

3 In 1997 the UK economy was beginning to overheat, with reports of skill shortages. What effect would you expect this to have on the current account?

4 Is your prediction confirmed by the subsequent data? Give reasons for your answer.

The exchange rate

Floating exchange rates respond to changes in the supply of and demand for the currency. If imports are rising, the supply of the currency increases and the exchange rate depreciates. This, in turn, will make imports dearer and discourage consumption of them. Changes in exports work similarly on the demand for the currency. (Refer to Module 3.1 page 205 to refresh your memory.) In theory, exchange rate flexibility irons out a trade deficit, given time.

So far, so good. But it has to be remembered that capital movements affect the exchange rate too. The UK, with an important capital market in the City of London, really notices the impact of capital movements on the pound.

Generally speaking, exchange rates are allowed to float, i.e. they are determined by market forces. This means that even if there is some inflation, competitiveness on world markets can be maintained by an exchange rate depreciation. However, within the euro zone, all member countries have a single currency and a single floating exchange rate with trading partners outside the zone. This means that inflation within one member country will cause it to lose competitiveness relative to other members and no exchange rate adjustment is possible.

Before the euro zone, many EU countries belonged to the European Exchange Rate Mechanism, which kept member currencies very close to each other. When the UK was inside the ERM, from 1990 to 1992, the exchange rate at which it went in was too high for the country's manufacturers to compete comfortably. When the UK came out, the pound dropped quite fast.

Take a look at Figure O2.25 and see the evidence. Then go back to Figure O2.21 (page 489) and see what was happening to economic growth. The depreciation made exporters very much more competitive and the result was several years of strong growth, especially in manufacturing.

Figure O2.25 The sterling index (1990 = 100)

Source: *National Institute Economic Review*, May 1999

Although the UK economy benefited from depreciation after 1992, many people would argue that a fluctuating exchange rate brings more problems than it solves. It can become very unstable and unpredictable, making business planning difficult. Furthermore, depreciation makes imports dearer, which itself raises the Retail Prices Index. It may be better to control inflation rather than to let it happen and then adjust through the exchange rate.

The exchange rate and macro-economic policy

The effects of the business cycle are complicated by the exchange rate. Some exchange rate changes are themselves a consequence of the cyclical changes. Equally, if the exchange rate changes for a specific reason, that will compound the way the economy is reacting. Macro-economic policy brings a third strand into the situation. Monetary policy and the exchange rate are very intimately linked. Changes in interest rates affect the decisions of people who hold large money balances.

Hot money means money which can move easily from one country to another. Its owners are primarily concerned with getting the best interest rate they can. If interest rates in London go up, hot money will flow on to the London money market and drive up the exchange rate.

Essentials

Hot money is money which moves around the world's financial centres in search of the best rate of return.

Quite often, capital flows are the dominant influence on exchange rates. Appreciation caused by a capital inflow can create big problems for exporters.

5 Monetary policy working

Asia and Europe

Shock waves in Asia

Riots in Jakarta

Bank close to collapse

During the Asian financial crisis, owners of hot money departed. They sold their Asian currency balances very fast indeed. What did they get in exchange for their Asian currencies? They got pounds, dollars, marks.... anything that they felt confidence in. A lot of Asian currencies depreciated very sharply.

A quick look at Figure O2.25 for the years 1997–9 makes the position clear from the UK point of view.

Your agenda

1 What effect would these changes have on UK exporters?

2 Explain the impact on the UK economy.

3 What was happening to inflation and to interest rates in 1997?

to appreciate. Then problems in the UK became more widespread. All UK exporters became less competitive, so many more businesses were fighting for orders. During 1998 an increasing number of manufacturing businesses announced cutbacks and in some cases closed down their factories. The service sector was not greatly affected.

Boom and bust at the same time

As 1998 wore on, two very different pictures emerged. The UK was becoming a two-tier economy. Manufacturing was increasingly afflicted and clearly going into recession. During the first quarter of 1999, manufacturing output fell by 0.3 per cent. Yet GDP as a whole continued to grow, albeit slowly for a short time. Services were doing well enough to keep the economy going.

The MPC grew worried again and started to cut interest rates in late 1998. By mid-1999 they stood at 5 per cent. Inflation was low. Unemployment was still falling, a bit.

Your agenda

1 Why did services do so much better than manufacturing?

2 Why did the MPC feel it was safe to cut interest rates at the end of 1998?

At the time that the Asian financial crisis began to be a problem in 1997, the UK economy was rapidly running into supply constraints. It seemed likely that imminent skill shortages would lead to accelerating inflation. The Monetary Policy Committee (MPC) of the Bank of England was worried. It needed to discourage borrowing, to slow the economy down before expectations of inflation made it hard to stop. It raised interest rates. Figure O2.23 page 495 has all the data.

As the Asian crisis unfolded, the first people to lose were the businesses which had important export markets in the Asian countries with difficulties. They found orders were drying up.

The hot money flowing out of the affected Asian countries was attracted by the relatively high interest rates on the London money market. The pound began

If inflation is rising, a floating exchange rate will depreciate. Depreciation brings competitiveness and can have positive effects, but they may not last too long. One reason for not letting inflation get out of control is that governments may prefer not to depreciate. Stable currencies can be a help to businesses. They make life more predictable.

If the MPC raises interest rates to choke off inflation, the result may be that sterling appreciates. Of course, this is partly how monetary policy works. The rise in the exchange rate makes exporting businesses less competitive. Orders fall and they will cut production. This reduces their demand for skilled labour and other resources which are scarce. The increased unemployment reduces pressure for pay increases, costs rise more slowly and inflation is damped down. Figure O2.26 summarises the story.

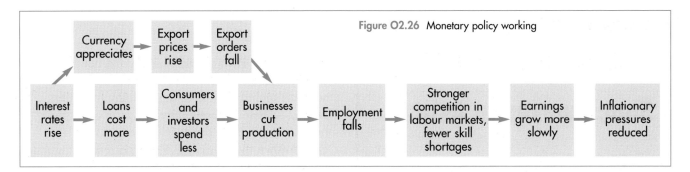

Figure O2.26 Monetary policy working

Recovery round the corner

Really, the recession in manufacturing didn't get very far. Despite the manufacturers' fears, by mid-1999, recovery was under way. Much of the service sector really had nothing to recover from. Manufacturers thought exchange rates might fall. Reports from Asia suggested that the worst was over. Profit margins improved.

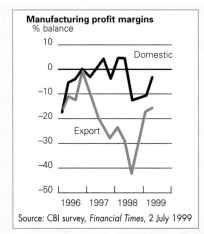

Figure O2.27 Manufacturing profit margins

Peter Lamble, managing director of Start-Rite shoes, was optimistic: 'We've seen exports increased to the Middle East and Australasia in the past six months, after suffering from the economic turmoil of last year. The further eastwards you go, the better it is. Things still aren't fantastic, but it's a lot better than last year. People who weren't interested in making orders then are now starting to reappear. Exports to Europe are still down, because of the weakness of the euro. But Start-Rite opted to cut its profit margins rather than reduce sales volume, in an effort to maintain its position

in overseas markets. If the euro's position is reversed, we pick up our margins straight away. Meantime the company has been helped because the strong pound meant cheaper raw materials.'

It is clear that some manufacturers have survived by cutting the labour force and keeping down wage growth. Productivity has increased in some sectors.

Meantime, in the service sector job creation continued as output carried on growing.

Your agenda

1 What was Start-Rite's response to the Asian crisis? Why?

2 If GDP starts to grow faster, what would you expect to happen next?

3 What would the policy response be?

4 Look at the data for subsequent years. What actually happened? How were businesses affected?

Is there a role for fiscal policy?

Monetary policy is not the only way to control the growth of spending. Tax increases can be used to reduce overheating. They cut disposable income and with it the spending power of all taxpayers. Consumption falls and with it, aggregate demand.

The snag is that recent governments have promised not to increase income taxes. They are unlikely to increase VAT either – it is already quite high. This rules out fiscal policy as a macro-economic tool. Other taxes might be increased, but their impact on spending will be limited.

This could change. Taxes in the UK are low by

European standards and could be raised. It is a little hard to imagine though. Many people might feel that if they pay more tax they want more public services. This won't work. If the tax revenue is immediately pumped back into, say, the NHS, spending will be unaffected overall. For tax increases to cut spending they have to be accompanied by a reduction in government borrowing.

Reducing government borrowing does sometimes mean that interest rates can be kept lower than they otherwise would be. Governments borrow by selling bonds. In order to encourage people to buy the bonds, interest rates have to be high enough to attract them. Selling bonds can push up interest rates generally.

6 Can we maintain stability?

How do they do it at the ECB?

Within the euro zone, all monetary policy is decided by the European Central Bank (ECB). Under the terms of the Maastricht Treaty, the ECB is charged with maintaining price stability. Euro interest rates are decided by a committee drawn from all member countries.

At the time of writing, the euro interest rate is lower than that of the UK. So are inflation rates. But unemployment is generally high. There is little doubt that the ECB will keep inflation under control. Inside the euro zone, the UK would be unlikely to experience higher inflation.

There have been suggestions that the MPC is a more flexible body than the committee of the ECB. It is really too soon to say what the implications of this are.

Your agenda

By the time you read this, our knowledge of the way the ECB works will be much greater than it is now. Find out how interest and inflation rates in the euro zone compare with the UK. If the UK is already in, find out how the euro zone compares with the USA. Explain any obvious differences.

One way to avoid exchange rate changes is to be inside Economic and Monetary Union (EMU). On joining, the pound will be fixed forever against the euro. If, after that, inflation accelerates in the UK, businesses will lose competitiveness and the government will not be able to change the exchange rate. UK businesses will therefore have to make quite sure that inflation does not accelerate. Not for long, anyway. EMU provides a massive incentive to control inflation and enforces exchange rate stability within the euro zone.

Any change in the value of the euro relative to the rest of the world will come about because of European conditions as a whole, and will not necessarily reflect UK trade with outside countries.

So, in the event of inflation in the UK, what could the government do? Well, it could raise tax rates. This would help to damp down demand, reduce supply constraints and diminish inflationary pressures. However, if the EU has set about harmonizing taxes, it might not be possible. Then, inflation in the UK would simply mean that UK companies had lost competitiveness

relative to the rest of the euro zone. Demand for their products would fall, they would contract output and lay off workers. Either earnings growth and costs would fall or unemployment would rise.

Achieving stability would mean making quite sure that inflation did not accelerate. At the moment that looks easy to arrange but things can change.

Why were earnings growing slowly in the UK in 1999?

To date, it appears that the UK managed to keep inflation down despite a historically low rate of unemployment and a good deal of talk about skill shortages. How can this be? All the ingredients for wage inflation seem to be present. There are two possible reasons why inflation remained low:

- Legislation designed to reduce the power of trade unions might be having an effect on pay negotiations. More people negotiate as individuals. The growing number of part-time and temporary workers have little bargaining power.

- A high pound means lower import prices. Imports figure quite large in the Retail Prices Index, as so many consumer goods are imported.

Work in progress

Q You now have all the equipment in place to look again at this question in the light of recent events. Had inflation really become less of a threat, or was it just a matter of time before it reappeared?

This enquiry contains two classic case studies. One is the 1988 boom and its aftermath. The other is the story of skill shortages in the 1990s. These two stories help to explain why monetary policy is seen as being so important in controlling the economy. The UK authorities may manage to avoid any significant further acceleration of inflation or they may not. If they do, it will be partly as a result of lessons learnt during previous periods of buoyant demand.

Retreat or recovery looks at the ways in which businesses and governments deal with recession. Businesses must look carefully at their strategy in order to avoid the worst impact of a shrinking economy. The government has a range of policy options which it can use in the circumstances. It needs to be clear about its rationale for those it chooses.

1 The downturn

Signs of worse to come?

The *CBI survey* showed that:

1991   18 per cent of firms in consumer services thought their businesses would shrink in the next six months.

1992   53 per cent of manufacturers' order books were below normal.

The *Chartered Institute of Purchasing and Supply*:

1991   recorded that manufacturing output and orders had fallen for the eighth month in a row.

The *Office for National Statistics*:

1990   revised its economic growth figures downwards from 0.5 per cent to 0.4 per cent.

1991   showed that growth in the past two quarters had partly come from increased stocks.

Your agenda

1 Explain the impact on the economy of each of these pieces of information. What would you expect to happen next?

2 These data show what was happening at the end of 1998. Find out what happened next. Can you explain why?

3 Track economic variables since then and explain the changes that have taken place.

All economies are subject to fluctuations which have impacts on people and business. When the business cycle moves into a downturn pressure is put on many sectors. Businesses that have been suffering in a very competitive market may finally go under in recession.

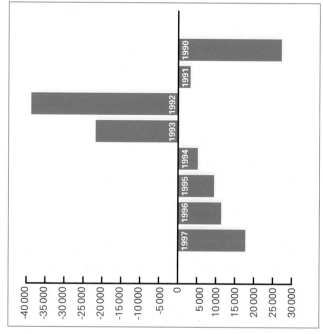

Figure O2.28 Registered businesses: net change, 1990–97
Source: ONS, *Regional Trends* 1999

As businesses close, the recessionary effects are increased. Demand is already falling and stocks held by businesses are rising, so the need for more production is diminishing. When businesses close, unemployment rises and demand will fall further because people have less to spend. The sequence continues as demand for many consumer goods falls. This means that an initial fall in demand has **multiplier** effects.

Essentials

The **multiplier** explains how an increase in spending has a greater impact on the economy than the initial amount spent. If more people are employed, they will have more to spend and therefore demand will increase. This will in itself create more employment and more people will be earning money… and so on.

Which businesses are vulnerable?

Many businesses survive recession but others fail. Why?

■ A high cost structure

Any business which has not been watching costs carefully will be vulnerable in recession. If costs have been allowed to rise during years of economic growth, once the downturn sets in the company's lack of competitiveness will be transparent. Orders will probably fall and it may be too late to retrieve the situation.

The high costs may have arisen from a variety of causes:

- A business may rely on resources from locations which are not in recession, so prices are still relatively high.

- A lack of investment will mean that the business has not embraced the latest technology.

- A lack of training may mean that the staff are not equipped to use the latest skills and technology.

It may be possible to change the source of inputs quickly in order to cut costs. Investment is however another matter. A business that is already in difficulties is unlikely to have financial resources to start investing. The bank will be unwilling to lend money for new equipment to a company which is in trouble for fear that it will be unable to repay the debt.

Even if investment is possible, there may be no time to train staff in the new skills which are necessary to use the new equipment.

■ Lack of flexibility

A business which cannot change quickly is more vulnerable than one which has developed working patterns that enable both products and people to change quickly.

Demand for luxury goods is often the first to fall in recession. A business may, for example, need to switch production from its top-of-the-range models to the more modest end of its output. Inability to do this will lead to stocks of expensive products rising, which ties

up a lot of money, while there may be a shortage of cheaper items for which demand is stronger.

A lack of flexibility is made worse in a company which does not keep a wary eye on market conditions. The type of data at the beginning of this section is constantly available. It is important to monitor changes in the economic climate as well as watching the patterns of orders received by the company.

■ Market focus

Any business with a market which is heavily concentrated in one particular country will be vulnerable. Not all countries follow the same path through the business cycle, so some may be in recession when others are booming. By selling to different countries, risks are spread.

Brazil was thought to be on the way to recovery when its economy succumbed again in 1998. The Asian financial crisis created problems and led to loss of confidence and collapsing demand there. Companies with a Brazilian focus therefore had to contend with a fall in demand and uncertainty about the future.

The pattern of the business cycle is not the only source of problems. Political upheaval can lead to economic crises. The Chinese, for example, were doing a roaring trade with Russians who were buying vast amounts of clothing, toys and shoes for their home market where such products were unobtainable. The visiting traders kept the hotels and restaurants busy as well as filling the cargo planes back to Russia. Political crises in the late 1990s threw the economy into free-fall and the Chinese were left with stockpiles of goods for which there was little demand in the home market.

■ Cash flow

Recession makes businesses particularly vulnerable to cash flow problems. When everyone is feeling the pinch, there is a strong temptation to leave bills unpaid for longer periods of time. A supplier company which relies on bills being paid on time in order to pay for raw materials, wages and everything else, will find its overdraft growing.

Cash flow can also be affected by rising stocks.

Goods which are sitting in the warehouse are not raising revenue and have storage costs. Budgets will probably have been set up on the basis of sales following a normal pattern. As recession sets in, demand and therefore orders will fall, so the budget will immediately become inaccurate.

If production and sales are not monitored carefully, the growing mismatch may not be noticed until it is too late. Even if the level of production is reduced, it will probably be difficult to cut costs proportionately because overhead costs are usually fixed, at least in the short term.

As the overdraft continues to grow, the bank may become impatient because it fears for the security of its loan. If it decides to call in the debt, the business will probably be forced to close.

Downturn hits the North East

The Siemens plant in the North East, which had cost US$650 million to build, was closed because of falling demand for semi-conductors. The price had fallen from $70 to $2, which made the plant non-viable. Despite the heavy investment, Siemens decided to cut its losses. Another effect of slowing economies was the closure of Grove Worldwide, a US company which made cranes.

In total, the region lost 4000 jobs through businesses shutting down or contracting. The Asian crisis was considered to be a cause of many of these closures.

Your agenda

1 How might recession in Asia affect the demand for semi-conductors?

2 Use demand and supply analysis to show why the price has fallen so dramatically.

3 Why do you think the UK plant was selected for closure in 1998 despite such heavy investment in only the previous year?

4 What impact will the loss of 4 000 jobs have on the region?

Not just their problem

Changes in the economic fortunes of other parts of the world can have knock-on effects in the UK. It is not just a case of UK businesses losing orders. The effects can be much more far reaching. The Asian financial crisis, for example, led to overseas businesses deciding not to go ahead with development plans or cutting back and closing factories in various parts of the UK.

Such actions can increase unemployment and reduce demand as well as having a negative effect on businesses which service the plant. The multiplier effect means that the impact of such changes has far-reaching effects on the local economy. An initial loss of jobs can be multiplied several times when the effect on local shops and other businesses are taken into account.

Inward investment is often attracted to parts of the country which have suffered from economic decline because the government offers grants (see Module 4.2, page 318).

What's the problem?

Recession first hits businesses which are inefficient and inflexible. Equally, it can undermine those which run on very tight margins because they have little room to cut back.

In cut-throat global markets, a lack of competitiveness will quickly lose markets for companies and countries. It is therefore essential that a business monitors its own internal activities as well as national and international economic movements.

2 Ahead of the game

Express Pizzas

Pizza Express has raced ahead. Despite the economic gloom of 1998, the company's half year profits leapt 40 per cent. Pre-tax profits rose from £9.4 million to £13.2 million in the second half of 1998.

Pizza Express has defied expectations with continuing growth. Admittedly, this year's 3 per cent increase in like-for-like sales was nowhere near last year's 12 per cent but their pizzas continue to be popular.

The company has set up franchise deals in South Africa, Spain, the Czech Republic, Hungary, Poland and North Africa. A joint venture in Japan is also on the cards.

The new pasta brands, planned for the home market, are another line of development. None of these ventures are expected to show results until 2001.

Your agenda

1 What is Pizza Express doing in order to spread risk?

2 How will these developments make the business less subject to changes in the economic climate?

3 What do you expect Pizza Express will have done before going ahead with these plans?

Managing strategy

Businesses that survive or succeed during recession rarely do so by chance. It takes foresight and planning to work out the path a company should take in the face of economic uncertainty. The range of data described in this option's enquiry 1 all contributes to the scene.

The culture and structure of an organisation will often determine how effectively it deals with the changing economic climate. The following four categories show some of the potential differences:

- *Incremental change* works in organisations which have standardised planning procedures. These are often large service and manufacturing companies. The environment is constantly being scanned for change and measures are taken to make small changes as and when necessary

- *Rational command* is generally the way that large companies work. Senior figures plan and direct strategy and create a strong vision or mission. The objectives of the company are clear to all and planning is carried out on this basis. The current environment is carefully researched and the future projected. When things do not go according to plan, senior management will review and redirect.

- *Muddling through* happens in smaller organisations, such as law firms and consultancies, in which the power is spread among more people. It often results in a more gradual strategic change and responsiveness rather than a pro-active approach.

- *Externally dependent* organisations have to work on strategy imposed from outside. Public sector organisations and large manufacturing companies are prone to such methods. Often a subsidiary company will have to follow the lead of the parent company. Such organisations are not very responsive to the changing external environment.

It is clear that a business which is in the habit of incremental change is better equipped for dealing with the challenges of recession because it will be constantly aware of changes in its markets and be able to adjust when necessary. However, the incremental change may be a technique that is more effective in a relatively stable environment.

Rational command can also be effective because the type of large plc that is organised on such a basis is able to employ specialists who can monitor the business environment and therefore contribute to the decision-making process. It may also take this sort of approach to deal with difficult decisions that can be necessary in a prolonged recession.

Businesses which will suffer particularly are those which 'muddle through' or are dependent on external forces for their decision-making. They will be unable to respond quickly and amend strategy to meet the changing environment.

The culture of the business is an important factor in the way these decisions are made. The business that adapts incrementally is likely to have a culture which is flexible and where people are working together as a team to meet the objectives.

Changing direction

Once a company is aware of the issue, it must set about making decisions about how to deal with it. A downturn in the economy will have been flagged in the press as the media have become much more aware of such potential changes in the economic climate.

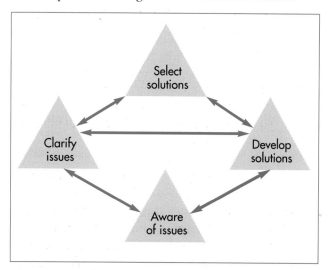

Figure O2.29 Making strategic decisions

Figure O2.29 shows how strategic decisions develop. First, the issue must reach a point where everyone is aware that something must be done about it. This may be an external factor such as a recession or an internal factor such as a reduction in sales. Whatever the decision, the same process is relevant.

All elements of the discussion are interlinked and feedback throughout is crucial because a possible range of solutions must be reviewed in order to come to a conclusion. The scale of change will depend upon the existing strength of the business and the issues to be dealt with. It may just require tightening up on current practice to ensure that the company maintains its competitive position, but at the other extreme, there may be a need for a more dramatic response.

A change in the paradigm can help. This means developing a completely new approach to the market place. It is needed when the external environment has changed to such an extent that the business cannot continue to function in the same way. For example, the move to e-commerce has meant that many organisations have had to look fundamentally at their **paradigm** because without change, they might not have survived.

Essentials

The **paradigm** is the pattern which underlies all decision-taking within the business. It reflects the experiences gathered over the years which give a business its character. It can be problematic if the environment changes but the paradigm stays the same.

Work in progress

Q What changes take place that might make a business review its paradigm? What might a business do about it?

Figure O2.30 shows three alternative routes for strategic change.

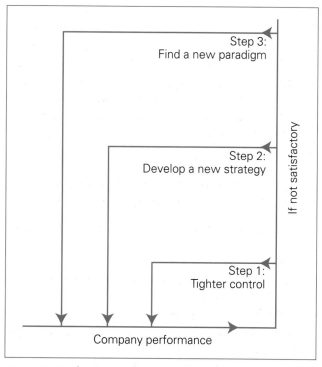

Figure O2.30 The process of strategic change

Cutting costs

Rover deal matches hours to sales

Siemens closes plant

DeVilbiss goes for cells

Centrica closes Energy Centres

Your agenda

1 At what stage is each of these businesses in the process of strategic change?

2 Which businesses are changing strategy?

3 Which businesses are improving productivity and which are making cuts?

4 Which strategies give long-run gains?

The first activity to be undertaken when troubles crop up is to review current activities. Figure O2.30 shows that this review should check that existing systems are working. It is easy for practices to slip over time and therefore it may be possible to cut costs by tightening up. Such changes can give a business a reasonably quick move to greater cost efficiency which may help in a difficult economic climate.

The review will not merely look at labour productivity but will need to survey all aspects of inputs and how they are used. A business should ask the following questions:

- Can the product be adjusted so as to be cheaper to produce?
- Will cost reduction help?
- Are raw materials and other inputs coming from the cheapest source?
- Is the process efficient?
- Is the relationship between labour and capital efficient?
- Is energy used effectively?
- Can the distribution process be more effective?
- Are there any other ways of maintaining sales?
- Is the business as a whole organised efficiently?

If, once these questions have been considered, the business has still not made an impact on the situation, it will be necessary to move to second-stage thinking and investigate the strategy. Each business will have its own opportunities in the light of its strategy, but there are a variety of common angles that might be considered in the search for survival.

How to survive

Business may use a variety of strategies to survive. Pizza Express succeeded in growing in a period that was difficult for many catering businesses. When recession strikes, eating out is one of the first activities that is cut from the domestic budget. Businesses also restrict the spending by employees on work-related entertaining, travel and subsistence. Pizza Express used two strategies:

- Diversification by setting up pasta restaurants. The business already had a good reputation so an alternative was likely to attract customers. As both pizza and pasta are regarded as inexpensive meals out, the restaurants are more likely to survive in a difficult economic climate.
- Exporting the concept through overseas franchising. By moving into overseas markets, the business was spreading its risks. Although recession can be a worldwide phenomenon, it is unusual for everywhere to suffer to the same extent at the same time. The decision to franchise was probably taken because it is difficult to control food outlets in international markets.

These two strategies often form the basis for surviving recession. It is well known that some products are more recession-proof than others. The greetings card industry is one example. However bad things get, we continue to buy birthday cards for our friends and relations because they are a small part of our total expenditure. Some products even sell more during recession. These include things which help businesses to be more efficient such as Internet technologies.

Both strategies draw on the ideas of Ansoff which were explained on page 462.

Work in progress

Q 1 What sort of products are likely to survive recession? Make a short list of examples and explain the ability of each one to survive.

2 What might a business that you know do to make itself more recession-proof?

A business which combines products which skim the market in a growing economy and others which survive well in a downturn can make the most of all situations. The merger of Chrysler, which makes cars for the mass market and Daimler-Benz, whose cars skim the market, exemplifies this.

The product range can be created by making strategic alliances with others or through developments within the business. The product portfolio can be the secret of success. Even if a 'cash cow' brings in less in a recession, it may allow the business to continue. Even if fighting for its life, a business should find time to develop the 'question marks' of the future and therefore create positive opportunities for the end of the recession.

Above all, there is a need for nimble decision-making. Whatever strategy is employed, changes need to be made quickly. This is why the rational command structure may be most appropriate in these circumstances. It can provide the necessary means for making swift changes.

Survival can be a mix of chance as well as good planning because some products and some markets can avoid the worst for unexpected reasons. While Japan's economy suffered dire recession in 1998, the luxury goods market would normally be expected to be hit hardest. In fact, it was in boom. Louis Vuitton, Calvin Klein and Ralph Lauren were all doing a roaring trade. This was put down to the fact that young Japanese men are becoming vain!

3 Efficient people?

Different sorts of deals

Crisp deals

A crisp factory in Yorkshire found that sales fluctuated considerably from month to month and year to year. To meet peak demand, it needed high staff levels, but at other times of the year, people would not have enough to do. It now works with contracts which are designed to allow flexibility and help it to match the size of the workforce to the demand for its product.

Many staff have a minimum number of hours but can be asked to do more when required. Others can be called in when needed.

Deals on wheels

Rover was in trouble. BMW, its new owner, was looking for increases in efficiency and productivity. There was a threat of closure hanging over the heads of the workforce at Longbridge, the Rover plant in Coventry, because BMW was unwilling to invest a further £2 billion unless changes were made.

The deal involved guaranteed basic pay at all times but no overtime and fewer bonuses. The workforce would be required to work longer hours when the order book is full and take paid time-off when work is short.

Zero deals

Oddbins, the wine shop chain, specialises in having staff who are young and full of helpful suggestions about what to buy. Keeping every shop fully staffed all the time is a challenge. The type of person who is interested in working for Oddbins is likely to take off to Australia – or some other wine producing country – to sample the output!

The company runs a scheme which employs people on a zero hours basis to meet these short-term needs. If you want to work, you ring round the shops in the area to see if they are short of staff. The shop may ring you to see if you want to work.

This strategy provides a flexible workforce of people who have already been interviewed and approved to fill such gaps.

Your agenda

1 How have each of these companies improved the relationship between costs and revenue?

2 What effect should this have on the price and sales of the product?

3 How does price elasticity of demand affect the need to cut costs?

4 Why is it particularly necessary for business to look for strategies to increase labour productivity in recession?

5 Are there any drawbacks for the workforce?

The search for flexibility

Companies have employed a variety of strategies to achieve flexibility. The traditional method of employing staff on permanent contracts for a regular number of hours per week is becoming less common. An increasing number of people are taken on in ways which leave the business in a position to adjust the amount of time required or review the situation after a short period of time.

- *Part-time working* allows a business to meet needs at peak times and therefore avoid being over-staffed at quiet times or, on lower staffing levels, providing an inadequate service.

  As the market has become more flexible with the advent of telephone banking and 24 hours a day shopping, part-time working developed an increasingly important position in the labour market.

- *Fixed hours contracts*, like Rover negotiated, mean that staff are expected to work on a flexible basis within the hours specified in the contract. This means that the workforce is available to put in more hours when the order book is full and have time off in quiet periods. Overtime payments become a thing of the past.

  Increased orders do not therefore mean increased costs because the workforce is flexible as to when the work is done. This sort of arrangement also allows the business to plan because it has a clear idea of its labour costs for the year.

- *De-layering* has been carried out by many big companies. It involves removing a layer of management to cut costs. As a result the organisation becomes flatter (see Module 2.1, page 84). This is often regarded at being beneficial in its own right because it assists in improving communications. It is aided by the introduction of more sophisticated information technology as this speeds up and personalises communication systems.
- *Outsourcing* involves buying in services rather than having in-house provision. This shifts the risk from the company as it can buy in services when required rather than having staff to provide them.

  A company which, for example, runs a number of conferences every year and employs staff to organise them might decide to hire the services of a company which specialises in conference organisation. This reduces the need for office space and other overheads. It also removes the long-term commitment to staff which can be costly when National Insurance and pension contributions are taken into account.

  Sometimes existing employees will leave the company but be re-employed as consultants on contracts for specific projects. This changes people's status: instead of being employees, they become self-employed.

  The main driving force for outsourcing is the desire for increased flexibility. A business that is in difficulties in a recession may decide, for example, to run three instead of four conferences in the course of the year. If the business is outsourced, it will have cut its costs by 25 per cent. If it employed staff to run the conferences, the cost would not have fallen nearly as much.

The increase in flexibility can make a business much more responsive to change. At whatever stage of the business cycle, a company will be better able to adapt. It will be able to deal with internal or external pressures more readily and maintain competitiveness.

Such practices often involve cultural change because the company can seem less cohesive if only core employees are on permanent contracts. If many of the people working for the business do not feel the same degree of commitment, motivation may be more difficult to achieve.

The big picture: short run

As businesses cut back during a recession, aggregate demand will fall. Figure O2.31 shows the outcomes. The effect of the fall will depend on the existing position of the economy. If a recession sets in when a boom has reached its peak, downward pressure on prices may occur before employment is hit. If recession is prolonged and turns into a slump, aggregate demand will have fallen so much that unemployment will have risen as businesses will be unable to sell their products. The shift of the aggregate demand curve from AD_1 to AD_2 to AD_3 shows these stages.

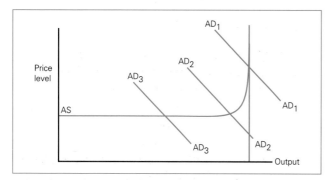

Figure O2.31 The short-run effect on aggregate demand and supply

The big picture: long run

By becoming increasingly flexible, businesses are probably becoming more competitive. As they work hard to reduce costs, demand for their products will, hopefully, rise. The ability to produce more efficiently can lead to an increase in demand abroad, if not yet at home. There will be a shift in the aggregate supply curve because the economy has become more productive. If home demand remains stable for a while, this enhances trading opportunities because there will be no pressure on prices in the domestic market. See Figure O2.32. Costs fall and output increases.

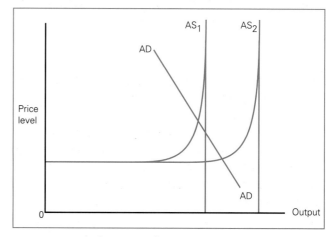

Figure O2.32 The longer-run effect on aggregate demand and supply

4 Shifting demand or supply?

Back to Barbour

Barbour reached a point where it could not sell all of the coats it produced. Its only solution was to cut back production which it did by closing two factories and making 83 people redundant. By doing so, it brought costs back into line and reduced output to meet sales.

Your agenda

1 Why did Barbour cut back on employment?

2 What does this tell you about the relationship between demand and employment?

3 If a government wants to raise the level of employment what might it therefore do?

On the demand side

There is only ever demand for labour because people want to buy the product of the work. In other words, the demand for labour is derived. If demand rises, employment rises and vice versa. Governments therefore have to find ways of increasing demand if they want to see employment increase.

Governments can use fiscal policy to regulate demand because it affects the amount of money people have in their pockets. The government has two choices to make if it wants to influence demand and therefore employment. It can:

Increase spending

or

cut taxes.

Both these alternatives can have the same effect because people will have more to spend. If the government spends more on roads, or hospitals, for example, it will create jobs and put money into the economy. People will have more money to spend on consumer goods and this will generate more employment. The multiplier effect operates because the initial injection of money into the economy has created a larger increase in incomes and output. The increase in demand has been multiplied.

Eventually, the effect will peter out because, in general, people always save a proportion of their income. Each time it reaches someone's wage packet it will diminish slightly. The effect is shown in Figure O2.33 where money is passed from person to person as it is spent. A little is left behind in each pocket.

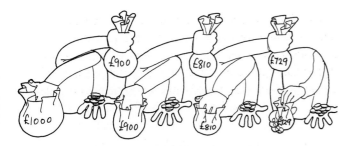

Figure O2.33 The multiplier effect

Figure O2.34 shows how aggregate demand can rise if government spending is increased. It shows that the government has to judge very carefully because increasing spending without caution can lead to overheating and inflation. The initial increase from AD_1 to AD_2 leads to more employment, but the move to AD_3 starts to cause inflation because aggregate supply has not shifted.

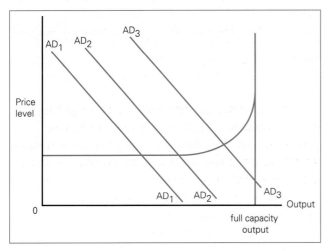

Figure O2.34 Increasing aggregate demand

Of course, governments have to be careful when putting such policies into practice because it is easy to go too far. At first, increased aggregate demand will lead to output and employment rising. Only later, perhaps after two or more years, will inflation start to accelerate. It all depends how close to full capacity output the economy was when expansion began. Time lags in the economy mean that the outcomes do not take effect immediately, so it takes a while to decide how well strategies have worked.

It is also true that some sectors will respond more quickly than others, so skill shortages may develop in some industries while others have yet to move.

■ What is the trade-off?

Any policy has a trade-off. If the government is to increase spending, the money must come from somewhere. There are two alternatives:

increase taxes

or

borrow.

Increasing taxes defeats the objective because it takes money out of people's pockets and reduces demand, so borrowing is the more common strategy. This allows the government to have a positive effect on employment without affecting demand immediately.

The drawback is that it will increase the public sector net cash repayment (PSNCR). This means that the government has to sell bonds in order to raise the money. This pushes up the demand for money available for borrowing and therefore puts pressure on interest rates. If the rates have to be increased, the cost of borrowing everything goes up. Mortgages, for example, become more expensive to repay. Investment too is more costly and the effect may be to reduce spending on new technologies and more efficient equipment.

■ Is there an alternative?

Taxation is a direct way of influencing how much people have to spend. By increasing it, demand can be expected to fall. Cutting tax rates generally increases demand. Both actions can therefore affect the demand for labour.

Cutting tax rates to stimulate demand has to be done with great care. The government must have a clear picture of the current state of the economy and how quickly it is expected to change. If tax rates are cut too far, the amount that people have to spend will grow fast and may lead to inflation because the economy cannot provide enough products to meet the increased demand.

If the government is to cut taxation in order to stimulate aggregate demand, it has to decide whether to cut expenditure or increase borrowing. With an aim of encouraging people to spend more, the latter is the more likely decision.

■ What is success?

If the policy works as planned, the unemployed will start to find jobs again, so GDP will start to rise and the economy will have turned the corner. If employment levels continue to grow, the upward climb from recession will be underway.

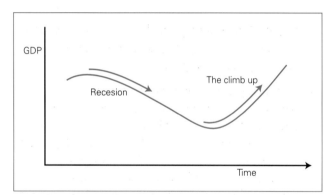

Figure O2.35 Climbing out of recession

The number of people on benefit will fall, revenue from taxation will begin to increase and the government can choose to spend money on other things or cut taxation. It may need to pay off some of the increased PSNCR which had risen while the government was funding the increased expenditure.

Work in progress

Q Draw flow diagrams to show the ways in which a government can stimulate demand. Use another one to show how it can go wrong. Use aggregate demand and aggregate supply diagrams to explain the stages of the flow diagram.

On the supply side

Policies which influence demand can be used in recessions, but the risk of inflation sometimes makes politicians very cautious. An alternative approach stems from the view that competition and incentives will keep both people and firms on their toes and therefore a more competitive economy will result. The measures which help are known as **supply-side policies**.

The objective is to increase the amount that the economy can produce so that more products are available but prices do not increase. More people will be employed as a result and the country's output will be competitive in overseas markets. Such policies are an essential part of dealing with a growing economy as they increase the potential output of the economy. In a recession, they help people to get more training and to ensure that businesses are working effectively.

Recession can lead to the shake out of inefficient businesses so that the economy is in a position to make the most of the upturn. The effect is the same as that shown in Figure O2.32. Many of the policies which improve competitiveness are known as supply-side policies because they aim to improve the ability of business to supply products at a cost which gives them a strong position in the market.

Essentials

Supply-side policies include all the measures which can increase the capacity of the economy to supply goods and services. Training, measures which make the labour force more flexible, competition policy and research and development are all important examples.

Supply-side policies which aim to raise employment are a mixture of carrots and sticks. Some are incentives, or carrots, which are designed to encourage businesses to employ more people or to make the labour force more employable. Other policies, or sticks, aim to stop people wanting to be unemployed. Many of the carrots aim to create a more flexible work force. This may come from making people able to move from one job to another easily because training has given them a variety of skills or enabled them to be retrained quickly. It also comes from making businesses able to employ people in a more flexible manner.

■ The carrots

- Training can be provided by governments or businesses. It needs to be well targeted to meet the demands of the economy. Programmes which are designed to make people employable directly affect the ability of the workforce to meet these demands. It can make people more flexible and therefore able to fit into the changing patterns of demand that emerge over time.

- Cutting the costs of employing people encourages business to increase the workforce. In countries where companies' social security payments are high, businesses have to have higher margins before more people are employed.

- Employment law protects people at work. If legal requirements are eased, companies may be more willing to take people on because it becomes easier to sack them if orders fall. If there are very high costs associated with making people redundant, managers will think twice before committing themselves to hiring more employees.

- Reducing red tape helps small businesses to be more efficient. Meeting the government's need for information and demonstrating that they are complying with legislation involves a great deal of paper work which has a substantial cost for any organisation. Small businesses, in particular, suffer because the time involved represents a higher proportion of resources.

- Encouraging research and development helps business to compete in the most effective way. It helps business to use resources effectively in order to add value to greatest benefit. In a high labour-cost economy, this is important. The UK cannot attempt to compete with the products of low labour-cost economies and must therefore seek products which require a high level of skill and sophistication.

- Taxation and its relationship to benefits can be a disincentive to work because a low paid job may be less financially rewarding than living on benefit. By altering this relationship people can be encouraged to work. Reducing tax rates at the bottom of the scale, for example, provides an incentive for people to take a job rather than stay on benefit.

■ The sticks

- Competition policy aims to create an environment in which no business can be protected from the rigours of the market. It attempts to prevent companies from creating situations which give them an unfair advantage over others and therefore means that efficiency may be reduced as the business does not have to work so hard to make a profit.

- Cutting benefits can push people into jobs that they would not have been prepared to accept if benefit levels had been higher. By reducing the length of time during which benefits are available, people will more quickly be put in a position of accepting almost any job.

- Weakening trade union power reduces the bargaining strength of the individual. If people have to negotiate on their own behalf rather than in groups, they are less likely to achieve high pay rates for everyone. This has been done by enforcing secret ballots on strike action and banning closed shops, where only union members can be employed.

■ What are the trade-offs?

Many supply-side policies reduce people's security. It seems ironic to make it easier for businesses to get rid of people when the objective is to increase employment, but they are much more likely to employ them in the first place if they know that there is flexibility.

Flexibility is often used in two different senses. The negative implication refers to the increased number of part-time employees and those working on short-term contracts who suffer. Such people may feel a lack of motivation because they no longer have the role they once did in an organisation. Equally, people whose work has been outsourced and are now running their own businesses based on contract work may find their motivation has increased because they are working for themselves.

The positive aspect of flexibility is that people in general become more employable and therefore are able to change roles as the economy changes. This is beneficial for each individual as well as for the economy.

The move to supply-side policies makes people more self-reliant because they have to be prepared to look after themselves. There are some members of society who find this very difficult and once benefits have run out may disappear from the statistics altogether. Those who drop out put themselves at risk in all sorts of ways. A system which endeavours to ensure that everyone has some kind of employment when benefits cease or can be given training, may reduce the impact.

5 What about the future?

Unemployment falls again

Year	Claimant count (% of work force)
1990	5.8
1991	8.1
1992	9.7
1993	10.3
1994	9.3
1995	8.1
1996	7.3
1997	5.5
1998	4.7
1999 est.	4.2

Figure O2.36

Source: *National Institute Economic Review*, May 1999

Output grows again

Year	GDP at constant prices (1995=100)
1990	92.3
1991	90.9
1992	91.1
1993	93.1
1994	97.4
1995	100.0
1996	102.5
1997	106.0
1998	108.5
1999 est.	110.3

Figure O2.37

No pressure on wages

Year	Average earnings growth rate (%)
1990	9.8
1991	8.1
1992	6.3
1993	3.3
1994	3.0
1995	2.3
1996	2.1
1997	4.4
1998	4.6
1999 est.	4.4

Figure O2.38

Your agenda

1 What contradictions can you see in the above data?

2 Can you think of any reasons which might account for these contradictions?

Economics is never an exact science. Because any interpretation depends on the actions of people, their responses must be built into any predictions. Data can be collected in all the usual ways and sometimes they will uncover changes which do not fit the model.

In the late 1990s the papers were full of headlines asking 'Is inflation dead?'. Economists had been expecting prices to start to rise in the usual cyclical way – but they did not (see Figure O2.39). What was happening?

Year	Retail prices index	Annual change (%)
1990	84.6	9.5
1991	89.6	5.9
1992	92.9	3.7
1993	94.4	1.6
1994	96.7	2.5
1995	100.0	3.4
1996	102.4	2.4
1997	105.6	3.1
1998	109.3	3.4
1999 est.	111.0	1.4

Figure O2.39 The pattern of inflation (1995 = 100)

Source: ONS, Monthly Digest of Statistics

One possible answer is that the labour market is really becoming more flexible. If people can move readily from one job to another, businesses can match their output to demand much more closely. This means that production can be achieved more efficiently and output can be adapted to meet the demand for new products.

Such a change could:

- reduce bottle necks in the labour market because people are better equipped to move from job to job, so pressure on wages is reduced

- reduce pressure on wage inflation because prices are not rising

- lead to reduced pressure on prices because goods and services can be produced more competitively, so inflation can be kept down

- allow unemployment to fall further before wages start to rise because existing staff have become more productive and firms can recruit more easily in a flexible market.

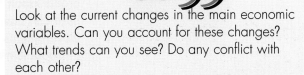

Point of view

Look at the current changes in the main economic variables. Can you account for these changes? What trends can you see? Do any conflict with each other?

Read a range of articles by the economics editors of the main broadsheet newspapers. You will find them on the papers' web sites. Do they agree with each other? If not explain their points of view. If you have queries, you could e-mail those that give you an address.

Businesses like a stable environment because it reduces uncertainty. However, in order to achieve reasonable stability internally, an organisation needs a culture that can deal with change. Yet change itself can have significant effects on the welfare of individuals. Governments, both national and EU, can try to protect businesses and individuals as they search for external stability.

1 A culture for change

Catching the imagination

Vivid Imagination makes toys. Not ordinary, average toys, but those which hit the headlines – the ones which always cause a storm at Christmas because every child in the country wants one.

The business specialises in catching the latest trends and must therefore always be on the look out for where the market is going next. It is a risky business. An average toy has a life of nine months, which is not long in a company which is working in an uncertain environment. Captain Scarlet was a winner with a life span of 18 months. He was just the start of a line of successes.

In such a volatile market, Vivid's key to success is its ability to move quickly. There are no tiers of decision-making. There is little formality – no one wears suits and even the finance director makes the tea.

It is a small company with only 35 staff and sales of £35 million. Every thing but core activities is outsourced. Vivid does not have packaging, warehousing or distribution facilities. It pays other companies to do these things. There isn't even any production from Vivid's Hong Kong subsidiary. It simply organises production in China. All this helps in such an uncertain market.

Now the company is looking for lines which give it a stable market that is less dependent on trends, fashions and whims.

Your agenda

1 Why is Vivid Imagination's market such a risky business?

2 Why is the ability to move quickly so important?

3 How do you think the company's structure and culture help to meet the needs of a market like this?

4 How does outsourcing allow the company to achieve sales of £35 million with a staff of 35?

5 How does outsourcing increase the company's flexibility?

6 What could Vivid do in order to reduce the element of risk?

A culture of change

Uncertainty is a constant challenge to business. There is always a possibility that the economic environment will move adversely. Even without any sign of recession though, the market for many products moves increasingly rapidly. Consumers are becoming more and more fickle as they seek the best way to maximise returns on their spending.

Meanwhile, computers, faxes, e-mail, video conferencing and many other electronic developments have speeded up decision-making and the conversion of decisions to action.

Traditional types of organisation may fail to meet the needs of businesses which face the need to change. The concept of decision-takers as a group of people at the top of a company is increasingly viewed as being flawed. These people may have long since left the commercial interface and may therefore hold views that have been overtaken by events.

There is an increasingly accepted perspective that the people with grass-roots experience of changes in the market need to be involved in decision-making in this fast moving world.

Businesses therefore have to be structured to move quickly and pre-empt or respond to change. They need systems in place which identify opportunities and threats and then build on employees' experience to come to rapid, effective conclusions.

The learning organisation

A learning organisation embodies the collective experience of everyone in the business. The competitive advantage which comes from experience cannot all be associated with any one individual. It is to be found in the combined expertise and understanding of the organisation as a whole.

The learning organisation is listening, challenging and flexible. This combination creates an environment in which a company is unlikely to become entrenched in systems or committed to products which no longer meet the needs of the market.

- *Listening* raises the awareness of changes that are taking place both inside and outside the company. A business that is constantly aware of the changes in the market will be able to stay at the forefront of change. Listening to people inside the company builds two sets of information into the process:
  - Their experiences in developing or selling the company's product.
  - Information about the way the company is functioning as an organisation.

The combination of these two sets of information can be used to build the bigger picture required to meet the needs of a changing market. Continuous improvement is usually an important element in this process.

- *Challenging* the perceived changes in the market and the decisions made within the business keeps everyone on their toes. It allows a permanent forum for discussion, which creates an environment in which no one person's views are sacrosanct. If a group of people make decisions

that cannot be challenged, a rigid environment has been created and this is not conducive to meeting the needs of a changing market and staying competitive.

- *Flexibility* in the way that the business is structured contributes to the development of a learning organisation. The ability to build multi-skilled teams that can work on current issues helps a business to identify the way the market is going and draw conclusions about the company's best response.

The sum total of knowledge held by people who work in an organisation is often greater than the formal knowledge held by the organisation itself. If the staff do not have an opportunity to contribute their knowledge, knowhow and skills, the company will be missing opportunities and not making the most of its market position.

The culture and structures within the organisation must therefore enable information to be shared. This can be done in a variety of ways:

- *De-layering* allows a more direct means of communication and therefore reduces the potential for ideas to get lost.

- *Multi-disciplinary discussion groups* are used to identify and highlight opportunities for greater effectiveness.

- *Suggestion schemes* can be used to feed practical ideas directly from the grass-roots to the upper echelons of the business.

- *Newsletters* and other forms of internal communication help to keep people involved and can provide opportunities for the expression of views.

An open, democratic approach to decision-taking may help everyone to participate and a greater spirit of democracy will result. This may help to avoid power play which can lead to the views of a dominant group outweighing those of others who might have made a useful contribution. Listening is therefore crucial in the opening up of the decision-making process.

The listening process may begin in one part of the business which changes to meet the needs of the market or moves ahead of the market in certain situations. If successful, the initiatives may be transferred to other divisions, or countries if the business functions on a larger scale. In this way all parts of the business will benefit from the early experience.

There is a drawback to this type of organisation however. By allowing incremental change to be the main device for moving ahead, the overall strategy may never be reviewed. It would seem, therefore, that businesses need a combination of approaches. An open environment in which people can challenge and feed in ideas, allied to a process of review of the overall strategy for the business, might achieve the best of both worlds.

Business structure and culture is rather like the spectrum of competition. The extremes are not very commonly found and reality lies somewhere in between.

There are probably rather more businesses at the autocratic extreme of the business organisation spectrum than there are at the learning end. Learning organisations need a common purpose among everyone involved and this can be hard to achieve, especially once a business grows beyond the size of Vivid Imagination.

Work in progress

If the suit fits...

Hugo Boss, the German fashion design company, has for a long time had a reputation for sharply tailored suits. The company has always done well among young executives seeking a rather macho image. This is not surprising for a company which sponsors motor racing and produces its own particular style of advertising. It already has its Hugo label for the younger end of the market. So where should it go from here?

As a menswear company, it could only reach half the fashion market, so it decided to try to attract the

other 50 per cent. After 12 years of experimenting, it finally went live with a range of women's work wear which sold well in the designer shops. This was a small-scale initiative and was only really intended to test the market. The chief executive, who is responsible for all the menswear, decided that women's wear would have to be made in a different environment. He knew he couldn't make clothes that he couldn't wear himself, but if he doesn't like the clothes which come from the Italian team, they won't go to market.

1 Why did Hugo Boss want to diversify?
2 What is the attraction of moving into women's wear?
3 Why was the chief executive so determined about the quality of the product?
4 What drawbacks are there to diversifying in this way if the company is looking for certainty?
5 Are there any other alternatives that might have been chosen?
6 What indication is there of the structure and culture of Hugo Boss? How do you think it has contributed to the process of change?

2 Managing change

Ford at the crossroads

Ford was getting left behind. Asia was the big new market and the company was not making the most of it. Its costs were high compared with other car firms. The only solution was to go global which was a challenge in a business that had been based on a continental structure. The individual divisions had been more or less independent of one another.

The concept of Ford 2000 grew from a meeting in London in 1997 and took just a year to come to fruition. A team of 24 of Ford's most respected people from both sides of the Atlantic were put together to carry out a feasibility study. Within two months it had reported and the decision to go ahead had been taken.

There were massive implications. Many businesses had failed in their attempts to go global because the workforce was left behind. This would mean 25 000 managers shifting to new roles or finding themselves working in a different hierarchy. Local bosses would suddenly lose their power and find that they were now just minions in a bigger organisation. Methods had to be devised to ensure the ongoing commitment of all these staff.

The changes became a reality for all Ford's employees at the Disneyworld conference centre. The chairman and chief executive, Alex Trotman, gave a dramatic presentation informing 2000 senior managers that Ford would never be the same again. The organisation chart was being torn up and the new structure would cut costs, raise efficiency and produce cars that would 'wow' the market. In the grand finale, Trotman was the first signatory on the Wall of Commitment where every delegate signed their allegiance to Ford 2000. The video of the rousing speech was subsequently shown to every single Ford employee around the world.

Within two years, Ford was working as a single worldwide organisation with four vice-presidents, each with global responsibility. Their key role involved spreading good practice to all corners of the business.

The new organisation had a range of targets including cutting costs and suppliers and reducing both development and delivery times. A key strategy was the setting up of multi-skilled groups to develop new products. If designers, engineers, and production experts work together, they are more likely to create cars that can be built and will sell than if they each work in isolation. It also freed the hands of managers to spend money when required instead of having to discuss the decisions with many tiers of management.

Your agenda

1 Why should going global cut costs?
2 What other gains were there likely to be?
3 What was happening to Ford's paradigm?
4 Why was the commitment of staff so important?
5 How would the strategies used assist the process of cutting costs?
6 How might motivation have been improved by the restructuring?
7 What effect does the creation of multi-skilled groups have on the culture of the business?
8 To what extent did Ford exhibit the traits of a learning organisation?
9 Find out whether Ford's restructuring did subsequently help it to compete in the international car market.

People can become very set in their ways. Change is often regarded as a threat because it means learning to do things in a different way. Staff who have felt secure and well equipped to carry out their roles must suddenly work with different objectives, with new people in a different sort of organisation. It is not, therefore, surprising that the introduction of change meets resistance.

The role of management is to find ways of making staff feel secure and helping them to accept change. First of all, management must be aware of the stages of the process and their objectives:

■ *Unfreezing the paradigm* must take place before change can begin. Staff who have been used to working in one way with a particular strategy have to be redirected. When change is being considered it is difficult to keep it under wraps within a business for very long. The merger between oil companies BP and Amoco was an exception as it came as a surprise to everyone. People who feel that change is underway but are not informed or involved will feel insecure. This can be very alienating and staff may feel inclined to seek other employment.

■ *Building a new paradigm* will need different approaches according to the nature of the organisation. The strategies used will depend on the nature of the change and the structure of the organisation. Consultation with the workforce is a different experience at Ford and Vivid Imagination because Ford has 320000 employees and Vivid has just 35. At Vivid, everyone can be involved and therefore the best strategy is probably to have open discussions about the nature of change. At Ford, very senior management can be involved and there may be a search for perspectives from below, but for change to take place on the scale envisaged the process of discussion may be largely cosmetic. An effective scheme of information provision may be more useful.

■ *Refreezing the paradigm* is the process of establishing the new strategy. When Alex Trotman stood on the stage at Disneyworld and led everyone to the Wall of Commitment, he was beginning to refreeze the paradigm in the minds of those senior managers. They then had to return to their plants and offices and continue the process. In their case it involved not only the move to the global business but also a shift to include aspects of a learning approach. The big picture had clearly been set down. At plant level, however, there were opportunities to contribute to the final shape.

In these final stages, there is often direction from the top because this will be the source of the new strategy. The fine-tuning may well take place in each sector of the business.

Getting the message

What do people need to know so that they can participate effectively in the change process? The detail can be overwhelming, so it is necessary to identify the right information for each group.

Communication must be appropriate for the circumstances. At Ford, the chairman appeared in front of all employees, either in person or on screen, because of the enormity of the events.

Small-scale change would need a lower-key approach or the significance of the change might become confused. The noticeboard or the company newspaper may be appropriate.

If people's individual positions are affected, they must be spoken to individually. If there are group changes, then the group is probably the vehicle for discussion.

Both before and after change takes place it is important that there are lines of communication running in both directions. In such circumstances rumour abounds and much can be misleading. Gossip can undermine the process and therefore needs to be counteracted.

Will there be job losses?

The greatest threat that hangs over people in times of change concerns the security of their jobs. Insecurity is the greatest threat to achieving a smooth transition from one paradigm to the next, so it must be handled with care.

Many companies that have dealt with job losses in times of change devised systems to assist people who were to be made redundant. Counselling and outplacement support are now common practice.

Doing this not only helps the individuals who are losing their jobs but demonstrates to the rest of the workforce that the organisation cares about their well-being. This makes people more willing to accept even painful change.

Looking ahead

Strategic change forms the big picture but it must be integrated with the operations of the business if it is to work in practice. The implications must be worked through and plans made for each section of the business to ensure that the strategy becomes reality.

As human resources are often the most valuable asset of a business, they must be integrated into the planning and outcomes of the process. If people are expected to change roles or ways of working, training will be an essential part of the development. The move, for example, from working as a production specialist to becoming part of an integrated team may take more skills than an employee currently has. This is inevitably a source of insecurity. The knowledge that training is an expected part of the package will help to ease the transition.

3 Planning for certainty

Japan's success stories

While Japan's economy was struggling with recession, a number of its companies established such firm foundations that the problems almost passed them by. These companies are not (yet) household names but they are notable because they performed well despite adversity.

Much of their success resulted from research and development leading to technical expertise. Many are doing well in export markets. Here are a few examples:

1 Noritsu Koki sells half the world's mini photo developing machines, which are used in processing shops.

2 Mabuchi Motor sells half the world's tiny electric motors that are used in computer drives.

3 Hoya has a huge market for optical glass because it has succeeded in reducing the production process from 26 to three days.

4 The pharmaceuticals company Takeda has a fast acting alternative to Viagra near production and a string of other new drugs following on.

Others have attained stability by being quick to respond to changing tastes:

1 Secom has gained 60 per cent of the market for security systems and is expanding abroad.

2 Kao has been profitable for 18 years by sticking to domestic cleaning products and cosmetics. With proportionately three times as many people in research and development as Proctor and Gamble, it has gained awards for Biore pore packs.

3 Rohm has added extra functions to its microchips and turned them into specialist products.

4 Yaoko, a supermarket chain, has added to its profits after freeing managers to make buying decisions to meet the needs of local customers.

Source: Adapted from *The Economist*, 26 June 1999

Your agenda

1 How does research and development assist in providing stability in the context of a fluctuating economic environment?

2 Explain the effect that research and development can have on the product life cycle and the product portfolio of a business.

3 Why is responding to consumer tastes important in the context of a fluctuating economic environment?

4 Use the Boston Matrix to explain the way in which a business needs to build a portfolio to create a secure position.

5 Why is it important for a business to have a clear understanding of its core competencies if it is to achieve long-run security?

6 What else might a business do in order to reduce uncertainty?

Many businesses want to build a sounder basis for dealing with the uncertainties of the market and the wider economy. To do this they must create a strategy which takes into account where the business is now, its strengths and weaknesses and where it wants to go.

In order to decide whether a plan makes sense, a series of questions must be posed:

Does the plan make sense?

Does it make the most of core competencies?

Will the portfolio provide long-run security?

Do new developments fit the portfolio?

Are new developments viable in the market place?

Will the plan improve or maintain the financial performance of the business?

The role of the product portfolio

Every company needs a mix of products at different stages of their life cycle. Vivid Imagination, for example, knew that its market was too volatile for comfort and sought products with a longer life cycle. This, in itself, increased the security of the company.

The standard product mix, which is exemplified by the Boston Matrix, tells a company how its situation compares with that standard. A dearth of products in any quadrant except for the dogs can lead to insecurity: it follows that there will be a shortfall at some point.

> **No question marks – future uncertainty**
> **No stars –   future uncertainty**
> **No cash cows –   current uncertainty**

Each of these quadrants has its uses either now or in the future. Without question marks and stars, the future is uncertain because the business is not investing for the future and therefore the income stream will eventually dry up. These products may carry risks but they also hold out the prospect of future growth. Unless the life cycle of the existing cash cows can be extended indefinitely, the business may have no reliable sales. They therefore support investment in question marks and stars. Without them, investment in the future will be constrained. Even dogs have their uses if they can be repositioned to achieve growth.

For greater security, a product portfolio would ideally include items which are not subject to the fluctuations of the market. A product which is income or price inelastic will be more resistant to uncertainty and therefore will continue to contribute revenue even in difficult conditions.

Obviously, few businesses achieve an even balance on a permanent basis, but the Boston Matrix is a useful tool for evaluating the situation and making decisions about how a business can plan to achieve the objective of increased certainty.

Planning the portfolio

■ Innovation

Corporate planning must be concerned with the future as well as the present if it is to try to reduce uncertainty. In some businesses the future is further away than in others. Ford, for example is trying to speed up the time a car takes to develop from a twinkle in a designer's eye to a showroom reality. This time period, however much it is shortened, will be much longer than the time it takes for Cadbury's, for example, to produce a new chocolate bar. It is therefore important for a business to ensure that it is looking at innovation in the long term if it is to build the portfolio that meets its needs.

Innovation is not simply a physical process but must be integrated into the business to ensure that the end result meets market requirements. It is therefore important to involve the marketing function as well as finance in order to produce the right product at the right price.

■ Research and development (R & D)

Successful R & D leads to innovation. It is a constant activity for the many businesses which exist in faster moving markets. It is particularly crucial in the market for consumer goods with short life cycles. The Walkman, CD or mini-disk player have been in a constant state of change ever since they were invented.

A company needs to have models at an early stage in their product life cycles, or ones which have been effectively extended, if it is to compete. The ability to skim the market comes from having new products which tempt the innovative purchaser. As product life progresses, the price tends to fall when an updated version is made available.

■ New opportunities

A business needs to look outwards for developments as well as inwards at its existing products. SWOT analysis will assist in the process of the search for new opportunities. By looking at its core competences, its areas of competitive advantage and the market environment, a business can identify new directions which will increase certainty. It does this in two ways:

- Risk spreading gives security because some areas are more vulnerable than others. Many fashion houses, for example, will have product ranges designed for the middle market as well as haute couture ranges. As car companies merge, there is often an upmarket range as well as more utilitarian vehicles.

- Adding value comes about by looking closely at ways to build on existing expertise. A business with a range of core competences may be able to put them to work in new ways which give higher returns. A book store which has great expertise in specialist books but one small outlet will increase its scope dramatically by developing e-commerce. A web site will widen its potential market very quickly while enabling customers to receive the book of their choice delivered to their door.

In the search for security and certainty, businesses have many strategies that can be used. It is not easy, however, because markets can move quickly and economic change can be unexpected. The extent of the impact of the Asian financial crisis in the late 1990s was largely unforeseen and therefore hit many very hard. However hard a business tries, such unpredictable circumstances can have a negative effect. Watching the future both inside and outside the business is therefore a critical element in reducing uncertainty.

In search of certainty

A home-grown market

What springs to mind when you hear someone is off to Leeds? Is it closed down textiles mills and drab back streets or a vibrant café society full of affluent young people? If yours was the first image, you are behind the times.

Leeds has become a vibrant business hub for the North. The trains to and from London are packed with well-dressed people with buzzing mobile phones. They are not just reporting that they will be home for dinner; they are busy doing deals and setting up meetings. But you don't have to travel to London for accountants, lawyers and all those businesses that build on a thriving economy. Leeds has both home-grown versions and most of the international names.

The business services sector has grown through the 1990s from 55 000 to 77 000 jobs. This represents 22 per cent of employment and one-third of the local gross domestic product. While UK employment grew by 1.5 per cent, the increase in Leeds was 2.3 per cent. £1.6 billion has been invested in the city in the same period. Much has gone into office development for this sector. The city's two universities attract thousands of overseas students every year.

Leeds has become a 24-hour city, brimming with cafés, clubs, restaurants and designer shops. The run-down riverside warehouses have been transformed into cool, spacious loft-style apartments which are for sale at prices that are not far behind those of London.

Your agenda

1 What effect have these changes had on the economy of Leeds?

2 What sort of products will the business sector employees be wanting to buy? How would a marketing expert classify them?

3 What effect does this growth have on companies that supply the business sector?

4 How do such changes affect the country's competitiveness. Why?

A source of competitiveness

Do you remember this?

Demand conditions: what is home demand like for the country's own products?

- **The composition of home demand**
  Customers who are ahead of the game lead businesses to anticipate international demand.

- **The size and pattern of growth of home demand**
  - A large home market gives economies of scale, although a small market can give an incentive to export.
  - Fast growing home demand means that firms invest in the latest technology.

- **Ways of accessing foreign markets**
  - Buyers who are multi-nationals will take products into foreign markets.
  - Training people from abroad will lead them to want the host countries' products.
  - Seeing new products in the movies works well.

In module 4.2 (How competitive?) the focus of discussion was on ways of creating a competitive economy. One of the factors was the effect of a dynamic home market on native business. Leeds is a prime example of how a thriving home market can assist the economy in pushing for competitiveness.

Young, affluent people demand the latest products which keep producers on their toes. They help create the vibrant market which puts business at the forefront of international competition. The USA has long been famed for this sort of market which has provided the foundation for innovation.

Figure O2.40 shows the changes that have taken place in the spending power of middle-income earners. As the 1990s have progressed, people have steadily become better off and therefore been in a position to help in the development of a strong home market.

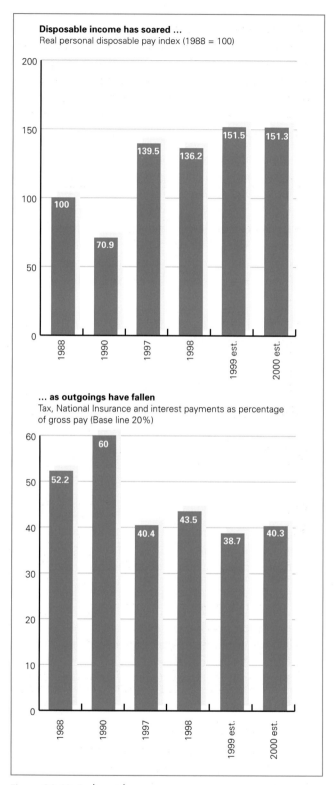

Disposable income has soared ...
Real personal disposable pay index (1988 = 100)

... as outgoings have fallen
Tax, National Insurance and interest payments as percentage of gross pay (Base line 20%)

Figure O2.40 Feeling richer

Source: Morgan, Stanley Dean Witter

If a business is searching for long-run stability, these developments are likely to be sources of success. There is, however, another side to the story. Cities like Leeds not only have great wealth but also appalling poverty. Two miles from the busy hub of the city are two estates where unemployment is rife and the new jobs in the business sector have little relevance.

What's happening to home demand?

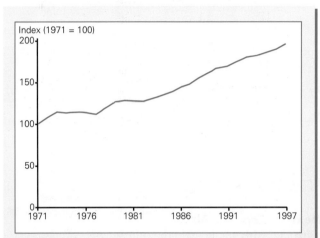

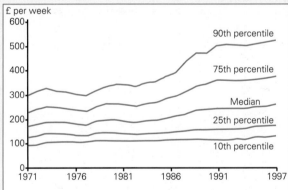

Figure O2.41 Real household disposable income, UK
Source: Institute for Fiscal Studies

Your agenda

1 What is the trend in real disposable income?

2 Does it ever fall? Why?

3 What changes have taken place in the relationship between the different percentiles?

4 What effect do the trends and fluctuations shown by the data have on business?

5 Why might the government try to adjust the relationship between the percentiles?

The size of incomes will determine how much people buy and therefore has a direct impact on business. One of the key determinants of income is the business cycle. In times of boom, disposable income will rise and in recession, it will fall or grow more slowly. There is therefore a strong incentive for government to smooth out the pattern as it provides greater security for people as well as a more stable environment for business. Figure O2.42 shows clearly how the business cycle can be tracked through unemployment figures.

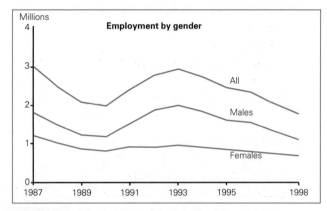

Figure O2.42 UK unemployment (Labour force survey)
Source: ONS, *Social Trends*, 1999

Behind the overall figures for disposable income in Figure O2.41 lies a much more informative picture of the way the economy influences people and businesses. This can be seen in the break down of the data. These are often shown in **percentiles**, **deciles** or **quintiles** as they help to show how earnings are distributed. Clearly, better-off people have benefited the most from rising incomes.

Essentials

Percentiles, deciles, quintiles are useful for making population comparisons. Percentiles divide the population into hundredths, deciles are tenths and quintiles are fifths.

If the rich are getting richer and the poor are getting relatively poorer, there will be changes in the pattern of consumption. Figure O2.43 shows the groups of people who are in each of the five percentiles. More lone parents are to be found in the poorest 20 per cent of the population than anywhere else. At the other end of the scale, 38 per cent of the top fifth are couples with no children. Only 3 per cent of one-parent families are among the wealthiest.

This pattern and any changes that are taking place will obviously impact on business. People in lower quintiles tend to spend a high proportion of their income whereas those in the higher quintiles save more. This is just one example of how the distribution of income can affect consumption. Figure O2.44 shows the variations that exist in the expenditure pattern of quintile groupings. Food, for example, takes a significantly higher proportion at the bottom of the scale than at the top.

Figure O2.43 Distribution of disposable income, UK

Source: ONS, *Social Trends*, 1999

	Percentage					
	Bottom fifth	**Next fifth**	**Middle fifth**	**Next fifth**	**Top fifth**	**All (millions)**
Pensioner couple	23	29	21	15	12	5.1
Single pensioner	25	33	21	13	7	4.1
Couple with children	19	17	24	22	17	17.2
Couple without children	10	11	16	26	38	10.5
One adult with children	42	35	14	6	3	4.6
One adult without children	18	17	19	22	24	8.2
All individuals	20	20	20	20	20	49.7

Figure O2.44 Household expenditure by income group, UK

Source: ONS, *Social Trends*, 1999

	Percentage					
	Bottom fifth	**Next fifth**	**Middle fifth**	**Next fifth**	**Top fifth**	**All**
Food	23	21	19	17	14	18
Housing	16	16	16	15	16	16
Leisure goods and services	13	13	15	16	16	16
Motoring and fares	11	13	17	17	18	16
Clothing and footwear	5	6	6	6	6	6
Fuel, light and power	7	6	5	4	3	4
Alcohol	4	4	4	5	4	4
Tobacco	4	3	2	2	1	2
Other goods and services	5	4	4	5	4	4
All household expenditure (£s per week)	163	208	292	376	518	311

Work in progress

Q Use the information in Figures O2.43 and O2.44 to consider the effects on business of both increasing poverty and increasing disposable income. Does a more equitable distribution of income provide a more stable environment for businesses?

How are people affected?

Who learns best?

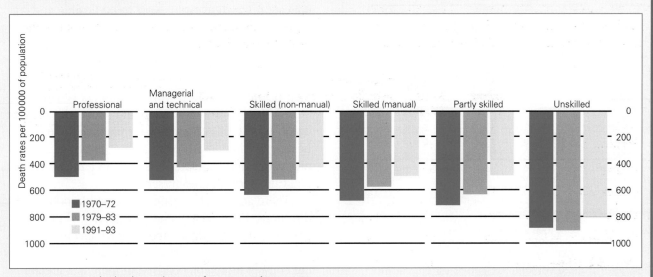

Figure O2.45 Standardised mortality rates for men aged 20–64

Source: Acheson Report, Department of Social Security, HMSO

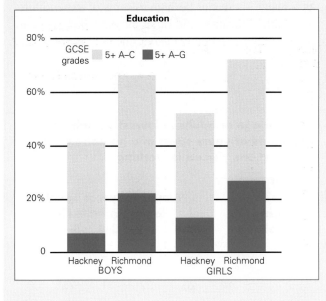

Figure O2.46 Educational achievement

Source: The Henley Centre (Taken from the Financial Times, 19.3.98)

There are strong links between low pay, educational success and state of health. The data in Figures O2.45 and O2.46 demonstrate some of these differences. Mortality figures improved significantly in the last 25 years of the twentieth century, but the gain was proportionately more significant in the more prosperous groups of the population.

There is some evidence that countries with a more equal distribution of income are healthier. It can therefore be assumed that a shift of resources to the less well off would lead to a general improvement in health.

Similar conclusions can be drawn about education. Even though London, as a whole, is the most affluent part of the UK, there are distinct differences within the city. Figure O2.46 shows just how great these can be. The relationship is clarified by the data in Figure O2.47: Richmond is very much more prosperous than Hackney.

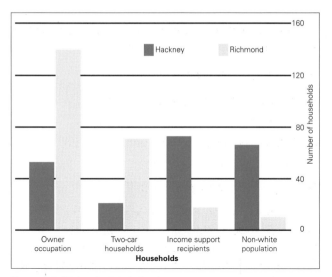

Figure O2.47 London's imbalances

Source: The Henley Centre (Taken from the Financial Times, 19.3.98)

The combination of poor health and low educational achievement has knock-on effects, not only for the individuals concerned but also for the economy as a whole. It has been demonstrated in Module 4.2 (page 324) that people with low levels of educational attainment are more likely to be unemployed than others.

As few people can now expect to stay in the same job for the whole of their working life, the need for education which allows people to be flexible and adapt to changing situations is an integral part of a growing economy. It is not enough simply to teach people lots of facts. They need to learn how to learn as well as to develop skills which allow them to put their personal toolkit to work in different situations.

Shortcomings in education and tendencies to poor health have cost implications for the government. A healthy, well-educated population is clearly more productive and generates less costs in terms of benefits and calls upon the health service.

There are therefore gains to be had in both directions. Better health and education could reduce government expenditure and improve incomes. The latter is also a double-headed gain because not only is the country more competitive but there is a greater potential for raising taxes on higher levels of earnings. As a result, there can be higher levels of expenditure on health, education and other factors which assist in developing a competitive economy.

4 Deep in poverty

Half the people in the lowest earning quintile are living on benefits and tend to stay in that quintile permanently. Others climb out when they get a job but may well fall back again if things go wrong. Families may fall into the bottom quintile when working children leave home. Women may find themselves in the same situation on separating from a partner.

The overwhelming factor which affects poverty is the ability to get a job and keep it. Figure O2.48 shows a correlation between these two factors. The more years spent in a working household, the less likely adults are to find themselves in the poorest fifth of the population.

To overcome poverty, it is therefore important to encourage people to find work. The move from benefit to work can be a difficult step to make for a variety of reasons:

Percentage of adults in lowest quintile by numbers of years spent in a household where at least one person is working.

Great Britain Years in working households	Number of years spent in lowest quintile (%)				
	None	1–2	3–4	5–6	All
None	33	22	17	29	100
1–2	20	22	31	26	100
3–4	21	43	27	9	100
5–6	78	17	4	1	100
Total	60	21	10	9	100

Figure O2.48 At the bottom of the heap

Source: ONS, *Social Trends*, 1999

- The level of education and training may be very low.

- Access to training may be difficult.

- Single parents can find childcare either difficult to find or too expensive.

- There may be few jobs available in the region.

- The jobs available may provide low wages.

- People may be better off on benefit than in low-paid jobs.

This combination can lead to people staying on benefits for many years. The link between taxation and benefits is responsible for providing little incentive to move into employment. Unemployed people with children will probably find that the benefits they receive are likely to be greater than earnings from a low-paid job. This is known as the **poverty trap**.

Essentials

The **poverty trap** becomes a problem when unemployed people are worse off or only marginally better off when working than when drawing benefits. They then have no incentive to work. High marginal tax rates on low wages make the problem worse. Tax and National Insurance contributions together can create high marginal rates.

Governments have looked at ways of reducing the effect of the trap. This can happen by:

- creating a lower initial tax band

- supplementing low pay according to the size and needs of the family

- helping employers to pay higher wages by giving them employment subsidies

- improving access to training.

All these strategies provide help for different groups of people. They all aim at assisting the transition for different people in different situations. Campaigners who are concerned about poverty argue that these measures do not do enough to help those people who, for a range of reasons, find it difficult to climb out of the bottom quintile. A lower tax rate does little to assist people who have no earnings.

Figure O2.49 shows the relationship between tax and benefits across the income groupings. People in the bottom fifth pay indirect taxes, such as VAT and excise duty, on their purchases, but they pay very little income tax. Taxes and benefits can be used to redistribute income and are one strategy in the battle against poverty.

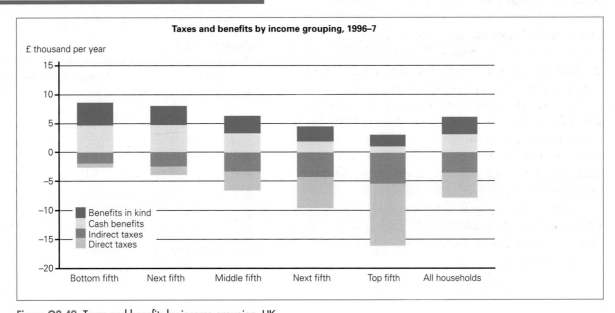

Figure O2.49 Taxes and benefits by income grouping, UK

Source: ONS, *Social Trends*, 1999

What can a budget do?

The 1999 Budget

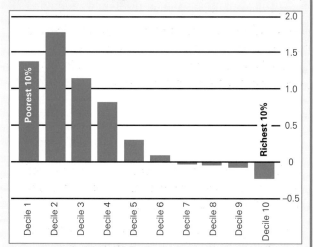

Figure O2.50 Winners and losers by income group

Source: Institute for Fiscal Studies

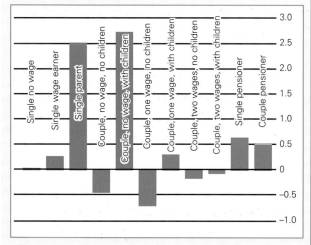

Figure O2.51 Winners and losers by household type

Vertical scale indicates Gains/losses (% change in disposabe income)

Source: Institute for Fiscal Studies

Your agenda

Figures O2.50 and O2.51 show the redistributive effects of the 1999 budget.

1 To what extent did the 1999 Budget redistribute income?

2 What impact would such changes have on the economy?

3 What kinds of measures can be used to achieve this effect?

One of the objectives of taxation is to redistribute income from the rich to the poor so that no one lives in a state of absolute poverty. It does not always work because there are always some people who do not fit into the system and therefore fall through the holes in the safety net. The redistributive effect of a Budget will also depend on the perspective of the government of the time. The 1999 Budget helped people on low incomes through the introduction of a 10 per cent tax rate band, improved family allowances and the Working Families' Tax Credit, which is aimed at helping the working poor. As well as improving real incomes for people on low pay, the latter measure helps to increase their incentive to work.

Governments have increasingly taken the line that it is better to encourage people into work than simply support them on benefits, and budgetary policies have reflected this. Most benefits are now means tested so they go to people who need them instead of providing blanket support for all.

Work in progress

Q To follow up changes that have taken place in government policy in this field, keep an eye on the Treasury and Department of Social Security web sites.

Figure O2.52 shows the maximum income levels for each decile at the time of the Budget referred to in Figures O2.50 and O2.51. The figures are adjusted according to the nature of the family.

Decile	Single	Couple with no children	Couple with two children
1.	4 610.55	7 609.10	11 109.29
2.	5 460.66	8 951.90	13 069.78
3.	6 265.20	10 271.48	14 996.36
4.	7 275.49	11 927.03	17 413.47
5.	8 455.03	13 860.70	20 236.62
6.	9 825.91	16 108.05	23 517.76
7.	11 690.81	19 165.27	27 981.29
8.	14 190.03	23 262.34	33 963.02
9.	18 150.41	29 754.77	43 441.96
10.	–	–	–

Figure O2.52 Maximum income by declile.

Source: Instute for Fiscal Studies via FT 10.3.99

Work in progress

Q Look at some adverts for jobs in the local and national press. Which quintile do they fit into? What do your answers tell you about the relationship between the type of employment and the distribution of income.

Some businesses will benefit when governments make genuine efforts to redistribute income. As poorer people spend a higher proportion of their income, any addition to their income will increase demand for goods and services and, in turn, aggregate demand. Equally, as the distribution of income across the country is unequal, improving the economic climate in poorer areas contributes significantly to growth.

5 What can the government do?

Regeneration for the regions

The poorest parts of Britain received £3.6 billion to help them climb out of the abyss. A combination of European and UK funding has created a package to help the poorest. The aim is to safeguard 118 000 jobs and assist with the training of 156 000 people.

The first tranche of money has come from the UK government's Single Regeneration Budget (SRB). This £1 billion will assist education, employment and crime prevention as well as fighting social exclusion and urban decay. The money will be spent by 2006 on 163 projects in eligible areas.

In Northumberland £15.6 million is being spent on improving job skills and raising employment levels. A Cornish project is putting £2 million into reducing social exclusion.

The second tranche comes from the EU's Objective 2 funding (see below) which is aimed at industrial, rural, urban and fisheries areas. The £2.6 billion, again, covers the seven-year period to 2006.

The poorest areas are able to claim up to 40 per cent of new investment. This is available in South Yorkshire, Cornwall, Merseyside and West Wales and the Valleys. In a further band, a 20 per cent contribution can be made.

A third tier has been introduced in which small and medium-sized businesses can receive help. There is also some funding for tourism projects.

The money is available in a smaller area of the UK than in previous years. The EU is preparing for the expansion of the Union and has decided that eligible areas must be reduced by 20 per cent. The UK government has drawn up a new map which must be approved by the European Commission.

Your agenda

1 What factor, in your view, contributes to the qualification of a region as an assisted area?
2 How does regional aid help:
   a the region
   b the economy?
3 Does regional aid help to provide a more stable environment for business? Give reasons.
4 Some people argue that regional aid is a waste of money because the market will deal with the problem. Explain this point of view and discuss any drawbacks.
5 Why does the expansion of the EU require a reduction in the areas receiving aid?
6 Why is regional policy particularly important within the euro zone?

Working in the regions

The EU's regional policy is made up of three objectives:

- *Objective 1* – to promote the development and structural adjustment of regions whose development is lagging behind.

- *Objective 2* – to convert the regions or parts of regions seriously affected by industrial decline.

- *Objective 3* – to develop human resources in areas not eligible for Objectives 1 and 2 assistance. It aims to help member states adapt and modernise their systems of education, training and employment.

Objectives 1 and 2 provide help with investment in regions which fall below a specific proportion of the average GDP of the EU. Investment takes the form of helping business, developing infrastructure as well as providing training for people.

Objective 3 is a relatively recent innovation. There is a growing appreciation that the development of people is a key element in economic growth. This has resulted in policies which aim to assist countries to raise the levels of attainment across the community.

In Module 4.2 (page 319), Liverpool was used as an example of the way in which regional policy can contribute to the economy. Apart from the straightforward economic gains, new initiatives can lift the attitudes of people in an area. From the developments of the old docks in Hull to the creation of a heritage centre at Wigan Pier, the concept of cultural change can be seen to work in communities just as in businesses.

EU member countries also have their own specific policies to help businesses with practical issues. The Department of Trade and Industry (DTI) runs a variety of programmes in the UK which aim to assist businesses with start-up, dealing with such areas as their finances and marketing. Small businesses are often run by people who have a skill to sell but lack business knowledge and skills. Many have gone under because they are unable to monitor their financial situation so cash flow, for example, has got the better of them. These schemes aim to help small and medium-sized enterprises.

Changes in these and other policies can be monitored on the DTI and the European Union's web sites.

One currency

The creation of the euro has been generally welcomed by many big businesses because of the opportunity to work in a stable currency area. Modules 3.1 and 4.2 showed the differing perspectives on the issue (pages 210 and 328). The combination of stability and reduced transactions costs has made the idea of one currency appealing to many. As Europe has become the focus for a high proportion of the UK's trade, this is a strong argument for businesses that seek stability. The knowledge that prices in Europe will not change is attractive.

The value of the euro beyond the euro zone is, however, subject to the fluctuations in foreign exchange markets. These fluctuations will reflect conditions in the euro zone as a whole rather than in individual countries. There is thus a trade-off between stability and flexibility. Price stability can be expected within the euro zone, but if businesses lose competitiveness exchange rates will not be able to adjust to reflect this.

It is quite likely that individual regions within the euro zone will from time to time find themselves losing competitiveness. With no exchange rate flexibility they will be forced to find ways of cutting costs and money wages may have to fall if employment is to be maintained.

The second trade-off is the constraint on economic policy. Once in the euro zone, a country must conform to certain macro-economic objectives. This may create difficulties for countries which are out of line with the rest.

The political agenda may prove to be a stronger driving force than the economic one. Until the currency is more firmly established, it is difficult to tell whether the gains will outweigh the losses for any particular country.

Point of view 66 99

'France's prime minister has proposed public works projects as an answer to unemployment. But such projects are financed either by raising taxes or by increasing the budget deficit. In the first case the number of jobs created by the additional public works will be smaller than that of the jobs lost in the rest of the economy. Governments which want to avoid this problem by deficit financing will run into the obstacle of EMU's anti-deficit rules.

European unemployment is a man-made disaster. Policy harmonisation would cause this blight to spread. At the European summit in Austria, the chancellor of that country, Victor Klima said that coordination of economic policies was 'the key to creating employment'. Such calls are usually supported by governments which espouse unsuccessful policies. They say they fear that tax rates will suffer a race to the bottom. Harmonisation, though, is more likely to result in a race to the top. Altogether, it would lessen the pressure to carry out necessary but unpopular structural adjustments to the welfare state.

In order to make the euro work, more flexibility in the labour market is needed since the instrument of devaluation no longer exists. Some governments are uneasy about this.'

(Frits Bolkestein, MP in the Netherlands. He has been leader of the Liberals, minister of foreign trade and defence.)

Source: *The Economist*, 22 May 1999 p.115 'The High Road that leads out of the Low Countries'

Your agenda

1 Explain how public works might reduce unemployment.

2 What are the drawbacks to this strategy?

3 Why is there an anti-deficit rule for members of the single currency? What effect can this have on the countries concerned?

4 Why might policy harmonisation in Europe cause unemployment to:
   a rise
   b fall?

5 Why does Frits Bolkestein believe that the welfare state needs reforming in Europe?

6 Review the passage and your answers and identify all the trade-offs in policy.

Competition, conflict or consensus?

Enquiry 1   Does the market motivate?

This enquiry examines the significance of market forces in shaping the economy. It explores the role of the producer in satisfying consumer demand, and the ways in which producers' rights can be protected when genuine new ideas are used. It goes on to investigate the ways in which businesses take care of their customers and the protection given to consumers by law. Lastly, it contrasts the experience of the emerging economies with that of traditional market economies.

1 Do markets encourage dynamism?

The Gunners are targeting the Net!

What a difference a year makes. In 1998 it was estimated that the UK Internet industry earned £350 million from subscription charges and advertising revenues. Earnings predictions for 1999 are estimated at £40 million. What has happened?

The answer is competition. In 1998 Internet service providers (ISPs) like Compuserve and AOL had the market cornered. In order to access the worldwide web users had to pay a subscription charge to an ISP. Customers complained about the cost of connection, pointing out that Internet users in the USA paid much lower connection charges, but if you wanted to use the Internet there was little alternative.

Dixons/Currys have transformed the market. Amid a fanfare of publicity they launched Freeserve. This was an ISP with no subscription charges *and* it could be set up by using a CD Rom available from any one of the group's stores. Within months Freeserve was able to claim half a million users, and traditional ISPs were starting to feel the pinch. Other firms were quick to recognise the potential of this market. Toys 'R' Us, Line One and Arsenal Football Club are all planning to offer free Internet access. Bury Football Club, although not in the same League as Arsenal, are also set to offer Internet access for a small charge.

Britain's newspapers are also seeking to exploit the potential of the web. Line One is backed by British Telecom, United News and Media and News International. Readers of the *Express*, *The Sunday Times* and the *Sun* will all be given CD Roms to enable them to connect to the Internet. Line One previously charged a subscription for its service, but in the light of market pressure it has been forced to admit that charging subscriptions is an 'unsustainable policy'.

It is apparent that with competition among ISPs increasing, the customer is the only one not likely to lose out, although industry analysts believe that some ISPs may find the competition too great, and may be squeezed out of the market.

Your agenda

1 How can a business support a free service? Where might revenue come from?

2 How would you expect the original Internet service providers to feel about the above events?

3 How are consumers affected by the changes?

4 What would you expect to happen next? List the possible consequences.

5 Is what happened here a good thing? For whom?

Entry into the business of providing Internet connections is easy. (This is true at the time of writing, although this particular scene changes by the month.) If someone is making a profit, market forces stimulate potential new entrants to offer a competing product. Barriers to entry are insignificant. Anyone who is making super-normal profit is likely to find that their prices are being undercut. To keep their place in the market they will have to reduce their prices too.

In the Internet example, there is a question about how far prices can be cut while still giving an adequate rate of return on capital invested in the business. By the time you read this you may know what happened next. Did the number of ISPs increase for a while and then drop back? Did prices fall, then eventually rise again, but not to the original level of a monthly subscription service? Or did something completely different happen? Perhaps some service providers merged, hoping to increase their market power.

The key factor here is what happens to consumers. Business dynamism of the sort described above can stimulate producers to innovate in ways which are highly beneficial to them. Firms may seek to exploit new technologies in order to gain a competitive advantage. New products can be developed. Perhaps even more importantly technological innovation can lead to improved products which work better and more reliably, or perhaps simply cost less. Process innovation leads to lower production costs. Use of technology in this way can enhance competitive advantage.

- Whenever something like this happens, standards of living are improving. People become better off because they can have more of the new or cheaper product.
- Alternatively, they can continue to buy the same quantity, but because it is cheaper, they have more money left over to buy other things.
- Either way, the consumer wins as real incomes rise.

Notice how vital competition is in this story. Consumers are better off because producers are having to compete in order to stay in the market. If they don't compete, they will exit from the market place. Survival means looking for ways to please the customer by adding value and establishing a competitive advantage.

Market forces

Markets are created by the existence of buyers and sellers. The buyers enter the market looking around at the products available. Given reasonably full information about what is available, they make an informed choice which reflects the satisfaction they expect to get. In this sense, they have consumer sovereignty: the capacity to determine what is produced by virtue of their demand for it.

Sellers are looking for opportunities to satisfy customer demand in profitable ways. They will come into the market looking for ways to add value and charge a higher price for the product. So long as the profits to be made reflect the opportunity cost of the resources employed, they will stay in the market. This means that they will need the rate of return on their capital to be at least as good as their alternative possibilities – the opportunity cost. If competition forces prices too far down, some businesses will exit from the market. These will probably be the ones with lower levels of technical efficiency: their costs will be higher. In the long run, the businesses which stay in the market will be those which can make at least a normal profit.

Work in progress

Q **1** Draw a supply and demand diagram which illustrates the events in the case study on Internet service providers. (You may prefer to draw a sequence of diagrams.)

2 How would you describe the ISP market? Which aspects of a perfectly competitive market, if any, does it illustrate?

3 What happens to consumer surplus when the free Internet providers enter the market? Draw a diagram to explain your answer.

4 What was the motive of the businesses which offered a free service?

This example illustrates the workings of the profit signalling mechanism in a way which is rather different from the conventional norm. Generally speaking, profit maximising businesses do not usually give things away, but the new providers of free services are all businesses which stand to gain from increased sales of their mainstream products. Internet services are complements to computers. Dixons is giving them away in rather the same way that shoe shops give you laces with a pair of boots. Arsenal's line must be slightly different: try working out the logic for yourself.

Innovation and investment

A cut-throat business

Just outside Reading, on the Basingstoke road, there was an old jam factory. Outside it, in 1998, security was very tight. The men who arrived each morning with stubble on their faces each showed their passes to the security guards. There was no clue outside the building as to what went on inside.

Shaving has been going on for thousands of years. Yet it has become a high technology business. The search for a performance razor can entail big research expenditures and years of development. But the potential market is massive and the profits can be very attractive.

Those men with the stubble were employed to test the new product. Gillette's objective was to make the Mach 3 into the most popular razor in the world by the end of the century. They spent US $750 million on the production facilities and a further $300 million on marketing. They called it the billion-dollar blade. It took seven years from prototype to production.

All this happened in Reading. The senior scientist at Gillette is John Terry, who now works from Boston but spent many years in Reading. He joined the team in 1962 with a doctorate in metallurgy. This is what he said about the technical development process:

People think that what we do in developing shaving systems is mundane compared to designing a rocket. There is remarkable sophistication in the technology that goes into a Mach 3 blade edge. We're making the sharpest thing that anyone makes, faster than anyone makes anything of that sort of precision.

Why all this secrecy? Producing razors is not especially difficult. What is difficult is finding the best technical solutions and producing a winning product. If competitors get a whiff of the processes and products being developed, they will copy the ideas in a flash. Industrial espionage is a real threat.

Time will tell how successful the Mach 3 is but it is clear that research and development is a core capability for Gillette.

Your agenda

1 What incentive did Gillette have for such a large investment?

2 The new razor is expected to be 30 per cent more expensive than the competition. Could Gillette be sure that it would sell?

3 What impact would a successful outcome have for Gillette, in terms of profitability, in the short and the long run?

New products and new technologies often require substantial investment, in research and development (R & D) and in production facilities. The risks are considerable. Yet businesses take risks of this kind all the time. Why do they do it?

The greater the risks, the better the prospects of long-term profit have to be in order to make the investment worthwhile. A diversified business can afford to make a range of investments, knowing that some will work better than others. So businesses which are making big investments in R & D have to be large to function competitively. What will happen to competition when the players in the field are big and powerful?

Profit maximising businesses will invest in order to stay competitive. They want product quality with cost-effectiveness. These are essential to their maintaining competitive advantage. However, what they want most of all is to soar ahead of the competition. This way they will be able to develop some market power. They will have a margin of safety which will bring higher profits in the future.

Big producers do sometimes compete very effectively, using their resources to invest in positive ways. Others may prefer not to rock the boat. They will avoid competing aggressively. There may be tacit agreement and stable price structures. In this case, the consumer faces a less satisfactory picture.

The Wilkinson view

There are 15.9 million men wet-shaving in the UK. Nine million of them are using Gillette products. The competition comes from Wilkinson Sword with 2.8 million and Bic with 2.6 million. Martin Harris, trade marketing manager at Wilkinson Sword, says, 'Gillette is claiming that the addition of a third blade is sufficient reason to add a 30 per cent premium to the price. That is unproven. They are certainly being adventurous.'

Your agenda

1 What did Martin Harris mean when he said that Gillette was being adventurous?

2 Calculate the market shares for Gillette, Wilkinson Sword and Bic.

3 How might Wilkinson Sword seek to hold its market share?

4 How does new product development of this kind benefit the customer?

5 Are any of the companies mentioned likely to go out of business? Give reasons.

6 Are producers in this industry acting in the consumer interest? Give reasons.

Answering to the market

Although most markets are very far from being perfect, market forces do still drive scarce resources towards the uses that consumers desire. Every day millions of decisions are made by consumers and producers in competitive markets. Each decision edges the current stock of resources into a better fit with the ever-changing contours of demand. It is a process that requires no commands from the government. Yet it is so complex that no single human organisation could be adequate to the task. It was this quality that Adam Smith celebrated in *The Wealth of Nations*, published in 1776.

The invisible hand

❝Every individual generally neither intends to promote the public interest, nor knows how much he is promoting it… He is in this case, as in many cases, led by an invisible hand to promote an end which is no part of his intention. Nor is it always the worse for society that it was no part of it. By pursuing his own interest he frequently promotes that of society more effectually than when he really intends to promote it. I have never known much good done by those who affected to trade for the public good. It is an affectation, indeed, not very common among merchants, and very few words need to be employed in dissuading them from it.❞
(Adam Smith, *The Wealth of Nations*, 1776.)

Work in progress

Q 1 Explain in your own words how market forces encourage the allocation of resources to move closer to allocative efficiency.

2 What incentives do businesses have to invest in extensive research and development?

3 What will happen to businesses which do not strive to compete with each other in producing what consumers want?

4 What happens to the consumer interest if businesses do not seek to compete strongly with one another?

Point of view ""

EasyJet objects

In January 1998 Stelios Haji-Ioannou, chairman of easyJet Airline wrote a long letter to the chairman of the Civil Aviation Authority (CAA). He expressed his concern at a plan hatched by BA to set up a low-cost carrier to compete with easyJet, Debonair, Ryanair and Virgin Express, as part of an operation code-named 'Operation Blue Sky'. Haji-Ioannou was convinced that the new airline called Go was part of a long-term strategy to eliminate low-cost carriers and raise fares. He was adamant that if BA was allowed to have its way, then consumers would be the losers. He sought action by the CAA to restrain the aggressive actions of British Airways. He argued that 'the opportunity and scope for BA to abuse its dominant position through the medium of Operation Blue Sky must be recognised by the regulators'.

The chairman of easyJet was convinced that Operation Blue Sky was a determined attempt to breach European anti-competition laws and in particular Article 86 of the EC Treaty. He believed that BA would use its dominant position to sell below the cost of production with the intention of removing competitors from the market.

BA could help Go by using its market muscle. The bulk purchasing power of BA would allow Go to secure preferential prices for:

- fuel
- insurance
- advertising
- landing fees
- spare parts
- credit card acquisition fees.

In addition, BA could raise the marketing profile of its subsidiary. It could provide free access to BA's vast management resources and could ensure preferential leasing rates for aircraft because it could act as guarantor.

Haji-Ioannou's concerns were heightened by an announcement that Go had been given £50 million and that BA did not expect Go to break even for three years.

Your agenda

1 Why was Mr. Haji-Ioannou so upset?
2 In what ways was the launch of Go threatening open competition?
3 Where is the consumer interest in a dispute of this type?
4 Evaluate the impact of BA's introducing a low-cost carrier service.

People want to travel. Holidays have a high income elasticity of demand. As incomes have risen, demand for air travel has risen faster. Airlines provide a wealth of examples as to how resources can be reallocated to meet changing consumer demands.

When the allocation of resources changes to reflect consumer demand, we can see consumer sovereignty working:

- EasyJet capitalises on the desire of consumers to travel in a cheap, no-frills environment. It caters for a different market segment. Entry into the airline business is possible, if perhaps not easy. Allocative efficiency improves as resources to satisfy increased consumer demand move into the business.
- Then a large and powerful business sets up in competition. On the face of it, this is also good for the consumer. But supposing the resources BA can command enable it to survive in a cost-cutting regime for longer than easyJet? BA can wait and watch while easyJet is forced to cut prices below its long run production costs. If easyJet then has to make an exit from the market, BA will be left in a strong position with less competition and better able to raise prices.

Markets create incentives for businesses to make profits by satisfying consumer demand. However, they also provide opportunities for businesses to exploit their power at the expense of the consumer. This underlines the importance of competition.

Work in progress

Q

1 Explain in your own words how markets work to bring consumers the goods and services they demand.

2 Show why competition is important to maintaining both technical and allocative efficiency.

3 Describe the process by which businesses are encouraged to innovate in a market system.

4 Explain using business and economic concepts that you have learned how a large business can dominate a market by using its size and resources to consolidate its position.

5 Explain the importance of competition policy.

2 How can creativity be rewarded?

L'Oreal

Until the 1960s L'Oreal operated mainly in France. The company started out in 1907 with the invention of the first synthetic hair dye. It gradually developed a large portfolio of hair-care products and cosmetics. Markets were expanded first in Europe, then in North and South America. Now the Asian market is seen as the area of expansion.

The company owns an amazing list of brands. Each one is aimed at a particular market segment. Lancôme, Laboratoire Garnier, Maybelline (in New York) and Elsève are all part of its empire. Then there are the prestige perfume brands such as Guy Laroche, Ralph Lauren, Helena Rubinstein and Paloma Picasso. There are many others.

Every time the company finds a formulation which works, it patents it. The company believes that there are three critical factors in its success. Research and development has a major role in the overall strategy. In 1995 the company registered 270 patents. The second critical factor is the communication of performance. This is achieved through advertising, samples and partnerships with retailers, hairdressers and journalists. The third factor is the internationalisation of its brands.

L'Oreal brands cover all segments of the cosmetics market. However, the company aims particularly at the customer who has an above-average income, is sensitive to style and fashion and attaches importance to the benefits of modern technologies.

Your agenda

1 Why would research be important for a company producing hair-care and cosmetics products?

2 Patents protect inventions from copying. Why would this be important to L'Oreal?

3 Why are brand names widely used for these products? Why does L'Oreal have separate names for its different brand ranges?

4 Some people say that all cosmetics products are much the same in terms of their ingredients. Is this view consistent with the features of L'Oreal's view of itself which are mentioned above?

Without **patents**, many companies would consider that there was little incentive to innovate. A patent gives legal monopoly protection to the inventor of a new product. The inventor must first register the patent. That means providing full details to the Patent Office, providing evidence of something original about the product and showing that it is the inventor's own idea.

■ Once the patent is granted, the inventor has a monopoly over production for the next 20 years. This provides an opportunity to make good profits which can be set against the cost of developing the new idea. Research is expensive and businesses need incentives to innovate. Many important new products have started with patent protection. Businesses which want to copy the invention during the life of the patent will have to find a different way of designing and making it.

■ Patent protection is valuable and all companies which use developing technologies take out patents all the time. However, if the patent is infringed, they will have to sue the company concerned. This means heavy legal expenses which small companies usually cannot face. For this reason, independent inventors and small businesses with new ideas often sell the patent to larger companies. They have the muscle to prevent infringement.

■ Patents can be registered internationally. A small company which has come up with an exciting invention might look to a venture capital fund to support it with finance for development. These are funds which specialise in lending to new and small businesses using risky new technologies. However, before they lend they always expect to see international patent protection in place.

Patents are a part of what is known as **intellectual property rights**. The other important category applies to all those ideas which are **copyright**. The copyright of the book you are reading is owned by the Nuffield Foundation, although most book copyrights are actually the property of the publisher. Almost always, when something is written down and made widely available, it is copyright. So brand names with their distinctive logos are copyright. Using another company's brand name usually provokes a swift response, with legal action not far behind. Other copyright items include all kinds of recorded music,

newspapers, magazines and photographs. Except under strict conditions, it is illegal to make recordings of your own from CDs or to photocopy books.

> ### Essentials
>
> **Patents** give the right to be sole user or producer of a new invention. Many patents relate not to a final product but to a way of producing it.

> ### Essentials
>
> **Intellectual property rights** are owned wherever there is a patent or some copyright material in the hands of a specific business or an individual.

> ### Essentials
>
> **Copyright** gives legal protection against copying to authors, composers and artists. It does not have to be registered and operates automatically. Infringements are pursued through legal action.

Pirate recordings are, of course, a real problem in the music industry. Some emerging economies have been rather casual about respecting intellectual property rights. Pirate copies of recordings and perfumes have become commonplace, especially in the Far East. The US government has been particularly active in international trade negotiations, in attempting to get governments to crack down on pirate producers.

Work in progress

Q **1** Supposing you make a cassette recording of your friend's new album. What are you stealing, and from whom?

2 For many years, pharmaceutical manufacturer Glaxo made enormous profits from sales of Zantac, a drug which effectively controlled stomach ulcers. Then the patent lapsed. Use economic theory to predict what happened to: (**a**) the price of the drug (**b**) Glaxo's profits.

3 Obviously, patents and copyright confer monopoly rights. Usually, we think of monopolies as being against the interests of the consumer. With patents and copyrights, most people think the consumer interest is well served, most of the time. Why is this?

Intellectual property rights protect people who have new ideas and encourage them to develop them. They are also a rich source of dispute and legal fees. They do not often favour the interests of the garden-shed inventor who has little knowledge of commercial practices.

There are some interesting issues developing in relation to copyright material on the Internet. In theory, all copyright material remains protected even when it is put on to web sites. In practice, it is quite difficult to enforce copyright laws in electronic contexts and it seems likely that the current position will change over a period of years.

Point of view

Pure genius

What is a new idea? Mehdi Norowzian makes TV commercials. In 1993 he had taken a suggestion along to the Guinness advertisers, showing a short film called 'Joy' featuring a young man dancing while he waited for his pint to settle. Later, Mr Norowzian was invited to make an advert but declined the offer.

Later still, Guinness came up with an advert called 'Anticipation'. This proved to be remarkably similar to some of Mr Norowzian's images. So Mr Norowzian sued Guinness. The judge found in favour of Guinness. He argued that the advert was not a copy of the original film, although this had clearly inspired it. He also ruled that the original film was not a dramatic work and was therefore not covered by the 1988 Copyright, Designs and Patents Act, which controls all intellectual property rights in the UK at the present time.

This legal decision was given in July 1998. Advertising agencies are now wondering where they stand. The ruling gives them some power, but it also discourages directors from bringing them new ideas on their own initiative. Could this reduce creativity? Should the law be changed?

Your agenda

1 Explain why books, pictures and music are protected by copyright law.

2 How important do you think copyright protection is in ensuring that resources are allocated in an efficient way?

3 What impact do intellectual property rights have on competition?

3 Does the customer count?

Cinemas

In 1984 the cinema business hit the buffers. Total cinema admissions dropped to 54 million. The next year, the first multiplex opened in Milton Keynes. Between 1984 and 1997 ticket sales increased from £103 million to £530 million. Non-ticket sales – all that popcorn and ice cream – increased even more. By 1997, there were over 1100 multiplexes. It is clear that people like their cinemas to be attractive places to visit. Many old 'fleapit' cinemas have closed down over the years.

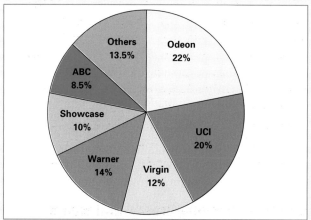

Figure O3.1 Cinema operators' percentage share of the market
Source: *Sunday Telegraph*, 25 January 1998 © Telegraph Group Limited, London 1999

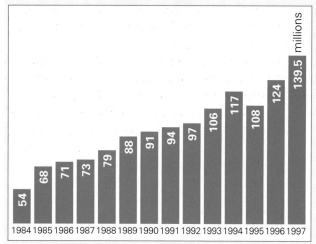

Figure O3.2 Cinema admissions, 1984–1997
Source: *Sunday Telegraph*, 25 January 1998 © Telegraph Group Limited, London 1999

By 1997 visits per head per year in the UK were standing at 2.2. This compared with five in the US. The UK has one cinema per 25000 people, whereas the USA has one per 9000 people, so there might be room for further growth. Most of the big operators are looking to big sound systems, wide screens, good confectionery, more space and improved customer service to attract more customers.

Richard Segal manages Odeon. He says, 'Multiplexes account for about one-third of our sites and half of our admissions. But we want multiplexes to account for two-thirds of our sites in time.'

A number of new operators are coming into the market. They are making planning applications but there is a shortage of out-of-town sites. Some planning authorities are concerned to breathe life into city centres. Meantime, it is expected that small operators will be taken over by the giants in the business.

Your agenda

1 To what extent are cinema operators reflecting consumer preferences by developing multiplexes?

2 Multiplexes have been very profitable. If more are built, would you expect that they will remain equally profitable in the future? Explain your reasoning. Use recent information on cinema attendances if you have it available.

3 Evaluate the extent of the cinema chains' market power. To what extent are they moulding consumer demand?

In a **laissez-faire economy** the allocation of resources is determined by market forces which reflect sellers' inclination to supply and buyers' to demand. Adam Smith's *The Wealth of Nations* (1776) is often quoted as the economics text that explained the role of the market in bringing buyers and sellers together. The invisible hand works to allocate resources in line with consumer demand. There are many buyers and sellers, which ensures that no one person is important enough in the market to manipulate the price. So the price will be kept down by competition, at a level which reflects the true opportunity cost of the resources used in production.

In practice, many markets are very different from this. In particular, it has become clear that there may not be many sellers. They can have influence over the market and can disadvantage the customers in terms both of a higher price and of reduced choice.

Essentials

A **laissez-faire economy** is one in which the allocation of resources occurs through the unfettered operation of market forces. It follows that government intervention is kept to an absolute minimum in such an economy.

Consumer-led markets

In an ideal world buyers would be powerful enough to influence producers to supply the goods and services that they want. In a consumer-led economy the producers have to respond to the wishes of the buyers in order to make a profit. In such a scenario consumers are sovereign and their wishes take precedence over the suppliers' wishes. Businesses must be market orientated if they are to survive.

An increase in consumer demand for a particular product will tend to mean that prices will rise. Producers will find that product more profitable. These profits will attract new entrants to the industry. Resources will move into production of the desirable product. As they do, competition will intensify and the price will be driven back down to the level at which it just covers the average total cost of production. Similarly, if consumer demand for a product falls, the price will fall and losses will be made. In time, producers will adjust by reducing output or going out of business altogether and the supply will again match demand at a price which reflects production costs. This process is summarised in Figure O3.3. You can see this

process at work in the cinema case study.

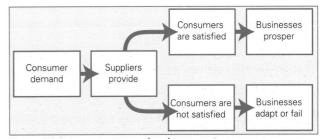

Figure O3.3 Consumer Demand and Business Success

In theory, therefore, suppliers have to respond to the demands of the consumers in order to stay in business. This implies that consumers have *all* the power in a market. Clearly, this is not the case. Suppliers have considerable scope to mould consumers' preferences and to control what is made available to them. Many examples were given in Module 4. However, in recent years competition among producers has sometimes led to the development of a much more market-orientated approach. When this happens, suppliers are acknowledging the force of consumer demand.

Defining consumer needs and wants

Consumer wants are unlimited. Although there are individuals who deliberately choose modest life styles, society as a whole is far from having achieved all that people want in material terms.

One of the tasks of any business, the marketing department in particular, is to turn consumers' wants into a demand for the company's products. If the company can successfully engineer this transformation from wants to demand the business is likely to succeed (Figure O3.4). At each stage in progressing from wants to demand to profits the marketing department can become involved.

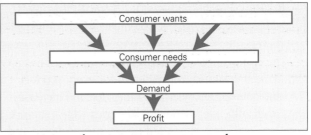

Figure O3.4 Transforming consumer wants into profits

For a marketing department there are three stages, which apply to all products, in trying to transform the wants or demands of consumers into profits for business. The stages are as follows:

- *Investigating* – to discover what benefits the consumers are seeking or if there are needs that have not been met. This involves market research.
- *Designing* – to develop a product or service that meets these identified needs. This involves product development which actively builds upon the market research.
- *Selling* – devising ways to persuade the consumer to buy the newly designed product. Segments will be identified and products designed to meet the needs of individual market segments.

The implication of this is that the marketing department will team up with other departments to ensure that the overall planning process is market orientated. Business strategies need to be backed up by a genuine knowledge of the true nature of the market.

Work in progress

In any supermarket you will find a bewildering choice of yoghurts. Some are supplied by major manufacturers. Others come from quite small businesses, sometimes built up by a single dairy farm.

Q

1 Why is the choice so large?

2 You are a dairy farmer with plans to start yoghurt production. What are the attractions of this course of action?

3 What will you need to do in order to ensure that the yoghurt sells?

4 Explain how an effective market research plan might be set up.

5 Are consumers sovereign? Provide arguments for and against this statement.

The complex balance between consumer sovereignty and marketing strategies is different for every product. Genuine attempts to meet consumer demand increase consumer influence. Marketing strategies which attempt to reduce competition can reduce consumer choice and limit consumer influence in the market place.

Customer service

Quick Snack

On the whole, rail travel and good refreshment facilities have not always gone together. So an early morning customer travelling on the first train may find little to attract. However, if you happen to pass through Doncaster at 8am, you will find on the platform a branch of Quick Snack which has definitely got things right. Cheerful and polite staff, a hot bacon and tomato baguette still crisp on the outside, good tea, fresh flowers on your table and perfect cleanliness are all to be found.

The company says that customer service is right at the heart of its business strategy. Without it, the quality of the product collapses. So it puts a great deal of effort into their training.

Your agenda

1 Why is training crucial in the provision of customer service?

2 How can customer service help to differentiate the product?

3 To what extent have market forces played a part in Quick Snack's approach to customer service?

4 Give two examples of companies you have come across which make customer service a high priority, and explain how they have achieved their reputation.

For some businesses, the care and attention which goes into **customer service** is crucial in defining the nature of their competitive advantage. Customer service covers all aspects of the way the business actually interacts with the customer. In the service sector it is often a central part of the product itself – as with Quick Snack. However, it can also be very important for some manufactures, especially where after-sales service is a significant element in the package.

Customer service can be a central aspect of market orientation. A business attitude which sees customer service as a major feature of the product itself can contribute greatly to competitive advantage.

The helpfulness of employees when faced with complaints plays a big part in retaining customers, even when things have gone wrong. The British Standards Institution recommends that businesses should turn customer complaints to their advantage. About 850 000 complaints are now made to Trading Standards departments each year. But recent studies have shown that only half the people who are dissatisfied in some way actually make a complaint. Usually, these people simply avoid the supplier in future but they may also tell others to do the same. It is clear that dealing effectively with complaints would be a powerful way to gain repeat sales and preserve customer loyalty.

Customers need easy access to staff who can help them. These staff need to have the power to take action to give customers redress: some delegation is required. If the employee who handles the complaint is empowered to take a quick decision as to how the customer can be compensated, there is less risk of losing business in the future. Training is obviously crucial to making the system work.

Properly handled, complaints provide vital information about customer preferences. This can be built into a system for monitoring the market and added to the information obtained from the rest of the market-research effort.

Comparing with substitutes

Flying again

Southwest Airlines is operating in a highly competitive business: US domestic flights. In order to carve out a market for itself, the company decided some time ago to concentrate on short-haul flights with an average distance of 425 miles. There are no meals, no in-flight films and no seating classes. What it offers is frequent flights with fares 60 per cent below competitors', to smaller, less-congested airports.

How did the company decide on this strategy? Instead of looking at the way competing airlines worked, it decided to look at their real substitutes. For their flights, the real competition is not other airlines but the car. People who choose to fly rather than drive will be giving up convenience in order to save time. Smaller airports allow time savings because they are not congested and subject to delay. Frequent flights mean people have a lot of choice about when to travel. Flying becomes a serious alternative, at those prices, to the convenience and freedom of driving. The company has been consistently profitable for 25 years.

Your agenda

1 Think of two other businesses which compete with a different product.

2 How does this affect the way they seek to meet customer needs?

3 Think of two examples of organisations which customers are often not happy with. How do you think they could compete better?

Businesses which make a general practice of serious study of customer needs can transform their approach. This aspect of marketing can have a highly beneficial impact on the extent to which customers get to determine for themselves what types of products they are going to consume.

The success of companies like Southwest has been used as an example for training purposes. As decision-takers become more aware of such strategies, we can expect that customers will, increasingly, count.

4 Are consumers protected?

Smoking or non-smoking?

Daniel Melitz asked for a non-smoking seat on his British Airways (BA) flight from London to Hong Kong. As a result, he expected to be able to spend the flight free from smoke – especially as he'd paid over £4 200 for his return club class fare.

But on the plane he found that although he was in a club class non-smoking seat, he was in fact sitting immediately in front of a smoking area. The flight was full so he could not move. He had to endure a cloud of smoke all through the twelve hour flight. Not only were the five people sitting behind him heavy smokers, but they kept swapping places with friends in no-smoking seats so they too could light up.

When Daniel got back to London he wrote to BA's chief executive. BA responded by sending him a bottle of champagne – but said it couldn't be held responsible for his uncomfortable journey. Further correspondence was getting nowhere, so Daniel asked Which Legal Service for advice.

We thought Daniel was right to expect a smoke-free flight as he'd booked a non-smoking seat, so we wrote to BA asking for compensation. But again, it refused. At this point we advised Daniel to issue a small claims summons against BA and let the judge decide the matter.

At the hearing, BA argued that it does not undertake to provide any particular seat on the plane. The judge agreed that this was a reasonable defence but added that it was also reasonable for Daniel to expect to be in a reasonably smoke free area. The judge ordered BA to pay Daniel £600 compensation.

When someone contracts to provide a service, you're entitled to expect them to perform the service reasonably well. But a supplier may be able to limit its obligations by including fair and reasonable terms of business in the contract. If possible read the small print before entering into an agreement.

Source: *Which? magazine*, November 1998

Your agenda

1 Would you expect Daniel to travel with BA again?

2 Why do you think BA resisted his claim in the early stages?

3 What impact does this type of case have on businesses?

The consumer can often have very little power or influence when compared with a business. Sometimes it is necessary for there to be a helping hand in the form of some protection from government. The law recognises that it is necessary to grant certain rights to the consumer and some responsibilities to businesses, in an attempt to redress the balance between individuals and firms. However, the law is not always easy to understand and individuals find it difficult to bring pressure to bear on companies.

The Consumers Association has been extraordinarily successful in raising standards of customer awareness among businesses. By exposing careless practice and poor design it has made it incumbent on businesses to strive for excellence and to ensure that they meet minimum standards. It is often the case that it can help consumers to secure the rights they have under consumer legislation.

Contract law

A contract is simply an agreement that is enforceable by law and is the main way in which people do business. This enables markets to function properly. Whenever consumers purchase products, or businesses arrange a sale, they are entering into a legally binding contract. Although this happens millions of times every day there is a set number of procedures that occur to ensure that there is a contract between both parties. For a contract to be in existence the following events must occur:

- An offer is made.
- This offer is accepted.
- Each party to the contract provides consideration.

For example, someone may offer a car for sale at £5000 and someone else will accept the offer. Both sides give up something in this arrangement (£5000 or the car) and as such, each provides consideration. If these three events occur, assuming both parties intend to make and are able to make a contract, both sides will be legally responsible for their part of the bargain. If one side then decides not to honour their commitment there is a breach of contract and legal remedies are available for the other party. The court decides what happens next and there are three possible remedies:

- Damages, where a sum of money is paid as compensation.
- Specific performance, where the offender is ordered to complete his or her part of the contract.
- Injunction, where the offender is prevented from doing something.

In addition to the legal remedies available in the event of a broken contract, there is a range of legislation aimed at protecting the consumer. These laws are considered necessary because of the unequal balance of power each side brings to the contract. Although few contracts end up being disputed in the courts, the existence of the law means that the vast majority of contracts are made in accordance with it.

Consumer protection legislation

The Sale of Goods Act 1979 gives consumers purchasing goods from a retailer some rights in the event of the goods not being of a suitable quality. The customer is entitled to a refund if the goods are:

- not as described
- not of merchantable (satisfactory) quality
- not fit for the purpose for which they were intended to be used.

These conditions do not give consumers the right to return something they do not like, but they do ensure that the customer receives the goods that have been paid for. These rights do not apply in a private sale.

The Trade Descriptions Act 1968 gives consumers protection against traders who mislead by applying a wrong description of goods for sale. In the event of a consumer suffering from a false description of goods, that causes him or her to purchase the goods, there is a remedy in the criminal courts.

The Consumer Protection Act 1987. Sometimes consumers are injured as a result of faulty products. This Act aims to ensure that producers insure their product against its potential for causing harm to consumers. The Act makes it a criminal offence to supply unsafe goods. This allows users of the product, even if they did not purchase it, to sue the manufacturer. The act is a response to an EU directive.

The Food Safety Act 1990. Under this Act, it is an offence for a person to sell food which carries a health risk. This means that anyone who prepares food or processes ingredients has a responsibility to take care. To enforce this Act officers have the power to inspect food which is for sale, has been sold or is in the process of preparation.

The above legislation has forced businesses to place more emphasis on quality control. It has greatly increased the level of accountability to customers. It has also given added impetus to businesses to set up customer service departments so that complaints can be dealt with before they become serious.

Regulation

In some markets regulation is used to protect the consumer. For example, the Civil Aviation Authority controls airline ticket sales. It makes tough rules for travel agents selling discounted tickets or cheap holidays. The objective is to prevent travellers from being stranded abroad. Tour operators which take out a licence contribute to a fund which is used to pay for return fares in the event of the operator going bankrupt. This is just one example of regulation.

5 Are markets better?

Jurassic Park in Siberia?

In the frozen wastes of Siberia an industrial dinosaur has been discovered alive and well. Back in the mists of time Soviet central planners with a sense of humour chose to site a steel plant in the middle of the Siberian wastes. It is difficult to find any economic logic to justify the decision to build a steel works so far removed from its market. The steel works is dependent upon raw materials shipped in from outside and must send its finished product by rail to distant markets.

The collapse of the Soviet Union should have marked the end of this behemoth. High transport costs, lack of investment and the loss of subsidised markets should have signalled the closure of the factory. However, the factory still stands. Smoke continues to spew out of its massive chimneys and trains regularly leave the railyards, laden with steel.

It doesn't matter that its customers don't have the cash to pay for its steel. A complex system of bartering has evolved. The company runs its own factory supermarkets which stock products given to the company by customers in exchange for steel. Employees are paid partly in cash and partly with electronic credits on a debit card which can be used to buy goods from the factory supermarkets. As one employee said, 'I don't mind being paid this way. If we insisted in being paid all in cash, we probably wouldn't get paid at all'.

Critics of the former state-run industries argue that such a complex system of bartering can only provide short-term protection for uneconomic factories. They argue that these industries can only survive in a market economy by cutting jobs, increasing productivity and streamlining production processes. This may be true, but the Siberian dinosaur still breathes fire, and its steel mills still roll. Most importantly, the steelworkers, unlike many Russian workers, still have cash in their pockets and bread on the table.

Your agenda

1 Why would the steel works not have been built in a market system?

2 What would you expect to happen to this factory over a period of time?

3 How has the factory survived so far?

Until 1989 a number of important economies operated with a system of central planning rather than with market forces. Russia and the other states which went to make up the old Soviet Union, the east European economies, China, Vietnam and Cuba all had communist governments and all their economic activity took place in the public sector. At the time of writing, only the last three remain communist. Even they have introduced a range of market incentives which mean that their private sectors are growing.

With a centrally planned economy, organisations are run in the public interest and profit is not a motivating factor. The government bureaucracy lays down targets and each production unit strives to meet the target. There are two snags with this approach:

- No one has an incentive to work hard.
- There is no role for the customer in deciding what is produced.

Over the long run, it became gradually clearer that the centrally planned economies were having difficulty in raising standards of living. By degrees, people living in eastern Europe became aware of the difference between their lives and life in western Europe. In particular, the East Germans began to watch West German TV and they could *see* the difference. The only way to preserve the system was by force, and President Gorbachov of the Soviet Union led the move to abandon force. As he did so, one communist party after another became fatally weakened.

The emerging economies, as they were called, did not find the changes easy. They had lived without market forces for many years and the transition process was painful. Large numbers of state-owned enterprises were unable to compete with western businesses because they lacked the experience of finding and implementing efficient production methods. Many simply collapsed. Shares in the state-owned enterprises were widely distributed, but many of them were closed down. Equipment was sold off. Many people were made redundant.

Figure O3.5 shows what happened to the countries in question. Although many of the emerging economies suffered at first from the transition to market economy status, there has been some recovery in recent years. Standards of living are rising in eastern

Europe, although income distribution is much wider now than under the old regimes. Some resourceful people have made fortunes because of the tremendous opportunities to meet unsatisfied demands. Others have had no opportunity to do anything but survive.

Russia and some of the other states of the former Soviet Union are having more difficulty. The absence of a system of business law at the time of transition made business life very difficult. We take for granted the laws which ensure that business is conducted in a reliable way and that debts can be collected. A poorly developed legal system makes business very risky.

Year	Czech Republic	Estonia	Georgia	Hungary	Poland	Romania	Russia	Slovak Republic	Ukraine
1989	1.4	−1.1	−4.8	0.7	0.2	−5.8	na	1.4	4.0
1990	−1.2	−8.1	−12.4	−3.5	−11.6	−5.6	−4.0	−2.5	−3.4
1991	−11.5	−13.6	−20.6	−11.9	−7.0	−12.9	−5.0	−14.6	−11.6
1992	−3.3	−14.2	−44.8	−3.1	2.6	−8.8	−14.5	−6.5	−13.7
1993	0.6	−9.0	−25.4	−0.6	3.8	1.5	−8.7	−3.7	−14.2
1994	3.2	−2.0	−11.4	2.9	5.2	3.9	−12.7	4.9	−23.0
1995	6.4	4.3	2.4	1.5	7.0	7.1	−4.1	6.9	−12.2
1996	3.8	3.9	10.5	1.3	6.1	4.1	−3.5	6.6	−10.0
1997	0.3	10.6	11.0	4.6	6.9	−6.9	0.8	6.5	−3.2
1998	−2.3	4.0	2.9	5.1	4.8	−7.3	4.6	4.4	1.7
1999	0.0	0.0	3.0	3.0	3.5	−4.0	0.0	1.8	−2.5

Figure O3.5 Growth rates in emerging countries (% change in GDP)
Source: EBRD Transition Report

Work in progress

1 Find out how the emerging economies are performing now.

2 If possible, select one emerging economy and find out what problems it still has.

3 Compare growth rates in one developed country, one developing country in Asia, Africa or Latin America and one emerging economy. What differences do you observe? What other differences are you now aware of?

China adopted a different strategy. The Communist Party retained political control but liberalised some areas of the economy. Many Chinese state-owned enterprises set up joint ventures with foreign companies. Many Chinese were permitted to set up small businesses, especially in retailing. Farmers were given incentives to produce and a big increase in agricultural production resulted. Most people now have enough to eat and growth rates have been impressive. (They may not be as big as the statistics tell us, but they are still high.) Officially, growth averaged 8 per cent per annum for 1985–95, compared with 5 per cent for the previous decade. In 1998 the Chinese government set about making its state-owned manufacturing sector subject to market forces, i.e. further state subsidies were ruled out for the future. The outcome of this is unknown at the time of writing.

Creating jobs and incomes

In the developed countries, from the Second World War onwards, there was a tendency for the role of the government in the economy to increase. Governments nationalised important industries, set up health care systems (such as the NHS in the UK) and intervened more by regulating various aspects of the economy. Some of the government interventions made a big difference to the welfare of many people. The welfare state, improved safety at work and so on had very beneficial consequences. Nationalisation was less successful. Too often, government interference made it difficult for good decision-making processes to develop. Market orientation was neglected as competition was reduced.

After 1980 there was a shift towards **economic liberalism**. In the UK this was associated with Prime Minister Thatcher. The objective was to encourage market forces to operate so that decisions would be taken on the basis of consumer demand and the need to increase efficiency. On the whole, competition received some encouragement and the resulting drive for efficiency had some effect in improving growth rates.

Essentials

Economic liberalism involves reducing the role of the government in the economy. Privatisation, deregulation, increased competition and putting public services out to tender all lead to the private sector taking over more economic activities and making them subject to market forces.

At the same time the European Union was creating opportunities for many companies to expand their markets, while increased imports from the EU created more competition and more choice for consumers. Similarly, trade negotiations through the World Trade Organisation have increased opportunities and competition worldwide.

In the UK economic liberalisation undoubtedly led to an increased pace of structural change. This meant that some people had to face redundancy and a period of unemployment. On the credit side, many people have experienced an improvement in both the quality and quantity of goods and services available to them since 1980. Large numbers of new businesses have been created and some of these have been very innovative and have created jobs.

There is absolutely no doubt that most organisations are now more market orientated than they used to be. Increased competition in many sectors has provided the motivation needed to study the customer's needs with some care. The Post Office is still in the public sector, but it has to compete with phones, faxes and e-mail and it must cover its costs. So it too must study the customer. We would find it hard not to conclude that the market does motivate.

Some of the change has come from the view prevailing in our society that everyone must be accountable for their actions. This attitude has definitely grown in strength and the rest of this option is very much concerned with different aspects of accountability.

Enquiry 2 **Who makes relationships?**

This enquiry has two themes: the way businesses work with each other and relationships between employers and employees. Both are important in creating dynamic and flexible business operations. Increasingly, links between businesses allow each to do things which could not be done without collaboration, so the line between competition and collaboration has become blurred. Similarly, employers and employees need to work together. Conflict has often given way to collaboration. Partnership has become critical to performance.

1 What are supply chains?

Li & Fung

Victor Fung's grandfather started Li & Fung in 1906. Then, no one in the factories of southern China spoke English. The US merchants who came to buy spoke no Chinese. His value added came from interpreting. He charged a fee for bringing buyers and sellers together.

In time, this kind of brokering became less profitable. Victor Fung decided to do things a little differently. He found that western companies buying in Hong Kong could manage on their own. But wages were rising there. They did not have the knowledge to buy what they needed in other Asian countries. Victor and his brother had that knowledge. They opened offices in Taiwan, South Korea and Singapore. In time they expanded all over the Far East.

Soon Li & Fung was able to put together packages, buying components from the cheapest and best sources for each input. It did this with radios. Then it shipped the components to the place where they could be assembled most cheaply, mainly in China. The finished product was shipped back to Hong Kong for testing and inspection.

Li & Fung call this dispersed manufacturing. The value chain is broken up into a series of processes. The company uses its specialist knowledge of Asian markets to place each process in the cheapest location. Its value added lies in knowing the best way to organise production. This is called supply chain management (Figure O3.6).

Companies can do this for themselves of course. But how long would it take them to gather the information

and experience needed to do it effectively? Li & Fung have 35 offices in 20 countries. It can help companies by organising new orders very quickly and maintaining some flexibility. This is important because so many businesses need to respond rapidly to changes in the market place.

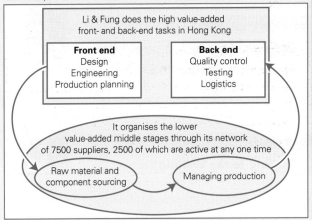

Figure O3.6 Supply chain management
Source: *Harvard Business Review*, September–October 1998

Your agenda

1 What is Li & Fung's product? How does it add value?

2 Why would many companies need help with supply chain management?

3 What advantages can Li & Fung offer them?

4 What particular possibilities would this way of outsourcing offer a UK business selling fashion clothing?

Global competition puts pressure on companies. One way to compete effectively is to focus on **core activities** and **outsource** the rest. So the business **sticks to the knitting**. It does what it does best: it produces the items in which it has a competitive advantage. Anything it needs which it does not itself produce cheaply, it buys from other companies. This is what is meant by focus: concentrating on the areas of greatest expertise within the company.

The business which concentrates on its core capabilities may require a great many suppliers. These need to be organised in a complex supply chain which is carefully coordinated. The businesses which participate in it will become interdependent. For each, future success will require continuing good relationships with each other.

> **Essentials**
>
> **Core activities** are those which the business sees as central to its main strategy. **Peripheral activities** are those which can be outsourced with advantage because they do not contribute in any crucial way to that strategy.

> **Essentials**
>
> **Outsourcing** means buying inputs from independent suppliers. These inputs can be goods, component parts for example, or services such as accountancy, canteen provision or design.

> **Essentials**
>
> **Sticking to the knitting** means concentrating on those areas of production where the business has a real competitive advantage. It implies that the business will seek focus rather than diversifying into areas it knows less well. The term was first popularised by Tom Peters, the management guru.

Setting up the supply chain requires knowledge. As you will, by now, have discovered, gathering information is a time-consuming and expensive activity. This is where Li & Fung makes its market. In a domestic setting, businesses base their knowledge of potential suppliers on past experience within their local or national market. But for many businesses sourcing inputs in the most efficient way requires international knowledge. This is more difficult to acquire.

One major advantage of outsourcing is that it makes the business much more flexible. Changes in the market place can lead to speedy adaptation. A major reason for this is that the big organisations which design and market the product are buying many of their inputs from smaller businesses. They need have no long-term obligations to these suppliers. The supplier businesses, in turn, may employ cheap labour on a part-time or short-term basis. If they run out of orders for any reason, they have little or no obligation to their employees.

> **Work in progress**
>
> Q **1** From your experience of businesses you have studied, describe a specific supply chain.
>
> **2** Why have supply chains tended to become longer in recent years?
>
> **3** What are the implications of this?

There are big issues here relating to security of employment and fair pay. Flexibility is an essential source of competitive advantage for businesses. Competition has brought improved real incomes for huge numbers of people all over the world. It remains the case that for many people, employment security has got worse rather than better. Yet the development of manufacturing in the poorer countries of the world has brought massive improvements in standards of living for the people who work there. There are significant gains, even though life is still difficult for so many.

Diversification, focus and outsourcing

There was a time when a dynamic company would diversify into new markets. It would look for new products and move in quite different directions from its past areas of expertise. The trouble with this approach is that some companies have found that their original products were the ones they really knew about. Diversifying spreads risks but can lead the company outside its area of expertise.

Hanson was the great prophet of diversification and the outstanding example of a conglomerate, the business with many unrelated products. Yet Hanson split itself into four groups in 1996, each taking in a group of related businesses with a much sharper focus. A number of its peripheral businesses were sold off.

This trend followed on the realisation that for most businesses, core activities were the ones which were most likely to be profitable in the long run. An important part of the process involved **divestment**. This meant that peripheral activities were hived off or sold as separate businesses. They then became suppliers to their previous owners.

Essentials

Divestment occurs when part of a business is sold off. It may be sold to its original managers, in which case it is a management buy-out.

Longman, the publisher of the book you are reading, did this. It had a printing plant in York which did a good deal of in-house printing for the company. This was clearly a peripheral activity for a major publisher. Longman's real expertise was in the commissioning, editing, designing and marketing of new books. So it sold the plant to its manager and it became York Publishing Services. That leaves Longman free to outsource its printing wherever it chooses and YPS free to take profitable business from anyone who needs books or pamphlets printed. Figure O3.7 shows how the supply chain looks. The author, editor and designer will all usually be freelance workers. The

printer will be a specialist business. Only the organisation, marketing and distribution will be carried out by the publishers themselves.

Figure O3.7 A publishing supply chain

This approach creates incentives for managers. Both the core and the peripheral business may be operated more profitably than before. But with a number of different yet interdependent businesses participating in the supply chain, good supplier relationships become vital to success.

Joint supply

Some products grow out of the same production process. Chemicals have by-products. Animal products are very varied. Saw mills produce planks and sawdust. The trends described are likely to mean that the main product and the by-product are processed and sold by separate businesses. You are not likely to go to the saw mill for supplies of gerbil bedding. By-products are sold on to the specialists who will be best able to market them.

2 Supplier relationships

Pritchards (printers) Ltd

In 1986 Pete Pritchard was, as he used to put it, 'making ends meet' with a small printing business outside Worcester. His main work was church magazines, catalogues and brochures, sports programmes and publicity for local shops. It was at this time that a small teachers' publishing cooperative called Pioneer asked him to print their first booklets intended for sale to schools. The material was an instant success and more titles followed. By 1989 Pete's business had doubled in size and three-quarters of his business was from Pioneer. Then, without warning, disagreement broke out among the cooperative's members and their most successful writer, Dave Atkins, decided to leave. Sales flagged and Pete's orders abruptly dropped away as Pioneer hurriedly tried to reduce its stocks.

However, Dave Atkins now set up as an independent publisher. He launched his own company, Trojan Publications, and came straight to Pritchards with plans for colour printing and higher volumes. Once more, Pete found himself investing in the needs of one customer. The computerised equipment necessary represented a major commitment. Fortunately, Trojan flourished and the orders rolled in. Indeed, so successful was the new company that in 1994 a major London publisher suddenly offered to buy Trojan for a substantial cash sum. Dave Atkins asked for time to consider. And Pete knew for sure that more than Trojan was at stake...

Your agenda

1 Many businesses sell their product to other businesses, rather than direct to the consumer market. What particular hazards do these companies face?

2 Why do some businesses seek close relationships with their suppliers?

3 Why have supplier relationships become crucial to many businesses as they have sought to increase their competitiveness?

During the 1990s many larger firms rethought the whole nature of their relationships with suppliers. There were two important trends:

- Many subsidiary enterprises have been sold or bought out by their managers. Some of these are unrelated to the major company's core business but many others become natural suppliers on achieving their independence.
- Businesses often now contract out many of the support services they need and parts of the production process that were previously provided in-house.

These changes are driven by the idea that true excellence is only likely to be achieved across a limited spectrum of fairly closely related activities. Put simply, there is no necessary reason for a domestic appliance manufacturer to assume that it will also prove to be a successful maker of security equipment or that it is best placed to write instruction manuals or run canteen services. Efficiency implies focus.

Although suppliers that emerge through divestment or contracting out must clearly operate in a competitive market, an element of goodwill often exists. The large firm may gain through a long and close relationship.

Traditionally, the purchasing department in a firm would be strongly cost-driven and inclined to perceive its task in very quantitative terms. Numerous orders might be put out to tender and, on the basis of competitive quotes, contracts might be awarded to hundreds of different suppliers. It was impossible to build up close relationships with so many suppliers. Besides, contracts would not necessarily be renewed if a rival firm could undercut the supplier on price. Thus any sense of accountability to a firm's suppliers was very limited or non-existent.

Supplying quality

Competitive pressures have pushed many firms towards rethinking the logistics of their production process and making quality an overriding priority. Just-in-time (JIT) stock control systems mean very tight schedules for input deliveries. Any significant error may disrupt an entire production process and with equally tight product delivery times, the failure may be transmitted to a customer. Lean manufacturing means that the whole chain of production and deliveries has to be extremely reliable and well coordinated. Collaborative relationships with suppliers are essential.

The search for ever higher quality has worked in the same direction. JIT production systems cannot depend on routine inspection. Components must automatically hit the specified standard with very few exceptions indeed. Meanwhile with the rising priority of quality within the marketing mix, the reputation of a firm may literally depend on consistently meeting the standard promised to consumers. The trend towards requiring zero defects has its origins here. The quality of one becomes the quality of all.

Work in progress

Q 1 What impact has lean production had on supplier relationships?

2 If a 'zero defects' policy is in place, whose responsibility is quality?

3 What problems can you see developing from these trends?

Quality in the final product depends not only on quality in production but also on the quality of relationships with suppliers. These links are very important to the business. In some companies they are being developed to the extent that a customer may actually provide training and expertise to assist a supplier.

This kind of relationship is only possible with a limited number of suppliers. Many firms are reducing their supplier base and shifting away from multi-sourcing towards single-sourcing of components and business services. The emphasis is moving from a simple contractual relationship based on lowest cost towards a long-term complex relationship based on a mutual commitment to efficiency and quality at a competitive but fair price.

Some firms are particularly dependent on the quality of a supplier's operations and may make the enforcement of high standards a condition of awarding contracts. This particularly applies to a retailer whose brand name is being directly applied to the output of its suppliers.

Point of view

Tomatoes and supermarkets

Some supplier relationships look distinctly less than equal. Consider the case of the tomato grower who built up a business on the basis of a long term contract with a supermarket chain. He built additional greenhouses. He was heavily reliant on the one buyer.

Then the buyer asked for discounts. The grower obliged, but the next time he was asked, he knew that further discounts would take his sales revenue below the level of his costs. He explained the situation to the buyer. A year later the supply contract was cancelled. Within another year the business was bankrupt.

Your agenda

1 Why was the supermarket chain able to treat the tomato grower in this way?

2 What would the attitude of the consumer be to this type of situation?

3 What types of businesses would be likely to find themselves in the tomato grower's situation?

4 What survival strategies might they adopt?

Collaborate or compete?

British Airways cooperates

Under BA's franchise arrangements passengers can fly with an independent airline which operates to BA's high standards of customer service quality and hospitality. Franchise partners specialise in specific routes and regions, enabling BA to extend its network by providing greater choice and flexibility. The franchised airlines fly under BA's name, livery and flight code. Inside the aircraft customers find the familiar BA cabin interior. Cabin staff are in BA uniforms. Customers gain from increased choice and guaranteed high standards of customer care. Who says BA isn't customer orientated?

Your agenda

1 What advantages does this arrangement have for BA?

2 How does the customer gain?

3 Why would BA use a franchise system as the basis for the relationship with its partners?

Increasing numbers of businesses are collaborating with one another because it allows them to create new opportunities. Effectively, they are using one another's core capabilities. This is another way in which business interdependency has tended to increase in recent years. Collaboration may be based on exploiting common strengths or providing complementary aspects of competitive advantage.

What happens, though, when the dominant company finds itself in some difficulty? BA faced some problems during the late 1990s, with falling profits. There were suggestions that perhaps the service it gave to its customers was not so brilliant as its advertising suggested. Where does that leave its franchisees? They have benefited from BA's marketing and brand image, but if the brand looks less successful than previously, the value of collaboration will diminish. Some business relationships may prove more durable than others.

Is collaboration anti-competitive?

Collaboration can be used to build up market power. Relationships which are good for businesses can also be a threat to their competitors. While sometimes the collaborating partners will decide on a full merger, for others it makes sense to retain some independence while working together on joint projects.

Point of view " "

Stifling competition

In a press release dated 19 August, 1997 BA chief executive Bob Ayling claimed that Richard Branson's airline, Virgin Atlantic, was afraid of competition. Richard Branson had criticised the proposed alliance between BA and American Airlines.

Government approval of the alliance was contingent upon all UK airports granting access to all US airlines. This move would allow Continental, US Airways, Delta, TWA and Northwest to fly into and out of Heathrow where Virgin is based. Bob Ayling argued that Virgin Atlantic opposed this measure because it would create additional competition. Ayling claimed that, 'basic economics spells out that more competition equals lower prices,' and that the new BA and American Airlines alliance would 'unlock new opportunities for competition'. He added that the real winners from the BA alliance would be the customer who would enjoy lower fares, greater choice and better services.

Sir Freddie Laker whose own budget airline Skytrain was forced out of business by BA in 1982 did not share Bob Ayling's optimism. He took out full-page adverts in all the national newspapers in order to express his opposition to the alliance.

He argued that BA and American Airlines wanted to form a monopoly which would allow them to squeeze other airlines out of the market enabling them to raise prices. In his advert, Sir Freddie outlined his reasons for opposing the agreement. He felt that the undertakings which the US and British governments required were likely to be ineffective. He pointed out that the two companies were seeking anti-trust immunity from the US government. Sir Freddie predicted that like all monopolies, 'BA and American [will] engage in jugular marketing and the other 'cartel' style price cutting, including dirty tricks of the kind that drove Skytrain out of business. Then, as before fares will skyrocket'.

As part of the deal BA would have to give up landing slots at Heathrow in order to allow new competitors access to the lucrative Atlantic route. Rather than give up transAtlantic slots BA has pulled out of less profitable routes affecting, among others, passengers in the Scottish Highlands who wanted to connect to Heathrow flights. The landing slots can be sold to rival airlines bringing in additional revenue for BA.

Sir Freddie urged the Prime Minister to intervene arguing that if the 'merger' was allowed, 'the British flying public [would] have to live with its dire consequences for many years to come'.

Your agenda

1 What effect would collaboration have on competition in this instance?

2 Why has BA developed a reputation for stifling competition?

3 Briefly outline the points of view of Bob Ayling, Richard Branson and Freddie Laker. Explain which you find the most reasonable and why.

4 Explain the consumer perspective on this situation.

3 Do employees participate?

New broom sweeps the floor at Rover

The British motor industry during the 1960s and 1970s was characterised by poor industrial relations. British Leyland, the nationalised motor manufacturer, was almost paralysed by powerful unions. Michael Edwardes, managing director of British Leyland, described the company as an 'industrial disaster'. Workers were taken on and laid off according to fluctuating demand. There were clear demarcations between management and workers. Land Rover, a subsidiary of British Leyland, even had seven different grades of dining room.

Times change. British Leyland is no more. The company survives under a new name, Rover. The company was sold in a deal which saw the government *paying* British Aerospace to 'buy' it. The new owners found the car industry not to their taste and sold the company to the German car manufacturers, BMW. New owners brought new approaches to labour relations. The new owners introduced a 'New Deal' called 'Rover Tomorrow' which guaranteed no compulsory redundancies and no more lay-offs.

Under the new owners, workers were encouraged to make suggestions on efficiency savings. If suggestions were implemented, then workers would be given financial rewards. William Britton, a foundry worker, received £5000 and a camcorder for designing a foundry tool which replaced three full-time jobs and saved the company £60000 annually. Those workers whose jobs disappeared were moved to new jobs elsewhere in the factory. Workers were guaranteed no redundancies. David Bower, personnel director at Land Rover, explained the management perspective, 'Workers have a role to play in the company's success. They do show flexibility and they do enjoy getting more involved.'

Production workers at the Solihull plant are now called 'Associates' and have become stakeholders in the success of the company. They are encouraged to identify waste and to identify ways of improving efficiency. In doing so, they benefit themselves and the company, gaining financial reward for their ideas, helping to guarantee a job for life (assuming, of course, that the business survives in its present form).

Workers are now encouraged to find and fix faults themselves using colour-coded cards. Cell production has been adopted. There is continuous testing in order to minimise the risk of product failure. Team leaders, paid a little more than team members, are encouraged to 'take ownership of problems' and to take responsibility if things go wrong. They have authority to call in suppliers to resolve problems when they occur. The advantage for the company is that it has helped to reduce an expensive management hierarchy and has raised employee morale. As far as David Bower is concerned, the new corporate culture is a strategy for business success and not an attempt at social engineering.

Your agenda

1 What benefits did Rover employees get from the new regime?

2 What benefits did the Rover management get from the arrangements?

3 In spite of these changes, productivity at Rover remains rather low in comparison to that of other car makers. Why might this be?

4 What has happened to Rover since the above changes were made?

There is no doubt that there has been a trend in management towards involving employees much more in the organisation of production. Cell production, improved quality assurance and teamwork are all strategies which encourage employees to feel involved in the production process and to recognise responsibility for progress.

Delegation is an important part of this process. The team leaders at Rover are being given more responsibility. They are encouraged to act more independently. Here, mutual trust is vital: without it, delegation simply leads to bad feeling. Delegation also requires that people in charge are prepared to trust their subordinates to take some of the decisions.

An important aspect of delegation is that the people who are actually responsible for doing the work are the ones who make decisions about how it should be done. Since they are the ones who are closest to the production process, they are in the best position to take the decisions.

This approach to production makes training of vital importance. People who are taking decisions need continuous updating, especially when they are going to be using new technologies. In this situation the concept of lifetime learning assumes enormous importance.

The concept of the **autonomous work group** develops these ideas to the full. A team of people will be given considerable responsibility for deciding how they will work. Timing, the allocation of different tasks and the way in which they are carried out, will be decided within the group. The members may decide for themselves whether they should have a leader, and if so, who it should be. Such a group is part of a highly decentralised system.

Essentials

The **autonomous work group** is given a large measure of responsibility for deciding how, when and by whom each task will be carried out.

Strategies for employee involvement

Decentralisation and delegation may play a major role in a corporate culture which involves employees. Other possibilities include the following:

- Suggestion boxes, in which employees are encouraged to put their ideas as to how production can be improved. In general, these have not been regarded by management specialists as very successful: they came to be thought of as token gestures. However, many businesses which started out with suggestion boxes have progressed to more effective ways of involving employees through delegation and autonomous group working
- Quality circles, in which employees collaborate to find ways of improving quality, encourage people to pool ideas and devise better methods of building quality into the whole production process.
- Employee share ownership schemes: employees can be given shares in the company which are financed from profits. Alternatively, they may be encouraged to buy shares out of their earnings. This does make them feel more involved in the long-term future of the business.
- Works councils, which provide a forum for discussion between employees and management.
- Representation on the board of directors, which allows for consultation at the highest level, although employee representatives are often welcomed only as observers and cannot then vote.

Participation

The divisional council

A divisional council is a works council representing the workforce. Communication operates on two levels, the management presents new ideas and policies that may be introduced and the workers can discuss their suggestions and grievances. A divisional council will operate as an alternative to a trade union. (Extract from company briefing)

Mansfield Products is a large electrical components manufacturer. The company operates a divisional council system, and membership of trade unions is actively discouraged. In addition to the council, the company offers a variety of vehicles for consultation and negotiation in the form of the health and safety committee, the social club committee and the pay advisory group. There is an open-door policy at management level.

Peter Harmer, the personnel manager, claims the divisional council is a forum for all levels of employees to raise topics that they feel may affect the operation of the business, or are a cause of concern for the employees. This, in turn, increases the involvement of employees in decision-making. Information is directed at a broader spectrum of people within the business and communications are improved.

Margaret Thomas, a divisional council representative, believes many positive decisions have been made at divisional council meetings. In the past ten years the company has introduced profit-related pay, share ownership and performance-related pay. Productivity in the company has improved. However, morale is still very low. There is a suggestion scheme operating within the company, but often many suggestions are not considered and workers feel undervalued. The divisional council is a place for discussion, but the workers do not often prevail when trying to influence policy.

Possible improvements for the future include more team briefings and management meetings. The senior management has become worried though because although many aspects of their approach seem to be working, the low morale identified by some representatives suggests that all is still not well. They have invited a consultant to examine the situation and make recommendations.

The following is an extract from the consultant's report:

The main problem with the company is its style of management. Many of the current schemes are paying lip service to prioritising and involving the workforce in decision-making. Many managers have an autocratic style and have built empires in each separate division. Without reform from senior management to restructure decision-making at every level, the schemes will not gain maximum benefit in terms of productivity and morale. Furthermore, although the company is in the manufacturing sector it has not kept fully up to date with new ideas about how to restructure production. The company still uses assembly-line production methods. It does use job rotation and it is committed to training, but it has not yet implemented just-in-time or Kanban. This means that much of the factory space is used for storage.

Your agenda

1 What positive steps have been taken to involve employees in the organisation of production?

2 Why have these strategies failed to overcome problems associated with low morale?

3 What kinds of action might now be necessary?

4 Why do you think the company discourages trade union membership?

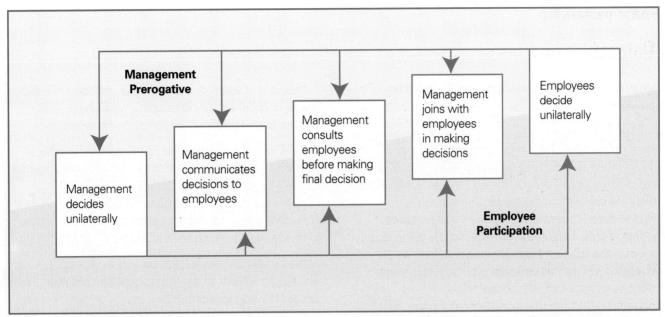

Figure O3.8 Relative employee participation

Employee participation covers a range of ways in which employees may be involved either directly or on a consultative level in the decision-making process. In some cases, it is possible for staff to work directly with management in tackling problems of joint interest. The objective is to find solutions which benefit all concerned. The basic concept has been the subject of debate and experiment for several decades. Figure O3.8 shows the range of ways in which managements seek to involve employees.

An open and democratic leadership style involves bottom-up as well as top-down communication. Managers may regularly take soundings among the workforce and encourage a flow of staff suggestions. Team briefings provide a planned and specific opportunity for managers to explain company policy, progress and general news.

The case study on the opposite page, based on a real company, shows how much hard work goes into effective employee participation. Very often it emerges that successful implementation of employee involvement strategies requires a whole package of measures and an overall approach which is open and receptive to change.

Share ownership

Unipart

John Neill, head of Unipart, last week won the battle to buy Railpart from British Rail.

Neill is a quietly spoken South African who coined the term 'stakeholder'. Neill was using the term back in 1987 when he led the controversial management buy-out of Rover's parts division for £50 million. Unipart has since been hailed as the model of a modern manufacturer, complete with library – *the Learning Curve*; a gym – *the Lean Machine*; and a technology room – *the Leading Edge*. Most important is a fully equipped lecture theatre where Neill regularly presents what he grandly calls his 'course' – a three-hour presentation on inspiration, motivation, the marvels of competition and naturally, stakeholding.

When the buy-out was announced, Neill made sure that the shares were spread around his staff. Today he owns 6 per cent of the company and almost half the shares are held by employees. 'Only three things give you control of your life – good health, a good education and capital,' says Neill. 'I gave employees the opportunity to have a stake in their business which, if successful, would mean they would have capital far beyond their expectations at the end of their careers.' Although he has resolutely resisted pressure to float Unipart, staff can sell their shares once a year and since 1987 the value has soared from 5p to £23.00.

Unions have no place in Unipart – the last trade union disappeared in 1992.

Profits to be announced this year should advance appreciably from last year's £31.5 million and company auditors, Coopers Lybrand, value the group at £264 million. The Railpart purchase, estimated at about £80 million, is key to Neill's strategy of applying what he has done with car parts and services to the privatised railways and protecting the company if the all-important contract with Rover is not renewed in 2002.

Neill has a vision of developing a company that could supply and deliver almost anything which has a part number to any customer, anywhere in the world.

Neill joined British Leyland (BL) in the 1970s, shortly after it was nationalised. He stayed however because his career was moving quickly. By the mid 1970s BL's market share had dropped from 50 to 35 per cent. 'I knew that unless we did something dramatically different, the future would be worse than the past.'

Neill's solution was to engage in a marketing campaign in order to develop a genuine consumer brand. His slogan was:

'CARS ARE ONLY PARTS'

He has achieved the remarkable in turning Rover parts division into a world-class company. 'He completely transformed the outlook of his team: it was a revolution,' said one founder investor. A former colleague adds, 'He recognised that people need to be inspired.'

Much has been made of his partnership with the Japanese and his espousal of Japanese management techniques. But they only go so far. 'I don't think you should ever guarantee people jobs for life. It is unrealistic,' he says, 'We do everything we possibly can to create the best possible future for our people, but that is not a guarantee.'

Your agenda

1 What strategies did John Neill use for motivating his workforce?

2 How has he increased efficiency?

3 To what extent can the company's success be attributed to employee shareholdings?

Owning shares in the company you work for can have a motivating effect. The usual approach is to offer share options to certain employees (although some businesses seek to spread share ownership more widely). Share options mean that employees get the right to buy shares at a fixed price, which will not be less than the current market price. The right may last for a number of years. If the share price rises during that time, the option becomes an increasingly valuable asset. The employee can take up the option and sell the shares on the Stock Exchange at a profit.

Being a shareholder does not confer power. Individual shareholders have little power anyway. But it does give the employee a more active stake in the business. Most large companies now offer share options to senior executives. Their use as rewards for large numbers of employees is less usual.

The learning organisation

'I only work here' is a traditional response from employees who feel confused, ignorant or helpless about the organisation within which they work. Although often said with a sense of humour, it is a symbolic and revealing remark about a place of work and employment. Above all, it is a statement of distance: there is an enormous gap between the employee and the organisation's management. 'No one tells me anything' is an employee remark of the same type. The feeling is that managers and owners are distant, remote, probably uninterested and unsympathetic. Such employees feel hired: they have sold their time and skills for money in a direct economic bargain.

This would be in sharp contrast to the style which might be encountered in businesses like Unipart. There, share ownership went hand in hand with continuous learning and aspects of lifestyle that were built into the corporate culture. The outcome would be one in which there is a perception of employees as 'the most important asset' of the business. This view is often quoted and sums up a cluster of different approaches involving motivation, delegation, training and rewards.

Delegation plainly requires that employees be able to take on responsibilities. This, in turn, requires training, but it also has implicit in the process a sense that employees are capable people who can be relied on. Good communications are essential.

Respect for individuals becomes important too. Without it there is no chance of creating the trust which is needed. Once all these elements in the culture are present, however, the business will think in terms of employee development. This means helping people to change the way they are, fostering talent, recognising strengths and creating opportunities to make them grow. Unipart exemplifies this approach.

Some of this development is going to be about improving technical knowledge and learning new processes. But some enlightened firms allow employees to develop skills which are not directly used in production. Here the emphasis is on the growth of the individual and the focus is partly on motivation and reward. Businesses which adopt this approach are the ones which take a long view of what is good for the company. Those that seek short-term profit above all else will probably not see it as advantageous.

4 The impact of the Social Chapter?

The Maastricht Treaty

The European Union adopted a Charter of Fundamental Social Rights at Strasbourg in 1989. A Social Action Programme was drawn up to implement the Social Charter. This guaranteed a range of basic rights for workers within the Union. These included a minimum wage for all employees, a maximum working week, minimum paid holiday, access to training programmes and the right to be informed and consulted regarding major company decisions.

All the EU member countries except the UK agreed to the Social Charter. The UK's reservations centred on the views of many business managers, which were put forward by bodies such as the Confederation of British Industry (CBI) and the Institute of Directors. The captains of industry were, in many cases, uncomfortable: they thought that the moves towards employee participation would raise costs of production and reduce their authority. They were also against the various improvements in working conditions, and the minimum wage, which were also thought likely to raise costs.

In 1992 the Social Charter was incorporated into the Social Chapter of the Maastricht Treaty, the agreement which set up the single market. The theory was that the single market provided an opportunity for member countries to trade with one another freely and on equal terms. This meant that all EU companies would be providing similar working conditions and would therefore have similar cost structures.

Still, the UK government was worried and negotiated the 'opt-out' clause. This allowed it to agree to everything in the Maastricht Treaty except the social provisions. The 1997 election brought change. The new Labour government immediately agreed to the Social Chapter. In fact, some businesses had already begun to implement the provisions and were not dissatisfied with the outcome.

Your agenda

1 Why were working conditions an integral part of agreement on the single market?

2 In what ways did the Social Chapter threaten some businesses?

3 Why do you think some UK businesses were implementing the Social Chapter before the UK government adopted it as policy?

The Social Chapter includes the following measures:

- the Works Council Directive
- the Working Time Directive
- the Parental Leave Directive
- the minimum wage.

The *Working Time Directive* has caused some new decisions to be made in relation to the hours worked by junior hospital doctors and transport workers. Employees are guaranteed a maximum working week of 48 hours.

The *Parental Leave Directive* now applies to both parents. There are also provisions for a minimum of four weeks' paid holiday a year and equal opportunities requirements are strengthened.

The European Works Council Directive

All businesses which are operating in two or more European countries must have works councils. In fact, a number of such businesses introduced works councils long before the UK adopted the Social Chapter. They had to, by virtue of their involvement in other EU countries. The objectives are to ensure that employees are given information and consulted. Employee representatives come from all countries involved, along with representatives from the management, at least once a year.

In setting up this requirement, the European Commission had one major concern. This was that when problems arose, multi-nationals were able to relocate part of their production in other EU countries. This significantly reduced the bargaining power of employees in any one country. With a works council, discussion can take place on job security generally. Health and safety and other matters affecting employee welfare can also be discussed.

Possible agenda items include:

- employment
- future investments or cutbacks
- training
- the introduction of new working practices
- the way the business is structured.

Pay and conditions issues relating to individual countries cannot be discussed. However, many businesses which are already experienced in organising these meetings find that they provide a useful means of communicating current trends and new ideas, as well as allowing employee anxieties to surface.

The minimum wage

The minimum wage had long been a part of Labour Party policy. Many European countries and the USA have had minimum wages for many years. Soon after the 1997 election, work began to determine what an appropriate level might be for it.

Businesses have often been dubious about minimum wages. The problem is that if they actually do raise wages, then costs rise too and there is potential for some loss of competitiveness. This may give employers an incentive to economise on the use

of labour which can mean that fewer jobs are available. Figure O3.9 shows the theoretical reasoning behind this argument. It predicts that a minimum wage set above the equilibrium level will reduce the availability of jobs.

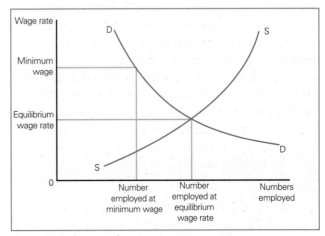

Figure O3.9 Theory and minimum wages

An added problem arose because many occupations attract different wage rates in different regions. A minimum wage which could significantly improve the welfare of low paid workers in London would be a very high wage in parts of Wales or northern England.

In the end, the UK minimum wage was set at £3.60, to take effect from April 1999. This meant that few people would benefit from higher wages in London and the South East, but wages could rise significantly elsewhere. Most businesses were relieved that the minimum had been set at a lower level than it might have been. The rate for 18–21 year-olds was set at £3.00.

> **A CBI survey**
> A survey conducted by the CBI in late 1998 led to the following findings:
> - Nearly three-quarters of employers believe government regulations on the minimum wage, working time and trade union recognition will not significantly affect their competitiveness.
> - Most employers thought that skill levels and management were the most important factors in determining productivity growth.
> - Interesting work is almost as important as pay in motivating workers.

Early indications about the effect of the minimum wage are mixed. The hotel and catering industry is nervous. Wages will be raised and costs will rise. It is not impossible that some hotels will go out of business, though much would depend on the state of demand. Evidence from the fast food chains suggests that they are still recruiting and little effect is expected.

There are possibilities that the minimum wage will improve the position of low paid people. Besides raising wages, it may improve incentives to work. It may also make employers think carefully about the use that is made of their employees and encourage them to invest in training. This would make low paid people more productive and their jobs would become more secure. An open question has emerged as to how frequently the minimum wage should be raised. Continued controversy can be expected.

Work in progress

At the time of writing, there is much activity as the provisions of the Social Chapter become law. The implications are only just beginning to be appreciated and further research will reveal more.

Q

1 Find out what difference the Social Chapter has made in a business you have studied.

2 Research the current situation with respect to the minimum wage. Has it been raised again since it was introduced? What, if any, impact has this had? When can employers pass the cost of higher wages on to customers in the form of higher prices?

3 How do average wages compare with the minimum wage in your region?

5 Are employees protected?

Unfair dismissal claims allowed after one year

In 1999 the law was changed. Until then, protection from unfair dismissal started after two years of employment. Under the new law, the qualifying period was cut to one year. The change was expected to lead to a large increase in the number of claims for unfair dismissal.

In 1998 40000 unfair dismissal cases were heard by the courts. The CBI said that employers were unenthusiastic about the change but could live with it. Most of them assess recruits' suitability for the job before one year is up. The CBI view is that it is important for there to be a period in which employer and employee can bring the job to an end without an expensive court case.

Your agenda

1 Why is it important for employees to be protected from unfair dismissal?

2 Why do employers often oppose employee protection measures?

3 How does employee protection affect flexible labour markets?

The relationship between the employers and the employees within any organisation is controlled mainly by their contract of employment. This has to conform to the current legal requirements. Most of the behaviour of people at work occurs without reference to their contracts, but if things start to go wrong, then the contract becomes important.

Employed people are entitled to receive a contract of employment within 13 weeks of starting work. It should include:

- the date work started
- the scale of pay
- when wages are paid
- hours of work
- holiday, sick pay and pension details
- length of notice to be given; disciplinary rules
- grievance procedures.

There are three types of employment contract – permanent, temporary and personal. Each type of contract gives the worker certain rights and responsibilities though the rights afforded to employees on temporary contracts are few because employers can include 'waiver clauses'. These clauses often deny the worker the right to claim redundancy pay or unfair dismissal if the contract is not renewed.

Flexible contracts

Many organisations now use contracts based on a minimum number of guaranteed hours of employment. This could be 20 or it could be zero hours. The idea is that the company can then ask its workers, often at very short notice, to work longer hours when there is work to do. In retailing an eight-hour contract is appearing, whereby employees are given work during the busy times in the week but may not be employed during week days when trade is slack. The difference between this and a Saturday job is that employees sign contracts to say they are available and prepared to work longer hours if called upon by the company. This increased flexibility is very beneficial for the company, but it leaves the employee very uncertain about what can be expected.

The move towards more flexible contracts of employment has reduced the protection granted to workers. The growth of temporary, casual and part-time employment has given Britain the highest number of part-time employees of any EU member country.

Redundancy

Redundancy can occur for the following reasons:
- the employer has ceased to carry on business
- the employer has ceased to carry on business in the place where the employee was employed
- the employer's need for employees to carry on work of a particular kind has ceased or diminished.

In these cases of unemployment the employee is entitled to a redundancy payment. Sometimes, there are disputes about whether a so-called redundancy is actually a case of unfair dismissal. The dividing lines are not always clear cut.

Equal opportunities legislation

Throughout the European Union there are regulations about the treatment of employees. UK legislation requires equal treatment of workers and ensures that there is no discrimination on the grounds of race or gender. However, it remains the case that, on average, women are paid less than men, even when doing a similar job. Their bargaining power in the labour market is generally less strong.

Any kind of discrimination indicates a market imperfection. It implies that:

- able-bodied white men face less competition than they would in a discrimination-free labour market
- their earnings will be higher than they need be, just as those of other groups will be lower than they could be.

Gender discrimination

The 1970 Equal Pay Act was introduced to end discrimination between men and women. It was amended in 1984 to enable men and women to claim equal wages for work of equal value done for the same employer or an associated employer. Figure O3.10 shows that there is still some discrepancy in the pay of men and women.

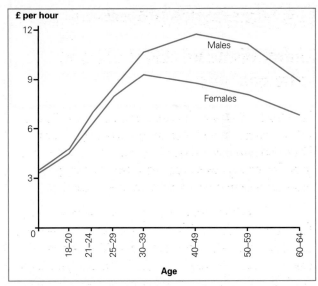

Figure O3.10 Hourly earnings by gender and age*, 1998
*Full-time employees on adult rates, all industries, Great Britain
Source: ONS, *Social Trends*, 1999

The Sex Discrimination Acts 1975 and 1986 declare that it is unlawful to be less favourably treated because of your sex or because you are married. Despite legislative protection, female employees remain at a real relative disadvantage. The principle of equal pay for equal work is often very difficult to ensure or to enforce. In addition, female employees are much more likely to occupy temporary or part-time posts which carry much reduced rights and low status. The Social Chapter may address this issue.

In general, women are less likely to be trade union members and some employers regard them as a soft option when looking for redundancies. Women also often find the pathways to promotion more difficult to ascend or find their routes blocked by subtle but deep-rooted prejudice. The proportion of the most senior positions in companies held by women remains extremely small. Despite this rather gloomy picture, the position is gradually improving, especially in some sectors.

Work in progress

Q **1** What obvious disadvantages will be encountered by employers who discriminate?

2 What further steps can be taken to counter discrimination?

3 Find a recent report of a case brought against an employer and explain what happened and the implications.

4 Evaluate the extent to which employees are currently protected.

Racial discrimination

The Race Relations Act 1976 outlaws all racial discrimination. It also established the Commission for Racial Equality which has direct responsibility for monitoring the effect of the Act. Despite the existence of the law, it is clear that discrimination still occurs; being a member of a racial minority reduces market power. The outcome is visible not so much in terms of lower pay, as is the case with women, as in higher unemployment.

Figure O3.11 shows the data. It is possible to argue that some of the differences in unemployment rates reflect the low level of skills in some ethnic groups. Recent research shows that this does not on its own explain all of the differences.

| | Percentage unemployed | | | | |
	16–24	25–34	35–44	45–59/64	All ages
White	13	6	5	5	6
Black	39	18	12	16	19
Indian	18	7	6	7	8
Pakistani/ Bangladeshi	29	16	13	26	21
Other groups	22	13	10	8	13
All ethnic groups	14	7	5	5	7

Figure O3.11 Unemployment by ethnic group, UK, 1998
Source: ONS, *Social Trends*, 1999

Recent research shows that ethnic minorities still face disadvantages. Not only are their rates of pay below average but they may experience all kinds of hidden or open discrimination when making applications for employment. Most companies claim to operate without any racial discrimination, but they cannot alter attitudes among their own personnel who may penalise members of ethnic minorities in ways that are difficult to expose or to eradicate. The same problems can arise for people who are disabled or who are known to be homosexuals.

The experience of negative discrimination is often humiliating and deeply frustrating. As well as any legal obligations, employers have a responsibility to ensure that everyone in the firm enjoys full respect and proper rights with fair rewards and prospects. Firms can also be argued to have a wider social and ethical duty to offer opportunities to all sectors of the community.

Hiring the best person for the job should be the most effective strategy. Businesses which have made progress in creating equal opportunities often believe in it as a way of improving performance.

6 How have trade unions changed?

Trade unions in Britain today

‘Unions are a counter-weight to employer and management power. By seeking to organise individuals at work into groups with a common interest, unions seek to avoid that power being used in arbitrary, exploitative or careless ways. Unions contribute to the dignity, self respect and standing of the individual workers. They seek to establish fair pay levels, to protect individuals, and solve by agreement, problems which inevitably occur at the workplace. Unions seek to regulate terms and conditions of employment through negotiations and agreements, handle differences through agreed procedures, involving conciliation and possible arbitration, and provide a means for workers to have a say in their employer's affairs.’

Norman Willis, General Secretary of the Trades Union Congress, 1991

The problem I have is how do we convince people that we are sincere, genuine; that we've changed?

Bill Morris, General Secretary, Transport and General Workers Union, 1999.

Opinion polls show that what most people really want is a satisfying job. They also want security. But the most important thing is a feeling that something has been accomplished. More money is not the most important factor. We should travel this route to create more wealth.

John Edmonds, General Secretary, General Municipal and Boiler Makers.

Your agenda

1 What is the role of a trade union?

2 Why have unions become less concerned with pay and more with working conditions?

3 How can trade unions foster good communications between management and employees?

Labour markets are subject to market forces, just as product markets are. The going wage is the equilibrium price of labour. If, for example, demand exceeds supply, then the 'price' will rise and more workers will enter the industry, so restoring equilibrium. If the market is very competitive, labour is treated rather like a commodity. When market forces turn in an unfavourable direction, then wages fall and people become unemployed. Significantly, there is no guarantee that the equilibrium wage level will even meet basic needs or that there will be any equity in the proportion of value added received by the workforce.

In the nineteenth century, large numbers of people were employed in conditions where they were at the mercy of such market forces. It is easy to see how and why trade unions developed. Workers had little if any protection from government. Acting singly, each worker was in a perfectly competitive framework, unable to influence the level of wages or conditions of service, but a combination of workers acting together could exercise selling power. Employers could be presented with minimum terms of employment which would be difficult to reject.

Naturally, trade unionism has often been unpopular with employers. After the Second World War, membership of trade unions grew and use of the strike weapon became more common. There seemed to be growing polarisation between the 'two sides' of labour and management. By the 1970s Britain had earned the reputation of being 'strike-prone' and the relative breakdown of industrial relations became a major subject of debate.

As the problem of industrial relations worsened in the 1970s, the then Labour government tried to bring unions, employers and the government closer together. In the event, this period ended in failure with the 'winter of discontent' in 1978–9 involving prolonged strikes in essential industries and public services. But one enduring outcome was ACAS (the Advisory, Conciliation and Arbitration Service) which is a state-funded but independent body offering advice to both sides on employment issues and able to provide unbiased help in settling disputes.

From 1979 successive Conservative governments aimed to create what they considered to be a fair framework of law within which employers and employees could strike what bargains they wished.

During the 1980s a series of Acts of Parliament forced unions to hold secret ballots before authorising a strike, made the extension of industrial action to a firm's customers or suppliers (secondary action) unlawful, and undermined 'closed shop' agreements by giving all employees the right not to join a union. These changes reduced the power of trade unions very considerably.

Trade unions and Europe

The Trades Union Congress (TUC), the parent body of all UK member unions, has for a long time had links with unions in other EU member countries. Community of interest has encouraged the union movement to be very positive in its attitude to European integration. The possibilities of collective bargaining at the EU level look quite promising. So far, this has focused mainly on working conditions. The European Trades Union Confederation (ETUC) has participated in negotiations on working hours and part-time work as well as fixed-term contracts. These have eventually led to the directives associated with the Social Chapter.

The ETUC is anxious to discuss with MEPs, with the European Central Bank and with Ecofin (the Council of the economic and finance ministers of all EU governments) the 'accountability of the ECB and how monetary convergence, economic stability and increasing economic growth can be most effectively used to attack unemployment' (TUC document, 'Preparing for the euro', 1999).

In the past, trade unions have generally played a more positive part in the business framework of other EU countries than they have in the UK. Trade union activity on an EU level offers a role to the TUC.

Your agenda

1 Why has the trade union movement generally looked positively on the EU?

2 What impact might economic and monetary union have on the trade union movement?

3 How do the provisions of the Social Chapter fit in with recent trends in management styles?

Meantime, deeper forces have been changing the climate of industrial relations:

- The number of workplaces employing very large numbers of manual (typically male) workers has declined steeply.
- Employment expansion has been in service industries and white-collar jobs where there are lower union membership rates and no tradition of militant attitudes.
- Casual and part-time employment has increased rapidly with much less opportunity or motivation for the confrontational approach.
- Persistent large-scale unemployment has meant that many workers are inclined to accept the terms of employment offered.

One effect has been a sharp drop in trade union membership – down by a third from 12 million in 1979 to 8 million (30 per cent of all employees) in 1997. The number of disputes has also fallen dramatically. A second trend relates to a new – and in many ways non-British – culture of employment. Incoming Japanese firms first popularised the concept of single union agreements where the workforce belongs to one union and the firm gives that union its official recognition. Some such unions have made 'no strike' agreements in return for long-term job security. This has often been associated with 'single status' in a workplace where all staff – manual and non-manual – enjoy the same rights and mix as equals. Faced with the changing realities of employment a 'New Unionism' has emerged. Unions have tended to stress their total service to members rather than a 'battle strategy' with employers.

Both trends may ultimately lead in the same direction. These radical shifts in management style have been spreading and represent a sea change in the concept of the 'employee' or 'worker'. The old image of the reluctant worker, unskilled and cash-paid is giving way to a picture of the committed staff member, highly skilled and with a personal 'rewards package'. The competitive necessity for rapid, pro-active change implies staff who are flexible, able to work as a team and unafraid to experiment. In this situation businesses often accept and may even welcome trade unions as a means by which groups can communicate and reach agreement.

Point of view

The state of industrial relations

The TUC's annual assessment of the state of industrial relations shows that disputes are increasingly likely to be settled before workers walk out. Even when ballots are held, the vote is often for disruption rather than strike.

In 1998 there were only 166 stoppages throughout the UK economy, the lowest since records began in 1891. Fewer ballots were held. The TUC General Secretary attributed the lack of militancy to a new mood of partnership. 'These figures should nail the myth that unions are adversaries and show good employers they have nothing to fear from a proper partnership with unions,' he said.

The BBC's employment correspondent pointed out 'global competition now makes workers think twice before walking out and jeopardising their employers' businesses and their own jobs'.

The regions with the highest number of days lost through industrial action in 1998 were Merseyside and Scotland. The lowest figures came from the South West, South East, Humberside and East Midlands.

Your agenda

1 Explain how a genuine partnership between trade unions and employers might affect the company and its employees.

This enquiry aims to uncover how and why firms disclose information of value to stakeholders. Legal obligations are examined as well as voluntary disclosure. Ways of interpreting information given by businesses are explored, as are ways in which information may be concealed.

1 What is statutory disclosure?

From sole trader to limited liability

Bob Philips was made redundant by a large engineering concern during the early 1990s recession. He had been with the company for a long time and received a substantial redundancy package. Soon afterwards, he discovered that a nearby newsagents was up for sale. He bought the business, including stock and goodwill, feeling confident that he could make it work.

To start with, Bob operated as a sole trader. He wanted to keep the business as simple as possible. He reckoned he could do the books himself. He had to keep accounts for tax purposes. His own income tax return would require full accounts of the sales revenue and the costs of everything he bought for the shop. The tricky bit was the VAT accounts, which required a quarterly return.

Things went well. With various good ideas, Bob saw sales rising in the first year. Three successful years later he saw another similar shop for sale just two miles away. He thought running two businesses would be less than double the effort. But at this point he would need a bank loan to make the purchase.

That meant constructing a business plan with forecast sales and profit and an estimated balance sheet. Then Bob realised that he really ought to have limited liability. The bank would want his own home to be the collateral on the loan, but he made extensive use of trade credit from his suppliers of foodstuffs and greetings cards. If he went bankrupt, he personally could be liable for these debts and could end up penniless, or worse. Limited liability would at least protect his personal property from his other creditors.

Limited liability meant facing the legal requirement to produce annual accounts. An accountant would be needed after all...

Your agenda

1 What are the advantages of limited liability over sole trader status?

2 Why are businesses required to keep accounts?

3 Which stakeholders have an interest in the accounts of: (**a**) a small business and (**b**) a plc?

Sole traders do not have to produce accounts except for tax purposes. Once a business becomes a company with limited liability, it needs to comply with legal requirements. The great majority of companies are 'private'. If, however, public limited company (plc) status is wanted, then the company must supply comprehensive details regarding its history, present circumstances and realistic prospects.

All companies must have two or more shareholders and must be registered with the Registrar of Companies. In fact, the formation of a limited company is fairly straightforward. Any group of two or more people can form a company to pursue a legal purpose. All that is required is a correct submission of documents to the Registrar. The company will receive a Certificate to Commence Trading and can then operate with limited liability and the letters 'Ltd' (if a private company) after its name. The firm is then subject to some important disclosure obligations.

The Annual Report and Accounts

All companies are required by law to send shareholders a copy of their accounts and directors' report every year. These must also be filed with Companies House and any member of the public – for a small fee – can obtain a copy.

- For many *private companies*, accounts consist of no more than a simple word processed or typed set of papers with little if any extra information. Small companies are allowed to send only abbreviated accounts to the Registrar. These are very basic and include only a condensed balance sheet plus a few simple details.
- By contrast, most *public companies* use their Annual Report and Accounts as a form of public relations exercise, with a glossy upbeat tone and the emphasis strongly on positive features of the firm's activities and performance. There is frequently quite a striking contrast between the serious and more substantial nature of the accounts themselves and the rather frothy commentary that often accompanies set-piece photographs of the company's management, employees, customers and products.

There is a great deal to be discovered from Annual Reports. Fascinating insights can be gained by using some simple skills of analysis.

The financial accounts are the only ones which must be made public. Management accounts, which are of immense importance to the successful running of the business, are usually kept confidential. They cover costs and revenues in a detailed and informative way, along with forecasts and plans for the future. They are likely to contain information which would not necessarily be flattering to the company. Similarly, confidential personnel records or the findings of expensive research and development will also be kept solely within the upper reaches of the company.

Work in progress

Obtain a copy of the Annual Report and Accounts of a company you know. Start by finding out what is happening to turnover and operating profit. If there have been major changes, look for signs of what actually happened. These may be in the chief executive or chairman's statements, or there may be information in the 'Notes to the accounts'. See if you can piece together the events of the past two years. Has the company experienced difficult trading conditions? If so, why? What impact have the changes had on the balance sheet and the profit and loss account?

The stakeholders versus the company

The directors of a company face many claims for the disclosure of information:

- Managers require information to make decisions.
- Employees need to evaluate job prospects.
- Lenders need to assess risk.
- Suppliers want assurance of payment and indications of future orders.
- Customers may want information about product availability or specification.
- The local community may want to know how the firm's plans will affect the local economy or the environment.
- If a firm grows large enough, there will be concern about its impact on the national economy or even the global environment.

Such claims for disclosure will be greater if the nature of the firm's business makes the stakeholder's interest more critical. For example, a car manufacturer such as Ford is a vital direct employer of manual labour and a large indirect employer via its component suppliers. A chemical-manufacturer such as ICI has potentially hazardous production operations with major implications for the health and safety of both its workforce and its local communities. Its processes and products also have serious environmental implications. It is easy to see that stakeholders have a deep interest in the extent and quality of disclosure by such firms.

In all matters of disclosure the directors (or owners) of a firm find themselves facing a dilemma. The claims of the various stakeholders are real but so too is the value of knowledge that has not been shared. For instance, plans for expansion would be very useful to the trade union and the local council, but they would also send signals to competitors that would entail losing the advantage of surprise in entering a new market.

Yet the spectrum of disclosure policy is very wide. At the heart of the decision making process, the directors have some difficult issues to resolve. Very often, they see their most fundamental obligation as being to the shareholders. In practice, this normally means making profit the priority, often with an emphasis on returns in the relatively short run. The information fed back to shareholders varies widely according to the size and status of the firm.

Firms' policies on disclosure vary greatly:

- Some firms provide the minimum of information. Many large, well established businesses see information as giving power and status and give out details very sparingly.
- Other firms are giving employees an increasing amount of tactical information as part of the effort to raise levels of commitment. This will be balanced by fuller disclosure to the media and public.
- Smaller businesses may give very full information to their relatively few shareholders.

Ultimately, the directors must strike a balance in their disclosure policy. Partly this will depend on the underlying beliefs and values of the managing director and the board. Beyond this point there is a calculation of net benefit in providing information to any stakeholder group. Would the loss of confidentiality in explaining strategic thinking to a trade union leader be justified by a possible improvement in industrial relations? Such decisions depend, in turn, on the firm's internal culture and the style of its leadership.

The legal requirements

The conventions associated with accounting help to ensure that the accounts provide a meaningful picture:

- From year to year, the accounts of the company must be consistent.
- They must be drawn up in accordance with the current rules.
- All potential losses and liabilities must be accounted for.
- All fixed assets must be depreciated.

The Accounting Standards Board lays down the procedures that firms should follow and checks that they are adhered to. The procedures are embodied in the Financial Reporting Standards which can be adjusted to reflect changing circumstances. The result is a set of rules which support the legal requirements enshrined in the Companies Acts.

2 What's in the Annual Report?

The Bluebird story

The following paragraphs formed the opening comments of the Chairman's statement for the year ended 31 December 1996 for Bluebird, a toy manufacturer.

‘Sales for the year were £67.7 million (1995 – £87.3 million) of which UK sales were £33.4 million (1995 – £37.5 million). Overseas sales were £34.3 million (1995 – £49.8). Group profit before tax and exceptional costs was £11.0 million (1995 – £17.8 million).The Board is recommending an unchanged final dividend of 6.75p per share which maintains the full year dividend at 9p.

Last year was difficult for Polly Pocket, after 1995 closed with excess stocks in many markets, which adversely affected our shipments. This overstocking position has been largely overcome and we anticipate consumer sales remaining strong in 1997. The performance overseas should benefit from Polly's continuing status as one of Mattel's long-term brands in a core category. Since its launch in 1990, Polly has grown to become the world's number 1 girls' collectable, and as a girls' toy brand, second only to Barbie.’ (Bluebird, *Annual Report and Accounts*, 1996.)

Bluebird Toys used to make Polly Pocket and Mighty Max. Manufacturing was based in Merthyr Tydfil and the head office was in Swindon. During the early 1990s recession, Bluebird had some problems. Toys can have a bad time if people are postponing non-essential purchases. But by 1994 the company was flourishing again: 60 per cent of its sales were overseas, primarily in North America. Marketing and distribution there were all undertaken by Mattel, the US toy giant.

Then in 1995 Christmas sales were disappointing. The year finished with the bad news of 'excess stocks'. The chairman went on to explain that the company was restructuring. During 1997 it would outsource distribution. It also planned to close down the last of its UK manufacturing operations and source everything in the Far East. However, overall the chairman remained optimistic. Here is his closing paragraph:

‘…we have had an excellent reaction to our new product ranges at the recent toy fairs. Stock levels in our warehouse are much closer to optimum. Product innovation and strong branding remain the essential requirements to develop further our main international ranges. We have a very focused, newly streamlined and cash generative business.’

Your agenda

1 Calculate the percentage decline in each of the following:
   a total sales
   b UK sales
   c export sales
   d group profit.

2 Why do you think that Bluebird maintained its dividends at the previous level?

3 What would you expect to happen next at Bluebird?

4 We know that the pound was rising as the chairman was writing his report. (In the year to June 1997, the sterling index rose by 16 per cent.) How would this be likely to affect Bluebird?

The exact content, format and running order in annual reports varies quite widely. Some companies offer 'financial highlights' or a section called 'the year at a glance'. These provide a brief but accessible summary of the results that are to be given in detail later.

The first substantial item is often the chairman's statement. This includes some observations about the performance over the year and the prospects ahead. It tends, as far as possible, to adopt an optimistic tone. At Bluebird the chairman started with the bottom line and the proposed dividend payments. This reflects the high priority often given in the Annual Report and Accounts (ARA) to shareholders' immediate objectives.

Some companies then take the opportunity to introduce the board of directors with brief biographical details. Executive directors have full-time specific roles within the company. By contrast non-executive directors are part time and bring an independent 'outsider' view to the company's affairs; they usually have wide experience of business management and often hold several non-executive directorships at the same time.

Others leave this information until later and continue with reports from their functional directors; a report from the chief executive is increasingly common. (The position chief executive is interchangeable with managing director, meaning the person with overall responsibility for the company's management and performance.)

The great majority of large firms then provide a 'review of operations' or similar coverage of their main trading activities. This is often a longer section with a good deal of glossy illustration. It is usually the most prominent part of an annual report, yet the least revealing. However, it does serve to give some general idea of the scope of the company's business operations. It may include or be followed by some information on the company's environmental policy and its active support for the community. A few firms issue a separate and much more detailed environmental report (see Enquiry 4, page 601). Generally, however, this section can be rather superficial.

Bluebird actually skipped most of these stages, reflecting its status as a medium sized company. It went straight from the chairman's report to the directors' report and then on to the main business of the accounts. What it did have was a section on corporate governance, with a long statement about its internal financial controls. There is at least a possibility that in view of the rather poor results summarised in the chairman's report, the board was expecting some criticism from shareholders and was anxious to present evidence of careful management.

⁹The group operates a comprehensive annual planning and budgeting system with an annual budget approved by the board. There is a financial reporting system which compares results with plan and the previous year on a monthly basis to identify any significant deviation from approved plans. Additional detailed financial reviews of the operating divisions are undertaken on a quarterly basis. Revised forecasts for the year are prepared quarterly.⁹ (Bluebird, *Annual Report and Accounts*, 1996)

The directors' report

The directors' report usually forms the opening of the serious financial reporting. It generally involves a structured statement featuring significant factual information about the company and its year. The tone is essentially formal and objective, since this is a legally required statement. It will include:

- comments on the company's progress and financial results, including an explanation of 'principal activities' in the year and any significant changes in their nature
- a restatement of the company's key policies with regard to such matters as employment, health and safety and charitable donations
- information on any acquisitions and disposals of shareholdings in other companies.

The report will also contain a statement of the directors' responsibility for the preparation and accuracy of the accounts. This is a legal requirement and is additional to the external check described in the auditors' report (see below). The directors may choose to highlight their responsibility in a separate statement.

The auditors' report is another legally required statement and states whether, in the opinion of an external accountant, the accounts represent a 'true and fair' view of the company's affairs. This report is not just a legal form of words. The auditors have a very serious responsibility to ensure that the accounts have indeed been properly prepared. This becomes painfully obvious when a company turns out to have been engaged in fraudulent activity.

Work in progress

Q Compare the Annual Report and Accounts that you obtained earlier in the enquiry with the norms described above. Which parts are largely froth or legal assurances and which parts reveal some interesting information?

3 What's in the Accounts?

Bluebird profit and loss for the year ended 31 December

	1996	1995
	£000	£000
Turnover	**67 651**	87 261
Cost of sales	**(45 358)**	(57 999)*
Gross profit	**22 293**	29 262
Other operating expenses	**(12 189)**	12 702)
Operating profit	**10 104**	16 560
Exceptional item	**(1 106)**	–
Profit before interest and tax	**8 998**	16 560
Interest receivable	**928**	1 264
Profit before tax	**9 926**	17 824
Profit after tax	**6 701**	11 808
Dividend	**(3 610)**	(4 396)
Retained profit	**3 091**	7 412
Earnings per share	**14.7p**	26.0p

Figure O3.12

Source: Bluebird, *Annual Report and Accounts*, 1996
*Amounts in brackets are subtracted from the total.

Your agenda

1 Explain how the events outlined in the chairman's statement can be seen in the profit and loss account.

2 What would your reaction be to this situation if you were: (**a**) a shareholder or (**b**) an employee of the company?

3 If you were Bluebird's banker, what further information would you want before assessing the situation?

4 Why are financial accounts subject to various legal requirements?

Many people have an almost instinctive feeling that company accounts are not only impenetrably difficult to understand but also bear little relationship to events in the real world. This perception is understandable but only partially justified. In fact, there is nothing particularly difficult about the basic principles of accounts. There are no mathematical barriers: simple arithmetic and a reasonable sense of logic are all that is necessary. Problems arise from:

● the lack of a consistent format for some statements
● the relative incompleteness of disclosure.

With a little practice, the published accounts of any public company can be made to reveal a great deal of interesting information. Accounts record the aggregate effect of numerous real events and transactions, each of which has been represented in terms of its financial value. Business is about the efficient use of resources to match demand. Accounts are simply the financial narrative that tells this story. As with any complex story, accuracy and objectivity are a problem. Published accounts are a summary, often of a very complex business scenario. As such, they are only the pinnacle of a vast edifice made up of financial and accounting records.

Work in progress

Q Use the Annual Report and Accounts you obtained earlier in this enquiry. Compare the layout and headings in those accounts with those presented here from the Bluebird accounts. What differences can you see? If you do not understand the differences, try using a good business dictionary to sort them out.

All companies (except those claiming 'small company' status) produce a profit and loss account and a balance sheet. These represent the core of a firm's financial disclosure.

Bluebird's profit and loss account confirms the gloomy view in the chairman's report. A number of Bluebird's stakeholders must have been feeling worried at this point. The exceptional item which is subtracted from operating profit relates to the costs of restructuring the business and outsourcing the product from overseas. This might be expected to help increase profitability in the long run.

The balance sheet

Bluebird balance sheet, 31 December

	1996 £000	1995 £000
Fixed assets		
Tangible assets	2691	8046
Current assets		
Stock	2595	3898
Debtors	11850	12554
Cash at bank	26267	34150
	40712	50602
Creditors		
Amounts falling due within one year	(22774)	(26268)
Net current assets	17938	24334
Total assets less current liabilities	20629	32380
Creditors		
Amounts falling due in more than one year	(96)	(118)
Net assets	20533	32262
Capital and reserves		
Share capital	6611	6589
Profit and loss account	13922	25673
Total capital and reserves	20533	32262

Figure O3.13

Source: Bluebird, *Annual Report and Accounts*, 1996

The big fall in fixed assets partly reflected the restructuring of production and the closing down of the Bluebird manufacturing plant at Merthyr Tydfil in South Wales. This information is in the notes to the accounts (see below).

Your agenda

1 What were the main changes in the balance sheet from 1995 to 1996?

2 How do these changes relate to the situation already described?

The balance sheet is intended to be a 'snapshot' view of the assets within a company and the means by which they have been financed. Essentially, there are two sections to a balance sheet under the most commonly used format specified by the Companies Act 1985. The first builds a total of the company's net assets. This value is the sum of the fixed and current assets less all the amounts owing to creditors of any kind. The second shows how the net assets have been funded by the shareholders.

Once an item which is owned by the business is included on the balance sheet, it is said to have been capitalised: it is therefore an asset. The fixed assets remain in the business on a long-term basis. Tangible assets represent the company's physical property and include land, buildings, equipment, fittings and vehicles. Some companies include **intangible assets** in their list of fixed assets. These are assets which do not have a physical presence but are based on attitudes or ideas. Brands are usually considered to be particularly important intangible assets.

Essentials

Intangible assets are not objects which can be used or felt, but they have value because they represent some advantage to the business. They include brands, patents, trade marks, copyrights and goodwill. Some brands are worth many millions of pounds.

The terms on the balance sheet

- *Current assets* are those which circulate through the day-to-day operation of the business. *Stock* includes raw materials, semi-finished and finished goods. *Debtors* are amounts owing to the business. Most of the firm's *cash* will actually be held at the bank.
- *Creditors* – amounts falling due within one year – are the sums that must be repaid by the business to outside parties over the coming 12 months. The item includes both loans falling due and trade creditors – outstanding debts that must be paid for goods or services received. These short-term creditors are also often called *current liabilities*.
- Current assets minus creditors (within one year) gives the *net current assets*.
- To this is added the value of *fixed assets* to find the *total assets less current liabilities*.

■ The next step is to subtract creditors – amounts falling due after one year – which take the form of longer-term loans. Also to be deducted are provisions for liabilities and charges. These include pension commitments, deferred taxation and any other charges such as the costs of business closures.

■ This gives *total net assets* (some companies do not actually include this literal heading). In effect, it is net of all liabilities to parties outside the company and therefore represents the assets belonging to the shareholders.

■ *Share capital and reserves* show the shareholders funds which balance net assets.

If this seems a little tricky, balance sheets can be revised by going back to Module 2, pages 113–120.

The Notes to the Accounts

Following the formal accounts are Notes to the Accounts. These are listed to correspond with a reference numbering system that runs alongside the accounting data. They enlarge on the headings concerned and provide additional information. Bluebird recorded the origins of its exceptional item in 1996: it represented the cost of restructuring production. Probably most of it was spent on redundancy money for people who had been part of the manufacturing and distribution sides of the business which were now to be outsourced.

The notes will probably include references to the shareholdings of each director, plus information on any share options to which they may have entitlement. Share options are rights to buy shares at a fixed price (not less than the current market price), usually over a period of between three and ten years after the date granted. As a form of executive incentive, these options can become very valuable indeed if the share price rises.

In the Bluebird notes to the accounts it is shown that performance-related bonuses for the executive directors were modest. Perhaps this is not surprising. However, they did receive substantial share options. The chief executive received 326 380. During 1996 the share price varied between 357p and 140p. Possibly these share options were not expected to be very valuable in the long run. Overall, directors'

emoluments were 13 per cent down on the 1995 level.

The published accounts are 'consolidated' meaning that they represent the aggregate of data from the parent company and all its subsidiaries. The parent company results are also shown separately. The later sections of the notes give details about subsidiaries.

Work in progress

Q Return to your selected example of an Annual Report and Accounts for a company you know. Where there are items that puzzle you, try looking up any relevant notes to the accounts.

Other Items

Many companies include a financial record or a five/ten year summary. This gives the key values from the profit and loss account, the balance sheet and other accounting data over the longer term period. This is very useful when assessing the firm's progress. In conjunction with the main accounting statements, it is the basis for using ratios to investigate performance.

A wide variety of further statistical and other information about the company may also be included at this stage in the report. There is no standard pattern or degree of disclosure and some companies provide far more detail than others. However, the section providing information for shareholders is generally fairly helpful and may include practical information on dividends and share dealing together with a breakdown of shareholdings by ownership type, size and value.

The last item in the Annual Report is traditionally the notice of Annual General Meeting (though it may appear earlier). This invites shareholders to attend the AGM and usually includes the formal agenda. Its significance is explored in Option 3, Enquiry 5.

Auditing the accounts

Auditing means checking that the accounts really are accurate. Once this process is complete, the auditors can state that in their professional opinion, the accounts represent a 'true and fair' view:

- 'True' in this context means complete and in accordance with all known and relevant facts.
- 'Fair' is more difficult to define but should mean first, that where approximations are necessary, they are as accurate as possible, and secondly that the impression to be reasonably inferred from the data is broadly realistic.

Achievement of these goals depends on proper standards in the accountancy profession and on general acceptance of certain common concepts and procedures. The consistency concept means that every item appearing in the accounts must be defined and treated in the same way between one period and the next.

Accountants must always be conservative or 'prudent'. Any likely loss is recognised and charged immediately; any likely profit is only recorded when it actually occurs. This may seem pessimistic but it ensures that unrealistic claims are avoided.

Other sources of information

Bluebird in the *Independent on Sunday*

On 7 December 1997 the *Independent on Sunday* ran an article featuring Action Man, the Teletubbies and ... Bluebird. They interviewed Chris Burgin, the chief executive. Here's what he said about the toy industry:

'Traditional toys are under huge pressure, and are a declining business, in the long term. Overseas sales are vital for a business like Bluebird. Tooling up costs for a toy that only shifts 100 000 units means each one may cost £2 before you get it into the shops. But if you can sell a million units, then your development cost comes down to 25p or so – a very different proposition.'

Your agenda

1 Explain why Bluebird needed overseas sales, using ideas and terminology that you have learnt on this course.

2 What sorts of products are competing with traditional toys?

Although the Annual Report and Accounts is the most important form of company disclosure, there are also other useful sources. Accounting information is much easier to handle if you know something about what is happening to the company. Information about companies may come from the press. If you see an interesting article in a newspaper, and can then look at the ARA, you may have an excellent opportunity to put together an informative picture:

- The AGM normally follows an agenda that is formal and routine, but there is often an extended statement by the chairman on the company's current position as well as the opportunity for shareholders to put direct questions to the board. This may be reported in the financial press.
- Marketing and sales information literature provide further information on a company's product range and general image. It is also often possible to visit the headquarters or an important site of the company concerned. This allows personal observations to be made about the physical assets, the workforce and general atmosphere, which can be surprisingly revealing.
- There are also certain legal requirements for the issue of information. The original prospectus, when a company issues shares to the general public, is very detailed concerning its management, financial record and future plans. There are also circulars that must be sent to shareholders when the firm makes significant acquisitions and disposals. If a take-over bid for a company is made and it is contested by the directors, then documents will be issued that defend the company's record and affirm its future prospects in more detail than would be available in the Annual Report. Section 5 of this enquiry examines some of this further information for Bluebird.

4 What does it all *mean*?

Bluebird – 1997

You may already have concluded that 1997 would be a make or break year for Bluebird. On the credit side, there was a good deal of new product development. The 1997 chairman's statement reported the introduction of the new Supermotion technology used to make Magical Moving Polly. Plans for 1998 included the introduction of this technology into the Disney Tiny Collection, Thomas the Tank Engine and Friends and Spider-Man ranges. Wombles products were well received at trade fairs and the launch of Super Striker was timed to coincide with the Soccer World Cup in 1998.

Meantime, turnover was down to £58.6 million and profit before tax and after exceptional costs was £9.9 million. No amount of new product development (NPD) could hide this story. Overseas sales were down from £34.3 million to £25.5 million.

The chairman said:

'Substantially all of the decline in turnover is explained by the reduction in sales of Polly Pocket and Disney-branded toys in North America. This decline was attributable to poor retail sales in the USA and the subsequent decision of our distributor, Mattel, to withdraw temporarily supply of those products in North America. This withdrawal was to reduce overstocking ahead of planned re-launches of both these ranges in 1999.'

Your agenda

1 What reasons can you discern for the worsening figures?

2 In the balance sheet, no provision was made for intangible assets. Intangibles do not have a physical existence, yet may be of great value. They include trademarks and brands. Do you think therefore that the balance sheet underrated Bluebird's assets?

3 How might Bluebird's performance be assessed objectively?

How can accounts be used to develop a picture of the company's strengths and weaknesses? In module 2, we used return on capital employed (ROCE) to measure efficiency. ROCE relates profit to the financial capital in use at the time. In this way, the income generated by the capital equipment can be compared over time. You can do this more easily if there is a financial record table in the back of the ARA. Bluebird's financial record is shown in Figure O3.14.

	1995 £000	1996 £000	1997 £000
Turnover	87 261	67 651	58 562
Operating profit	16 560	10 104	5 290
Earnings per share	26.0p	14.7p	10.3p
Dividend per share	9p	9p	9p
Balance sheet			
Total fixed assets	8 046	2 691	2 593
Net current assets	24 334	17 938	17 492
Total assets less current liabilities	32 380	20 629	20 085
Net assets	32 262	20 533	20 004
Shareholders' funds	32 262	20 533	20 004
Long-term loans	118	96	81
Capital employed	32 380	20 629	20 085

Figure O3.14 Bluebird financial record, 1997

Source: Bluebird, *Annual Report and Accounts*, 1996 and 1997

A particular ratio for a single year is of little value in isolation. It is the trend pattern in ratios over a period that can be revealing. Even then, some basis for comparison with other companies is very helpful. Here it is often most fair and effective to evaluate other companies in the same business sector, if possible with similar size, product mix and markets.

Work in progress

Q **1** Calculate ROCE for Bluebird for the three years concerned.

2 What conclusions can you draw?

3 How do these figures compare with ROCE's in two other companies for which you have data? Use Kingfisher (page 119) and the company whose accounts you looked at earlier in this enquiry, unless you have others available.

4 Using any one set of accounts, evaluate their usefulness to each of the company's stakeholder groups. Then look at the accounts for a second company. How do they compare in this respect?

It is useful to remember when calculating ROCE that capital employed is the same as total assets less current liabilities, i.e. all the assets of the business minus its short-term loans.

Bluebird's ROCE looks extraordinarily healthy for a company with some problems. However, the direction of change is clear. We can now go on to examine two further ratios which may help to clarify the position.

Asset turnover and acid test ratios

Ratios are often the best available means of analysing a company's performance and possible prospects. With care, it is possible to use them to penetrate the gloss on published accounts. If some ratios are supplied by the company it may be valuable to identify and calculate others. If none are offered it is all the more interesting to explore. Indeed, some firms may supply ample 'financial record' data when times are good and then abruptly drop the practice when losses break out.

The asset turnover ratio shows the relationship between the value of sales and the value of resources necessary to achieve those sales. It shows how efficiently the business is using its resources. Another way of looking at it is to regard it as the number of pounds worth of sales which has been generated by each pound's worth of investment.

$$\text{Asset turnover} = \frac{\text{Turnover}}{\text{Total assets less current liabilities}}$$

The acid test ratio shows the number of times by which very liquid assets (excluding stock) exceed short-term liabilities. It measures liquidity. Stocks are excluded because they can be hard to sell and turn into cash. The other current assets – bank balances and debtors, the amounts owed to the business – are much more liquid. In this ratio, they are being compared with the short term loans outstanding, which have to be repaid soon. It is called the acid test ratio because it will show whether there is a serious risk of the company's running out of cash.

$$\text{Acid test ratio} = \frac{\text{Current assets less stock}}{\text{Current liabilities}}$$

Work in progress

Q **1** Calculate the asset turnover ratios for Bluebird for 1995–7.

2 Calculate the acid test ratios for 1995 and 1996. (The ratio for 1997 hardly changed.)

3 Why might these ratios be unreliable indicators of Bluebird's performance?

Obviously, the level of the asset turnover ratio varies depending on the type of business. You can see at once that a window cleaner might have quite a high asset turnover ratio. A business with higher fixed assets might have a lower ratio. However, there is nothing about Bluebird's asset turnover ratio to arouse anxiety. In fact, it seems very high. Could it be that Bluebird had a lot of cash but lacked the strategic impetus to form a dynamic plan for the future?

Generally speaking, a fairly average acid test ratio might be around 1.0. This indicates that there are enough current assets to cover outstanding debt. Here too, Bluebird seems comfortable, although it is possible that continued trading after 1998 might not have been quite so positive in this respect. Nevertheless, the ratios show that although there had been a rapid fall in profitability, the company was still trading successfully and had a sound basis for recovery if sales could be made to rise to former levels.

For individual businesses, comparing ratios over time can reveal trends which are not exposed in a casual look at the accounts. When making comparisons between businesses, it is important to compare companies with similar products which are also similar in scale. The supermarket chains provide interesting possibilities.

Inflation and accounts

The issue of inflation needs recognition. Since accounts use money values and relate to periods of time, there is an obvious problem in ensuring consistency and compatibility. 'Turnover and profit up by 5 per cent' is a statement which requires that we know the rate of inflation before we decide how impressive the growth

is. Similarly, fixed assets can be measured in a variety of ways and if inflation is significant, this may matter. The balance sheet may refer to the original cost, or to today's value in today's money, or to replacement cost. These questions have serious implications for the idea of a 'true and fair view'.

This problem was particularly acute in the 1970s when inflation rates were often very high – with a peak of 24.9 per cent in 1975. Even over the 1980s retail prices more than doubled – or the value of money more than halved. However, since 1991 the inflation rate has been relatively low so this aspect of accounting is currently less problematic.

5 What happened next?

Bluebird, 1998

Bluebird wasn't looking for a buyer. Nevertheless, in January 1998 Guinness Peat Group (GPG) announced its intention of making an offer. Within two days the Board of Bluebird had written to the shareholders as follows:

*The Board believes that the GPG offer is nothing more than opportunistic and significantly undervalues Bluebird. As at the end of 1997, net cash is estimated to amount to in excess of £19 million (equivalent to approximately 46p per Bluebird share). Shareholders should note that at the close of business today the mid market price of a Bluebird share was 112p which is significantly above the offer price of 101p.

Shareholders are advised to take no action for the present. Your Board will be writing to you after the receipt of the formal offer document.*

GPG had already acquired 23 per cent of Bluebird's shares, mostly at less than the current price. The formal offer followed in February. The chairman wrote again to shareholders as promised:

*The Board continues to believe that the GPG offer significantly undervalues Bluebird ... Given GPG's

belief that "the intrinsic value of each Bluebird share is more that 101p" it is the opinion of the Board that the offer is a cynical move to put Bluebird in play rather than a serious attempt to gain control of the company at 101p per share.*

The GPG offer set out reasons why shareholders should sell. It pointed to the recent low in the share price of 81p; uncertainty as to Mattel's plans for the US market; the deterioration of its profit and cash positions; overall it emphasised the trends with which you are now familiar. On the credit side, it noted that sales were satisfactory outside North America and that Mattel's relaunch plans looked encouraging.

Your agenda

1 If Bluebird's sales outlook seemed satisfactory, why had the share price fallen so much from its peak of nearly 400p in late 1995?

2 Why did the fall in the share price make Bluebird vulnerable to a serious take-over bid?

3 What would you expect to happen next?

Bluebird produced a flashy, colourful document for shareholders. The cover featured Wallace and Gromit, the Wombles, Thomas the Tank Engine and numerous other characters carrying a banner, saying 'REJECT THE OFFER'. Inside, the important elements of Bluebird's brand management strategy were outlined. Temporary difficulties were admitted, but the tone was very upbeat. GPG replied with a news release in early March which claimed that Bluebird had given no specific plan for improving profitability. It claimed that Mattel's promises of a relaunch in the USA were nothing more than 'vague intentions'.

By 24 March, GPG had received acceptances representing only 0.05 per cent of the share capital. From then on, the pace heated up. On 30 March Mattel made an offer of 111p. This time the board supported the offer. The chairman wrote to shareholders saying 'a great deal of the potential value in Bluebird depends on the successful relaunch of our products in North America. This offer removes any risk or uncertainty for our shareholders as to the outcome of these relaunches'. The chairman recommended shareholders to sell. He pointed out that Mattel was thinking about manufacturing Polly Pocket for the North American market itself. It was also hoping to restrict Bluebird margins in other markets where it distributed Bluebird products. This was likely to lead to significant reductions in Bluebird's profits.

GPG was not finished yet. In mid-May it increased its offer to 116p. Mattel countered with 116.5p. Both were described as final offers and Mattel won the bidding war. With hindsight, it is clear that Mattel's withdrawal from the North American market in 1997 had been a crucial factor in the outcome.

Most of the Bluebird management and workforce departed. The Bluebird range was added to Mattel's. This substantially reduced overhead costs.

Valuing intangibles

A good deal of the Bluebird case study is about intangible assets. Here the intangibles are the brands. These brands had their 'collectable' quality: a first branded toy might lead to buying more to make a collection. This is obviously potentially very valuable. But children are fickle and toys are subject to fashions. Remember the tamagotchi? It was a big hit all over the world in summer 1997. Six months later it had lost its trendiness altogether. Action Man has been a big seller for more than 30 years. How can a brand name which may or may not keep its attractions be valued? Yet, in the end, what Mattel bought was a set of brands.

The Accounting Standards Board now has a new standard for dealing with intangibles. Some observers consider that this will force managers to think more carefully about how the brands should be maintained and managed.

What are the lessons?

Businesses which are involved in possible merger negotiations have to reveal much more about themselves than is usually their habit. Media coverage is often very full. The arguments can provide a good opportunity to investigate the way the relevant businesses operate.

Studying the accounts from the run up to the negotiations can reveal much of the background. Contrasting business situations can be explored. We get a chance to see how the accounts illuminate the story.

Economics and business consist of a serial with unlimited episodes. Always watch for news when a story is unfolding. However, for Bluebird, it was the last episode.

6 Disclosure or window dressing?

A cookery lesson at the carpet shop

Boxing Day tended to be a busy day for Floors Unlimited. Boxing Day was the day that the firm cooked its books. For five years the company broke its own accounting rules by recording carpets as paid for, before they had even been delivered. When the practice was discovered in 1996, the managing director John Somers and the finance director Richard Lewis denied any knowledge of what had been going on. Richard Lewis has since resigned and the managing director has been sacked.

Floors Unlimited's auditors responded to the public uproar by questioning what they could possibly do to detect fraud when people lie. The incident was not the work of a couple of rogue managers. Documents leaked to a national newspaper by a former employee of Floors Unlimited reveal a systematic guide on how to cook the books. The whole process was managed like a military operation.

Phase 1: Sales figures to be submitted at 11.30 am, 2.00 pm, and 4.00 pm.

Phase 2: Employees told to book uncompleted sales figures under Interest Free Credit (IFC) – this compares with a normal processing time of one week.

Phase 3: All IFC applications, including those which had been turned down by head office, were to be included in sales figures as paid and stocks were adjusted.

Phase 4: All approved IFC sales had to be recorded on the computer and given a serial number. Staff were instructed to type in 0000000. This fooled the computer into thinking that a deal had been done.

Phase 5: Carpets which had been ordered as part of an insurance claim, but which had not been fitted, should be recorded as having been fitted and recorded in sales figures as, 'Goods Delivered but Not Paid for' (GDNP). This would flatter the sales figures.

Phase 6: The week after the accounting year-end, figures should be adjusted back. IFCs should be declared void and the figures for GDNP should be adjusted downwards. Stock levels would also be adjusted upwards at the same time.

The chairman of Floors Unlimited confirmed that the 'vast majority' of its 2000 workers knew what was going on but denied that board members knew anything. It seems that if you want to know what's going on in the company, then the shop floor rather than the boardroom is the place to be.

Your agenda

1 In what ways were: (a) managers and (b) shareholders likely to be misled by the fraudulent practices described here?

2 What decisions might have been taken on the basis of the faulty evidence?

3 What motives would the perpetrators have had for their fraudulent behaviour?

The published accounts of a company are the key public 'window' through which stakeholders may hope to see the reality of the firm's affairs. In practice, the window is often steamy or carefully 'dressed'! Because there were so many perfectly legal ways in which such effects could be achieved, pressure in the past built up for some fairly fundamental reforms in the rules for financial reporting.

Legal strategies for improving the appearance of the accounts are termed **window dressing**. However, some illegal strategies are also used from time to time. The momentum for reform has been greatly increased by various corporate scandals. The case study above is a fictitious example of the sorts of outcomes which are possible.

Essentials

Window dressing means presenting company accounts in ways which make the accounts look healthier than they really are. Many cases of window dressing are really just putting the best construction on the facts. Others may go close to being fraudulent by manipulating the accounts so as to conceal a bad situation.

The Accounting Standards Board has tackled a number of problems, but despite this progress, there are still ways for companies to improve the appearance of their accounts:

- The balance sheet can be 'massaged'. If the 'book' value of the company in terms of its net assets is looking rather low, then it may be possible to capitalise some brands under the 'intangible fixed assets' heading and so make the company a less obvious target for take-over.
- Acquisitions and disposals of subsidiaries raise particular problems. When another firm is acquired, its assets must be consolidated in the buyer's balance sheet at their 'fair value' and not their book value. When the fair value is less than the purchase price, the difference is 'goodwill'. This may be depreciated over a period through charges to the profit and loss account. Many companies show any profit arising from the disposal or sale of a fixed asset as a gain to the profit and loss account. This may give an artificially inflated impression of the firm's underlying profitability.
- Another useful accounting device for some companies is the practice of capitalising certain expenses. This means that a cost, instead of being deducted as an expense in the profit and loss account, is treated as an addition to assets on the balance sheet. For example, suppose that a property company is developing a new site which was purchased with a loan. The interest on this loan may be added to the value of 'stock' or developments-in-progress – rather than being treated as an expense. This practice can have a striking affect on an assessment of the firm's financial stability.
- Less spectacular, but still significant, are the opportunities for companies to 'stage manage' accounting data. The reporting date can be chosen to reveal an unrealistically low level of stock (for example a retailing group reporting just after Christmas). Events – such as large orders or asset sales – can be slowed or accelerated to fall either side of the reporting date.

Point of view 66 99

Coca-Cola's empire

In the late 1980s, Coca-Cola's managers decided to remove its capital intensive bottling plants from the main company and set them up independently as Coca-Cola Enterprises. The bottling operations are less profitable than the parent company and the subsidiary has more debts. The effect on Coca-Cola's accounts has therefore been very positive.

Some financial analysts are not impressed by this, and the US Financial Accounting Standards Board is concerned too. Coca-Cola's accounts are fully in line with the legal requirements, but is the company sticking to the spirit of the rules?

Coca-Cola's sales in 1997 were US$18.9 billion; Coca-Cola Enterprises' sales were $11.3 billion. The market value of Coca-Cola was $203 billion, and of Coca-Cola Enterprises, $13 billion. How could there be such a big difference? The answer is that Coca-Cola Enterprises has a huge debt burden. This means that the parent company is able to provide much higher returns for investors. Critics of Coca-Cola say it has increased its recorded profits by selling to its bottling company. These sales could not lead to increased profits if the two companies' accounts were amalgamated.

Coca-Cola made the following statement in its defence:

'The company is in absolute accordance with the accounting rules. Federal securities regulators were informed of the accounting system in 1986, when Coca-Cola Enterprises became a separate company. They did not object. The two companies are independent. Coca-Cola has a minority stake, 44 per cent in the bottling company. Because Coca-Cola does not control the bottler, it does not have the option of consolidating financial statements. This is an old, worn-out point of view, totally without merit, said Laura Asman, spokeswoman for Coca-Cola Enterprises, and our company's performance for our shareholders speaks for itself.'

Critics say that the board of Coca-Cola Enterprises is controlled by people with strong connections to the parent company.

Your agenda

1 What motives would Coca-Cola have for hiving off less profitable operations to Coca-Cola Enterprises?

2 In what ways does its strategy mislead the public?

3 What consequences are likely to flow from this approach?

What do accounts tell us?

It has been argued that ARAs give a very partial picture of company performance. They are constructed by people who are obsessed with the rules and financial techniques. Professors Hugh Davidson (Cranfield University) and Roger Hussey (Bristol Business School) have set out the following arguments for disclosing a much wider range of information:

'Profitable growth is usually achieved by being in the right markets, developing strong customer franchises, allocating resources to areas of best return and exploiting the skills of people. Investors require additional information on these aspects of company activities to give balance to their investment decisions. Concentrating further on the accounts will not achieve this.

The most important areas of information are market trends, brand share and investment levels. Investors need to know how companies define their markets and the quality of future prospects. They need figures for market share for the past few years. They need to know how the company is building its profits, whether by customer growth or cuts in investment. They need to know about R & D, advertising and training and development.'

Published accounts provide many insights, but they need to be interpreted with great care, and whenever possible, a knowledge of the company background and recent events.

This enquiry investigates the extent to which government and business are accountable. It examines the issue of environmental responsibility and considers how businesses can become more accountable. The role of stakeholders and pressure groups, international efforts to protect the environment and possible future developments are all explored.

1 What's the problem?

Union Carbide and Bhopal

In 1984 the US multi-national, Union Carbide, was well regarded in Bhopal, India. Its fertiliser plant, providing valuable employment, was almost entirely managed by local staff. Around the plant was a large shanty town.

In December 1984 water seeped into one of the processing tanks at the plant resulting in a chemical reaction which led to a discharge of poisonous cyanide gas. The gas spread across the surrounding residential area. More than 2500 people were killed and many more suffered painful and disabling injuries.

The US firm was heavily criticised. Local residents had not been properly informed about the potential risks posed by the chemical plant. Staff had been inadequately trained and emergency procedures had not been properly developed.

Your agenda

1 Why do you think the plant in Bhopal was inadequately prepared for this event?

2 Why do you think businesses might be more concerned about the external effects of their activities at plants in the developed world than those in the developing world?

3 Apart from the business, who might be held responsible for such disasters?

4 What effects can such disasters have on a business?

The decisions taken by governments and business influence our daily lives to an extent which few of us fully appreciate. They affect:
- the quality of air that we breathe
- the quality of water that we drink
- the quality and safety of food that we eat
- the quality of the environment that we enjoy.

In extreme cases, decisions taken by business may affect our life expectancy. Firms are usually profit maximisers – they seek to minimise private costs and maximise profit. For many firms externalities are not a major consideration. Successive governments have included in their manifestos the target of long-term economic growth. It has been a central tenet of government policy – embraced by developed and developing countries alike – and has created costs for society.

Society is as much a stakeholder in business decisions as the consumer is. The 'environment lobby' expresses the concerns of many people who are personally worried about the environmental impact of economic development and who wish to influence the agenda of business. Pressure on business to consider externalities when making business decisions is mounting. This pressure comes from environmental activists, pressure groups, ethical investors, NIMBY's ('I don't care what you do as long as its Not In My Backyard!') and governments.

The challenge facing government and business is to achieve continuing economic growth in order to satisfy the pressure for ever-increasing standards of living, while conserving scarce economic resources and maintaining employment levels in a way that is sustainable in the long term. Satisfying all these demands at once presents an enormous challenge to government and business in the developed world.

The challenge for countries in the developing world is much greater. Living standards are far behind those in the developed world, population is expanding much more rapidly and there is far greater pressure to raise incomes and ignore the social and environmental costs. This poses a moral dilemma for multi-nationals, international financial institutions and governments of the developed world. Should they:

support the dash for growth in order to raise living standards in the developing world

or

withhold technical and financial support unless environmental and economic externalities are accounted for?

What on earth can we do?

Working together

"We inhabit a single planet but several worlds. There is a world of abundance where plenty brings pollution, there is a world of want where deprivation degrades life. Such a fragmented planet cannot survive in harmony with nature and the environment or indeed with itself. It can assure neither sustained peace nor sustainable development. We must therefore ensure that the affluence of some is not derived from the poverty of many."
(Narashimo Rao, Prime Minister of India, speaking at the Rio Summit, 1992)

Agenda 21

◆ Allocating international aid to programmes with high returns for poverty alleviation and environmental health, such as providing sanitation and clean water, reducing indoor air pollution and meeting basic needs

◆ Investing in research and development to reduce soil erosion and degradation and put agricultural practices on a sustainable footing

◆ Allocating more resources to family planning and to primary and secondary education, especially for girls

◆ Supporting governments in their attempts to remove distortions and macro-economic imbalances that damage the environment

◆ Providing finance to protect natural habitat and bio-diversity

◆ Investing in research and development of non-carbon energy alternatives to respond to climate change

◆ Resisting protectionist pressures and ensuring that international markets for goods and services, including finance and technology remain open

Source: *World Development Report, 1992*

Your Agenda

1 Why might 'the affluence of some be derived from the poverty of many'?
2 How does each of the points in Agenda 21 contribute to achieving sustainable growth?
3 Why is it difficult to achieve agreement on an international basis?
4 How might Agenda 21 affect the activities of business?

The United Nations Conference on Environment and Development (UNCED) in Rio de Janeiro in June 1992, better known as the 'Earth Summit', brought heads of government together to discuss global environmental issues and culminated in the signing of five separate agreements which were endorsed by most of the participating governments.

Principal items on the summit agenda were:

- poverty
- environmental destruction
- gaining international agreement for the concept of **sustainable development**.

Essentials

Sustainable development involves using resources in a way which does not destroy future potential. It has a range of interpretations as some people believe that our stock of resources should be left unchanged and others consider that the exact nature of resources is less important as long as future potential is maintained.

One of the major themes of the Rio Earth Summit was the widening gap between those living in rich, western industrialised economies and those living in the 'majority world.' Agenda 21 was the product of the Earth Summit. It sets objectives for all countries in the search for sustainable growth.

There are widely varying views on the success or failure of the Earth Summit. It has variously been described as both an abysmal failure and an outstanding success.

One of the outcomes of the summit was Local Agenda 21 which sought to recognise that there was a diverse group of stakeholders who were interested in the environmental agenda. It encourages local authorities to work in partnership with the local community, with industry and with other groups to address local environmental issues. Figure O3.15 shows the potential links. They give a framework for looking at the environmental agenda for businesses and communities as well as governments.

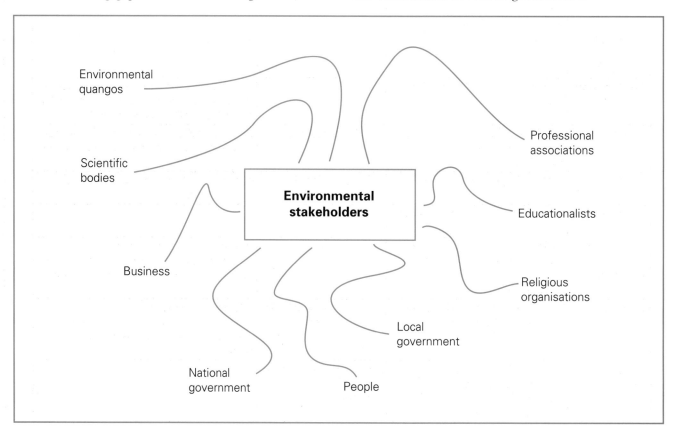

Figure O3.15 Local stakeholders

2 What's been achieved?

The European dimension

	Goal	Progress	Outlook
Climate change	'no exceeding of natural absorption capacity of planet earth'		Increased global economic activity, increased contribution from transport sector and limited impact of energy saving and reduction programmes require intensified effort
Carbon dioxide (CO_2)	2000 – stabilise at 1990 levels Progressive reductions at the horizons 2005 and 2010	On target	Will meet target
Methane (CH_4) and Nitrous oxide (N_2O)	1994 – identify and apply controlling measures	Delays in adopting strategy	Progress report forecasts increase in methane emissions
Ozone depletion	'working towards ultimate goal of no emissions of ozone depleting substances'	Phased out CFCs and halons by 1996	Concern is now whether less-developed countries will be able to reduce consumption of ozone depleting substances
HCFCs	1995 – limit consumption to 2.6 per cent of 1989 CFC level	Achieved	
CFCs, carbon tetrachloride, halons, 1.1.1 trichloroethane	Phase out before 1996 except for some essential uses	Achieved	
Acidification	'no exceeding of critical loads and levels'		Expected acid deposition levels in 2000 will fall. But in northern Europe and Alpine region critical loads will still be exceeded
Oxides of nitrogen	1994 – stabilisation at 1990 levels 2000 – 30 per cent reduction on 1990 levels	1994 target reached	Target for 2000 unlikely to be achieved due to increase in private cars and road transport in freight
Oxides of sulphur	2000 – 35 per cent reduction on 1985 levels	Achieved in 1994	Reduction of 50 per cent on 1985 levels likely by 2000
Ammonia (NH_3)	Variable targets in accordance with problems identified in regions		
Volatile organic compounds, e.g. petrol vapour	1996 – 10 per cent reduction of manmade emissions on 1990 levels 1999 – 30 per cent reduction on 1990 levels	Data not complete	Mobile sources account for 50 per cent of VOC emissions. Expected increase in use of cars will not facilitate achievement of targets
Dioxins	2005 – 90 per cent reduction on 1985 levels of dioxin emissions of identified sources	Full data not available in all member states	Potential for 80 per cent reduction by 2005. Much rests on reduction of emissions from waste incineration and other combustion processes
Heavy metals	1995 – at least 70 per cent reduction from all pathways of cadmium (Cd), mercury (Hg) and lead (Pb) emissions	Most North Sea countries achieved 50 per cent reduction	

Figure O3.16 EU progress

Source: EU website, http://www.europa.eu.int

The activities of the European Union are carried out by 'directorate generals'. The one responsible for the environment is DG X1. The organisation has set targets which reflect the measures of Agenda 21. Figure O3.16 shows the degree to which the targets will be achieved. In some areas the targets have been met quickly. Others are proving more elusive. There is a clear indication of the link between economic growth and pollution. The use of the car and the production of waste are both factors which increase as countries get richer.

Although the carbon dioxide target is likely to be met, it has proved impossible to introduce an energy carbon tax which would reduce levels further. Richer areas of the community have a better record as the poorer regions have less efficient energy use. The EU's Structural Fund is assisting in the development of energy efficient infrastructure programmes.

There is still much to be done, but the EU has the environment high on the agenda. It is working on integrating its environmental policy through all the departments or directorate generals. However, there is still some evidence of reluctance to co-operate among member governments.

What about the UK?

Local Agenda 21
Characteristics of a Sustainable Society:
Checklist for Local Authorities

A sustainable society seeks to:

Protect and enhance the environment
- use energy, water and other natural resources efficiently and with care minimise waste, then re-use or recover it through recycling, composting or energy recovery, and finally sustainably dispose of what is left
- limit pollution to levels which do not damage natural systems
- value and protect the diversity of nature

Meet social needs
- create or enhance places, spaces and buildings that work well, wear well and look well
- make settlements 'human' in scale and form
- value and protect diversity and local distinctiveness and strengthen local community and cultural identity
- protect human health and amenity through safe, clean, pleasant environments
- emphasise health service prevention action as well as care
- ensure access to good food, water, housing and fuel at reasonable cost
- meet local needs locally wherever possible
- maximise everyone's access to the skills and knowledge needed to play a full part in society
- empower all sections of the community to participate in decision-making and consider the social and community impact of decisions

Promote economic success
- create a vibrant local economy that gives access to satisfying and rewarding work without damaging the local, national or global environment
- value unpaid work
- encourage necessary access to facilities, services, goods and other people in ways which make less use of the car and minimise impacts on the environment
- make opportunities for culture, leisure and recreation readily available to all

Source: Department of the Environment, Transport and the Regions web site, http://www.environment. detr.gov.uk

Your agenda

1 How do these strategies contribute to the EU's contribution to Agenda 21?

2 How can a community's stakeholders contribute to achieving these objectives?

3 What has been done, by whom, in your local area to meet the objectives of Agenda 21?

In recent years the UK government has sought to address environmental issues. Support has been given to environmental initiatives and the government has accepted EU targets for the reduction of airborne pollution. Local Agenda 21 is being put into practice across the country and measures for the national agenda have been established.

A variety of practical strategies have been put in place in order to achieve these local, national and international objectives. The following are examples of the use of planning controls:

- Out-of-town shopping developments have been blocked.
- Targets have been set for the number of new houses to be built on brownfield sites.
- Local authorities are being challenged to identify new ways of halting the population migration from North to South and revitalising decaying towns and cities.

On the transport front, the government has developed proposals for Transport 2000, a commitment to develop an integrated transport system and to encourage greater use of public transport. The Labour government has embraced new technology. A number of ministerial cars were converted to gas to make them more environmentally friendly. Transport is an area in which the market can be used to influence people's habits:

- The Conservative government offered a tax incentive for motorists who switched from leaded to unleaded petrol and toyed with the idea of road pricing.
- The Labour government committed itself to road pricing.

An important consideration in introducing a road-pricing scheme is whether it will be politically acceptable. The problem with road pricing is that it tends to divert traffic off toll roads and on to secondary roads. This has happened in France and Spain where the average charge is 5p and 10p per mile respectively.

Attempts to increase taxes and duty on petrol and diesel have had a mixed response. Analysts have calculated that the elasticity of demand for petrol is 0.05. This means that increasing the tax on petrol will raise more revenue for the government but will not significantly reduce road usage. Tax increases on diesel have caused resentment among road hauliers who have organised moving traffic jams around big cities in order to highlight their cause.

The green lobby argues that the present transport policy, based on free access to roads, is unsustainable. Official forecasts that road traffic will double over the next 30 years have produced almost universal agreement that the supply of road space cannot be increased to meet demand. The government has recognised this argument and has made a commitment not to plan any new roads and to review those already approved. This decision has implications for industry, the attraction of inward investment, employment and international competitiveness.

This point is highlighted in Wales. North and South Wales are separated because of poor road and rail communications. This has hampered not only the economic integration of Wales but also the development of the economically disadvantaged Mid-Wales. GDP levels, average incomes and employment levels are all below levels for the rest of the UK. An improved North–South road link would provide a stimulus to the Welsh economy, but it will not be built. This has implications for the government's targets of 4 per cent per annum economic growth in the Welsh economy.

Work in progress

 1 Suggest a strategy for achieving higher employment and higher incomes in Wales.

2 The Welsh economy has in recent years become dependent upon inward investment for its job creation. Can this strategy be justified on environmental grounds? Explain your point of view.

3 Wales has just been identified as an area needing special assistance by the European Union. The funding can only be spent on infrastructure and/or job creation. How would you spend this money? Why?

What's the cost of a green future?

Government measures are already affecting British manufacturers and could have an impact on the comparative advantage of UK manufacturing. The 1998

Budget included proposals for an energy tax, in order to encourage greater energy efficiency and to help the UK meet targets for the reduction of carbon-dioxide emissions. The proposed tax would increase the cost of gas by 50 per cent.

As an example of the possible impact, we can consider the effect of the tax on British Steel. British Steel's energy costs would rise by £200 million a year. Such a significant increase in costs would force British Steel to seek efficiency gains by cutting its labour costs at a time when it is already cutting the workforce by more than 3000 employees a year. It will be a test of the government's commitment to green taxes if it is prepared to accept the social costs of factory closures in areas such as Scunthorpe and Port Talbot that are already economically disadvantaged.

On a commercial level firms are seeking to re-educate consumers to recycle waste and to accept products which are more environmentally friendly. Firms are increasingly seeking to acquire international environmental standards such as ISO, or to set up their own systems of environmental audit.

Businesses often do recognise that an ethical and environmentally responsible attitude can be popular with stakeholders. Problems arise when the interests of different stakeholder groups conflict; when the desire to profit maximise, to increase incomes and achieve economic growth conflicts with ethical and environmental considerations.

What about Rio?

The trade-offs in meeting the targets have proved problematic for some countries. Five years after the Rio Earth Summit a meeting was held in New York. At the meeting President Clinton admitted the USA was a major polluter. Although the USA has only 4 per cent of the population, it produces more than 20 per cent of the world's greenhouse gases. He added that the USA needed to persuade the US people and Congress that climate change was a real and pressing problem. Despite this assertion the US government stated that it was not prepared to commit itself to targets for the reduction of greenhouse gases.

President Clinton recognised the USA's great love affair with the automobile by stating that he was not prepared to commit himself to any measure which would put a single cent on the price of a gallon of petrol or any measure which would reduce the living standards of US people.

The New York Summit was described by Steve Howard, Senior Forests Officer with the World Wide Fund for Nature, as a meeting which focused on process rather than substance (there was plenty of 'talk-talk' and little constructive action). He believed that there were pressing issues which could have been addressed under existing commitments and conventions:

'…since Rio we've seen the rate of deforestation in the Amazon go up by one third … We've seen the Philippines become a net importer of timber because its forests are in fragments … we could be a generation that sees a 20–30 per cent reduction in biodiversity.'

Two key factors make the achievements of the targets difficult:

- The USA was hindered by domestic political problems and voter resistance to an attack on its consumerist culture.
- Developing countries were angered that development priorities – alleviation of poverty, education and healthcare – which were a prerequisite for their support for environmental agreements, had not been supported by the developed world. In fact, since the Rio Summit global aid budgets have been reduced.

The failure of northern industrialised countries to deliver on promises made at Rio has fuelled resentment among developing countries that they are being told how they can exploit their resources and expand their economies but at the same time are not being given assistance to address pressing poverty issues. The EU, for example, has reduced foreign aid by 25 per cent.

Developing countries ask why they should not use their resources to earn money to help economic development when they have such pressing problems. Timber is always in demand, but countries are being asked to restrict logging in order to maintain the forests and reduce global warming. The trade-off is lost income which could help to improve living standards for the population.

Point of view

Should the developing world be expected to sacrifice economic growth for the environment?

3 Putting on the pressure

Where are the pressure points?

Brent Spar: no slick solution

Brent Spar was to be 'retired' in 1991 after 15 years' service. It was an enormous floating storage tank which acted as a loading facility for tankers. It was, in effect, a giant metal iceberg floating in the North Sea – its six storage tanks lay hidden below the surface. The Spar weighed the equivalent of 2000 double-decker buses. It was longer than a football field floating on its end, and its oil storage tanks could comfortably hold the equivalent of four Big Bens.

The physical size of Brent Spar was one of the arguments used by Shell UK for sinking it rather than attempting to bring it ashore and salvaging it. Several consultancy firms established that sinking the Brent Spar in the deep waters of the North Atlantic was the Best Practicable Environmental Option (BPEO). The UK government supported this plan.

Shell argued that its proposal would have only minimal impact on marine life. It marshalled the support of independent scientists and oceanographers, environmentalists, conservationists and fishermen for its view. It has continued to deny the assertion made by pressure groups that the Brent Spar was a 'toxic time bomb'.

The summer of 1995 saw a wave of public outrage at the proposals for dumping the Brent Spar. Members of the pressure group Greenpeace occupied the platform in order to prevent the dismantling operation proceeding. There were protest marches across Europe and German motorists organised a boycott of Shell filling stations. A petrol station was damaged in an arson attack.

Greenpeace attacked Shell in the media, highlighting the large quantities of toxic residues which could leak into the sea, damaging the marine environment (Greenpeace subsequently admitted that these figures were inaccurate). Faced with widespread condemnation Shell decided to abandon the deepwater disposal plan. The UK government assisted Shell in obtaining a licence from the Norwegian authorities to anchor the Spar in the deep waters of Erfjord.

In order to find a long-term solution for the disposal of Brent Spar, Shell invited contractors to come up with ideas for re-using or salvaging it. The winning proposal was to incorporate it into a quay for a new roll-on roll-off ferry.

Learning the hard way

'Brent Spar taught us that finding solutions to environmental and economic problems requires a shared understanding of complex technical and scientific issues. In that spirit we will continue to work with others, to build bridges with our critics in the environmental lobby, to share expertise, and to apply the lessons of Brent Spar to future decisions and activities. At Shell UK, we do not believe that there is such a thing as a "black and white" issue.'

Source: Shell web site

What about the stakeholders?

'We have to face daily the practical challenge of juggling competing interests, of balancing conflicting demands, and of satisfying the needs of different stakeholder groups.'

Source: The Shell UK Report to Society

Trade-offs

'The dilemma is that people want to flick a switch and have clean, cheap power, but at the same time, they want nature to be untouched.' (Heinz Rothermund, managing director of Shell Expro, in a speech to the Society of Petroleum Engineers, 1997.)

Your agenda

1 What type of pressure group is Greenpeace?

2 What do you think its objectives are?

3 What strategies did Greenpeace and other interest groups use in order to achieve their objectives?

4 Do you think the ends justified the means? Explain your point of view.

5 Before deciding to dump Brent Spar in the North Atlantic, Shell went through a process of consultation. What more could Shell have done in order to have avoided the disruption to its commercial interests?

6 The case study provides evidence that Shell has sought to minimise external costs. Find out what Shell has done to internalise other external costs involved in the production and distribution of oil.

The Brent Spar case study highlights the way that pressure groups can influence the decisions of business and of governments. Pressure groups are usually formed to campaign on a specific issue. They seek to influence government policy and the policy decisions of the business community. Groups such as Friends of the Earth, Greenpeace and the League Against Cruel Sports allow people to express their opinion on specific issues. Pressure groups themselves can be categorised into three broad groups as shown in Figure O3.17.

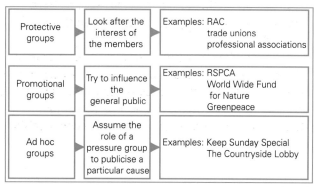

Figure O3.17 Types of pressure group

Many pressure groups are concerned with environmental issues. Individuals who are strongly interested join pressure groups as a way of influencing the strategic decisions made by companies and as a way of influencing government environmental policy.

There is a much larger group of people, who are concerned enough to alter their buying habits and cut down on consumption of environmentally unfriendly products, particularly when pressure groups raise issues of concern to consumers.

Genetically modified (GM) foods are a case in point. Pressure groups have fanned consumer concerns about safety of GM foods. They have expressed concern about the damage that these products may cause to public health and the potential loss of bio-diversity. The fact that GM soya products went on sale unnoticed some five years before the media concern intensified highlights the effectiveness of pressure groups in influencing consumer concerns.

Influencing consumers

Oil spill in the Shetlands

Date: Tuesday, 5 January, 1993

Location: Garth Ness, Quendale Bay, Shetland Islands

Culprit: MV *Braer*, Liberian-registered oil tanker

Cause: Vessel lost power and grounded while attempting to take a short cut through a narrow channel in rough seas

Short-run effects
◆ Some 84 500 tonnes of light crude oil were released into the marine environment.

◆ Hundreds of tonnes of fuel oil were also released.

◆ Evaporation of the light crude oil caused eye irritation and headaches and nausea.

◆ Sea spray carried oil on to land, coating habitation, pasture, crops and livestock.

◆ Large numbers of heavily oiled birds were washed ashore.

◆ Concern was expressed about the impact on fish farmers and fishermen.

The pressure group response
Extensive press releases and sound-bites demanded immediate government intervention to clean up the mess and an insistence that there should be tighter control on the routes used by oil tankers and that tankers should be built with double hulls, in order to reduce the potential of oil spillages when vessels grounded. The World Wide Fund for Nature produced a special marine fact sheet highlighting the environmental impact and outlining its proposals for tighter controls. Readers were encouraged to write to the Minister of Transport in order to encourage the government to take further action.

Long-run effects
Puffins gather on the cliff tops feeding their young with sand eels caught from crystal clean waters. Meanwhile gannets plummet like dive-bombers into the sea in pursuit

of fish for their young. Seagulls wheel and screech around the cliff face. Below the bobbing heads of seals can be seen among the breaking wave crests.

This idyllic spot is Quendale Bay, scene of an ecological disaster following the grounding of the MV *Braer*. The events described took place less than six months after the disaster.

Official statistics reveal that of the 800 or so otters that could have died following the disaster, only four did so – two died as a result of natural causes, while the other two died as a result of road accidents. The oil spill did claim the lives of 12 seals and porpoises. Estimates of tens of thousands of birds killed contrast with an official count of 1 542 dead birds. Bobby Tulloch, a Shetlands naturalist, recalled, 'Even a month after what was supposed to be our worst-ever disaster it was as if it had never happened… we went to look at the damage, we wondered what the fuss had been about.' It is apparent that the knee-jerk reaction about devastation and environmental catastrophe was an overstatement of the reality.

Some businesses which operate in environmentally sensitive areas are concerned that they are subject to punitive and restrictive measures following an 'incident' as a result of pressure brought to bear on government agencies by environmentalists who overstate the environmental impact.

Your agenda

1 Why might pressure groups overstate the impact of an 'environmental disaster' such as that caused by the MV *Braer*?

2 What drawbacks are there to exaggerating the impact of such events?

3 What effect would legislation requiring all oil tankers to have double-hulls have on:
   a the motor industry
   b the oil industry
   c commuters?
   Use appropriate diagrams to support your answer

Pressure group influence on consumer tastes and preferences has focused the attention of producers on the environmental impact of their products. However, the ability of consumers to influence producer decisions depends on the quality and reliability of information which consumers receive.

The decision to dismantle the redundant Brent Spar oil storage platform and dump it in the North Atlantic caused a wave of public protest across Europe. Eventually, the oil company agreed to dismantle and remove the rig. Only much later did the environmental groups concede that information, which had been influential in their campaign, was inaccurate and misleading.

The MV *Braer* disaster provides a further example of the way in which pressure groups use a situation to make a point. One of the most significant criticisms levied at pressure groups is that they distort the decision-making process and prevent rational decisions being taken.

Putting the point

Pressure groups need to find the most effective way of achieving their agenda. They will generally use one of the following methods of persuasion in order to achieve their stated objectives.

■ **Consultancies**
Trade organisations often ask MPs to 'promote their interests'. Trade unions have a long tradition of sponsoring Labour MPs who are sympathetic to their aims. MPs now have to register their interests so that everyone is aware of their motives.

■ **Paid lobbyists**
In recent years there has been a proliferation in the number of professional lobbyists who are prepared to canvass MPs for their support on a particular topic or issue.

■ **Influencing public opinion through the media**
Pressure groups have become increasingly sophisticated in the use of staged events which gain public attention through the media. 'Swampy' became a minor celebrity following his tunnelling exploits at Manchester Airport, while tree protesters on the route of the Newbury bypass also managed to gain sustained media attention. The strategy can be extremely effective.

■ **Influencing the experts**

Governments rely heavily on 'experts' when making technical decisions. Pressure groups can influence the outcome of the decision-making process by seeking to win over experts. They can do this in a number of ways. Pressure groups and businesses with special interests often fund research but sometimes it is criticised on the basis that 'they would say that, wouldn't they'.

■ **Public demonstration**

Demonstrations can be effective in attracting public attention to a particular issue and they are often the most visible method of protesting. Marches against the community charge (poll tax) were seen as a highly visible demonstration of public disquiet about a regressive tax.

■ **Law breaking**

In the most extreme cases, pressure groups may resort to civil disobedience, violent acts and terrorism. Animal rights activists have on occasions been characterised as 'the loony fringe' for firebomb attacks on furriers. They have attacked mink farms: at one point thousands of mink were released into the wild, causing significant damage to the local ecosystem.

The impact of pressure groups

Pressure groups have forced businesses to confront the following questions:

● What are the environmental consequences of their business activity?
● What are the potential long-term implications for their business decisions?
● Do the company accounts reflect the full costs of production?
● Who pays for environmental protection?

The importance of the 'green' lobby has increased and its concern about such issues as global warming, acid rain, toxic waste and the loss of the tropical rain forest has been recognised by the business community. For some firms the response was little more than a promotional gimmick, but other firms have shown a genuine commitment to manufacturing goods and providing services which were genuinely 'green'.

One of the most interesting examples of pressure group activity concerns a different ethical issue. A leading manufacturer of baby milk has experienced sustained criticism and lobbying from pressure groups for its decision to market its product in the third world. Lobbyists pointed out that mothers in the third world did not have access to clean water or facilities for sterilising bottles. As a result, disease among young babies increased.

Stories of mothers mixing baby milk with water from muddy puddles prompted a backlash against the company in developed countries. Its 'bottom line' was affected as consumers boycotted its products. The manufacturer was forced to spend a significant amount of time and money countering the stories and eroding the effects of the boycott on its profits.

4 What is the business response?

The *Exxon Valdez* experience

In March, 1989 the *Exxon Valdez* oil tanker ran aground in Prince William Sound, Alaska. The resulting oil spillage caused massive environmental damage. More than 1000 miles of coastline was contaminated with oil. Only 25 per cent of the migratory salmon population returned to the area the following season. In all, 33 species were directly affected by the disaster. According to conservationists 300000 birds and 3000 sea otters were killed by the oil. The spill also had a significant impact on the Alaskan economy which is heavily dependent upon Alaska's fisheries.

In total, 11.2 million gallons of oil were spilled from the *Exxon Valdez*, necessitating a massive operation to recover or disperse the leaked oil: 11000 people and 1400 vessels were involved in the clean-up operation, which lasted for more than four years.

Increasingly, international law has recognised the principle of 'the polluter pays'. Exxon has certainly had to pay. It paid US$2.2 billion for the clean-up operation. A further $300 million was paid to 11000 people and businesses. Criminal and civil cases were instituted against the company. Exxon agreed to pay $900 million over ten years in settlement of the civil claim. Under the criminal plea agreement, Exxon paid a fine of $250 million. Amazingly, the US government agreed to waive $125 million of the criminal fine because of Exxon's cooperation during the cleanup. The captain of the *Valdez*, who was intoxicated at the time of the accident, was found guilty of the negligent discharge of oil and was sentenced to collect rubbish along the roads of Anchorage.

Cleaning up its act

Following the *Exxon Valdez* disaster, Exxon decided it was time to clean up its act and improve its public image. A number of measures were put in place to improve oil spill prevention. Tanker routes were modified to take them away from environmentally sensitive areas. Drug and alcohol testing was introduced for employees. Training for captains and pilots was improved and new technology was introduced to assist with navigation and oil storage.

Exxon supported the creation of oil spill response centres worldwide. Over 1,000 Exxon staff are seconded to oil spill response teams. The company developed 'Corexit 9500' the world's most effective oil spill dispersant. Additional investment has been made into new oil spill detection technology.

The *Valdez* disaster prompted the development of the Valdez Principles which are gradually being accepted by environmentally aware firms.

The Valdez Principles

◆ Minimise and strive to eliminate the release of any pollutant that may cause environmental damage to the air, water or earth or its inhabitants.

◆ Safeguard habitats in rivers, lakes, wetlands, coastal zones and oceans to minimise contributions to the greenhouse effect, depletion of the ozone layer, acid rain or smog.

◆ Minimise the creation of waste, especially hazardous waste, and wherever possible recycle materials.

◆ Dispose of all wastes through safe and responsible methods.

◆ Minimise the environmental health and safety risks to employees and the communities in which they operate by employing safe technologies and operating procedures and by being constantly prepared for emergencies.

◆ Sell products or services that minimise adverse environmental impacts and that are safe as consumers commonly use them. Inform consumers of the environmental impacts of their products or services.

◆ Take responsibility for any harm the firm causes to the environment by making every effort to fully restore the environment and to compensate those persons who are adversely affected.

◆ Disclose to employees and to the public incidents relating to their operations that cause environmental harm or pose health or safety hazards.

◆ Commit management resources to implement the Valdez Principles.

◆ Monitor and report upon implementation efforts, and sustain a process to ensure that the board of directors and chief executive officer are kept informed of and are fully responsible for all environmental matters.

◆ Conduct and make public an annual self-evaluation of progress in implementing these principles and in complying with laws and regulations throughout the company's operations.

◆ Work towards the timely creation of independent environmental audit procedures, which will be completed annually and make the results available to the public.

Your agenda

1 How were the externalities which resulted from the disaster internalised?

2 What has Exxon done to reduce the external effects of all its activities?

3 What differences can the Valdez Principles make to levels of business responsibility generally?

4 To what extent do you think that these principles have been accepted?

5 What incentives do businesses have to adopt ethical principles?

Ten years ago business ethics meant dealing with other businesses in an honest and trustworthy manner. The general perception was that businesses operated to serve shareholders' interests. The notion that businesses had obligations to all their stakeholders was very much a minority view.

Times have changed. Businesses often realise that a good reputation will increase shareholder value rather than threaten returns.

Modern-day companies can no longer ignore the interests of employees, the community and the environment in which they operate. The stakeholder view of the firm (see Figure O3.18) recognises the complex interrelationship between firms and those who have an interest in the success or failure of the organisation. It also shows the wider community of interest in a business's activities. The media, for example, are not really stakeholders in the true sense, but they have to be taken into account if a business wants to present its activities in a positive light.

Individual businesses

Retailers have responded to the 'green' consumers who have used consumer sovereignty to influence corporate behaviour. Tesco has initiated an environmental campaign called 'Tesco Cares'. A range of products has been labelled as conforming to environmentally friendly criteria. Bottle banks and paper banks have been sited at the majority of its stores. Reclamation schemes for aluminium and plastics have also been piloted. Organic products have gained greater prominence in-store and the firm has expanded its range of 'welfare friendly' meats. Other supermarkets have followed Tesco's example: Sainsbury's operates a bag recycling scheme and Asda operates a 'shopping bag for life scheme.'

Firms such as Haden McLellan have successfully exploited waste management opportunities, carving a business opportunity out of recycling industrial paint sludge into filler and paint for cars. Where government legislation has been rigorously enforced, firms have exploited commercial opportunities. Johnson Matthey (one of only four catalytic converter manufacturers worldwide) has seen its business expand following changes in EU regulations which required all new cars to be fitted with catalytic converters.

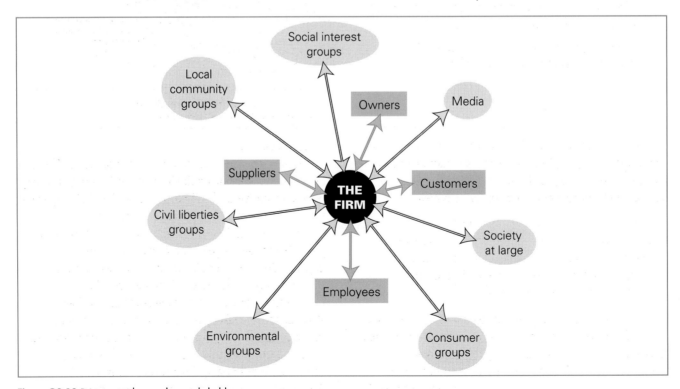

Figure O3.18 Primary and secondary stakeholders

5 Can the costs be counted?

Sainsbury's view

Sainsbury's produces an annual Environment Report which is made available with its Annual Report and Accounts. This details its environmental policies and assesses its progress towards the achievement of defined goals. Sourcing of food and DIY products, transport, energy use and waste management are all covered. Failures are mentioned as well as successes. Taken as a whole, the report presents a full environmental audit.

Various measures of performance are presented. Figure O3.19 shows some progress in reducing fuel use and emissions of delivery vehicles.

Independent accountants will verify and confirm environmental accounts just as they compile and audit financial accounts.

Source: Adapted from Sainsbury's web site, http://www.j-sainsbury.co.uk

Your agenda

1 Why is it important that businesses develop ways to measure their environmental impact?

2 How would you expect an annual environmental account to affect the company's policy?

3 How might the environmental report affect company performance generally?

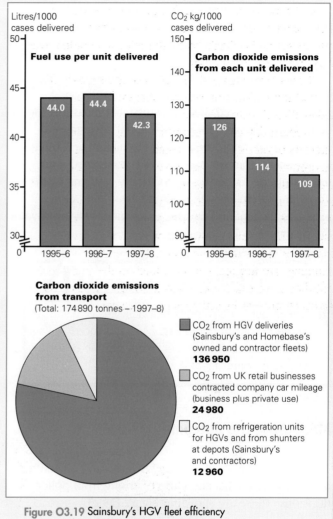

Figure O3.19 Sainsbury's HGV fleet efficiency
Source: Sainsbury's Environmental Report 1988

The government can set the agenda for environmental awareness, but people and businesses have to put it into practice. Shifting attitudes have led business to take a much more open view of its activities.

•There is a growing external pressure on companies to report on broader social, ethical issues in addition to financial performance.• (Price Waterhouse Coopers, the company that carried out the verification on Sainsbury's environmental report.)

Environmental accounting is not easy, but ways are being developed to put money values on environmental resources which are damaged or used up. Assessing the impact of decisions taken by government and business is central to the process of making informed policy decisions.

Some companies do an environmental audit. This can be similar to Sainsbury's Environmental Report but it may be less extensive and still be helpful in highlighting areas for improvement. The essential feature of an environmental audit is that it measures as accurately as possible the full range of the firm's environmental impacts. The audit should become the basis for an environmental policy which identifies specific performance targets and sets dates for their achievement. This has to be backed by an appropriate management system, a training programme and a communication plan.

Ecobalance research is one way of assessing the environmental impact of a product from its development to its final disposal. One application of this type of research occurred in Germany where a study was conducted to measure the energy efficiency of using plastic bags in comparison to using recycled paper bags. The study revealed that it was better to use plastic bags, providing they were re-used, than it was to use recycled paper bags.

Benefit and damage assessment contribute to the decision-making process where big construction projects are involved. Benefit assessment measures the benefit in monetary terms of the social advantages accruing from 'improvements' in the natural and built environment. Damage assessment is concerned with measuring the money losses to society resulting from these 'improvements'. As environmental legislation increases, benefit and damage assessment will improve the quality of policy decisions.

Work in progress

Q   Check out the environmental activities of a range of large companies. Most put such information on the Internet. Rank them in order of green commitment.

Measuring the outcome

There are a number of strategies which can be used to measure the benefits and damage arising from policy decisions. These are shown in Figure O3.20.

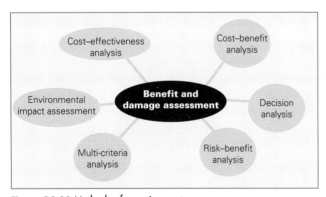

Figure O3.20 Methods of counting costs

■ Cost–benefit analysis (CBA)

This looks at the monetary value of benefits in order to compare them with the monetary value of costs (which should reflect the value to society of the resources being used up) in any project or activity. The requirement for a policy to be worth proceeding with is that benefits are greater than costs. Cost–benefit analysis therefore supports the drive towards economic efficiency. Cost–benefit analysis tries to weigh the costs and benefits which are implicit in people's economic choices.

The basic rule of CBA is that a policy or activity is desirable if benefits exceed costs. However, there are many criticisms of CBA which revolve around the difficulty of putting money values on things that are difficult to quantify.

■ Decision analysis

This can be used to work through the impact of various decisions. Values can be attached to the potential results of the alternative strategies in order to quantify the impact of changes or policies. A decision tree with various branches can be followed through to assess the expected values of particular choices. Clearly, the values ascribed to different alternatives may depend on subjective estimations of possible effects.

■ Risk–benefit analysis

This is simply cost–benefit analysis transferred to risky events such as nuclear accidents, health risks from chemicals on the soil, etc. For example, if the government or a business organisation takes no action to reduce the amount of chemicals in drinking water the risks or costs might be the cancers that result. The benefits of 'no-action' are the avoided resource costs of removing the chemicals.

■ Multi-criteria analysis

This analysis can be used when there are a number of outputs which stem from a particular policy or activity which are measured using different units. It therefore becomes necessary to attach a 'weighting' to the importance of each of the outputs. For example, if reduced accidents are more important than gains in scenic beauty, then they will be given a higher weighting. The weights then play the part of prices reflecting the relative importance of each of the outputs considered.

■ Environmental-impact assessment

This involves identifying and measuring the impacts of actions which are either harmful or beneficial. It is particularly concerned with environmental decision-making. The assessment may or may not involve ascribing monetary values to the environmental impacts of activities or policies.

■ **Cost-effectiveness analysis**
This involves measuring costs in money terms but not benefits. Such a technique can be used to decide which might be the most appropriate choice from a number of options, but it cannot measure whether the benefits to society outweigh the costs.

Is everyone more ethical?

Ethical considerations have certainly climbed the corporate agenda, partly in response to the activities of pressure groups and partly in response to the success of other companies which have adopted a more ethical approach. There is some quantitative data to suggest that businesses really have become more ethical.

People are becoming increasingly interested in questioning the agenda of businesses in which they invest. The Ethical Investment Research Service (EIRS) reports that the amount invested in ethical funds has doubled in the last three years. It estimates current investment at £1.5 billion.

The New Economics Foundation estimates that 384 000 consumers in the UK regularly buy goods produced according to fair trade principles. The Foundation reports that two-thirds of all the companies listed in the Financial Times Stock Exchange Index now undertake some type of environmental reporting. This trend reflects the growing conviction in the business community that ethical behaviour represents good business practice. Firms like the Co-operative Bank, Ben and Jerry's Ice Cream and The Bodyshop have all found that an ethical approach is attractive to their customers, who would rather give their business to companies which can make them feel that they are minimising the effect of consumption.

Ed Mayo, director of the New Economics Foundation, believes that the growth of the private sector and the reduction of the public sector has focused attention on business: 'Once it could get away with saying business is business, but people are no longer willing to accept that.' Now that companies have put ethical considerations on the corporate agenda, campaigners have learnt that targeting companies can be a highly effective strategy. Public awareness of sensitive issues can be harnessed as a powerful tool against commercial interests. Firms that ignore consumer reaction do so at their peril.

6 Is the ethical approach secure for the future?

The Body Shop: Part 1

The Body Shop's approach to ethical accountability is founded on communication. Good communication is seen as being central to ensuring that the company gains stakeholder support for its initiatives.

Mission statement   Our reason for being

To dedicate our business to the pursuit of social and environmental change

To creatively balance the financial and human needs of our stakeholders: employees, customers, franchisees, suppliers and shareholders.

To courageously ensure that our business is ecologically sustainable: meeting the needs of the present without compromising the future.

To meaningfully contribute to local, national and international communities in which we trade, by adopting a code of conduct which ensures care, honesty, fairness and respect.

To passionately campaign for the protection of the environment, human and civil rights, and against animal testing within the cosmetics and toiletries industry.

To tirelessly work to narrow the gap between principle and practice, whilst making fun, passion and care part of our daily lives.

Between August and December 1993 an intensive series of 44 Company Values Meetings was held at The Body Shop's head office. All staff had an opportunity to discuss The Body Shop's values and what they meant to them. The process of consultation resulted in the Company adopting 32 objectives.

In 1996 The Body Shop published a statement of its ethical performance. This 'Values Report' was made up of a guide to the audit and disclosure process and a report on the firm's ethical performance in relation to the environment, animal protection and social issues.

Stage 1: monitoring performance

In order to monitor performance Values Watch, a small watchdog group, was set up to question, challenge and pursue.

A social audit has also been initiated by the company in order to examine The Body Shop's relationship with key stakeholders including employees.

Staff consultation has been undertaken on two levels – using focus groups and a UK company-wide staff survey in order to ascertain the views of the workforce.

Staff were asked to gauge company performance against statements drawn from The Body Shop's mission statement. Staff were also given the opportunity to make additional comments. Results of the survey were used to clarify company policy initiatives.

Stage 2: communication

Departments hold regular meetings to discuss departmental and company issues. Departments have a Department Environment Adviser (DEA). A DEA's role is to disseminate information on the company's environmental initiatives. He or she also assists in the development of new policy initiatives.

Departments also have a communicator who is responsible for facilitating communication between departments.

Stage 3: implementation

The Body Shop's principles regarding animal protection, environmental protection and human rights are all taken into consideration and exert a strong influence on the firm's relationship with suppliers. The Bodyshop has produced a 'Trading Charter'. Central to the company's policy is a commitment not to test products or ingredients on animals. Twice a year The Body Shop's Animal Protection Department sends out a declaration form to each of its suppliers, requiring them to certify that products supplied to The Body Shop meet with the company's purchasing code. If the supplier does test an ingredient on animals, then it will be de-listed automatically.

In the past The Body Shop has withdrawn products from sale when it has been unable to find a supplier to comply with its purchasing rule. In order to ensure that the firm's purchasing policy is rigorously monitored and enforced the Body Shop has sought to achieve ISO 9002 (an international quality control standard).

The Body Shop is committed to a long-term goal of achieving fully sustainable operations. Meeting this objective involves the firm in monitoring the ecological and life cycle impact of its products and their packaging. The firm's policy seeks to encourage stewardship. Suppliers must complete a questionnaire which examines their approach to environmental management and auditing. Suppliers are then graded on a scale of (0–5).

The Body Shop also has a commitment to developing long-term relationships with communities in need as part of its commitment to Trade Not Aid, working with cooperatives, family businesses and tribal councils. By developing these links the company hopes to benefit the wider community providing healthcare, education and supporting projects which local producers feel will be of benefit.

Source: The Body Shop, 1999 Annual Report and Accounts

Your agenda

1 Why are monitoring and communication so important to The Bodyshop?

2 What do you understand by the term 'stewardship'?

3 What are the benefits of a Trade Not Aid programme to people from developing countries?

4 What are the benefits of its ethical policy to companies such as The Body Shop?

Measuring, monitoring and sustainable development

Sustainable development is development which can be achieved without destroying the resources upon which further growth depends. One way of moving towards the long-term goal of sustainable development is by measuring resource depletion, measuring product and waste output and monitoring the effect that industrial activity has on the environment.

The International Chamber of Commerce has sought to introduce a business charter which focuses on sustainable development through a commitment to continuous improvement. The charter targets a number of key areas and is a benchmark against which firms who have a genuine environmental commitment can measure their performance:

- *Environmental management* – creating policies, programmes, procedures and practices for achieving environmentally sound operations for the company.
- *Integrated management* – so that environmental policy becomes an integral part of normal business operations. Such a strategy is likely to require the integration of management systems for environment, quality, customer satisfaction, health and safety of staff.
- *Continuous improvement* – using customer expectations, community expectations, legal regulations as a focus for continuous improvement of the organisation's environmental performance. In addition, there should be a commitment within the organisation to develop new tools, management techniques and production processes in order to improve efficiency and environmental performance.
- *Staff education and training* – to engender an environmental awareness and to encourage employees to act in an environmentally responsible manner.
- *Prior assessment* – a commitment to assess the environmental impact of new projects, new products and new commercial activities. This commitment to assessing the environmental impact of corporate decisions should also extend to corporate decisions relating to the closure of facilities and ending production
- *Products and services* – companies should conduct

a review of the life cycle of products and services
in order to assess their environmental impact.
Consideration should be given as to whether goods
and services:

– are 'fit for purpose'
– are efficient in their consumption of resources
– can be re-used.

Goods should be:

– recyclable
– if not recycleable, disposed of safely.

■ *Facilities and operations* – encouraging the use of
renewable resources, minimising waste generation
and the emission of pollutants and responsible
management of land resources

■ *Contractors and suppliers* – should be seen as an
integral part of a company's operations. Businesses
should use their influence with suppliers and
contractors to adopt sound environmental practice

■ *Responsiveness to concerns* – encouraging
communication between the organisation and:

– employees
– stockholders
– stakeholders
– society.

■ *Reporting and compliance* – companies should
identify targets for areas of business activity such
as recycling, emissions and efficient use of
resources. Performance should then be monitored
and results distributed to stakeholders

Accountability and sustainability are desirable goals
for firms. It is worth considering what happens when
there are conflicting objectives. Within The Body Shop
there has been considerable tension between Anita
and Gordon Roddick and the large institutional
shareholders over the profit performance of the
company. In 1999 changes were made to the senior
management structure. The decision to outsource
production suggests a subtle change in The Body
Shop's relationship with its stakeholders.

The Body Shop: Part 2

When Anita Roddick wanted to replace herself as chief executive of The Body Shop she appointed a head-hunter. The head that he returned with was that of Patrick Gournay, a senior executive with the French food group Danone. When she wanted to interview him she booked him into The Body Shop's Oxford Street store for a massage. After all, she reasoned, he ought to know something about the products. When he was appointed he was given a clear and unambiguous brief – turn the company around.

The Body Shop's profits for the last full year of trading were flat (£38million) and the share price which peaked in the early 1990s at 370p had fallen back to 88p. The company's fortunes had been affected by the Asian economic crisis and copycat stores in the USA coupled with heavy discounting. High street chains such as Boots and Superdrug had moved into what had been a niche market. There is also a suggestion that its range of 'earth friendly' products might be slightly 'naff'.

Gournay announced his master plan:
◆ The company's factory at Littlehampton would be sold, casting uncertainty over the jobs of the 550 employed there.
◆ Franchising operations would be reviewed.
◆ A loyalty scheme would be introduced in order to tempt back shoppers.
◆ The corporate structure would be reorganised into four regions (Asia, the USA, Europe and the UK).

The decision to sell the Littlehampton factory raised a number of questions. Would the decision affect the company's approach to ethical trade with 'the majority world'? Could The Body Shop ensure that contractors supplying products would produce to Body Shop standards?

Gournay's response to these questions was to point out that a third of the company's products was already outsourced. He pointed out that its environmental audit would ensure that suppliers maintained ethical standards. Despite these reassurances an uneasiness remained. Would the new suppliers be so much more efficient or simply better at cutting costs? If they were better at cutting costs, who would lose out? Would it be the employees (lower wages) or the materials suppliers (lower commodity prices)?

Of course, the City liked the changes and The Body Shop share price rose 5p, buoyed up by news of job cuts. The Littlehampton factory was sold to Pac Creative, a South African personal care company in August 1999.

Gournay rejected the idea that The Body Shop's goal of increasing profits was incompatible with its ethical stance. He rejected the suggestion made in one national newspaper that The Body Shop should 'spend more money promoting its products and less time getting its customers to save the whale'. He maintained that, 'We have our values, our campaigns, our fair trade policy on one side and we have our products on the other. The opportunity we have is to bridge the two'. The company intended to achieve this by revamping the stores, introducing new packaging and introducing a loyalty scheme. Mass marketing would be a last resort. There was concern that improving the returns to shareholders might be at the expense of other stakeholders.

Source: The Body Shop, 1999 Annual Report and Accounts

Your agenda

1 Why did the company decide to undergo a radical restructuring?

2 Briefly explain how the proposed changes might affect The Body Shop's relationships with stakeholders.

3 How would outsourcing help the Body Shop's profitability? Why did the announcement of job cuts cause share prices to rise?

4 Does an ethical agenda compromise shareholder value? Explain your point of view.

This enquiry focuses on the issues of responsibility and accountability. The increased awareness of consumers and the activities of interest groups have prompted organisations to review their attitudes towards their stakeholders. The enquiry explores the ways businesses seek to become more responsible as well as some of the less obviously ethical practices which persist.

1 Shareholders or stakeholders?

Partnership

The Co-operative Bank recognises the pressures that modern businesses are facing:

◆ increasing competition
◆ the pressure on business from consumers to act with integrity
◆ legislative pressure to 'respect the limited capacity of our environment to produce resources and absorb waste'
◆ the pressure from shareholders to ensure that firms increase shareholder value.

The Co-operative Bank's response to the changing commercial world is to 'move towards a new model for a successful business; one based upon a wider, longer term, more *inclusive* view of the purpose for which an organisation exists'. Its Partnership Approach reflects this commitment which is based on sound commercial reasoning. The Co-operative Bank believes that recognising 'mutually advantageous Partnerships' is its most effective long-term strategy for ensuring the success of the organisation.

The Partnership initiative is seen to be a part of a natural progression in the development of a socially responsible company, and is a natural development from its mission statement, its ethical policy and its ecological mission statement. It is a recognition of the crucial role of interdependence in creating long term sustainable success. In effect, the Partnership initiative forms the final piece of a jigsaw, presenting a *coherent* and *inclusive* corporate strategy. (Figure O3.21)

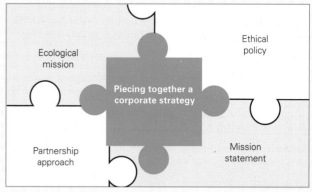

Figure O3.21 The Co-operative bank's corporate strategy

The bank has a commitment to ensure that it respects the needs of all its interest groups at all times and that, 'where necessary it achieves a balance between them'. In return, the bank expects its Partners to fulfil their responsibilities to the bank itself. Where there are conflicting objectives, then the bank will seek to negotiate compromise and achieve a reconciliation. For the bank this is the very essence of Partnership. It believes that it is impossible to achieve sustainable long-term success at the expense of others. In order to fulfil its long-term objectives the bank has sought to learn from its partners through a process of communication and consultation.

Your agenda

1 What form might the consultation process take?
2 What benefits might the bank expect to gain from this process?
3 How might the bank justify the additional cost of this consultation process to its shareholders?

The traditional perception of business is that it seeks to embrace the 'shareholder concept'. This means that the business places the shareholders' interests at the top of its priority list. Everything that managers do should be in the best interests of shareholders. If shareholders want short-run profit maximisation at the expense of long-term growth, then it is the responsibility of business managers to deliver. Will Hutton, in his book *The False Economy,* has condemned British managers for their preoccupation with short-run profits, arguing that merger mania and the desire to maximise · shareholder value has forced firms to act against the long-term best interests of the shareholders.

The underlying principle of the 'shareholder concept' is that managers are employed to manage on behalf of shareholders. The needs, desires and aspirations of other interest groups should not take precedence over shareholder interests.

The decisions that firms make actually influence a diverse group of individuals, groups and organisations. Those affected are frequently referred to as stakeholders. Stakeholders affect and are affected by the firm's decisions. Stakeholder groups have their own objectives which may or may not be compatible with those of the business. The task, and it is a difficult one, is to balance these competing objectives.

The alternative view to the 'shareholder concept' is the 'stakeholder concept' and this has gained currency in recent years. The 'stakeholder concept' recognises that managers have a responsibility to take account of the interests of several groups. The underlying assumption behind this concept is that firms can benefit significantly from the development of a cooperative approach towards stakeholder groups, incorporating their needs into the decision-making process. The Co-operative Bank case study highlights the philosophy behind such an approach. The benefits might include:

● improved retention and motivation of staff
● firms becoming more attractive to ethical investors
● closer relationships with suppliers, leading to better quality service
● improved public relations, resulting in more favourable media coverage
● a reduction in the disruption of commercial activities by pressure groups.

While businesses have increasingly sought to develop a cooperative alliance with stakeholders, not everyone is satisfied. Some firms have encountered some resistance from shareholders because of their concerns about the impact of such an approach on profitability, share price and dividends. Meantime, expectations placed on firms have increased. For example, the oil producer Shell has been vilified for its links with the Nigerian government, because of its abuse of human rights.

In reality, it may be impossible to satisfy the demands of all stakeholders. The senior management must attempt to prioritise competing demands. Inevitably, there will be opportunity costs. The previous enquiry highlighted how these opportunity costs may affect competing groups and the ways in which the various interest groups respond.

Work in progress

Q **1** An increasing number of firms are adopting the stakeholder approach. What is their motivation?

2 Why might firms find difficulty in changing from a profit/shareholder first culture to a stakeholder culture? How could they facilitate such a change?

3 Consider what effect the business cycle may have upon a firm's commitment to the stakeholder approach.

Accepting a commitment to doing business in responsible ways can, in fact, be very attractive to customers – if combined with a continuing dialogue with a range of stakeholder groups, it has the potential to create some genuine sensitivity to the needs of all the people affected by the business.

Point of view

Clearing the air

Early in 1999 Nike received a rare pat on the back for its endeavours to improve working conditions at its factories in Asia. Dara O'Rourke, an environmental researcher at the University of California, applauded the giant sportswear company for making substantial improvements to the air quality and working conditions at a shoe-making plant in Vietnam.

It was Mr O'Rourke who had first revealed that poor ventilation, exposure to hazardous chemicals and inadequate safety and equipment training were putting the workers at risk. In an unprecedented move, Nike let him into the factory to ensure that changes really had been made.

Global Exchange, a human rights group that had been a severe critic of Nike's employment practices in Asia, described the decision to allow an independent observer to visit the site as 'an astounding transformation for a company that once treated independent monitoring as a public relations exercise'.

After years of enduring hostile publicity over pay and working conditions at its Asian factories, the praise made a welcome change for Nike. Criticism of working conditions in factories belonging to Nike's suppliers in China, Thailand, Indonesia and elsewhere began in earnest in 1995. The anti-Nike campaign steadily picked up speed as pressure groups and labour activities identified the Oregon-based company as, if not the only or worst culprit among multi-national shoe and garment companies, at least the biggest and easiest target in the war against low wages, child labour and poor working conditions in developing countries.

Initially, Nike adopted an aggressively defensive posture that only added fuel to the fire. It stated that the wages of its Asian workers, which might seem obscenely low by US standards, were well above the local average. This cut little ice with consumers who were told that $150 trainers were being made by people earning $1.50 a day.

But as the negative publicity started to take its toll, Nike began to address the issue directly. The company joined Apparel Industry Partnership, a group of clothing manufacturers committed to eradicating the use of sweatshops by enforcing an industry-wide code of conduct in overseas factories.

Nike commissioned an independent survey of conditions at some of its factories abroad, an initiative greeted with some scepticism by its critics. But it was at the local level that Nike was forced into taking the most direct action. It severed contracts with factories that paid below minimum wage levels.

Press for Change, a group which monitors workers' rights in Asia, regards some of Nike's efforts to improve conditions as mere 'window-dressing', although it did welcome the recent improvements in Vietnam. Its main criticism of Nike is the company's reluctance to allow local workers' rights groups more of a say in changing the labour practices of Asian manufacturers. 'Nike should be sitting down with the people who have fought for years for what they consider to be living wages.'

Nike believes strongly that the changes it has made and the new policies it has adopted are having meaningful impact on the lives of the 350 000 workers who make their products in Asia. Its ultimate aim, it says, is to 'build and manage an aggressive corporate responsibility agenda'.

Press for Change says changes were made not because Nike eagerly embraced new thinking about the social role of companies in developing countries, but because publicity about working conditions was beginning to inflict real damage on the Nike brand. 'They saw some pretty scary market research that twelve-year old girls in focus groups were talking about these labour abuses… and realised they could not continue the way they were going.'

Source: Adapted from *Responsible Business*, an FT Guide, June 1999

Your agenda

1   What evidence is there that Nike made improvements mainly in response to customer pressure?

2   Does it matter why Nike began to make improvements?

3   What effect would you expect the changes to have on Nike's sales?

2 Business in the community

Scope for big business

The relationship between a company and its key stakeholders, which is based on the exchange of different types of capital (financial, natural, human's social, political) and different types of product and service, can be mutually beneficial and reinforcing when the company is competitive, profitable and able to create shareholder value, as well as recognising the importance of societal value creation.

Figure O3.22 Virtuous circle of shareholder and societal value creation
Source: *Building Competitiveness and Communities*, Jane Nelson, the Prince of Wales Business Forum, 1998

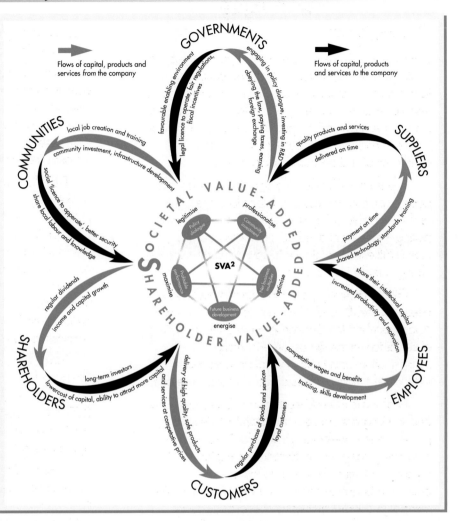

Your agenda

Explain in your own words the underlying messages to businesses contained in Figure O3.22.

Golf day triumph

Lewes Golf Club raised more than £3000 for St Peter and St James Hospice at its annual charity day.

Twenty-seven teams of four entered the competition and the club provided its course free of charge. The Hospice was delighted with the outcome.

Source: *The Sussex Express*, 27 August 1999

Your agenda

1 What advantages are there in this type of activity for the golf club?

2 Find two examples of similar activities in your own neighbourhood, identifying any special reasons why the local business was ready to contribute to a community activity.

Small businesses everywhere sponsor activities for local good causes and involve themselves directly in community activities. Sponsoring a local football team, providing waste bins in high streets and supporting mini-enterprise projects in schools are just three examples. Small businesses often see clearly that they want the support of local people and act accordingly. They themselves have a stake in the community and collaboration seems to come naturally.

The Prince of Wales Business Leaders Forum, the World Bank and the United Nations Development Programme have been instrumental in creating the Partners in Development programme which highlights the many ways in which businesses can contribute to the community. It identifies sources of leadership challenge for businesses. These are:

■ societal value-added
■ shareholder value-added.

The elements in this approach are shown in Figure O3.22. From this starting point the Partnership identifies a range of strategies which benefit the community. In sum, these 'optimise positive economic, social and environmental impacts and minimise negative ones'. The important practical implications are that businesses will be:

● generating investment and income
● creating jobs
● developing human resources
● providing appropriate products and services
● building local business systems
● sharing international standards and business practices
● supporting technology development and transfer
● establishing physical and institutional infrastructure.

3 What can a social audit achieve?

Auditing a pharmaceuticals company

Novo Nordisk is a Danish company manufacturing pharmaceutical products in a number of locations in eight countries. It is a market leader in treatments for diabetes. It has done some pathbreaking work with its social audit, quoted below.

'Building credibility requires transparency in the data and information we put forward in our social report. However, given the nature of the information in a report such as this, traditional methods of auditing may not be the most suitable way to review our social report. Independent auditors drawn from the accountancy profession and from the New Economics Foundation have been invited to provide their comments on this report, based on cooperation with our Internal Audit. The starting point for this process is that organisations need to develop policies, procedures, and credible public reporting covering all of its relationships, and based on an inclusive dialogue with stakeholders.

The first social report accurately reflects where the company is today. It highlights its stated and underlying values, its focus on nurturing its employees, and its stated commitment to taking practical steps to making these values relevant in its relationships with other stakeholders.'

These are Novo Nordisk's ambitions:
◆ To clarify key policy areas bearing on social performance, such as human rights, and to establish strategic indicators relevant to each area.
◆ To extend the process of social accounting to external and non-Danish stakeholders, particularly those in developing countries where employees' and other stakeholders' rights and opportunities may be relatively limited.
◆ To open up more of a two-way dialogue with stakeholders and their representatives that seeks to understand and respond where possible to divergent values, situations and interests.
◆ To work with stakeholders in establishing further quantitative indicators, and in particular to provide more effective performance benchmarks.
◆ To begin the task of integrating social accounting and reporting with the economic and environmental dimensions of the company's performance.
◆ To establish and publish more systematic social performance targets and to ensure that performance against these targets is externally verified and the results made publicly available.

Your agenda

1 In your own words, explain the company's priorities.

2 How can a social audit enhance company performance?

3 To what extent will stakeholders benefit from this process?

4 The last point above mentions 'systematic social performance targets'. Why are these important?

Social auditing is an extension of the concepts of stakeholders and partnership and builds on the principles of transparency and accountability. **Social audits** allow firms to measure their progress towards responsible decision-taking. They recognise the responsibility of firms to provide information and the right of society to have access to information about the environmental and social impact of commercial activities.

The audit process allows the values and expectations of internal stakeholders (employees) to be considered alongside those of external stakeholders (shareholders and the community). Communication between stakeholders is encouraged. As in the case of The Bodyshop (see Enquiry 4, page 604) the audit process encourages communication between management and employees, encouraging trust and mutual respect.

In order for social auditing to be effective there must be a clearly defined corporate vision, with well-publicised aims and objectives and well-defined corporate values. This documentation provides a benchmark against which the company can measure its performance. The social audit cycle is shown in Figure O3.23. Note the similarity between this cycle and the consultative approach adopted by The Body Shop. Novo Nordisk plans to benchmark its progress against that of other concerned businesses in the international arena.

Essentials

Social audits highlight the progress, or lack of it, of a business which is committed to acting responsibly towards all its stakeholders. They complement the information contained in conventional annual financial reports.

Figure O3.23 shows how a social audit operates through three assessment loops. Central to the assessment procedure are the core values of the organisation, which should be expressed in the organisation's value framework. This should be published. The organisation's success in meeting these core values is judged in a consultation process with stakeholders and experts.

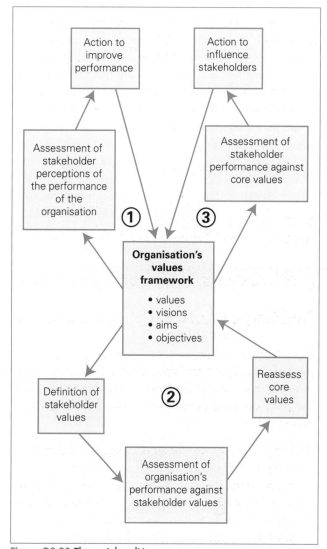

Figure O3.23 The social auditing process

Source: Richard Welford, *Hijacking Environmentalism*, Earthscan Publications, 1997

If the company performance is found to be unsatisfactory, then strategies will need to be implemented to improve performance (loop 1). While this process is ongoing the firm should compare its core values with those of its stakeholders (loop 2). This part of the process is to further clarify stakeholders' values (through a process of consultation) and to enable the organisation to compare its performance against them. Where there are omissions, then core values can be revised and the value framework modified to reflect this.

The final loop in the diagram highlights the education process needed when the organisation finds that its core values are superior to those of its stakeholders. If this is the case, then the firm will seek to raise the standards of stakeholders to those of the organisation. The audit system can only function if the audit process is undertaken on a regular basis and if the system of two-way communication is maintained between the firm and all its stakeholders.

The value of social auditing can be measured not simply in the improvement of environmental and ethical standards but also in the 'green marketing of the company'. The process of social auditing also allows firms the opportunity to become facilitators of change. Social auditing can be seen as an incremental process by which the organisation seeks to contribute towards environmental, social and ethical goals. It is at the very heart of the movement towards the assumption of corporate responsibility for the wider impact of commercial activities.

Mission statements

Successful organisations need to develop a collective view which can be presented as a set of corporate aims. These are beneficial to the firm as they help to build team spirit and foster commitment to the organisation. Corporate aims form the basis for corporate goals, which are the intermediate targets which must be realised if the firm is to achieve longer-term aims. The success or failure of each individual decision can be measured by the extent to which it contributes towards achieving corporate aims.

The **mission statement** is a management tool which can provide a focus for the organisation. Stakeholders within the organisation will be helped to identify more closely with it. A mission statement should provide a shared sense of purpose which directs and stimulates the organisation. It should include four basic elements: purpose, strategy, values and standards of behaviour, as shown in Figure O3.24.

> **Essentials**
>
> **Mission statements** provide an explanation of the main aims of the company. They can give employees a clear view of the importance of objectives such as quality and customer service, thus defining their role in achieving them.

A social audit can reveal information which is then used to change core values. The organisation may react with a new mission statement which highlights the change.

> **Work in progress**
>
> **Q** Examine two mission statements and consider the following points:
>
> **a** Do they highlight the company's purpose, values, standards, behaviour and strategy?
>
> **b** Are the mission statements likely to engage (gain the support and commitment of) the firms stakeholders?
>
> **c** Consider whether you feel that firms actually meet the objectives outlined in their mission statements. Justify your conclusions.

> **Purpose**
>   Why does the company exist?
> **Values**
>   What does the company believe in?
> **Standards and behaviour**
>   Company policies and standards of behaviour expected of company employees
> **Strategy**
>   Corporate plans to develop the competitive position of the company

Figure O3.24 The Mission Statement

The mission statement should identify the stakeholder 'needs' which will be considered when a strategic plan is developed. In reality, the responsibility of balancing the conflicting demands of different stakeholder groups may be a difficult if not impossible task.

4 The rewards of responsibility

Bonanza

In 1997 UK captains of industry were able to secure an 18 per cent pay rise. Meantime, average earnings were rising at 4.4 per cent. The government had asked for moderation: inflation looked as though it might be about to accelerate. The Chancellor feared that big pay rises for top executives might set a bad example and precipitate similarly large wage demands. He said, 'It would be the worst of short-termism to pay ourselves more today at the cost of higher interest rates, fewer jobs and slower growth tomorrow. All of us must show greater responsibility'.

The very highest paid executives secured much more than 18 per cent. Figure O3.25 shows how much more. Pay negotiators at two water companies were known to be making comparisons.

Name	Company	% pay increase
Robert Mendelsohn	Royal & Sun Alliance	89
Sam Chisholm	BSkyB	78
John Brock	Cadbury Schweppes	78
Bryan Langton	Bass	63
Tom Vyner	Sainsbury	58
John Stewart	Woolwich	53
Sir Richard Sykes	Glaxo Wellcome	53
Sir Peter Bonfield	BT	46
David Thomas	Whitbread	45
Chris Gent	Vodaphone	43
John Strickland	HSBC	43

Figure O3.25 The biggest increases

Source: The *Guardian*, 22 July 1998

Your agenda

1 Why might the companies in Figure O3.25 want to give such large pay increases?

2 How could companies justify giving bigger pay awards to executives than to less-elevated employees?

3 Was the Chancellor's anxiety justified? Explain your reasoning.

Corporate pay became a cause for public concern with news of the pay deal awarded to Cedric Brown, then chief executive of British Gas. Cedric Brown's pay increased by 75 per cent in 1995 and the total pay bill for executive directors at British Gas rose by 54 per cent. News of the pay rises came at a time when British Gas was shedding 25 000 workers. The task of defending the pay award fell to British Gas's US Chairman who earned £450 000 for his part-time post. He argued that the salary of Cedric Brown represented the going rate for someone of his calibre.

The problem behind this argument is that there is no market for top executives. For markets to function there need to be willing buyers and sellers and near perfect knowledge. Dealing must be transparent and buyers and sellers must have the option of looking elsewhere. The reality of executive appointments is very different. Moving down the management hierarchy, it is possible to find a ready market for marketing, finance or personnel executives, but for the most senior jobs in an organisation the situation is very different. Boards seeking to appoint senior managers must seek a complex blend of management skills, contacts and technical knowledge. Such appointments are of necessity secretive and likely to include delicate negotiations on pay and remuneration packages.

A further difficulty is that the market for top executives is an international one. Executive pay has been rising in the USA as well as in Europe. The skills needed by multi-national organisations are quite scarce. So it is easy for those who are believed to have them to demand high pay and get their way.

Setting executive pay

Companies devolve responsibility for setting pay to a committee of **non-executive directors**. They are supported in their deliberations by specialist pay consultants. The chairman can tell shareholders that executive compensation is decided by an impartial independent group. The problem is that non-executive directors have their own agenda – they have their own pay to consider. Influencing pay awards to directors can indirectly influence their own remuneration by raising the going rate. The specialist advisers are merely recycling information about pay awards at other firms – quite often they themselves may have acted as advisers in setting those pay rates. What is evident is that pay at this level is not entirely market determined.

The Greenbury Report

Sir Richard Greenbury was appointed to review executive salaries and benefits after the British Gas episode described above. His report came out in 1997 and set out guidelines for executive salaries and benefits. The committee of 11 industrialists and representatives from financial institutions criticised the way that executives in some privatised companies set their remuneration.

The recommendations of the report included proposals that:

- share option profits should be taxed as income rather than as capital gains
- there should be full disclosure by public companies on executive pay and that they should adhere to the new code of best practice
- the Stock Exchange should require listed companies to make full disclosure and give shareholders an annual statement about compliance with the new code
- no share options should be granted for at least six months after privatisation; water and energy companies should review pay packages and if changes are made they should be reported to the next AGM.

Sir Richard Greenbury noted that the principles behind the proposals were total transparency, greater responsibility and accountability. He also noted that the best way to make further progress on reforming executive pay was to link rewards to both personal and company performance in order to ensure that interests of directors and shareholders are aligned.

The problem with linking pay to company performance is that, as *Business Week* notes 'boards are setting easier hurdles for payouts, while at the same time increasing the pot of money available for bonuses'. This defeats the attempts to increase accountability. Some firms, Boots the Chemist among them, have sought to abandon stock options.

Work in progress

Q How has the pay of top managers changed in the past two years? Have increases been greater than those for employees? Are these issues still creating problems? If so, why?

5 Who has the power?

The role of non-executive directors

Lord MacLaurin was appointed to the board of Guinness in 1986 at the insistence of the Bank of England which was concerned at the way that Guinness was being managed by the chief executive Ernest Saunders. The principal criterion for his appointment was that he had 'Scottish connections'. He found the experience an enlightening one. On his first visit to the headquarters of Guinness he found Ernest Saunders urbane, vain and something of a puzzle. He asked Saunders for copies of recent board minutes. He was told that Saunders never kept any! Next, MacLaurin asked for copies of any records he held of meetings with his executive team. Saunders informed him that weekly meetings were held but that no records were kept. This encounter left MacLaurin astonished. How could Saunders run a multi-million pound company without keeping a single record or minute of any meetings with executives or board members?

The other non-executive directors all agreed with Lord MacLaurin that there was something very odd going on at Guinness. The only thing that they didn't know was what precisely was going on. It was not until 1 December, 1986, when the Department of Trade and Industry (DTI) moved into the offices of Guinness to investigate, that Ernest Saunders's skilful manipulations began to be uncovered. At a meeting the following day MacLaurin pressed Saunders about the DTI investigation:

MACLAURIN: Is there any reason why the DTI and the Fraud Office should be interested in your own or Guinness's affairs?

SAUNDERS: Absolutely nothing

MACLAURIN: Is there anything that you want to tell us?

SAUNDERS: I can assure you and the other non-executive directors that there is nothing I know of that could cause the interest of the DTI and the SFO (Serious Fraud Office).

Within a month, Saunders's deception had been uncovered. Saunders had operated on the principal that

if you tell a lie, tell a big one and stick to it.

The illegal share dealing orchestrated by Saunders to ensure the take-over of Distillers was revealed by Olivier Roux, a confidant of Saunders who turned whistle-blower. Saunders and his accomplice had bought 78 million Guinness shares at a total cost of £257 million, in order to increase the Guinness share price. Despite the scale of the operation the non-executive directors had little idea of what had been going on. At a special board meeting they called for Saunders and Roux to be suspended. The rest of the board disagreed.

The following day another non-executive director received a letter from a director who had not attended the meeting. It accused the non-executive members of being more interested in their personal interests than those of the company and that if they made any adverse public comments, then they would have to bear 'the full responsibility for any adverse effects upon the Company – its share prices, its liability to legal action by other parties and its overall trading interests'. Saunders finally resigned on 9 January, 1987 and subsequently served a prison sentence for his part in the Distillers affair.

For MacLaurin the Distillers episode highlighted the value of non-executive directors, providing that they do not see the role as 'money for old rope'. The non-executive directors questioned, investigated and sought to uncover wrong-doing and then set about clearing up the mess left in Saunders's wake. It would be nice to think that all non-executive directors were as conscientious.

Source: *Tiger by the Tail*, Ian Maclaurin, 1999, Macmillan

Your agenda

1 Why do companies appoint non-executive directors?

2 What additional powers might have helped the Guinness non-executive directors to uncover the share manipulation earlier?

The function of non-executive directors is to provide unbiased advice. They are therefore independent of the senior management of the company. They can scrutinise company policy, give objective advice and help to moderate the actions of powerful executive directors.

Non-executive directors are expected to do much more than simply advise on executive pay. They should have the expertise to evaluate all aspects of the management of the business. In particular, they should be able to discourage dubious business practices. They might have been able to ring the alarm bell when Robert Maxwell took money for himself from his newspaper company's pension fund, leaving thousands of retired employees without the pensions they had themselves paid for.

By bringing in experience from other areas of business, non-executive directors can strengthen the expertise available when decisions are taken. However, if they are reluctant to use their powers to 'rock the boat', their effectiveness may be reduced.

Non-executive directors and pay

Increasingly, pressure is being placed on executive bodies to consider the morality of directors' costs. This pressure is gaining momentum across Europe and the USA and there are ripples appearing in the British pond. Trade unions and institutional investors are scrutinising executive pay more closely. Boards have always had the ability to increase the pay of directors, giving them a larger slice of the corporate cake. Traditionally, there was an element of restraint in setting pay levels, but this restraint has been relaxed and top managers have felt free to use their positions for self-enrichment.

Legislation to limit pay awards may appear attractive but is unlikely to be effective. Calls from the Prime Minister for senior managers to exercise restraint are likely to fall on deaf ears. Curbing management pay can only be achieved by shareholders exerting their power and influence. The indication is that insurance companies and other institutional investors may be ready to act.

On the other hand, executive pay is partly a matter of basic economics. If there is a shortage of skilled managers to manage international businesses, then the price which firms will have to pay in order to attract those skills will inevitably rise. As globalisation of markets increases, then it must be expected that British firms will have to increase salaries in order to compete in the international market place for scarce executive talent. International pay awards will inevitably affect pay levels in the UK for top managers.

Point of view

Self interest...

Non-executive directors hold the keys to the corporate cash box. The difficulty that they face is in devising meaningful criteria on which to base executive pay. One of their other responsibilities is to curb the excesses of top executives.

However, as *Forbes* magazine notes, 'Big corporations have been showering more and more goodies on their board of directors. Is it any wonder some of these boards have dithered in the face of obvious mismanagement?'. Concern has been expressed that non-executive directors who are very ready to dip into corporate coffers in order to reward top executives are very reluctant to address such issues as poor strategic management and a lack of basic common sense.

There appears to be a correlation between length of tenure in office and the over-payment of chief executive officers who believe 'that what's good for me is good for the company'. If non-executive directors are to do their job properly they must challenge this view. They must recognise that morale within the company is affected by their actions. Increasing the pay differential between senior managers and the workforce can have a negative effect on the morale of employees and on the firm's long-term objective of sustaining and optimising the performance of the company.

...or a simple case of supply and demand?

A report by independent advisers Monks Partnership in May 1999 concluded that senior management pay was continuing to rise fast because of a reported shortage of able people. The top 20 per cent of company directors saw their average earnings rise by 21 per cent during the previous year. Monks Partnership concluded that the rapid growth of executive pay might be due to difficulties in recruiting people who have the skills and experience to manage complex businesses in an increasingly competitive international market place.

Your agenda

1 Why should non-executive directors be responsible for setting executive pay?

2 To what extent would you expect there to be a close correlation between executive pay and corporate performance?

3 What criteria might non-executive directors use in order to determine pay awards?

4 Why might executive pay rises affect employee morale?

5 What are the drawbacks to being a top executive?

Do shareholders have power?

By law, shareholders are all invited to an Annual General Meeting (AGM) of the company. This is the opportunity for the senior managers to meet shareholders and report on the performance of the company. It also gives shareholders the chance to ask pertinent questions about the performance of the company. So what is achieved at the AGM? The truth is, very little. Many people think that most AGMs are an expensive waste of time. Those who turn up often have an axe to grind and little real power with which to affect corporate policy. It takes something special to attract media attention to AGMs.

The run-up to an AGM is likely to be filled with a series of meetings to agree the text of the chairman's address to shareholders; meetings with media consultants to ensure that the presentation is slick and professional and careful preparation of answers to possible difficult questions.

Yet difficult questions are rarely asked. Institutional investors usually do not attend AGMs and the floor of the meeting is likely to be dominated by private shareholders, who are likely to ask questions about the environment, employee issues or consumer-related matters. Paul Myners, chairman of Gartmore investment fund managers, notes that private shareholders tend to avoid questions on important issues such as the company's corporate strategy or the financial management of the company. He asserts that AGMs can never be an effective forum if major shareholders do not attend.

One of the reasons that so few large institutional investors attend AGMs is that they have access to senior executives at other times and are likely to have their own one-to-one meetings with the company. This allows them to discuss company performance frankly and make criticisms where appropriate.

Ratner and the prawn sandwich

Although the biggest issues are usually not discussed at AGMs, there are occasions when they do generate a little excitement. Gerald Ratner developed a very successful chain of jewellery shops during the 1980s. It was positioned in the budget sector of the market, with an accurate understanding of customers' needs. In April 1991 Ratner addressed an audience at the Institute of Directors' Annual conference at the Albert Hall. In an impetuous and infamous burst of humour he boasted that his firm 'sold jewellery for the price of a prawn sandwich – and it lasts about as long'.

An amazed and delighted press seized on the story and featured other injudicious remarks ('Some of our products are absolute crap'). Among consumers, amusement soon turned to anger and the company's sales plummeted. The next AGM was very stormy indeed. Shareholders demanded to know why Ratner had ridiculed the company's products, wiping millions off the share value. He resigned in 1992.

Your agenda

1 What does this episode reveal about shareholder power?

2 Why are so few AGMs as interesting?

Pressure groups in the AGM

An increasingly common phenomenon has been the practice of hijacking AGMs by particular interest groups which have sought to dominate the agenda with their own concerns. Animal rights groups, environmental activists or individuals with a grievance can all gain admission to the AGM providing they buy at least one share. Companies have sought to minimise the effectiveness of these groups in a number of ways. One possible if rather extreme solution is to close the AGM to the media, denying the protest group publicity for its cause.

Rio Tinto Zinc (RTZ) has had many of its meetings disrupted by environmental protesters. It is perhaps unique in having its own protest group called Partizans. The persistent disruption of the AGM prompted RTZ to pre-empt questions and provide detailed written answers in advance of the meeting. RTZ found that the strategy reduced the disruption caused by Partizan and forced the protest group to become much more specific about the questions they asked.

Paul Myners is one of a group of influential people proposing change in the structure of AGMs. One suggestion is to abandon the notion of an Annual General Meeting unless 10 per cent or more of the shareholders want one. Instead, there could be General Meetings every three years, encouraging institutional investors to attend. A second suggestion is that the meeting should become more informative, advising shareholders of company plans in more detail. Questions which are of 'limited interest' to the majority of shareholders could be passed to the relevant director to deal with after the meeting. The answers could then be made available to shareholders interested in the response. Such changes, if implemented, may keep more shareholders awake during the AGM.

AGMs have the potential to encourage a stronger degree of accountability if shareholders will make effective use of them. However, this takes time and thought which most shareholders might find it hard to give.

6 Are there signs of improvement?

Germany

Ekkehard Wenger, Professor of Banking and Finance, is the German advocate of shareholders' rights. He attended his first annual meeting in 1987 and has been making the life of senior managers difficult ever since. His questioning attitude has ruffled the feathers of many senior executives. The chief executive of Daimler even had him thrown out of one meeting. Wenger's activities have prompted a new law in Germany which bans insider trading and which requires banks and companies to disclose equity stakes. He has now been joined in his crusade to make German business more accountable to share holders by a number of new shareholder groups. Wenger says that in the past Annual General Meetings of German firms have tended to be 'a form of cabaret'. The activities of Wenger and other shareholder activists promise to make the annual meetings of German firms a lot more interesting.

Your agenda

1 Why would it be in the public interest to use AGMs to raise issues relating to business responsibility?

2 What other measures might increase accountability?

Shareholders across Europe are becoming more militant as they seek to influence corporate decisions. Increasingly, shareholder activists are putting pressure on senior managers in order to increase profits and dividends, to remove ineffective managers, to end executive pay schemes which are not linked to performance and to encourage social responsibility. In a number of instances shareholders have formed shareholder-defence committees in order to fight for their rights in the courts. The privatisation which swept Europe in the 1980s and early 1990s created a new pool of investors who are learning to flex their collective muscles.

In practice, minority shareholders have few rights. Assets can become trapped in underperforming companies. Company reports are often misleading, denying shareholders a true picture of the company's performance. Voting rights are heavily weighted in favour of existing executives. They know that large blocks of shares rest in the hands of institutional investors (such as insurance companies) which may be reluctant to support radical change.

One reason for the changes has been the increasing investment in Europe by US organisations that demand greater accountability, greater transparency and greater returns than some European firms have been accustomed to.

France has been one of the first countries to feel the wind of change. Over the past 15 years the French government has sought to reduce its role in the economy by disposing of state-owned industries. France does not have the large institutional investors to be found in the UK. Instead, shares in privatised companies have been bought by industrial holding companies creating a number of interrelated companies whose boards are dominated by a small and powerful group of executives.

This cosy arrangement has been broken by a number of vocal shareholders, forcing out senior executives and making the companies more accountable to their shareholders. The share price and earnings have been given greater prominence in order to satisfy disgruntled shareholders.

In Germany corporate boards have also found themselves under attack over the way that they appoint chief executives. The system of appointment has been criticised following the spectacular failure of several companies, including one which required a US$2.5 billion rescue package. Even Daimler has been criticised after it warned of severe losses only weeks after promising a rosy future at an annual meeting.

Dissatisfaction with the present systems has prompted many European countries and the EU to consider legislation to make firms more accountable, discourage such practices as cross-shareholding and limit the number of boards which executives can sit on.

Changing patterns of ownership

Mergers and acquisitions have affected the relationship between firms and their stakeholders and have significant implications for individuals who have an interest in the firms affected. Mergers and acquisitions almost inevitably lead to shifts in corporate focus and new attitudes to corporate responsibility. There are numerous examples of family firms firmly rooted in local communities which are rationalised after a merger. Employment may be greatly reduced or the production may cease in that location, in the interest of cutting costs.

The impact of factory closures on local communities is immense and long term. The traditional coal-mining, steel-producing and ship-building areas show the social dislocation caused by mergers, acquisition and closure. The corporate buzz words of synergy, economies of scale, rationalisation and the maximisation of shareholder values have alternative meanings. For employees and local communities affected, they mean structural unemployment, occupational immobility, social exclusion and depressed standards of living.

A peculiary British disease

There is one issue which finds itself at the centre of agreement among industrialists, trade unionists, journalists and economists. That is the chronic and persistent under investment in the UK economy. UK economic performance has been plagued by short-sightedness and a lack of innovation. Why is this? What can be done to address the situation?

The Bank of England is convinced that the blame for under investment rests with industry. In a study conducted by the Bank, the majority of firms surveyed set a threshold of 20 per cent nominal rates of return as their criterion for approving investment projects. More than 40 per cent of the firms required a three-year investment payback. A separate survey by the CBI has confirmed these findings. Therefore, in order to gain approval for an investment project, managers must demonstrate that a project can achieve this level of return. Some managers may massage their financial projections in order to show a better rate of return for investments. This may explain why forecast projections of growth are often far higher than actual growth rates for UK firms.

Performance-related pay can mean that managers sacrifice long-term investment projects in order to meet short-term performance targets. In both cases, decision takers are likely to make too few investments which require a focus on the more distant future. Social responsibility often requires a long view and the UK has not scored well in this area. The disease of short-termism can be very damaging.

Some evidence for this view may be seen in Figure O3.26. Research and development spending is just one aspect of investment, but it is important for long-term business success and economic growth rates in developed countries.

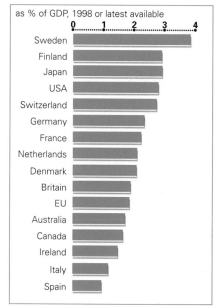

Figure O3.26
Research and development spending
Source: *The Economist*, 28 August 1999

A conclusion

Although many businesses are still driven by the profit motive alone, many others have embraced the need for social responsibility as an essential feature of business life. This is despite the increase in competitive pressures which has also been a feature of recent years. As students you are in a good position to examine the behaviour of individual companies and evaluate current trends, keeping in mind that each business is unique in its way, and looking beyond the obvious and superficial observations to explore the underlying realities.

Social responsibility does not have to detract from the value of the business to shareholders. Responsible decision-taking encourages people both within the business and outside it to value its activities.